OXFORD EARLY CHRISTIAN STUDIES

General Editors

Gillian Clark   Andrew Louth

THE OXFORD EARLY CHRISTIAN STUDIES series includes scholarly volumes on the thought and history of the early Christian centuries. Covering a wide range of Greek, Latin, and Oriental sources, the books are of interest to theologians, ancient historians, and specialists in the classical and Jewish worlds.

AMBROSE
De officiis

Edited with an Introduction,
Translation, and Commentary by
IVOR J. DAVIDSON

Volume I
Introduction, Text,
and Translation

OXFORD
UNIVERSITY PRESS

OXFORD
UNIVERSITY PRESS

Great Clarendon Street, Oxford OX2 6DP

Oxford University Press is a department of the University of Oxford.
It furthers the University's objective of excellence in research, scholarship,
and education by publishing worldwide in

Oxford New York

Athens Auckland Bangkok Bogotá Bombay Buenos Aires Calcutta
Cape Town Chennai Dar es Salaam Delhi Florence Hong Kong Istanbul
Karachi Kuala Lumpur Madrid Melbourne Mexico City Mumbai
Nairobi Paris São Paulo Singapore Taipei Tokyo Toronto Warsaw

with associated companies in Berlin Ibadan

Oxford is a registered trade mark of Oxford University Press
in the UK and in certain other countries

Published in the United States
by Oxford University Press Inc., New York

British Library Cataloguing in Publication Data

Data available

Library of Congress Cataloging in Publication Data

Data applied for

Set ISBN 0-19-924578-9
Volume 1 ISBN 0-19-827023-2
Volume 2 ISBN 0-19-827024-0

1 3 5 7 9 10 8 6 4 2

Typeset in Imprint
by Joshua Associates Ltd., Oxford
Printed in Great Britain
on acid-free paper by
Biddles Ltd., Guildford & King's Lynn

For Julie,
sine qua non

PREFACE

Though Ambrose's *De officiis* has long been recognized as one of the major bequests of Latin patristic literature, its students have laboured under two significant disadvantages: first, the absence of a readable modern English translation of the text, and secondly the lack of a study which locates the treatise meaningfully in its original socio-cultural context. In a modest way, the present work is offered as a corrective to both of these deficiencies.

The Translation is intended to render Ambrose accessible to modern readers, and thus to signal the enduring significance of *De officiis* as a testament to the synthesis of intellectual influences which characterized late antiquity. Translating Ambrose into modern idiom while remaining faithful to the nuances of his philosophical inheritance is not especially easy, despite the apparent simplicity of his language; too often the results can be stilted or wooden, and thus of limited value in widening Ambrose's potential readership today. The version offered here naturally aspires to be true to the original, and to convey the texture of the classical and biblical registers with which Ambrose is working. It also acknowledges that not all of the author's complex range of semantic evocation can be caught in English (far less in an entirely consistent fund of modern English equivalents), and that one of the hallmarks of his style is the practicality of his tone. Ambrose writes as a preacher, and a certain discursiveness and rhetorical energy are never far away as he presses upon his readers the applications of his ideals or the splendour of their biblical exemplars. These features deserve to be captured to some extent in translation. Sometimes this means that the interpretation is fairly full or idiomatic by the standards of some patristic translations, but I leave it so in the belief that Ambrose's primary concern is to communicate in practical (and sometimes fairly unpolished) terms, and that, for him,

episcopal *auctoritas* and a rich pastoral immediacy are not at odds.

The Introduction and Commentary seek to explain the social, cultural, and theological factors which give the work its particular flavour. While they uncover an even greater density of Ciceronian evocation than has hitherto been noticed in Ambrose's Latin, they also endeavour to assess his text not just as a literary puzzle but also as an expression of its author's larger ecclesiastical strategy in the Milan of the 380s. I seek to describe and analyse Ambrose's moral message within the specific circumstances of his effort to placard the superiority of his Nicene faith over all its competitors, pagan and Christian. On the assumption that the intellectual stratigraphy of Ambrose's language can only be appreciated by quoting directly from his chief sources, Cicero and Scripture, the Commentary is based upon the Latin text and contains a fair degree of Latin citation, but I hope its more general analysis renders it still useful for readers without the language. To facilitate the latter's access, I have for the most part ignored matters philological and syntactical, though I offer a brief overview of the work's Latinity in the Introduction, which refers interested readers to further specialized tools.

The work has had a lengthy gestation, and I have accumulated many debts. Ambrose has occupied my attention in a lot of places: Glasgow, Edinburgh, St Andrews, Oxford, Mainz, Heidelberg, Melbourne, and Dunedin, and I have cause to be grateful to scholars and librarians in all of them. I should like to thank the editors of the Oxford Early Christian Studies series, Andrew Louth and Gillian Clark, for their willingness to accommodate an unusually large study within the series, and for the generosity with which they reviewed this one. I am also much indebted to Roger Green for his appreciative comments and valuable suggestions. David Wright and George Newlands appraised an earlier version of the work, and both have extended much valuable encouragement and friendship over the years. I am grateful to my father for his interest in the project over even longer, and thankful, too, to the colleagues, students, and friends with whom I have been able to discuss aspects of the work in detail. I am also glad to acknowledge the

financial assistance of a number of research grants from the University of Otago.

My debts to the remarkable florescence of Ambrose scholarship in recent years will be obvious, and are too extensive to justify individual acknowledgements. I am all too conscious of the many areas into which further delving would have brought additional insights, and can only say that such wisdom as has been captured is in no small measure attributable to the labours of those who have toiled in related fields. It is encouraging to note the enduring interest in Ambrose and his world, and to see the extent to which the study of late antiquity has become a truly multi-disciplinary affair. The present study was completed in late 1999, and I have not been able to incorporate literature published since then. Maurice Testard's text has since seen the light of day in another place, the CCL, and there are on-going developments of relevance in the study of the virtues and passions in ancient philosophy which may yet shed further light on elements of Ambrose's moral vision.

At Oxford University Press, I should like to extend particular thanks to Hilary O'Shea, whose early enthusiasm for the project and patience in overseeing its delivery proved a great source of encouragement to me. I am grateful also to Enid Barker, to Georga Godwin, and, in particular, to Georga's successor, Lucy Qureshi, for exemplary work on a complex text. The typescript had a meticulous copy-editor in Nigel Hope, whose attention to detail saved me from many inconsistencies; Leofranc Holford-Strevens performed a similar service for the indexes.

My two greatest debts come last. The first is to Peter Walsh, who oversaw the original (and somewhat different) study from which these volumes ultimately derive, and who has shown far more patience than he could have expected to require in awaiting its sequel. It was his inspiring teaching and gracious expression of considerable learning which first helped kindle my enthusiasm for patristic Latin, and—while the errors that remain in what follows are of course all mine—there is possibly more of his influence in this work than even he may discern. The second is to my wife Julie, who has known more than anyone else the cost of this enterprise, and has sacrificed much for it over many years and in two hemispheres. Its dedication to

her is a testimony of my love and gratitude—and, I trust, a pledge that there can indeed (in some sense at least) be life after Ambrose.

I. J. D.

Dunedin
July 2001

CONTENTS

ABBREVIATIONS

References to periodicals follow the style of *L'Année philologique*; exceptions are either specified in full or can be identified in the list below. Abbreviations for classical texts follow the conventions of C. T. Lewis and C. Short, *A Latin Dictionary* (repr. Oxford, 1984) and H. G. Liddell, R. Scott, and H. S. Jones, *A Greek–English Lexicon*, 9th edn. (Oxford, 1940, suppl. E. A. Barber *et al.*, 1968–96); in the case of Christian authors and scriptural books the forms should be self-explanatory (with OT references, I adopt the traditional style of the Latin Bible: '1–2 Ki.' = 1–2 Sam.; '3–4 Ki.' = 1–2 Ki.; references to Pss. use the Vulg. enumeration); on biblical citations, see Introduction, n. 291. For references to Ambrose's works, see separate list below. Other standard abbreviations are as follows:

AA.SS.	*Acta Sanctorum* (Antwerp, 1643–1770; Brussels, 1780–6, 1845–83, 1894– ; Tongerloo, 1794; Paris, 1875–87)
ABD	*The Anchor Bible Dictionary*, 6 vols. (New York, 1992)
ACW	Ancient Christian Writers (Westminster, MD and London)
AmbrEpisc i–ii	G. Lazzati (ed.), *Ambrosius Episcopus: Atti del Congresso internazionale di studi ambrosiani nel XVI centenario della elevazione di sant'Ambrogio alla cattedra episcopale*, 2 vols. (Milan, 1976)
Ambroise de Milan	Y.-M. Duval (ed.), *Ambroise de Milan. XVIᵉ Centenaire de son élection épiscopale. Dix études* (Paris, 1974)
BA	Bibliothèque Augustinienne (Paris)
Banterle	G. Banterle, *Sant'Ambrogio: Opere Morali I–I Doveri*, Sancti Ambrosii

Episcopi Mediolanensis Opera, 13 (Milan and Rome, 1977)

Bar-Kochva — B. Bar-Kochva, *Judas Maccabaeus: The Jewish Struggle against the Seleucids* (Cambridge, 1989)

Barry — M. F. Barry, *The Vocabulary of the Moral-Ascetical Works of Saint Ambrose: A Study in Latin Lexicography* (Washington, DC, 1926)

Becker — M. Becker, *Die Kardinaltugenden bei Cicero und Ambrosius: De officiis* (Basle, 1994)

Biermann — M. Biermann, *Die Leichenreden des Ambrosius von Mailand. Rhetorik, Predigt, Politik* (Stuttgart, 1995)

Biondi i–iii — B. Biondi, *Il diritto romano cristiano*, 3 vols. (Milan, 1952–4)

Brown, *Body* — P. Brown, *The Body and Society: Men, Women and Sexual Renunciation in Early Christianity* (New York, 1988)

Brown, *Power* — P. Brown, *Power and Persuasion in Late Antiquity: Towards a Christian Empire* (Madison, WI, 1992)

Bürgi — E. Bürgi, 'Prolegomena quaedam ad S. Ambrosii episcopi Mediolanensis libros de officiis tres', in *75 Jahre Stella Matutina*, i (Feldkirch, 1931), 43–68

Cavasin — A. Cavasin, *Sant'Ambrogio, Dei Doveri degli ecclesiastici* (Turin, 1938)

CCL — *Corpus Christianorum, series Latina* (Turnhout and Paris)

Claus — F. Claus, 'De opvatting van Ambrosius over de navolging in de "De officiis"', *Handelingen XXVI der Koninklijke Zuidernederlandse Maatschappij voor Taal- en Letterkunde en Geschiedenis* (1972), 63–72

Colish i–ii — M. L. Colish, *The Stoic Tradition from*

ecclésiastique, ed. A. Baudrillart *et al.*
(Paris, 1912–)

Draeseke   J. Draeseke, 'M. Tulli Ciceronis et Ambrosii episcopi Mediolanensis De officiis libri III inter se comparantur', *RFIC* 4 (1876), 121–64

DSp   *Dictionnaire de spiritualité*, ed. M. Viller *et al.* (Paris, 1937–)

DTC   *Dictionnaire de théologie catholique*, ed. A. Vacant, E. Mangenot, and E. Amann, 15 vols. (Paris, 1903–50)

Dyck   A. R. Dyck, *A Commentary on Cicero, De Officiis* (Ann Arbor, MI, 1996)

Emeneau   M. B. Emeneau, 'Ambrose and Cicero', *The Classical Weekly* 24/7 (1930), 49–53

Ewald   P. Ewald, *Der Einfluss der stoisch-ciceronianischen Moral auf die Darstellung der Ethik bei Ambrosius* (Leipzig, 1881)

Faust   U. Faust, *'Christo servire libertas est': Zum Freiheitsbegriff des Ambrosius von Mailand* (Salzburg, 1983)

Fenger   A.-L. Fenger, *Aspekte der Soteriologie und Ekklesiologie bei Ambrosius von Mailand* (Frankfurt and Berlin, 1981)

Förster   Th. Förster, *Ambrosius, Bischof von Mailand: Eine Darstellung seines Lebens und Wirkens* (Halle, 1884)

Gaudemet   J. Gaudemet, *L'Eglise dans l'empire romain (IVe–Ve siècles)* (Paris, 1958)

Gauthier   R.-A. Gauthier, *Magnanimité: Idéal de la grandeur dans la philosophie païenne et dans la théologie chrétienne* (Paris, 1951)

Graumann   T. Graumann, *Christus interpres: Die Einheit von Auslegung und Verkündigung in der Lukaserklärung des Ambrosius von Mailand* (Berlin and New York, 1994)

Griffin and Atkins   M. T. Griffin and E. M. Atkins (eds.),

	Cicero: On Duties (Cambridge, 1991) [translation by Atkins; introduction and annotation by Griffin]
Gryson, *Prêtre*	R. Gryson, *Le Prêtre selon saint Ambroise* (Louvain, 1968)
Gryson, 'Typologie'	R. Gryson, 'La Typologie sacerdotale de saint Ambroise et ses sources', Th.D. Diss. (Université Catholique de Louvain, 1966)
Guthrie i–vi	W. K. C. Guthrie, *A History of Greek Philosophy*, 6 vols. (Cambridge, 1962–81)
Hagendahl	H. Hagendahl, *Latin Fathers and the Classics: A Study on the Apologists, Jerome, and other Christian Writers* (Gothenburg, 1958)
Hahn	V. Hahn, *Das wahre Gesetz: Eine Untersuchung der Auffassung des Ambrosius von Mailand vom Verhältnis der beiden Testamente* (Münster, 1969)
Hill	C. Hill, 'Classical and Christian Traditions in Some Writings of Saint Ambrose of Milan', D.Phil. Diss. (University of Oxford, 1979)
Hiltbrunner	O. Hiltbrunner, 'Die Schrift "De officiis ministrorum" des hl. Ambrosius und ihr ciceronisches Vorbild', *Gymnasium* 71 (1964), 174–89
Holden	H. A. Holden, *M. Tulli Ciceronis De Officiis libri tres, with Introduction, Analysis and Commentary*, 3rd edn. (Cambridge, 1899)
Homes Dudden i–ii	F. Homes Dudden, *The Life and Times of St Ambrose*, 2 vols. (Oxford, 1935)
Humphries	M. Humphries, *Communities of the Blessed: Social Environment and Religious Change in Northern Italy*, AD 200–400 (Oxford, 1999)
Ihm	M. Ihm, *Studia Ambrosiana, Neue*

	Jahrbücher für klassische Philologie, Suppl. Bd. 17 (1890), 1–124
Jacob	C. Jacob, *'Arkandisziplin', Allegorese, Mystagogie: Ein neuer Zugang zur Theologie des Ambrosius von Mailand* (Frankfurt, 1990)
Johanny	R. Johanny, *L'Eucharistie, centre de l'histoire du salut chez saint Ambroise de Milan* (Paris, 1968)
Jones i–iii	A. H. M. Jones, *The Later Roman Empire, 284–602: A Social, Economic, and Administrative Survey*, 3 vols. + maps (Oxford, 1964)
Kellner	J. B. Kellner, *Der heilige Ambrosius, Bischof von Mailand, als Erklärer des alten Testaments. Ein Beitrag zur Geschichte der biblischen Exegese* (Regensburg, 1893)
Klein	R. Klein, *Die Sklaverei in der Sicht der Bischöfe Ambrosius und Augustinus* (Stuttgart, 1988)
Krabinger	J. G. Krabinger, *S. Ambrosii episcopi Mediolanensis De Officiis Ministrorum* (Tübingen, 1857)
Lenox-Conyngham	A. Lenox-Conyngham, 'Ambrose and Philosophy', in L. R. Wickham and C. P. Bammel (eds.), *Christian Faith and Greek Philosophy in Late Antiquity: Essays in Tribute to George Christopher Stead, VChr*, suppl. 19 (Leiden, 1993), 112–28
Lizzi	R. Lizzi, *Vescovi e strutture ecclesiastiche nella città tardoantica (L'"Italia Annonaria' nel IV–V secolo d. C.)* (Como, 1989)
Löpfe	D. Löpfe, *Die Tugendlehre des heiligen Ambrosius* (Sarnen, 1951)
LP	*Le Liber Pontificalis*, ed. L. Duchesne, 2 vols. (Rome, 1886–92)
LXX	Septuagint [see Introduction, n. 291]

McLynn	N. B. McLynn, *Ambrose of Milan: Church and Court in a Christian Capital* (Berkeley and Los Angeles, 1994).
Madec	G. Madec, *Saint Ambroise et la philosophie* (Paris, 1974)
Maes	B. Maes, *La Loi naturelle selon saint Ambroise de Milan* (Rome, 1967)
Markschies	C. Markschies, *Ambrosius von Mailand und die Trinitätstheologie: Kirchen- und theologiegeschichtliche Studie zu Antiarianismus und Neunizänismus bei Ambrosius und im lateinischen Westen (364–381 n. Chr.)* (Tübingen, 1995)
Mohrmann	C. Mohrmann, *Etudes sur le Latin des chrétiens*, 4 vols. (Rome, 1961–77)
Monachino	V. Monachino, *S. Ambrogio e la cura pastorale a Milano nel secolo IV* (Milan, 1973)
Moorhead	J. Moorhead, *Ambrose: Church and Society in the Late Roman World* (London and New York, 1999)
Morgan	R. Morgan, *The Imagery of Light in St Ambrose's Theology* (Melbourne, 1998)
Morino	C. Morino, *Church and State in the Teaching of St Ambrose*, ET (Washington, DC, 1969)
Muckle	J. T. Muckle, 'The De Officiis Ministrorum of Saint Ambrose: An Example of the Process of the Christianization of the Latin Language', *MS* 1 (1939), 63–80
Nec timeo mori	L. F. Pizzolato and M. Rizzi (eds.), *Nec timeo mori: Atti del Congresso internazionale di studi ambrosiani nel XVI centenario della morte di sant'Ambrogio, Milano, 4–11 aprile 1997* (Milan, 1998)
Niederhuber	J. E. Niederhuber, *Des heiligen Kirchenlehrers Ambrosius von Mailand, Pflichtenlehre und ausgewählte Kleinere-*

	schriften, Bibliothek der Kirchenväter, 3/32 (Kempten and Munich, 1917)
Niederhuber, *Eschatologie*	J. E. Niederhuber, *Die Eschatologie des heiligen Ambrosius: Eine patristische Studie* (Paderborn, 1907)
Niederhuber, *Reiche Gottes*	J. E. Niederhuber, *Die Lehre des hl. Ambrosius vom Reiche Gottes auf Erden: Eine patristische Studie* (Mainz, 1904)
NT	New Testament
Oberhelman	S. M. Oberhelman, *Rhetoric and Homiletics in Fourth-Century Christian Literature: Prose Rhythm, Oratorical Style, and Preaching in the Works of Ambrose, Jerome, and Augustine* (Atlanta, GA, 1991)
OCD	*The Oxford Classical Dictionary,* 3rd edn., ed. S. Hornblower and A. Spawforth (Oxford, 1996)
OCT	Oxford Classical Texts (Oxford)
ODCC	*The Oxford Dictionary of the Christian Church,* 3rd edn., ed. E. A. Livingstone (Oxford, 1997)
O'Donnell i–iii	J. J. O'Donnell, *Augustine, Confessions: Introduction, Text, and Commentary,* 3 vols. (Oxford, 1992)
OT	Old Testament
Palanque	J.-R. Palanque, *Saint Ambroise et l'empire romain. Contribution à l'histoire des rapports de l'Eglise et de l'Etat à la fin du quatrième siècle* (Paris, 1933)
Paredi	A. Paredi, *Saint Ambrose: His Life and Times,* ET (Notre Dame, IN, 1964)
Pétré	H. Pétré, *Caritas: Etude sur le vocabulaire latin de la charité chrétienne* (Louvain, 1948)
PG	*Patrologia Graeca,* ed. J.-P. Migne (Paris, 1857–66)
Pizzolato	L. F. Pizzolato, *La dottrina esegetica di sant'Ambrogio* (Milan, 1978)

PL	*Patrologia Latina*, ed. J.-P. Migne (Paris, 1844–64)
PLRE	A. H. M. Jones, J. R. Martindale, and J. Morris, *The Prosopography of the Later Roman Empire*, 4 vols. (Cambridge, 1980–92)
P-W	A. Pauly, *Realenzyklopädie der klassischen Altertumswissenschaft*, ed. G. Wissowa and A. Kroll (Stuttgart, 1893–)
RAC	*Reallexikon für Antike und Christentum*, ed. T. Klauser, E. Dassmann, *et al.* (Stuttgart, 1950–)
Ramsey	B. Ramsey, *Ambrose* (London and New York, 1997)
Ring	T. G. Ring, *Auctoritas bei Tertullian, Cyprian und Ambrosius* (Würzburg, 1975)
Sauer	R. Sauer, *Studien zur Pflichtenlehre des Ambrosius von Mailand*, Diss. (Würzburg, 1981)
Savon	H. Savon, *Ambroise de Milan (340–397)* (Paris, 1997)
Savon, 'Intentions'	H. Savon, 'Les Intentions de saint Ambroise dans la préface du *De officiis*', in M. Soetard (ed.), *Valeurs dans le stoïcisme, du portique à nos jours: Textes rassemblés en hommage à Michel Spanneut* (Lille, 1993), 155–69
SCh	*Sources Chrétiennes* (Paris)
Schmidt	T. Schmidt, *Ambrosius, sein Werk De officiis libri III und die Stoa* (Augsburg, 1897)
Seibel	W. Seibel, *Fleisch und Geist beim heiligen Ambrosius* (Munich, 1958)
SP	*Studia Patristica* (Berlin; Kalamazoo, MI)
Steidle, 'Beobachtungen'	W. Steidle, 'Beobachtungen zu des Ambrosius Schrift, De Officiis', *VChr* 38 (1984), 18–66

Steidle, 'Beobachtungen 2'	W. Steidle, 'Beobachtungen zum Gedankengang im 2. Buch von Ambrosius, De Officiis', *VChr* 39 (1985), 280–98
Stelzenberger	J. Stelzenberger, *Die Beziehungen der frühchristlichen Sittenlehre zur Ethik der Stoa: Eine moralgeschichtliche Studie* (Munich, 1933)
SVF	H. von Arnim (ed.), *Stoicorum Veterum Fragmenta*, 3 vols. (Leipzig, 1903–5); indices as vol. 4 by M. Adler (Leipzig, 1924)
TDNT	*Theological Dictionary of the New Testament*, ed. G. Kittel and G. Friedrich, ET, G. Bromiley, 10 vols. (Grand Rapids, 1964–76)
Testard i–ii	M. Testard, *Saint Ambroise: Les Devoirs: Texte établi, traduit et annoté*, 2 vols. (Paris, 1984–92)
Testard, 'Aveu'	M. Testard, 'Jérôme et Ambroise. Sur un "aveu" du *De officiis* de l'évêque de Milan', in Y.-M. Duval (ed.), *Jérôme entre l'Occident et l'Orient: XVIe centenaire du départ de saint Jérôme de Rome et de son installation à Bethléem. Actes du Colloque de Chantilly 1986* (Paris, 1988), 227–54
Testard, '*Conscientia*'	M. Testard, 'Observations sur le thème de la *conscientia* dans le *De officiis ministrorum* de saint Ambroise', *REL* 51 (1973), 219–61
Testard, 'Etude'	M. Testard, 'Etude sur la composition dans le *De officiis ministrorum* de saint Ambroise', in Y.-M. Duval (ed.), *Ambroise de Milan. XVIᵉ Centenaire de son élection épiscopale. Dix études* (Paris, 1974), 155–97
Testard, 'Observations'	M. Testard, 'Le *De officiis* de saint Ambroise. Observations philologiques

	et historiques sur le sens et le contexte du traité', *RecAug* 28 (1995), 3–35
Testard, 'Recherches'	M. Testard, 'Recherches sur quelques méthodes de travail de saint Ambroise dans le *De officiis*', *RecAug* 24 (1989), 65–122
Thamin	R. Thamin, *Saint Ambroise et la morale chrétienne au IVe siècle: Etude comparée des traités 'Des Devoirs' de Cicéron et de saint Ambroise* (Paris, 1895)
TLL	*Thesaurus Linguae Latinae* (Leipzig, 1900–)
Toscani	G. Toscani, *Teologia della Chiesa in sant'Ambrogio* (Milan, 1974)
TRE	*Theologische Realenzyklopädie*, ed. G. Krause, G. Müller, *et al.* (Berlin and New York, 1976–)
TU	*Texte und Untersuchungen zur Geschichte der altchristlichen Literatur* (Leipzig; Berlin)
Vasey	V. R. Vasey, *The Social Ideas in the Works of St Ambrose: A Study on De Nabuthe* (Rome, 1982)
Vermeulen	A. J. Vermeulen, *The Semantic Development of* Gloria *in Early-Christian Latin* (Nijmegen, 1956)
Vescovi e pastori i–ii	*Vescovi e pastori in epoca teodosiana. In occasione del XVI centenario della consacrazione episcopale di s. Agostino, 396–1996. XXV Incontro di studiosi dell'antichità cristiana, Roma, 8–11 maggio 1996*, 2 vols. (Rome, 1997)
VL	*Vetus Latina* [see Introduction, n. 291]
Vulg.	Vulgate [see Introduction, n. 291]
White	C. White, *Christian Friendship in the Fourth Century* (Cambridge, 1992)
Williams	D. H. Williams, *Ambrose of Milan and the End of the Nicene–Arian Conflicts* (Oxford, 1995)
Winterbottom	M. Winterbottom, 'The Text of

	Ambrose's *De Officiis*', *JThS* NS 46 (1995), 559–66
Zelzer, 'Beurteilung'	K. Zelzer, 'Zur Beurteilung der Cicero-Imitatio bei Ambrosius, De officiis', *WS* 90 (1977), 168–91
Zelzer, 'Randbemerkungen'	K. Zelzer, 'Randbemerkungen zu Absicht und Arbeitsweise des Ambrosius in De Officiis', *WS* 107/8 (1994–5), 481–93

Note on Cicero Citations

Citations of Cicero, *De officiis* are from *M. Tulli Ciceronis De officiis recognovit brevique adnotatione critica instruxit* M. Winterbottom, OCT (Oxford, 1994). Citations of Cicero, *Laelius: De amicitia* are from *M. Tulli Ciceronis scripta quae manserunt omnia*, fasc. 47: *Cato Maior; Laelius recognovit* K. Simbeck (with *De gloria, recognovit* O. Plasberg), Bibliotheca Scriptorum Graecorum et Romanorum Teubneriana, 47 (Stuttgart, 1961), though sometimes with altered punctuation. The quotation from Cicero, *De finibus* in the commentary on 2.4 is from *M. Tulli Ciceronis De finibus bonorum et malorum libri quinque recognovit brevique adnotatione critica instruxit* L. D. Reynolds, OCT (Oxford, 1998).

ABBREVIATIONS AND EDITIONS
OF OTHER WORKS BY AMBROSE

Abr.	*De Abraham*, CSEL 32.1.501–638
Apol.	*De apologia prophetae David*, CSEL 32.2.299–355
Apol. alt.	*Apologia David altera*, CSEL 32.2.359–408
Bon. mort.	*De bono mortis*, CSEL 32.1.703–53
Cain	*De Cain et Abel*, CSEL 32.1.339–409
Elia	*De Elia et ieiunio*, CSEL 32.2.411–65
Ep(p)./Epp. extra coll.	*Epistulae/Epistulae extra collectionem*, CSEL 82.10/1–4. Enumeration follows this edition; Maurist edition references are given in square brackets. *Ep.* 75a = *Sermo contra Auxentium* [21a]
Ex.	*Exaemeron*, CSEL 32.1.3–261
Exc. fr.	*De excessu fratris sui Satyri*, CSEL 73.7.209–325
Exh. virg.	*Exhortatio virginitatis*, PL 16.351–80
Expl. Ps.	*Explanatio Psalmorum XII*, CSEL 64.6.3–397
Expos. Ps. 118	*Expositio Psalmi CXVIII*, CSEL 62.5.3–510
Fid.	*De Fide ad Gratianum*, CSEL 78.8.3–307
Fug.	*De fuga saeculi*, CSEL 32.2.163–207
Hymn(s)	*Hymn(s)*, ed. J. Fontaine (Paris, 1992)
Iac.	*De Iacob et vita beata*, CSEL 32.2.3–70
Inc.	*De incarnationis dominicae sacramento*, CSEL 79.9.225–81
Inst. virg.	*De institutione virginis*, PL 16.319–48
Interp.	*De interpellatione Iob et David*, CSEL 32.2.211–96
Ios.	*De Ioseph*, CSEL 32.2.73-122
Is.	*De Isaac vel anima*, CSEL 32.1.641–700
Luc.	*Expositio evangelii secundum Lucam*, CCL 14.1–400

Myst.	*De mysteriis*, SCh 25 bis
Nab.	*De Nabuthae historia*, CSEL 32.2.469–516
Noe	*De Noe et arca*, CSEL 32.1.413–97
Ob. Theod.	*De obitu Theodosii*, CSEL 73.7.371–401
Ob. Val.	*De obitu Valentiniani*, CSEL 73.7.329–67
Paen.	*De paenitentia*, SCh 179
Parad.	*De paradiso*, CSEL 32.1.265–336
Patr.	*De patriarchis*, CSEL 32.2.125–60
Sacr.	*De sacramentis*, SCh 25 bis
Spir.	*De Spiritu Sancto*, CSEL 79.9.15–222
Tob.	*De Tobia*, CSEL 32.2.519–73
Vid.	*De viduis*, PL 16.247–76
Virg.	*De virginibus*, ed. I. Cazzaniga (Turin, 1948)
Virgt.	*De virginitate*, ed. I. Cazzaniga (Turin, 1954)
Acta conc. Aquil.	*Acta concili Aquileiensis* from *Gesta episcoporum Aquileiae adversum haereticos Arianos*, CSEL 82.10/3.315–68

Citations of Paulinus of Milan, *Vita Ambrosii* (Paul. *VA*) are from the edition by M. Pellegrino, *Paulino di Milano: Vita di S. Ambrogio* (Rome, 1961).

Introduction

I. TITLE

For the last three centuries, Ambrose's most influential moral work has generally been called *De officiis ministrorum*. This title was used in the late seventeenth century by the Maurist editors, who maintained that it was based on evidence *ex manuscriptis fere omnibus ac notae melioris*.[1] The validity of their claim has been assumed by a majority of modern students,[2] and many works of reference continue to cite the treatise by this name.

The assumption is mistaken, for three reasons. First, in the two primary families of manuscripts the text is consistently entitled *De officiis*, not *De officiis ministrorum*. In the third family, both names can be found within the same manuscript, and in several cases it is clear that the longer title is simply a corrective gloss on the shorter.[3] Secondly, other early Christian writers refer to the work simply as *De officiis*: Augustine, *Ep.* 82.21: *nisi forte nomen te moveat, quia non tam usitatum est in ecclesiasticis libris vocabulum officii, quod Ambrosius noster non timuit, qui suos libros utilium praeceptionum plenos 'de officiis' voluit appellare*; Cassiodorus, *Inst.* 1.16.4: *utiles etiam sunt ad instructionem ecclesiasticae disciplinae memorati sancti Ambrosii de officiis melliflui libri tres*; and the Carolingian *vita Ambrosii*, 16: *primam itaque ecclesiasticorum ordinum institutionem et catholicae vitae formulam in*

---

[1] PL 16, 21–2; cf. 25–6 n. 1.

[2] e.g. Förster, 176; Palanque, 453.

[3] For details, see Testard i. 49–52. The majority of Renaissance editors also support the shorter title: Testard, 'Etude', 195 n. 83, and 157–9 (curiously, Testard retains the form *De officiis ministrorum* in the title of that essay, though he abandons it in later work).

libris suis, quos 'de officiis' praenotavit, luculenter inseruit et evidenter expressit.[4]

Finally, the language of the text itself indicates that Ambrose is writing *de officiis: successit animo de officiis scribere* (1.23); *videamus utrum res ipsa conveniat scribere de officiis* (1.25); *de officiis adgrediamur dicere* (1.65); *accidit ut scripturi de officiis* (1.231); *superiore libro de officiis tractavimus* (2.1); *sermo de officiis* (2.25). The *officia* which he prescribes certainly relate in the first instance to clerics: *ad officia ecclesiae* (1.184); *ad officium ecclesiae* (1.186); *in ecclesiastico . . . officio* (1.218); *officium sacerdotis* (2.69); *ecclesiastici ordinis officium* (3.58); *in sacerdotis officio* (3.59).[5] But the *officia* of the clerical life are pointedly compared with the responsibilities enjoined upon those who engage in the service of the *saeculum* (e.g. 1.186). Ambrose is thinking above all of the advice given in his literary model, the *De officiis* of Cicero [Introduction III]: he aims to construct a distinct alternative to the ethical principles of secular philosophy, and to show that Christian morality is established on quite different grounds (1.27–9). The retention of Cicero's title is part of this deliberate contrast between Christian and pagan versions of *officia*.

The title *De officiis ministrorum* has proved convenient for the purposes of distinguishing Ambrose's treatise from its Ciceronian forebear, but it lacks any serious support, and tends to obscure Ambrose's clear intentions for his work: it deserves to be laid to rest.[6]

---

[4] In Courcelle, *Recherches*, 59.

[5] It is a mistake, then, to object to the longer title on the grounds that the substance of the work is not primarily aimed at an ecclesiastical readership, as some nineteenth-century critics, exaggerating the weight of the Stoic influence in Ambrose's intellectual message, sought to do: e.g. Ewald, 15 n. 1; Schmidt, 11 n. 1. On the other hand, R. O. Gilbert, in his edition in Bibliotheca Patrum Ecclesiasticorum Latinorum selecta, VIII/1 (Leipzig, 1839), was apparently so convinced of the ecclesiastical nature of the work that he entitled his volume *Sancti Ambrosii episcopi Mediolanensis De officiis clericorum libri tres*, while inexplicably printing the words *De officiis ministrorum* at the top of his text (26). But Ambrose's language in 1.86, *unde prudenter facitis convenire ecclesiasticis, et maxime* **ministrorum officiis** *arbitror*, the sole textual foundation for the addition of *ministrorum*, cannot provide the basis for a title: Ambrose is simply sounding a familiar note about the high standards of *officia* required of those consecrated to ministerial office.

[6] So also Claus, 65–6; Sauer, 4, 213 n. 36; Banterle, 16.

II. DATE

Ambrose's writings are notoriously difficult to date.[7] This is partly because they often amount to or incorporate revised versions of sermons: do identifiable historical references tell us when the texts were edited into their final form, or do they hint merely at the provenance of individual oral sections? Even where the works do not derive from a homiletic base, their chronological context can be equally elusive. In the case of *De officiis*, there is insufficient evidence to support the widely held theory that the text was pieced together out of earlier addresses [Introduction V], but here too it is impossible to pin down a precise date of writing; we can only establish a broad period within which the work is likely to have originated.

Even at that, the reliable markers are few. We have no information as to when the treatise was first in circulation. Judging by the thematic parallels between *De officiis* and Jerome's *Epistle* 52 to Nepotian,[8] it is possible that Jerome had read Ambrose's work when he composed his *libellus* on the clerical life in 393, but there is no way of proving this conclusively [Introduction VIII]. Within the text itself, some supposed clues to chronology are simply irrelevant. 1.245 has sometimes been thought to allude to the overthrow of statues of Maximus in the late summer of 388, but the language is much too general to bear such a specific construction.[9] Linguistic

[7] See H. Savon, 'Quelques remarques sur la chronologie des œuvres de saint Ambroise', *SP* 10 (1970), 156–60; M. Zelzer, 'Zur Chronologie der Werke des Ambrosius. Überblick über die Forschung von 1974 bis 1997', in *Nec timeo mori*, 73–92.

[8] See I. J. Davidson, 'Pastoral Theology at the End of the Fourth Century: Ambrose and Jerome', *SP* 33 (1997), 295–301. I follow the dating of *Ep.* 52 proposed by P. Nautin, 'Etudes de chronologie hiéronymienne (393–397)', *REAug* 20 (1974), 251–3, also adopted by S. Rebenich, *Hieronymus und sein Kreis: Prosopographische und sozialgeschichtliche Untersuchungen* (Stuttgart, 1992), 202 n. 382, *contra* F. Cavallera, *Saint Jérôme: sa vie et son œuvre*, 2 vols. (Louvain and Paris, 1922), i. 183 n. 2; ii. 44; J. Labourt, *Saint Jérôme: Lettres* ii (Paris, 1951), 171 n. 2; and J. N. D. Kelly, *Jerome: His Life, Writings, and Controversies* (London, 1975), 190 n. 59, who say 394. Jerome writes *Ep.* 52 *post annos decem* (52.17.1) since the time of *Ep.* 22 (384), but this is by inclusive reckoning.

[9] See commentary ad loc., *pace* Palanque, 526.

parallels with other Ambrosian works also prove nothing about the relative chronology of any of the texts in question. The use of similar language in, say, *De Iacob et vita beata*, or *Expositio Psalmi 118*, or *De Interpellatione Iob et David*, or *De Elia et ieiunio*, indicates only that Ambrose, like the rest of us, was in the habit of repeating ideas and phrases; in itself it tells us nothing about the order in which he wrote any of these passages.[10]

Certain other historical allusions can only be identified very tentatively. 2.136–9 responds to Arian criticism of the author's decision to sell church plate to ransom prisoners *Illyrici vastitate et Thraciae* (2.70). This may well refer to the aftermath of the battle of Adrianople in August 378, when the ravages of the victorious Goths extended to the foot of the Illyrian Alps, and Milan proved a haven for refugees; nevertheless, certainty on the matter is not possible, since captives were ransomed throughout the late 370s.[11] 2.150–1 narrates a *recens exemplum* of an attempt by the civil authorities to confiscate property which a widow had entrusted to the care of the church at Pavia, and it is said that the emperor himself was involved in the affair. Valentinian II was at Pavia in the spring of 386, and this offers a possible setting; but again we cannot be absolutely sure, and there is no likelihood of taking the matter further.[12]

An approximate *terminus post quem* can be established on the basis of just two passages. In 1.72, Ambrose speaks of a man who 'deserted the faith' *Arianae infestationis tempore*. This is almost certainly a reference to Ambrose's confrontation with his homoian opponents in 385–6, and most probably to its

[10] *Pace* e.g. W. Wilbrand, 'Zur Chronologie einiger Schriften des hl. Ambrosius', *HJ* 41 (1921), 1–19, at 14–15, on *Expos. Ps. 118*. 5.27 and *Off.* 2.26. Homes Dudden ii, 683 n. 6 rightly warns against inferring chronological relationships from the similarities between *Off.* 1.202–3 and *Iac.* 2.42, 45–58.

[11] The period after Adrianople almost certainly witnessed greater numbers of such transactions, however, and does make for a likelier context.

[12] Palanque, 526, is wrong to locate the affair in the context of the arbitrary exactions of the usurper Maximus during his occupation of Italy in 388, in view of Ambrose's references to *praeceptis imperialibus* and to the *imperator*; see Homes Dudden i. 119–20; ii. 694–5; McLynn, 286 n. 139.

crisis-point in the spring of 386.[13] In 3.49–51, there is an anonymous attack on a certain urban prefect of Rome for his mismanagement of a recent temporary food shortage in the city. There is a strong probability that the target of the censure is Q. Aurelius Symmachus, who served as prefect in 384;[14] it is also likely that some of the Italian *corporati* whose case Ambrose champions against the prefect's unjust treatment had made their way to Milan, where they had backed the bishop (and suffered for it) in the stand-off in 386. If these identifications are correct, Ambrose certainly cannot have written *De officiis* prior to the summer of 386.[15] If it is right to suppose that *Arianae infestationis tempore* in 1.72 is not a likely turn of phrase to describe events which had taken place only a matter of weeks or months before, it may be better to assume that he composed the work later than that.

Overall the likeliest setting for the writing of *De officiis* is some time in the late 380s, the period of Ambrose's greatest literary activity. In its attempt to subsume and renovate classical stereotypes under the authority of a triumphant biblical gospel, the work epitomizes its author's quest in these years to demonstrate the cultural pre-eminence of his Christian message. *De officiis* belongs in a time of social consolidation; more exactly than that we cannot say.

[13] See McLynn, 158–219, especially 181 ff. For further discussion, see commentary ad loc.

[14] This happened *proxime* (3.49), picking up *nuper* in Cicero, *Off.* 3.47. Testard i. 46 n. 2, argues that this *proxime* (and the similar *recens* in 2.150), may simply indicate the time at which Ambrose composes these particular passages, rather than revealing the date of the work as a whole. Testard is assuming, however, that *Off.* comprises various disparate texts which have been redacted into a final version, a theory for which evidence is lacking. The Roman famine described in 3.46–8 can be placed in 376.

[15] In 1.78, Ambrose speaks of his earlier exposition of Noah's ark as a picture of the human body in *Noe* 13–30: if, as some scholars have thought, *Noe* contains allusions to Adrianople, the death of Valens, and the Gothic ravages, that treatise can possibly be dated to the autumn of 378, but in any case there is little doubt that it was published prior to 386, perhaps in 384 (Palanque, 499–500; Homes Dudden ii. 681, say late 378; O. Bardenhewer, *Geschichte der altchristlichen Literatur* iii: *Das vierte Jahrhundert mit Ausschluss der Schriftsteller syrischer Zunge* (Freiburg, 1923), 511, suggests 378 or 379; others are less sure: K. Schenkl in CSEL 32.1, xii, considers 384 more likely, and Savon, 'Quelques remarques sur la chronologie', 157–8, rejects Palanque's dating without committing himself).

III. MODEL

(i) Cicero: background, sources, argument

Ambrose's literary model, the *De officiis* of Cicero, was produced at the end of the ambitious series of philosophical works
which Cicero wrote between late 46 and December 44 BC. In
these essays Cicero sought to bring together the fruits of his
lifelong interest in Hellenistic philosophy, and to make a name
for himself as the initiator of an independent Roman tradition
of philosophical thinking by attempting to render conceptual
ideas which had long been mediated in Greek into the less
flexible structures of the Latin language.[16] The death of his
daughter Tullia in February of 45 BC had intensified his
resolve, as he had given himself more and more to philosophy
in a quest for personal consolation.[17] Cicero's rapid programme
of writing, covering epistemology, natural philosophy, and
ethics, was driven by an urgent practical concern: to sketch
an intellectual stance that would prove morally responsible
amidst the ambiguities of life in the turmoil threatening the
Roman Republic. *De officiis*, written in the autumn of 44 BC,[18]
reflects Cicero's anxiety over the political crisis then facing
Rome. The assassination of Julius Caesar earlier that year,
legitimate tyrannicide though it was in Cicero's eyes, had not
brought the restoration of the Republic which he so desired,
and the likelihood of civil war was increasing.[19] The treatise is

[16] On the rationale behind the philosophical texts, cf. Cicero, *ND* 1.6–9;
Div. 2.1–7; *Off.* 2.2–8. See further J. G. F. Powell (ed.), *Cicero the Philosopher: Twelve Papers* (Oxford, 1995), 1–35.

[17] On the practical focus which Cicero's quest to deal with his grief lent to
his writing, see A. Erskine, 'Cicero and the Expression of Grief', in S. Morton
Braund and C. Gill (eds.), *The Passions in Roman Thought and Literature*
(Cambridge, 1997), 36–47.

[18] The earliest reference to work on *Off.* 1–2 is from 28 Oct. 44 BC (*Att.*
15.13.6). These books were completed by 5 Nov. (*Att.* 16.11.4). *Off.* 3 was
delayed as Cicero waited for some writings of Posidonius, but he had received
one of them by mid-November (*Att.* 16.14.4). The work must almost
certainly have been finished by 9 Dec., since Cicero had by then returned
to Rome from Puteoli (*Fam.* 11.5.1).

[19] Cicero had returned to Rome in the late summer of 44 BC, hoping that a
compromise was possible between Antony and the 'Liberators' (*Att.* 16.7;

addressed to Cicero's son, Marcus, who at the time of writing was aged twenty-one and studying oratory and philosophy at Athens, under the tutelage of the eminent Peripatetic, Cratippus. He was a young man of whom much was expected, but he had given his father cause for concern, having scarcely proved a model student.[20] Shunning the dialogue-form, Cicero confronts his son bluntly: Marcus may be an independent adult with ideas of his own, but he evidently needs to be taught philosophy before he can discuss it. At a critical age, on the verge of a career which would inevitably be measured with reference to his father's, Marcus was in line for some heavyweight paternal guidance.[21] But Cicero was also determined to make his voice heard among all young Romans with aspirations to a public life. For all the gathering storm-clouds, he hoped there might yet be a renaissance of sound leadership, if the rising generation could acquire a due sense of social responsibility and demonstrate a proper dedication to noble causes like advocacy and popular generosity—the sort of activities which had traditionally promoted the *right* kind of political *gloria*. *De officiis* is designed as a kind of 'manual of civic virtue',[22] the advice of a self-consciously illustrious elder to all potential young leaders in an age of upheaval, explaining how the old political values might yet flourish once more.

In his earlier philosophical texts, Cicero had sought to establish that human beings were free but socially responsible

Fam. 10.1.1), but his expectations were short-lived. Witnessing Antony's increasingly desperate attempts to preserve his own power by capturing the favour of Caesar's veterans against the threat from his formidable rival Octavian, Cicero had launched into his series of notorious *Philippic Orations* denouncing Antony—the course which would ultimately lead to his proscription and death. *Off.* was produced in the same weeks as the impassioned *Phil.* 2. On the context, see T. N. Mitchell, *Cicero, the Senior Statesman* (New Haven, CT and London, 1991), 273 ff.

[20] Cf. e.g. *Att.* 6.1.12; 13.1.1; *Fam.* 16.21.6. See Dyck, 10–16; and M. Testard, 'Le fils de Cicéron, destinataire du De officiis', *BAGB* 1962, ii. 198–213. *Off.* was delivered as a substitute for a disciplinary visit which Cicero had had to abandon in the summer of 44 BC when he returned to Rome (*Off.* 3.121).

[21] In *Part. Or.*, Marcus is given the role of an enquiring pupil; in *Off.*, though he is now decided in his Peripatetic sympathies, he is still to be instructed: 1.1–4; 3.5–6, 121.

[22] R. Syme, *The Roman Revolution* (Oxford, 1939), 145.

moral agents. Even if, as the Academics said, they could never be absolutely certain as to the reliability of the knowledge on which their choices must be founded, they were capable of behaving honourably on the basis of probabilities.[23] The contours of such behaviour were now, for Cicero, best delineated by Stoicism, and particularly by the 'middle' Stoa, which shared something of the pragmatism to which he himself inclined and of the Peripatetic teaching to which Marcus was being exposed at Athens. *Officia* is Cicero's equivalent of the Stoic καθῆκον, rendered conventionally as 'duty' though more literally as 'appropriate/fitting action' and so 'proper function' or 'good form'.[24] The root idea is not a Kantian notion of an absolute imperative to do something that is ethically required; it is rather the obligation to do that for which one can give a reasonable defence, and hence to act in a way that is appropriate or natural to one's constitution, first as a human being, and then, in middle Stoicism, as a specific individual in specific circumstances.[25] Cicero's rendering of the singular Greek καθῆκον with the Latin plural, *officia*, seems to reflect a typically Roman conviction that duties to state, family, friends, neighbours, allies, inferiors, and enemies are like a web of commitments of varying intensity, a complex of responsibilities determined by degrees of relationship and circumstance.

The primary model for Cicero's *De officiis* was a treatise by Panaetius of Rhodes (*c*.180–109 BC), περὶ τοῦ καθήκοντος, written around 139/8 BC, and now lost.[26] Panaetius' work set out to discuss appropriate action in three stages. In order to act well, Panaetius argued, it was necessary to ask, first, whether a

[23] H. A. K. Hunt, *The Humanism of Cicero* (Melbourne, 1954), sees a deliberate progression in the philosophical texts from Cicero's refutation of theological determinism to his presentation of a socially focused ethic of appropriate action. Cicero himself says little to indicate that he is following such a systematic strategy; Hunt pays too little attention to the personal and political dimensions. Nevertheless, there are some significant thematic connections between *Off.* and the preceding texts on rhetoric and philosophy. P. Mackendrick, *The Philosophical Books of Cicero* (London, 1989), 253, is right to regard *Off.* as in some sense 'part of a conscious overall plan'.
[24] 'Proper function' is used by A. A. Long and D. N. Sedley, *The Hellenistic Philosophers*, 2 vols. (Cambridge, 1987), i. 359–68; ii. 355–64; Dyck, 3–8 and *passim*, prefers 'appropriate action'.
[25] The principle can also be applied to animals (*DL* 7.107).
[26] It was still extant in the mid-2nd cent. AD: Aulus Gellius, *NA* 13.28.1.

particular course is morally good (καλόν) or not; secondly, whether it is beneficial or expedient (συμφέρον) or not; and thirdly, what one should do when the morally good and the beneficial or expedient appear to conflict (Cicero, *Off.* 1.9; 3.7). Panaetius' text comprised three books, but although the author lived for thirty years after stopping work on it he never dealt with the third question, on the apparent conflict between virtue and expediency (Cicero, *Att.* 16.11.4; *Off.* 3.7–16, 33–4). Cicero retained the three-book framework, translating καλόν with *honestum* and συμφέρον with *utile*, but to him it made more sense to devote one book to each of the three core questions, so he compressed the material which Panaetius covered in three books into two, and devoted the third to the theme left unfinished by Panaetius (*Att.* 16.11.4; cf. Pliny, *NH, praef.* 22–3). He expressed admiration for Panaetius' attractive style and practical good sense (*Fin.* 4.79 (also 4.23); *Off.* 2.35; cf. Seneca, *Ep.* 116.5), but insisted that his imitation was not slavish (*Off.* 1.6–10, 152–61; 2.60; 3.7–16). The Panaetian model ultimately proved inadequate, not only because it failed to treat the question of the relationship between the honourable and the beneficial, but also because its division of the first two topics was not comprehensive. In the first place, Cicero contended, it is not enough simply to ask if something is 'honourable' or not, for there will be occasions when two courses of action are *both* 'honourable': we must therefore be prepared to compare them, and to enquire which is the *more* honourable. Similarly, there may be two actions *both* of which are 'beneficial', and we need then to ask which is the *more* beneficial (*Off.* 1.10; 2.9). Supplementary sections were accordingly appended to his books 1 and 2, dealing with these issues (*Off.* 1.152–61 and 2.88–9).

For the third book, Cicero had planned to make use of a discussion of duty by another middle Stoic, Panaetius' distinguished pupil and his own former teacher, Posidonius of Apamea (135–50 BC). He requested a summary of Posidonius' work from his friend, Athenodorus Calvus (*Att.* 16.11.3; cf. 16.14.3–4), but it apparently proved a disappointment, touching only briefly on the relationship of the honourable and the beneficial (*Off.* 3.8). However, its discussion of duties for particular circumstances seems to have provided him with

some practical illustrations (cf. *Off.* 1.159). There are also traces of some influence on Cicero from another of Panaetius' pupils, Hecato of Rhodes, in the third book (*Off.* 3.63, 89), but Cicero depended more upon his own resources in that section than in either of the first two books (*Off.* 3.34).[27]

Cicero's treatment of the honourable in book 1 is organized around the four cardinal virtues of prudence, justice, courage, and temperance, the traditional Socratic canon which was maintained by Stoicism.[28] Cicero does not, however, present these virtues in consistently Stoic terms; he gauges their significance according to a criterion of practical usefulness. His thrust is the inculcation of practical virtue, and so the exhortation in the case of the first virtue is not to be diverted from a life of action by a desire for learning: practical wisdom takes priority over theoretical knowledge. Justice, which Cicero regards as the most important source of duty (an Aristotelian preference), is twofold in nature. Its first part, justice proper, consists in not doing harm unless one is harmed, and in maintaining the *suum cuique* principle: public goods must be treated as public, private as private. There is a fundamentally social criterion to be observed when it comes to acquiring property, say, or honouring public commitments, or dealing with enemies, or waging war, or protecting the oppressed: the public good must come first. The other aspect of justice is beneficence or generosity. Here, justice must ensure that giving harms no one, and that it is proportionate to the means of the giver and the merits of the recipient. Goodwill, the motivating factor, is measured in terms of a person's obligations to those who love him, to those to whom he is indebted, to those from whom he desires a return of favour, and, more broadly, to those with whom he has a clear social relationship—which is, in reality, the entire human race. On the Stoic principle of οἰκείωσις, fellow-human beings, fellow-citizens, family, friends, and compatriots are all part of a single nexus.

Courage, too, is viewed in social terms. One should aspire to be free from the passions of desire, fear, pain, pleasure, and anger, and the quality of one's magnanimity ought to be tested

---

[27] On the sources generally, see M. Testard, *Cicéron: Les Devoirs*, 2 vols. (Paris, 1965), i. 25–49; on Panaetius, see Dyck, 17–29.

[28] See commentary on 1.115.

by a vigorous participation in public life. Physical courage is inferior (though physical training has its own worth), and discretion is necessary in martial contests, so that the desire for glory does not come before the good of the state. More important is the demonstration of inner strength by political conduct which is free from partisanship, self-seeking, vindictiveness, and anger; moderation and humility should be shown in success. Temperance consists of modesty and propriety (doing what is seemly, or *decorum*). The latter means following nature's norm in the subjection of the appetites and passions to reason. But this process should take due account of individual endowments and circumstances, say in the choice of a career, and each person needs to behave according to the standards appropriate to his age, which will differ in old age and youth. Modesty is important in physical appearance, self-control, formal speech, and informal conversation. The casuistry and aesthetic orientation with which Cicero works—seemliness involves being *seen* to do the right thing in a given context— are strongly Panaetian. When it comes to his own comparison of the virtues in order to determine which conduct is most conducive to the fulfilment of social duty, Cicero argues that wisdom and courage must serve the cause of justice, and temperance must exercise control over the action thus undertaken in the interests of justice.

The upshot of Cicero's presentation of the *honestum* is that virtue is no longer seen in classical Stoic terms as simply the supreme and sole good: it is thought of, rather, in a practical sense, as the standard by which the benefit of social *utilitas* is measured and attained. In book 2, Cicero lays the foundations for a direct equation of virtue with expediency: behaviour which is honourable assists in attaining to that which is practically advantageous. The greatest benefit is to acquire the help and support of one's fellow-men, and this is obtainable when the virtues co-operate effectively. A person's interests are promoted by winning goodwill, affection, and esteem for behaving in a just fashion, and not—as tyrants like Julius Caesar suppose—by holding people in fear. One important benefit which comes from this right perception of usefulness is friendship. Another is glory, which follows when one is trusted and admired, and when one enjoys a good reputation for

military service, personal character, association with the great, and eloquence. Also useful is the prudent display of beneficence, whether it be with money and public entertainments, or generosity with one's legal services, especially to defend people in court. Advantages flow from service to the state, from the care of the populace in such matters as taxation and legislation, and from the avoidance of greed in public office. In the calculus of *utilia* with which the book ends, Cicero urges his readers to weigh the merits of practical advantages one against another, thus comparing, say, health with wealth, and glory with riches. For the Stoics, such *utilia* were *adiaphora*, morally neutral, and capable of classification only as more or less to be preferred in specific circumstances according to the sole criterion of the *honestum*. For Cicero, beneficial things are valid ends in themselves, and the benefit of society is the most important end of all.

Book 3 develops the argument begun in book 2 to its logical conclusion. Since the honourable and the beneficial are so closely associated, what is dishonourable cannot be beneficial, and there can be no real conflict between virtue and usefulness. The *formula* for resolving apparent cases of conflict is that it is contrary to nature to secure a benefit for oneself at someone else's expense. Personal gain that is contrary to the laws of nature, or contrary to reason, or attained at the expense of the interests of society, cannot be beneficial. Immorality is contrary to nature. Justice never conflicts with what is genuinely beneficial, but only with *apparent* advantage. In business, law, and politics, we must shun fraud and maintain good faith (though *fides* may be broken where the consequences of keeping it would be dishonourable—say in the case of certain oaths). The argument is illustrated with copious *exempla*, some of them presumably suggested by Posidonius and Hecato, others drawn from Roman history.

Cicero insists that he has exercised his own *iudicium* with regard to Panaetius (*Off.* 1.6), and the most striking illustration of this lies in his distinctive way of resolving the apparent tension between the honourable and the beneficial. For Panaetius, the honourable was the *solum et summum bonum*. Though he evidently never executed his plan to compare this with the beneficial, Panaetius implicitly signalled the fact that the two

could not conflict, because all the categories of the beneficial
were technically neutral, and at best only means to the end of
virtue under certain conditions (which Panaetius himself was
concerned to explore); virtue was the sole end in itself. To
Cicero, however, the beneficial is equated with practical
advantage as a goal in its own right, and the honourable
course is that which promotes the ultimate end of the public
good. Private advantage cannot conflict with the common weal
because human beings are by nature social beings. The
honourable and the beneficial converge not because virtue is
the supreme determinant of what is preferable, but because the
interests of the community and the interests of the individual
are governed alike by natural law. Cicero professes to reject the
traditional Stoic image of the *honestum* as an unrealistic ideal,
unattainable by the ordinary person, and to discuss instead
media officia, the duties by which most people can attain to the
goal of the public good. Ironically, his method of reconciling
the *honestum* with the *utile* evokes a political vision of a Roman
society which seems as utopian as the orthodox Stoic pattern
itself.[29]

(ii) Ambrose and Cicero

The fourth century might well be designated the *aetas Ciceroniana* of later Latin.[30] The study of Cicero's writings was an
essential part of the standard school curriculum, and all the
great literary names, pagan and Christian, reveal an intimate
grounding in his works and his style. Ambrose, educated in
'the liberal arts' at Rome,[31] was a typical product of that

[29] I am indebted to MacKendrick, *The Philosophical Books of Cicero*, 232–
49; Griffin and Atkins, pp. xxi–xxviii. On the deviation of Cicero from
Panaetius, see Colish i. 145–52. For a discussion of the extent to which
source-criticism can illuminate our evaluation of Cicero's text, see Dyck, 18–
21, 28.

[30] E. K. Rand, *Founders of the Middle Ages* (Cambridge, MA, 1928), 255.
See also J. T. Muckle, 'The Influence of Cicero in the Formation of Christian
Culture', *Transactions of the Royal Society of Canada*, ser. 3, 42/2 (1948),
107–25.

[31] Paulinus, *VA* 5. On what this involved, see the classic treatment of H.-I.
Marrou, *A History of Education in Antiquity* (London, 1981); for an outstanding assessment of the professional process in this period, see R. A. Kaster,

tradition. He quarries Cicero extensively in the homilies which
make up his *De excessu fratris*, where pagan *consolatio* motifs sit
side by side with scriptural patterning, and his *œuvre* as a whole
is replete with Ciceronian reminiscences.[32] As his use of
praeteritio[33] in the present work implies (3.71, 87; also 2.30;
3.66, 70), *De officiis* in particular was a staple text, and he could
expect many of his addressees to have a reasonable awareness of
its argument. For his copious allusions and verbal echoes,
Ambrose did not need to have Cicero at his elbow; he could
rely on his memory of a classic he had known since boyhood.[34]
Already exploited in the service of a Christian apologetic by
Lactantius in his *Divine Institutes,*[35] as a discussion of ethical

Guardians of Language: The Grammarian and Society in Late Antiquity
(Berkeley and Los Angeles, 1988). On Ambrose, see the basic survey of G. L.
Ellspermann, *The Attitude of the Early Christian Latin Writers toward Pagan
Literature and Learning* (Washington, DC, 1949), 113–25.

[32] On *Exc. fr.*, see Y.-M. Duval, 'Formes profanes et formes bibliques dans
les oraisons funèbres de saint Ambroise', in M. Fuhrmann (ed.), *Christianisme
et formes littéraires de l'Antiquité tardive en Occident*, Fondation Hardt,
Entretiens sur l'Antiquité Classique, 23 (Geneva, 1977), 235–301; H. Savon,
'La Première Oraison funèbre de saint Ambroise (*De excessu fratris* i) et les
deux sources de la consolation chrétienne', *REL* 58 (1980), 370–402; Biermann, 24–44. In general, see Madec, 141–66; M. L. Ricci, 'Fortuna di una
formula ciceroniana presso sant'Ambrogio (a proposito di *iustitia*)', *SIFC* 43
(1971), 222–45; L. Alfonsi, 'Ambrogio "Ciceronianus"', *VChr* 20 (1966), 83–
5; Hill, 144–207; M. Zelzer, 'Ambrosius von Mailand und das Erbe der
klassischen Tradition', *WS* 100 (1987), 201–26. In *Off.* alone, Ambrose
evokes *Amic.*, *Sen.*, *Fin.*, *Rep.*, and very probably *ND* and *Tusc.*, too, as
well as *Cat.*, *Planc.*, and *Verr.*: cf. 1.43, 77, 94, 126, 127, 135, 167, 207; 2.4,
100, 106; 3.2, 20, 125–38. On *ND*'s influence in the Fathers, see I. Opelt,
'Ciceros Schrift *De natura deorum* bei den lateinischen Kirchenvätern', *A&A*
12 (1966), 141–55.

[33] The rhetorical technique of claiming that one will 'pass over' a subject,
only to mention it dismissively just the same: see H. Lausberg, *Handbuch der
literarischen Rhetorik*, 2 vols. (Munich, 1960), i. 436–7.

[34] On the techniques involved in Roman literary education, see H. Blum,
Die antike Mnemotechnik (Hildesheim, 1969).

[35] See N. E. Nelson, 'Cicero's De Officiis in Christian Thought: 300–1300',
in *Essays and Studies in English and Comparative Literature* (Ann Arbor, MI,
1933), 59–160. See also R. A. Greer, 'Cicero's Sketch and Lactantius's Plan',
in A. J. Malherbe, F. W. Norris, and J. W. Thompson (eds.), *The Early
Church in its Context: Essays in Honor of Everett Ferguson* (Leiden, 1998),
155–74. Augustine, on the other hand, has few references to *Off.*: M. Testard,
Saint Augustin et Cicéron, 2 vols. (Paris, 1958), i. 214.

principles Cicero's *De officiis* was not just one obvious model among others: it was known as no other Latin work on the subject would have been.

Ambrose makes no secret of the fact that he is using Cicero. On the contrary, he underlines the fact that he is continuing an established tradition by taking up the theme of duties, the same subject to which Cicero had devoted his energies. Just as Panaetius and his 'son' (Posidonius) wrote on duties among the Greeks, and as Cicero did among the Latins, so he himself, he says, may write on duties as a bishop (1.24).[36] Cicero is mentioned by name only five times in all of Ambrose's extant works, and all five references (to *Tullius*) occur in *De officiis*: two in 1.24, and one apiece in 1.43, 82, and 180. The choice of the Ciceronian topic of *officia* is explicitly defended by appeal to scriptural authority (1.23–5).

Cicero's style of writing as father to son is directly imitated: *Et sicut Tullius ad erudiendum filium, ita ego quoque ad vos informandos filios meos; neque enim minus vos diligo quos in evangelio genui, quam si coniugio suscepissem* (1.24). Ambrose addresses his spiritual 'sons', offering them fatherly guidance (1.1, 2, 23–4, 72, 184; 2.25, 134, 149, 152–6; 3.132, 139). They are members of the Milanese clergy, whose ranks clearly contain a high proportion of young men (cf. 1.65–6, 81, 87, 212, 217–18; 2.97–101). Just as Cicero could follow the Roman tradition of expressing paternal *auctoritas* in literary form,[37] Ambrose is able to evoke the examples of apostolic spiritual fatherhood to be found in the New Testament, which had come to be used conventionally to define the relationship between bishops and their subordinates.[38] This facilitates the incorporation of important didactic material from texts like the Pastoral Epistles (cf. 1.183–5, 246–8). Ambrose may modestly disclaim any title to share in the glory of Christ's apostles (1.3), but he can also speak in quasi-apostolic terms of 'passing on' valuable teaching to his charges (1.2–3),[39] and, like Paul to Timothy, can

[36] There is no evidence that he knows of Panaetius' and Posidonius' works except from Cicero.
[37] See F. J. Lemoine, 'Parental Gifts: Father-Son Dedications and Dialogues in Roman Didactic Literature', *ICS* 16 (1991), 337–66.
[38] See commentary on 1.24.
[39] 'Passing on' or 'handing down' here is also evocative of Ciceronian

entrust his work to his spiritual offspring as a deposit to be guarded (3.139).[40]

Ambrose emphasizes the fact that he is addressing clerics in particular (cf. 1.86, 175, 184–6, 217–18; 2.25). Nevertheless, it is clear that, like Cicero, he envisages a much wider readership for his work than just this 'filial' constituency. Some of his material, such as his condemnation of speculation by grain-merchants in times of food-shortages (3.37–44), or his section on the banishment of foreigners from a city during a famine (3.45–52), is not of obvious or primary relevance to ecclesiastics. Other arguments, while within the possible parameters of teaching addressed to clerics, are also clearly intended for more general consumption: examples include passages on the greed of merchants (1.242–5), or on fraud in business-contracts (3.57–75).[41]

The threefold structure which Cicero takes from Panaetius is maintained by Ambrose. He clearly outlines the division of the material into the *honestum*, the *utile*, and the relationship of the two, and he alludes to Cicero's two supplementary themes, the respective comparisons of *honesta* and of *utilia* (1.27), though these additional questions receive very little explicit treatment in the substance of books 1 and 2. He refers to the distinction between *medium officium* and *perfectum officium* (1.36–7; cf. 3.10), but, as with *officium* itself (1.25), he seeks scriptural authority for the terminology, and, unlike Cicero, he insists that it is perfect, not 'middle', duty with which he is concerned (3.10–12). The discussion of the honourable in book 1 is broken down into an analysis of the cardinal virtues (1.115 ff.),[42] though not before some lengthy preambles, which help to set the scene by clarifying the key spiritual assumptions which underpin the ethic that will follow. Ambrose intends to distinguish his theological framework

idiom: see commentary ad loc. Both registers are probably in Ambrose's mind.

[40] The belief that the Pastoral Epistles are deutero-Pauline was unknown to Ambrose. In order to avoid embroiling him anachronistically in a later scholarly debate, the wording of the commentary simply assumes his perspective, without implying anything in particular about its accuracy.

[41] On the likely readership of the work, see further Introduction VI.

[42] For critical literature on Ambrose's presentation of the virtues, especially the essential analysis by Becker, see commentary on 1.115.

from Cicero's right from the start, and to that end he spends time stressing the importance of modesty and self-control (1.1–22, 31–5), establishing the nature of divine providence and the purpose of temporal suffering (1.40–64: God brings faithful sufferers to glory in a future life), and underscoring the centrality of modesty in the behaviour of the spiritual servant (1.65–114).

The definitions of the virtues are infused with fair amounts of Stoic thinking, especially in the case of courage and temperance, but scriptural motifs and illustrations are dominant. Ambrose endorses the Stoic premiss that the virtues are in the end a unified package; the expression of each one mutually implies the presence of the others and indicates an overall orientation towards the good. But they are far more than a matter of general rational self-mastery and of living life in accordance with nature, however significant such ideas continue to be; they are ways of expressing the potency of divine grace at work in the life of the believer (cf. 1.116–21). Prudence, for Ambrose as for Cicero, is essentially practical rather than speculative, but the most practical knowledge of all is for him the knowledge of God; the piety of faith is the *primus . . . officii fons* (1.126), and so it, not justice, is the most important of the virtues (1.122–9). Justice is divided into strict justice (1.131–42) and kindness (1.143–74), as in Cicero, and Ambrose similarly ranks kindness above the basic *suum cuique* principle; but he focuses his exposition of kindness on an appeal to Christian charity, in which right intentions and the following of a Christlike pattern are critical. On courage (1.175–209), spiritual valour and resolve in the face of circumstantial adversities are said to be more significant than physical or martial bravery, though Ambrose does not resist the temptation to celebrate the military glories of biblical characters and the physical courage of the martyrs. His main focus is on the control of the passions and the despising of externals (1.178–95): he combines Stoic ideals of rational triumph over irrational forces with biblical images of perseverance in hope of eschatological reward. Modesty has already dominated a substantial section of book 1 (65–114), and the treatment of temperance recapitulates and expands upon some of its core aspects (1.210–51). As in the Panaetian-Ciceronian

vision, the visibility of propriety is vital: the respectability of preserving a due *ordo . . . vitae* (1.211), characterized by harmony, sobriety, tranquillity, and due measure in both the parts and the whole of one's deportment, and determined in detail according to context and personal constitution, is funda-mental to the task of being seen to do the right thing. The inner soundness of a heart devoted to *honestas* is evidenced outwardly by conduct that observes the vital principle of the *decorum* (1.219–22). Such behaviour is a sign of right order, not just internally, as it was for the orthodox Stoic sage, or horizontally, as it was for Cicero, but also vertically, between the ethical agent and God, both in this life and in a life to come.

In book 2, Cicero's social focus is retained, but the *utile* is defined neither as a neutral 'preferable' nor as positive worldly advantage but as that which contributes to the attainment of eternal life (where the vision of human community is realized *par excellence*). Faith and works are the means by which the Christian operates in this world, for they are the way to the *summum bonum* of eternal blessedness—a way which involves suffering, privation, and self-denial in the here and now, but one which is already marked by existential happiness in the midst of (and even because of) these realities (2.1–21). Indi-vidual *utilia* include many of Cicero's categories, such as the values of showing prudent generosity, extending hospitality, offering good counsel, keeping the right company, and treating people fairly and sincerely, but all are structured around a principle of serving Christ (cf. 2.24) and of obtaining the *vita aeterna* for oneself and commending it to others (cf. 2.27: *Quid etiam hoc utilius quo regnum caeleste acquiritur?*). In practical terms, the most useful thing of all is to be loved (2.29–39), which implicitly means showing God's own *caritas* to human-kind. If the *honestum* is determined ultimately with reference to knowing and honouring God, the *utile* is deemed to consist in acting in a way that will reflect divine priorities and draw others to God. All the means by which reputation is won and maintained—and Ambrose has a considerable interest in tem-poral and societal image—are meant to be seen as slanted towards this final redefining of what is beneficial as eternal and other-worldly.

Book 3 follows Cicero in arguing for and illustrating the

truth that dishonourable conduct cannot be beneficial, and that
the honourable end must be sought by honourable means. But
whereas for Cicero the honourable is aligned with the advantage of pursuing whatever promotes the interests of human
cohesion and equity, for Ambrose the honourable is about
rightly relating to and mirroring the character of God, through
whose design the ultimate interests of the individual and the
interests of the universal human family which the individual is
called to serve are consonant. The Christlike course (cf. 3.13,
15, 27, 36) and the law of nature are one. The good of
humankind as a whole is naturally furthered by the observance
of justice, the protection of the vulnerable, and the preservation
of what is right and true: in the perspective of faith, these ends
are synonymous with the working out of redemption for both
individual and society. The key note is the supremacy of the
honourable, rather than a comparison of the honourable and
the beneficial. There is in the end no difference between the
honestum and the *utile* because both can only be understood
with reference to the purposes of God and the task of bringing
people to appreciate them in this world and the next. If
Cicero's desire to expound a relevant ethic of 'middle' duty
remains wedded to an idealistic conception of political possibilities, Ambrose's effort to issue practical advice involves an
unabashed appeal to perfection as the only applicable target for
the moral agent called to dedicated Christian service.[43]

IV. THEMES AND PERSPECTIVES

Ambrose may sketch a somewhat different way of resolving the
apparent difference between virtue and expediency, but he
clearly follows Cicero in his choice of title, ethical categories,
style of address, and basic structure. How in detail does he
handle his subject? A number of his techniques are worth
noting.
1. Ambrose goes to some lengths to justify his adoption of the
classical subject-matter and terminology by appealing to the

[43] For a more detailed analysis of what Ambrose's argument implies in
terms of ethical substance, see Introduction VII (ii); on his theological
presuppositions as they contrast with Cicero's position, see Introduction VI.

authority of the Scriptures. The theme of *officia* is not just of relevance to the pagan philosophers; it is appropriate to Christians as well, because the Bible itself uses the word *officium* (1.25). Not only so, but the standard by which *officium* is measured biblically is quite different—the good of eternal life rather than the good of present gain (1.28–9). The middle-Stoic distinction between *medium officium* and *perfectum officium* can be found in the gospel story of Jesus's response to the rich young man who had kept the divine commandments but lacked the self-sacrificial spirit which is the essence of the perfection to which the spiritual leader must aspire (1.36–7). 'Seemliness', that essential component of a virtue that is visibly 'right', is also anchored in a number of biblical verses: Ambrose can cite both Latin (*decorum, decet*) and Greek (πρέπον, πρέπει) to reinforce the point, and to parade his textual learning (1.30, 221, 223–4). The same holds good for the *honestum* (1.221) and the *utile* (2.23–7), and Cicero's attempt to explain the difference between *honestum* and *decorum* can be bettered in a differentiation established in the Scriptures (1.221). Secular philosophy's speculations on what might be said to constitute the *vita beata* must be corrected by attentiveness to the Bible's definitions of blessedness, spelt out in the Psalms and the Wisdom literature and illustrated in the characters of the champions of the faith (2.1–21).

Some of the efforts to find scriptural authentication involve fairly desperate contrivance (cf. 1.25, 36–7 especially), but what clearly matters to Ambrose is that the all-important *auctoritas* is duly invoked for the relevant ethical prescriptions (1.36, 131, 151; 2.3, 5, 65, 113; cf. 1.106).[44] *Quae in scripturis non repperimus, ea quemadmodum usurpare possumus?*, he asks (1.102), and the implied answer is an essential key to his didactic method. Whatever thematic inspiration comes from Cicero or, through him, from Greek philosophy, it is the wisdom of the divine Word that is the regulative principle: the language must be sanctioned in Holy Writ. It is, we are told, through reflection on a Psalm that the idea of taking up the whole subject of duties comes to birth in Ambrose's mind (1.23); it is appropriate, then, that the substance of his teaching is presented as both consonant with and anchored in the

[44] See Ring, 183–96.

repository of the divine Spirit's disclosure. After all, the bishop is simply a humble student-teacher of the Bible himself (1.3).

2. As part of his determination to ground the philosophical themes in the Bible, Ambrose constantly insists that biblical truth and biblical exemplars are intrinsically superior to anything offered by the classical tradition. There are two sides to this claim. There is first the supposition that 'earlier' means 'better', or at least more deserving of praise for originality. Thus the psalmist's injunctions to 'keep your tongue from evil, and your lips from speaking guile' and to 'seek peace and pursue it' (Ps. 33: 14–15) are to be credited as the first expressions of a sentiment which orators like Cicero have subsequently enunciated, about avoiding excesses in rebukes (1.92). The morass of secular theorizing can be escaped (cf. 2.8) by going back to the Old Testament: *redeamus ad nostrum Moysen, atque ad superiora revertamur, ut quanto praestantiora tanto antiquiora promamus* (3.92). There are inevitably some potentially awkward chronological constraints to such a process. The teaching of Jesus on the blessedness of eternal life is naturally more profound than any pagan conceptions of the *vita beata*, but *ne aestimetur hoc recens esse*, Ambrose is obliged to cite propositions about faith and good works drawn from the 'prophet' David (2.6). David's prophetic role as psalmist in fact proves remarkably convenient, for he neatly fits into history even before the Presocratics (1.31). In general, appeal to Old Testament material is of course safer (cf. 1.43–4; 94; 2.48; 3.2, 80); go back as far as Abraham, and the details are bound to pre-date any of the philosophers known to the classical world (1.118).

The other side of the logic is the assumption that the pagans plagiarized from the Old Testament Scriptures. This claim will be familiar to anyone who has read the second- and third-century Apologists, who inherit it from the Alexandrian Jewish tradition. It is very common in Ambrose, whose debts to Philo in particular are substantial.[45] The five-year rule of silence

---

[45] See commentary on 1.31. On Ambrose and Philo, see E. Lucchesi, *L'Usage de Philon dans l'œuvre exégètique de saint Ambroise. Une 'Quellenforschung' relative aux commentaires d'Ambroise sur la Genèse* (Leiden, 1977); H. Savon, *Saint Ambroise devant l'exégèse de Philon le Juif* (Paris, 1977); D. T. Runia, *Philo in Early Christian Literature: A Survey* (Assen and Minneapolis,

which Pythagoras imposed on novices in his community
followed, we are told, the example of David, who kept quiet
when abused by the scoundrel Shimei (1.31). The Stoics'
teaching that the earth's produce is designed for all human
beings alike, and that people have a responsibility to help one
another, is derived from verses in Genesis and the Psalms
(1.132–5). For other examples, cf. 1.79–80, 92, 126, 141, 180
(also 2.43).

3. Ambrose almost always avoids explicitly attributing sentiments to Cicero or to classical thinkers: he adopts their
language, but scarcely ever cites the source. Only two of the
five mentions of Cicero's name (1.82 and 1.180) are in the
context of reference to specific passages of Cicero's text, and
only the first of these is accompanied by a *direct* reference (the
second comes after an allusion which has not been expressly
signalled). The normal practice, as elsewhere in Ambrose's
writings,[46] is not to name the source, but to employ vague
plurals. Examples include the following: *aestimaverunt . . .
aiunt . . . haec illi* (1.27); *illi aestimaverunt; illa* (1.29); *oratores
saeculi* (1.92); *ferunt gentiles* (1.94); *saeculares viri* (1.102);
illorum (1.118); *tractant* (1.122); *ab huius saeculi . . . sapientibus*
(1.126); *vocant* (1.130); *quod putant philosophi; dicunt . . . illi*
(1.131); *putaverunt . . . aiunt* (1.132); *quod si hi qui ad
capessendam rem publicam adhortantur aliquos, haec praecepta
dant . . .* (1.186); *ferunt* (1.207);[47] *hi qui foris sunt* (1.252);[48]
sapientum definitione (2.43); *nonnulli . . . putant* (3.8); *feruntur*
(3.26); *quaerunt aliqui* (3.27); *ut philosophi disputant* (3.29); *illud
quod memorabile habetur apud philosophos* (3.80); *in spectatis et
eruditis viris* (3.81); *mirantur* (3.83); *memorabile ferunt rhetores*

1993), 291–311: Savon in particular stresses Ambrose's creativity in his
application of Philonic material.

[46] Cf. the passages documented by Madec, 349 ff. Ambrose refers to Vergil
as *quidam poeta* (*Abr.* 1.82; cf. 2.4), and to Cicero as *quidam saecularium doctor*
(*Virg.* 3.25), just as Augustine speaks of *Aeneae nescio cuius errores* (*Conf.*
1.13.20) and *librum cuiusdam Ciceronis* (*Conf.* 3.4.7). On the question of
whether Augustine's feigned ignorance in itself implies dissociation from
pagan authors, see M. Testard, *Saint Augustin et Cicéron*, 2 vols. (Paris, 1958),
ii. 11–19, though Testard's argument that there is nothing pejorative about
the phrases seems to me to go too far.

[47] Referring not to Cicero's *Off.*, but to his *Amic.* 24.

[48] Hiding Cicero behind a NT phrase: see commentary ad loc.

(3.91); *quaestiones philosophorum; illi . . . tractant* (3.97); *sunt enim pleraeque philosophorum quaestiones* (3.126). The vagueness often occurs when Ambrose is alluding to Ciceronian *exempla*. He can mention a story from Cicero without naming the author at all, as in 3.71: *quid mihi tractare de Syracusano illo amoeno secretoque secessu . . .?*; or 3.87: *illud Graecorum*; cf. also 3.66 and 3.70. In 2.30, he refers obliquely to a passage from Cicero simply with *legimus*.

The ancient world took a far freer approach to the citing of sources than would ever be tolerated in modern times, and the deployment of generalizing plurals such as *alii* to refer to sources is common in classical literature, not least in historiography. It was not regarded as careless or dishonest, nor did it necessarily betoken a hostile spirit. Ambrose regularly cites exegetical authorities in precisely this manner, often with either approval or no sharp dissent,[49] while contributing his own particular shape to their material.[50] We should not assume, then, that his failure to name his source at every turn in *De officiis* makes him either a shameless plagiarist[51] or an invariable opponent of Cicero's ideas.

Nevertheless, it comes as no surprise to find that Ambrose regularly *is* negative about the values and assumptions of the classical world in general, and about a number of the Ciceronian-Panaetian perspectives in particular. Again and again he sets up antitheses between classical sentiments or illustrations and the teaching and exemplars of the Bible and Christian history. Many of the oblique references to Cicero and the classical tradition are accompanied by sharp adversatives:

---

[49] Cf. 1.15, referring to variant texts of Ps. 90: 3. For some examples where Philo is cited in a similar fashion, see Lucchesi, *L'Usage de Philon dans l'œuvre exégètique de saint Ambroise*, 25.

[50] A classic illustration can be found in *Virg.*: see Y.-M. Duval, 'L'Originalité du "De virginibus" dans le mouvement ascétique occidental: Ambroise, Cyprien, Athanase', in *Ambroise de Milan*, 9–66. Further on Ambrose's creativity, see n. 45 above on Philo; G. Lazzati, *Il valore letterario della esegesi ambrosiana* (Milan, 1960), 66–71 (on Basil); also P. Courcelle, *Recherches sur les Confessions de saint Augustin*, 2nd edn. (Paris, 1968), 93–138 (on Platonist sources).

[51] Hagendahl, 347–72.

haec illi . . . nos autem (1.27–8); *illi . . . nos . . .* (1.29); *Tullius . . . nos
certe* (1.82–3); *multa . . . dant praecepta saeculares viri, quae nobis
praetereunda arbitror* (1.102); *sed hoc artis est; nos autem artem fugimus*
(1.116); *dicunt . . . illi; apud nos* (1.131); *ut non hominum opinionibus
aestimandum relinqueretur, sed divino iudicio committeretur* (2.3); *philosophi . . . scriptura autem divina* (2.4–5); *quaerunt aliqui . . . mihi
quidem* (3.27); *illi . . . tractant; noster iste* (3.97).

Sometimes, Ambrose completely repudiates a classical idea in
favour of a higher, Christian, principle. The philosophers may
say that the principle of never doing anyone harm can be set
aside if one has been provoked by an injustice; the gospel
allows no exception to the rule at all (1.131).[52] It may be a good
thing for a *sapiens* to survive even at the expense of someone
else's life, but Christ has set the *vir Christianus* the example of
individual pacifism and self-denial in all circumstances (3.27).
On a number of occasions, while there is no explicit rejection of
the secular view, arguments from lesser to greater are used in
comparison of classical and Christian standards. If there are
laws forbidding men who engage in military service for the
emperor to get involved in trade or embroiled in lawsuits, how
much more should soldiers of the faith, who serve the true
Imperator, abstain from such activities (1.185; cf. 1.186)?
Injustice is offensive in any circumstances; it is doubly appal-
ling in the community of those who are called to epitomize
fairness and the denial of self-preferment at others' expense
(2.124). Success by fraudulent means is improper for athletes
whose concern is victory in the stadium; how much more so for
those who run in the true race of life (3.26; cf. also 3.65)?
Behind such injunctions lies the conviction that, at best, the
classical norms or the conventions of civilized society represent
only the minimum level to which the ecclesiastical servant
should aspire: in practice, the faithful soldier of Christ must
aim higher still. Even where there is no outright contrast
drawn, Ambrose is still concerned to articulate an ethic
which goes beyond the mores of the secular world.
4.   One of the most important insights into Ambrose's perspective is to be found in his choice of *exempla*. The *auctoritas*
of the Scriptures yields concrete paradigms in the lives of the

---

[52] Cf., however, 1.177 and see commentary ad loc.

heroes and heroines of the faith (plus, for warning's sake, a few of its villains), whose characters are displayed in the biblical narratives. In the *exempla maiorum*, there is a model for Christian conduct: *sit igitur nobis vita maiorum disciplinae speculum* (1.116). This kind of reverence for the protagonists of antiquity and the corresponding exploitation of their stories for moralistic purposes are both natural enough to a mind shaped by Roman culture. What is striking in *De officiis* is the way in which Ambrose transfers the traditional veneration of the ancestral and the national to a spiritual and ecclesial context, and endeavours thus to present a new version of the classical thesis, one that is grounded in the story-line of the Bible rather than in the history and legends of antiquity.[53] The church is visualized as the spiritual offspring of the people of God in the Hebrew Scriptures. The apostle Paul himself had maintained that Abraham was the father of believing Gentiles as well as of Israel, and that the ancient Israelites were the ancestors of the Corinthians;[54] so Ambrose can speak with pride of the *populus patrum* (1.139, 197, 246; 2.10, 130; 3.5, 69, 92; cf. also 3.103), of the *patres* (2.63; 3.99–100, 108), and of *nostri* or *maiores nostri* (1.118, 175; 3.53, 98; cf. 3. 111, 117). The heroic exploits of spiritual progenitors like *noster Moyses* (3.92) are celebrated in *scripturae nostrae* (1.133, etc.), or *nostri libri* (1.92), or simply *in nostris* (1.221).

There is no question in Ambrose's mind that these biblical records offer anything other than reliable historical accounts: the fictitious tales of classical mythology are contrasted with the veracity of these events in real history (3.29, 32). Ancient Israel and fourth-century Milan are linked in one great sweep of salvation-history. In accordance with a preference manifested throughout his works, and reflecting the influences of his chief exegetical guides in Greek, Ambrose draws upon the Old Testament in particular: the patriarchs, Moses, David, Solomon, Job, Elijah, Elisha, and Daniel are his favourite exemplars. From the New Testament, Jesus himself is inevitably the supreme model, the climactic antitype of the Old Testament figures whose virtues, however great, were still marred by various imperfections. Paul, typically cited simply as *apostolus*,

[53] See Zelzer, 'Randbemerkungen', 483–4.
[54] Cf. Rom. 4: 11–12, 16–18; Gal. 3: 6–9; 1 Cor. 10: 1.

is, equally inevitably, the next in importance. But the Old
Testament narratives remain dominant. Their heroes regularly
serve to illustrate the same particular virtues. So, for instance,
when Ambrose speaks of patience, we come to expect that the
stock example will be Job (1.113, 195; 2.20); when he mentions
chastity, it will be Joseph (1.66, 76; 2.59); on careful speech, it
will be David (1.6–7, 9–10, 21, 31, 34, 236–8); and on wisdom,
Solomon (2.51–3; 3.12) or Daniel (2.11, 48, 55, 57; 3.12).

Ambrose's method thus implies two somewhat distinct
hermeneutical frameworks. On the one hand, he assumes that
older means better [Introduction IV.2] and he is determined to
trace his ethical principles in examples which pre-date the
putative claims of the philosophers or the anecdotes of the
pagan past. This assumption presumably lies behind his
particular fondness for the Old Testament narratives. On the
other hand, he works with the typical Christian claim that there
is some kind of essential progress in divine revelation between
the Old Testament and the New, and that the Old Testament
stories come from the age of the 'shadow', whereas the gospel
dispensation is the era of the 'image' (1.239). At times there is a
logical tension between these two perspectives, such as when he
tries to claim that David did not fall behind Paul as a moral
paragon (1.236). It is not clear, however, that Ambrose himself
was troubled by this apparent oddity: in his mind, there
appeared to be no problem in maintaining a classical fascination with antiquity, while assuming the truth of a larger
theological claim, that the Christian age represents fuller
insight. Read with Christian spectacles, the Old Testament
stories could tell whatever ethical stories their interpreter
wished to narrate [see also Introduction IV.5].[55]

In the great majority of cases, the biblical *exempla* directly
replace Cicero's illustrations from Roman and Greek history
and mythology. So, in 2.81, Aratus of Sicyon in Cicero's
account becomes in the equivalent passage Joseph (who also
replaces M. Octavius in 2.80); in 2.93–4, Rehoboam substitutes
for Julius Caesar; and in 3.77–81 the tragic consequences of
rash oaths or vows are illustrated not with Sol and Phaëthon or
Agamemnon and Iphigenia, but with Herod and John the
Baptist, and with Jephthah and his daughter. Cicero's com-

[55] See Hahn, especially 196 ff., 454 ff.; also Pizzolato, 43–87.

mendations of the charity of ransoming prisoners of war are
echoed, but the Christian version adds its own touches, about
the need to save women from *turpitudo* (2.70, 136, 138) and to
deliver children from the pollution of idolatry (2.136). Like
Cicero, Ambrose has a particular concentration of illustrations
in book 3, and it is only here that he retains any significant
number of classical examples. The stories of Scipio Africanus
(3.2); Gyges (3.29–36); Canius and Pythius (3.71–2); Damon
and Phintias (3.80–1, 83); the Athenians' rejection of a dishonourable stratagem (3.87); and Fabricius' response to a
deserter's ignoble proposal (3.91) remain; but only Scipio
and Gyges are mentioned by name. With the rest, Ambrose
declines to identify the Ciceronian source explicitly: the allusions are meant to be noticed by the reader unassisted. Book 3
repeatedly underscores the superiority of the scriptural material (3.1–7, 29–36, 67, 69–75, 77–85, 86–7, 91–7).[56] In books 1
and 2, there are a couple of allusions to Ciceronian references:
to the tradition that fathers and sons do not bathe together
(1.79), and to the advantages of an affable style in the letters of
kings to their sons (2.30). Two passages mention classical
stories which are drawn not from Cicero's *De officiis* but from
elsewhere in his philosophical writings (1.94; 1.207); in both
cases, the characters are named.

Alongside the biblical illustrations, Ambrose weaves in
stories from Christian history and personal reminiscences.
This lends a certain vividness to the text: its *Sitz im Leben* is
obvious. But the treatise should not simply be read superficially as a potential source of information about Ambrose's
church: far more importantly, it enables us to glimpse his
overarching episcopal strategy. It is designed to convey a

---

[56] Thamin, 249, suggests that Regulus, the dominant exemplar in Cicero,
Off. 3 (99–115), is replaced by Job as the hero of Ambrose's book 3. Regulus,
however, is referred to only once by Cicero prior to book 3 (*Off.* 1.39),
whereas Job appears frequently in Ambrose's text (1.39, 41–6, 61, 113, 148,
164, 167–8, 180, 195; 2.20) before being mentioned at the close of book 3
(3.131, 138). It is possible that Moses is the substitute for Regulus in book 3,
though in a much shorter section than its Ciceronian equivalent, in 3.92–5.
Ambrose's favourite biblical hero in *Off.* may well be David, who appears
again and again throughout the work, and dominates the opening sections of
books 1 and 3; he is clearly presented as the author's model: 1.1–2; cf. 2.32 and
see commentary ad loc.

specific personal and ecclesial image, and modern readers must apply a certain hermeneutic of suspicion if they are to penetrate behind the allusions to the realities of the text's social context. Ambrose can refer to incidents which he expects his clergy to remember, like his rejection of an applicant to the clergy and the man's subsequent abandonment of 'the faith'—or departure from the Nicene ranks—*Arianae infestationis tempore* (1.72), or the desertion of an inherited member of the clergy when faced with trial before the episcopal tribunal for financial misconduct (1.72). References like these, brief as they are, inform us not just about Ambrose's standards of discipline and his effort to present a visually impressive church hierarchy; they also allow us to glimpse the tensions that were all too real in his political situation. When he mentions his support of a bishop of Pavia in his resistance of a demand to surrender a sum of money which a widow had deposited with the church (2.150–1), the intention is to exemplify the point that the church has an obligation to maintain a faithful watch on the property of the vulnerable against even the severest of secular pressures. Read with a more critical eye, however, the rhetoric can be taken as an indication of the dominance of Ambrose's influence in the North Italian ecclesiastical scene: not the least part of the said bishop's heroism, as it is presented, consists in the fact that he had the sense to take Ambrose's advice. Here is Ambrose the authority figure, deferred to by a brother bishop, belligerent in the face of challenge from the civil powers.[57]

When Ambrose illustrates the practice of ransoming prisoners of war by referring to his sale of church plate (2.70–1, 136–43), he is openly attempting to justify his conduct in the face of homoian criticism. When he appeals to the example of St Lawrence (2.140–1), he is not simply introducing another pious tradition from Christian martyrology: he is deliberately citing illustrious precedent for his own behaviour, and presenting himself as a follower in this line of spiritual champions who have been prepared to risk all in fulfilment of their devotion to charity to Christ's poor. Cicero refers to two historical incidents to illustrate the practice of the expulsion

---

[57] Yet also an Ambrose who treads a narrow line between boasting of his own defiance of secular authorities and warning his addressees against behaving *insolentius* towards the powers that be (1.208).

of *peregrini* (ξενηλασία) in *De officiis* 3.47. Ambrose also has two stories on the same theme, developed at much greater length, contrasting honourable and dishonourable treatment of *peregrini* by urban prefects in recent situations of corn-shortage at Rome (3.45–52). In the first incident, a Christian prefect behaved magnificently, organizing a subscription to support the vulnerable; in the second, the official overreacted and banished the *peregrini* from Rome when help was shortly at hand. The later official is very probably Q. Aurelius Symmachus, Ambrose's pagan adversary in the Altar of Victory dispute in 384, with whom he maintained an officially civil relationship, based upon the formalities of upper-class *amicitia*; each needed the other to further his respective interests in Rome and Milan.[58] Ambrose does not need to name him: the allusion would be obvious to a contemporary. This apparently unspecific illustration thus amounts to a thinly-veiled swipe at a formidable sparring-partner and correspondent. What is more, there is a strong likelihood that the commercial *peregrini* who are depicted as so mistreated by Symmachus were associated with the very Milanese businessmen who had been caught up in Ambrose's cause against the homoians in 386: when the bishop's supporters are wont to profit from just the same kind of capitalization on shortages which he has previously condemned (3.37–44), he can well turn a blind eye.[59]

These subtleties in the illustrations of the work are features to which we need to be alert. But the vital feature that needs to be appreciated is Ambrose's effort to translate the Ciceronian themes into an extensive scriptural tableau, and his sustained concentration on the lives of biblical characters as illustrations of philosophical points. The moralistic significance of the *exempla maiorum* mentioned in 1.116 is the closing note of book 3. The author claims to have put together a *series . . . vetustatis quodam compendio expressa* of the words and deeds of characters from Scripture, and he commends the study of these models to his addressees (3.139). The ultimate worth of the work lies not in its style, he says (cf. the dismissal of *ars* in 1.116; also 1.29), nor in its conformity to the framework of a

---

[58] For some shrewd assessment, and refutation of the traditional theory that Ambrose and Symmachus were blood-relations, see McLynn, 263–75.

[59] See commentary on 3.45–52.

philosophical genre, but in the stock of *exempla* which it
modestly presents for the faithful reader to imitate. When
Cicero's themes are forgotten, it is these biblical patterns
which really matter.[60]

5. The centrality of Scripture for Ambrose, even where he is
developing ethical arguments which are obviously rooted in the
classical tradition, will come as no surprise to those who have
looked elsewhere in his corpus: the Bible is always *the* formative source for him. But Ambrose does not explain biblical
texts in the kind of systematic fashion we expect of a modern
commentator; he quotes and paraphrases them copiously and
discursively, using them as scaffolding for more immediate
(and generalized) arguments on contemporary moral themes.
His exegetical works, a large proportion of which originated as
sermons, are exegetical in the strict sense only secondarily: they
are first and foremost pastoral extemporizations, ranging across
a much wider textual canvas than just the biblical passage
around which they are structured. *De officiis* reveals the very
same approach. Scriptural texts are presented as a mosaic of
(generally brief) stories and quotations illustrative of or providing validity for points and themes which have occurred to
Ambrose under the influence of Cicero or some other source.
Arguments flow along in a rather meandering style, punctuated
again and again by direct challenges and exhortations to the
reader—implicit appeals to both the moral attractiveness and
the sheer reasonableness of the behaviour revealed by scriptural characters. Tenuous associations of ideas are often
provoked by a sudden recollection of a biblical verse.
Ambrose's memory of scriptural narratives can be conveniently
selective or partial, as in 1.91–2 on Jacob, or in 1.237 on
David's pardon of Shimei, or just plain inaccurate, as in
1.42; and such lapses or sleights of hand can sometimes be
crucial to a point.

[60] Further on *exempla*, see Thamin, 244–9; Madec, 177–86; Sauer, 192–
201; C. Dantu, *La Place et le rôle de l'Ecriture dans le De officiis ministrorum
d'Ambroise* (Dijon, 1970); F. E. Consolino, 'Gli *exempla maiorum* nel *De officiis*
di Ambrogio e la duplice eredità dei cristiani', in *La tradizione: forme e modi.
XVIII Incontro di studiosi dell'antichità cristiana, Roma, 7–9 maggio 1989*
(Rome, 1990), 351–69. More generally, see M. E. Mohrmann, 'Wisdom and
the Moral Life: The Teachings of Ambrose of Milan', Ph.D. diss. (University
of Virginia, VA, 1995).

At one level, Ambrose regards Scripture as basically per-spicuous: it is a series of stories to be told rather than a text to be deconstructed. His references to Greek renderings, to vari-ants, to etymologies, and to exegetical authorities are designed as much to convey an impression of his own intellectual credentials as to shed genuine light on his subject-matter—though the fact that the Bible's language affords such scope for extensive discussion and celebration is meant to be seen as a testimony to its inexhaustible spiritual profundity. In the early days of his episcopate, Ambrose was all too sensitive to the charge that he had little formal preparation for his responsi-bilities as a teacher (*Virg.* 1.1–4; 2.1–5; cf. *Off.* 1.1–4), and he made sure that his ongoing endeavours in study remained visible to his public (cf. Augustine, *Conf.* 6.3.3). *De officiis* contains its fair share of passages where Ambrose airs the fruits of his scholarship. We have mention of textual variants, gleaned from Origen's *Hexapla*, in 1.15. There are some typical references to the meaning of Hebrew names in 1.91 and 1.246 (and a conflation of Hebrew and Greek words in 1.141), and other forays into etymology, evocative ultimately of Stoic assumptions that language is grounded in nature, occur in 1.26, 78; 3.112; note also the famous *homo–humus–humanus–humanitas* derivation in 3.16 and 3.45.[61] Ambrose's preference was to study the Old Testament in Greek,[62] and he quotes a verse in Greek in 1.30. The Greek of the New Testament appears in 1.221, and in 2.26 we are given different Latin renderings of an Old Testament verse. None of these touches adds any particular clarity to the text in question: they are there simply to parade knowledge (in the case of 1.30 and 1.221, they also facilitate strained parallels with or justifications of Cicero-nian vocabulary).

It is not that Ambrose naively underestimates the potential problems of the interpretative process, or fails to appreciate the layers of meaning that may be inherent in the language of biblical texts. On the contrary, the fondness he shows for

[61] See in general I. Opelt, 'Etymologie', *RAC* vi. 797–844; on Ambrose, see Kellner, 43–57; Gryson, *Typologie*, 151–63; commentary on 1.91.

[62] *Expos. Ps. 118*.12.45; the scepticism of S. Giet, 'De saint Basile à saint Ambroise. La condamnation du prêt à intérêt au IVe siècle', *RSR* 31 (1944), 95–128, about Ambrose's proficiency in Greek is misplaced.

spiritual exegesis implies an obvious desire to emphasize the
range of truths which can be fathomed in the scriptural
witness, and his control of verbal imagery to that end can
be quite remarkable.[63] *De officiis* offers a number of examples
of his interest in an allegorical or spiritual understanding of
Old Testament texts: e.g. 1.11 (Eccli. 28: 28–9); 1.80 (Ex. 28:
42–3); 1.78 (an exposition of Noah's ark as a symbol of the
human body, as sketched already in *De Noe* 13–30); and
1.162–5 (Prov. 23: 1–3). Typological exegesis in particular,
learnt above all from his reading in Philo and Origen, gives
Ambrose an interpretative key with which to unlock the Old
Testament, and a way of demonstrating the continuity of
God's purposes as one grand, connected design. The basic
assumptions can be seen in the *umbra–imago–veritas* scheme of
1.239, where a Stoic–Platonist conception of moral progress is
fused with a Christian perspective of salvation-history as
pivoting upon the Christ-event and oriented towards eschatological fulfilment.[64] More specific manifestations of the same
principle are to be seen in the presentation of Solomon as a
type of Christ in 2.51–3, and the association of his sword of
judgement with the sword of the Spirit in 2.47. Moses is
another type of Christ in 3.95, and the transformation of his
rod into a serpent is visualized as a symbol of the incarnation
and the cross in 3.94. The sacred fire which the fathers hid
when carried off into exile was in fact the fire of the Holy
Spirit, and several types of Christian baptism can be found in
Old Testament passages (3.98–110).[65] As Christian exegetes

[63] Cf. *Expl. Ps. 36.1*: *omnis Scriptura divina vel naturalis vel mystica vel moralis est*; also *Luc.*, prol. 1–4; *Is.* 23–30; *Expos. Ps. 118.1.3*. See generally Kellner, 31–40, 57–65, 65–74; P. de Labriolle, 'Saint Ambroise et l'exégèse allégorique', *Annales de philosophie chrétienne* 155 (1908), 591–603 (repro-duced essentially in id., *The Life and Times of St Ambrose* (St Louis, MO and London, 1928), 137 ff.); R. H. Malden, 'Saint Ambrose as an Interpreter of Holy Scripture', *JThS* 16 (1915), 509–22; Pizzolato, *passim*. On the artistry with which Ambrose's method can work, see H. Savon, 'Maniérisme et allégorie dans l'œuvre d'Ambroise de Milan', *REL* 55 (1977), 203–21. For Augustine's impressions, cf. *Conf.* 5.13.23–14.24; 6.4.6.

[64] See commentary on 1.233. On the tensions between this progress ideal and Ambrose's predilection for OT texts, see Introduction IV.4.

[65] Ambrose does not distinguish between apocryphal or deutero-canonical literature, such as Macc., Tob., Dan. 13, Judith, Wisd., and Eccli., and other OT material (cf. Homes Dudden ii. 558 n. 6). Throughout the commentary,

had so often claimed, Noah's ark was a type of the church (1.78).

In the end, Ambrose's policy of assembling vast *catenae* of citations is calculated to invest his language with the texture of the Bible itself, and to lend pastoral immediacy to his work: it is by immersion in the sheer breadth of sacred Scripture, and in the glories of its rhythms, that his addressees, like their teacher, will become what God intends them to be. The quotations, the allusions, and the narrative *exempla* are all about *sounding* biblical, and about being formed after a biblical pattern.[66]

V. COMPOSITION

Superficially, Ambrose maintains the basic anatomy of Cicero's text. The classical order of the three books is preserved, and material is generally maintained in the 'right' places: Ambrose avoids transferring major subject-matter from book 1 of Cicero, say, to book 2 in his own text.[67] On closer examination, however, it is quickly apparent that Ambrose takes considerable liberties with Cicero, and that he shows more enthusiasm for extolling scriptural examples than he does for constructing a careful philosophical argument. There are virtually no *exact* quotations; only (at best) very close reminiscences and endless verbal echoes, many of them doubtless subconscious[68] and in no specific logical sequence. There is also a decreasing amount

references to these texts are described as 'biblical' or 'scriptural', since that is what they are for him; nothing in particular is implied about the reliability of his view of canonical boundaries.

[66] G. Nauroy, 'L'Ecriture dans la pastorale d'Ambroise de Milan', in J. Fontaine and C. Pietri (eds.), *Le Monde latin antique et la Bible: La Bible de tous les temps*, ii: (Paris, 1985), 371–408, an excellent analysis. On the impact on Ambrose's style, see also G. Lazzati, 'Esegesi e poesia in sant'Ambrogio', *Annuario della Università Cattolica del Sacro Cuore* (1958), 75–91; id., *Il valore letterario della esegesi ambrosiana* (Milan, 1960), esp. 58–102; J. Huhn, 'Bewertung und Gebrauch der heiligen Schrift durch den Kirchenvater Ambrosius', *HJ* 77 (1958), 387–96.

[67] Though there are many verbal echoes and certain repeated ideas which do cross boundaries: see e.g. commentary on 1.126, 166, 254; 2.120–1; 3.34, 134.

[68] Especially in the case of the casual usage of single words or cognate forms.

of concentrated Ciceronian evocation as the work progresses: Scripture becomes more and more dominant; the contrasts drawn in book 3 between pagan and biblical models are direct rather than allusive; the narratives of scriptural stories become longer, and the classical vocabulary, while still very significant, is more sporadic and casual.[69]

Large sections of Ambrose's argument contain none of the fundamental Ciceronian philosophical terminology. Neither *honestas* nor *honestus* nor *honeste* appears in 1.1–26, 29–73, 103–22, 126–51, 153–74, 223–57; *utilis* is found only once in 2.98–156 (*utile* in 2.138), and neither *utilitas* nor *utilis* is mentioned after 3.90 (thereafter the honourable is presented as the only standard).[70] The treatment of Cicero's supplements to the Panaetian structure, the comparison of *honesta* and the comparison of *utilia*, respectively, is in each case very slender indeed. 1.252–9 corresponds superficially to Cicero, *Off.* 1.152–61, but contains only one explicit reference to a calculus of *honesta*, where it is said simply that when faced with a choice of two honourable courses, one should opt for *id quod honestius est* (1.258). In 2.22 and 2.28, Ambrose implies that a ranking of differing *utilia* is necessary, and we might suppose that 2.136–51 covers this; yet there is only one brief reference to *utile*, in 2.138. Furthermore, in 2.22 it is suggested that a calculus of *utilia* in book 2 will correspond to the distinction between the *honestum* and the *decorum* in book 1 (1.219–21), rather than (as it should) to the classification of *honesta* in book 1. Apart from the terse references to *honesta* and *honestius* in 1.258, the philosophical language is missing from the close of all three books: in every case, Ambrose addresses his clerics directly and in broader terms, without mentioning the Ciceronian theme at all.

Some passages which are essentially biblical in content are linked into the Ciceronian themes by the insertion of just one or two Ciceronian words. For example, in 3.98–124 there is no substantive evocation of Cicero, except in the link-passages,

---

[69] As far as Cicero's *Off.* is concerned, at any rate; the allusions to *Amic.* in 3.125–38 are of course another matter (though they too amount to *ad hoc* reminiscences, not systematic evocation of that work's arguments); see commentary ad loc.

[70] Testard, 'Etude', 173 n. 37, 179 n. 52; Testard misses *utile* in 2.138.

3.98, 110–11, 118, and 124, which attempt to tie in biblical stories by mentioning the *honestum/honestas* and the *decorum*. 3.103–10 constitutes what Ambrose himself calls an *excursus* (3.110) on types of Christian baptism to be found in the Old Testament; the only obvious connection to the ethical theme is the brief reference to *honestas* in the final paragraph, 3.110.

The arrangement of specific themes often bears only a loose resemblance to Cicero's. This is most striking in book 1. The cardinal virtues, which are introduced early on by Cicero (*Off.* 1.15), are not delineated by Ambrose until 1.115 (Ambrose is conscious of this obvious difference in 1.116). Nevertheless, before he gets to that point, he discusses modesty and seemliness in conduct and speech in 1.65–114, and thus anticipates material which might seem to belong better in the treatment of the fourth virtue, temperance, in 1.210–51. Both 1.65–114 and 1.210–51 echo a single Ciceronian section on temperance, *Off.* 1.93–151, yet Ambrose divides the classical themes between two passages which occur at some distance from each other. This leads to some apparent anomalies or repetitions. Anger is discussed twice, in 1.90–7 and in 1.231–8; the twin *motus* of the soul, reason/thought and appetite, appear in 1.98; 1.105–14; and 1.228–30; and *sermo* is mentioned briefly again in 1.226, having already been explored in 1.99–104.

Within each book, there are sections which do not obviously pick up Cicero at all. In book 1, for instance, Ambrose discusses the virtues of silence as opposed to speech (1.5–22, 31–5); talks about divine providence and theodicy (1.40–64); and outlines duties which are specific to clerics, particularly deacons (1.246–51). 2.1–21, on the *vita beata*, finds no parallel in Cicero.[71] 3.125–38, on the delights and the obligations of *amicitia*, goes far beyond Cicero's reference to the theme in *Off.* 3.43–6; Ambrose exploits the much fuller characterization offered by Cicero in the *De amicitia*.

There are a number of places where Ambrose appears to misunderstand, or fails to recollect accurately, what Cicero

---

[71] Cicero, *Off.* 2.6, has the phrase *ad bene beateque vivendum*, with reference to the practical quest of the philosophers, but no more is said about the *vita beata* by Cicero in his introduction to book 2. Cicero had already discussed the subject at a popular level in *Par.* 6–19, and more elaborately in *Fin.* and *Tusc.* 5.

says. In 1.105–14, for example, he is inspired by Cicero, *Off.*
1.141–2, which summarizes the criteria to be observed in
seemliness of *actio* (outlined already by Cicero in *Off.* 1.126–
40). At 1.105, Ambrose treats Cicero's summary as if it were a
divisio of points to be dealt with, which for Cicero it is not, and
then attempts to illustrate these points with biblical examples
in the paragraphs which follow. Then, having listed in 1.105
the three points made by Cicero in *Off.* 1.141, Ambrose in
1.106 treats a phrase from Cicero, *Off.* 1.142 (*de ordine rerum et
de opportunitate temporum*) as if it were a fourth point, which in
Cicero it is not.[72] Again, in Cicero, *Off.* 2.31–8 three ways of
gaining glory are mentioned: by winning people's goodwill
(*Off.* 2.32); by inspiring their faith (*Off.* 2.33–4); and by
earning their honour and admiration (*Off.* 2.36–8). In 2.40,
Ambrose conflates this three-point scheme with the larger
threefold division which occupies Cicero throughout *Off.*
2.23–85 (on three ways to gain people's support and esteem),
of which *Off.* 2.31–8 is just a small part (namely a subsection of
one way to acquire support: through the acquisition of glory).
Ambrose confuses what Cicero says about maintaining power
by love rather than fear in *Off.* 2.23–9, a passage which he
evokes in 2.29–39, with what he says about goodwill as the first
way to glory in *Off.* 2.32, and from 2.41 onwards he mixes up
two different plans.[73]

At several points, the sequence of thought between passages
is not very clear, and Ambrose senses a need to comment on his
arrangement. He defends the order in which he has developed
material in 1.23, 116, and 231, and in 1.47, 81;[74] 3.110. Other
claims are simply inconsistent. In 3.132, he says he has
narrated earlier the story of the three Hebrew youths from

---

[72] See commentary on 1.106. The illustration of the points in the ensuing
paragraphs is patchy and artificial, too: 1.110 has a four-point scheme; 1.111
has three points; 1.112 and 1.114 allude to two; 1.113 has none.

[73] See commentary on 2.29–39, 40, drawing on Testard, 'Etude', 176–9.
The attempt of Steidle, 'Beobachtungen 2' to defend the coherence of
Ambrose's argument is not very convincing, save in so far as Steidle rightly
underlines Ambrose's preoccupation with the *utilitas* of clerical self-commendation as a dominant theme throughout much of the book.

[74] In 1.81, the treatment of *verecundia* is not over, contrary to what
Ambrose implies: it continues in 1.85–9, and the intervening section, 1.81–
4, is really on the same lines (*verecundia* is mentioned in 1.83).

Daniel 3, yet no such passage has appeared. In 2.25, he maintains that he is addressing his 'sons', not avaricious merchants, yet in 3.37–44 he condemns those who seek to capitalize on food-shortages by selling grain at exorbitant prices, and in 3.45–52 he deprecates the banishment of *pere-grini* from a city during a time of famine: the later passages at least are obviously aimed at a wider circle than just clergy.[75]

It seems clear from such features that Ambrose cannot have composed his work with a copy of Cicero before him.[76] As we have seen, that is no surprise, given the widespread knowledge of Cicero among men of his class. Many scholars have gone further, however, and argued that *De officiis* was not produced in the first instance as a written text at all, but began life as a series of homilies. Ambrose first preached on a number of moral themes loosely based upon his memory of Cicero, it is said, and the transcripts of these sermons were then lightly edited and strung together into a published version.[77] Others have been less sure that the process was so clear-cut, but have perceived a homiletic dimension none the less: Ambrose may have written the work in book-form for the most part, they say, but made use of sermonic material as well, in the form of stenographers' copies or his own rough notes; the overall operation was hurried, and so the adherence to the Ciceronian template is haphazard.[78] It has been suggested that Ambrose wrote the bulk of the text but then delivered it to his clergy as a series of lectures.[79] A number of scholars have even sought to identify passages which they suggest have been incorporated

[75] Ambrose also reverses the order in which the source-passages occur: 3.37–44 is inspired by Cicero, *Off.* 3.50–3, and 3.45–52 by Cicero, *Off.* 3.47.

[76] *Pace* e.g. Paredi, 316; E. G. Weltin, *Athens and Jerusalem: An Interpretative Essay on Christianity and Classical Culture* (Atlanta, GA, 1987), 16.

[77] e.g. the Maurist editors in PL 16, 21–2; Draeseke, 131–2; Ihm, 27; Thamin, 216–17; Schmidt, 12–13; O. Bardenhewer, *Geschichte der altchristlichen Literatur* iii: *Das vierte Jahrhundert mit Ausschluss der Schriftsteller syrischer Zunge* (Freiburg, 1923), 529; Bürgi, 58; Palanque, 452–5; Homes Dudden ii. 694; Muckle, 64; Coyle, 225; Paredi, 316; H. von Campenhausen, *The Fathers of the Latin Church* (London, 1964), 123; Oberhelman, 39–41.

[78] Testard, 'Etude', 'Recherches' (especially 86 here), 'Observations'; also Testard i. 21–39. Testard, 'Etude', is approved by Banterle, 12–13; cf. also Moorhead, 157 (and 134).

[79] Crouter, 171–82.

more or less untouched from oral addresses.[80] One obvious example of such haste can, it is said, be seen in the introductory section, 1.1–22, where Ambrose confesses his inability to undertake the task of teaching and goes on to commend the spiritual virtues of silence: this piece must, it is claimed, have stemmed from an independent homily, probably preached when Ambrose was new to the episcopate; it has simply been prefixed to the body of the text, which begins properly at 1.23.[81]

At first sight, the signs do seem confusing. On the one hand, there are a whole string of references to Ambrose writing and to the work being read in book-form: *ad vos filios meos scribens . . . de officiis scribere* (1.23); *non alienum duxi nostro munere ut etiam ipse scriberem* (1.24); *scribere de officiis . . . quasi adhortaretur ad scribendum* (1.25); *scriptionis nostrae . . . deinde qui illa non legunt, nostra legent si volent* (1.29); *scripsimus* (1.162); *pulchre autem et hoc accidit ut scripturi de officiis, ea praefationis nostrae adsertione uteremur . . .* (1.231); *superiore libro de officiis tractavimus* (2.1); *superiore libro* (2.22); *in hoc libro* (3.29); *supra scripsimus* (3.77); *his tribus . . . libris* (3.139). On the other hand, in addition to the meandering style and the structural anomalies we find a number of phrases which might look as though they belong in a transcript of an oral piece rather than in a written treatise. In two places, Ambrose mentions a Scripture-reading which his addressees (or strictly 'addressee'—the verbs are singular) have (has) heard that day: *audisti hodie lectum* (1.13); *sicut audisti hodie legi* (1.15). In 2.25, *ad filios sermo est, et sermo de officiis* might be thought to imply that Ambrose is speaking rather than writing. And again, it seems odd that the only doxology to be found in the text comes at the end of book 2: if the work is written, might we not expect this language either at the close of book 3 or perhaps at the end of every book?[82]

Despite the apparent ambivalence of such data, there is in

---

[80] See e.g. Thamin, 216–17; Palanque, 452–5, speculating about such sections as 1.40–64, 246–51; 2.1–21; 3.125–38.

[81] Emeneau, 49–50; Palanque, 453–4; Homes Dudden ii. 694.

[82] The liturgical phrase printed at the end of book 1 in the PL text and translated in versions based upon it is not Ambrose's, but a medieval scribal addition; see commentary ad loc.

fact no reason to believe that *De officiis* as a whole began life as anything other than a book,[83] and no reason to doubt Ambrose when he tells us he is writing it. The roughness of the work's style in no way necessitates the conclusion that the author must first have delivered his material in oral form. It is no surprise that Ambrose's enthusiasm for biblical narratives often interrupts the flow of ostensibly Ciceronian moral points, or that his attempts to evoke classical philosophical nomenclature can sometimes look strained. Ambrose is a spiritual teacher articulating *ad hoc* practical advice, not an ethical theorist developing a careful intellectual case. He weaves together a variety of didactic approaches—philosophical *disputatio*, scriptural *expositio*, and pastoral *exhortatio*[84]—but, as the overall informality and spontaneity of his style suggest, the last two matter far more to him than the first. Ambrose is also an ancient author, for whom (as his scriptural references equally show) approximate paraphrase rather than exact quotation of well-known texts in the public domain was normal,[85] and whose ideas of structural arrangement were far more fluid than those which might be deemed desirable today.[86]

Besides, nowhere does Ambrose suggest that his ambition is to produce an exact Christian mirror-image of Cicero. All he says is that he too is entitled to write on *officia* (1.24); he simply points up the tradition which he is following, and Cicero's obviously prominent place within it. As we have seen, he imitates Cicero's paternal *persona*, and seeks to justify his

[83] Cf. W. G. Rusch, *The Later Latin Fathers* (London, 1977), 56. I therefore withdraw statements I myself have made to the contrary in some earlier published work.

[84] Testard i. 36–7; 'Etude', 195–6.

[85] On published texts as *publica materies*, see H. Hagendahl, 'Methods of Citation in Post-Classical Latin Prose', *Eranos* 45 (1947), 114–28, at 118.

[86] Cicero's style also appears free by modern standards. Repetition, for example, is not just Ambrose's trait: he may have two passages on the honouring of oaths (1.255 and 3.77–9), or the maintenance of deposits (1.254 and 2.144–51), or the benefits to be gained by the young in keeping older company (1.212; cf. 1.87; and 2.97–101); but in each of these cases so has Cicero. Ambrose is not the only one to digress and then call himself back to a theme: *sed iam ad proposita pergamus* in 2.21 evokes Cicero, *Off.* 2.8; and *ut ad propositum redeamus* in 3.32 echoes Cicero, *Off.* 2.35 and 3.39. Expressions like *quem paene praeterieram* in 2.59 are also common enough in classical authors where the tone is informal.

application of the philosophical vocabulary; but he also develops a series of contrasts, intending his work to be a very
different version of the same theme. Cicero's model is vital,
in so far as it is the outstanding representative of its kind, but
Ambrose never promises to set out a section-for-section parody
of it. The aim of *his* work is, we are told, practical usefulness,
not literary impression (1.116; 3.139), and he expects his
approach to be seen as distinct (cf. particularly 1.116; also
1.23, 231–2).

None of this, perhaps, excuses the overall diffuseness of
Ambrose's writing. Taken together, however, such features
forbid us to overstate the significance of it. If we cannot fault
Ambrose for failing to do something which he does not claim to
be attempting (and which he would doubtless have considered
unnecessarily restrictive as a literary exercise),[87] we certainly
cannot draw conclusions about how he composed on the basis
of a false expectation that he ought to be following Cicero's
lead at every turn. Many of the weaknesses in his style may
have as much to do with haste and spontaneity as anything else.
Ambrose had to fit his literary activity into a demanding
schedule of other commitments. No doubt, like all authors,
he was sometimes interrupted, and had to pick up the thread of
his argument after some sort of interval; he may simply have
had neither opportunity nor motivation to iron out every
technical crease.

The direct textual 'evidence' usually adduced in support of a
theory of homiletic provenance for the work is at best incon-
clusive and at worst irrelevant.[88] Nothing decisive can be

[87] Testard, 'Recherches', 66–8.

[88] When Ambrose says that he has today read or meditated on a certain
passage of Scripture (1.23 and 1.25), there is clearly no reason to believe that
he must be speaking, as opposed to writing. This is perhaps particularly true
when, as in 1.23, it is a Psalm to which he refers: since the Psalms were an
important part of the daily office, Ambrose might presumably have happened
to ponder verses from one Psalm or another on any given day. When he refers
to scriptural texts that his addressees have read, using expressions like *legimus*
(1.25, 80, 140; 2.101, 145; 3.103, 118); *legisti* (2.109; 3.42); *cum legerimus*
(3.103); or *cum legeris* (3.106), this plainly need not mean that the readings had
taken place in an immediate liturgical context, only that the biblical passages
are familiar. Despite peculiar suggestions to the contrary in some quarters
(Palanque, 437, 452–3), vocatives like *filii* and *fili* are every bit as likely to
appear in a written as in an oral text; so too are idioms such as *meministis* (1.72;

inferred from the use of *sermo* in 2.25: the word may well be
standard for a homily, but it can also describe a written piece
produced in conversational style and initially read as a literary
performance.[89] Book 2 may be the only book to end with a
doxological phrase, but the immediate context in 2.152–6,
which is in any case a mosaic of scriptural texts, contains two
brief allusions to Cicero.[90] If Ambrose went to the trouble of
inserting Ciceronian vocabulary into material deriving from an
independent sermon, we might expect him to have made a
more consistent job of it, rather than managing only a couple of
fleeting echoes. It was not unusual for a portion of a work to be
released for circulation prior to the completion of the whole: [91]
while there is no other evidence that *De officiis* 1–2 were
published prior to *De officiis* 3, such an occurrence is not
inherently impossible, and might afford some explanation for
the sole appearance of a doxology at the end of book 2.[92] But
perhaps Ambrose simply felt moved to include one at that

2.150), or *ad vos loquebar* (1.81; cf. *loqui* in 1.143, 235; 2.69; 3.63). Certain
passages may be similar to sections in other works which are generally held to
be sermonic in origin (e.g. 1.202–3 resembles *Iac.* 2.42, 45–58; 2.26 is similar
to *Expos. Ps. 118*.5.27; and 3.107–8 is close to *Elia* 83), but this no more
establishes parallel methods of composition than it proves anything about the
relative chronologies of the texts [Introduction II]: any writer might make use
of or recycle in print material that he elsewhere presents orally, and vice versa.
Attempts to infer a homiletic genesis from the Latinity of the text are also
flawed [Introduction IX].

[89] Horace could call both his *Satires* and his *Epistles sermones*, and the
dialogical texts of Cicero and others regularly use the word for the convention
of a literary conversation.

[90] Both of which have been overlooked by all scholars to date.

[91] e.g. Augustine made the first thirteen books of *CD* available to the monks
Peter and Abraham in 417, long before the treatise was finished (*Ep.* 184A),
and his *Doctr. Chr.* appears to have circulated for a time in only two books (cf.
Retract. 2.30, and see W. M. Green, 'A Fourth-Century Manuscript of Saint
Augustine?', *RBén* 69 (1959), 191–7. Sometimes portions of texts were
purloined and circulated against an author's wishes, as happened with parts
of Augustine's *Trin.* (*Ep.* 174; cf. *Retract.* 2.41); cf. also Tertullian, *Adv.
Marc.* 1.1.

[92] Interestingly, Palanque, 454, canvassing the supposed evidence for a
sermonic base for the work as a whole, mentions the theory that books 1 and 2
were originally homiletic and that book 3 was written as a supplement for the
published version, to parallel Cicero's three-book structure. He dismisses the
idea, on the grounds that the Ciceronian evocation pervades all three books.

point. We are presumably safe in assuming that he produced his text in stages; perhaps the completion of book 2 brought its own sense of exultation.

The only details which might conceivably point to any prior oral stage for any part of the text are the two brief references to liturgical readings said to have been heard *hodie* in 1.13 and 1.15. One possible explanation is to say that Ambrose simply uses these as a literary device: they are an affectation, not a genuine relic from a homily. There are two problems with this. First, phrases such as *audisti hodie lectum* are usually treated as reliable testimony of sermonic provenance elsewhere, so why not here?[93] Secondly, what purpose would be served by the use of just two phrases as a literary device? They appear in close proximity early in the work, and no similar expression occurs anywhere thereafter. It is a strange device that is used so sparingly, and without more obvious effect where it is applied. Another possibility is that the two expressions are simply a slip, made by an author who spends a good deal of his time composing for audiences rather than readers. This theory might be strengthened if we suppose that Ambrose might have *dictated* some or all of his work rather than written it with his own hand:[94] speaking to a *notarius*, does he simply

---

[93] For a few examples, see A. Paredi, 'La liturgia di sant'Ambrogio', in *Sant'Ambrogio nel XVI centenario della nascita* (Milan, 1940), 69–157, at 73–6.

[94] The idea of an author invariably writing in private at his desk is inappropriate in antiquity. Both Jerome and Augustine relied heavily on the services of amanuenses (not surprisingly, they were easier to come by in Hippo than in the Judaean desert): E. P. Arns, *La Technique du livre d'après saint Jérôme* (Paris, 1953), 37–79; and especially H. Hagendahl, 'Die Bedeutung der Stenographie für die spätlateinische christliche Literatur', *JbAC* 14 (1971), 24–38; R. J. Deferrari, 'St Augustine's Method of Composing and Delivering Sermons', *AJPh* 43 (1922), 97–123, 193–219 (Augustine typically dictated treatises and letters, but preferred the extempore form in preaching). Ambrose claims to have preferred to write with his own hand, and we are told that he often wrote far into the night: *Ep.* 37 [47].1–2, evoking Quint., *Inst.* 10.3.18 ff.; *Ep. extra coll.* 11 [51].14; Paulinus, *VA* 38 (see also Hagendahl, 'Die Bedeutung der Stenographie', 36–8), but he certainly did employ secretaries as well: cf. Paulinus, *VA* 42.1, where he is described as dictating *Expl. Ps. 43*; there is no indication that there was anything unusual about this practice (*pace* Homes Dudden ii. 489). Sometimes Ambrose's compositions were also proof-read for him by faithful associates such as Sabinus of Piacenza: *Ep.* 32 [48].2–3.

forget that readings which have been part of the lectionary on that particular day will not have been heard *hodie* by subsequent readers of a published text?

Alternatively, Ambrose may be making use of some kind of homiletic material *in and around these points*. The two references occur in the introduction to the work (1.1–22). It is highly unlikely that the whole of that passage derives from an independent sermon preached early in Ambrose's episcopate, since there are numerous deliberate allusions to Cicero woven into the language, contrasting the Christian approach with the classical one: 1.1–22 as it stands is integral to the text.[95] At the same time, much of the section (1.5–22) is structured loosely around an exegesis of some verses from Psalm 38, which Ambrose claims inspired him to take up the theme of *officia* (1.23). It is quite possible that 1.5–22 does exploit some kind of sermonic treatment of the Psalm, which in turn is indebted to Origen; the same material is evidently used also in 1.233–45.[96] Ambrose has clearly not just inserted an independent exposition of the Psalm into the body of his text, but he may be drawing upon ideas which he had developed elsewhere in a sermon. For some reason, his editorial process seems not to have been very thorough, and liturgical references which made sense only in a different treatment have escaped excision.[97] Whatever the explanation, though, the presence of the two small phrases in 1.13 and 1.15 is insufficient evidence on which to construct a theory of oral origins for even the entire *praefatio* of 1.1–22, far less for the treatise as a whole.

The ultimate problem with positing a sermonic provenance for *De officiis* is in many respects the most basic: what kind of audience could be envisaged for a series of homilies based upon

[95] For details, see commentary on 1.1–22, and esp. I. J. Davidson, 'A Tale of Two Approaches: Ambrose, *De officiis* 1.1–22 and Cicero, *De officiis* 1.1–6', *JThS* NS 52 (2001), 61–83.

[96] See commentary ad loc.

[97] The first references to writing or to the work being read cluster around the section which follows (1.23–5, 29); another reference to writing occurs in 1.231, where the exegesis of Ps. 38 appears again, in 1.231–45. On the whole subject, see further commentary on 1.1–22. There are other extended references to scriptural passages in e.g. 1.153–7 (2 Cor. 8), 162–5 (Prov. 23: 1–3; note the reference to writing in 1.162); and 3.103–10 (on OT baptismal types), which again might possibly reflect earlier formulations.

Cicero? Ambrose could hardly have expected an average congregation to appreciate what he was up to when he obliquely criticized Cicero's *exempla* and echoed tiny—yet vital—phrases from his arguments. The bishop's normal weekly audiences in his basilica numbered anything up to 3,000, and certainly included some important intellectuals, such as the *grammaticus* Verecundus,[98] educated courtiers like Ponticianus,[99] and former officials like Nicentius;[100] but they must also have consisted of hundreds of people far less cultivated than these.[101] It stretches the bounds of credibility to picture such individuals making sense of sermons preached on material directly indebted to a text of classical philosophy.[102] Nor is it likely that Ambrose could have preached this way within his *presbyterium*. His clerical body doubtless included some who knew their Cicero well enough to discern obvious reminiscences in a written work; but it was hardly a learned society, capable of tracing a random pastiche of allusions and nuances as they came from the lips of a speaker. Ambrose's evocation may be uneven, but he requires the differences between Cicero's vision and his own to be clearly identifiable. Crudely executed in literary terms his effort may appear; but it was as readers, not hearers, that his first addressees must have encountered it.[103]

---

[98] Augustine, *Conf.* 8.6.13; 9.3.5.

[99] Ibid. 8.6.14–15.

[100] Ambrose, *Ep.* 70 [56].8; Paulinus, *VA* 44.

[101] See further R. Macmullen, 'The Preacher's Audience [AD 350–400]', *JThS* NS 40 (1989), 503–11.

[102] A. Ebert, *Allgemeine Geschichte der Literatur des Mittelalters im Abendlande* i, 2nd edn. (Leipzig, 1889), 162; M. Schanz, *Geschichte der römischen Literatur bis zum Gesetzgebungswerk des Kaisers Justinian* iv/1 (Munich, 1914), 340.

[103] While Testard's work (especially 'Etude'; 'Recherches'; Testard i. 21–39; also 'Saint Ambroise et son modèle cicéronien dans le *De officiis*', in R. Chevallier (ed.), *Présence de Cicéron: Hommage au R. P. M. Testard* (Paris, 1984), 103–6) tends to overstate the disorganization of *Off.*, the dense efforts of Steidle, 'Beobachtungen' and 'Beobachtungen 2', to argue that the text is constructed with great care seem to me to go too far. The commentary seeks to steer a middle course between exaggerating the structural weaknesses and ignoring the definite problems. For studies of other editing processes in Ambrose, see G. Nauroy, 'La méthode de composition d'Ambroise de Milan et la structure du *De Iacob et vita beata*', in *Ambroise de Milan*; id., 'La Structure du *De Isaac vel de anima* et la cohérence de l'allégorèse d'Ambroise

VI. PURPOSE OF THE WORK

Quot interpretes, tot sententiae: even a cursory survey of the history of scholarship on *De officiis* reveals a vast range of assessments as to what Ambrose was aspiring to achieve. The treatise has variously been taken as proof that Ambrose was a fraudulent plagiarist, a creative genius, an unreconstructed Roman chauvinist, a proto-Marxist, a Stoic masquerading as a Christian, a cultural apologist, a philosophical bridge-builder, a detester of all philosophy, and, last but not least, a spiritual giant whose gracious humility and self-effacement render his achievement in ennobling pagan virtue all the more remarkable. The sheer range of judgements is intriguing in itself, and it is worth glancing at a few of them, at least in summary form.[104]

One theory is that Ambrose remained at heart a traditional Roman, who so admired the ideals of gentlemanly conduct

de Milan', *REL* 63 (1985), 210–36; also M. Roques, 'L'Authenticité de l'*Apologia David altera*: histoire et progrès d'une controverse', *Augustinianum*, 36 (1996), 53–92, 423–58. Ambrose did sometimes take considerable care, such as in the case of his epistles, which seem to be deliberately organized into a collection of ten volumes, nine 'private' and one 'public', in imitation of Pliny's model: see M. Zelzer, '*Plinius Christianus*: Ambrosius als Epistolograph', *SP* 23 (1989), 203–8; though the thesis has been challenged by H. Savon, 'Saint Ambroise a-t-il imité le recueil de lettres de Pline le Jeune?', *REAug* 41 (1995), 3–17.

[104] For an outline taxonomy, and analysis in broadly similar terms to what follows here, see I. J. Davidson, 'Ambrose's *De Officiis* and the Intellectual Climate of the Late Fourth Century', *VChr* 49 (1995), 313–33, esp. 314–15. Some of the literature is canvassed by M. Grazia Mara in A. di Berardino (ed.), *Patrology*, intro. J. Quasten, *Patrology* iv: *The Golden Age of Patristic Literature* (Rome, 1986), 166–7; E. Dekkers, *Clavis Patrum Latinorum*, 3rd edn. with A. Gaar (Turnhout and Steenbrugge, 1995), 44. For surveys covering various periods, see especially Crouter, 375–404; Sauer, i–vi; Colish ii. 58–9; A. Nawrocka, 'L'Etat d'études concernant l'influence de l'éthique de Cicéron sur l'éthique de saint Ambroise', *Helikon* 28 (1988), 315–24; Becker, 9–13. On the work of Ewald (n. 106) and of Thamin (n. 115), see H. Savon, 'Les Recherches sur saint Ambroise en Allemagne et en France de 1870 à 1930', in J. Fontaine, R. Herzog, and K. Pollmann (eds.), *Patristique et Antiquité tardive en Allemagne et en France de 1870 à 1930: influences et échanges. Actes du colloque franco-allemand de Chantilly (25–27 octobre 1991)* (Paris, 1993), 111–28, esp. 112–20.

advocated by Cicero that he simply reiterated them with little substantive modification. The result is an ethical prescription more classical than Christian.[105] The Stoic influence, mediated through Cicero, is so strong that a truly Christian moral spirit is obscured.[106] In effect, *De officiis* symbolizes the conquest of the Christian church by the ethics of the Stoa.[107]

Then again, Ambrose's handling of his sources has been viewed completely the opposite way. For many critics, Ambrose overwhelmingly Christianizes his Stoic-Ciceronian inheritance. The outward classical framework may remain the same, but it has been given a new, Christian content.[108] We have paganism at its noblest, allied to the higher ethic of

[105] Emeneau, *passim*, esp. 53: 'Ambrose may be considered the last of the Roman Christians, the last of those who, nurtured on pagan ideals, could not be possessed of true Christianity.'

[106] Ewald, *passim*, esp. 32–3, 87–8; Th. Zielinski, *Cicero im Wandel der Jahrhunderte*, 2nd edn. (Leipzig and Berlin, 1908), 131–40.

[107] E. Hatch, *The Influence of Greek Ideas and Usages upon the Christian Church* (London, 1888), 168–70; A. Harnack, *History of Dogma* v (London, 1898), 49 n. 3; K. Lake, *Landmarks in the History of Early Christianity* (London, 1920), 9–10.

[108] This is the assessment of a large group of critics; for simplicity's sake I list them together, though their emphases, their levels of engagement with the text, and their scholarly sophistication vary considerably: F. Spach, *Etude sur le traité de saint Ambroise, 'De Officiis Ministrorum'* (Strasbourg, 1859), 47–51; D. Leitmeir, *Apologie der christlichen Moral. Darstellung des Verhältnisses der heidnischen und christlichen Ethik, zunächst nach einer Vergleichung des ciceronianischen Buches 'De officiis' und dem gleichnamigen des heiligen Ambrosius* (Augsburg, 1866); H. H. Scullard, *Early Christian Ethics in the West, from Clement to Ambrose* (London, 1907), 101–3, 183–7, 233–8, 270–8; L. Visconti, 'Il primo trattato di filosofia morale cristiana (il De Officiis di s. Ambrogio e di Cicerone)', *Atti della Reale Accademia d' Archeologia, Lettere e Belle Arte di Napoli* 25/2 (1908), 44–61; P. Canata, *De S. Ambrosii libris qui inscribuntur De officiis ministrorum quaestiones* (Modena, 1909), especially 38, 52; F. Wagner, *Der Sittlichkeitsbegriff in der hl. Schrift und in der altchristlichen Ethik* (Münster, 1931), 219–34; C. N. Cochrane, *Christianity and Classical Culture* (Oxford, 1940), 373–4; Homes Dudden ii. 502–54, esp. 551–4; Paredi, 316–20; J. Gaffney, 'Comparative Religious Ethics in the Service of Historical Interpretation: Ambrose's Use of Cicero', *Journal of Religious Ethics* 9 (1981), 35–47; G. Verbeke, *The Presence of Stoicism in Medieval Thought* (Washington, DC, 1983), 48; M. Zelzer, 'Ambrosius von Mailand und das Erbe der klassischen Tradition', *WS* 100 (1987), 201–26, at 208–9; C. Rossi, 'Il De officiis di Cicerone e il De officiis di Ambrogio: rapporti di contenuto e forma', in F. Sergio (ed.), *'Humanitas' classica e 'sapientia' cristiana: scritti offerti a Roberto Iacoangeli* (Rome, 1992), 145–62; Ramsey, 53.

Christ.[109] A supernatural foundation has been laid;[110] and entirely new senses have been injected into classical terminology.[111] Ambrose has elevated the old patterns of morality to a new dimension, and in varying degrees accentuated the differences between the two in order to assert the superiority of the Christian paradigm.[112] Behind the façade of a shared inheritance, the substance of the edifice is entirely new.[113]

In each case, the thinking behind the work has also been subjected to conflicting interpretations. Some argue that Ambrose was an inept plagiarist, who clumsily constructed a mosaic of pagan sentiments and attempted, with little success, to give it a Christian veneer.[114] On this reading, what we have is an awkward juxtaposition of pagan and Christian ideas, either because Ambrose remained insensitive to the distinctions between them or, more likely, because he was incapable of harmonizing them better. Ambrose effected an 'intellectual coup d'état' of Ciceronian ethics, but did not see any need to produce a significant constitutional rearrangement in his new territory.[115] The Stoic content remains more prominent than any reasonable Christian reader would consider desirable, it is said, and more prominent than the author himself could surely have wished had he enjoyed the benefit of any critical distance from the implications of his cultural syncretism.[116] But

[109] J. W. C. Wand, *The Latin Doctors* (London, 1948), 21.

[110] J. T. Muckle, 'The Influence of Cicero in the Formation of Christian Culture', *Transactions of the Royal Society of Canada*, ser. 3, 42/2 (1948), 107–25, at 113–18.

[111] Muckle [1939], *passim*; cf. also more generally M. Badura, *Die leitenden Grundsätze der Morallehre des hl. Ambrosius* (Prague, 1921), 22–47.

[112] F. Bittner, *De Ciceronianis et Ambrosianis Officiorum Libris Commentatio* (Braunsberg, 1849); F. Hasler, *Über das Verhältnis der heidnischen und christlichen Ethik auf Grund einer Vergleichung des ciceronianischen Buches 'De Officiis' mit dem gleichnamigen des heiligen Ambrosius* (Munich, 1866), 18–48; Draeseke, *passim*; J. Reeb, *Über die Grundlagen des Sittlichen nach Cicero und Ambrosius: Vergleichung ihrer Schriften De officiis* (Zweibrücken, 1876), 30 ff.; G. Nosari, *Del preteso stoicismo ciceroniano nei libri 'De officiis' di s. Ambrogio* (Parma, 1911), 27–40; Löpfe, 153–5; Coyle, *passim*.

[113] Hiltbrunner, especially 178, 182.

[114] Hagendahl, 347–72.

[115] Thamin 1 ('un vrai coup d'Etat intellectuel'), 201–309; E. K. Rand, *Founders of the Middle Ages* (Cambridge, MA, 1928), 79–83, esp. 82.

[116] Again, the nuances vary somewhat, but see Schmidt, *passim*; Stelzenberger, 491–502 (cf. also 129–34, 175–8, 234–42, 335–40); von

Ambrose has equally been seen as an heir to a certain Christian apologetic tradition. The claim in this case is that he judiciously selected from Cicero ideas which to him were not at odds with his Christian beliefs and which fitted his social context, and carefully combined them with ethical ideals drawn from the Scriptures. The aim of this intellectual eclecticism was to produce a deliberate blend of the old and the new, a judicious harmony of sacred wisdom and classical insight, in order to appeal to a philosophically sophisticated readership.[117]

But, again, it has been suggested that Ambrose deliberately contrasted the Christian ethical spirit with Cicero's pagan ethos in order to point up the excellence of scriptural truth. The two thought-worlds are set in sharp antithesis, and there is sustained polemic against paganism. Ambrose intended to show that pagan ideas were at worst erroneous and at best derivative from Scripture; the Bible stands supreme as the source of wisdom.[118] This implies an attempt to replace Cicero's treatment of *officia* with a new, Christian, exposition of the theme.[119]

Other scholars have sought to move the debate on from such preoccupation with possible ideological programmes by arguing that Ambrose's method was governed by pragmatism. He was more interested in offering utilitarian guidance than he was in achieving any sort of intellectual *tour de force*. This meant that he was prepared to use whatever he felt was practically useful for his immediate pedagogical purposes as a pastor, without troubling himself about potential clashes of philosophical assumptions or seeking to present a systematic

Campenhausen, *The Fathers of the Latin Church*, 123–4. For similar appraisals of Ambrose more generally, see also M. Pohlenz, *Die Stoa* i (Göttingen, 1948), 445–7; F. Flückiger, *Geschichte des Naturrechtes* i: *Altertum und Frühmittelalter* (Zurich, 1954), 360–77.

[117] Zelzer, 'Beurteilung', *passim*; J. L. Womer (ed.), *Morality and Ethics in Early Christianity* (Philadelphia, 1987), 27. Cf. also Hill, 38–90, 144–207.

[118] P. de Labriolle, 'Le "De officiis ministrorum" de saint Ambroise et le "De officiis" de Cicéron', *Revue des cours et conférences* 16/2 (1907–8), 177–86 (= de Labriolle, *The Life and Times of St Ambrose*, 186–204); Lenox-Conyngham, esp. 119–20; Savon, 'Intentions', *passim*; Savon, 246–50.

[119] Sauer, 202–7; cf. also Zelzer, 'Randbemerkungen', *passim*; A. Michel, 'Du De officiis de Cicéron à saint Ambroise: la théorie des devoirs', in *L'etica cristiana nei secoli III e IV: Eredità e confronti* (Rome, 1996), 39–46.

contrast of secular and Christian agendas. Ambrose was quite capable of distinguishing *verba* from *res* in accordance with his own moral and spiritual convictions, while remaining firmly opposed to the general world of secular 'philosophy'.[120] In the process, he was also creative, able simultaneously to de-Stoicize the Ciceronian virtues in certain crucial respects while in others treating them in a more integrally Stoic manner than Cicero himself; he was thus able to effect an amalgam which was distinctively stamped by his own style.[121]

For all the voluminous literature, quite a lot of the analysis of *De officiis* has been rather shallow, and critics have sometimes revealed almost as much about their own philosophical prejudices or confessional perspectives as they have about Ambrose himself.[122] If we are trying to gauge Ambrose's *aims*, virtually all of the judgements can in the end be reduced to two opposing views. Either (1) Ambrose wished to produce a positive synthesis of Ciceronian Stoicism and Christian ethics, as an ambitious sort of apologetic exercise or in a pious attempt to elevate the pagan virtues by applying them creatively to a different context; or (2) he sought to replace Cicero's work by transforming its content, and thus to write a new account of *officia* for a new age, informed by quite different, and palpably superior, values. In either case, his *aims* need to be differentiated from his *results*. There can be no dispute that Ambrose produced a text which retains a great deal from Cicero, for all his professed disdain for secular philosophy. The extent to which his effort constitutes an intellectual, literary, or moral success or failure is not the point. A conceptual amalgam of old and new was perfectly standard in the context of the late Roman world to which Ambrose belonged, and modern

---

[120] Madec, 80–5, 161–6, 344–5.

[121] Colish ii. 58–70; ead., 'Cicero, Ambrose, and Stoic Ethics: Transmission or Transformation?', in A. Bernardo and S. Levin (eds.), *The Classics in the Middle Ages* (Binghamton, NY, 1990), 95–112.

[122] Certain late nineteenth- and early twentieth-century German Protestant readings appear fixated on the Stoic influences, which perhaps reflects the concern of some contemporary liberalism to demonstrate the corruption of the Christian gospel by patristic philosophizing; Catholic scholars, on the other hand, tended to depict Ambrose as a saintly genius who wonderfully baptized classical morality into a new existence—without much reference to the political dynamics of his time. Cf. Crouter, 375–404.

labels such as 'plagiarism' and 'originality' cannot be reliably applied to ancient literature, for the conventions of *imitatio* that prevailed in antiquity directly encouraged the copying of admired forms.[123] Whether Ambrose created a masterpiece or a monstrosity is not the issue; the question is whether he wished to present his Christian faith as the cultural heir of classical antiquity by adapting a pagan classic to a new spiritual context, or whether his intention was to use his Ciceronian model as a framework within which to articulate a quite different message. Did he want to point up intellectual continuities, or did he aim to supersede his classical archetype?

A positive synthesis?

On the face of it, if Ambrose was approaching a pagan source in a generous spirit he was following a tradition that stretched back through the Alexandrians to the Apologists, to Philo the Jew, and possibly even to some of the New Testament authors themselves.[124] In the strategy of, say, a Clement of Alexandria, Christian thinkers could repudiate the errors of pagan theology and ethics while at the same time making positive overtures about the value of Greek philosophy as a preparation for the gospel of true wisdom. The personal intellectual pilgrimages of men such as Clement had left them with a determination to show that conversion to the faith was eminently reasonable, and that it did not require an automatic or absolute denigration of secular learning.

Unlike some of these earlier churchmen, Ambrose had never been a professional scholar; but he was certainly no philosophical ignoramus. Quite naturally for a man of his class and education, he had a grasp of the concepts and vocabulary which

---

[123] See D. A. Russell, 'De Imitatione', in D. West and A. J. Woodman (eds.), *Creative Imitation and Latin Literature* (Cambridge, 1979), 1–16. On *imitatio* and *Off.*, see Claus, *passim*.

[124] Consider such classic passages as Acts 17; Rom. 1; and perhaps Acts 14: 8–20; all of which must of course be measured alongside 1 Cor. 1: 18–2: 5 and Col. 2: 8; consider too Jn. 1: 1–18, and the influence of Platonist idealism in Heb. (however it is assessed). Philosophical insights may be exploited, while 'philosophy' as a way of salvation is firmly condemned. On the second- and third-century context, H. Chadwick, *Early Christian Thought and the Classical Tradition* (Oxford, 1966) is still the best introduction.

made up the intellectual currency of his time. Source-criticism
of works which stem from sermons which he preached in the
mid-380s, *De Isaac vel anima*, *De bono mortis*, and *De Iacob et
vita beata*, has revealed his knowledge of Platonist ideas and
texts, especially those of Plotinus,[125] whom he had almost
certainly read for himself in some measure. Such findings
have helped to dispel any illusions that his intellectual range
was narrow. Some of his knowledge may possibly have been
acquired under the tutelage of his presbyter (and eventual
successor) Simplicianus, who in the 350s had been instrumen-
tal in the conversion of the great Neoplatonist rhetor, Marius
Victorinus, at Rome.[126] It may have come through contact with
a wider 'Platonist circle' (so-called) in Milan of which Simplicianus and other leading intellectuals such as the former
courtier Manlius Theodorus formed a nucleus. But it is more
likely that he had come into contact with Neoplatonist ideas on
his own earlier on, prior to his election as bishop.[127] In any

[125] See esp. P. Courcelle, *Recherches sur les Confessions de saint Augustin*
(Paris, 1968), 93–138; also id., 'L'humanisme chrétien de saint Ambroise',
Orpheus 9 (1962), 21–34; 'Anti-Christian Arguments and Christian Platon-
ism', in A. Momigliano (ed.), *The Conflict between Paganism and Christianity
in the Fourth Century* (Oxford, 1963), 151–92, especially 165; 'Deux grands
courants de pensée dans la littérature latine tardive: Stoïcisme et néo-
Platonisme', *REL* 42 (1964), 122–40; L. Taormina, 'Sant'Ambrogio e
Plotino', *MSLCA* 4 (1953), 41–85; A. Solignac, 'Nouveaux parallèles entre
saint Ambroise et Plotin: le "De Iacob et vita beata" et le Περὶ Εὐδαιμονίας
(*Ennéade* I, 4)', *Archives de Philosophie* 20 (1956), 148–56; P. Hadot, 'Platon et
Plotin dans trois sermons de saint Ambroise', *REL* 34 (1956), 202–20;
H. Dörrie, 'Das fünffach gestufte Mysterium. Der Aufstieg der Seele bei
Porphyrios und Ambrosius', in A. Stuiber and A. Hermann (eds.), *Mullus:
Festschrift Theodor Klauser* (Münster, 1964), 79–92. For a prudent overview
of the whole subject, see Madec, 60–71.
[126] Augustine, *Conf.* 8.2.3–5. On the difficulties which attend our knowledge of Simplicianus' movements prior to Ambrose's tenure in Milan, see
McLynn, 36, 54; Williams, 117–19; Markschies, 79–83; Savon, 52–4.
[127] Courcelle, *Recherches*, 9–16, argues that one of the ways in which,
according to Paulinus, Ambrose attempted to avoid ordination was, *philoso-
phiam profiteri voluit* (Paulinus, *VA* 7), should be read as a declaration of
interest in Neoplatonism; cf. Madec, 24–5 n. 8; Zelzer, 'Beurteilung', 178. (On
these expedients generally, see Y.-M. Duval, 'Ambroise, de son élection à sa
consécration', in *AmbrEpisc* ii. 243–83.) For a classic (and disputed) account of
Christian Neoplatonism in Milan, see P. Courcelle, *Les lettres grecques en
Occident de Macrobe à Cassiodore* (Paris, 1948), 119–29; cf. A. Solignac in *Saint
Augustin*, Les Confessions, BA 14 (Paris, 1962), 529–36; Madec, 60–71.

event, the fact remains that the Ambrose of the mid- to late
380s had already shown himself quite capable of evoking
fashionable philosophical language. His scholarly activities
were to be seen by everyone, and the learning which fortified
his pulpit style was meant to be obvious to discerning ears.[128]

De officiis, of course, draws not so much on the Platonist
tradition[129] as on Panaetius' Stoicism, as mediated by Cicero.
Stoicism, especially the more eclectic versions of it represented
by the middle and late Stoa, had long appeared particularly
congenial to Christianity. Christian and Stoic views seemed to
overlap somewhat in several areas of psychology and ethics,
and there were evident, if superficial, similarities in certain
aspects of their theological 'physics', such as the importance
both traditions attached to the Logos and to divine providence.
A galaxy of writers from both sides—Musonius Rufus, Epicte-
tus, Justin Martyr, Tatian (for all his virulent anti-Hellenism),
Tertullian, Clement of Alexandria, and others—had high-
lighted and in some cases built upon these apparent parallels.
Tertullian's famous *Seneca saepe noster*;[130] the late fourth-
century forged correspondence between Paul and Seneca (not
to mention the real Paul's evocation of Stoic ideas);[131] or
Jerome's reference to the *Stoici, qui nostro dogmati in plerisque
concordant*[132] all testify to the acknowledged points of contact

---

[128] Cf. Augustine, *Conf.* 5.12.23. Very curiously, Augustine seems to have
failed to spot the Platonist allusions, despite his emerging interest in Platonist
ideas: J. O'Meara, 'Augustine and Neo-Platonism', *RecAug* 1 (1958), 91–111,
at 100, *contra* Courcelle, *Recherches sur les Confessions de saint Augustin*,
133–8.

[129] Though there is certainly clear evidence of its influence: see e.g. the
introductory commentary on 1.233–9; 2.1–21.

[130] Tertullian, *Anim.* 20.1; cf. Lactantius, *Inst.* 1.5; 6.24.

[131] On the forged letters, see the text edited by A. Kurfess in E. Hennecke
and W. Schneemelcher, *New Testament Apocrypha* ii (London, 1965), 133–41;
also J. N. Sevenster, *Paul and Seneca* (Leiden, 1961). On Paul, cf. his use of
Aratus in the much-discussed Acts 17 passage; also his use of Stoic language
in Romans: see e.g. S. K. Stowers, *The Diatribe and Paul's Letter to the
Romans* (Chico, CA, 1981); G. Bornkamm, *Early Christian Experience*
(London, 1969), 47–70, 105–11.

[132] Jerome, *In Isaiam* 4.11.6. Jerome also included Seneca in his catalogue
of celebrated writers (*Vir. illustr.* 12), on the assumption that the pseudonym-
ous correspondence between Seneca and Paul was genuine. Jerome could,
however, also see Pelagian teachings as partly rooted in Stoic ethics: *Ep.*
133.1.

between the two traditions.[133] Ambrose was hardly breaking new ground, then, if he saw scope for the assimilation of Stoic thinking on, say, nature as an ethical norm (cf. 1.33, 77–8, 84, 123–5, 127, 132, 135, 223; 3.15–28);[134] or the unimportance of wealth (1.118); or the image of human society as a body (cf. 2.135; 3.17–19); or the triumph of the sage/spiritual leader over external problems (cf. 1.178–95; 2.10–21).[135] He was simply picking up the same kinds of compatibilities that were noted and developed by other Christian spokesmen in the early centuries.

Should *De officiis* be seen, therefore, as an attempt to stage an intellectual marriage between Cicero and Christ, and thus to evolve a protreptic for the Christian way by endorsing the highest moral insights of the Stoic tradition? This theory has attracted no shortage of supporters; but, as an overall assessment of Ambrose's motives, it does not do justice to three layers of evidence: first, to Ambrose's implied aims;[136] secondly, to his overall treatment of philosophy and philosophers; and thirdly (and most importantly), to the bigger picture of his cultural context in the West at the end of the fourth century, to contemporary Christian attitudes to classical literature, and to the likely readership of the work.

---

[133] For a brief overview, see C. Tibiletti, 'Stoicism and the Fathers', in A. di Berardino (ed.), *Encyclopedia of the Early Church*, 2 vols. (Cambridge, 1992), ii. 795–7; for detail, Pohlenz, *Die Stoa*, i. 400 ff.; M. Spanneut, *Le Stoïcisme des Pères de l'Eglise, de Clément de Rome à Clément d'Alexandrie* (Paris, 1957); id., *Permanence du stoïcisme, de Zénon à Malraux* (Gembloux, 1973); id., 'Les normes morales du stoïcisme chez les Pères de l'Eglise', *Studia Moralia* 19 (1981), 153–75; Colish ii. *passim*.

[134] See Maes, 6–8, 123–38, 152–62.

[135] See Pétré, 275–93.

[136] That is, his aims as implied by the language of the text. I assume a 'critical-realist' hermeneutic: grammatical-historical scholarship can uncover prima facie evidence of authorial intention, and though we can never be *absolutely* sure of the reliability of such clues, we should naturally treat them as significant to the interpretative process. I thus disown postmodernist strategies which assume that meaning may be created by the reader without constraints from the words of the text. As will be clear from what follows, I also assume that exploration of an author's socio-historical context can illumine his/her work and may corroborate a particular reading of it. Naturally I wish to avoid the 'intentionalist fallacy' of locating the author's own aims somewhere outside the text.

Replacement by transformation

(i) The clear implication of the perspectives outlined in
Introduction IV is that Ambrose wishes to produce a Christian
replacement for Cicero. By taking Cicero's title, structure, and
general themes, and imitating his father-to-son style, he draws
attention to his adherence to a specific textual model, but the
tone in which he handles Ciceronian arguments and illustrations is clearly negative. The authority of the Scriptures
offers a far higher pattern of duties than that offered by the
saeculum. The sustained antitheses, the charges of pagan
plagiarism of biblical truth, and the depreciation of classical
exempla all combine to press this point. If Ambrose had
wanted to build bridges, he might surely have contrived a
more positive and obvious parallelism between his mental
world and that of Cicero. His implied aims simply do not fit
that bill.

(ii) Ambrose refers to a number of secular thinkers, from a
range of schools: Panaetius (1.24, 31, 180); Zeno (2.4, 6); the
Stoics in general (1.132–3; 2.4); Aristotle (1.31, 48, 50, 180; 2.4,
6); the Peripatetics (2.4, 6); Pythagoras (1.31); and the Epicureans (1.47, 50; 2.4). In every case, they are cast in an adverse
light when contrasted with Scripture. Even where he mentions
Plato in an apparently neutral tone in 1.43, he goes on in the
following paragraph to argue that Plato was anticipated by Job;
in 3.30–1, Plato's story of Gyges and the ring is contrasted with
the *vera exempla* (3.32) of the Bible. The edges are blurred
between the different schools of thought: there is one basic
dichotomy between *ipsi* and the truth (1.47–50). Ambrose can
pass almost imperceptibly from speaking of the mistaken ideas
of popular sinful opinion to the falsehoods of the philosophers
(cf. 2.1–4). The most explicit statement of all comes in 2.8: *et
quoniam sola rerum scientia explosa est vel quasi inanis secundum
philosophiae disputationes superfluas vel quasi semiperfecta sententia, consideremus quam enodem de eo scriptura divina absolvat
sententiam, de quo tam multiplices et implicatas atque confusas
videmus quaestiones esse philosophiae.* Verbal evocation of Cicero
there may be,[137] but by no stretch of the imagination can this

---

[137] See commentary ad loc.

sentence be taken to imply a conciliatory spirit: it is an unmistakable antithesis of two approaches to wisdom.[138]

This effort to contrast the simple truth of the Christian Scriptures with the involved debates and erroneous opinions of philosophy is in keeping with Ambrose's approach throughout his works. His invariable assumption is that the *sapientia* revealed in the Scriptures is the original and the definitive disclosure of ultimate reality, that everything worth knowing is contained there, and that the best thoughts of the pagans have simply been stolen from that source.[139] By implication, Christians who find anything of value in secular philosophy are only reappropriating what is their own by right. Intensive analysis of his *œuvre* has yielded documentation of the ways in which his writings and sermons habitually set the Bible and Christian belief over against pagan *philosophia*.[140] Just as the philosophers are wrong about cosmogony (*Ex* 1.1–4), so they are wrong about ethics as well (*Off.* 2.4–6, 8);[141] indeed, philosophy *per se* is always inferior, and its abstractions are always overly complicated when cast in the pure light of Scripture.

Clearly we must not conflate what Ambrose says about 'philosophy' as a generalized phenomenon with what he may have believed about the particulars of individual philosophical standpoints. As his allusions to Platonist texts imply, Ambrose could assimilate certain ideas while repudiating the larger pagan realm to which they belonged. Significant philosophical influences also weighed upon him from his reading in authorities such as Philo and Origen, who were themselves shot through with Platonist and other assumptions. In terms of his Roman Stoic inheritance, similarly, Ambrose obviously owed his classical matrix much more than he was able to

---

[138] Lenox-Conyngham, 119, suggests that the general passage from which the sentence comes reveals Ambrose's purpose in the work more clearly than any other.

[139] S. V. Rovighi, 'Le idee filosofiche di sant'Ambrogio', in *Sant'Ambrogio nel XVI centenario della nascita* (Milan, 1940), 235–58.

[140] Madec, *passim*. The one apparent exception to a pejorative depiction of *philosophia* is *Virgt.* 48, where the word seems to designate the way of Christian asceticism.

[141] On the physics of *Ex*, see J. Pépin, *Théologie cosmique et théologie chrétienne (Ambroise, Exam. I.1.1–4)* (Paris, 1964).

recognize or prepared to admit.[142] Nevertheless, there is a clear
thread of polemic running right through his works, not just
against the corrupt intellectual world from which the errors of
the pagans originate, but also against example after example of
their falsehood. Even where his reproduction of philosophical
idioms can be shown to be more delicate, his motive is evidently not to trace points of commonality but to set particular
aspects of Christian doctrine in greater relief, and to show that
the Bible is best (while airing his knowledge in the process).
The fragments of his lost work, *De sacramento regenerationis
sive de philosophia*, show him proclaiming that the *true* 'philosophy' is to be attained only through baptism and resurrection
to new spiritual life in Christ.[143] Of course, polemic and
borrowing could coexist in the service of positive synthesis in
early Christian rhetoric,[144] but such an approach does not
square with Ambrose's style. For him there could be no
ideological merger, for any such compound would perforce
adulterate the clarity of the one true gospel.[145]

(iii) The greatest problem of all with the idea that Ambrose
was labouring to span two thought-worlds is that it makes no
sense in his cultural context. Scholars who have imagined that
Ambrose inhabited the same kind of world as a Justin Martyr
or a Clement of Alexandria have ignored the intellectual
paradigm-shift which had taken place over the course of the
fourth century. The conflict of ideologies presented so starkly
in Tertullian's notorious *quid ergo Athenis et Hierosolymis?* was
now no longer relevant, for all the church's enduring rhetoric
against the *saeculum*;[146] the alternative to Tertullian's fervid

[142] See these and other qualifications or criticisms of Madec's analysis in
H. Savon, 'Saint Ambroise et la philosophie à propos d'une étude récente',
RHR 191 (1977), 173–96; Hill, 38–90, esp. 80–3; Zelzer, 'Beurteilung', 175 ff.
Madec essentially restates his case in summary form in '"Verus philosophus
est amator Dei." S. Ambroise, s. Augustin et la philosophie', *RSPhTh* 61
(1977), 549–66. For a survey of some other relevant material on the subject,
see A. Pastorino, 'La filosofia antica in sant'Ambrogio (Rassegna bibliografica)', *BStudLat* 7 (1977), 88–104.
[143] See Madec, 247 ff.
[144] See Zelzer, 'Beurteilung', *passim*; Hill, 38–90.
[145] Lenox-Conyngham, 128. Cf. *Bon. mort.* 45, on the philosophers, who
should have stuck with the simple truth of what they lifted from the Bible:
Utinam non superflua his et inutilia miscuissent!
[146] Tertullian, *Praescr. haer.* 7.9 is in context part of a denunciation of

antagonism was no longer a quest for *rapprochement*, but a demonstration of the social triumph of the gospel over the pagan world.[147]

Ambrose had received a traditional Roman education within a Christian family; talk of ecclesiastical affairs as well as the reading of classical literature had been part of his childhood experience. Groomed according to the fastidious (if to us rather quaint) standards of deportment deemed essential to upper-class *Romanitas*, he had worked hard to belong among a social élite.[148] He had served as an advocate and *consularis* in an imperial system whose make-up would have been quite unimaginable to earlier generations of churchmen. Cicero's textbook image of a gentleman's personal and civic obligations depicted

philosophically inspired heresy, not of classical literature as such, but it clearly sums up the tensions at work in the mind of one who, for all his puritanical zeal, remained deeply indebted to both classical style and classical philosophy. By the time he wrote *Pall.* 6.4, however, Tertullian could envisage the elevation of the philosopher's *pallium* when donned by the Christian. See generally J.-C. Fredouille, *Tertullien et la conversion de la culture antique* (Paris, 1972), 301–57.

[147] See especially C. Gnilka, *Chrêsis: Die Methode der Kirchenväter im Umgang mit der antiken Kultur* (Basle, 1984), on the assimilation and reshaping of literature as a spiritual conquest; also R. A. Kaster, *Guardians of Language: The Grammarian and Society in Late Antiquity* (Berkeley and Los Angeles, 1988), 70–95. These sketches offer a more nuanced account of the fourth-century situation than does, say, R. A. Markus, 'Paganism, Christianity and the Latin Classics in the Fourth Century', in J. W. Binns (ed.), *Latin Literature of the Fourth Century* (London, 1974), 1–21, who does not say enough about Christian attempts to purify and integrate pagan ideas in new forms. For a typology of evolutionary attitudes to secular culture, see A. M. Wolters in W. E. Helleman (ed.), *Christianity and the Classics: The Acceptance of a Heritage* (Lanham, MD, 1990), 195–201.

[148] By background, Ambrose belonged on the margins rather than at the heart of the senatorial aristocracy; he could not take his social status for granted simply on account of his father's high office (McLynn, 33); see further S. Mazzarino, *Storia sociale del vescovo Ambrogio* (Rome, 1989), 75–82. Of course, a certain early self-consciousness may very probably have helped to form the very obsession with image which *Off.* and other texts reveal. Intriguingly, the teenage Ambrose is said to have aped the mannerisms of the clergy who visited his family home in Rome (Paulinus, *VA* 4; 9.4): for the young Ambrose, it seems, one of the authoritative role-models of a certain idealized adult behaviour had perhaps been the ecclesiastic (others would of course view the Roman clergy's preoccupation with style a different way: cf. Jerome, *Ep.* 22.28; and *Ep.* 52.6).

exactly the kind of model which he himself had striven to emulate, and naturally he found a lingering appeal in its exposition of manners. As bishop of Milan, Ambrose inhabited a cosmopolitan world. He was surrounded by the complex society of the Western imperial court, with its fluid assortment of local gentry, ambitious functionaries, political movers and shakers, military personnel, and enterprising businessmen. The city attracted men of letters, teachers, rhetoricians, poets, and thinkers from all over the empire. Its Alpine hinterland contained large estates owned by retired grandees and dignitaries, who would profess to pass their time as cultivated gentlemen of leisure, indulging their tastes for literature and ideas.[149] Ambrose's most pressing task was to convince this complex and image-conscious world that his church constituted the heart of the region's social order, and that it was only by the strength of its pulse that everything else in the political, economic, and cultural life of northern Italy was sustained. To persuade an educated but impressionable onlooker like the young professor Augustine, halting between pagan and Christian philosophical opinions and ready to be swayed by an aura of intellectual weight combined with social bearing, it was necessary for the Nicene community to be seen to be invested with finesse and assurance, and for its episcopal figurehead to appear as the natural leader of his society.[150] Ambrose was no crass lowbrow, incapable of passing himself off in polite company: he affected to be every inch the urbane, thinking churchman, at ease at the highest tiers of the pyramid, indispensable to the cohesion of an entire social world.

For Ambrose, this preoccupation with ecclesial prestige called not for overtures on possible links between the gospel and secular philosophy, but for a bold annexing of cultural capital, and a determination to prove that the intellectual achievements of the classical world had been overtaken by

---

[149] J. Matthews, *Western Aristocracies and Imperial Court, AD 364–425* (Oxford, 1975), 183–6. On nobility and landownership more generally, see M. T. W. Arnheim, *The Senatorial Aristocracy in the Later Roman Empire* (Oxford, 1972), 143–54.

[150] On Ambrose's strategic 'missionary' activity here, see J. Mesot, *Die Heidenbekehrung bei Ambrosius von Mailand* (Schöneck-Beckenried, 1958), 118–32, especially 126 ff.

the superiority of the Christian message. Pagan literature presented deeply formative patterns of thought and behaviour, but it had been eclipsed by a new Christian culture, which transcended the moral framework within which these patterns had arisen. Ambrose typified a rationale which can be identified in many leading figures in Latin Christianity in and around his time. In the stock idea of *spoliatio*, the argument that the wealth of secular literature could be plundered and revamped by the Christian;[151] in the example of the gentleman scholar Paulinus of Nola adapting the genres of classical poetry to articulate an urbane Christian message for a network educated enough to appreciate the dramatic variations he was working upon the substance of the old forms;[152] or in the famous case of Jerome vowing in his dream in *Epistle* 22 to temper his enthusiasm for the classics and devote himself wholeheartedly to sacred texts, then later reaching a gentler solution in *Epistle* 70, where he could claim that the much-loved books of his youth might in fact be useful, provided they were appropriately sanitized[153]—a clear trend can be discerned. For all of these writers, it was ultimately no longer necessary to choose between compromise on the one hand versus puritanism on the other. Correct use of the literature of the pagan past meant taking over some of its models and showing not that their ideas were always wrong or sometimes right, but that the context in which they belonged had been left behind. It was precisely by reworking the old patterns and setting their contents in sharp relief that the traditional structures could be shown to be *passé*.

The Christian *De officiis* is thus designed to be a sign of Ambrose's church's relationship to the *saeculum*.[154] Its moral foundations are meant to be seen as entirely different from those of its pagan ancestor. Ambrose presupposes a story of creation and fall (e.g. 1.132–7, 169), of divine omniscience and

---

[151] See R. Holte, *Béatitude et sagesse: saint Augustin et le problème de la fin de l'histoire de l'homme dans la philosophie ancienne* (Paris, 1962), 111–24.

[152] For some examples, see P. G. Walsh, 'Paulinus of Nola and the Conflict of Ideologies in the Fourth Century', in P. Granfield and J. A. Jungmann (eds.), *Kyriakon: Festschrift Johannes Quasten*, 2 vols. (Münster, 1970), ii. 565–71.

[153] See Hagendahl, 318–28. Lenox-Conyngham, 128, speaks of Ambrose engaging in a similar sort of 'religious homoeopathy'.

[154] McLynn, 255–6.

providence (1.40–64, 124),[155] of redemption in Christ, of regeneration, faith, repentance, self-denial, spiritual progress, prayer, sacraments, and final judgement (e.g. 1.28–9, 39, 58, 124, 147, 188, 218; 2.15–21, 96, 126; 3.11, 36). *Humilitas* and *castitas*, both of them indispensable to the Ambrosian ethic, are no virtues to Cicero; nor, of course, is the disposition that is now said to be the starting-point for all wisdom: the fear of God (1.1). Asceticism, self-sacrifice, and poverty belong to an entirely distinct *Weltanschauung*. The very obviousness of these points can actually blind us to the extent to which their significance dominates the panorama and is critical to the attempted transformation of the classical landscape. Ambrose depicts scriptural figures as paragons of various virtues which in subtle ways remain rooted in classical soil [Introduction VII (ii)], but he means these exemplars to be seen as exponents of an ultimately far more dazzling morality, for their actions are deemed to be energized by divine power and oriented towards heavenly reward. *Illi autem praesentibus, nos futuris militamus. Unde quo praestantior causa, eo debet esse cura adtentior* (1.218). Ambrose has a theocentrism and a soteriological-eschatological reference-point which are altogether foreign to Cicero.[156] He may sanction the Stoic axiom that life must be lived in accordance with nature (cf. 1.33, 77–8, 84, 123–5, 127, 132, 135, 223; 3.15–28), but he also subscribes to a biblical view of nature as fallen and dependent upon divine grace in order for virtue to become a reality.[157] To one whose convictions are informed by the Sermon on the Mount, right *motives* are crucial in actions, as is the awareness that God is our judge (cf. e.g. 1.146–7). The law of nature is the law of God imprinted on the human heart, fashioned as God's image;[158]

---

[155] And not, of course, the impersonal cosmic force of Stoic thought, but an omniscient God who deals personally with human beings in reward and judgement.

[156] Hill, 186–204, esp. 203. However, Homes Dudden ii. 551–4, over-simplifies a number of the ethical differences between the two perspectives.

[157] On the tensions between these two conceptions of nature's ethical status, see Homes Dudden ii. 520; Colish ii. 52–4, 61–70; Stelzenberger, 175–8.

[158] See S.-E. Szydzik, '*Ad imaginem Dei': Die Lehre von der Gottebenbild-lichkeit des Menschen bei Ambrosius von Mailand* (Berlin, 1961), 34–75. Löpfe, 72–7, wrongly argues that the picture is entirely biblical; a more balanced

scriptural precept and natural law are visualized as co-ordinate authorities (1.135).

Another more subtle area of creativity is the semantic development Ambrose brings to Ciceronian nomenclature under the influence of the Bible. This is not the matter of his attempts to validate his use of philosophical terminology by far-fetched appeals to scriptural verses. It is rather his way of lending particular nuances to classical vocabulary by pervasive allusion to biblical usages. There is frequent ambivalence between the Ciceronian and the scriptural senses of, for example, *fides* (1.140, 142, 145–6), or *gloria* (1.175, 177, 179, 187, 194–6, 208; 2.2, 14, 81, 90, 153, 156; 3.36, 48, 56, 89–90), or *iustitia* (1.39, 110, 117, 142, 186, 259; 2.35); Ambrose can slide from one register to another and back again within a few sentences. For him the moves are easy—even sometimes, it seems, unthinking—so closely bound is he to two conceptual worlds. Even if the referential renovation is incomplete, it is nevertheless part of an overall attempt to Christianize classical categories by pointing beyond the Ciceronian nuances to profounder understandings of what faith or glory or justice *really* means.[159] Through it all, the intellectual confidence of Ambrose's view of things is unmistakable. For him, the *simplicitas* of revelation outshines all the *ars* of the world (cf. 1.29, 116; 3.139), and the Christian conceptions of moral principles possess a clarity and a depth which render the older construals irrelevant.

For whom, then, was *De officiis* written? The question has surprisingly seldom been asked by scholars; it seems that most of Ambrose's interpreters have been too preoccupied with tracing his echoes of Cicero and the Bible to think about the obvious issue of his social milieu.[160] In the first instance, he must have in mind his immediate clerical body. There seems no good reason to doubt the reality of his dedication of the

account of the dual influences of Scripture and Stoicism is given by Maes, 6–8, 123–38, 152–62; see also K. Zelzer, 'L'etica di sant'Ambrogio e la tradizione stoica delle virtù', in *L'etica cristiana nei secoli III e IV: eredità e confronti* (Rome, 1996), 47–56. More generally, cf. M. Spanneut, 'La notion de nature des stoïciens aux Pères de l'Eglise', *RecTh* 37 (1970), 165–73.

[159] Muckle, *passim*.
[160] Cf. McLynn, 256 n. 18.

work to his *filii*. Just as Cicero thinks not only of Marcus but of
a potential élite of politically ambitious young men, Ambrose
sees *his* young men as a new élite, who have a responsibility to
propagate a Christianity which will appeal to civilized tastes
and ensure that his church strikes the right social note.[161]

But the treatise is also designed to reach a much larger
readership than simply the Milanese *presbyterium*. Ambrose
personally exercised a considerable influence over ecclesiastical
affairs across northern Italy. He not only sought to ensure the
widest possible spread of officials committed to Nicene theology; he also shaped liturgical practices and influenced the roles
played by such clergy in their local communities. In *De officiis*
Ambrose aims to substitute for the Ciceronian political counsel
a new vision of the glories of spiritual leadership, which will be
studied by ecclesiastics throughout these neighbouring territories.[162] The words of 1.29 are telling: *deinde qui illa non
legunt, nostra legent si volent, qui non sermonum supellectilem
neque artem dicendi sed simplicem rerum exquirunt gratiam*. Here
is surely more than an expression of modesty about style,
conventional or otherwise. Ambrose wants his work to be
read *instead of* the pagan—Cicero's—account of duties: he
aspires to replace the celebrated classical handbook with a
guide that is inspired by and targeted at a changed world.

De officiis very probably attracted some lay Christian readers
as well. Influential laypeople had a vital part to play in the
Christianizing of their social peers and in the steady transformation of regional power-structures, not least on town-
councils and in the country areas where they held their estates.
Two of Ambrose's letters (*Epp.* 44 [68] and 48 [66]) are
addressed to a distinguished layman, Flavius Pisidius Romulus, the holder of his own former post of consular of Aemilia-
Liguria in 385/6,[163] and there must have been other prominent
lay-Christians likely to read his literary offerings, who were
perhaps particularly eager to gauge his ability to handle the
awkward questions of applied ethics. It is not for nothing that

---

[161] R. A. Markus, *Christianity in the Roman World* (London, 1974), 121.
[162] See Introduction VII (ii).
[163] Romulus, on retreat at his country estate at a time of considerable
tension in Milan, had written to Ambrose seeking explanations of conundra in
OT texts. See Matthews, *Western Aristocracies and Imperial Court*, 193–5.

Ambrose has so much to say about the responsibilities of merchants and those involved in financial activities (cf. 1.242–5; 3.37–52, 57–75); at the same time, it may also not be for nothing that his comments on greed and exploitation of the poor remain general: his concern is to excoriate the evils perpetrated by his church's enemies, not to upset the sensibilities of its rather useful friends. It was not only the clergy who had an obligation to conduct themselves in a manner pleasing to God and calculated to promote the Nicene cause; the onus was upon all believers in positions of influence to do likewise.[164] In his broad-brush-stroke delineation of moral philosophical *topoi*, spiritually focused yet perhaps seldom directly unsettling to the comfortable ways of traditionally minded aristocrats, Ambrose is painting an image of Christian respectability which is meant to impress and inspire those whose public commitment to (or acquiescence in) his church's cause mattered greatly.

But Ambrose undoubtedly has in his sights a very different group of potential readers, too—non-Christian *litterati* among the intelligentsia of Milan and Rome. Such 'leisured sophisticates'[165] would undoubtedly have been keen to observe the intellectual stance adopted by any prominent churchman venturing a transformation of a central text from the classical canon. It has been plausibly suggested that Q. Aurelius Symmachus himself, a dedicated Ciceronian, was envisaged as a reader, and that he is meant to recognize himself as the anonymous target of the invective in 3.45–52.[166] It is certainly hard to imagine a single one of Ambrose's publications more likely to elicit interest among a secular literary world which would normally have paid scant attention to the appearance of such perceived trivia as mere expositions of Scripture or contentious dogmatic treatises. Those whose memories retained a reasonable stock of Cicero's language, and whose libraries allowed them ready reference to his text, could reflect in detail on Ambrose's reworking of the old themes, and see what he was up to in his virtuoso repackaging of aspects of their ethos for a new context.

[164] See generally P. Brown, *Authority and the Sacred: Aspects of the Christianisation of the Roman World* (Cambridge, 1995), 18–26. On the diffusion of Christianity in the frontier zones of the North Italian countryside, see Humphries, 175–84.   [165] McLynn, 255–6.   [166] Ibid. 272–3.

Many of these recipients must have been disappointed by what they read. Ambrose does not offer a systematic response to Cicero, but a hastily constructed and somewhat untidy synthesis, pervaded by what, to such readers, were the unappealing textures of biblical authority. Nevertheless, his message is perfectly clear. Pagan onlookers are to appreciate that ecclesiastical officialdom is interested in gentlemanly behaviour, but that it consciously pursues far higher goals besides, for it knows that *its* duty is owed in the first instance to God. The Ciceronian norms fall short of the standards prescribed and exemplified in the Scriptures. The clergy is not so much a *continuation* of a classical élite, in fact, as its superior successor. Ambrose is not interested in forging artificial correlations, but in demonstrating a wholesale takeover. In a mature Christian empire, he makes bold to say, the pagan account of *officia* ought really to have a *raison d'être* no longer.[167]

VII. CONSTRUCTING AN ECCLESIAL COMMUNITY: AMBROSE'S ETHICAL VISION

(i) Ambrose's episcopate prior to *De officiis*

One of the most significant achievements of Ambrosian scholarship in recent years has been to demonstrate that Ambrose's establishment of a Nicene hegemony[168] in Milan was a much more complex process than has traditionally been assumed. The simplistic picture painted in Paulinus' *Vita* and other conventional accounts, in which Ambrose stamped his orthodoxy upon his church right from the start, is now widely recognized to be unreliable. Ambrose in fact spent much of his episcopate struggling against an assortment of powerful enemies, and the influence which he came to exercise in the

---

[167] Homes Dudden ii. 502, is right, then, to say that Ambrose's project is 'bold', but wrong to suggest that it represents an 'attempt to combine' the old and the new. At ii. 554, Homes Dudden admits that Ambrose makes 'no serious attempt' to harmonize the two sets of ideas, the Christian and the Stoic. On the combination of *traditio* and *renovatio*, see Hill, 301–2.

[168] Or perhaps 'neo-Nicene': for a reassessment of the creativity of Ambrose's mediation of the doctrinal inheritance, see Markschies, esp. 84–212.

political developments of his time depended on a good deal of opportunism and strategic posturing. The stereotypical image of Ambrose the spiritual giant reducing his opponents to silence and bringing emperors to their knees is only one dimension of the story; behind it lies the far more prosaic reality of a figure who had to labour against serious odds, to manoeuvre his way out of many a tight corner, and to improvise in the face of often significant opposition. Sanctity of character, intensity of conviction, and intellectual gifts all remain relevant categories in any summary of Ambrose's qualities, but political astuteness, an ability to work on popular emotions, and a genius for creating the impression that he was most in control when it was least true were also vital weapons in his arsenal.[169]

Ambrose had inherited a volatile clerical community, in which a clear majority of his staff remained in sympathy with the homoian Arian theology of his predecessor, Auxentius. In his early years he had to concentrate a good deal of his energy on symbolic gestures in an attempt to consolidate his public position while he devoted himself to acquiring some of the necessary tools for his job. The gifts of presentation and rhetorical persuasion which he had developed as an advocate and administrator had to be put to new uses in the forging of an appropriate episcopal *persona*. All the while, he had to contend not just with divided loyalties within his own order but with rival forces outside it. His footsteps were dogged by the activities of men like Iulianus Valens, a homoian cleric who had come to Milan *c*.375 from his native Poetovio,[170] and the

---

[169] See the ground-breaking studies by McLynn and Williams, *passim*; also, very briefly, Humphries, 119–26, 149–53. In fear of overstating the political side, some scholars continue to opt for a fairly conventional characterization, along the lines of e.g. Homes Dudden or Paredi: C. Pasini, *Ambrogio di Milano: Azione e pensiero di un vescovo* (Milan, 1996); Ramsey, 1–54; and (to a lesser extent) Savon, *passim*. In the process, these latter approaches seem to underestimate the significance of Ambrose's political acumen for the very distinctiveness they seek to celebrate. For an outline attempt to steer a middle way between Ambrose the stained-glass hero and Ambrose the Machiavellian, see I. J. Davidson, 'Ambrose', in P. F. Esler, *The Early Christian World*, 2 vols. (London and New York, 2000) ii. 1175–1204; also, at a basic level, Moorhead, *passim*.

[170] See Williams, 137; Markschies, 134–42.

machinations of the anti-pope Ursinus, who was also in the city around this time, apparently stirring up hard-line Nicene elements to protest against Ambrose's failure to remedy the Arian tenor of his clergy.[171] The strength of these hostile forces continues to be underestimated by one or two scholars,[172] but it was in fact considerable. Dissident household meetings seem to have been held, with distinct liturgies and apparent plots against the bishop. When Ambrose intervened in a local synod at Sirmium, more than five hundred miles away, to ensure the election of a Nicene candidate as bishop in late 377 or early 378, it implied that he was prepared to take stronger action against Arians elsewhere than he was yet in a position to do on his own territory.[173] When he first met the young Gratian in Milan in the summer of 379, in the aftermath of the crushing defeat suffered by the Roman forces the previous year at Adrianople, he managed to prevail upon him to resist overtures from the dissidents,[174] but the pressure from them remained significant. When Ambrose sold church plate to finance the ransom of prisoners of war from the Goths, the Arian protest was clearly severe indeed: Ambrose refers to it in *De officiis*, still evidently determined to justify his behaviour (2.70–1, 136–43).[175]

While still in Illyricum, Gratian had written to Ambrose inviting him to explain his theological position. The publication of *De fide* 1–2, the bishop's first extended manifesto against the logic of Arian theology, did little to commend his grasp of contemporary doctrinal issues.[176] He refused to make any

---

[171] Ursinus himself was no Arian, but Ambrose pictures Valens and him in an unholy alliance: *Ep. extra coll.* 5 [11].3.

[172] e.g. P. I. Kaufman, 'Diehard Homoians and the Election of Ambrose', *JECS* 5 (1997), 421–40, who resists the picture of an organized opposition at the time of Ambrose's elevation and in his early years.

[173] It also aroused the wrath of Justina, the fiercely pro-Arian mother of the young Valentinian II, who would yet seek her revenge.

[174] *Ep. extra coll.* 12 [1].2.

[175] It was in fact no wonder that the homoians protested vociferously: Ambrose had not broken up and sold any old vessels, but chalices donated by homoian families; see commentary ad locc.

[176] *Pace* Homes Dudden i. 195, who hails *Fid.* as 'a really valuable contribution to constructive theology', R. P. C. Hanson, *The Search for the Christian Doctrine of God: The Arian Controversy 318–381* (Edinburgh, 1988), 669, suggests a very different verdict on Ambrose's achievement: 'too often

ultimate distinctions between the beliefs of the homoians and the positions of far more extreme Arians, and chose to vilify all Arian theologies as more or less equally terrible. He depicted Adrianople and the Gothic ravages of the Danubian provinces as divine judgements on Arian strongholds, and promised that theological orthodoxy and imperial security were all of a piece: fidelity to the true faith would grant Gratian victory in his forthcoming campaign against the Goths.[177] But his enemies were not to be shaken by his audacious attempt to pass himself off as personal spiritual adviser to the emperor. When Gratian showed the text to the ablest of the Illyrican homoians, Palladius of Ratiaria,[178] Palladius responded with a sharp rejoinder, rebutting Ambrose's caricature of his position and inviting him to engage in an open debate with him.[179] On the basis of *De fide* 1–2, he must have been confident of his chances of victory.

The ensuing *De fide* 3–5 and the three books *De Spiritu Sancto* which Ambrose wrote in late 380 and early 381 were produced by a man under some pressure. At the same time as he faced the potentially serious challenge of a direct engagement with Palladius, Ambrose refers in *De Spiritu Sancto* 1 to a recent decision by the emperor to rescind an order to sequestrate a basilica.[180] The incident, perhaps sparked by the arrival of Justina and her entourage in Milan,[181] may imply that the local homoians had been emboldened to press their case that worship in private was no longer good enough: they wanted

his arguments are, as rational discussion, beneath contempt'. For a more positive analysis of Ambrose's grasp of the metaphysical dynamics, see Markschies, 165–212, esp. 197 ff.

[177] *Fid.* 2.136–43. Scholarly opinion is divided on the dating of *Fid.* 1–2: the traditional setting of autumn 378 is defended by Williams, 129–30 n. 8; Savon, 88–91; G. Gottlieb, *Ambrosius von Mailand und Kaiser Gratian* (Göttingen, 1973), 49–50, dates it to the aftermath of Gratian's second visit to Milan in the spring of 380; McLynn, 102 n. 90, opts for 380, but prior to Gratian's second meeting with Ambrose.

[178] See M. Meslin, *Les Ariens d'Occident, 335–430* (Paris, 1967), 111–34.

[179] Palladius, *Apol.* 81–7.

[180] *Spir.* 1.19–21. See D. H. Williams, 'When did the Emperor Gratian Return the Basilica to the Pro-Nicenes in Milan?', *SP* 24 (1994), 208–15.

[181] Justina is traditionally said to have been a refugee from the Gothic invasion of Illyricum after Adrianople (e.g. Palanque, 60); McLynn, 122, however, suggests that she arrived in Milan during the winter of 380/1.

churches of their own, where they could establish their presence publicly as an official opposition.[182] Though the basilica
in this case was 'restored', the confrontation was a portent of
further troubles ahead. As for Palladius, however, when he
finally got his meeting with Ambrose at the council of Aquileia
in September 381, Ambrose succeeded in stitching up the
whole process. He had persuaded Gratian that there was no
need to assemble a large gathering of Eastern clergy,[183] since
the dispute was a private one between himself and his Illyrican
brethren. Surrounded by a group of staunch supporters from
northern Italy and Gaul, Ambrose orchestrated an overwhelm-
ing condemnation of Palladius and of his prominent colleague,
Secundianus, bishop of Singidunum, and swiftly followed it up
with appeals to both Gratian and Theodosius to act decisively
against the Arians of both West and East, first by legally
enforcing the deposition of Palladius and Secundianus from
their sees, then by removing other menaces, such as the
presence of Iulianus Valens in northern Italy. A potentially
awkward theological *contretemps* was turned into a major political gain.[184]

The early 380s saw Ambrose as an often-effective[185] lobbyist
at the court of Gratian. His political influence was evident upon
Gratian's downfall, too, when he went in person to Trier to
appeal to Maximus for peace, while forces loyal to Valentinian
were mustering under the Frankish general, Bauto, and appeals

---

[182] See H. O. Maier, 'Private Space as the Social Context of Arianism in
Ambrose's Milan', *JThS*, NS 45 (1994), 72–93.

[183] The East had had its own council a matter of months before at
Constantinople. Theodosius, having removed the homoian bishop Demophi-
lus, had called this meeting to elect a Nicene successor. This had evidently
caused considerable embarrassment to Gratian, who had already made plans
for the staging of a general council later in the year.

[184] See Williams, 154–84.

[185] But by no means always: when the supporters of the controversial
Spanish ascetic, Priscillian of Avila, lobbied the court for justice in their fight
with their ecclesiastical opponents, Ambrose's antagonism to their cause was
drowned out by the agencies of the *magister officiorum*, Macedonius, who
evidently resented the influence which the bishop had come to exercise on too
many occasions; see H. Chadwick, *Priscillian of Avila: The Occult and the
Charismatic in the Early Church* (Oxford, 1976), 111–69. On Priscillianism
more widely, see also V. Burrus, *The Making of a Heretic: Gender, Authority,
and the Priscillianist Controversy* (Berkeley and Los Angeles, 1995).

were being made to Theodosius to act against the usurper. In the end, on that occasion, no fighting took place, for Theodosius was persuaded to grant recognition to Maximus in return for the assurance that Valentinian's court was legitimate. Ambrose nevertheless called in the debt for his diplomatic efforts in 384, in his passionate protest against the persuasive appeal to Valentinian by Symmachus to restore the pagan symbol of the Altar of Victory to the senate-house in Rome.[186] He warned Valentinian—a teenage ruler of obvious vulnerability—that he would face the full opposition of his bishop if he chose to heed the pagans' case: the threats worked, and Symmachus' petition was rejected.

Nevertheless, it was only a matter of time until Ambrose's troubles intensified again. The machinations came not only from Justina, but from a complex alliance of hostile forces, in which the lead was taken by the local homoians themselves, who experienced something of a revival in their fortunes from around late 384.[187] The catalyst seems to have been the arrival of (Mercurinus) Auxentius,[188] a former protégé of Ulfila, the homoian[189] 'apostle' to the Goths during the reign of Constantius II. As bishop of Durostorum on the Lower Danube, Auxentius had been recognized by Palladius as a potential challenger to Ambrose, and after being removed from his see by Theodosius he found refuge in Milan, probably in the

---

[186] See R. Klein, *Der Streit um den Victoriaaltar: Die dritte Relatio des Symmachus und die Briefe 17, 18 und 57 des Mailänder Bischofs Ambrosius* (Darmstadt, 1972); K. Rosen, 'Fides contra dissimulationem: Ambrosius und Symmachus im Kampf um den Victoriaaltar', *JbAC* 37 (1994), 29–36, citing the extensive earlier literature.

[187] On the homoian 'revival', see Williams, 185–210. For some possible qualifications of Williams' handling of the evidence, see McLynn's review of Williams in *JThS* 48 (1997), 270–3, at 272.

[188] Ambrose, *Ep.* 75a [*C. Aux.*].22 claims that Auxentius changed his name from Mercurinus to Auxentius on his arrival in Milan in order to evoke the authority of the Auxentius who had been the bishop's predecessor; more probably the pagan-sounding Mercurinus had already been dropped earlier; see McLynn, 183 n. 92.

[189] M. Simonetti, *La crisi Ariana nel IV secolo* (Rome, 1975), 442–3, 460 n. 5, suggests he was an 'anomoian' Arian, who believed that Christ the Son was 'unlike' God the Father, but this view has not commanded much support; on his life and activity see P. J. Heather and J. F. Matthews, *The Goths in the Fourth Century* (Liverpool, 1991), 133–53.

second half of 384. He spearheaded an assault which proved to be the most serious of Ambrose's career.[190]

Once more, the focal point of the confrontation was the question of private space for worship. In the spring of 385, Ambrose was summoned to the imperial palace to be informed that the emperor wished to have a cathedral in which the court might celebrate worship (presumably at Easter) led by homoian clergy: one of the bishop's basilicas (probably the Basilica Portiana, just outside the city-walls), was to be handed over forthwith.[191] The ultimatum was a rebuttal of Ambrose's earlier attempt to dominate Valentinian (although, by way of diplomacy, it was delivered courtesy of a special invitation to the bishop to attend the imperial consistory). Ambrose had, however, apparently informed his supporters that he had been called to the palace, and the meeting was interrupted by a crowd clamouring that the churches of God must remain inviolate. Fearing a public riot, the court had little option but to back down.

The victory was, however, only temporary. On 23 January of the following year, a law was issued (*C.Th.* 16.1.4) requiring freedom of worship for those who followed the (Arian) faith as specified at the councils of Rimini (359) and Constantinople (360). The language of the directive warned that there would be firm retaliation against any who resisted or claimed that such freedom was theirs alone; any such responses would be treated as treasonous. The law was clearly targeted at Ambrose, and aimed to prevent him from staging another popular show of resistance. In all probability, as Ambrose himself contended,[192] it was framed with the direct involvement of Auxentius. It amounted to an implicit legal validation of the homoian community which had opposed the bishop from the start. The crisis which followed at Easter 386, when the law was invoked against Ambrose, has been subjected to intense scholarly scrutiny, and this is not the place to rehearse the disputed details of its chronology and topography.[193] Suffice it

---

[190] See Williams, 202–10.　　　　　　[191] *Ep.* 75a [*C. Aux.*].29.

[192] *Ep.* 75a [*C. Aux.*].16, 22, 24.

[193] For an exemplary study, see in particular J. H. Van Haeringen, 'De Valentiniano II et Ambrosio: Illustrantur et digeruntur res anno 386 gestae', *Mnemosyne* 3 (1937), 152–8; 28–33; 229–40, largely followed by A. Lenox-

to say that in Ambrose's refusal to give up any church to the imperial authorities, either the Basilica Portiana or (even less likely) his own Basilica Nova itself, on the grounds that they were all alike divine property, he managed to secure his most enduring triumph over his enemies. By a skilful if impromptu combination of brinkmanship, demagoguery, and exploitation of popular emotions, he engineered a remarkable coup, resisting both the surrender of property and open debate with Auxentius. The *populus Dei*, locked inside its sanctuary, sang its hymns and prepared to face martyrdom in fidelity to its cause, while the forces of Satan—the imperial troops dispatched to forestall public disorder—prowled at the doors.[194]

Aside from his obvious inside knowledge of developments at the palace and his clever manipulation of crowds during the Easter crisis, two things in particular saved Ambrose in the awkward stalemate which ensued after the withdrawal of the troops. The first was political uncertainty. While the stand-off was taking place, there were veiled threats from Maximus at Trier, who protested to the court in Milan about its reprehensible harassing of a catholic bishop and his pious followers, whose cause was as great as God himself.[195] There were also renewed problems on the Danube frontier, which made the dispute over the tenancy of a church building, no matter how symbolic, seem trivial by comparison. The second and climactic saving grace for Ambrose came with the completion in June 386 of a magnificent new basilica, the most impressive example yet in the large-scale church-building programme in which the bishop had been engaged for several years.[196] At the dedication ceremony, Ambrose pledged that the building (where he himself planned to be buried; already it was being dubbed the Basilica Ambrosiana) would be

Conyngham, 'The Topography of the Basilica Conflict of AD 385/6 in Milan', *Historia* 31 (1982), 353–63; G. Gottlieb, 'Der Mailänder Kirchenstreit von 385/386: Datierung, Verlauf, Deutung', *MH* 42 (1985), 37–55; Savon, 201–22. G. Nauroy, 'Le fouet et le miel. Le combat d'Ambroise en 386 contre l'arianisme milanais', *RecAug* 23 (1988), 3–86, is also perceptive, but differs in various respects.

[194] For an outstanding sketch of the psychology of the situation and the theatricality of Ambrose's behaviour, see McLynn, 158–219.

[195] Theodoret, *HE* 5.14.

[196] And engaged controversially at that: see commentary on 2.111, 142.

decorated appropriately if the remains of some martyrs could
be discovered. Next day, he led his people to the memorial to
the celebrated martyrs Nabor and Felix nearby in the Hortus
Philippi, and gave his clerics orders to start digging in its
vicinity. Not surprisingly, they soon discovered remains,
which were claimed to be those of Gervasius and Protasius,
who were believed to have been martyred under Nero; the
names were attested by a 'demon' being exorcized from an
elderly woman. Amidst great rejoicing from the bishop's supporters, the skeletons were solemnly transported to the new
church for reinterment; en route, even fleeting contact with the
bones is said to have proved sufficient to heal all kinds of
diseases among the attending crowds.[197]

Ambrose's opponents alleged that the spectacle was staged
by the bishop,[198] and for all his protests about their impiety[199]
they may well have been right. But whatever the identity of the
relics, their discovery and ceremonial transference had a
significant impact upon the Milanese community. Ambrose
had provided a spectacular distraction from the tensions of the
previous weeks; he had also signalled that, even if his foes had
him killed, they would not be able to remove what he stood for:
a martyred bishop would be commemorated in noble company
in a vast new shrine. His tactics presupposed the growing
significance of the cult of the martyrs in the late fourth century,
and its ability to evoke powerful passions in a people already
stirred by religous fervour.[200] He could readily connect the
inventio, the demonic testimonies, and the miraculous healings
with fidelity to a theological cause, and thus foster the idea that
here was reward for spiritual steadfastness.[201] In the end,
hopelessly outstaged by the excitement the bishop had
inspired, the court gave up in its pursuit of its cause. The
January law may or may not have been formally repealed; it
was certainly dropped in practice. Rather than risk a further

[197] See McLynn, 209–19; Williams, 219–23, both citing the earlier literature on the subject.

[198] Paulinus, *VA* 15.

[199] *Ep.* 77 [22].16–23.

[200] See P. Brown, *The Cult of the Saints: Its Rise and Function in Latin
Christianity* (Chicago, 1981), 36–7; Humphries, 54–6.

[201] See E. Dassmann, 'Ambrosius und die Märtyrer', *JbAC* 18 (1975),
49–68.

outbreak of potentially more serious anarchy, and increasingly preoccupied elsewhere with the problem of Maximus, Valentinian was advised to abandon the campaign his mother had supported. His regime was left fatally wounded by its encounter with Ambrose's intransigence, and within a matter of months the emperor and his retinue were in flight from Maximus' invading forces. While in retreat at Thessalonica, Valentinian repudiated his past homoian allegiances (perhaps in the wake of his mother's death); Theodosius, the swift victor over Maximus in the summer of 388, accompanied him back to Milan, where he was reconciled with Ambrose. Theodosius meanwhile sought to assert his own right to govern the West, remaining in Italy for three years while Valentinian was dispatched to Gaul.

Ambrose never had quite the same relations with Theodosius' court that he had with either Gratian's or Valentinian's, and his fabled ascendancy over Theodosius was hardly as his hagiographers pictured it.[202] Nevertheless, the advent of Theodosius guaranteed the political triumph of catholicism in the North Italian context. For all the political problems which lay around the corner for Ambrose in the early 390s (and he managed to die before things became even worse), he had at last entered upon a phase in which his version of the Nicene faith had achieved a major bridgehead.

(ii) *De officiis* as moral manifesto

All of this background is essential for an understanding of the context of *De officiis*. The once uncertain and unwilling bishop had evolved a reputation as an urbane and powerful preacher, and proved himself well capable of impressing the eyes and ears of a discerning society. He had made converts and allies in

---

[202] Two famous incidents in particular have conventionally been taken to show Ambrose's power over Theodosius: first, his belligerent protest against Theodosius' response to the Christian burning of a synagogue at Callinicum in December 388, and second, his even more famous staging of the spectacle of the emperor submitting to public penance to atone for the massacre of up to 7,000 innocents at Thessalonica in 390. In each case, however, the dynamics of the encounters were far more subtle than the traditional versions imply, and Theodosius was looking after his own interests as well: see McLynn, 298–309 and 315–30.

important circles of business life and bureaucracy, and established himself as a chief civic benefactor and rhetor, protector of the weak, pastoral counsellor, and symbolic linchpin of an otherwise loosely united social world. To a degree that no Western bishop before him had known, he had gained access to the ear of emperors and a degree of leverage in the affairs of their courts.[203] He had become a go-between on political business and a sponsor of the causes and careers of diverse associates and contacts, not least from Rome itself.[204] He had steadily transformed the physical landscape of his city by encircling it with a string of new churches which symbolized the social prestige of the Nicene cultus, its viability as an alternative to conventional symbols of civic cohesion, and its successful colonization of suburbia.[205] Across northern Italy as whole, his church had come to provide effective leadership for a disparate collection of bishoprics spread over a considerable area. When Ambrose assumed office, each of these sees had still been defined very much by its own traditions and practices, and there was little if any sense of their belonging to a coherent group, all articulating the same social and intellectual message. Under his direction, Milan became a mediator of the authority of the church of Rome yet also the figurehead for a proudly particular northern tradition.[206] The obvious political instability of the 380s made this quest for unity all the more pertinent. Ambrose capitalized on a *Zeitgeist* which reflected ongoing uncertainty every bit as much as cultural sophistication. In a time in which ecclesiastical progress had as much to do with

[203] See generally A. Piganiol, *L'empire chrétien (325–395)*, 2nd edn. (Paris, 1972), 269–73.

[204] For some examples of the ties of *amicitia* in this official context, see McLynn, 256–75.

[205] McLynn, 226–37; R. Krautheimer, *Three Christian Capitals: Topography and Politics* (Berkeley and Los Angeles, 1983), 69–92; Humphries, 196–202. On the symbolism of constructing physical expressions of orthodoxy to supplant the influences of earlier heresy, see R. Sörries, *Auxentius und Ambrosius. Ein Beitrag zur frühchristlichen Kunst Mailands zwischen Häresie und Rechtgläubligkeit* (Dettelbach, 1996); on churches as markers of spiritual power more generally, see D. Janes, *God and Gold in Late Antiquity* (Cambridge, 1998).

[206] See e.g. his defence of the non-Roman practice of baptismal 'footwashing' in *Sacr.* 3.4–7. On the delicate dynamics of loyalty to Rome and the consolidation of northern authority, see Humphries, 157–8.

social and political impact as with theological acuity, his
brilliance consisted in his ability to convince people that the
interests of the empire were inextricably bound up with the
security of the catholic faith. He himself may not have been as
secure as his rhetoric and gestures were designed to imply, but
he had by now negotiated the most difficult stages of his
mission to persuade his immediate world of the potency of
his message.

Ambrose writes as one who has come a long way from his
early vulnerability; but he also remembers the ebb and flow of
his fortunes in recent years, knows that his achievements have
been hard-won, and senses that every advantage deserves to be
pressed. It is clear that he no longer has to make do with an
inherited retinue: he has by now been able to staff his church
with officials whose loyalties are much safer. Some, like the
cleric whose 'cocky' gait had debarred him from being allowed
to precede the bishop in official processions, had resigned their
charge (in his case allegedly *pecuniae studio*, to avoid being
arraigned before his master's tribunal: 1.72); others had
perhaps been replaced more directly. Now Ambrose's spiritual
'sons' (1.1, 2, 23–4, 72, 184; 2.25, 134, 149, 152–6; 3.132, 139)
are said to have been chosen by him (1.24), and to be dear to
his heart (1.24; 2.155). Some of this language is no doubt
conventional, but it is evident that Ambrose has a particular
focus on the duties and dangers facing younger men (cf. 1.65–
6, 81, 87, 212, 217–18; 2.97–101), which may suggest that at
least part of his retinue, particularly in its junior ranks,
consisted of a new, hand-picked generation of suitably malle-
able material. Like Rome, Carthage, Poitiers, Vercelli, and
other major churches, Milan had evolved a kind of mini-
seminary system, in which young men could be trained from
boyhood to be the spiritual leaders of the future.[207] From this

---

[207] A. G. Hamman, 'La formation du clergé latin, dans les quatres premiers
siècles', *SP* 20 (1989), 238–49. One example of a presbyter who had been in
the church since childhood (probably as a reader: see commentary on 1.65)
and was ordained by Ambrose was Horontianus (*Ep.* 18 [70].25), to whom a
number of the bishop's letters are addressed (*Epp.* 21–3 [34–6], 29 [43], 31
[44], 18–19 [70–1], 20 [77], 66 [78]). Cf. also Paulinus' reference to the
deacons Castus and Polemius, *nutriti ab Ambrosio* (*VA* 46). The *monasterium*
which Augustine discovered outside the walls of Milan (*Conf.* 8.6.15; *Mor.*
1.70) offered another example of Ambrose's control. It consisted of a group of

school of virtue, Ambrose is aspiring to raise men after his own pattern.

At the same time, it is clear that Ambrose is still sensitive about the need for fidelity to his cause. It can be no accident that he makes so many references to the evils of deserting the faith or giving up when circumstances are tough (1.72, 188, 256; cf. also 3.126): doubtless the temptations of alternative careers, and perhaps of alternative ministries in rival theological circles, had proved too great for some. The bishop's critics still rankle: Ambrose is concerned to justify his disposal of church funds in the face of homoian censure (2.136–43). The clergy may be called *ad pacis negotia* (1.175), but the *militia Dei* (1.185–7) requires the tenacity and fortitude of an army in order to withstand external assaults and pressures: the legions of the Lord's anointed must stick together. There must be a preparedness to face danger (cf. 1.175–209; 3.56, 82–5, 88, 90, 124).[208] Ambrose has a good deal to say on the importance of the believing community existing as a family (1.24, 170; 2.152–6; 3.132) and as a body (2.134–5; 3.18–19) which coheres in the mutual affection and respect of its members, as each man prefers his neighbour to himself. *Una est domus quae omnes capit* (1.88), he contends; unity and peace are crucial within it (2.134, 155; 3.19). The *amicitia* of the brotherhood is not just a precious gift: it is a spiritual *desideratum* as well (3.125–38), demonstrating a maturity of faith that will be honoured by God and men. The rupturing of friendship is depicted as a terrible thing, akin to Judas' betrayal of Christ in the upper room (3.137). Sincerity, truthfulness, and honesty are vital (2.96, 112–20).

---

ascetics under the supervision of one of the bishop's presbyters. Indirectly, episcopal authority thus held sway beyond the immediate bounds of the ecclesiastical establishment as well as within them. Some of the former residents of the monastery nevertheless ended up renegades in Ambrose's eyes: the heterodox Jovinian (who denied that celibacy was superior to the married state), and two of his disciples, Sarmatio and Barbatianus, were ex-Milanese monks (on the latter pair, see *Ep. extra coll.* 14 [63].7–9; *Expl. Ps.* 36.49).

[208] Some similar sentiments are to be found later in a short epistle written to his clergy probably during Eugenius' occupation of Milan in 394 (*Ep.* 17 [81]): Ambrose encourages them not to think of giving up or retiring from the ministry on account of their difficult circumstances.

The grounding of the clergy's unity is said to be love (1.24; 2.155), but there is a strong emphasis on the responsibilities of the participants as a privileged group. These men are not just the bishop's choice; they have been chosen by God, and entrusted with the awesome task of guarding the divine mysteries (1.250–1). Obligation to the Lord comes before duty even to parents (1.257–8). What this means in practice, inevitably, is obedience to the bishop (2.123), for it is he who is the representative of divine authority, the *paterfamilias* of a new household whose smooth running depends upon the submission of its members to the firm direction of its head. However carefully cultivated Ambrose's *persona* of *humilitas* may be as a foil for Ciceronian assurance (1.1–4), his teaching is invested with a firm authority, for it takes its voice from the divine Scriptures: it is a deposit of faith, passed on to be guarded and pondered (1.2–3; 3.139), not quibbled with. When the episcopal mind determines what the biblical ethic entails in the particulars of the Milanese context, a brief *non probo* (1.84; cf. 1.74) carries an air of finality about it. Young men must show respect for their elders (1.65); the *honestum* is what is *probabile* in their leader's eyes (1.75, 144; 3.125; cf. 1.150; 3.45), whose tersely prescriptive *volumus* (2.96) must be heeded. There must be no unseemly ambition and arrogance among the clergy (2.119, 123); the bishop ensures fulfilment and the best use of resources by allocating each man to the role to which he is best suited (1.216; 2.134). The episcopal *sacerdos*, for his part, must of course be just in his treatment of his subordinates, and not grow jealous if a lesser cleric earns special esteem (2.121–2). Excommunication for misdemeanours is always to be regarded as a last resort, an expedient to be used sorrowfully only if penance has failed to bring about amendment of character (2.135). Control is tight nevertheless.

Beneath the rhetoric, the modern reader can sense the realities of an ecclesiastical structure which, for all the reforms, still creaked under the strain of inevitable personality clashes, ambitions, and petty jealousies. The clerical *ordo* was in reality as subtly graded as the hierarchy of any town council, with its own fairly rigid *cursus honorum*.[209] No doubt there were junior

---

[209] See generally Gryson, *Prêtre*, 120–30. Of course, Ambrose's own elevation illustrated the possibilities for exceptions to the rules; yet his

clerics desperate for the added prestige and power which came
with promotion, and no doubt there were senior clerics
determined to hold on to these privileges for themselves at all
costs, while all the time the temptations of the world and the
blandishments of alternative ecclesial communities posed their
own dangers for them all.

Ambrose's strict standards imply that he had no shortage of
candidates all the same: any church which could reject men on
the grounds of gait (1.72) clearly did not find it difficult to meet
its staffing requirements.[210] As a metropolitan see, Milan, like
Rome, attracted plenty of young men from a wide variety of
backgrounds who were willing and ready to be nurtured on the
bishop's ideals. They were not only locals: there is reference to
at least one African as a member of the clergy,[211] and there may
well have been others from similar contexts, given Ambrose's
ability to import virgins from as far afield as Mauretania.[212] If
the city's bureaucratic machine could attract careerists from all
over the empire, so, in some measure, could its church order.
As in government, so in ecclesiastical officialdom: a period of
service at Milan was seen as a stepping-stone to promotion, and
this must have helped with recruitment. A number of
Ambrose's men were apparently of some kind of independent
means, capable at least of living off their *agelluli*, and thus
saving the church the cost of supporting them (1.185; cf.
1.152). Ambrose was scarcely one to miss an opportunity to
raise the social tone of his *presbyterium*, either: when in 395 he
heard that the wealthy aristocrat and literary scholar Paulinus
(future bishop of Nola) had embraced Christianity and
renounced his wealth in order to pursue the service of God,
he eagerly invited him to join the Milanese ranks; had Ambrose
succeeded in persuading him, it would naturally have been a
significant coup.[213]

A number of Ambrose's trainees went on to hold episcopal

enduring sensitivity to his irregular initiation highlights in itself the perceived
importance of normal processes.

[210] Brown, *Body*, 357; McLynn, 285 n. 134.

[211] Paulinus, *VA* 54.1.

[212] *Virg.* 1.57, 59. It is possible that some of these North African virgins
were in fact slaves recruited from Ambrose's family estates: McLynn, 67–8.

[213] Paulinus, *Ep.* 3.4.

office elsewhere: Felix of Bologna was a direct export from Milan,[214] as was Theodulus, a former *notarius* who ended up in charge at Modena.[215] Nor did Ambrose hesitate to intervene in appointment processes, imposing favoured candidates upon neighbouring sees, presumably because they reflected the appropriate 'Milan style', even if they had not necessarily been under his direct tutelage: Felix of Como, Gaudentius of Brescia, Vigilius of Trent, and Chromatius of Aquileia were all installed with his active support and were recipients of detailed advice on the obligations of their ministry.[216] Among his last achievements was his effort to ensure the consecration of a former Milanese, Honoratus, at Vercelli, in 396, even visiting in person when his extensive letter on the matter failed to produce the desired result among the local clergy.[217] Since Ambrose was probably not a 'metropolitan' in an official sense,[218] his heavy-handedness could at times incur resentment, but, as he had proved at Aquileia in 381,[219] the more loyal satellites he had, the better for him personally, and the faster his ecclesial vision would spread. Opposition to his teaching or his methods undoubtedly existed in his region, and may have been more widespread than the one-sided evidence from his own writings implies; nevertheless, he succeeded in building up a considerable network of like-minded

---

[214] Paulinus, *VA* 46. [215] Paulinus, *VA* 35.

[216] Note too Anemius of Sirmium, in Ambrose's first controversial intervention in 377/8 (Paulinus, *VA* 11). Felix: A., *Ep.* 5 [4]; Gaudentius: Gaud. Brix. *Serm.* 16; Vigilius: A., *Ep.* 62 [19]; Chromatius: A., *Ep.* 28 [50] (probably). The Constantius of A., *Ep.* 36 [2] was probably installed at Claterna.

[217] *Ep. extra coll.* 14 [63]; and see Lizzi, 46–50: after Honoratus' appointment, the see was very quickly broken up into smaller bishoprics, probably with Milan's encouragement. Paulinus, *VA* 40, says that Ambrose grieved to hear of the death of a good bishop partly because it was so difficult to find 'worthy'—or perhaps 'appropriate' or 'tractable'?—candidates.

[218] See E. Cattaneo, 'Il governo ecclesiastico nel IV secolo nell'Italia settentrionale', *AAAd* 22 (1982), 175–87. Humphries' study marks a deliberate attempt to view North Italian church history in a way that is *not* dominated by Ambrose's official influence as a presupposition (see esp.17–18).

[219] Cf. also his invocation of the bishops' authority in the aftermath of the council, in *Ep. extra coll.* 9 [13]. For other appeals to the implicit backing of his episcopal colleagues in his defiance of or challenge to the civil powers, cf. e.g. *Epp.* 72 [17].10, 13; 75 [21].17; 74 [40].29 (McLynn, 281 n. 122).

supporters, men with whom he kept in regular contact and over whom the authority of his sacred learning and the force of his personality maintained a steady hold.[220] This influence was clearly a matter of some pride to Ambrose, as witness his reference to his instructions to his brother in Pavia in 2.150–1.

De officiis needs to be seen as part of Ambrose's quest to ensure that both locally and throughout northern Italy his church comprised 'a loyal and efficient corps of subordinates, moulded in his own image'.[221] The treatise gives advice of relevance to a range of ecclesiastical grades, from the most junior, like readers, psalm-leaders, and exorcists (1.216), right up to bishops. Instructions concerning the responsibilities of those in higher orders are doubtless aimed not just at the work's wider ecclesiastical readership but also at still junior clerics who might attain such office in the future. The most frequent reference is to *sacerdos*, or to *sacerdotium*. Sometimes it is the bishop's role that is in mind (1.216; 2.121–2; cf. also 1.205–6); the *episcopus* is explicitly mentioned in 1.87, 246; 2.69, 123, 134–5. Usually, however, *sacerdos* depicts the priest or presbyter (1.80, 152, 249; 2.69, 76, 78, 87, 111, 125; 3.58–9). *Minister* and *ministerium* appear often: occasionally the reference is to the diaconate (2.121–2, 134; cf. 1.205, 207), but more often it is general, covering the clergy as a whole (1.86, 152, 247, 249; 2.25, 101, 149; 3.58); other general terms are *clericus* (2.111, 134, 150) and *ecclesiastici* (1.86). Presbyters are mentioned in 1.87 and 2.121–2, and 1.246–59 is directly addressed to 'Levites' or deacons.[222] In practice, few distinctions are made according to the rank or ministry, current or potential,

---

[220] For examples of expository letters sent to clerics, cf. those to Irenaeus: *Epp.* 4 [27], 6 [28], 11–13 [29–31], 14 [33], 15 [69], 16 [76]; 54 [64], 63 [73], or those to Sabinus: *Epp.* 27 [58], 32–3 [48–9], 34 [45], 37 [47], 39 [46], 40 [32]. On the whole subject, see Lizzi, 15–57; ead., 'Ambrose's Contemporaries and the Christianization of Northern Italy', *JRS* 80 (1990), 156–73; W. H. C. Frend, 'St Ambrose and other Churches (except Rome)', in *Nec timeo mori*, 161–80; Humphries, 147–53; and especially M. Zelzer, 'Vescovi e pastori alla luce delle lettere ambrosiane', in *Vescovi e pastori* ii. 559–68. On opposition to Ambrose, see McLynn, 287–8; Humphries, 152–3.

[221] McLynn, 253.

[222] The office of *dispensator*, spoken of in 2.69, is part of the diaconate. On the terminology in general, see further R. Gryson, 'Les degrés du clergé et leurs dénominations chez saint Ambroise de Milan', *RBén* 66 (1966), 119–27; id., *Prêtre*, 133–45.

of the addressees. Just as in his letters Ambrose aspires to place ecclesiastical correspondents and aristocratic friends in the same social category by addressing them in very similar terms,[223] so in *De officiis* he magnifies the spiritual privileges of all who are called to the service of the church, and makes much of the responsibilities of even quite junior clerics (cf. 1.246–59). They are all encouraged to project the church's authority with a uniform sense of assurance, and to manifest alike the virtues of *primarii viri* (2.67).

Ambrose provides an authoritative construal of what is and is not ethically appropriate for those whose social grooming has in most cases been considerably less exacting than his own. He seeks to weld a community that will present to a watching world an ideal of harmony, equity, self-denial, and dignity. The church is to be the *forma iustitiae* (1.142), where the abuse of *aequalitas* is terrible precisely because it is unexpected (2.124). Ecclesiastics need to cultivate a good reputation in society at large (1.227, 247; 2.29–39): it is vital that their deeds, words, and personal integrity are well thought of not just within the confines of the believing community but also among *hi qui foris sunt* (1.247).[224] The stated motivation is pious—*laus enim Domini ubi munda possessio et innocens familiae disciplina* (1.247)—but the pragmatism behind it is clear. Details like *incessus* (gait) matter in part because the bishop's retinue has to know how to behave itself when he visits the palace.[225] The clergy need advice about how to speak, what to wear, how to respond to social invitations, what to do about visiting women, or how to spend their leisure-time, because the eyes of the world—and in particular the discerning world of a political metropolis—are upon them. There must be nothing 'rustic' about God's servants (cf. 1.84, 104): they need to reflect a sanctified variant on traditional *urbanitas*.[226] Civilized behaviour correlates, in the end, with spiritual and theological soundness (cf. 1.72). What the *vir optimus* thinks matters a

---

[223] See Lizzi, 15–36.

[224] A Ciceronian principle lurks behind a NT phrase; see commentary ad loc.

[225] Cf. Paulinus, *VA* 35.

[226] For the context, see E. S. Ramage, *Urbanitas: Ancient Sophistication and Refinement* (Norman, OK, 1973), esp. 52–76.

great deal (1.227); the *minister altaris* is to be *seen* to display
appropriate virtues (1.247).[227] Of course, many of Ambrose's
putative addressees might seldom if ever come into direct
contact with the upper échelons of society, but their public
style must evince the kind of dignity that will make the
possibility of such intercourse seem credible, to make it *look*
as if they might well belong in the sphere in which gentlemen
of distinction would operate. And for those who might have to
assert their place in the closely knit and competitive communities of provincial towns, and become part of the alliances
which had to be nurtured in these sees between senior clergy
and local notables, it was necessary to learn the right steps to
social acceptability and maximum political effectiveness. The
church's success depended heavily upon winning financial and
cultural support from regional élites. Ambrose may praise the
virtues of Christlike self-effacement and of not seeking to
'shine' in this world (3.36), but the motif of self-commendation
runs all the way through the exposition of the *utile* in book 2.[228]
Unlike monks, who could practise their spiritual discipline in
the shelter of a cloistered asceticism, clergy had to carry out
their duties *velut in quodam theatro*, a spectacle to all: [229] it was
vital to render a convincing performance, by living in a way
which signalled dissociation from the world while nevertheless
avoiding social ineptitude.[230]

Although Ambrose's aim is to demonstrate the pre-eminence
of the Christian image of duty, his ethic implicitly assumes the
validity of a plethora of classical stereotypes. Core elements of
the prescribed *habitus* can be traced back to ideals of the
classical *vir publicus*, though they are applied in and to a
quite distinct social context. Ambrose's key assumption is an
ancient one: that *virtus* was, as its etymology suggested, about
'manliness'. To do the right thing was to manifest a character
that was truly *virilis*; to create an impression of effeminacy,

---

[227] Cf. the stress on the visibility of the ethic of temperance in 1.219–25,
and the reference to 'raising' Christ's image in 1.245.

[228] See commentary on 2.29–39.

[229] *Ep. extra coll.* 14 [63].71.

[230] For an attempt to expound Ambrose's paradigm in terms of a discourse
of clerical 'performativity', see I. J. Davidson, 'Staging the Church? Theology
as Theater', *JECS* 8 (2000), 413–51. Much of this section covers themes
explored in that article.

conversely, was to betray a lack of moral fibre. A real man had to exclude from his character all tell-tale traces which might convey the idea that he was subject to the kind of tempers and weaknesses which afflicted women, who were assumed to be intrinsically weaker creatures.[231] Deportment encoded the complex realities of social structure: a gentleman walked, talked, and carried himself in a way that distinguished him from the crowd and demonstrated his inner rectitude. His masculinity was the badge of his status, something to be achieved and proved rather than assumed; it required serious effort.

Such assumptions fuelled a widespread fascination with physiognomy in classical antiquity, where numerous writers had issued extensive advice to aspiring public men on how to demonstrate their credibility as social leaders and how to avoid conveying inappropriate messages by the 'wrong' kind of body-language. In the second and third centuries of the Christian era, these ideas were widely shared in both pagan and Christian moralizing. The deliberate fashioning of sexual and social identity through rhetorical performance was a vital part of the so-called Second Sophistic, where the orator, like his classical forebears, was scrutinized for manliness of gait, gesture, facial expression, and voice.[232] Christian moralists

[231] Brown, *Body*, 11; cf. also Moorhead, 60–2. On the psychology of 'ocular' culture, or the ensuring of conformity to particular ethical constraints by the subjecting of individual agents to unrelenting societal surveillance, see E. Clark, 'Sex, Shame and Rhetoric: En-Gendering Early Christian Ethics', *JAAR* 59 (1991), 719–45.

[232] The investigation of this side of ancient ethics has been a major achievement of recent scholarship at the interface of Classics and Social Anthropology. See, *inter alia*, M. W. Gleason, 'The Semiotics of Gender: Physiognomy and Self-Fashioning', in D. M. Halperin, J. J. Winkler, and F. I. Zeitlin (eds.), *Before Sexuality: The Construction of Erotic Experience in the Ancient Greek World* (Princeton, NJ, 1990), 389–415; ead., *Making Men: Sophists and Self-Presentation in Ancient Rome* (Princeton, NJ, 1995); C. Edwards, *The Politics of Immorality in Ancient Rome* (Cambridge, 1993), esp. 63–97; J. Bremmer and H. Roodenburg, *A Cultural History of Gesture, from Antiquity to the Present Day* (Cambridge, 1991), chs. 1–2; F. Dupont, *Daily Life in Ancient Rome* (Oxford and Cambridge, MA, 1993), 239–58; T. S. Barton, *Power and Knowledge: Astrology, Physiognomics, and Medicine under the Roman Empire* (Ann Arbor, MI, 1994), 95–131; E. Gunderson, 'Contested Subjects: Oratorical Theory and the Body', Ph.D. Diss. (University of California, Berkeley, CA, 1996); A. Richlin, 'Gender and Rhetoric: Producing

such as Clement of Alexandria readily transmuted such
assumptions into their own context: Clement's *Paidagogos*
(like *De officiis*, in direct debt to Stoic sources) is full of
advice about avoiding effeminacy and embodying virtue by
moving, appearing, and sounding the right way. Much of it
might be equally at home in a non-Christian manual of
etiquette. Virtue was not so much about internalized principles: it was about an interconnected web of social signs. This
logic persisted in the fourth and fifth centuries: a curiosity
concerning the import and interpretation of the *verba visibilia*
conveyed by visual and aural symbolism continued to exercise
some of the greatest Christian minds.[233]

Ambrose's ideal community is to be characterized by a whole
series of habits, gestures, and relationships generated by classical perceptions of manhood and respectability. Just like his
classical predecessors, Ambrose is fascinated by body-language
as an eloquent index of character (1.71), indicative of just how
well or otherwise the 'womanish' passions are being restrained
by 'masculine' rationality (cf. 1.97–8, 228–9).[234] When the
'inner man' is suitably modest and humble (1.13, 19, 65, 89,
237; 2.67, 87, 90, 119, 122–3, 134; 3.36, 133), it will be obvious
in the 'outer man''s physical deportment (1.72–5) and in the
clothing he wears (1.83). His voice will not be contrived,
effeminate, or uncouth (1.84): it will be simple, clear, manly,
and unaffected (1.104; cf. 1.84), a testimony to his *verecundia*
(1.67).[235] Whether the context be formal *tractatus* or informal
conversation, his speech will be redolent of the Scriptures
(1.99–101). He will neither engage in nor will he listen to
immodest talk (1.76, 86), and he will avoid jokes and improper

Manhood in the Schools', in W. J. Dominik (ed.), *Roman Eloquence: Rhetoric
in Society and Literature* (London and New York, 1997), 90–110.

[233] Cf. Augustine, *Doctr. Chr.* 2.3.5. For some seminal discussions of
Augustine's remarkable theorizing on the whole subject of signs in *Doctr.
Chr.* 2, see R. A. Markus, 'St Augustine on Signs', *Phronesis* 2 (1957), 60–83;
B. D. Jackson, 'The Theory of Signs in St Augustine's *De Doctrina
Christiana*', *REAug* 15 (1969), 9–49; scholarly interest in the field shows no
signs of abating.

[234] Though in 1.228–9 *ratio* is personified as a *bona domitrix*.

[235] On the classical background, see A. Rousselle, 'Parole et inspiration: le
travail de la voix dans le monde romain', *History and Philosophy of the Life
Sciences* 5 (1983), 129–57.

stories (1.102–3; cf. 1.85, 88, 184). Flattery will no more be proffered (1.226; 2.96, 112–20; 3.134–5) than it is invited (1.88, 209, 226; cf. 2.66). The individual's entire language will be affable (1.226; 2.96), wholesome, and blameless (2.86). Self-control will characterize his personality, for angry words are a failure of *decorum* (1.5–22; 90–7). To say nothing at all may well be a mark of spirituality, especially in response to provocation; the conscience may speak eloquently in secret, and a person may engage in the best form of address, namely prayer to God, when silent with those around him (1.5–22, 31–5, 68, 234, 236; cf. 3.1–7).

In much of this besides the references to prayer and the Scriptures, Ambrose is mirroring the traditional icon of the public figure. The cleric is to be urbane, assured, in control of his emotions, calm and steady in all situations, the epitome of self-mastery (cf. 1.181–2). However cultivated his image, it is essential that his behaviour does not *appear* contrived (cf. 1.73, 75, 84, 101, 104); the qualities implied by his deportment must seem natural, not 'put on'.[236] But the outward conduct of the spiritual leader must be more than simply circumspect: it must be identifiably better than anything achieved by his peers. Even at their best, the conventions of civilized protocol represent only a minimum standard; in practice, the faithful soldier of Christ must aim higher still (cf. 1.185–6; 2.124; 3.26, 65).

The middle-Stoic/Ciceronian distinction between *medium officium* and *perfectum officium*, Ambrose argues, is akin to the difference between a basic heeding of the divine command-ments and an actual emulation of God's own perfection through asceticism and sacrificing one's interests for the sake of others (1.36–7). The lower standard of the *medium officium* may be achieved by the many; the *perfectum officium* is attain-able only by the few (3.10; cf. 3.12; also 1.16, 125, 184, 217–18). The Panaetian idea of different contexts for duty is effectively recast as a twofold standard of Christian morality, and thus Ambrose anticipates a major trajectory of Western moral theology.[237] There is a higher path for the select ones who are called by God to spiritual leadership. By combining

---

[236] Ambrose is also alert to the dangers of artificiality and insincerity more generally: cf. 2.112–20; 3.58.

[237] Stelzenberger, 237.

the Stoic ideal with the images of the *athleta Christi* (1.183, 238; cf. 1.59–60) and the *miles Christi* (1.185–7, 238; cf. 1.218), Ambrose's ethic seminally transfers an element of the Stoic framework into the context of spiritual service. The philosophical sage is rhetorically reincarnated as the holy man, distinct from the ordinary achievers of even the larger Christian community.[238] In evoking the ideal of a special 'primary' group who are summoned to an exemplary life of special sanctity and self-giving, Ambrose is spelling out a process of not simply Christianization, but 'hyper-Christianization'.[239] In the end, *medium officium* is actually irrelevant, for it is synonymous with an attitude of greed and selfishness which cannot see beyond the present world: nothing less than perfection will do (3.12).

Ambrose goes beyond invoking the rituals of stylized good conduct; he transposes them. A whole new degree of moral integrity is required. Clerics are not to be taught how to behave at secular dinner-parties; they are to turn down their invitations to them in the first place. Such occasions are unsuitable settings for those consecrated to a life of purity and self-denial: they are full of temptations to engage in excessive eating and drinking, and people inevitably find themselves in situations where they overhear unsavoury *fabulae* (1.85–6). Christ's servants should generally avoid dangers such as wine in any case (1.247). Visits to Christian homes can be equally perilous for young men, if the homes in question are those of widows or virgins. These trips should take place only when there is good reason for it (such as, presumably, in a case of illness), and even then a junior cleric ought to be accompanied by elders (1.87); there must be no cause for suspicion. True to classical (and biblical) form, the company of older men is always desirable for the young anyhow (1.212; 2.97–101; cf. 1.65–6).

Ambrose inherits the typical Roman preoccupation that

[238] Cf. 3.27, where the *sapiens* of the classical illustration is equated with the man of faith: *vir Christianus et iustus et sapiens*. On this process more generally, see P. Cox, *Biography in Late Antiquity: A Quest for the Holy Man* (Berkeley and Los Angeles, 1983). On the necessary ethical differential between the spiritual leader and the *populus Dei* as a whole, cf. e.g. 1.184, 249.

[239] See P. Brown, 'Christianization and Religious Conflict', in A. Cameron and P. Garnsey (eds.), *The Cambridge Ancient History* xiii: *The Late Empire, AD 337–425* (Cambridge, 1998), 632–64, at 655–6.

otium should not be squandered on indolence but used profit-
ably; but he fleshes out the principle in a new way. Instead of
the literary or cultural pursuits of the classical gentleman at
ease, the ideal now is spiritual activity, and the paragon is the
holy man who never wastes a moment without engaging in
meditation upon and communion with the God to whom he
must give account (3.1–7).[240] The great spiritual responsibility
of the cleric is the study of the Scriptures, and the obligation to
model himself upon the examples of the saints (1.88, 116, 165;
3.139). Prayer, a discipline in which modesty is essential (1.70),
is communion with Christ (1.88). Fasting is another important
exercise for those called to a lifelong service of self-denial
(2.122; 3.10).

The area where the transformation of the classical ideal is
most obviously radical is in Ambrose's insistence on celibacy
(cf. 1.68–9, 76–80; 2.27). Sexual propriety is no longer a case
of showing mere discretion or restraint of appetite, as it was
for the *adulescentes* to whom Cicero addressed himself: the
Christian élite must abstain completely. Ambrose's demands
for *ascesis* directly confront secular ideals of moral behaviour;
they invite the recognition that the manhood of the Christian
official is, contrary to all preconceived ideas of strength and
weakness, superior to that of his pagan competitor, because it
consists in a transcendence of the physical desires which afflict
even the strongest of men. No Roman gentleman had ever
been bound to such a rigorous commitment; Ambrose
requires of his leading men an absolute sexual *integritas*
(1.249; 2.27) which traditionally would have been expected
only of women.[241] On the one hand, then, Christian leadership is about conventional stereotypes of assertive masculinity; on the other, the discourse of idealized Christian
maleness is subtly 'feminized' as part of an appeal to cultural
resistance.[242] These men are *ministri altaris Christi* (1.247),

[240] See further C. Somenzi, 'Ambrogio e Scipione l'Africano: la fondazione
cristiana dell' "otium negotiosum"', in *Nec timeo mori*, 753–68.

[241] Brown, *Body*, 359.

[242] On the background here, see A. Cameron, *Christianity and the Rhetoric
of Empire: The Development of Christian Discourse* (Berkeley and Los Angeles,
1991), 165–88; on Ambrose, see V. Burrus, '"Equipped for Victory":
Ambrose and the Gendering of Orthodoxy', *JECS* 4 (1996), 461–75.

and the sacraments cannot be administered with an 'impure' body (1.249). To 'keep the body untainted, and to maintain one's honour unsullied and undefiled' (2.27) is for them essential to the preservation of a higher degree of *decorum*. Clergy who are married at the time of ordination must observe a strict *continentia* (1.249; cf. 1.256),[243] and those who have been married more than once, even if their second marriage was contracted subsequent to baptism (so that, technically, their first union did not count), are barred from ordination altogether (1.248). This of course highlights the arduousness of the clerical calling for the young (1.218; cf. 3.10). Ambrose builds up an aura of mystique around the church's leaders. They are a body of noble sufferers, gladly taking up their cross in obedience to their Lord's command, surrounded by a viciously hostile world.[244] They are the guardians of the deep things of God, summoned not only to deny themselves but also to guard the mysteries of the faith—the spiritual secrets known to those who have been initiated by baptism (cf. 1.170)—from the prying eyes of the unworthy, whose unholy *curiositas* is a mark of their spiritual impotence (1.251).

Other forms of self-denial are also pressing. The Christian vocation is also to poverty, which is regarded as an advantage in the quest for *beatitudo* and eternal reward (2.15–21; cf. 1.59). Riches, ephemeral tokens at best, are to be despised rather than desired (1.23, 137, 182, 184–5, 192–3, 241–6; 2.25, 66–7, 89, 108, 129–33; 3.57–8), and greed is never to be countenanced within the *presbyterium* (1.137–8, 193, 195; 2.24–6, 62, 66, 89, 108, 128–33; 3.37). Practices like angling for inheritances are profoundly disgraceful (3.57–8). Contentment with one's resources is crucial (1.185). Some ecclesiastics may retain a proportion of their assets so as not to be an unnecessary financial burden upon the church (1.152), while others make do with their benefice (1.185).

Money is to be used especially for works of *misericordia*

---

[243] We may guess that quite a large number fell into this category, hence the concession of continence as the next best thing to life-long celibacy.

[244] Cf. the celebration of the exemplary courage of the martyrs in 1.202–7. On the impact of such language on early Christian self-imaging, see J. Perkins, *The Suffering Self: Pain and Narrative Representation in the Early Christian Era* (London and New York, 1995), 200–14.

(1.38, 148, 253; 2.69, 126–7), and that to the point of sacrifice (1.151; 2.136). A number of conventional examples of the vulnerable and the deserving are cited: widows and orphans (1.63, 144; 2.70–1, 150–1); the aged and the infirm (1.158); prisoners (2.70–1, 109, 136–43); blood-relatives (1.150); the victims of robbery (1.158); those who have lost their inheritance through no fault of their own (2.69), especially those of good birth who feel embarrassment at having fallen upon hard times (1.148, 158; cf. 2.76)—another illustration of Ambrose's own prejudices; debtors (1.253; 2.71; cf. 1.168); and fellow-believers generally (1.148). People who have shown kindness are to be repaid with generous interest (1.160–2). Hospitality is another crucial service (1.167; 2.103–8; cf. 1.39, 86). It is naturally quite appropriate to spend money on church-buildings (2.110–11), as Ambrose himself did so heavily. There are, however, specific ground-rules for giving: clerics need to beware of professional beggars (2.76–7); and charity must be prudent, gradual, and in response to genuine need, not just a case of pouring out resources in one great act of expenditure (1.149–50; cf. in general 1.143–59; 2.76–8, 109–11). Alms must never be given for the sake of display (1.147; 2.76, 102; cf. 2.122–3), and should ideally be done in secret (1.147; 2.2–3). Christ's kenotic example is fundamental (1.151). In reality, however, Ambrose deliberately promotes the image of the churchman as benefactor and protector of the disadvantaged. In a fundamentally patronal society, the bestowal of *beneficia* always involved specific social dynamics. By implicitly absorbing such dependants into his retinue, the cleric, and especially the bishop, is seen as the bestower of bounty, a kind of quasi-imperial patron scattering gold to the needy as a sign of his status. Classical euergetism is recast as Christian almsgiving.[245] In an urban centre of considerable wealth, Ambrose could work hard to promote private generosity among his well-heeled constituents as well as among his clergy; but the facilitating of such largesse was also a matter of control, a practical way of corroborating the rhetoric of power which pervaded the spiritual message.[246]

[245] Cf. *Ep.* 75a [*C. Aux.*].33, cited by P. Brown, *Power*, 97.
[246] On euergetism and almsgiving, see P. Veyne, *Bread and Circuses* (London, 1990), 19–33; on the scarcity of evidence as to how much was

Some of the social injustices or moral crimes which Ambrose mentions, such as avarice and excess, are obviously stylized, the standard targets of classical satire exploited by influential Christian sources like Basil.[247] Others presumably do indicate genuine problems in contemporary society. Why warn about charlatan mendicants if they were not a real nuisance, or tell clerics to steer clear of *omnis usus negotiationis* (1.185) if none of them was dabbling in a little commercial activity on the side?[248] Nevertheless, there can be little doubt that Ambrose's denunciations are selective. In a region filled with the country estates of wealthy aristocrats, he condemns farmers who capitalize on grain-shortages (3.37–44), but proceeds to complain about injustice inflicted on *peregrini* at Rome who must have been doing that very thing (3.49–52). Many of Ambrose's regular hearers were drawn from the ranks of the rich speculators who were most likely to be guilty of such sins, and this imposed practical constraints upon his and his clergy's freedom to specify their transgressions: much of the rhetoric remains general out of pragmatic necessity. Ambrose finds it safer to reiterate traditional criticisms of evils such as money-lending (2.111; 3.20, 41)[249] and commercial avarice (1.243; cf. also his conservative respect for inherited property in 2.17; 3.63), and to parrot Stoic platitudes about the whole world being the country of the wise man (2.66), or about the wise and just man having the riches of the entire world (1.118),[250] or to hold out

actually changed by ecclesiastical donation, see C. Pietri, 'Les Pauvres et la pauvreté dans l'Italie de l'Empire chrétien', in *Miscellanea Historiae Ecclesiasticae*, 6, Bibliothèque de la *Revue d'histoire ecclésiastique*, 67 (Brussels, 1983), 267–300.

[247] Cf. the set-piece diatribes against greed, drunkenness, and usury, respectively, in *Nab.*, *Elia*, and *Tob.*

[248] I thus opt for a *via media* between Vasey's apparently unquestioning acceptance that Ambrose takes a serious and consistent ideological position on every social issue to which he alludes, however tangentially (cf. 19–20: *Off.* 'is by far the most useful of all Ambrose's works to sound the depths of his spirit on social questions'), and McLynn's extreme scepticism (244–51) about deriving any reliable indications of current social conditions from anything that Ambrose says.

[249] See commentary on 2.111.

[250] His ideas on slavery are partly rooted in Stoic principles that true freedom is detachment from outward circumstances (such as physical bondage), and that slaves share an intrinsic dignity and deserve to be treated

conventional Christian promises of eternal reward for the blessed poor (1.28–9, 45–6, 59).

The direction of fourth-century society was more and more being determined by episcopal power-brokers like Ambrose, who in many respects had emerged as a new class of imperial administrators, functioning as arbiters in civil disputes, counsellors on practical affairs covering everything from marriage arrangements to financial dealings, intermediaries between government and people, and spokesmen for whatever *ad hoc* range of interests might be perceived to be of value to their local churches' social cause. In the fragmented world of late antiquity, great differences often existed in the methods adopted by such bishops; within formal parameters of professed conciliarity, individual churchmen tended to cultivate their own manifestations of the *ecclesia catholica* as best their specific circumstances allowed. In building up the disparate fiefdoms which we tend to regard, anachronistically, as a coherent entity labelled 'the Western church', the political power and freedom of speech exercised by bishops was ever more obvious.[251] Ambrose discharged his role with all the aplomb of a former advocate and administrator, hearing legal cases, interceding on behalf of people convicted of civil offences, and acting as a general champion of the weak against the strong. He is clearly concerned to ensure that the next generation learn to use the system to their church's best

humanely (the latter obviously reinforced by biblical anthropology): see Klein, 9–51, esp 17–27.

[251] On the context, see e.g. W. Eck, 'Der Einfluss der konstantinischen Wende auf die Auswahl der Bischöfe im 4. und 5. Jahrhundert', *Chiron* 8 (1978), 561–85; H. Chadwick, 'The Role of the Christian Bishop in Ancient Society', in H. C. Hobbs and W. Wuellner (eds.), *The Role of the Christian Bishop in Ancient Society* (Protocol of the 35th Colloquy, Center for Hermeneutical Studies, Berkeley and Los Angeles, 1980), 1–14; F. D. Gilliard, 'Senatorial Bishops in the Fourth Century', *HTR* 77 (1984), 153–75; G. W. Bowersock, 'From Emperor to Bishop: The Self-Conscious Transformation of Political Power in the Fourth Century AD', *CPh* 81 (1986), 298–307; Cameron, *Christianity and the Rhetoric of Empire*, 123–41; Brown, *Power*, chs. 3–4; P. I. Kaufman, *Church, Book, and Bishop: Conflict and Authority in Early Latin Christianity* (Boulder, CO and Oxford, 1996); E. Rebillard and C. Sotinel (eds.), *L'Évêque dans la cité du IVe au Ve siècle. Image et authorité* (Rome, 1998); Humphries, chs. 4–7; and many of the studies in *Vescovi e pastori*.

advantage. This means that there must be scrupulous justice in all affairs that touch directly upon society at large. When vulnerable parties such as widows and orphans deposit property with the church for safekeeping, they have a right to expect that it will be preserved with proper care, and jealously guarded against encroachments by secular authorities (2.144–51; cf. 1.254). When bishops are involved in adjudicating in civil cases, they must show no partiality to the rich and powerful (the accusation that they did was obviously common), and there must be no condoning of evil (2.124–5). Sordid financial disputes may be turned down (2.125; 3.59), but not a *causa Dei* (2.125). The bishop is visualized as a kind of reincarnation of the Old Testament counsellor and judge; his place is at the centre of his community, where his leadership skills can be recognized, where everyone can see that he is a man of prudence, a reliable strategist forging a destiny for the masses who depend upon his wisdom. But more lowly clerics also need to be approachable (2.61), and able to offer good counsel to all who seek it (2.41–89); they must be known to be morally upright and wise (2.60–3).

The man of God ought to be useful to all, and harmful to no one (3.58; cf. 1.26). From time to time he will find himself engaging in an act of direct *intercessio* on behalf of a condemned person (2.102; cf. 1.138); when he does, the motive must never be to further his own glory. As for the civil authorities, there is precedent for disobedience of imperial orders in certain cases of principle (2.150–1), but it is wrong to provoke persecution by being abusive towards the *potestates* (1.208; cf. 1.187). The opportunity to die a glorious death (for the sake of truth or justice) is, all the same, a chance for spiritual honour not to be missed: it should be seized eagerly (2.153). In reality, the prospect of martyrdom for most of Ambrose's addressees was slim,[252] but that, to him, was no reason not to build up the sense of importance, the image of daring, attaching to the clerical role. The clergy are to perform a delicate balancing-

---

[252] Though the missionary activities of Ambrose's disciple Vigilius of Trent (A., *Ep.* 62 [19]), who prosecuted his ministry with more zeal than tact, led to a few deaths not long after Ambrose's passing in 397, and Vigilius himself suffered a martyr's fate in *c*.405; see Lizzi, 59–70, 86–96; Humphries, 181–3.

act. On the one hand, the Nicene community and the Roman empire are seen as co-terminous and interdependent (cf. 1.144), and so the imperial system is naturally to be used to best effect.[253] On the other, the church always has to transcend its social milieu, to be qualitatively different in its mores. It must be ready to challenge the failings of its culture with a fearless prophetic voice. Fearless—but not reckless. Spiritual leadership offered a vantage-point from which to look down on the kind of values cherished by the crowd (cf. 1.184, 192; 2.66—a mélange of Stoic and biblical ideas), but it had to learn ways of articulating its denunciations which commended the cause of Christ's kingdom rather than jeopardizing it.

The pervasive antitheses of church and *saeculum*, truth and error, soul and body, the rigid asceticism, and the moral puritanism of Ambrose's Christianity—the mindset that has aptly been described as a 'siege mentality'[254]—are thus only one side of the picture; the other is an activism which aspires to take over and to realign the structures of the world's authorities.[255] The resulting spirituality is both austere and dynamic: it characterizes a lifestyle that is simultaneously other-worldly yet rather uninterested in a contemplative theology as an end in itself. Ambrose could preach disengagement from (even 'contempt for': 1.242) the world while sketching a moral vision that would have a deliberate influence on the course which that world would take.

To ask what the precise ratio of classical or Stoic ideology to Christian content is in the overall message is potentially to lose

[253] On the importance of the stability of the *patria*, ranked next in importance to God himself, cf. 1.127, 129, 254; 3.23, 127; on barbarians as beyond the pale, cf. 2.70–1, 136; 3.84. Though the church comes before the Roman people (*Tob.* 51), patriotism is perfectly appropriate (*Luc.* 4.47), and imperial fidelity to Nicene theology leads to military success; Arianism is synonymous with barbarism (*Fid.* 2.136–42): see commentary on 1.144; 2.70–1. On the importance of society generally, cf. 1.134–5. Ambrose shares Cicero's anti-Epicurean sentiments about the importance of political activity (3.23), and his acceptance of the principle of a just war (1.176–7).

[254] M. Meslin, *Les Ariens d'Occident, 335–430* (Paris, 1967), 51, cited by Brown, *Body*, 348.

[255] On these juxtapositions at the level of both verbal and visual representation in general, see the brilliant analysis of Cameron, *Christianity and the Rhetoric of Empire* (though sadly Cameron makes few references to Ambrose); also Brown, *Power, passim*.

sight of the pragmatism that dominates Ambrose's perspective. Obviously, a great deal of what he advocates remains explicitly indebted to classical traditions, Stoic ones in particular. But, as his depiction of philosophy as a whole leads us to expect, he tends to generalize Stoic assumptions about the virtues and the passions, and (as too many of his interpreters have neglected to see) he shows little appreciation of the ways in which Cicero's own model of duties differs from orthodox Stoicism's picture of the ideal attained by an austere, self-sufficient sage.[256] In certain places, Ambrose can actually sound *more* authentically Stoic than Cicero does, even if his claims to authority are expressly biblical.[257] In others, there is an obvious tension between a view of the passions which is predicated on an autarkic psychology and an anthropology which, in elevating the soul over the body, sees physical suffering (both the pain of outward circumstances and the cost of voluntary asceticism) as productive of eternal advantage.[258] The question of whether nature is an ideal ethical teacher or a force whose wilder excrescences need to be curbed is never fully settled, especially given that for Ambrose the issue was complicated by theological discussions about the relationship between nature and grace (cf. 1.24). Ambrose imbibed an intellectual infusion drawn from an assortment of sources, and for him there was no incentive to identify all the constituents—to highlight the differences, say, between Cicero and Panaetius, or between Panaetius and earlier Stoicism—far less to talk positively about the relationship of any such authorities to Christian ideas. He was interested in promoting the practical relevance of ideals that to him were fundamentally scriptural, not in analysing the ingredients in the cultural inheritance which led him to construe these patterns in the way that he did.

Of course, divested of the *exempla*, the scriptural terminology, and the spiritual reference-points, some of Ambrose's

---

[256] Far too many students of Ambrose have treated 'Stoicism' as if it were a monolithic entity somehow transmitted in pristine form by Cicero, without reference to either the different stages within the ancient tradition or Cicero's creativity with regard to Panaetius.

[257] See e.g. on private property in 1.132. For another strongly Stoic-sounding phrase, cf. 2.18 on the role of virtue in obtaining the *vita beata*.

[258] See commentary on 2.1–21.

advice might perhaps sound at home in pagan antiquity. But, crucially, such a dismantling of his vision would dissolve the cultural specificity of his work and miss its purpose as an expression of his quest to assert the moral supremacy of his Christian way. Ambrose's drama was a success precisely *because* it integrated traditional cultural prejudices and ideals within a new spiritual setting. To judge from his ministry as a whole, it was this particular combination of classical patterns of social respectability with other, very different, ideas—the convergence of, say, *gravitas* with *humilitas*; the fusion of the Roman man of action with the priest and the Levite; the transformation of the political leader into the one who denies himself, beats his body into submission, blesses his enemy, and is prepared to lay down his life for his friend—that made such a striking impact in the context of late fourth-century Italy. That is not to suggest that the synopsis of the plan presented in *De officiis* is all thought through in any systematic sense, or to imply that Ambrose makes his case as well as he might *vis-à-vis* Cicero. Far less is it to say that his patterns are easily transferable to any modern context: the *ecclesia* evoked by Ambrose's stagecraft would cut a strange figure indeed anywhere today. Nevertheless, for all the rawness of its rhetorical depiction in *De officiis*, in the Milan of the late 380s the image seemed to belong. Ambrose was in the business of constructing a community for his own times.[259]

---

[259] There is a considerable literature on Ambrose's clerical teaching, much of it inattentive to the social dynamics of the late fourth century. The best survey is Gryson, *Prêtre*, especially 235 ff., 295 ff. A. Bonato, 'L'idea del sacerdozio in s. Ambrogio', *Augustinianum* 27 (1987), 423–64 is helpful on the fusion of classical morality and spiritual typology; see also F. E. Consolino, *Ascesi e mondanità nella Gallia tardoantica: Studi sulla figura del vescovo nei secoli IV–VI* (Naples, 1979), 23–37; E. L. Grasmück, 'Der Bischof und sein Klerus. Ambrosius von Mailand: De officiis ministrorum', in A. E. Hierold, V. Eid, *et al.* (eds.), *Die Kraft der Hoffnung. Gemeinde und Evangelium. Festschrift für Alterzbischof DDr. J. Schneider zum 80. Geburtstag* (Bamberg, 1986), 84–97; G. Coppa, 'Istanze formative e pastorali del presbitero nella vita e nelle opere di sant' Ambrogio', in F. Sergio (ed.), *La formazione al sacerdozio ministeriale nella catechesi e nella testimonianza di vita dei Padri* (Rome, 1992), 95–132; Moorhead, 157–81 (a summary of themes); I. J. Davidson, 'Social Construction and the Rhetoric of Ecclesial Presence: Ambrose's Milan', *SP* 38 (2001), 385–93. From the earlier literature, consult the following: J. Lécuyer, 'Le sacerdoce chrétien selon saint Ambroise',

VIII. THE INFLUENCE OF *DE OFFICIIS*

The precise impact of *De officiis* upon Ambrose's contemporaries is difficult to gauge. Its message was presumably read and absorbed by its intended clerical recipients throughout northern Italy, but we have no evidence of references to the work from Ambrose's immediate context. For a treatise which has been said to constitute 'the first manual of Christian ethics',[260] certainly the first in the Western church,[261] we have surprisingly few clues about its initial reception.

Like most literary projects in antiquity, the work was probably launched into the public domain with the support of the author's friends, particularly wealthy friends, through whose agencies it would be copied and distributed fairly rapidly.[262] However, possibly the earliest indication of a

Revue de l'Université d'Ottawa 22 (1952), 104*–126*; J. Huhn, 'Der Kirchenvater Ambrosius im Lichte der Pfarrseelsorge', *Anima* 10 (1955), 136–50; F. Spedalieri, 'S. Ambrogio e l'eccellenza del sacerdozio', *La civiltà Cattolica* 91/4 (1940), 321–31; Fr. Weiss, 'Der hl. Ambrosius an die Priester', *Schweizerische Kirchenzeitung* 126 (1958), 310–12; Homes Dudden i. 122–6; Morino, 23–8; Monachino, 32–44; G. Ceriani, 'La spiritualità di sant'Ambrogio', in *Sant' Ambrogio nel XVI centenario della nascita* (Milan, 1940), 159–207, especially 163–8. On Ambrose's practical activity: W. Wilbrand, 'Ambrosius von Mailand als Bischof', *TG* 33 (1941), 190–5; J. Huhn, *Ambrosius von Mailand, ein sozialer Bischof: Das Vorbild unserer Zeit* (Fulda, 1946), 40–8 (and 11–27 on *Off.*). On *Off.* specifically: Th. Förster, *Von den Pflichten der Geistlichen (De Off. Min.). Ein Beitrag zur Pastoraltheologie von Ambrosius, Bischofs von Mailand* (Halle, 1879); Förster, 176–82; B. Citterio, 'Spiritualità sacerdotale nel "De officiis" di s. Ambrogio', *Ambrosius* 32 (1956), 157–65 (bk. 1); 33 (1957), 71–80 (bks. 2–3). On the weaknesses of a good deal of the older material, see Gryson, 'Typologie', i–xi; also B. Studer, 'Il sacerdozio dei fideli in sant'Ambrogio di Milano (Rassegna bibliografica 1960–1970)', *VetChr* 7 (1970), 325–40.

[260] Homes Dudden ii. 502; cf. Krabinger, iv: *hoc unicum ethicum Christianae enchiridion*, echoed by Draeseke, 129: *tamquam unicum ethicae Christianae enchiridion*; E. Dassmann, 'Ambrosius', *TRE* ii. 362–86, at 374.

[261] As a systematic account, at least; individual moral themes had of course been treated by Tertullian, Cyprian, and Lactantius.

[262] Paulinus of Nola was a particular advocate for Ambrose's texts, as he was for the writings of Sulpicius Severus (*Dial.* 3.17) and Augustine (*Ep.* 31.7). On the relationship between Ambrose and Paulinus, cf. Ambrose, *Ep.* 27 [58]; Paulinus, *Ep.* 3.4. On Paulinus as a possible reader of *Off.*, see below. Ambrose's sister Marcellina evidently played a part in the publicizing of

Christian reading may be glimpsed, ironically enough, in the writings of someone who was no friend of Ambrose. Jerome's famous *Epistle* 52, a *libellus* on clerical conduct written in 393 to Nepotian, the nephew of his old associate Heliodorus of Altinum, evinces a number of thematic parallels with *De officiis*. It is possible that these parallels simply reflect a series of contemporary commonplaces on clerical behaviour, but the degree of similarity in Jerome's counsel may just imply that he had read Ambrose's work, if only out of an instinctively critical curiosity.[263] Paulinus of Nola probably knew *De officiis*, if we may judge from one or possibly two allusions in his *Epistle* 24, probably written in 400.[264] Given his sponsorship of other Ambrosian texts, the chances of his having read this one are high; its classical-sounding title would have been sure to appeal to his literary tastes, and its attempt to transform a traditional form paralleled some of his own efforts to remodel the genres of Roman poetry.[265] The first definite reference to Ambrose's

Virg. at Rome (cf. *Virg.* 2.3, 5; also Jer., *Ep.* 22.22). For an excellent account of contemporary publishing practices, see H. Y. Gamble, *Books and Readers in the Early Church: A History of Early Christian Texts* (New Haven, CT and London, 1995), 82–143, especially 132–40.

[263] For some suggested parallels, see I. J. Davidson, 'Pastoral Theology at the End of the Fourth Century: Ambrose and Jerome', *SP* 33 (1997), 295–301. Testard, 'Aveu', 238 ff., argues for linguistic parodies of *Off.* 1.3–4 (*discere . . . docere*) elsewhere in Jerome's letters, but this has been rightly challenged by N. Adkin, 'Jerome, Ambrose and Gregory Nazianzen (Jerome, *Epist.* 52, 7–8)', *Vichiana* 4 (1993), 294–300, on the grounds that the antithesis is common, even proverbial, in a number of authors; see commentary ad loc. J. Fontaine, 'L'Apport de la tradition poétique romaine à la formation de l'hymnodie latine chrétienne', *REL* 52 (1974), 318–55, at 337 n. 1, suggests that Jerome's famous rhetorical question in *Ep.* 22.29.6 ('How can Horace belong with the Psalter, or Vergil with the gospels, or Cicero with the Apostle?') could be one of his anonymous shafts at Ambrose—Horace and the Psalter referring to his hymns, Vergil and the gospel to his epigrammatic inscriptions for religious edifices in Milan (the authenticity of which is disputed: PL 17, suppl. 1, 585–9), and Cicero and the Apostle to *Off.* However, as Testard, 'Aveu', 232–3 points out, the idea falls down on the chronology: Jerome's *Ep.* 22 (early 384) is too early for him to know of *Off.*

[264] According to P. G. Walsh, *Letters of St. Paulinus of Nola*, 2 vols. (Westminster, MD and London, 1967), ii. 313 n. 30 and 314 n. 68, Paulinus, *Ep.* 24.7, evokes 1.183 and *Ep.* 24.13, is similar to 1.193–4. The first suggestion is stronger than the second.

[265] See n. 262 above.

work comes, however, in Augustine, *Epistle* 82, from *c*.404: *nisi forte nomen te moveat quia non tam usitatum est in ecclesiasticis libris vocabulum officii, quod Ambrosius noster non timuit, qui suos libros utilium praeceptionum plenos 'De officiis' voluit appellare.*[266] Augustine's words are spare: he mentions Ambrose's work to justify the use of the secular term *officiosus* in a Christian context, but says nothing about its content except that it is 'full of useful teachings'. Oddly, he does not even mention Ambrose's attempt to find authority for the word *officium* in the Bible (1.25), which might have been an obvious point in support of his own case. Overall, there is little evidence that the work made a very significant impression upon Augustine: nowhere else does he mention it at all.

Ambrose's former deacon and *notarius*, Paulinus, is likely to have referred to *De officiis* in composing his *Vita*, perhaps around 412–13.[267] Paulinus does not directly quote the work, but his language in a number of places hints at a familiarity with Ambrose's presentation of the clerical *persona*[268] and his knowledge of other Ambrosian texts renders it highly probable a priori that he knew this one as well. We then have no explicit evidence of other allusions to *De officiis* prior to Cassiodorus, who says this: *utiles etiam sunt ad instructionem ecclesiasticae disciplinae memorati sancti Ambrosii De officiis melliflui libri tres.*[269] Again the reference is a basic one. In their life of Caesarius of Arles, produced in the late 540s, a group of Gaulish clerics describe their hero as selling church plate to ransom captives, and the language is evocative of *De officiis*

---

[266] *Ep.* 82.21.

[267] The date is controverted: I tentatively follow E. Lamirande, 'La Datation de la "Vita Ambrosii" de Paulin de Milan', *REAug* 27 (1981), 44–55 (cf. McLynn, 370 n. 40; Ramsey, 195), though O'Donnell ii. 342 and n. 4 points out that if Augustine commissioned the work in the early 420s this would fit in with his repeated appeals to Ambrose's authority at that period. The traditionally accepted date is *c*.422.

[268] Cf. e.g. some of the details mentioned in *VA* 38–41. For studies of the text and its author, see the edition by M. Pellegrino, *Paulino di Milano: Vita di s. Ambrogio* (Rome, 1961) and especially E. Lamirande, *Paulin de Milan et la 'Vita Ambrosii'. Aspects de la religion sous le Bas Empire* (Paris and Montreal, 1983).

[269] *Inst.* 1.16.4. On Cassiodorus and Ambrose generally, see F. Weissengruber, 'Benützung des Ambrosius durch Cassiodorus', in *AmbrEpisc* ii. 378–98.

2.136–43.[270] For major evocation, however, we have to wait until the early seventh century, and Isidore of Seville, who cites several passages of *De officiis* both in his *Originum Libri* and in the work known traditionally as *De ecclesiasticis officiis*, though originally called *De origine officiorum*.[271] The author of a Carolingian *Vita Ambrosii* testifies to the function and eloquence of Ambrose's treatise, but, not unsurprisingly in a biographical sketch, does not quote it: *primam itaque ecclesiasticorum ordinum institutionem et catholicae vitae formulam in libris suis quos de officiis praenotavit luculenter inseruit et evidenter expressit.*[272] Quotations can, however, be found in Hincmar of Reims (*c*.806–82), in his letters *Ad episcopos* and in his *De regis persona*. One tenth-century author who was evidently fond of the work was Atto of Vercelli (*c*.885–961): his *De pressuris ecclesiasticis*, written against royal infringement of clerical rights, cites a number of examples of Ambrose's wisdom.[273]

The compilers of the *florilegia* of the Middle Ages often include citations of *De officiis* among their *sententiae patrum*. In the ninth century, the most significant source is Florus, deacon of the church of Lyons (d. *c*.860). From the eleventh and twelfth centuries, references can be found in the *Collectio Canonum* of Cardinal Deusdedit, the *Decretum* of Ivo of Chartres (*c*.1040–1115), the *Polycarpus* of Gregory of St Chrysogonus, and the *Collection in Three Books*, the major source for the celebrated *Decretum* of Gratian of Bologna (d. *c*.1160). There are, besides, an anonymous twelfth-century *Patristic Prologue*, and two contemporary manuscripts on

---

[270] *Vita Caesarii* 1.32–3. See further W. Klingshirn, 'Charity and Power: Caesarius of Arles and the Ransoming of Captives in Sub-Roman Gaul', *JRS* 75 (1985), 183–203.

[271] *Pace* A. C. Lawson, 'The Sources of the "De ecclesiasticis officiis" of St Isidore of Seville', *RBén* 50 (1938), 26–36, at 27; Hiltbrunner, 178, Isidore's title is not inspired by Ambrose. On the original title of *De origine officiorum*, see CCL 113, Introduction, 14*–15*, 119*–121*. For ease of reference only, citations of this text in the commentary preserve the traditional designation.

[272] *Vita Ambr.* par. 16, in Courcelle, *Recherches*, 59.

[273] Examples from Hincmar, Atto, and others are recorded in the *testimonia* in Testard i–ii. On the possible influence of *Off.* in the exposition of the cardinal virtues in the Carolingian period, see S. Mähl, *Quadriga Virtutum: Die Kardinaltugenden in der Geistesgeschichte der Karolingerzeit* (Cologne, 1969), 7–15.

clerical life and canon law, which contain frequent allusions.[274]

The most extensive twelfth-century reference is by Bernard of Clairvaux (1090–1153): his *Tractatus de ordine vitae* paraphrases and quotes whole passages of *De officiis*, particularly from book 1.[275] The English Cistercian, Ælred of Rievaulx (*c.*1110–67), uses Ambrose as well as Cicero in his celebrated characterization of friendship in *De spiritali amicitia*, book 3.[276] Peter Lombard (*c.*1100–60), cites in his *Sentences* just a single maxim: *adfectus tuus nomen imponit operi tuo* (1.147). This saying turns out to be a favourite with authors of this period.[277] It is no surprise that the greatest number of quotations in the next century are to be found within the vast compass of Thomas Aquinas' *Summa Theologiae*; there is a real sense in which Ambrose, along with Lactantius before him and Augustine after him, constitutes one of the headwaters of the methodology elaborated by the medieval giants of moral theological synthesis.[278]

It is impossible to know just how thoroughly *De officiis* was actually *read* over the immediate centuries after its publication. Quotations, and the lack of them even more so, are ambivalent sources of information. The scarcity of allusions from the later

---

[274] For some of the references in the documents of canon law, see C. D. Fonseca, 'Gli "Excerpta Ambrosii" nelle sillogi canonicali dei secoli XI e XII', in *AmbrEpisc* ii. 48–68, esp. 56–7 nn. 18–21; also G. G. Picasso, 'Gli "Excerpta Ambrosii" nelle collezioni canoniche dei secoli XI e XII', in *AmbrEpisc* ii. 69–93. See in general Testard i. 55–9, to which I am indebted; also 57 and 60 on a few other authors. The two anonymous manuscripts are: (i) Vatican, Ottobonianus lat. 175; (ii) Bononiensis 2535. On Florus, see *TRE* xi. 221–4; on Deusdedit, *DTC* vi/1. 647–51; on Ivo of Chartres, *TRE* xvi. 422–7; on Gratian, *TRE* xiv. 124–30.

[275] Text in PL 184.

[276] Examples can be traced in critical texts, such as that in *Corpus Christianorum, continuatio mediaevalis*, 1 (Turnhout, 1971), 287–350; see also A. Squire, *Ælred of Rievaulx: A Study* (London, 1969), 98–111.

[277] The *testimonia* are recorded by Testard i. 166.

[278] See especially M. Omberti Sobrero, *L'etica sociale in Ambrogio di Milano. Ricostruzione delle fonti Ambrosiane nel 'De iustitia' di san Tomaso, II.II, qq. 57–122* (Turin, 1970), especially 83–94, 95–161, 234–65, 267–337; also Th. Deman, 'Le "De officiis" de saint Ambroise dans l'histoire de la théologie morale', *RSPhTh* 37 (1953), 409–24, especially 422–4. On the general context, see R. Crouse, '"Summae auctoritatis magister": The Influence of St Ambrose in Medieval Theology', in *Nec timeo mori*, 463–71.

patristic age may suggest that the work was not exactly pored
over, even in the libraries of Monte Cassino and the other
emerging centres of clerical learning; by the same token, the
fact that it was often quoted in the High Middle Ages does not
necessarily mean that it was carefully perused even then. In a
great many cases, especially with the *florilegia*, it very probably
was not, for compilations tended simply to borrow stock
excerpts from one another. Nevertheless, scholars such as
Bernard, Ælred, and Thomas, who reveal more detailed awareness of the work's contents, must almost certainly have had
access to it. *De officiis* never rivalled Gregory the Great's *Liber
regulae pastoralis* (*c*.590) as a manual of pastoral theology, but,
to judge by the considerable proliferation of manuscripts
dating from the eighth to the twelfth centuries, it was widely
circulated.[279] The Carolingian *Vita Ambrosii* (16) speaks of it as
a seminal work on ecclesiastical *ordines*; perhaps some of
Ambrose's advice was heeded by those who occupied these
ranks even where his words were not actually quoted.[280]

Augustine's reference to the work indicates admiration that
Ambrose (with customary intellectual assurance) 'was not
afraid' to bring into widespread ecclesiastical usage the secular
word *officium*. *Officium* was used to translate both λειτουργία (cf.
1.25) and λατρεία in Christian Latin, and the primary force of
Ambrose's use of the word continues to be the Ciceronian
sense of moral duty or obligation. Nevertheless, even if Augustine exaggerates the significance of Ambrose's semantic
achievement, it is quite probable that Ambrose *encouraged*
the use of *officium* in a church context. 'Obligation to' the
church very easily came to mean specific 'office' within the
church, just as *officium* had covered both ideas in the secular
domain classically; the philosophical term readily took on more
precise functional overtones. In an indirect way, then,
Ambrose may have helped to inspire the linguistic usage of

---

[279] For some examples, see Testard i. 60–94. For a comparison of
Ambrose's pastoral counsel with Gregory's, and with John Chrysostom's in
On the Priesthood, see R. Pastè, 'Il sacerdozio negli scritti di tre Padri della
Chiesa', *SC* 54 (1926), 81–106, 271–85, 334–59. It is not clear whether
Gregory himself had read *Off.*: Moorhead, 214.

[280] On the Carolingian *vita*, see Courcelle, *Recherches*, 49–121 (text and
sources), 123–53 (analysis).

the huge number of medieval liturgists who wrote works *de officiis*.[281]

Given its classical background, it was inevitable that *De officiis* should rise to particular prominence during the Renaissance. Cicero's *De officiis* was then studied and imitated more heavily than it had been during the Middle Ages, and Ambrose's work offered an obvious Christian conversation-partner. The fifteenth and sixteenth centuries saw the publication of numerous editions, at Rome, Milan, Basle, Paris, and Louvain, as Christian humanists like Zell, Valdarfer, Paderborn, Amerbach, Gillot, and especially the great Erasmus himself felt the obvious appeal of a text which epitomized the interface of classical and Christian learning. At least some passages were referred to by the magisterial Reformers.[282] A number of translations appeared throughout Europe in the sixteenth, seventeenth, and eighteenth centuries, in French, Italian, and Spanish.[283] English translations can be traced from at least the early seventeenth century, and the work was certainly known in English-language circles long before then, since Ambrose was read in England in Anglo-Saxon times.[284]

---

[281] For examples such as Isidore of Seville's *De officiis VII graduum*, John of Avranches' *De officiis ecclesiasticis*, William of Auxerre's *Summa de officiis ecclesiasticis*, and Guy of Orchelles' *Summa de officiis ecclesiae*, see C. Vogel, *Medieval Liturgy: An Introduction to the Sources* (Washington, DC, 1986), 11–16.

[282] On Luther and Calvin e.g. see commentary on 2.70. On Luther's knowledge of Ambrose generally, see F. Buzzi, 'La recezione di Ambrogio a Wittenberg', in *Nec timeo mori*, 569–83, esp 571–6; J. Irmscher, 'Ambrogio nel giudizio dei riformatori tedeschi', in *Nec timeo mori*, 633–8.

[283] e.g. French versions were published at Rouen in 1606 (Tigeon), Paris in 1689 (Abbé de Bellegarde) and 1691 (id.); Italian at Florence in 1558 (Cattani) and *sine loco* in 1578 (Filimusi); Spanish at Toledo in 1534 (Gracian) and Madrid in 1789 (Aldarete). On Ambrose during the Renaissance, see generally P. Cherubelli, 'Sant' Ambrogio e la rinascita: fonti manoscritte, edizioni a stampa e iconografia del santo nel secoli XIV, XV e XVI—Saggio', in *Sant'Ambrogio nel XVI centenario della nascita* (Milan, 1940), 571–91, esp. 575 ff.

[284] R. Humfrey, *Christian offices crystall glasse. In three bookes. First written in latine, by . . . saint Ambrose . . ., whereunto is added his conviction of Symmachus the Gentile* (London, 1637); C. Fitzgeffrey, *Compassion unto captives, chiefly towards our bretheren and country-men who are in Barbarie: urged and pressed in three sermons on Heb. xiii.3. Whereunto are anexed an Epistle of St. Cyprian concerning the redemption of the bretheren from the*

The fundamental edition of the Benedictines of St Maur was published in Paris between 1686 and 1690, reprinted twice at Venice before the end of the next century, and by Migne in 1845.[285] The first attempt to produce a modern critical text was made by Krabinger in his Tübingen edition of 1857; the work suffers from many faults, but it constitutes a commendable effort to do what no one had done before, and it provided a platform for a number of modern studies and translations. The nineteenth and twentieth centuries saw translations into a wide range of vernaculars, including Italian, German, French, Russian, Polish, and Romanian.[286] In English, the only modern rendering of the whole treatise to date has been that of De Romestin in the series *A Select Library of Nicene and Post-Nicene Fathers of the Christian Church* (New York, 1887–92; Oxford, 1890–1900; several reprints). Modern critical scholarship should obviously be distinguished from work which has been 'influenced' by *De officiis*, or from basic translations of it, but the many literary and philosophical studies of the text published over the last 150 years, however varied their

---

bondage *of the barbarians; and a passage concerning the* . . . *benefits of Compassion, extracted out of St Ambrose, his second Booke of Offices, c. 28* (London, 1637). On the general context, see M. Vessey, 'English Translations of the Latin Fathers, 1517–1611', in I. Backus (ed.), *The Reception of the Church Fathers in the West, from the Carolingians to the Maurists*, 2 vols. (Leiden, 1997), ii. 775–835. On the earlier centuries, see D. A. Bankert, J. Wegmann, and C. D. Wright, *Ambrose in Anglo-Saxon England, with Pseudo-Ambrose and Ambrosiaster* in *Old English Newsletter*, Subsidia, 25 (1997).

[285] PL 16, 25–194.

[286] Versions can be traced in P. F. Beatrice, R. Cantalamessa, *et al.* (eds.), *Cento anni di bibliografia Ambrosiana (1874–1974)* (Milan, 1981), and in *Bibliographia Patristica* and *L'Année Philologique* for the years since 1974. The best known of the modern translations are: in Italian, those of Cavasin (Turin, 1938) and Banterle (Milan, 1977) (the latter, based on a slightly revised version of Krabinger's text, is superior), and in German, that of Niederhuber (Kempten and Munich, 1917). The most significant of the older German versions are: Ph. Lichter, *Drei Bücher von den Pflichten* (Coblenz, 1830); C. Haas, *Die Pastoralschriften des hl. Gregor d. Gr. und des heiligen Ambrosius von Mailand—Des heiligen Ambrosius Schrift von den Pflichten der Seelsorger* (Tübingen, 1862); F. X. Schulte, *Ausgewählte Schriften des heiligen Ambrosius, Bischofs von Mailand* (Kempten, 1871–7). In French, Testard's edition (1984–92) is by far the most careful.

quality, testify to a continuing interest in Ambrose's achievement and the puzzle of how to assess it.

A comprehensive survey of the *Nachleben* of *De officiis* would require the investigation of a huge quantity of medieval, Renaissance, and modern literature. Such a study is clearly beyond the scope of an introductory sketch like this. Even a brief overview, however, suggests that Ambrose's use of Cicero may in reality have proved the primary obstacle to any prospect of his establishing his Christian *De officiis* as a central didactic text in Western clerical formation. The Ciceronian template lent the work a particular structure which has naturally intrigued Renaissance and modern students of late antiquity. But it also ensured that the work never was to be a definitive pastoral guidebook, for, despite all the changes, *De officiis* remained synonymous with a cultural context far broader than clerical formation, and far more tied to the ancient world than some later Christian sensibilities could accommodate. It is no surprise that the medieval church found the much more explicitly ecclesiastical idiom of Gregory's *Pastoral Rule* to be of greater practical value for the changed structures of its political and social world.

Ambrose must have known that any aspiration to supersede Cicero's text (cf. 1.29) could never be realized; his profession of that aim is a gambit indicating a wider desire to transform the intellectual property of the *saeculum*, not a genuine expectation that Christians would never again glance at Cicero. As long as Ambrose's text is studied, so must its classical archetype be: in fact, if we read Ambrose carefully, we must reread Cicero even more carefully, to catch the tiny echoes which lurk in so many unexpected places. The *Quellenforschungen* of Renaissance and modern scholarship on Ambrose have been inevitable. But the student of Ambrose's treatise is not faced with just a dry exercise in textual comparison. There is a compelling fascination about the work as a window on the psychology of a figure who, for all his faults, played a unique role in the shaping of the Western church. It is for that reason above all that *De officiis* deserves continued attention.

IX. LATINITY

Cassiodorus speaks warmly of Ambrose's *De officiis melliflui libri tres*,[287] but the author himself makes no claims for his style. The work is to be read by those *qui non sermonum supellectilem neque artem dicendi sed simplicem rerum exquirunt gratiam* (1.29). *Ars* is shunned in favour of the moralistic worth of biblical *exempla* (1.116), and it is these models that are said to constitute the real value of the treatise, *etsi sermo nihil deferat gratiae* (3.139). The literary quality of Ambrose's writings could certainly both disappoint as well as please his contemporaries,[288] and on the basis of the published versions of his sermons it is not always easy to see quite why his listeners found his pulpit manner so compelling.[289] *De officiis* looks as if it was written fairly quickly, and offers less polished prose than we might perhaps expect in a work destined to be compared with a distinguished classical exemplar. For

---

[287] *Inst.* 1.16.4.

[288] Pelagius says that Ambrose *scriptorum inter Latinos flos quidam speciosus enituit* (cited in Augustine, *Grat. Christ.* 43), and Augustine praises his style (*Doctr. Chr.* 4.21.127–22.133), while Jerome, notoriously, scoffs at it (*Interpr. Did. Spir. Sanct.*, praef.; cf. also *Hom. Orig. in ev. Luc. transl.*, prol.; *Vir. illustr.* 124; for other similar derision, and assessment of it, see A. Paredi, 'S. Gerolamo e s. Ambrogio', in *Mélanges Eugene Tisserant*, 5, *Studi e Testi*, 235 (Vatican City, 1964), 183–98; also G. Nauroy, 'Jérôme, lecteur et censeur de l'exégèse d'Ambroise', in Y.-M. Duval (ed.), *Jérôme entre l'Occident et l'Orient* (Paris, 1988), 173–203; Testard, 'Aveu'). There were of course other considerations besides the stylistic in such judgements. Edward Gibbon offers a memorable verdict on Ambrose's notorious *Ep. extra coll.* 11 [51] to Theodosius on the aftermath of the massacre at Thessalonica in 390: 'His epistle is a miserable rhapsody on a noble subject. Ambrose could act better than he could write. His compositions are destitute of taste, or genius; without the spirit of Tertullian, the copious elegance of Lactantius, the lively wit of Jerom [*sic*], or the grave energy of Augustin [*sic*]' (*The History of the Decline and Fall of the Roman Empire, Volume the Third*, ii (1781), ed. D. Womersley (London, 1994), 59 n. 96).

[289] Cf. Augustine, *Conf.* 5.13.23–14.24; also *C. Iul. Pelag.* 2.11; Cassiodorus, *Inst.* 1.1 and 1.20. Marcellinus calls Ambrose *orator catholicus* (*Chron.* s.a. 398), and Paulinus speaks of an Arian critic who had a vision of an angel whispering into the bishop's ear as he preached (*VA* 17). See Homes Dudden ii. 454–76; C. Killian, 'Saint Aurelius Ambrosius: Orator Catholicus', *CB* 46 (1970), 38–40, 46–7.

Ambrose, conveying a suitably impressive vision of practical morality takes priority over the objective of earning literary approval from the armchair aesthetes who formed one element of his readership. Rhetorical eloquence, in his view, is a distraction from the exposition of vital truth. The 'right' use of language is not simply a matter of clear communication: it is an ethical responsibility, part of the Christian's overall obligation to act in a way that will earn divine approval (cf. 1.8).[290] All *sermo*, Ambrose argues, whether it be the *colloquium familiare* of everyday discourse or formal *tractatus disceptatioque fidei atque iustitiae* (1.99), should be gentle, attractive, and measured. It ought to avoid emotional extremes; informal conversation and official homiletic exercises alike should be devoted to the Scriptures and to spiritual matters (1.99–100). In articulating the faith (*tractatus*), *oratio* is to be *pura, simplex, dilucida atque manifesta, plena gravitatis et ponderis, non adfectata elegantia sed non intermissa gratia* (1.101). Given the close interlacing of oral and written styles in Ambrose, how does the Latinity of *De officiis* measure up against its author's own standards?

The dominance of Scripture is certainly inescapable. *Saturemur in verbo Dei* (1.164), Ambrose exhorts his addressees: he himself reflects the results of such mimesis on every page. We have vast *catenae* of biblical quotations, paraphrases, and echoes, cited from memory of 'Old Latin' versions and his own rendering of the Greek of the Septuagint and the New Testament.[291] But it is not just in these obvious ways that the

---

[290] See T. Graumann, 'St Ambrose on the Art of Preaching', in *Vescovi e pastori* ii. 587–600, esp. 587–90.

[291] There is much dispute over how to establish his Old Latin text, not least because he very probably worked with far more than a single version. Ambrosian manuscripts are bedevilled by the glosses of medieval scribes who knew only the Vulgate. The only major attempt at reconstruction, R. W. Muncey's *The New Testament Text of Saint Ambrose* (Cambridge, 1959) is vitiated by numerous textual errors, inadequate discussion of corruption in Ambrosian manuscripts, and a multitude of neglected Ambrosian citations; see the critical reviews of G. G. Willis in *JThS* NS 11 (1960), 172–6, and J. Duplacy, 'Citations patristiques et critique textuelle du Nouveau Testament: A propos d'un livre récent', *RSR* 47 (1959), 391–400. On some aspects of the basic problem, see H. J. Frede, 'Probleme des ambrosianischen Bibeltextes', in *AmbrEpisc* i. 365–92. On Scripture in *Off.*, see generally C. Dantu, *La Place et le rôle de l'Ecriture dans le De Officiis Ministrorum de*

text is invested with Scripture: Ambrose's vocabulary is profoundly influenced by biblical semantics. Words like *salus, gratia, gloria, fides, iustitia,* and *humilitas* take on completely different nuances from those intended by Cicero and the classical tradition. We find an entire specialized Christian nomenclature for soteriology (e.g. *redemptio, remissio, propitiator*), or for church, liturgy, and sacraments (e.g. *ecclesiasticus, exorcizare, communio, oratio, lavacrum*). There are several words derived directly from Greek and Semitic roots (e.g. *parabola, evangelista, byssus, sabbatum, manna, paradisus*). There is also plenty of more general 'late' vocabulary (e.g. *emundatio, exaltare, opertorium, protectio*), influenced by biblical texts. Ambrose's syntax, too, typical of the prose style of its time, is affected not only by colloquial usages but also by Greek constructions common in the Bible, such as the use of *quod/quia/quoniam/ut* after *verba sentiendi et dicendi,* where classical Latin generally employs an accusative and infinitive sequence; or the use of the nominative with the infinitive in indirect statements.[292]

Ambrose is also of course the product of a traditional classical education. His mind is steeped in the language of the two giants of his school curriculum, Cicero and Vergil. Besides the explicit allusions to Cicero, he displays a general fondness for vocabulary used frequently by Cicero (and not necessarily in his *De officiis*).[293] Vergilian echoes abound, often delivered subconsciously in the midst of the narration of biblical stories (cf. 1.32, 49, 55, 177, 198; 2.21, 49, 74, 82, 114; 3.30, 34, 41, 98, 100, 113).[294] Language reminiscent of Lucretius (1.55–6, 96,

saint Ambroise (Dijon, 1970). The commentary signals relevant variants, and refers where appropriate to the *Vetus Latina* of B. Fischer *et al.* (Freiburg, 1949–) ('VL' is also used to refer where appropriate to P. Sabatier's *Vetus Italica* (Reims, 1743–9; Paris, 1751) or to A. Jülicher's *Itala* (Berlin, 1938–63)) or to the *Septuaginta,* ed. A. Rahlfs (Stuttgart, 1935, 1979), but for the average reader's convenience quotations are given from R. Weber (ed.), *Biblia Sacra iuxta Vulgatam versionem,* 3rd edn. (Stuttgart, 1983). The translation of course seeks to render the biblical verses as Ambrose gives them.

[292] Some examples are explored by P. Canata, *De syntaxi ambrosiana in libris qui inscribuntur 'De officiis ministrorum'* (Modena, 1911).

[293] See Barry, 232–54, and e.g. commentary on 1.75, 85; 2.130, 136.

[294] See generally Ihm, 80–94, and especially M. D. Diederich, *Vergil in the*

192), Horace (1.198; cf. also 2.64), and Ovid (1.20, 176) can
also be found, and the *color poeticus* of the style of Ambrose the
hymn-writer and composer of inscriptions is evident in his use
of words (e.g. *illecebrosus, maestificare, moderamen, obumbrare*)
which are often poetic in origin.[295] As well as using some rare
words (e.g. *arbitra, averruncare, coniventia, domitrix, emolere,
invecticius*), Ambrose occasionally mints some vocabulary of
his own (e.g. *effluescere* (2.109); *irrutilare* (2.139)). Phrases
from Terence (2.69, 106, 147)[296] and Sallust (1.138, 177; 2.2)
are further evidence of the literature which has shaped his
mind. Scriptural stories are sometimes elaborated in terms
reminiscent of poetic scenes (cf. 2.145–8; 3.62). We also
encounter traditional images like those of the Titans (1.177)
and the *negotiatores* of Tyre (2.67); descriptions of the seafaring
merchant (1.243), the spendthrift heir (1.244; 2.69), and the
inheritance-hunter (3.57) likewise evoke classical characteriza-
tions. Ambrose retains his interest in a game which had long

Works of St Ambrose (Washington, DC, 1931), though Diederich's treatment
of *Off.* (76–8) is not exhaustive.

[295] See esp. J. Fontaine, 'Prose et poésie: l'interférence des genres et des
styles dans la création littéraire d'Ambroise de Milan', in *AmbrEpisc* i. 124–
70; id., 'En quel sens peut-on parler d'un "classicisme" ambrosien?', in *Nec
timeo mori*, 501–10; also J. Den Boeft, 'Ambrosius Lyricus', in J. den Boeft
and A. Hilhorst (eds.), *Early Christian Poetry: A Collection of Essays* (Leiden,
1993), 77–89. On the possibilities of influences on Ambrose's vocabulary from
his background in legal procedure, see J. Gaudemet, 'Droit séculier et droit de
l'Eglise chez Ambroise', in *AmbrEpisc* i. 289–90 (cf. Vasey, 79–81): caution is
needed here, however, since the use of words like *possidere, hereditas,* and
spoliare clearly no more requires technical legal knowledge in Ambrose than
the use of their equivalents by a modern English writer does today. For
further discussion of Ambrose's vocabulary in general, exploring its fondness
for Greek derivatives, adjectives in *-bilis,* and verbs in *-esco,* see Barry, *passim*;
Bürgi, 49 ff.; I. Gualandri, 'Il lessico di Ambrogio: problemi e prospettive di
ricerca', in *Nec timeo mori*, 267–311. P. Canata, *De S. Ambrosii libris qui
inscribuntur De Officiis Ministrorum quaestiones* (Modena, 1909), ch. 4, is
unreliable. The new *Thesaurus Sancti Ambrosii* in the CETEDOC series of
CCL (Turnhout, 1996), superseding the basic word-list compiled by O. Faller
(ed. L. Krestan), *Wortindex zu den Schriften des hl. Ambrosius* (Beihefte zum
CSEL, Heft 4, Vienna, 1979), is likely to prove an invaluable resource for a
new generation of Ambrosian scholarship.

[296] See also on 3.45, though the main source for the *homo-humanus* motif
there is Cicero. On Ambrose's knowledge of comedy generally, see Courcelle,
Recherches, 41–8.

appealed to the Romans—speculating about the origins of words. He is interested in the spiritual significance of biblical names, naturally, but he is equally fond of explaining the etymology of everyday terms (1.26, 78; 3.16, 112).[297]

Ambrose is a master of 'the alchemy of imagery'.[298] There are too many examples to cite them in full here, but the cluster of images in 1.11–16 is perhaps one particularly striking instance—a mosaic of language drawn from the worlds of horticulture; warfare; rivers; bits, bridles and reins; doors and locks; weights and measures; metal-refining; medicine; and hunting. Some of the metaphors and similes Ambrose uses, such as favourite images like the Christian as athlete, come directly from Scripture; others are inspired by his reading of poetry; and still others doubtless are original to his own fertile imagination for the vivid phrase; for examples, cf. 1.20, 32–3, 48, 85, 90, 93, 165, 167, 181, 192, 203, 212, 220, 228, 245, 259; 2.1, 7, 21, 60–2, 64, 112, 113, 135; 3.17–19.[299]

For all Ambrose's disavowal of rhetorical adornment, his text is liberally sprinkled with rhetorical flourishes. There are plenty of passages which might lend themselves to effective oral delivery, such as the characterization of the provocative *peccator* in 1.17–20; or the exchange of words between spiritual athletes and their worldly spectators in 1.59–62; or the dialogue between Sixtus II and his archdeacon Lawrence in 1.205–7 (very probably drawn from an independent *passio Laurentii* tradition); or the judgement-day rebukes of those who have placed too much value on personal riches in 1.63 and 2.137–8; or the depiction of Abraham and Isaac on Mount Moriah in 1.119; or the *controversia* between the speculating farmer and the person who accuses him of dishonesty in 3.38–40. There are favourite interjections such as *quid loquar?* (1.203, 204, 248; 2.11, 20, 56, 84; 3.66, 73; cf. *quid loquamur?* in 2.100); effect can

[297] See G. Bartelink, 'Sprachliche und stilistische Bemerkungen in Ambrosius' Schriften', *WS* 92 (1979), 175–202, at 197 ff.

[298] Brown, *Body*, 363.

[299] One type is studied by M. T. Springer, *Nature-Imagery in the Works of St Ambrose* (Washington, DC, 1931), esp. 71–84; however, Springer pays too little attention to the biblical inspiration of many of the images she records. For a study of Ambrose's language at work in exposition of Scripture's hidden wisdom, see H. Savon, 'Maniérisme et allégorie dans l'œuvre d'Ambroise de Milan', *REL* 55 (1977), 203–21.

be built up by short, punchy clauses which convey tension (as strikingly in 1.119), or by extended series of rhetorical questions (e.g. 1.48–50, 52, 55–7, 87–8, 117, 120, 122–3, 137–8, 195, 243–5; 2.10–11, 20, 27, 56–7, 59–62, 84; 3.7, 24, 28) or exclamations (e.g. 1.87, 121, 195; 2.31–2, 58, 74–5; 3.60, 85). One technique of which Ambrose is especially fond is apostrophe: over and over, we find him one minute addressing a plurality of persons, the next introducing a direct question or challenge to an imaginary individual, or anticipating some putative objection to which, naturally, he has just the right answer: e.g. *habes* (1.34, 37, 117, 162, 202, 221, 224, 237); *vides* (1.46; 3.44); *intueris* (1.46); *vide* (1.118, 183, 237); *adverte* (1.108, 110, 119, 223); *considera* (1.184; 2.52; 3.16, 108, 127); *cognosce* (2.52); *intellege* (2.52); *disce* (1.249); *introspice* (1.46); *interroga* (1.46); *adde* (1.171); *tolle* (1.167); *finge* (3.18); *da* (3.18); *pone* (2.20; 3.22); *puta* (2.21); *nega, si potes* (1.45); *forte dicas* (1.60); *o homo* (1.156; 2.52; 3.16).[300] The skilled communicator's ability to frame memorable one-liners is evident in such neat *sententiae* as *tuus denarius census illius est* (1.38); *si lapides teras, nonne ignis erumpit?* (1.93); *adfectus tuus nomen imponit operi tuo* (1.147); *melius est hic esse in humilitate, ibi in gloria* (3.36). And all the standard rhetorical tricks, from anaphora, asyndeton, and antithesis to alliteration and assonance, can be found by the attentive reader.[301] In general, however, *De officiis* reveals only a slight tendency to accentual prose rhythms: the rhetorical impact is delivered quickly and naturally, without studied

[300] There is no obvious pattern of sections containing only plural or only singular styles of address; Ambrose regularly moves from one to the other within a paragraph or a few sentences, all within a clear thematic unit: cf. e.g. 1.7, 13, 86, 88, 93, 143, 221, 223; 2.39–40, 77, 125–6, 137; 3.18, 47, 59, 129–30, 132. He also varies the way in which he refers to himself, using now the singular, now the royal plural: cf. e.g. 1.1–4, 23–5. On the technique of *hypophora/subiectio* (anticipating and answering an imaginary interlocutor), see H. Lausberg, *Handbuch der literarischen Rhetorik*, 2 vols. (Munich, 1960), i. 381–2.
[301] For some examples, see Bürgi, 57–68. On Ambrose's techniques elsewhere, see e.g. G. M. Carpaneto, 'Le opere oratorie di s. Ambrogio', *Didaskaleion* 8 (1930), 35–156, esp. 117–39; and particularly M. Testard, 'Observations sur le rhétorique d'une harangue au peuple dans le *Sermo contra Auxentium* de saint Ambroise', *REL* 63 (1985), 193–209, a very useful study.

polish.[302] As the style of the translation seeks to convey, Ambrose's tone on the whole remains fairly informal, even intimate, even when dealing with its most solemn themes: no-nonsense didacticism there may be, but the reader is invited to yield directly to the beauty and plausibility of the moral imperatives which are unfolded from the biblical picture-book. Sentence structure is either simple, with runs of short sentences and clauses strung together, or typical of the instinct-ive orator, tends to spin off into involved exuberant flourishes. The mood of pastoral appeal is frequently sustained by a liberal use of connectives, which again often seem to invite a vivid rendering. Ambrose is invariably the preacher, commending in his own natural and discursive way the practical good sense of a vision that for him is divinely inspired.

Overall, the Latinity of *De officiis* is typical of Ambrose. In his preoccupation with biblical images, his style is baptized into an idiom self-consciously different from that of his

---

[302] Oberhelman, 21–62, esp. 40–1 and n. 84: *Off.* evinces only a slight tendency to accentual rhythms, and in general seems to steer clear of prose rhythm altogether; there is none of the carefully wrought *cursus mixtus* prose that we find in, say, *Fid.* or *Spir.*, treatises which in their final form were designed for the eyes of an emperor. The only examination of this aspect of Ambrose's Latinity prior to Oberhelman is the thesis of M. R. Delaney, *A Study of the Clausulae in the Works of St Ambrose* (Washington, DC, 1934). Delaney's work is beset with errors and methodological illogicalities; with typical selectivity, she looks at only book 2 of *Off.* See Oberhelman, 21–2; Testard i. 41 n. 3. Oberhelman's research has shown that Ambrose generally avoided the use of elaborate prose rhythm when preaching but tended to embellish his language this way when revising for publication (one of the striking differences between the stenographic record of the homilies preserved in *Sacr.* and their redacted version in *Myst.* is the latter's use of prose rhythm as well as more complex vocabulary and syntax). It would be quite wrong, however, to assume that the text of *Off.* might similarly have been sermonic in origin simply because it lacks formal prose rhythm. In the absence of any other compelling evidence for an oral provenance for the work [Introduction V], all we can say is that, for one reason or another, Ambrose never polished his Latin that way in this case. Oral performance of written texts was a (or the) primary means of publication right into Christian times, and (as the burgeon-ing discipline of rhetorical criticism is exploring in both classical and biblical studies) rhetorical conventions shape all kinds of ancient literature. A piece of prose may well be 'rhetorical' in a host of ways, but that certainly does not mean that it must first have been delivered orally. On the whole subject, see M. Banniard, Viva voce. *Communication écrite et communication orale du IVe au IXe siècle en Occident latin* (Paris, 1992).

classical inheritance. At the same time, he is always the literate communicator, who can never shed the influence of the poetry and prose-texts over which he had pored in his schooldays, and who is well able to use to maximum effect some of the oratorical devices which he had practised to exploit as an advocate and which still come naturally to him as a preacher. The function of Ambrose's poetic language, rich imagery, and eloquence is, however, more than merely ornamental. As he sees it, it is a way of imitating the *gratia* of Scripture itself, which conveys its delights in a quite different way from the techniques of rhetorical *ars*. Since scriptural inspiration lies at the core of properly Christian speech, the use of language that is *suavis* and *dulcis* is, for Ambrose, a way of opening up the delights of God's word, and thus of communicating to parched souls the refreshing grace of revealed truth. It is about facilitating the mediation of a message which purports to carry a divine authority.[303] In words as in ideas, he works hard to show how different he is, not how traditional, and his sustained attempt to sound like the Bible is a central plank in that strategy; yet all the while the echoes of tradition abound. Ambrose's Latin bespeaks his quest to transform the conventions of one world in living for another.[304]

---

[303] On the ambiguities of *gratia* as artificial adornment versus *gratia* as a spiritual gift (1.29, 101, 103), see Graumann, 'St Ambrose on the Art of Preaching', 593 ff.

[304] The quality of many of the analyses of Ambrose's Latinity is poor. For a survey of the general literature, consult G. Sanders and M. Van Uytfanghe (eds.), *Bibliographie signalétique du latin des chrétiens* (Turnhout, 1989), 4–7.

Text and Translation

Text

All modern students of Ambrose are indebted to the pioneering work of Testard, whose Budé text (1984–92), the basis of a new edition to appear in CCL, constitutes the first critical edition of *De officiis* since that of Krabinger in 1857. Testard is however a conservative editor, who leans heavily upon French manuscripts; a wider textual survey has yet to be completed. A new text, with more extensive apparatus, has been in preparation for CSEL for several years, but a thorough recension is a very large task, and publication is still some way off. I print a working text which follows Testard's Budé version quite closely but differs from it in a number of places, often, but not always, in agreement with the suggestions of M. Winterbottom in 'The Text of Ambrose's *De Officiis*', *JThS* ns 46 (1995), 559–66. In the interests of space, and to avoid the clutter of unimportant material which affects much of Krabinger's edition and some of Testard's, I dispense with an apparatus criticus. The commentary records variants where they have seemed worth a mention, but does not always venture a full defence of the adopted text.

Pending the publication of a fuller recension, Testard i. 60–87 should be consulted on the manuscript traditions and the relationships between them. Of the chief manuscripts, PVMA constitute the primary family, EW the second, and CONB the third.

MANUSCRIPTS

P   Paris, Bibliothèque Nationale, Lat. 1732, fos. 4–89^v (8th century). Missing 1.1–43; 3.131–9.
V   Vatican Library, Lat. 266, fos. 131–95^v (9th century).

M　Montpellier, Faculty of Medicine Library, 76, fos. 1–72^v (10th–11th centuries). Missing 3.125–39; lacuna at 2.112–13.

A　Vatican Library, Lat. 282, fo. 56^v col. 2–fo. 103 col. 1 (11th–12th centuries).

E　Munich, Bibliothek National, Lat. 14641, fos. 48^v–128 (9th century).

W　Würzburg, University Library, M p. th. fo. 7, fos. 1^v–69^v (9th century).

C　Paris, Bibliothèque Nationale, Lat. 18064, fos. 1–111 (9th century).

O　Paris, Bibliothèque Nationale, Lat. 17361, fos. 1–92^v (9th century). Missing 1.1–9; 3.117–39; lacunae at 1.120–31; 3.50–62.

N　Vatican Library, Lat. 293, fos. 1–94^v (9th century).

B　Berlin, Bibliothek National, Theol. Lat., fo. 45 (Rose 284), fos. 1–131 (9th century).

EDITIONS

Zell	U. Zell (Cologne, *c*.1470)
Gering	U. Gering (Paris, 1472)
Lignamine	J. P. de Lignamine (Rome, 1473)
Valdarfer	C. Valdarfer (Milan, 1474)
Paderborn	J. von Paderborn (Louvain, 1480)
Scinzenzeler	U. Scinzenzeler (Milan, 1488)
Amerbach	J. de Amerbach (Basle, 1492)
Marchand	G. Marchand (Paris, 1494)
Langendorf	J. P. de Langendorf (Basle, 1506)
Erasmus	D. Erasmus (Basle, 1527; Paris, 1529)
Erasmus–Gelen	D. Erasmus and S. Gelen (Paris, 1539)
Erasmus–Gelen–Coster	D. Erasmus, S. Gelen, and F. Coster (Basle, 1555)
Gillot	J. Gillot (Paris, 1569)
Monte Alto	F. de Monte Alto (Rome, 1579–87)
Maurists	Maurists (Paris, 1686–90, repr. Venice, 1748–51, 1781–2)

Krabinger	J. G. Krabinger (Tübingen, 1857)
Banterle	G. Banterle (Milan and Rome, 1977), based on Krabinger
Testard	M. Testard (Paris, 1984–92)

LIBER PRIMUS

I **1.** Non adrogans videri arbitror si inter filios suscipiam adfectum docendi, cum ipse humilitatis magister dixerit: *Venite, filii audite me: timorem Domini docebo vos.* In quo licet et humilitatem verecundiae eius spectare et gratiam. Dicendo enim *timorem Domini*, qui communis videtur esse omnibus, expressit insigne verecundiae. Et tamen cum ipse timor initium sapientiae sit et effector beatitudinis, quoniam timentes Deum beati sunt, praeceptorem se sapientiae edocendae et demonstratorem beatitudinis adipiscendae evidenter significavit.

2. Et nos ergo ad imitandam verecundiam seduli, ad conferendam gratiam non usurpatores, quae illi Spiritus infudit sapientiae, ea per illum nobis manifestata et usu comperta atque exemplo, vobis quasi liberis tradimus; cum iam effugere non possimus officium docendi quod nobis refugientibus imposuit sacerdotii necessitudo. *Dedit* enim *Deus quosdam quidem apostolos, quosdam autem prophetas, alios vero evangelistas, alios autem pastores et doctores.*

3. Non igitur mihi apostolorum gloriam vindico (quis enim hoc nisi quos ipse Filius elegit Dei?) non prophetarum gratiam, non virtutem evangelistarum, non pastorum circumspectionem; sed tantummodo intentionem et diligentiam circa scripturas divinas opto adsequi quam ultimam posuit apostolus inter officia sanctorum; et hanc ipsam ut docendi studio possim discere. Unus enim verus magister est qui solus non didicit quod omnes doceret; homines autem discunt prius quod doceant et ab illo accipiunt quod aliis tradant.

4. Quod ne ipsum quidem mihi accidit. Ego enim raptus de tribunalibus atque admininistrationis infulis ad sacerdotium, docere vos coepi quod ipse non didici. Itaque factum est ut prius docere inciperem quam discere. Discendum igitur mihi simul et docendum est quoniam non vacavit ante discere.

II **5.** Quid autem prae ceteris debemus discere quam tacere, ut possimus loqui, ne prius me vox condemnet mea quam

BOOK ONE

1. I shall not appear presumptuous, I trust, if I adopt the approach of
a teacher when addressing my own sons, for the master of humility
himself has said: 'Come, my sons, listen to me: I will teach you the fear
of the Lord'. We can see in these words the humble modesty that he
showed, and his grace as well. In speaking of 'the fear of the Lord', he
was referring to something which seems to be found in people everywhere, and it was clear proof of his modesty. But, more than that, since
that same fear is the beginning of wisdom and the attitude of mind that
guarantees happiness—for only those who fear God know what
happiness is—he also made it plain that he was a sound teacher of
the ways of wisdom and a reliable guide in the quest for happiness.

2. Well, keen to imitate his modesty, though hardly presuming to
measure up to his grace, we are passing on to you, as to our own
children, the same truths that the Spirit of wisdom imparted to him.
They have been revealed to us through him and we have learnt them
by practice and example. No longer is it possible for us to escape our
obligation to teach: reluctant as we are, it has been laid upon us as part
of the responsibilities which the priesthood has brought us, for 'God
gave some to be apostles, some to be prophets, others evangelists, and
yet others pastors and teachers'.

3. I make no claims, of course, to the glory of the apostles—whoever
could, other than those whom the Son of God himself chose? Nor do I
claim to have the grace of the prophets, or the power of the evangelists,
or the vigilance of the pastors. My wish is only to attain to the attention
and diligence towards the divine Scriptures which the apostle ranked
last of all among the duties of the saints. This is all I desire, so that, in
my endeavour to teach others, I might be able to learn myself. For
there is only one true Master, who never had to learn all that he taught
everyone else: in this he is unique. Ordinary men must learn beforehand what they are to teach, and receive from him what they are to
pass on to others.

4. In my own case, not even this was allowed. I was snatched into the
priesthood from a life spent at tribunals and amidst the paraphernalia
of administrative office, and I began to teach you things I had not
learnt myself. The result was that I started to teach before I had
started to learn. With me, then, it is a matter of learning and teaching
all at the same time, since no opportunity was given me to learn in
advance.

5. What is it that we need to learn before everything else? Surely it is
to be silent, so that we are able to speak as we ought. Otherwise, I stand

absolvat aliena? Scriptum est enim: *Ex verbis tuis condemnaberis*. Quid opus est igitur ut properes periculum suscipere condemnationis loquendo, cum tacendo possis esse tutior? Complures vidi loquendo peccatum incidisse, vix quemquam tacendo; ideoque tacere nosse quam loqui difficilius est. Scio loqui plerosque cum tacere nesciant. Rarum est tacere quemquam cum sibi loqui nihil prosit. Sapiens est ergo qui novit tacere. Denique sapientia Dei dixit: *Dominus dedit mihi linguam eruditionis quando oporteat sermonem dicere*. Merito ergo sapiens qui a Domino accepit quo tempore sibi loquendum sit. Unde bene ait scriptura: *Homo sapiens tacebit usque ad tempus*.

6. Ideo sancti Domini, qui scirent quia vox hominis plerumque peccati adnuntia est et initium erroris humani sermo est hominis, amabant tacere. Denique sanctus Domini ait: *Dixi: custodiam vias meas ut non delinquam in lingua mea*. Sciebat enim et legerat divinae esse protectionis ut homo a flagello linguae suae absconderetur et a conscientiae suae testimonio. Verberamur enim tacito cogitationis nostrae opprobrio et iudicio conscientiae; verberamur etiam vocis nostrae verbere cum loquimur ea quorum sono caeditur animus noster et mens consauciatur. Quis autem est qui mundum cor a peccatorum habeat colluvione aut non delinquat in lingua sua? Et ideo, quia neminem videbat sanctum os seruare posse ab immunditia sermonis, ipse sibi silentio legem imposuit innocentiae ut tacendo culpam declinaret quam vix effugere posset loquendo.

7. Audiamus ergo cautionis magistrum: *Dixi: custodiam vias meas*, hoc est: mihi dixi, tacito cogitationis praecepto indixi mihi ut custodirem vias meas. Aliae sunt viae quas debemus sequi, aliae quas custodire: sequi vias Domini, custodire nostras ne in culpam dirigant. Potes autem custodire si non cito loquaris. Lex dicit: *Audi, Israel, Dominum Deum tuum*. Non dicit: *loquere*, sed *audi*. Ideo Eva lapsa est, quia locuta est viro quod non audierat a Domino Deo suo. Prima vox Dei dicit tibi: *Audi*. Si audias, custodis uias tuas, et si lapsus es, cito corrigis. *In quo enim corrigit iuvenior viam suam nisi in*

condemned by my own voice before anyone else can raise his to acquit me, for it is written: 'By your own words you will be condemned'. Why run the risk of being condemned by speaking when you do better to stay silent? Many is the person I have seen fall into sin by speaking, but scarcely ever have I seen anyone do so by staying silent. The reason is this: it is far harder to know how to stay silent than it is to know how to speak. I realize that most people speak simply because they have no idea how to be silent. It is a rare thing for anyone to keep silent, even when there is nothing to be gained by speaking. It is a wise person indeed who knows how to keep silent. The wisdom of God has put it this way: 'The Lord has given me a tongue full of instruction, to know when I ought to speak a word.' A person deserves to be called 'wise' if he has been taught by the Lord when it is right to speak. The words of Scripture say it so well: 'The wise man will keep silent until the right time.'

6. So, the saints of the Lord, recognizing that man's voice is so often the messenger of sin and that man's speech is the beginning of human error, were glad to stay silent. The saint of the Lord affirms it: 'I have said: I will guard my ways, so that I will not offend with my tongue'. He knew, you see, he had read it for himself, that it is only through divine protection that man can be hidden from the scourge of his own tongue and from the witness of his own conscience. For we are chastised by the silent reproach of our own thoughts and by the judgement of our own conscience; we are chastised, too, by the cutting blow which our own voice can inflict, when we say things at whose sound our own spirit is pierced and our own mind is grievously wounded. Which of us has a heart that is untainted by the pollution of sins, or which of us does not offend with his tongue? He could see that it was impossible for anyone to keep his mouth pure from the pollution that speech brings, and so he imposed a law of innocence on himself by staying silent. If he kept silent, he thought, he might manage to avoid fault; if he spoke, he would almost certainly never escape it.

7. Let us hear, then, what this master of caution had to say: 'I have said: I will guard my ways'. What he meant, in other words, was this: 'I have said to myself, I have laid it upon myself by silently establishing it as a rule in my own mind, that I will guard my ways'. There are certain ways we ought to follow, and others we ought to guard: we should follow the ways of the Lord, and guard our own ways, so that they do not lead us into sin. You can guard them if you do not rush to speak. The Law says: 'Hear, O Israel, the Lord your God'. It does not say: 'Speak'; it says: 'Hear'. This was why Eve fell: she spoke to her husband things that she had not heard from the Lord her God. This is

custodiendo verba Domini? Tace ergo prius et audi ut non delinquas in lingua tua.

8. Grave malum ut aliquis ore suo condemnetur. Etenim si pro otioso verbo reddet unusquisque rationem, quanto magis pro verbo impuritatis et turpitudinis? Graviora sunt enim verba praecipitationis quam otiosa. Ergo si pro otioso verbo ratio poscitur, quanto magis pro sermone impietatis poena exsolvitur?

III **9.** Quid igitur? Mutos nos esse oportet? Minime. *Est enim tempus tacendi et est tempus loquendi.* Deinde si pro verbo otioso reddimus rationem, videamus ne reddamus et pro otioso silentio. Est enim et negotiosum silentium, ut erat Susannae, quae plus egit tacendo quam si esset locuta. Tacendo enim apud homines, locuta est Deo, nec ullum maius indicium suae castitatis invenit quam silentium. Conscientia loquebatur ubi vox non audiebatur, nec quaerebat pro se hominum iudicium quae habebat Domini testimonium. Ab illo igitur volebat absolvi quem sciebat nullo modo posse falli. Ipse Dominus in evangelio tacens operabatur salutem omnium. Recte ergo David non silentium sibi indixit perpetuum, sed custodiam.

10. Custodiamus ergo cor nostrum, custodiamus os nostrum; utrumque enim scriptum est: hic, ut os custodiamus; alibi tibi dicitur: *Omni custodia serva cor tuum.* Si custodiebat David, tu non custodies? Si immunda labia habebat Esaias qui dixit: *O miser ego quoniam compunctus sum quia, cum sim homo et immunda labia habeam*; si propheta Domini immunda habebat labia, quomodo nos munda habemus?

11. Et cui nisi unicuique nostrum scriptum est: *Saepi possessionem tuam spinis . . . et argentum et aurum tuum adliga, et ori tuo fac ostium et vectem, et verbis tuis iugum et stateram?* Possessio tua mens tua est, aurum tuum cor tuum est, argentum tuum eloquium tuum est: *Eloquia Domini, eloquia casta, argentum igne examinatum.* Bona etiam possessio mens bona. Denique possessio pretiosa homo mundus. Saepi ergo hanc possessionem et circumvallato cogitationibus, munito sollicitudinibus, ne in eam irruant et captivam ducant irrationabiles corporis

the very first word God utters to you: 'Hear'. If you hear, you guard your ways; and if you have fallen, you soon make amends. For 'how does a young man amend his life, other than by paying heed to the words of the Lord?' First and foremost, then, be silent, and hear, and this way you will not offend with your tongue.

8. It is a serious evil for a person to be condemned by his own mouth. After all, if each of us must give account for every idle word we have spoken, how much more for every word that is unclean and shameful? Words uttered in foolish haste are more serious than words uttered idly. So, if an account is going to be demanded of us for every idle word, how much more will we be punished for talk that is ungodly?

9. What then? Am I suggesting that we should behave as though we **III** were dumb? Far from it. For 'there is a time to be silent and a time to speak'. Besides, if we must give an account for every idle word, we need to make sure that we do not find ourselves having to account for idle silence as well. For there is another kind of silence as well, one that is characterized by activity. The silence of Susanna was an example of it. She achieved more by keeping silent than she would have done if she had spoken. In keeping silent before men, she spoke to God, and she devised no greater proof of her chastity than this silence. Her conscience spoke when her voice was not heard; she sought no judgement at the hands of men, for she had the Lord himself as her witness. It was by him that she wanted to be acquitted, for she knew that he could never be deceived in any way. The Lord himself, we read in the gospel, kept silent, yet accomplished the salvation of us all. David was right, then, not to impose a perpetual silence on himself, but only to keep a guard on his words.

10. So let us guard our heart, let us guard our mouth. We can find both of these injunctions in the Scriptures. In the present passage, we are told to guard our mouth, and in another place you are enjoined to 'Guard your heart with all watchfulness.' If David made sure to guard his heart, do you not think you should guard yours? If Isaiah had unclean lips—for he could say, 'Wretched man that I am! I am cut to the heart! Here am I—a mere man, with unclean lips!'—if the prophet of the Lord had unclean lips, how can ours be clean?

11. And for whose benefit was that other command recorded in the Scriptures: 'Hedge your property with thorns . . .; bind fast your silver and your gold; make door and bar for your mouth, and yoke and balance for your words'? It was for each one of us, was it not? Your property is your mind, your gold is your heart, your silver is your word: 'The words of the Lord are pure words, like silver tested by fire.' A good mind is good property. Indeed, a man that is without sin is valuable property. Hedge this property, then, and enclose it in the

passiones, ne incursent motus graves, ne diripiant vindemiam eius transeuntes viam. Custodi interiorem hominem tuum, noli eum quasi vilem neglegere ac fastidire quia pretiosa possessio est; et merito pretiosa, cuius fructus non caducus et temporalis sed stabilis atque aeternae salutis est. Cole ergo possessionem tuam, ut sint tibi agri.

12. Adliga sermonem tuum ne luxuriet, ne lasciviat et multiloquio peccata sibi colligat. Sit restrictior et ripis suis coerceatur. Cito lutum colligit amnis exundans. Adliga sensum tuum, non sit remissus ac defluus, ne dicatur de te: *Non est malagma apponere neque oleum neque adligaturam.* Habet suas habenas mentis sobrietas quibus regitur et gubernatur.

13. Sit ori tuo ostium ut claudatur ubi oportet et obseretur diligentius ne quis in iracundiam excitet vocem tuam et contumeliam rependas contumeliae. Audisti hodie lectum: *Irascimini et nolite peccare.* Ergo etsi irascimur, quia adfectus naturae est non ⟨nostrae⟩ potestatis, malum sermonem non proferamus de ore nostro ne in culpam ruamus; sed iugum sit verbis tuis et statera, hoc est humilitas atque mensura, ut lingua tua menti subdita sit. Restringatur habenae vinculis, frenos habeat suos quibus revocari possit ad mensuram, sermones proferat libra examinatos iustitiae, ut sit gravitas in sensu, in sermone pondus, atque in verbis modus.

IV 14. Haec si custodiat aliquis, fit mitis mansuetus modestus. Custodiendo enim os suum et retinendo linguam suam nec prius loquendo quam interroget et expendat atque examinet verba sua, si dicendum hoc, si dicendum adversus hunc, si tempus sermonis huius, is profecto exercet modestiam ac mansuetudinem et patientiam, ut non ex indignatione et ira in sermonem erumpat, non alicuius passionis indicium det in

proper manner, with serious thoughts; protect it with every kind of care, to ensure that the irrational passions of the body do not burst into it and take it captive, to ensure that strong emotions do not assault it and plunder its harvest, seizing what they can as they pass on their way. Guard your inner man; do not neglect or despise this part of you as if it did not matter, for it is a valuable property—and I mean genuinely valuable, since its fruit is not perishable and temporal, but has to do with a salvation that is lasting and eternal. Look after your property carefully, then, so that you find yourself with cultivated fields.

12. Keep your conversation tightly bound, so that it does not run riot or get out of control, and does not amass sins for itself by constant loose talk. It should be properly restrained, and confined within its own banks: a river that overflows soon gathers mud. Keep your thinking tightly bound; do not let it become slack or fall adrift, in case it should be said of you: 'Neither poultice nor oil nor bandage can be applied.' A sober mind holds reins of its own, and uses them to give direction and maintain control.

13. You should keep a door over your mouth so that it is closed when it ought to be, and make sure that it is fastened carefully; otherwise, someone will provoke you to say something in anger and you will start to return insult for insult. You have heard these words read today: 'Be angry and do not sin.' So, even if we are angry—since anger is a natural emotion, and not something we can control completely—we must not allow any kind of evil language to come out of our mouth, otherwise we shall fall into sin. Rather, you should use a yoke and balance to weigh your words—in other words, show humility and due measure in what you say—so that your tongue remains under the authority of your mind. Your tongue needs to be restrained with a firm rein; it needs to feel the pull of its own bridle, calling it back to a measured pace. All its language needs to be carefully weighed in the scales of justice. This way, there will be gravity in the thoughts you express, weight in the substance of what you say, and due measure in the words you use to say it.

14. If a person guards these things, he soon becomes mild and gentle IV and modest. For in guarding his mouth, restraining his tongue, and being careful not to say anything before he has carefully examined and weighed and measured his words ('Should I make such a remark?', he will ask himself; 'Is it appropriate for me to go ahead and contradict that person? Is it the right moment to come out with this kind of comment?') he really is practising modesty, gentleness, and patience. And here is the result. He does not go and blurt something out in a fit of indignation or anger. He does not betray passion in the words he

verbis suis, non ardorem libidinis flammare in sermone suo
indicet et inesse dictis suis stimulos iracundiae, ne sermo
postremo, qui commendare interiora debet, vitium aliquod
esse in moribus aperiat et prodat.

15. Tunc enim maxime insidiatur adversarius quando videt
nobis passiones aliquas generari: tunc fomites movet, laqueos
parat. Unde non immerito, sicut audisti hodie legi, propheta
dicit: *Quia ipse liberavit me de laqueo venantium et a verbo
aspero.* Symmachus *irritationis verbum* dixit, alii *perturbationis.*
Laqueus adversarii sermo noster est, sed etiam ipse non
minus adversarius nobis. Loquimur plerumque quod excipiat
inimicus et quasi nostro gladio nos vulneret. Quanto tolerabilius est alieno gladio quam nostro perire!

16. Explorat ergo adversarius nostra arma et concutit sua tela.
Si viderit moveri me, inserit aculeos suos ut seminaria
iurgiorum excitet. Si emisero verbum indecorum, laqueum
suum stringit. Interdum mihi quasi escam proponit vindictae
possibilitatem ut, dum vindicari cupio, ipse me inseram
laqueo et nodum mortis adstringam mihi. Si quis ergo hunc
adversarium sentit praesentem esse tunc magis custodiam
adhibere debet ori suo ne det locum adversario; sed non
multi hunc vident.

V **17.** Sed etiam ille cavendus est qui videri potest, quicumque
irritat, quicumque incitat, quicumque exasperat, quicumque
incentiva luxuriae aut libidinis suggerit. Quando ergo aliquis
nobis conviciatur, lacessit, ad violentiam provocat, ad iurgium
vocat, tunc silentium exerceamus, tunc muti fieri non eru-
bescamus. Peccator est enim qui nos provocat, qui iniuriam
facit et nos similes sui fieri desiderat.

18. Denique si taceas, si dissimules, solet dicere: 'Quid taces?
Loquere si audes; sed non audes, mutus es, elinguem te feci'.
Si ergo taceas, plus rumpitur: victum sese putat, irrisum,
posthabitum atque illusum. Si respondeas, superiorem se

uses, or give an indication in his choice of language that there is a flame of desire blazing within him, or that, deep down, it is a sense of bitter outrage that is spurring him on to say what he does. In short, he makes sure that his language, intended as it is to commend his inner nature, does not reveal the existence of some fault in his character and parade it for all to see.

15. For this is the very moment when the enemy lies in wait for us— when he spots that passion of one kind or another is being brought to the birth within us. This is the very moment when he kindles his wood and sets his snares. No wonder, then, the prophet says, in the words you have heard read today: 'Because he has delivered me from the snare of the hunters and from the word that is harsh.' Symmachus' text read: 'the word that provokes'; others have: 'the word that disturbs'. Our own language is the enemy's snare, but our language is also no less of an enemy to us in its own right. Too often we say something that our foe is able to intercept, and it is as if he is able to wound us with our own sword. It is far more bearable to perish by someone else's sword than by our own!

16. Here then is the enemy, spying out our armour and rattling his weapons. If he sees that I am disturbed, he plants his sharp spikes into me, determined to stir up the first seeds of strife. If I let slip an unseemly word, he draws his snare tight around me. Sometimes he sets before me, like bait, the possibility of revenge, so that in my desire to get even with somebody I step into the snare myself and draw the deadly knot around my own neck. So, if a person senses that this enemy is near, it is at that moment above all that he needs to set a guard on his mouth, so as not to give the enemy an opportunity. But not many see him.

17. But we need to beware also of the kind of enemy who *can* be seen—   V and here I mean anyone who winds us up, anyone who incites us, anyone who annoys us, or anyone who spreads before our eyes the sort of things which tempt us to self-indulgence or lust. As soon as someone insults us, or irritates us, or provokes us to violence, or invites us to get involved in a fight, it is then especially that we need to exercise silence, and it is then especially that we should feel no shame about behaving as though we were dumb. For the person who provokes us and does us an injury is a sinner, and his great desire is that we should become like him.

18. Of course, if you do keep silent, if you do pretend not to hear, he will probably say something like this: 'Why are you silent? Speak, if you dare! Ah, no, you don't dare, you're dumb: I've knocked you speechless.' So if you keep silent, he explodes all the more: he thinks he has been beaten and mocked and belittled and laughed at. If you reply,

factum arbitratur quia parem invenit. Si enim taceas, dicetur: 'Ille conviciatus est huic, contempsit iste'. Si referas contumeliam, dicetur: 'Ambo conviciati sunt. Uterque condemnatur, nemo absolvitur'. Ergo illius est studium ut irritet, ut similia illi loquar, similia agam; iusti est autem dissimulare, nihil loqui, tenere bonae fructum conscientiae, plus committere bonorum iudicio quam criminantis insolentiae, contentum esse gravitate morum suorum. Hoc est enim *silere a bonis*, quia bene sibi conscius falsis non debet moveri nec aestimare plus ponderis in alieno esse convicio quam in suo testimonio. **19.** Ita fit ut etiam humilitatem custodiat. Si autem nolit humilior videri, talia tractat et dicit ipse secum: 'Hic ergo ut me contemnat et in conspectu meo loquatur talia adversum me quasi non possim ego ei aperire os meum? Cur non etiam ego dicam in quibus eum maestificare possim? Hic ergo ut mihi iniurias faciat quasi vir non sim, quasi vindicare me non possim? Hic ut me criminetur quasi ego non possim graviora in eum componere?'

20. Qui talia dicit non est *mitis atque humilis*, non est sine temptatione. Temptator eum exagitat, ipse ei tales opiniones inserit. Plerumque adhibet hominem atque apponit nequam spiritus qui haec illi dicat; sed tu in petra fixum vestigium tene. Etsi servus convicium dicat, iustus tacet; etsi infirmus contumeliam faciat, iustus tacet; etsi pauper criminetur, iustus non respondet. Haec sunt arma iusti ut cedendo vincat, sicut periti iaculandi cedentes solent vincere et fugientes gravioribus sequentem vulnerare ictibus.

VI **21.** Quid enim opus est moveri cum audimus convicia? Cur non imitamur dicentem: *Obmutui et humiliatus sum et silui a bonis*? An hoc dixit tantummodo, non etiam fecit David? Immo et fecit. Nam cum ei conviciaretur Semei filius, tacebat David et quamvis saeptus armatis, non retorquebat convicium, non ultionem quaerebat eo usque ut dicenti sibi Sarviae filio, quod vindicare in eum vellet, non permiserit. Ibat ergo tamquam mutus et humiliatus, ibat tacens nec movebatur,

he imagines that he has got the better of you, because he has found someone just like himself. If you keep silent, people will say: 'That man was insulting, but this man just despised him.' If you return the abuse, they will say: 'They were both trading insults. The one is as guilty as the other: neither of them can be absolved.' All the man wants, then, is to provoke me to speak and behave as he does himself. The task of the just man, though, is to pretend that he hears not a word of it, to say nothing, to hold on to the reward of a good conscience, to leave the last word to the judgement of the good rather than to the arrogance of his attacker, and to be content with the dignity of his own demeanour. His role, in fact, is 'to keep silent about his good deeds', for the person who has a good conscience never needs to be disturbed by any false charges, or to imagine that someone else's insults count for more than the witness of his own heart.

19. The result is, he guards his humility. If, however, he has no wish to come across as quite so humble, he starts to think differently, and he says to himself: 'So, is this character going to slight me and say things like this to my face, as if I can't open my mouth to him? Why shouldn't I say something myself to make him suffer for it? Is he to do me this injury, as if I'm not a man myself, as if I'm somehow not quite capable of getting even with him? Is he going to throw accusations at me, as if I can't come up with far more serious charges against him?'

20. Anyone who speaks like this is not 'gentle and humble', nor is he free from temptation. The tempter is rousing him: it is he himself who instils such ideas in him. Very often the spirit of evil uses a man as his agent, and makes him say things like that to the other person. But as for you—keep your foot firmly planted on the rock. Even if it is a slave who does the insulting, a just man keeps silent; even if it is a poor person who slanders him, a just man makes no reply. These are the weapons of the just man: by giving way, he wins the battle. Think how those who are skilled with the javelin often end up winning the battle just when they give way, inflicting far more serious wounds on a pursuing force even as they flee.

21. Why should we be disturbed when we hear people insulting us? **VI** Why not imitate the one who could say: 'I held my peace, I humbled myself, and kept silent about my good deeds'? Do you think that David just said this, but did not actually put it into practice? Far from it. Think of the time when the son of Shimei insulted him: David kept silent, and though he had armed men all around him, he would not return the insult and would not seek any revenge. And not only so— when the son of Zeruiah said to David that he wanted to take revenge on his behalf, he would not allow him to do it. So he went on, like someone who was dumb and humiliated, he went on in silence and was

cum vir appellaretur sanguinis qui erat conscius propriae mansuetudinis. Non ergo movebatur conviciis cui abundabat bonorum operum conscientia.

22. Itaque is qui cito iniuria movetur, facit se dignum videri contumelia dum vult ea indignus probari. Melior est itaque qui contemnit iniuriam quam qui dolet: qui enim contemnit quasi non sentiat, ita despicit; qui autem dolet quasi senserit . . .

VII **23.** Neque improvide, ad vos filios meos scribens, huius psalmi prooemio usus sum. Quem psalmum propheta David sancto Idithun canendum dedit, ego vobis tenendum suadeo delectatus eius sensu profundo et virtute sententiarum. Advertimus enim ex his quae breviter libavimus, et silendi patientiam et opportunitatem loquendi et in posterioribus contemptum divitiarum, quae maxima virtutum fundamenta sunt, hoc psalmo doceri. Dum igitur hunc psalmum considero, successit animo de officiis scribere.

24. De quibus etiamsi quidam philosophiae studentes scripserint, ut Panaetius et filius eius apud Graecos, Tullius apud Latinos, non alienum duxi nostro munere ut etiam ipse scriberem. Et sicut Tullius ad erudiendum filium, ita ego quoque ad vos informandos filios meos; neque enim minus vos diligo quos in evangelio genui quam si coniugio suscepissem. Non enim vehementior est natura ad diligendum quam gratia. Plus certe diligere debemus quos perpetuo nobiscum putamus futuros quam quos in hoc tantum saeculo. Illi degeneres nascuntur frequenter, qui dedeceant patrem; vos ante elegimus ut diligamus. Itaque illi necessitate diliguntur, quae non satis idonea atque diuturna est ad perpetuitatem diligendi magistra; vos iudicio, quo magnum caritatis pondus ad vim diligendi adiungitur: probare quos diligas et diligere quos elegeris.

VIII **25.** Ergo quoniam personae conveniunt, videamus utrum res ipsa conveniat scribere de officiis et utrum hoc nomen

not disturbed when he was called a bloodthirsty man, for he knew in himself his own gentleness. He was not disturbed in the slightest by these insults, for his conscience bore ample testimony to the good works he had done.

22. The truth is, a person who is readily disturbed by an injury succeeds only in making it look as if he deserves the abuse—and this at the very time when he is keen to prove that he does not. So, the individual who despises an injury is a better person than the one who is annoyed at it, for the one who despises it as if he does not feel it thus looks down on it, whereas the one who is annoyed at it as if he does feel it. . . .

23. It was not without careful consideration that I made use of the VII opening words of this Psalm in writing to you, my sons. I urge you to hold fast to this Psalm, which the prophet David gave to Jeduthun to sing, for I have been delighted by the profound truth it expresses and the powerful sentiments it contains. From the few verses we have sampled already, we have seen that the Psalm affords instruction on the kind of patience we require to remain silent and on the importance of waiting for the right occasion to speak. In later verses, it tells us how to despise riches as well. These things are the major foundations of all virtues. It was while I was meditating on this Psalm, then, that the idea came to me to write about duties.

24. Although various devotees of philosophy have written about duties—Panaetius and his son among the Greeks, for instance, and Cicero among Latin writers—it seemed to me that I would not be venturing beyond my own realm if I undertook to write about them myself as well. In the same way that Cicero wrote to instruct his son, I too am writing to mould you, my sons; for I do not feel any less love for you as children whom I have begotten in the gospel than I would if I had fathered you literally in marriage. Nature is no stronger than grace when it comes to love. In fact, we ought to have all the greater love for those who, we trust, will be with us for ever than we do for those who are with us in this world only. Here, people often have sons who turn out to be a disappointment, the kind who disgrace their father; but with you it is different: we have chosen you beforehand, to love you. Children who disappoint are still loved, but the love stems from a sense of obligation, and that is hardly an adequate or enduring basis for teaching the kind of love that will last. You, though, are loved on the basis of deliberate judgement, and this adds to love's force the great weight of real affection: it means that you truly approve of those you love and you truly love those you have chosen.

25. Since the characters are suitably cast for their respective roles, let VIII us think about the suitability of the topic itself. Is it an appropriate

philosophorum tantummodo scholae aptum sit an etiam in scripturis reperiatur divinis. Pulchre itaque, dum legimus hodie evangelium, quasi adhortaretur ad scribendum, sanctus Spiritus obtulit nobis lectionem qua confirmaremur etiam in nobis officium dici posse. Nam cum Zacharias sacerdos obmutuisset in templo et loqui non posset, *Factum est* inquit, *ut impleti sunt dies officii eius; abiit in domum suam* Legimus igitur officium dici a nobis posse.

26. Nec ratio ipsa abhorret, quandoquidem officium ab efficiendo dictum putamus quasi efficium, sed propter decorem sermonis una immutata littera officium nuncupari; vel certe ut ea agas quae nulli officiant, prosint omnibus.

IX **27.** Officia autem ab honesto et utili duci aestimaverunt et de his duobus eligere quid praestet; deinde incidere ut duo concurrant honesta et duo utilia, et quaeratur quid honestius et quid utilius. Primum igitur in tres partes officium dividitur: honestum et utile et quid praestantius. Deinde haec tria in quinque genera diviserunt: in duo honesta et duo utilia et eligendi iudicium. Primam pertinere aiunt ad decus honestatemque vitae, secundam ad vitae commoda copias opes facultates; de his eligendi subesse iudicium. Haec illi.

28. Nos autem nihil omnino nisi quod deceat et honestum sit futurorum magis quam praesentium metimur formula; nihilque utile nisi quod ad vitae illius aeternae prosit gratiam definimus, non quod ad delectationem praesentis. Neque aliqua commoda in facultatibus et copiis opum constituimus sed incommoda haec putamus si non reiciantur: eaque oneri cum adsunt, aestimari magis quam dispendio, cum erogantur

theme for us to write about 'duties'? Is the word fit only for the schools of the philosophers, or can it be found in the divine Scriptures as well? Well now, a wonderful thing happened just this day while I was reading the gospel. As though he was encouraging me to write on the subject, the Holy Spirit brought before me a reading which confirmed my view that we too are able speak of *officium*, or 'duty': when Zacharias the priest had become dumb in the temple and was unable to speak, 'it came to pass,' Scripture says, 'that the days of his *officium* were completed; he went away to his own house'. From what we read here, then, it is clear that we too are able to speak of *officium*, or 'duty'.

26. Reason itself has no difficulty with this, either. For the word *officium*, 'duty', is, we believe, derived from *efficere*, 'to achieve', as though it were *efficium*, 'achievement'; but, in the interests of euphony, one letter has been changed, and it is now known as *officium*. Alternatively, you can think of it this way: you should behave in ways that are harmful (*officiant*) to no one but helpful to all.

27. The philosophers have held that duties derive from two sources: IX one is the need to do what is 'honourable' and the other is the need to do what is 'beneficial': we must choose, they said, whichever of these two carries greater weight. But then it also occurred to them that there could be two honourable or two beneficial courses open to us at the same time, so they argued that what we must then do is enquire which is the *more* honourable and which is the *more* beneficial in each case. So, in the first place, duty gets divided into three constituents: there is the honourable course, the beneficial course, and whichever of the two carries more weight. But then they have further divided these three categories, to make five: there may be two courses, both of which are honourable, and two, both of which are beneficial, and there is the question of how to choose between them. They say that the first two are all about doing what is 'seemly' and honourable in life, while the second two are connected with things which are 'advantageous' to life—resources, wealth, and opportunities. The question of how to choose between them comes last. This is what these people claim.

28. For ourselves, we have no interest in anything unless it is seemly and honourable, and we measure that by the standard of the future, not the present. Nor do we recognize anything to be beneficial unless it helps us attain the grace of eternal life; we do not give this name to the sort of thing which merely contributes to the enjoyment of our present life. Nor do we hold that there are any advantages to be had in the possession of opportunities or the resources of wealth; in fact, we deem things like these to be disadvantages if they are not cast aside, and for us it is more of a burden to have them than a loss to give them away.

29. Non superfluum igitur scriptionis nostrae est opus, quia officium diversa aestimamus regula atque illi aestimaverunt Illi saeculi commoda in bonis ducunt, nos haec etiam in detrimentis, quoniam qui hic recipit bona, ut ille dives, illic cruciatur, et Lazarus, qui mala hic pertulit, illic consolationem invenit. Deinde qui illa non legunt, nostra legent s volent, qui non sermonum supellectilem neque artem dicend sed simplicem rerum exquirunt gratiam.

X **30.** Decorum autem in nostris scripturis primo constitui loco quod Graece πρέπον dicitur, instruimur et docemur legentes *Te decet hymnus, Deus, in Sion*, vel Graece: Σοὶ πρέπει ὕμνος, ὁ Θεὸς, ἐν Σιών. Et apostolus ait: *Loquere quae decent sanam doctrinam*. Et alibi: *Decebat autem eum per quem omnia et propter quem omnia, multis filiis in gloriam adductis, ducem salutis eorum per passionem consummari*.

31. Numquid prior Panaetius, numquid Aristoteles, qui et ipse disputavit de officio, quam David, cum et ipse Pythagoras, qui legitur Socrate antiquior, prophetam secutus David legem silentii dederit suis? Sed ille ut per quinquennium discipulis usum inhiberet loquendi; David autem non ut naturae munus imminueret sed ut custodiam proferend sermonis doceret. Et Pythagoras quidem ut non loquendo loqui doceret; David ut loquendo ⟨minus⟩ magis disceremus loqui. Quomodo enim sine exercitio doctrina aut sine usu profectus?

32. Qui disciplinam bellicam vult adsequi, cotidie exercetur armis et tamquam in procinctu positus proludit proelium et velut coram posito praetendit hoste, atque ad peritiam viresque iaculandi vel suos explorat lacertos vel adversariorum declinat ictus et vigilanti exit obtutu. Qui navem in mari regere gubernaculis studet vel remis ducere prius in fluvio praeludit. Qui canendi suavitatem et vocis adfectant praestantiam prius sensim canendo vocem excitant. Et qui viribus

29. It can hardly be irrelevant, therefore, for us to set about the business of writing on this theme, for we measure duty by a standard quite different from the one that the philosophers apply. They consider the advantages of this world to be good things, whereas we regard them as loss: for the person who receives good things in this world, like the rich man did, ends up tormented in the next, while Lazarus, who endured such terrible evils here, finds consolation over there. From now on, those who choose not to read the works of these people will be able to read ours if they so wish—those who are looking not for ornate language or verbal artistry but for the simple grace of things as they really are.

30. Conduct which is 'seemly', or 'fitting', called in Greek *prepon*, is X accorded a place of prime importance in our Scriptures. We are taught this in the clearest of terms when we read: 'A hymn of praise is fitting for you, O God, in Zion', or, as the verse is in Greek: *Soi prepei hymnos, ho Theos, en Sion.* And the apostle says: 'Speak things which befit sound doctrine'; and, in another place: 'It was fitting for him, through whom are all things and for whom are all things, to make perfect the captain of their salvation through suffering'.

31. Take Panaetius, or take Aristotle, who also spent time discussing the subject of duty—neither of them lived before David, did he? Why, Pythagoras himself, who, we read, pre-dated Socrates, simply followed the prophet David when he imposed a law of silence on his disciples. But Pythagoras did it in order to deny his pupils the complete use of speech for five years, whereas David's law of silence was designed not to violate the gift of nature but to teach us to take care over the words we utter. Again, Pythagoras' intention was to teach his pupils to speak by becoming used to the experience of not speaking, while David's objective was to show us that by speaking less we would learn how to speak more appropriately. After all, how can anyone learn anything without practising, or make progress without applying himself?

32. The man who wishes to acquire expertise in warfare spends time every day in practice with his weapons: he rehearses the whole scenario of a battle, imagining that he is there in the line of conflict, and he takes up his stance as though an enemy really were in position in front of him. To develop skill and strength at throwing the javelin, say, he will put his muscles to the test; or perhaps he will learn to dodge blows from opponents and to escape by keeping a sharp eye out. The person who is keen to take the helm of a ship or to guide it with oars out on the high seas first rehearses on a river. People who aspire to sing with great melody and show that they have the sweetest of voices first develop their voices by singing just a little at a time. And those who seek to win

corporis legitimoque luctandi certamine coronam petunt quo-
tidiano usu palaestrae durantes membra, nutrientes patientiam, laborem adsuescunt.

33. Haec ipsa natura nos in parvulis docet, quod prius sonos
meditantur loquendi ut loqui discant. Itaque sonus exercitatio
quaedam et palaestra vocis est. Ita ergo et qui volunt discere
cautionem loquendi, quod naturae est non negent, quod
custodiae est exerceant, ut qui in specula sunt, speculando
intendant, non dormiendo. Omnis enim res propriis ac
domesticis exercitiis augetur.

34. Ergo David tacebat non semper, sed pro tempore; non
iugiter neque omnibus sed irritanti adversario, provocanti
peccatori non respondebat. Et, sicut alibi ait, loquentes
vanitatem et cogitantes dolum non audiebat quasi surdus, et
quasi mutus non aperiebat illis os suum; quia et alibi habes:
Noli respondere imprudenti ad imprudentiam eius ne similis illi
fias.

35. Primum igitur officium est loquendi modus. Hoc sacrificium laudis Deo dependitur, hoc reverentia exhibetur cum
scripturae divinae leguntur, hoc honorantur parentes. Scio
loqui plerosque cum tacere nesciant. Rarum est tacere quemquam cum sibi non prosit loqui. Sapiens, ut loquatur, multa
prius considerat: quid dicat, et cui dicat, quo in loco et
tempore. Est ergo et tacendi et loquendi modus; est etiam
factis modus. Pulchrum igitur tenere mensuram officii.

XI 36. Officium autem omne aut medium aut perfectum est,
quod aeque scripturarum auctoritate probare possumus.
Habemus etenim in evangelio dixisse Dominum: *Si vis in*
vitam aeternam venire, serva mandata. Dicit illi: Quae? Iesus
autem dixit illi: Non homicidium facies, non adulterabis, non
facies furtum, non falsum testimonium dices, honora patrem e

a crown by proving their physical strength in an official contest with proper rules toughen up their limbs by practising day after day on the training-ground, and build up their stamina by becoming used to the experience of fatigue.

33. Indeed, nature herself teaches us this lesson if we consider little children, for they first study the sounds of speech in order to learn to speak. The sound of language is like a kind of practice-area or training-ground for the voice. In the very same way, people who want to learn caution in speaking must never try to deny what is natural, but they need to practise at the side that is amenable to careful attention. Think of men who are on look-out duty: they concentrate by looking out, not by going to sleep! Every procedure is improved by the performance of its own particular and special exercises.

34. So, David did not keep silent at all times, but only when the circumstances called for it. He did not refuse to give a reply as a matter of regular habit or in response to everyone who ever spoke to him: he only responded this way when an enemy goaded him or a sinner provoked him. It was just as he tells us himself elsewhere: he acted as though he was deaf, and refused to hear, and he acted as though he was dumb and refused to open his mouth, but he did it with those who were speaking vain words and plotting deceitfully against him; for you find it is also said in another place: 'Do not answer the fool according to his folly, or you will become like him.'

35. The very first duty, then, is to show due measure in the business of speaking. That way, a true sacrifice of praise is offered to God; that way, proper reverence is shown when the divine Scriptures are read; that way, parents are honoured. I realize that most people speak simply because they have no idea how to be silent. It is a rare thing for anyone to keep silent, even when there is no gain in speaking. A wise person, before he speaks a word, first asks himself a series of questions. What should he say? To whom should he say it? Where, and when? There is, then, such a thing as due measure which we need to observe both in our silence and in our speech. Due measure needs to be seen in our actions as well. It is a splendid thing to preserve the kind of measure that is appropriate to the duty you are seeking to fulfil.

36. Every duty is either 'middle' or 'perfect'. We can prove this just as **XI** readily from the authority of the Scriptures. Here we find that the Lord himself said in the gospel: '"If you wish to reach eternal life, keep the commandments." The young man said to him: "Which ones?" Jesus replied to him: "You shall not commit murder; you shall not commit adultery; you shall not steal; you shall not bear false witness; honour your father and mother; and you shall love your

matrem, et diliges proximum tuum sicut te ipsum. Haec sunt media officia, quibus aliquid deest.

37. Denique, *Dicit illi adulescens: Omnia haec custodivi a iuventute mea: quid adhuc mihi deest? Ait illi Iesus: Si vis perfectus esse, vade, vende omnia bona tua et da pauperibus et habebis thesaurum in caelo et veni, sequere me.* Et supra habes scriptum ubi diligendos inimicos et orandum dicit pro calumniantibus et persequentibus nos, et benedicere maledicentes: hoc nos facere debere si volumus perfecti esse sicut Pater noster qui in caelo est, qui super bonos et malos solem iubet radios suos fundere et pluviae rore terras universorum sine ulla discretione pinguescere. Hoc est igitur perfectum officium, quod κατόρθωμα dixerunt Graeci, quo corriguntur omnia quae aliquos potuerunt lapsus habere.

38. Bona etiam misericordia, quae et ipsa perfectos facit, quia imitatur perfectum Patrem. Nihil tam commendat Christianam animam quam misericordia, primum in pauperes, ut communes iudices partus naturae quae omnibus ad usum generat fructus terrarum, ut quod habes largiaris pauperi et consortem et conformem tuum adiuves. Tu nummum largiris, ille vitam accipit; tu pecuniam das, ille substantiam suam aestimat. Tuus denarius census illius est.

39. Ad haec plus ille tibi confert cum sit debitor salutis. Si nudum vestias, te ipsum induis iustitiam; si peregrinum sub tectum inducas tuum, si suscipias egentem, ille tibi acquirit sanctorum amicitias et aeterna tabernacula. Non mediocris ista gratia: corporalia seminas et recipis spiritalia. Miraris iudicium Domini de sancto Iob? Mirare virtutem eius qui poterat dicere: *Oculus eram caecorum, pes claudorum. Ego eram infirmorum pater, velleribus agnorum meorum calefacti sunt humeri eorum. Foris non habitabat peregrinus, ostium autem meum omni venienti patebat.* Beatus plane de cuius domo numquam vacuo sinu pauper exiuit; neque enim quisquam magis beatus quam qui intellegit super pauperis necessitatem et infirmi atque inopis aerumnam. In die iudicii habebit salutem a Domino quem habebit suae debitorem misericordiae.

XII 40. Sed plerique revocantur ab officio dispensatricis misericordiae dum putant hominis actus non curare Dominum aut

neighbour as yourself." ' These are 'middle' duties, in which there is something lacking.

37. Then 'the young man said to him: "All these things I have kept from my youth; what do I still lack?" Jesus said to him: "If you wish to be perfect, go, sell all your goods and give to the poor, and you will have treasure in heaven; then come, follow me." ' We find the same principle recorded earlier on as well, in the passage where the Lord tells us that we should love our enemies, and pray for those who slander and persecute us, and bless those who curse us. This is how we are to behave, he says, if we wish to be perfect like our Father in heaven: he commands the sun to shed its rays on the good and the evil alike, and makes the whole earth grow rich with rain and dew, with no distinction at all. This, then, is 'perfect' duty, called by the Greeks *katorthoma*: it sets right any duties which may have fallen short of the mark in one way or another.

38. Mercy is a good thing, as well, for it too makes people perfect in imitation of this perfect Father. Nothing commends the Christian soul so much as mercy. First and foremost, it must be shown towards the poor: you should treat nature's produce as a common possession; it is all the fruit of the ground, brought forth for the benefit of all alike. You should give what you can to a person who is poor, and offer assistance to one who is by nature your brother and your fellow. You give just a coin or two: he receives life. You pass on mere money: he considers it his fortune. It is only cash to you, but it is wealth to him.

39. In return for your help, he confers more upon you than you do upon him, for he owes you his salvation. If you clothe the naked, you put a robe of righteousness on yourself. If you take a stranger under your roof, or if you help somebody in need, such a person brings you the friendship of the saints and the tabernacles that are eternal. That is surely no bad return—you sow bodily seeds and you reap spiritual fruits! Do you marvel at the judgement the Lord passed on holy Job? You should marvel, instead, at the man's virtue, in that he could say: 'I was the eye of the blind and the foot of the lame. I was a father to the weak; their shoulders were kept warm with fleeces from my lambs. No stranger was ever left outside: my door was open to everyone who came.' Here was a man who was happy in the truest sense: no poor person ever left his house with his pockets empty. No one is more truly happy than the one who gives thought to the needs of the poor and the hardship of the weak and helpless. On the day of judgement, he will receive salvation from the Lord: the Lord will owe it to him for the mercy he has shown.

40. But many people are put off the duty of showing mercy through **XII** giving, for they imagine that the Lord has no concern for man's

nescire eum quid in occultis geramus, quid teneat nostra conscientia, aut iudicium eius nequaquam iustum videri, quando peccatores divitiis abundare vident, gaudere honoribus, sanitate, liberis; contra autem iustos inopes degere, inhonoros, sine liberis, infirmos corpore, luctu frequenti.

41. Nec mediocris ea quaestio, quandoquidem tres illi reges amici Iob propterea eum peccatorem pronuntiabant, quia inopem factum ex divite, orbatum liberis ex fecundo parente, perfusum ulceribus, inhorrentem vibicibus, exaratum vulneribus a capite usque ad pedes videbant. Quibus hanc sanctus Iob proponit adsertionem: Si ego propter peccata mea haec patior, *Cur impii vivunt? Inveteraverunt autem et in divitiis semen eorum secundum voluntatem, filii eorum in oculis, domus ipsorum abundant, timor autem nusquam: flagellum autem a Domino non est in ipsis.*

42. Haec videns infirmus corde exagitatur et studium avertit suum. Cuius dicturus sermones ante sanctus praemisit Iob dicens: *Portate me, ego autem loquar, deinde ridete me. Nam etsi arguor, quasi homo arguor. Portate ergo onus sermonum meorum.* Dicturus enim sum quod non probo, sed ad vos redarguendos proferam sermones iniquos; aut certe quia ita est versus: *Quid autem? Numquid ab homine arguor?* Hoc est: homo me non potest redarguere quia peccavi, etsi argui dignus sum, quia non ex evidenti culpa me arguitis sed ex iniuriis aestimatis merita delictorum. Videns ergo infirmus abundare iniustos successibus prosperis, se autem atteri, dicit Domino: *Discede a me, vias tuas scire nolo; quid prodest quia servivimus ipsi, aut quae utilitas quia occurrimus ipsi? In manibus eorum omnia bona, opera autem impiorum non videt.*

43. Laudatur in Platone quod in Politia sua posuit eum, qui contra iustitiam disputandi partes recepisset, postulare veniam dictorum quae non probaret, et veri inveniendi atque examinandae disputationis gratia illam sibi impositam personam dicere. Quod eo usque Tullius probavit ut ipse, in

actions, or that he does not know what we do in secret—even though our own consciences retain this knowledge—or that his judgement is anything but just. Everywhere they look they see people who are sinners living in luxury and enjoying all sorts of honours, good health, and children, while those who are just seem to be forever in need, always the ones deprived of all the honours, childless, weak in body, and beset with one sorrow after another.

41. Well, we can hardly dismiss this as a trivial objection. Think of those three leaders, Job's friends, and the conclusion to which they came. Their verdict was that Job must have sinned greatly when they saw that he had been reduced from riches to poverty, from being a fruitful parent to one bereft of children, covered in sores, bristling with weals, and a mass of cuts and wounds from head to foot. Holy Job put the following challenge to them: 'If I am suffering these things on account of my sins,' he said, '"Why are the ungodly still alive at all? Yet they have managed to live to a goodly old age; their offspring are as rich as they could wish; their sons are there before their eyes; their houses lack for nothing; and fear has no place within their hearts: the scourge of the Lord is not upon them."'

42. When a weak person sees this, he is shaken in his heart, and he allows his enthusiasm to wane. Holy Job was about to voice the thoughts of such an individual, so he prefaced his remarks like this: 'Bear with me, and I too shall speak; then laugh at me if you will. For even if I am accused, it is as a man that I am accused. So bear with me, burdensome though my words may be to you.' In other words, what he was saying was: 'I'm about to voice thoughts of which I do not approve, but my aim in saying these wicked things is simply to show you that you're wrong.' To quote the verse properly, his actual words were: 'What then? Is it by a man that I am accused?' In other words, he said, 'No man can prove to me that I have actually sinned, even if I am worthy of the accusation. You are not accusing me on the basis of obvious guilt; you are calculating from my misfortunes that what I am receiving must be the just reward for my transgressions.' So, when a weak person sees the wicked enjoying all the prosperity they could desire while he himself is worn down with troubles, he says to the Lord: 'Depart from me: I do not want to know your ways. What good does it do us that we have served him, or what use is it that we have come to him? All the good things are in the hands of the ungodly. As for their works—he never sees them.'

43. People praise Plato for the way he put things in his *Republic*: the character who has been given the task of arguing against justice asks to be pardoned for saying what he does: he does not approve of it personally, he says, but claims that the role has been imposed upon

libris quos scripsit de Republica, in eam sententiam dicendum putaverit.

44. Quanto antiquior illis Iob, qui haec primus repperit nec eloquentiae phalerandae gratia sed veritatis probandae praemittenda aestimavit! Statimque ipse quaestionem enodem reddidit, subiciens quod *exstinguatur lucerna impiorum et futura sit eorum eversio*, non falli Deum doctorem sapientiae et disciplinae sed esse veritatis iudicem; et ideo non secundum forensem abundantiam aestimandam beatitudinem singulorum sed secundum interiorem conscientiam quae innocentium et flagitiosorum merita discernit, vera atque incorrupta poenarum praemiorumque arbitra. Moritur innocens in potestate simplicitatis suae, in abundantia propriae voluntatis, sicut adipe repletam animam gerens. At vero peccator, quamvis foris abundet et deliciis diffluat, odoribus fragret, in amaritudine animae suae vitam exigit et ultimum diem claudit, nihil eorum quae epulatus fuerit referens boni, nihil secum auferens nisi pretia scelerum suorum.

45. Haec cogitans, nega, si potes, divini esse iudicii remunerationem. Ille suo adfectu beatus, hic miser; ille suo iudicio absolutus, hic reus; ille in exitu laetus, hic maerens. Cui absolvi potest qui nec sibi innocens est? *Dicite*, inquit, *mihi ubi est protectio tabernaculorum eius? Signum eius non invenietur*. Vita etenim facinorosi ut somnium: aperuit oculos, transivit requies eius, evanuit delectatio. Licet ipsa quae videtur, etiam dum vivunt, impiorum requies in inferno sit: viventes enim in inferna descendunt.

46. Vides convivium peccatoris: interroga eius conscientiam. Nonne gravius omnibus foetet sepulcris? Intueris laetitiam eius et salubritatem miraris corporis, filiorum atque opum abundantiam: introspice ulcera et vibices animae eius, cordis maestitudinem. Nam de opibus quid loquar, cum legeris: *Quia non in abundantia est vita eius*, cum scias quia, etsi tibi videatur dives, sibi pauper est, et tuum iudicium suo refellat? De multitudine quoque filiorum et de indolentia quid loquar, cum se ipse lugeat et sine herede futurum iudicet, cum

him purely in order to elicit the truth and to explore the argument. Cicero was so impressed by this idea that he felt he should make the same point himself in the work he also wrote on *The Republic*.

44. Look how holy Job predates all of them, who first discovered all this. Nor was it simply to embellish an argument that he thought he should offer such excuses: it was to establish the truth. And he unravelled the mystery himself without further ado, when he added this: 'The lamp of the ungodly is snuffed out, and their destruction is yet to come.' God is not deceived, he said, and he is the one who teaches us wisdom and gives us instruction: he is the judge of truth. An individual's happiness is not to be measured by the level of affluence he enjoys on the outside, but by the state of his conscience within: this is the faculty that distinguishes what the innocent and the guilty deserve; this is the true, the incorruptible judge when it comes to deciding whether they merit reward or punishment. The innocent person dies with his honesty intact, enjoying the riches of his own free spirit, with his soul satisfied as though with fat. As for the sinner—he may be outwardly so affluent and wallowing in every kind of pleasure and fragrant with the richest of perfumes, but he ends his life in bitterness of soul, and finishes his last day deriving no benefit from all the things on which he has gorged himself, taking nothing with him but what his crimes deserve.

45. Consider this, and deny, if you can, that recompense is for God to determine. The one man is happy in his own spirit, the other is miserable; the one is innocent in his own eyes, the other is guilty; the one rejoices when the hour of his death comes, the other is distraught. How can someone be acquitted in his neighbour's judgement, if he is not innocent even in his own? 'Tell me,' Job says: 'Where is the protection of his tents? Not a trace of him will be found.' The truth is, the life of the criminal is like a dream: he has opened his eyes: his calm repose is gone, his pleasure has vanished. They may appear to live a life full of repose, but it is the repose of the wicked in hell, for even while they live they are plunging deeper and deeper into hell.

46. You look longingly at the sinner, there at his sumptuous dinner: try examining his conscience. It smells worse than any grave! You gaze at his happiness, wishing it were yours, you marvel at the health of his body, at all the children and all the riches he has: try looking more closely, at the sores and weals to be found on his soul, and at the sadness that there is in his heart. As for his riches—what is there to say? You have read it for yourself: 'For a man's life does not consist in the abundance of his possessions.' You know that though he may look rich to you, he is poor in his own eyes, and his own judgement gives the lie to yours. And what about his host of children, or his freedom from

imitatores sui successores suos esse nolit? Nulla enim hereditas peccatoris. Ergo impius ipse sibi poena est, iustus autem
ipse sibi gratia; et utrique aut bonorum aut malorum operum
merces ex se ipso solvitur.

XIII **47.** Sed revertamur ad propositum, ne divisionem factam
praeteriisse videamur, qua occurrimus opinioni eorum qui
videntes sceleratos quosque divites laetos honoratos potentes,
cum plerique iustorum egeant atque infirmi sint, putant vel
Deum nihil de nobis curare, ut Epicurei dicunt, vel nescire
actus hominum, ut flagitiosi putant, vel si scit omnia, iniquum esse iudicem ut bonos egere patiatur, abundare improbos. Nec superfluus velut quidam excursus fuit, ut opinioni
huiusmodi ipsorum adfectus responderet, quos beatos iudicamus, cum ipsi se miseros putent. Arbitratus enim sum quod
ipsi sibi facilius quam nobis crederent.

48. Quo decurso, proclive aestimo ut refellam cetera, et
primo eorum adsertionem qui Deum putant curam mundi
nequaquam habere, sicut Aristoteles adserit usque ad lunam
eius descendere providentiam. Et quis operator neglegat
operis sui curam? Quis deserat et destituat quod ipse con-
dendum putavit? Si iniuria est neglegere, nonne est maior
iniuria fecisse, cum aliquid non fecisse nulla iniustitia sit, non
curare quod feceris summa inclementia?

49. Quod si aut Deum creatorem suum abnegant aut ferarum
et bestiarum se haberi numero censent, quid de illis dicamus
qui hac se condemnant iniuria? Per omnia ire Deum ipsi
adserunt et omnia in virtute eius consistere, vim et maiesta-
tem eius per omnia elementa penetrare, terras caelum maria
et putant iniuriam eius si mentem hominis, qua nihil nobis

pain? He is all anxious within himself, and he comes to the conclusion that he will end up without an heir, for he is determined that the people who inherit his wealth must not be the kind who will copy his ways. In the end, the sinner finds he has no legacy at all. So the godless person is his own punishment, while the just person is his own reward. Each of them finds within himself the appropriate recompense for his works, whether good or evil.

47. But let us get back to our theme: we do not wish to give the XIII impression that we have announced an outline plan only to ignore it by venturing off the point in order to respond to the sort of views held by some people. Some, when they see those who are dishonest enjoying riches, happiness, honours, and privileges, while as often as not the just are weak and in need, conclude that God must have no concern for us at all. This is what the Epicureans say. Alternatively, they imagine that God has no knowledge of men's actions. This is what the wicked think. Or again, if God really does know everything, they say, he must be an unjust judge, since he allows the good to suffer so much deprivation while the evil have more than enough. Our digression to consider these challenges could scarcely be called pointless, for we found the answer to such views in the feelings of the individuals concerned: *we* may consider them to be happy, but actually, in themselves, they feel that they are utterly miserable. I thought they would find it easier to believe themselves than to believe us.

48. With this steep descent negotiated, I believe it should be easy for me to refute the other remaining points. There is, first, the argument of those who think that God has no concern whatsoever for this world. Aristotle, for example, maintains that God's providence descends only as far as the moon. Tell me this: what kind of worker is going to neglect or show no concern for his own work? Who is going to abandon and forsake the very thing he decided to make in the first place? If it is wrong to neglect something, must it not then be a greater wrong to have brought it into existence to start with? There is nothing wrong with choosing not to bring something into existence, but surely if you *have* elected to bring an object into existence you show remarkable callousness if you then show no concern for it?

49. As for those who deny that God is their creator, or believe that they should simply be numbered with the wild animals and the beasts—what do we say to people who condemn themselves with this insult? They themselves maintain that God pervades everything, that everything subsists in his power, and that his might and majesty penetrate all the elements—the earth, the heavens, and the seas. Do they then imagine that it is insulting for him to penetrate the mind of

ipse praestantius dedit, penetret et divinae maiestatis ingrediatur scientia?

50. Sed horum magistrum velut ebrium et voluptatis patronum ipsi qui putantur sobrii irrident philosophi. Nam de Aristotelis opinione quid loquar, qui putat Deum suis contentum esse finibus et praescripto regni modo degere, ut poetarum loquuntur fabulae, qui mundum ferunt inter tres esse divisum, ut alii caelum, alii mare, alii inferna coercenda imperio sorte obvenerint, eosque cavere ne usurpata alienarum partium sollicitudine inter se bellum excitent? Similiter ergo adserit quod terrarum curam non habeat, sicut maris vel inferni non habet. Et quomodo ipsi excludunt quos sequuntur poetas?

XIV **51.** Sequitur illa responsio utrum Deum, si operis sui cura non praeterit, praetereat scientia. Ergo: *Qui plantavit aurem, non audit? Qui finxit oculum, non videt, non considerat?*

52. Non praeteriit haec vana opinio sanctos prophetas. Denique David inducit eos loquentes quos superbia inflatos adserit. Quid enim tam superbum quam cum ipsi sub peccato sint, alios indigne ferant peccatores vivere, dicentes: *Usquequo peccatores, Domine, usquequo peccatores gloriabuntur?* Et infra: *Et dixerunt: Non videbit Dominus neque intellegit Deus Iacob.* Quibus respondit propheta dicens: *Intellegite nunc insipientes in populo et stulti aliquando sapite. Qui plantavit aurem, non audit? Et qui finxit oculum, non considerat? Qui corripit gentes, non arguit, qui docet hominem scientiam? Dominus scit cogitationes hominum quoniam vanae sunt.* Qui ea quaecumque vana sunt deprehendit, ea quae sancta sunt nescit et ignorat quod ipse fecit? Potest opus suum ignorare artifex? Homo est et in opere suo latentia deprehendit: et Deus opus suum nescit? Altius ergo profundum in opere quam in auctore: et fecit

man—which is quite the most outstanding endowment he has given us—and for the knowledge of his divine majesty to enter there?

50. In any case, the philosophers who are considered to be of sober mind laugh at the one who taught these people to think this way: he was just a drunkard, they say, a man who championed sensual pleasure. And what about Aristotle's views? He thinks that God is content to stay within his limits, that he lives within the prescribed bounds of his kingdom. This is the selfsame picture that the poets give us in their tales. They tell us that the universe has been divided between three beings, and their respective dominions have been determined purely by the way the lots have fallen, so that one has control over the heavens, another over the sea, and another over the lower regions. They also say that each of these three has to be careful not to stir up a war with his fellows by seizing responsibility for the areas which do not belong to him. This is just what Aristotle is saying when he claims that God has no concern for the earth, and none either for the sea or for the lower regions. How can the same people pretend to shun the poets, when they follow their paths so closely?

51. The next question we must answer is this: if it is not beyond God **XIV** to have a concern for his own work, is it beyond him to have a knowledge of that work? This is how we find it put: 'He who formed the ear, does he not hear? He who fashioned the eye, does he not see, does he not take notice?'

52. This futile idea was not beyond the experience of the holy prophets; they too encountered it. For example, David gives us the words of people who, he tells us, are puffed up with pride. And what greater pride could there be than this—people in the grip of sin themselves, claiming that other sinners have no right to live, and saying: 'How long will sinners boast, Lord, how long?'? Then further on we read this: 'And they have said: "The Lord will not see, and the God of Jacob takes no notice."' This is what the prophet says in reply: 'Pay heed now, you senseless ones among the people, and you fools, be wise at last. He who formed the ear, does he not hear? And he who fashioned the eye, does he not take notice? He who corrects the nations, does he not judge us critically, the one who teaches man knowledge? The Lord knows the thoughts of men, that they are futile.' This One who observes all that is futile—does he not know what is holy, and has he no knowledge of what he himself has made? Can a craftsman be ignorant of his own work? A craftsman is a mere man, and he can look into the hidden depths of his work: does God then have no knowledge of *his* work? If so, there is a greater profundity in the work than in its creator. Did God make something superior to himself, something whose value he, the creator, does not know, and of

aliquid quod supra se esset cuius meritum ignoraret auctor, cuius adfectum nesciret arbiter? Haec illi.

53. Ceterum nobis satis est ipsius testimonium qui ait: *Ego sum scrutans corda et renes*. Et in evangelio quod ait Dominus Iesus: *Quid cogitatis mala in cordibus vestris?* Sciebat enim quod cogitarent mala. Denique evangelista testatur dicens: *Sciebat enim Iesus cogitationes eorum*.

54. Quorum non poterit satis ⟨nos⟩ movere opinio si facta eorum consideremus. Nolunt supra se esse iudicem quem nihil fallat, nolunt ei dare occultorum scientiam qui metuunt occulta sua prodi. Sed etiam Dominus sciens opera eorum tradidit eos in tenebras: *In nocte, inquit, erit fur. Et oculus adulteri servavit tenebras dicens: Non considerabit me oculus, et latibulum personae posuit suae*. Omnis enim qui lucem fugit, diligit tenebras studens latere, cum Deum latere non possit, qui intra profundum abyssi et intra hominum mentes non solum tractata sed etiam volvenda cognoscit. Denique et ille qui dicit in Ecclesiastico: *Quis me videt? Et tenebrae operiunt me et parietes, quem vereor?*, quamvis in lecto suo positus haec cogitet, ubi non putaverit comprehenditur. *Et erit,* inquit, *dedecus quod non intellexerit timorem Dei*.

55. Quid autem tam stolidum quam putare quod Deum quidquam praetereat, cum sol qui minister luminis est etiam abdita penetret et in fundamenta domus vel secreta conclavia vis caloris eius irrumpat? Quis neget verna temperie tepefieri interiora terrarum quas glacies hiberna constrinxerit? Norunt ergo arborum occulta vim caloris vel frigoris, adeo ut radices arborum aut urantur frigore aut fotu solis virescant. Denique ubi clementia caeli adriserit, varios terra se fundit in fructus.

56. Si igitur radius solis fundit lumen suum super omnem terram et in ea, quae clausa sunt, inserit nec vectibus ferreis aut gravium valvarum obicibus, quominus penetret, impeditur, quomodo non potest intelligibilis Dei splendor in cogitationes hominum et corda semet, quae ipse creavit, inserere? Sed ea quae ipse fecit non videt, et fecit ut meliora sint quae facta sunt et potentiora quam ipse est qui ea fecit, ut possint,

whose condition he, the judge, is unaware? This is what these people are suggesting!

53. For us, though, it is enough to go by the testimony of the one who says: 'I am he who searches heart and reins.' And in the gospel the Lord Jesus says: 'Why do you harbour evil thoughts in your hearts?' For he knew that they were harbouring evil thoughts. The evangelist himself bears witness to this, when he says: 'For Jesus knew their thoughts.'

54. These people's views will not disturb us if we examine their actions. They are not prepared to have a judge who is superior to themselves, one whom nothing whatsoever can deceive; they are not prepared to grant him the knowledge of secrets, for they are worried that their own secrets will be divulged. But the Lord himself, knowing their works, delivered them over to darkness. 'In the night,' he says, 'he will be a thief. And the eye of the adulterer has waited for darkness, saying: "No eye will notice me; he has placed a veil over his face."' Everyone who flees the light loves darkness, eager to avoid detection; but no one can possibly avoid the detection of God, for whether it be in the innermost depths of the abyss or in the innermost places of the hearts of men, he knows all things—not only what goes on but even what is planned. Again, take the case of the man in Ecclesiasticus who says: 'Who sees me? The darkness and the walls hide me: of whom should I be afraid?' He may think like this when he is lying on his bed, but he finds himself caught just where he never imagined it. 'And it will be to his shame,' Scripture says, 'that he did not know the fear of God.'

55. What could be so stupid as to suppose that anything could pass God by? The sun itself, the supplier of light, penetrates every nook and cranny, and the force of its heat breaks into the foundations and the innermost recesses of a house. Who would deny that the mildness of spring weather warms the inner depths of the earth, even when they have been fastened firmly together by the winter's ice? The hidden parts of trees can feel the force of heat or cold so acutely that the roots of the trees end up withered by the cold or become vibrant thanks to the warmth of the sun. And then, when heaven smiles indulgently, the earth pours forth all manner of crops.

56. Well, if a single ray of the sun can pour its light over all the earth and reach into parts which are hidden from our sight, its penetration prevented neither by iron bolts nor by the barriers of heavy doors, how can the brilliance of the divine intelligence possibly fail to reach into the thoughts of men and into the very hearts which God himself has created? Are we really to believe that God does not see what he has made, that he has made everything that is made to be better and more

quando volunt, cognitionem sui operatoris latere? Tantam ergo virtutem et potestatem inseruit mentibus nostris ut eam comprehendere, cum velit, ipse non possit?

XV 57. Duo absolvimus et, ut arbitramur, non incongrue nobis huiusmodi cecidit disputatio. Tertium genus quaestionis residet huiusmodi: cur peccatores abundent opibus et divitiis, epulentur iugiter, sine maerore, sine luctu, iusti autem egeant et adficiantur aut coniugum amissione aut liberorum? Quibus satisfacere debuit illa evangelii parabola, quod dives bysso et purpura induebatur et epulas copiosas exhibebat cotidie, pauper autem plenus ulcerum de mensa eius colligebat reliquias. Post obitum vero utriusque, pauper erat in sinu Abrahae requiem habens, dives autem in suppliciis. Nonne evidens est meritorum aut praemia aut supplicia post mortem manere?

58. Et recte, quia in certamine labor est, post certamen aliis victoria, aliis ignominia. Numquid, priusquam cursus conficiatur, palma cuiquam datur aut defertur corona? Merito Paulus: *Certamen*, inquit, *bonum certavi, cursum consummavi, fidem servavi; quod reliquum, reposita est mihi corona iustitiae, quam reddet mihi Dominus in illa die, iustus iudex, non solum autem mihi sed etiam his qui diligunt adventum eius. In illa*, inquit, *die reddet*, non hic. Hic autem in laboribus, in periculis, in naufragiis, quasi athleta bonus decertabat, quia sciebat quoniam per multas tribulationes oportet nos introire in regnum Dei. Ergo non potest quis praemium accipere nisi legitime certaverit, nec est gloriosa victoria nisi ubi fuerint laboriosa certamina.

XVI 59. Nonne iniustus est qui ante dat praemium quam certamen fuerit absolutum? Ideoque Dominus in evangelio ait: *Beati pauperes spiritu quoniam ipsorum est regnum caelorum.* Non dixit: *Beati divites*, sed *pauperes*. Inde incipit beatitudo iudicio divino ubi aerumna aestimatur humano. *Beati qui esuriunt quia ipsi saturabuntur. Beati qui lugent quoniam ipsi consolationem habebunt. Beati misericordes quoniam ipsis*

powerful than he is himself, its maker—so that, whenever it wishes, it can escape the knowledge of the One who gave it its origin? Has he then planted in our minds a force and a power so great that when *he* wishes to comprehend *them* he cannot do it?

57. We have now dealt with two of the points, and, if we may say so, **XV** the argument has not gone too badly for us so far. There remains a third challenge, and it is this: why is it that sinners get to live in luxury and wealth, always going from one banquet to another, never knowing sorrow and never knowing grief, while the just are forever in need and constantly afflicted by loss of one kind or another, either of wives or of children? The great parable told in the gospel ought to have been answer enough for those who reason this way. There was a rich man: he went around in fine linen and purple, and held vast banquets every day of his life. And there was a poor man: he was covered in sores, and all he had was the scraps he gathered from the rich man's table. But look at what happened to each of them after death: the poor man found himself in Abraham's bosom, enjoying rest, while the rich man woke up in torments. Surely this should be sufficient to convince us that it is after death that our just deserts await us—whatever they be, whether rewards or torments.

58. And this is only right, for while a contest is going on there is hard work for everyone, and after the contest there is victory for some and disgrace for others. No one is ever given the palm or awarded the crown before the course is completed, is he? How appropriate Paul's words are: 'I have fought the good fight, I have finished the course, I have kept the faith; now there is laid up for me a crown of right-eousness, which the Lord, the righteous judge, will confer upon me on that day, and not only upon me, but also upon those who love his coming.' It is 'on that day' that God 'will confer' it upon him, he tells us; not here. Here, he endured all kinds of labours, dangers, and shipwrecks, and fought on to the end like a good athlete, for he knew that we must go through many tribulations to enter the kingdom of God. So, no one can receive the prize unless he has competed according to the rules, and there is no glory in victory except where the contests have cost real effort.

59. It is quite unjust, surely, for anyone to award a prize before a **XVI** contest has been completed? This is why the Lord says in the gospel: 'Blessed are the poor in spirit, for theirs is the kingdom of heaven.' He did not say: 'Blessed are the rich,' but 'Blessed are the poor.' So, in the judgement of God, blessedness, or true happiness, begins in the very place where, in the judgement of men, there is nothing but misery. 'Blessed are those who hunger, for they shall be filled. Blessed are those who mourn, for they shall receive comfort. Blessed are the

miserebitur Deus. Beati mundo corde quoniam ipsi Deum vide-
bunt. Beati qui persecutionem patiuntur propter iustitiam quo-
niam ipsorum est regnum caelorum. Beati estis cum vobis
maledicent et persequentur et dicent omne malum adversum vos
propter iustitiam. Gaudete et exsultate quoniam merces vestra
copiosa est in caelo. Futuram, non praesentem, in caelo, non in
terra mercedem promisit esse reddendam. Quid alibi poscis
quod alibi debetur? Quid praepropere coronam exigis antequam vincas? Quid detergere pulverem? Quid requiescere
cupis? Quid epulari gestis antequam stadium soluatur?
Adhuc populus spectat, adhuc athletae in scammate sunt, et
tu iam otium petis?

60. Sed forte dicas: Cur impii laetantur? Cur luxuriantur?
Cur etiam ipsi non mecum laborant? Quoniam qui non
subscripserint ad coronam, non tenentur ad laborem certaminis; qui in stadium non descenderint, non se perfundunt oleo,
non oblinunt pulvere. Quos manet gloria, exspectat iniuria.
Unguentati spectare solent, non decertare, non solem aestus
pulverem imbresque perpeti. Dicant ergo et ipsi athletae:
Venite, nobiscum laborate. Sed respondebunt spectatores:
Nos hic interim de vobis iudicamus, vos autem sine nobis
coronae, si viceritis, gloriam vindicabitis.

61. Isti igitur qui in deliciis, qui in luxuria rapinis quaestibus
honoribus studia posuerunt sua, spectatores magis sunt quam
proeliatores. Habent lucrum laboris, fructum virtutis non
habent. Fovent otium, astutia et improbitate aggerant divitiarum acervos; sed exsolvent, seram licet, nequitiae suae
poenam. Horum requies in infernis, tua vero in caelo;
horum domus in sepulcro, tua in paradiso. Unde pulchre
vigilare eos in tumulo Iob dixit, quia soporem quietis habere
non possunt quem ille dormivit qui resurrexit.

62. Noli igitur ut parvulus sapere, ut parvulus loqui, ut
parvulus cogitare, ut parvulus vindicare ea quae sunt poster-
ioris aetatis. Perfectorum est corona. Exspecta ut *veniat quod*
perfectum est, quando non *per speciem in aenigmate*, sed *facie*
ad faciem formam ipsam redopertae veritatis possis cognos-
cere. Tunc qua causa ille dives fuerit qui erat improbus et

merciful, for God will show mercy to them. Blessed are the pure in heart, for they shall see God. Blessed are those who suffer persecution for the sake of righteousness, for theirs is the kingdom of heaven. Blessed are you, when men speak ill of you, persecute you, and say all kinds of evil things against you for the sake of righteousness. Rejoice and be glad, for rich is your reward in heaven.' It was a future reward, not a present one, that he promised would be given: it was in heaven, not on earth. Why are you demanding something in one place that is due in another? Why are you so impatient to get the crown before you have won the battle? Why are you so keen to wipe away the dust, why are you so keen to rest? Why are you set on joining the celebration feast before the course has been completed? The people are still watching, the athletes are still in the arena, and are you already asking for a rest?
60. But maybe you will say: 'Why are the wicked so pleased with themselves? Why is it that they have enough and to spare? Why are they not labouring along with me?' Why? It is because those who have not entered their names in the competition for the crown are not obliged to endure the labour of the contest. Those who have not gone down into the arena do not anoint themselves with oil, they do not smear themselves with dust. For everyone for whom glory is reserved, there is also pain awaiting. People who go around delicately perfumed spend their time watching, not fighting, or enduring the sun, the heat, the dust, and the rain. The athletes could well say to them: 'Come now, how about sharing the labour with us?' But the spectators would reply: 'No, for now we are here to judge you. But you are the ones who will get the glory of the crown, if you win—not us.'
61. So then, people who have devoted their energies to indulging in pleasures, or to living an extravagant lifestyle, or stealing from others, or making easy profits, or chasing honours, are spectators rather than combatants. They may have the advantage of no exertion, but they do not have the reward that virtue brings. They cherish the leisure that they enjoy, and through sharp practice and dishonesty they heap up great piles of riches for themselves. But, however belatedly, they will pay the penalty for their wickedness. Their rest is in hell, yours is in heaven; their home is in the grave, yours is in paradise. Job put it so well: even in the tomb, he said, they must be watchful, for they are unable to enjoy the peaceful sleep slept by the one who has risen again.
62. So then, stop judging like a child, speaking like a child, thinking like a child, and behaving like a child, by laying claim to things which belong to an age yet to come. The crown is for those who are perfect. Wait 'till that which is perfect comes', when not 'through a glass obscurely' but 'face to face' you are able to recognize the actual form of the truth, which at present is hidden. Only then will it be revealed to

raptor alieni, qua causa potens alius, qua causa ille abunda-
verit liberis, ille fultus honoribus, revelabitur.

63. Fortasse dicatur raptori: Dives eras: qua causa aliena
rapiebas? Egestas non compulit, inopia non coegit. Nonne
ideo te divitem feci, ut excusationem habere non possis?
Dicatur etiam potenti: Cur non adfuisti viduae, orphanis
quoque iniuriam patientibus? Numquid tu infirmus eras?
Numquid non poteras subvenire? Ideo te feci potentem, ut
non inferres violentiam sed repelleres. Non tibi scriptum est:
Eripe iniuriam accipientem? Non scriptum est: *Eripite pauperem et egenum de manu peccatoris liberate?* Dicatur etiam
abundanti: Liberis et honoribus te cumulavi, salubritatem
corporis concessi tibi; cur non secutus es praecepta mea?
Famulus meus, *quid feci tibi aut quid contristavi te?* Nonne
ego tibi liberos dedi, honores contuli, salutem donavi? Cur me
negabas? Cur aestimabas quod ad scientiam meam quae
gereres non pervenirent? Cur tenebas dona mea, despiciebas
mandata mea?

64. Denique de Iuda proditore haec colligere licet, qui et
apostolus inter duodecim electus est et loculos pecuniarum
quas pauperibus erogaret, commissos habebat, ne videretur
aut quasi inhonorus aut quasi egenus Dominum prodidisse.
Et ideo ut iustificaretur in eo Dominus, haec ei contulit, ut
non quasi iniuria exasperatus sed quasi praevaricatus gratiam,
maiori esset offensae obnoxius.

XVII **65.** Quoniam igitur et poenam improbitati et virtuti fore
praemium satis claruit, de officiis adgrediamur dicere quae
nobis ab adulescentia spectanda sunt, ut cum aetate accrescant
simul. Est igitur bonorum adulescentium timorem Dei
habere, deferre parentibus, honorem habere senioribus, castitatem tueri, non aspernari humilitatem, diligere clementiam
ac verecundiam, quae ornamento sunt minori aetati. Ut enim

you why one man who was corrupt and stole from others was rich, or why another man exercised such power and influence, or why this one had so many children, or why that one was bolstered by all sorts of honours.

63. It may well be that it will be said to the one who stole: 'You were rich: why did you steal from other people? You were not forced into it by any kind of need, or driven to it by any kind of shortage. I made you rich for this very reason, did I not, so that you should have no excuse?' It may well be said to the one who had a position of power and influence: 'Why did you not come to the aid of that widow, or those orphans who suffered injustice? It wasn't that you were too weak to do anything, was it? It wasn't that you were in no position to offer help, was it? I gave you all that power for a purpose—so that you would not inflict violence on people but drive it away from them. Was it not for you that it was written: "Rescue the person who is experiencing injustice"? Was it not written: "Rescue the poor man and set the needy man free from the hand of the sinner"?' And it may well be said to the one who had so much: 'I lavished upon you the gifts of children and honours. I allowed you bodily health. Why did you not follow my precepts? My servant, what have I ever done to you? What grief have I ever caused you? Was it not I who gave you the children, brought you all the honours, and granted you the well-being you enjoyed? Why did you deny me? Why did you imagine that your behaviour did not come to my knowledge? Why did you hold on to my gifts, but despise my commandments?'

64. We can see that this is so from the case of the traitor Judas. He was chosen as an apostle, one of the Twelve, and had charge of the money-bags, to make the payments to the poor; this way, no one could think that it was a man who had been deprived of all honour, or one who was in genuine need, who had betrayed the Lord. And the Lord granted Judas all these privileges precisely so that he might be justified in him, for if it transpired that the traitor had not been provoked by any kind of injustice but had deliberately sinned against grace he would be guilty of an even more terrible crime.

65. Since there is plenty of evidence, then, that there will be **XVII** punishment for wicked behaviour and reward for virtue in a coming day, let us now start to discuss the actual subject of duties. There are various obligations which we need to observe from the days of our youth, so that they will develop as we grow older. Young men who are of good character need to maintain a fear of God, submit to their parents, respect their elders, and keep a close watch on their chastity. They should not despise humility, but love gentleness and modesty of character—these things are an adornment

in senibus gravitas, in iuvenibus alacritas, ita in adulescentibus verecundia velut quadam dote commendatur naturae.

66. Erat Isaac Dominum timens, utpote Abrahae indoles,
deferens patri usque eo ut adversus paternam voluntatem
nec mortem recusaret. Ioseph quoque, cum somniasset quod
sol et luna et stellae adorarent eum, sedulo tamen obsequio
deferebat patri, castus ita ut ne sermonem quidem audire
vellet nisi pudicum, humilis usque ad servitutem, verecundus
usque ad fugam, patiens usque ad carcerem, remissor iniuriae
usque ad remunerationem. Cuius tanta verecundia fuit ut,
comprehensus a muliere, vestem in manibus eius fugiens
vellet relinquere quam verecundiam deponere. Moyses
quoque et Ieremias, electi a Domino ut oracula Dei praedi-
carent populo, quod poterant per gratiam, excusabant per
verecundiam.

XVIII **67.** Pulchra igitur virtus est verecundiae et suavis gratia, quae
non solum in factis sed etiam in ipsis spectatur sermonibus,
ne ⟨ultra⟩ modum progrediaris loquendi, ne quid indecorum
sermo resonet tuus. Speculum enim mentis plerumque in
verbis refulget. Ipsum vocis sonum librat modestia ne cuius-
quam offendat aurem vox fortior. Denique in ipso canendi
genere prima disciplina verecundiae est; immo etiam in omni
usu loquendi, ut sensim quis aut psallere aut canere aut
postremo loqui incipiat, ut verecunda principia commendent
processum.

68. Silentium quoque ipsum, in quo est reliquarum virtutum
otium, maximus actus verecundiae est. Denique si aut infan-
tiae putatur aut superbiae, probro datur; si verecundiae, laudi
ducitur. Tacebat in periculis Susanna et gravius verecundiae
quam vitae damnum putabat nec arbitrabatur periculo
pudoris tuendam salutem. Deo soli loquebatur, cui poterat
casta verecundia eloqui; refugiebat ora intueri virum. Est

to a person's early years. In the same way that old men ought to show gravity, and youths display energy, in young men the quality that commends itself is modesty—it is as though nature herself had endowed things this way.

66. Isaac maintained a fear of the Lord, showing that he was worthy to be called a son of Abraham, and he was so submissive to his father that he did not hesitate to face even death itself if it meant going against his father's wishes to refuse. Joseph, too—he had seen the sun, moon, and stars all bowing down to worship him in a dream, yet he submitted to his father with a ready devotion. He was so chaste that he would not listen to a single word if it was not pure. He was so humble that he endured slavery; so modest that he ran for his life; so patient that he put up with prison; and so ready to forgive those who had treated him unjustly that he even did them good in return. Here is the measure of his modesty: there he was, with a woman with her arms around him, and he resolved to leave his cloak in her hands and run for his life rather than surrender his modesty! Moses, too, and Jeremiah, were both chosen by the Lord to declare the oracles of God to their people, yet they sought to excuse themselves from the task: their grace rendered them capable of doing it, yet their modesty made them resist.

67. What a beautiful virtue modesty is, then; how delightful and full **XVIII** of grace it always is. It can be seen not just in what people do, but also in what they say. It guarantees that you never go beyond the measure that is appropriate when you speak and that your language never drops an unseemly note. The image of our spirit is so often reflected in the words that we use. Moderation balances even the sound of the voice, so that if a person has a voice that is a little on the strong side it will not offend anyone's ear. In the art of singing, the very first rule people have to learn is the importance of modesty. Indeed, this applies not just in singing, but in any vocal process: a person always has to start off in the same gradual manner, whether he is going to intone a psalm, or sing, or indeed speak. The idea is that if you begin modestly, you will commend what is to follow.

68. Silence, too, that disposition which offers space for all the other virtues, is a marvellous expression of modesty. Of course, if our silence is taken to be the silence of childishness or pride, it deserves to be criticized; but if it is the silence of modesty, it is a cause for praise. Susanna kept silent even in the midst of great dangers: to her, it was a more serious calamity to lose her modesty than to lose her life, and she was firmly resolved not to preserve her overall safety at the expense of her chastity. It was to God alone that she spoke: chaste and modest as she was, she was able to lift her voice to him, though

enim et in oculis verecundia ut nec videre viros femina nec videri velit.

69. Neque vero quisquam solius hanc laudem castitatis putet. Est enim verecundia pudicitiae comes, cuius societate castitas ipsa tutior est. Bonus enim regendae castitatis pudor est comes, qui, si praetendat et ⟨praecaveat⟩ quae prima pericula sunt, pudicitiam temptari non sinat. Hic primus, in ipso cognitionis ingressu, Domini matrem commendat legentibus et, tamquam testis locuples, dignam quae ad tale munus eligeretur, adstruit: quod in cubiculo, quod sola, quod salutata ab angelo tacet et mota est in introitu eius, quod ad virilis sexus speciem peregrinatur aspectus virginis. Itaque quamvis esset humilis, prae verecundia tamen non resalutavit nec ullum responsum retulit nisi ubi de suscipienda Domini generatione cognovit, ut qualitatem effectus disceret, non ut sermonem proferret.

70. In ipsa oratione nostra multum verecundia placet, multum conciliat gratiae apud Deum nostrum. Nonne haec praetulit publicanum et commendavit eum, qui nec oculos suos audebat ad caelum levare? Ideo iustificatur magis Domini iudicio quam ille Pharisaeus, quem deformavit praesumptio. Ideoque oremus *in incorruptione quieti et modesti spiritus qui est ante Deum locuples,* ut ait Petrus. Magna igitur modestia quae eum sit etiam sui iuris remissior, nihil sibi usurpans, nihil vindicans et quodam modo intra vires suas contractior, dives est apud Deum, apud quem nemo dives. Dives est modestia quia Dei portio est. Paulus quoque orationem deferri praecepit *cum verecundia et sobrietate.* Primam hanc et quasi praeviam vult esse orationis futurae, ut non glorietur peccatoris oratio sed quasi colorem pudoris obducat, ⟨et⟩ quo plus defert verecundiae de recordatione delicti, hoc uberiorem mereatur gratiam.

71. Est etiam in ipso motu gestu incessu tenenda verecundia. Habitus enim mentis in corporis statu cernitur. Hinc *homo*

she shrank from looking at the face of any man—for there is also a modesty to be found in the eyes, where a woman prefers not to see or be seen by men.

69. But no one should suppose that it is only chastity that earns this kind of praise. Modesty also acts as a companion to purity, and in its company chastity itself is all the more secure. Shame makes a good companion and guide for chastity: when it is always on the lookout and on its guard against the first signs of danger, it ensures that purity suffers no violation. This shame is the first thing that strikes us when we encounter the mother of our Lord, and it commends her to everyone who reads her story; it is like a reliable witness, testifying that she was indeed worthy to be chosen for the great task appointed to her. Here she is, in her chamber, and on her own; she keeps silent when the angel greets her and is distressed when he comes into the room; and, chaste virgin that she is, she blushes at the sight of a member of the opposite sex. She was humble, yes, but such was her modesty that she did not return his greeting or make any response to him—not until she heard that her mission was to conceive and bear the Lord himself; and even then she spoke only to ask how this amazing thing could be so, not to talk for the sake of talking.

70. If we ask how we should pray ourselves, a spirit of modesty is a most pleasing quality here too, and one that wins us great favour with our God. What was it that made the publican better in God's sight and rendered him so commendable? It was his modesty, of course: he would not even dare to lift his eyes to heaven. This was why in the Lord's judgement it was he, not the Pharisee, who was justified, for the Pharisee marred his own claims by his presumption. This is also the reason why we should pray 'in the incorruptibility of a quiet and moderate spirit, for this is of great value in the sight of God,' as Peter says. Moderation is a great thing, then: it is not interested in asserting any rights of its own, it makes no claims for itself, it makes no assumptions, and by one means or another it confines itself entirely within the limits of its own resources; yet it is rich in the sight of God—and in his sight no one is rich. Moderation is rich, because it is the portion of God himself. Paul also taught us that prayer should be presented 'with modesty and sobriety'. His desire was that this should come first—that it should be, if you like, a signpost to the kind of prayer that is to follow: that the sinner's prayer should not be boastful, but should as it were veil itself with a blush of shame. The more a person is inclined to modesty as he recollects his faults, the more abundant the favour he merits.

71. Modesty ought to be maintained in all our physical movement as well, in the way we carry ourselves, and in the way we walk. It is from

cordis nostri absconditus aut levior aut iactantior aut turbidior, aut contra gravior et constantior et purior et maturior aestimatur. Itaque vox quaedam est animi corporis motus.

72. Meministis, filii, quemdam amicum, cum sedulis se videretur commendare officiis, hoc solo tamen in clerum a me non receptum, quod gestus eius plurimum dedeceret; alterum quoque, cum in clero repperissem, iubere me ne umquam praeiret mihi, quia velut quodam insolentis incessus verbere oculos feriret meos. Idque dixi cum redderetur post offensam muneri. Hoc solum excepi, nec fefellit sententia: uterque enim ab ecclesia recessit, ut qualis incessu prodebatur, talis perfidia animi demonstraretur. Namque alter Arianae infestationis tempore fidem deseruit, alter pecuniae studio, ne iudicium subiret sacerdotale, se nostrum negavit. Lucebat in illorum incessu imago levitatis, species quaedam scurrarum percursantium.

73. Sunt etiam qui sensim ambulando imitantur histrionicos gestus et quasi quaedam fercula pomparum et statuarum motus nutantium; ut quotienscumque gradum transferunt modulos quosdam servare videantur.

74. Nec cursim ambulare honestum arbitror, nisi cum causa exigit alicuius periculi uel iusta necessitas. Nam plerumque festinantes anhelos videmus torquere ora; quibus si causa desit festinationis necessariae, naevus iustae offensionis est. Sed non de his dico quibus rara properatio ex causa nascitur, sed quibus iugis et continua in naturam vertit. Nec in illis ergo tamquam simulacrorum effigies probo nec in istis tamquam excursorum ruinas.

75. Est etiam gressus probabilis, in quo sit species auctoritatis, gravitatisque pondus, tranquillitatis vestigium, ita tamen si studium desit atque adfectatio sed motus sit purus

the attitude of the body that the condition of the spirit is gauged. This is the evidence upon which people form their opinions of 'the hidden man of our heart', concluding that here is someone who is rather fickle, perhaps, or boastful, or prone to get upset—or, alternatively, that this is a person who is altogether firm and steady, pure, and mature. The movement of the body thus acts as a kind of voice for the soul.

72. You will recall, my sons, a certain friend of ours. He appeared to commend himself by carrying out his duties with due care, yet I still refused to admit him into the body of the clergy. I had one reason only, and it was this: he carried himself physically in a way that was totally unseemly. You will recall another man, too. He was already a member of the clergy when I first encountered him, but I issued instructions that he was never to walk in front of me, for the cocky way in which he walked was—to be frank—painful for me to behold. And I said just that when he was restored to his office after committing his offence. I had no other reason but this to reject these men; but I did not prove mistaken in my judgement, for both of them went on to leave the church: they showed themselves to be every bit as faithless in spirit as their style of walking had suggested. One deserted the faith at the time of the Arian onslaught; the other was so keen on money that he was prepared to say he was not one of us, so as to escape being judged by his bishop. The hallmark of the fickleness inside these men was plain in the way they walked—they had all the appearance of wandering jesters.

73. On the other hand, there are people who walk so slowly that they appear to be imitating the sort of contrived movements which actors make, or even the motions of statues nodding on litters at processions: with every step they take they look as though they are observing some vague, imaginary rhythm.

74. Nevertheless, I do not think it is honourable to walk too hurriedly, either, unless it is essential to do so in some situation of danger or where there is a legitimate necessity. So often we see people hurrying along, puffing and panting, their faces all distorted with the exertion they are putting themselves through. If there is no necessary reason for their haste, they are giving reasonable grounds for offence. I am not speaking here about people who occasionally have good reason to hurry, but about those to whom constant and persistent haste has become second nature. So, on the one hand, I do not approve of people looking like statues, nor, on the other, of people virtually tripping over themselves in a mad rush to dash about their business.

75. There is, though, another type of gait, one of which we can approve, which gives an impression of authority, of firmness and gravity, and a sense of calm purpose. The important thing is to keep

ac simplex: nihil enim fucatum placet. Motum natura infor-
met. Si quid sane in natura vitii est, industria emendet; ut ars
desit, non desit correctio.

76. Quod si etiam ista spectantur altius, quanto magis cavendum est ne quid turpe ore exeat; hoc enim graviter coinquinat
hominem. Non enim cibus inquinat sed iniusta obtrectatio,
sed verborum obscenitas. Haec etiam vulgo pudori sunt. In
nostro vero officio nullum ⟨sit⟩ verbum quod inhoneste cadat
aut incutiat verecundiam. Sed non solum nihil ipsi indecorum
loqui sed ne aurem quidem debemus huiusmodi praebere
dictis, sicut Ioseph, ne incongrua suae audiret verecundiae,
veste fugit relicta; quoniam quem delectat audire, alterum
loqui provocat.

77. Intellegere quoque quod turpe sit, pudori maximo est.
Spectare vero, si quid huiusmodi fortuito accidat, quanti
horroris est! Quod ergo in aliis displicet, numquid potest in
se ipso placere? Nec ipsa natura nos docet, quae perfecte
quidem omnes partes nostri corporis explicavit ut et necessitati consuleret et gratiam venustaret? Sed tamen eas quae
decorae ad aspectum forent, in quibus formae apex, quasi in
arce quadam locatus et figurae suavitas et vultus species
emineret, operandique usus esset paratior, obvias atque aper-
tas reliquit; eas vero in quibus esset naturale obsequium
necessitatis, ne deforme sui praeberent spectaculum, partim
tamquam in ipso amandavit atque abscondit corpore, partim
docuit et suasit tegendas.

78. Nonne igitur ipsa natura est magistra verecundiae? Cuius
exemplo modestia hominum, quam a modo scientiae quid
deceret appellatam arbitror, id quod in hac nostri corporis
fabrica abditum repperit, operuit et texit; ut ostium illud
quod ex transverso faciendum in arca illa Noe iusto dictum
est, in qua vel ecclesiae vel nostri figura est corporis, per quod

studied effort and affectation out of it, and to allow your movement to be natural and simple; for no kind of falsehood can ever be pleasing. Let nature herself shape your movement. If, of course, there is some flaw in the style nature has given you, then by all means try to put it right with a little hard work: it is artificiality that needs to be kept out of things, not an appropriate measure of correction.

76. If we can explore the theme of modesty a little further, I would say this: we must take even more care to ensure that nothing shameful ever comes out of our mouth, for that is something that brings serious defilement to a man. It is not food that pollutes; it is the unjust disparagement of other people, it is the use of language that is foul. Even the common crowd holds that it is shameful to behave that way. In our office, then, not a word should slip out dishonourably, or in a way which offends modesty. Indeed, not only ought we to refrain from saying anything unseemly ourselves; we should never even lend an ear to talk like that. That was what Joseph did: he turned and ran for his life, leaving his cloak behind, rather than listen to proposals which affronted his modesty. For if one person shows that he likes to hear such things, he incites another to come out with them.

77. To know about what is shameful is a great disgrace, too. Actually to pay close attention to such a thing, if it should happen by accident, is dreadful! How can it give us any pleasure to find in ourselves the very behaviour which it gives us no pleasure to encounter in other people? Does not nature herself teach us? She arranged all the parts of our body perfectly, ensuring both that our needs were provided for and that we were given the most attractive appearance possible. She did it, though, in a particular way, namely by leaving open and on display only the parts which it would be seemly for others to see. At the head of these, the crown of our beauty—placed at the top like a kind of citadel—the pleasantness of our overall physical form, and the features of our face are prominent, and their practical purpose is ready to hand. But, when nature came to the parts which were designed only to serve our needs, she either tucked them out of the way, so to speak, by concealing them in the body itself, or else she taught us persuasively to cover them up, so that they would not present an unsightly spectacle.

78. Nature herself, then, is a teacher of modesty, is she not? Following her example, human moderation (the word 'moderation', *modestia*, took its name, I believe, from *modus*, which suggests the due measure of the knowledge of what is seemly) has chosen to hide and conceal the parts which it has found already hidden in the way our body is constructed. Think of the door that the just man Noah was told he had to construct in the side of the ark: it can be taken as a figure of the church, but it can also be taken as a figure of our body, for it is through

ostium egeruntur reliquiae ciborum. Ergo naturae opifex sic nostrae studuit verecundiae, sic decorum illud et honestum in nostro custodivit corpore ut ductus quosdam atque exitus cuniculorum nostrorum post tergum relegaret atque ab aspectu nostro averteret, ne purgatio ventris visum oculorum offenderet. De quo pulchre apostolus ait: *Quae videntur,* inquit, *membra corporis infirmiora, necessariora sunt et quae putamus ignobiliora esse membra corporis, his abundantiorem honorem circumdamus et quae inhonesta sunt nostra, honestatem abundantiorem habent.* Etenim imitatione naturae industria auxit gratiam. Quod alio loco etiam altius interpretati sumus, ut non solum abscondamus ab oculis, verum etiam, quae abscondenda accipimus, eorum indicia ususque membrorum suis appellationibus nuncupare indecorum putemus.

79. Denique si casu aperiantur hae partes, confunditur verecundia, si studio, impudentia aestimatur. Unde et filius Noe Cham offensam retulit, quia nudatum videns patrem risit; qui autem operuerunt patrem acceperunt benedictionis gratiam. Ex quo mos vetus et in urbe Roma et in plerisque civitatibus fuit ut filii cum parentibus puberes vel generi cum soceris non lavarent, ne paternae reverentiae auctoritas minueretur; licet plerique se et in lavacro quantum possunt tegant ne vel illic, ubi nudum totum est corpus, huiusmodi intecta portio sit.

80. Sacerdotes quoque veteri more, sicut in Exodo legimus, bracas accipiebant, sicut ad Moysen dictum est a Domino: *Et facies illis bracas lineas ut tegatur turpitudo pudoris. A lumbis usque ad femora erunt et habebit ea Aaron et filii eius cum intrabunt in tabernaculum testimonii et cum accedent sacrificare ad aram Sancti; et non inducent super se peccatum ne moriantur.* Quod nonnulli nostrorum servare adhuc feruntur, plerique spiritali interpretatione ad cautionem verecundiae et custodiam castitatis dictum arbitrantur.

XIX **81.** Delectavit me diutius in partibus demorari verecundiae quia ad vos loquebar, qui aut bona eius ex vobis recognoscitis

the same kind of 'door' that the residue of the food we ingest is discharged. Now it was the One who fashioned nature herself who took such pains to preserve our modesty, and it was he who took such care to safeguard what is seemly and honourable in the design of our body. He placed behind our back all the different passages and tracts which come from our stomach, and put them there out of our sight; he did it to spare our eyes the embarrassment of having to look on when our bowels are being purged. The apostle makes this point so well when he says: 'Those members of our body which seem weaker are all the more necessary; and to those members of our body which we regard as less honourable we show greater honour; and those of our members which are less honourable in fact possess greater honour.' It is indeed by imitating nature that hard work has enhanced the attractiveness that the body already has. I have already explained all this at greater length elsewhere, pointing out that we not only hide from our eyes the parts that have been given us to be kept hidden, but also think it unseemly even to mention the names of these members or to speak of their functions.

79. If these parts are exposed accidentally, it is a violation of modesty; if it is done deliberately, people regard it as gross indecency. This was why Noah's son Ham incurred such resentment from his father—he laughed when he saw him naked. The sons who covered their father, however, received the favour of his blessing. It was as a result of this that the ancient custom arose, observed in the city of Rome and in many other states as well, that adult sons never bathed with their fathers, or sons-in-law with their fathers-in-law, to ensure that the proper respect due to the authority of fathers was not undermined. In actual fact, most people cover themselves as much as they can even when they are in the bath, so that even there, where almost their entire body is bare, their private parts at least are not uncovered.

80. There was another ancient custom, too, for we read in *Exodus* that the priests were given breeches. This was what the Lord instructed Moses: 'And you shall make for them linen breeches, so that their shame is covered against all disgrace. The breeches shall extend from the loins right to the thighs, and Aaron and his sons shall wear them when they enter the tent of the Testimony and when they approach the altar of the Holy One to offer sacrifice; and they shall not bring sin on themselves, lest they die.' There are a number of our brothers who are said to observe this practice still, but most interpret it spiritually, believing that the point of the injunction is the general need to preserve modesty and protect chastity.

81. I have been delighted to spend so long on modesty and its various **XIX** obligations, because it is you that I have been addressing: you either

aut damna ignoratis. Quae cum sit omnibus aetatibus personis temporibus et locis apta, tamen adulescentes iuvenalesque annos maxime decet.

82. In omni autem servandum aetate ut deceat quod agas et conveniat et quadret sibi ordo vitae tuae. Unde Tullius etiam ordinem putat in illo decore servari oportere idque positum dicit *in formositate ordine ornatu ad actionem apto*, quae difficile ait loquendo explicari posse, et ideo satis esse intellegi.

83. Formositatem autem cur posuerit, non intellego, quamvis etiam ille vires corporis laudet. Nos certe in pulchritudine corporis locum virtutis non ponimus, gratiam tamen non excludimus, quia verecundia et vultus ipsos solet pudore offundere gratioresque reddere. Ut enim artifex in materia commodiore melius operari solet, sic verecundia in ipso quoque corporis decore plus eminet, ita tamen ut etiam ipse non sit adfectatus decor corporis, sed naturalis simplex neglectus magis quam expetitus, non pretiosis et albentibus adiutus vestimentis sed communibus, ut honestati vel necessitati nihil desit, nihil accedat nitori.

84. Vox ipsa non remissa, non fracta, nihil femineum sonans, qualem multi gravitatis specie simulare consuerunt, sed formam quamdam et regulam ac sucum virilem reservans. Hoc est enim pulchritudinem vivendi tenere, convenientia cuique sexui et personae reddere. Hic ordo gestorum optimus, hic ornatus ad omnem actionem accommodus. Sed, ut molliculum et infractum aut vocis sonum aut gestum corporis non probo, ita neque agrestem ac rusticum. Naturam imitemur: eius effigies, formula disciplinae, forma honestatis est.

XX **85.** Habet sane suos scopulos verecundia, non quos ipsa invehit sed quos saepe incurrit; sed ne in intemperantium incidamus consortia, qui sub specie iucunditatis venenum infundunt bonis. Hi si assidui sunt et maxime in convivio ludo ac ioco enervant gravitatem illam virilem. Caveamus

recognize its virtues for yourselves or you have no experience of the kinds of damage it can suffer. It is appropriate for all ages, persons, times, and places, undoubtedly, but it is particularly seemly for young men and for those in their early adult years.

82. Whatever your age, you should see to it that you behave in a way that is seemly and appropriate, and make sure that there is order and equilibrium in your life. This is why Cicero also thinks it is necessary to maintain order in the context of doing what is seemly, and he says that this consists in 'physical beauty, order, and style that is suited to action'. He admits that it is difficult for these qualities to be explained in words, and so it is sufficient, he says, if they are understood.

83. Why he has given a place to physical beauty, I cannot understand, though it is true that he also praises bodily strength. We for our part certainly do not want to locate virtue in the beauty of the body. Nevertheless, we have no wish to exclude physical grace, seeing that modesty tends to spread over our features themselves with a blush of shame and manages to make them more graceful. Just as a craftsman tends to work better when his material is more suitable, so modesty too is all the more conspicuous when it is evinced in the body's own attractiveness—so long as this attractiveness of the body is in no way contrived, but is natural and simple, casual rather than carefully produced, and promoted not by the wearing of expensive or brightly coloured garb but by plain, ordinary clothes. This way, there is no neglect of what is honourable or necessary, but equally there is no pretension towards display.

84. The voice itself should not be soft or feeble, and should not sound at all effeminate, or convey the sort of tone that many people who pretend to seriousness are inclined to put on. It ought to preserve a specific accent, pitch, and manly timbre. You maintain the true beauty of your life by rendering the qualities that are appropriate for your own sex and personality. This is the best order by which to manage your deportment generally, this is the sort of style that is right in every activity. But just as I do not approve of a tone of voice or a bodily movement that is soft or effete, I equally do not approve of the kind that is coarse or uncouth. Let us imitate nature: her image is the rule by which our conduct should be governed, and the model for what is honourable.

85. Modesty has its own dangers, of course. It does not bring them on **XX** itself, but it often meets with them. All the same, we must make sure not to fall into the company of people who show no ability to control themselves, for they inject poison into those who are good, all under the guise of harmless pleasure. If good men become too closely involved in their ways—especially in their lavish dinners, their fun

itaque ne, dum relaxare animum volumus, solvamus omnem harmoniam, quasi concentum quemdam bonorum operum: usus enim cito inflectit naturam.

86. Unde prudenter facitis convenire ecclesiasticis, et maxime ministrorum officiis arbitror, declinare extraneorum convivia, vel ut ipsi hospitales sitis peregrinantibus vel ut ea cautione nullus sit opprobrio locus. Convivia quippe extraneorum occupationes habent, tum etiam epulandi produnt cupiditatem. Subrepunt etiam fabulae frequenter de saeculo ac voluptatibus: claudere aures non potes, prohibere putatur superbiae. Subrepunt etiam praeter voluntatem pocula. Melius est tuae domui semel excuses quam alienae frequenter; et, ut ipse sobrius surgas, tamen ex aliena insolentia condemnari non debet praesentia tua.

87. Viduarum ac virginum domos nisi visitandi gratia, iuniores adire non est opus, et hoc cum senioribus, hoc est cum episcopo, vel si gravior est causa, cum presbyteris. Quid necesse est ut demus saecularibus obtrectandi locum? Quid opus est ut illae quoque visitationes crebrae accipiant auctoritatem? Quid si aliqua illarum forte labatur? Cur alieni lapsus subeas invidiam? Quam multos etiam fortes illecebra decepit! Quanti non dederunt errori locum et dederunt suspicioni!

88. Cur non illa tempora quibus ab ecclesia vacas, lectioni impendas? Cur non Christum revisas, Christum adloquaris, Christum audias? Illum adloquimur cum oramus, illum audimus cum divina legimus oracula. Quid nobis cum alienis domibus? Una est domus quae omnes capit. Illi potius ad nos veniant, qui nos requirunt. Quid nobis cum fabulis? Ministerium altaribus Christi, non obsequium hominibus deferendum recepimus.

89. Humiles decet esse, mites decet, mansuetos, graves,

and games, and jocular banter—they undermine all their natural manliness and seriousness. We need to take care, then, that in our desire to relax our spirit we do not shatter the overall harmony of our character or, as it were, introduce a jarring note into the symphony of our good works. There is no doubt about it: habit soon alters nature.

86. Since this is the case, you will behave with the kind of wisdom appropriate to ecclesiastics—and especially appropriate, I think, to the duties of ministers—if you steer clear of dinner-parties held by people outside the church—either so that you can show hospitality to travellers yourself, or simply to ensure by your discretion that you do not give any occasion for scandal. The point is, dinners with those outside bring their own engrossments, not to mention the fact that they instil a fondness for eating large meals. Stories to do with the world and its pleasures often creep in, too: it is not possible for you to close your ears to them, and if you forbid them it is construed as a sign of pride on your part. Drinks also creep in, in far greater quantities than you would wish. Better to give the excuse once and for all that you would rather stay in your own home, than to be always making excuses for spending time in other people's. Besides, you may well leave the table quite sober yourself, but it cannot be right to bring criticism on yourself for being present where others have over-indulged.

87. There is no reason for younger men to go near the houses of widows and virgins, unless they are on an official visit. Even this should be done in the company of older men—namely, the bishop, or, if the situation is that serious, with the priests. Why should we give worldly people occasion to criticize us? Why should such visits take on some significance by their frequency? What if one of these women were by chance to fall? Why should you come under reproach because someone else has fallen? Think how many men there are, strong men, too, who have been taken in by charms like these! Think how many there are who have given no occasion for any kind of transgression, but have given plenty of occasion for suspicion!

88. Why not employ those periods, when you are free from church responsibilities, in reading? Why not go to see Christ again, speak to Christ, listen to Christ? We speak to him when we pray, we listen to him when we read the divine oracles. What have we to do with other people's homes? There is one home that contains us all. Rather, let those who need us come to us. What have we to do with stories? We have received a ministry to serve at the altars of Christ, not a responsibility to pay homage to men.

89. It is seemly for us to be humble, it is seemly for us to be meek and gentle and serious and patient, and to preserve due measure in everything we do: then we shall not betray any kind of fault at all in

patientes, modum tenere in omnibus, ut nullum vitium esse in moribus vel tacitus vultus vel sermo adnuntiet.

XXI **90.** Caveatur iracundia aut, si praecaveri non potest, cohibeatur; mala enim illex peccati indignatio est, quae ita animum perturbat ut rationi non relinquat locum. Primum est igitur, si fieri potest, ut morum tranquillitas usu quodam adfectione proposito in naturam vertat. Deinde, quoniam ita plerumque motus infixus est naturae ac moribus ut evelli atque evitari non queat, si provideri potuerit, ratione reprimatur. Aut si prius occupatus fuerit animus ab indignatione quam consilio prospici ac provideri potuerit ne occuparetur, meditare quomodo motum animi tui vincas, iracundiam temperes. Resiste irae si potes, cede si non potes, quia scriptum est: *Date locum irae.*

91. Iacob fratri indignanti pie cessit, et Rebeccae, id est patientiae, instructus consilio abesse maluit et peregrinari quam excitare fratris indignationem et tunc redire, cum fratrem mitigatum putaret. Et ideo tantam apud Deum invenit gratiam. Quibus deinde obsequiis, quantis muneribus fratrem ipsum reconciliavit sibi, ut ille praereptae benedictionis non meminisset, meminisset delatae satisfactionis!

92. Ergo si praevenerit et praeoccupaverit mentem tuam iracundia et ascenderit in te, non relinquas locum tuum. Locus tuus patientia est, locus tuus est ratio, sapientia est locus tuus, locus tuus sedatio indignationis est. Aut si te contumacia respondentis moverit et perversitas impulerit ad indignationem, si non potueris mitigare mentem, reprime linguam tuam. Sic enim scriptum est: *Cohibe linguam tuam a malo, et labia tua ne loquantur dolum.* Deinde: *Inquire pacem et sequere eam.* Pacem illam Iacob sancti vide, quanta! Primum sedato animum; si non praevalueris, frenos linguae impone tuae. Deinde reconciliationis studium non praetermittas. Haec oratores saeculi de nostris usurpata in suis posuere libris; sed ille sensus huius habet gratiam qui prior dixit.

our character, either by the silent expression we wear or by the words we say.

90. Anger must be avoided, or, if it cannot be prevented, it must be **XXI** kept within proper limits. An indignant temper is a lure towards evil, that draws people into sin: it so disturbs the spirit that it leaves no room for reason. Our first aim, then, must be to ensure that, if at all possible, calmness of temperament becomes second nature to us: this can only be achieved through sheer practice, endeavour, and resolve. The second aim—for passion is often so fixed in our nature and character that it simply cannot be uprooted or avoided—must be to ensure that, if it can be foreseen, it is checked by reason. But if the spirit has already been seized by indignation before it has proved possible to foresee this outcome and to take precautions against it by applying careful thought to the matter, think about how you can overcome the passion of your spirit, and how you can temper your anger. Resist anger, if you can; draw back from it, if you cannot, for it is written: 'Give place to anger.'

91. Jacob dutifully drew back from his brother when he was indignant with him, and, following the advice of Rebecca—or of patience, in other words—he decided it would be better to go away and live in another country than to stay and fan the flames of his brother's indignation; he would then return once he felt sufficient time had elapsed for his brother to have calmed down. This was how he found so much favour with God. And look at the amazing offers of submission he then made, and all the gifts he presented to win his brother round again! His brother never gave a thought to the blessing that had been snatched from him prematurely; all he could think of was the compensation offered to him.

92. So, if anger has already come upon you and if it has already seized your spirit and welled up inside you, do not abandon your place. Your place is patience, your place is reason, your place is wisdom, your place is to settle the feeling of indignation. Say someone has annoyed you by talking back to you in an arrogant manner, and driven you to indignation by acting in a way that is perverse: if you find that you are unable to calm your spirit, hold your tongue. This is what is written: 'Restrain your tongue from evil, and your lips from speaking guile.' And again: 'Seek peace, and pursue it.' Look at the peace holy Jacob found! In the first place, try to settle your spirit. If you cannot manage this, place a bridle on your tongue. Finally, never forget that you should be eager for reconciliation. The orators of the secular world have set out these ideas in their books as well, but they simply took them over from ours: the credit for grasping the principle here belongs to the person who enunciated it first.

93. Vitemus ergo aut temperemus iracundiam, ne sit eius aut in laudibus exceptio aut in vitiis exaggeratio. Non mediocre est mitigare iracundiam, non inferius quam omnino non commoveri; hoc nostrum est, naturae illud. Denique commotiones in pueris innoxiae sunt quae plus habent gratiae quam amaritudinis. Et si cito pueri inter se mouentur, facile sedantur et maiore suavitate in se recurrunt; nesciunt se subdole artificioseque tractare. Nolite hos contemnere pueros, de quibus Dominus ait: *Nisi conversi fueritis et efficiamini sicut puer iste, non introibitis in regnum caelorum.* Itaque ipse Dominus, hoc est *Dei virtus*, sicut puer, *cum malediceretur, non remaledixit*; cum percuteretur, non repercussit. Ita ergo te compara ut quasi puer iniuriam non teneas, malitiam non exerceas: omnia a te innocenter proficiscantur. Non consideres quid ab aliis in te revertatur. Locum tuum serva, simplicitatem et puritatem tui pectoris custodi. *Noli respondere* irato ad iracundiam eius sive *imprudenti ad imprudentiam*. Cito culpa culpam excutit: si lapides teras, nonne ignis erumpit?

94. Ferunt gentiles, ut in maius omnia verbis extollere solent, Archytae Tarentini dictum philosophi quod ad vilicum suum dixerit: *O te infelicem, quam adflictarem nisi iratus essem!* Sed iam David et armatam dexteram in indignationem compresserat. Et quanto plus est non remaledicere quam non vindicare! Et bellatores adversus Nabal ad ultionem paratos Abigail deprecatione revocaverat. Unde advertimus tempestivis quoque intercessionibus non solum cedere nos sed etiam delectari oportere. Eo usque autem delectatus est ut benediceret intervenientem, quod a studio vindictae revocatus foret.

95. Iam dixerat de inimicis suis: *Quoniam declinaverunt in me iniquitatem et in ira molesti erant mihi.* Audiamus turbatus in ira quid dixerit: *Quis dabit mihi pennas sicut columbae et volabo et requiescam?* Illi ad iracundiam provocabant, hic eligebat tranquillitatem.

96. Iam dixerat: *Irascimini et nolite peccare.* Moralis magister, qui naturalem adfectum inflectendum magis ratione doctrinae

93. Let us then avoid or temper our anger, so that it does not detract from our good qualities or swell the list of our faults. It is no small achievement to succeed in calming your anger—it is as good as not being disturbed in the first place. The first is up to us, the second depends on our nature. Think of the fits of temper children have: they are harmless, and there is really more pleasantness than bitterness about them. True, children are easily provoked into quarrelling with one another, but they are calmed down readily enough and soon revert to their normal selves, more agreeable than they were before; they do not know how to behave deceitfully and artfully. Never despise these children, for the Lord says of them: 'Unless you are converted and become like that child, you shall not enter the kingdom of heaven.' So the Lord himself, the very 'power of God' himself, behaved just like a child: 'when evil was spoken of him, he spoke no evil in reply', and when people struck him he did not strike them back. Set your mind on being like that—so that, like a child, you keep no record of injuries and display no malice, and so that whatever it is you set about you do it in an innocent fashion. Never think about what others may do to you in return. Keep your place, guard the simplicity and the purity of your heart. Never reply to an angry person according to his anger, or to a foolish person according to his folly. One fault quickly forges another. If you rub stones together, is it not inevitable that fire breaks out?

94. The pagans—who are forever exaggerating everything they speak of—make much of a saying of the philosopher, Archytas of Tarentum, some words that he uttered to his bailiff: 'You wretch, what a hiding I'd give you if only I weren't so angry!' Already long before this, though, David had restrained his hand, though he was armed and ready to satisfy his feelings of indignation. It is a far greater thing to refuse even to utter an evil word in reply than it is to refuse to settle a score physically. And think of Abigail: with her strong pleas, she managed to dissuade the warriors who were all set to take revenge on Nabal. We learn from this story not just that we should yield to timely petitions, but something else as well—we should actually be glad to hear them. So glad was David that he gave his blessing to this woman who had intervened, because she had dissuaded him from his thirst for revenge.

95. Already he had said of his enemies: 'Since they have turned evil on me and in their anger they have sorely provoked me.' Let us hear what he said when he was roused to anger: 'Who will give me wings like a dove, and I shall fly away and be at rest?' They were provoking him to anger, and all he was asking for was tranquillity.

96. Already he had said: 'Be angry, and do not sin.' Here is a master of morality, who knows that we must never try to destroy our natural

quam exstirpandum noverit, moralia docet; hoc est: Irascimini ubi culpa est cui irasci debeatis. Non potest enim fieri ut
non rerum indignitate moveamur; alioquin non virtus sed
lentitudo et remissio iudicatur. Irascimini ergo ita ut a culpa
abstineatis. Vel sic: Si irascimini, nolite peccare sed vincite
ratione iracundiam. Vel certe sic: Si irascimini, vobis irascimini quia commoti estis, et non peccabitis. Qui enim sibi
irascitur quia cito motus est, desinit irasci alteri; qui autem
vult iram suam iustam probare, plus inflammatur et cito in
culpam cadit. *Melior est* autem, secundum Salomonem, *qui
iracundiam continet quam qui urbem capit*, quia ira etiam fortes
decipit.

97. Cavere igitur debemus ne in perturbationes prius incidamus quam animos nostros ratio componat; exanimat enim
mentem plerumque aut ira aut dolor aut formido mortis et
improviso percellit ictu. Ideo praevenire pulchrum est cogitatione quae volvendo mentem exerceat ne repentinis excitetur commotionibus sed iugo quodam rationis et habenis
adstricta mitescat.

XXII 98. Sunt autem gemini motus, hoc est cogitationum et
appetitus: alteri cogitationum, alteri appetitus; non confusi
sed discreti et dispares. Cogitationes verum exquirere et quasi
emolere muneris habent; appetitus ad aliquid agendum impel-
lit atque excitat. Itaque ipso genere naturae suae et cogitationes tranquillitatem sedationis infundunt et appetitus
motum agendi excutit. Ita ergo informati sumus ut bonarum
rerum subeat animum cogitatio, appetitus rationi obtemperet
(si vere ut illud decorum custodiamus, animum volumus
intendere) ne rationem excludat rei alicuius adfectus, sed
ratio quid honestati conveniat examinet.

99. Et quoniam ad conservationem decoris spectare diximus
ut sciamus in factis dictisve qui modus (prior autem ordo
loquendi quam faciendi est) sermo in duo dividitur: in
colloquium familiare et in tractatum disceptationemque fidei

feelings but seek to modulate them by a gradual process of learning—here is one to give us moral instruction. What he means is this: 'Be angry where there is something wrong, something which actually deserves your anger.' In reality, it is impossible for us not to be moved by feelings of indignation at some things—or at any rate, if we do respond that way, people do not see it as a virtue, only as a sign of apathy and indifference. Be angry, then, but in such a way that you keep clear of sin. Or look at it like this: if you are angry, do not sin, but overcome your anger with reason. Or at least like this: if you are angry, be angry with yourselves that you have ended up so agitated, and you will not sin. You see, a person who is angry with himself for being quickly aroused ceases to be angry with his neighbour, while one who wants to prove that his anger is just becomes all the more incensed, and soon falls into sin. 'Better is he who contains his anger,' Solomon tells us, 'than he who captures a city', for anger can ensnare even the bravest of men.

97. We need to take great care, then, that we do not give in to our passions before reason has had a chance to compose our spirits. Very often, anger or distress or the fear of death can paralyse the mind and strike it with some unforeseen blow. It is therefore a good policy to seek to prevent such things by giving careful thought to them in advance, by giving them the kind of reflection which exercises the mind, and so ensures that it is not excited by sudden fits of agitation, but rather becomes tame—held in, as it were, by the yoke and the reins of reason.

98. There are two ways in which the spirit can be moved: by thought **XXII** and by impulse. One way is a matter of thought, the other of impulse; they do not overlap, but are quite distinct and dissimilar. The function of thought is to seek out the truth and, if you like, to grind it down, while impulse drives us on and urges us to action of one kind or another. The very nature of each of them confirms it: thought diffuses a calmness and stillness over us, whereas impulse stirs us into motion and activity. This is the way we are formed, so that the thought of good things comes naturally to our mind, and impulse submits to reason—so long as we are genuinely keen to concentrate our mind upon ensuring that what we do is seemly. This way, our attachment to a particular object does not mean that reason is banished from the scene; instead, reason weighs up which course of action will be most conducive to maintaining honourable standards.

99. As we have said, we must seek to preserve what is seemly, so that we will appreciate the significance of due measure in whatever we do or say. Good order in what we say comes before good order in what we do. Speech can be divided into two types: there is informal discourse,

atque iustitiae. In utroque servandum ne sit aliqua perturbatio, sed tamquam mitis et placidus et benevolentiae plenus
et gratiae sine ulla sermo ducatur contumelia. Absit pertinax
in familiari sermone contentio; quaestiones enim magis
excitare inanes quam utilitatis aliquid adferre solet. Discep-
tatio sine ira, severitas sine amaritudine sit, monitio sine
asperitate, hortatio sine offensione. Et sicut in omni actu
vitae id cavere debemus ne rationem nimius animi motus
excludat sed teneamus consilii locum, ita etiam in sermone
formulam eam teneri convenit ne aut ira excitetur aut
odium, aut cupiditatis nostrae aut ignaviae aliqua exprima-
mus indicia.

100. Sit igitur sermo huiusmodi de scripturis maxime. Quid
enim? Magis nos oportet loqui de conversatione optima,
adhortatione observationis, disciplinae custodia. Habeat
caput eius rationem et finis modum. Sermo enim taediosus
iram excitat. Quam vero indecorum ut cum omnis confabu-
latio habere soleat incrementum gratiae, habeat naevum
offensionis!

101. Tractatus quoque de doctrina fidei, de magisterio continentiae, de disceptatione iustitiae, adhortatione diligentiae;
non unus semper, sed ut se dederit lectio, nobis et adripien-
dus est et prout possumus prosequendus: neque nimium
prolixus neque cito interruptus neque vel fastidium derelin-
quat vel desidiam prodat atque incuriam. Oratio pura simplex
dilucida atque manifesta, plena gravitatis et ponderis, non
adfectata elegantia sed non intermissa gratia.

XXIII 102. Multa praeterea de ratione dicendi dant praecepta saeculares viri, quae nobis praetereunda arbitror, ut de iocandi
disciplina. Nam licet interdum honesta ioca ac suavia sint,
tamen ab ecclesiastica abhorrent regula, quoniam quae in
scripturis non repperimus, ea quemadmodum usurpare possumus?

and there is preaching and discussion of matters of faith and justice. In both cases, we must see to it that there is no trace of passion in anything we say, and ensure that our speech is conducted in a manner which is mild and peaceful, full of goodwill and pleasantness, and free from any kind of insulting language. There should be no stubborn arguing when we are conversing informally, for more often than not talk like that only stirs up pointless questions rather than contributing anything of any benefit. We should discuss things without showing anger, and talk about serious matters without displaying bitterness; we should give people warnings without being harsh about it, and offer them encouragement without causing offence. After all, in every action of our life we must take great care to ensure that our spirit does not become overly excited and that reason is not banished from the scene, and we must maintain a place for careful thought instead. Well, we should follow the same rule in all our speech as well, to ensure that neither anger nor hate is aroused, and that we never give the slightest sign of being covetous or lazy.

100. It follows that speech of this sort should be concerned with the Scriptures above all. Why so? Because we ought to spend more time talking about the very best standards of behaviour, about how to encourage one another to live carefully, and about how to preserve right principles. Such discourse should begin with a proper purpose and end when it has reached its due measure. Talk that goes on and on only arouses anger. Conversation is generally meant to make company more agreeable—so it can hardly be seemly if all it does is make people feel sick and tired!

101. Preaching, too—whether it be about the doctrine of the faith, or about the teaching of self-control, or the discussion of issues to do with justice, or encouraging people to show diligence in what they are doing—should not always take exactly the same form. Rather, as a reading suggests itself, we should take it up and develop it as far as we can. Our exposition should not be excessively lengthy, but nor should it be broken off too soon: it ought to leave behind neither a sense of distaste nor an impression of carelessness and inattention. Our language should be pure, simple, clear, and plain, full of seriousness and dignity; it should not be studied with elegance, but nor should it be bereft of a touch of appeal.

102. The men of the world give plenty of other guidelines on how to **XXIII** speak as well, but I think we can pass these by. One example is their advice on the subject of jokes. The fact is, jokes can sometimes be honourable and pleasant, but they remain quite at odds with the rule of the church: if we do not find things in the Scriptures, how can we possibly make use of them?

103. Cavenda enim etiam in fabulis, ne inflectant gravitatem severioris propositi. *Vae vobis qui ridetis, quia flebitis,* Dominus ait; et nos ridendi materiam requirimus ut hic ridentes, illic fleamus! Non solum profusos sed omnes etiam iocos declinandos arbitror, nisi forte plenum urbanitatis et gratiae sermonem esse non indecorum est.

104. Nam de voce quid loquar? Quam simplicem et puram esse satis arbitror; canoram autem esse naturae est, non industriae. Sit sane distincta pronuntiationis modo et plena suci virilis, ut agrestem ac subrusticum fugiat sonum, non ut rhythmum adfectet scaenicum sed mysticum servet.

XXIV 105. De ratione dicendi satis dictum puto; nunc de actione vitae quid congruat consideremus. Tria autem in hoc genere spectanda cernimus. Unum, ut rationi appetitus non reluctentur; hoc enim solo modo possunt officia nostra illi decoro convenire. Si enim appetitus rationi oboediat, facile id quod deceat in omnibus officiis conservari potest. Deinde, ne maiore studio quam res ipsa est quae suscipitur vel minore, aut parvam magno ambitu suscepisse aut magnam inferiore destituisse videamur. Tertium, de moderatione studiorum operumque nostrorum. De ordine quoque rerum et de opportunitate temporum non dissimulandum puto.

106. Sed primum illud quasi fundamentum est omnium, ut appetitus rationi pareat. Secundum et tertium idem est, hoc est in utroque moderatio. Vacat enim apud nos speciei liberalis, quae pulchritudo habetur, et dignitatis contemplatio. Sequitur de ordine rerum et de opportunitate temporum. Ac per hoc tria sunt quae videamus utrum in aliquo sanctorum consummata possimus docere.

107. Primum ipse pater Abraham qui ad magisterium futurae

103. We need to beware of jokes even when telling stories, in case they distract people from grasping the more serious and profound point we want to make. 'Woe to you who laugh, for you shall weep,' says the Lord. And what do we do? We go about looking for things to laugh at! So we laugh in this world and weep in the next. As I see it, it is not just immoderate jokes that we should shun: it is jokes of all kinds—except that it is not unseemly, perhaps, for our language to be full of elegance and pleasantness.

104. What shall I say about the voice? As I see it, all that matters is that it is plain and clear; a melodious tone is nature's gift to bestow, not the product of effort. Its pronunciation should of course be distinct, and it should possess a thoroughly manly timbre, so that it avoids sounding in any way coarse or uncouth. The aim is not to affect a cadence which is theatrical but to preserve a pace which is appropriate for speaking of the mysteries.

105. I think we have said enough by way of rules about how we should **XXIV** speak; let us now consider what is appropriate when it comes to the way we act in life. We find that there are three principles which need to be observed here. First of all, impulse must never resist reason, for only in this way can our duties conform to a standard that is seemly. If impulse obeys reason, it is a simple thing to preserve a seemly standard in every duty we undertake. Secondly, we must never set about any task with either a greater or a lesser degree of enthusiasm than the business itself deserves—otherwise it will either look as if we have set about a small task with great show or as if we have given up on something important without trying hard enough at it. Thirdly, there is a need to show moderation in the tastes we have and in the things we do. There is an additional principle as well, which I think we must not ignore: it is the question of how to order our affairs the right way and how to get our timing right in everything.

106. But the first point is really the foundation of all the others, and it is this: impulse must obey reason. The second and the third points are effectively one and the same: we are talking in both cases about the need to show moderation. With us, there can be no place for thinking about whether or not we are always presenting the appearance of a gentleman (some people take that as true beauty), or for dwelling on what our public standing might be. The one remaining point is the issue of how to order our affairs the right way and how to get our timing right in everything. These are the three principles, then: let us take any one of the saints, and see if we can show that his life illustrates all of them to perfection.

107. Take, first, our father Abraham himself—a man who was moulded and shaped to be an object-lesson for generations to come.

successionis informatus et instructus est, iussus exire de terra sua et de cognatione sua et de domo patris sui, nonne multiplicatae necessitudinis praestrictus adfectu, tamen appetitum rationi oboedientem praebuit? Quem enim terrae suae, cognationis, domus quoque propriae gratia non delectaret? Et hunc ergo mulcebat suorum suavitas, sed imperii caelestis et remunerationis aeternae consideratio movebat amplius. Nonne considerabat uxorem imbecillam ad labores, teneram ad iniurias, decoram ad incentiva insolentium, sine summo non posse duci periculo? Et tamen subire omnia quam excusare consultius diiudicavit. Deinde cum descenderet in Aegyptum, monuit ut diceret se sororem esse, non uxorem ipsius.

108. Adverte quanti appetitus. Timebat uxoris pudori, timebat propriae saluti, suspectas habebat Aegyptiorum libidines, et tamen praevaluit apud eum ratio exsequendae devotionis. Consideravit enim quod Dei favore ubique tutus esse posset, offenso autem Domino etiam domi non posset ' illaesus manere. Vicit igitur appetitum ratio et oboedientem sibi praestitit.

109. Capto nepote non perterritus neque tot regum turbatus populis bellum repetit; victoria potitus praedae partem cuius ipse fuit auctor, recusavit. Promisso quoque sibi filio, cum consideraret emortui corporis sui vires depositas, sterilitatem coniugis et supremam senectutem, etiam contra usum naturae Deo credidit.

110. Adverte convenire omnia. Appetitus non defuit sed repressus est; animus aequalis gerendis, qui nec magna pro vilibus nec minora pro magnis duceret; moderatio pro negotiis; ordo rerum, opportunitas temporum, mensura verborum.

He was told to set out and leave his own land, his own family, and his own father's house. He had all kinds of attachments and close ties around him, did he not? Yet he showed that his impulse was subject to reason. What person would not take a pleasure in the comforts of his native soil, and his family, and his own home? The joys of his own surroundings held a powerful attraction for him; but thinking about the authority of the heavenly command and contemplating the prospect of an eternal reward moved him far more. Think of the challenge he faced: how could he take his wife along with him without putting her in extreme danger? He could see it all quite clearly, could he not? She was so frail in the face of the terrible hardships they would have to undergo, so vulnerable in the face of the violent attacks they would encounter, and so beautiful that she would arouse the lusts of men who would not hesitate to assault her. Yet he determined that he would rather face all these things than make excuses for disobeying God's will. In the end, when he was going down into Egypt, he advised her to say that she was his sister, not his wife.

108. Look at the kind of impulse he must have felt. He was afraid for the honour of his wife, he was afraid for his own safety, he had suspicions about the lusts of the Egyptians—yet, for all that, reason, or the obligation to honour the vows he had made to God, prevailed with him. So long as he enjoyed God's favour, he believed, he would be quite safe whatever the circumstances; but if he offended the Lord he felt sure that he would not remain unharmed even if he stayed at home. And so it was that reason overcame his impulse and rendered it obedient.

109. When his nephew was taken prisoner, he showed not a trace of terror or anxiety at the sight of the hordes which all those kings had at their command—he went back to war. When he had secured victory over them, he declined a share of the spoils, though it was thanks to him that they had been won at all. And when a son was promised to him—yes, he thought of the fact that his own strength was spent, that his body was worn out, and that his wife was infertile and so far on in years—yet, even so, though it seemed so contrary to the ways of nature, he believed God.

110. Look how well it all came together. There was no lack of impulse, but it was put in check. His spirit was well suited to the tasks he had to complete, for he did not treat important things as worthless or regard trivial things as important. He showed moderation in all his dealings; he ordered his affairs the right way; he made sure that his timing was right in everything he did; and he showed due measure in the language he used. He was outstanding in the faith he had, exceptional in the

Fide primus, iustitia praecipuus, in proelio strenuus, in victoria non avarus, domi hospitalis, uxori sedulus.

111. Sanctum quoque eius nepotem Iacob delectabat domi securum degere, sed mater voluit peregrinari ut daret fraternae iracundiae locum. Vicit appetitum consilii salubritas. Exsul domo, profugus a parentibus, ubique tamen convenientem mensuram negotiis tenuit et temporibus opportunitatem reservavit. Acceptus domi parentibus, ut alter maturitate provocatus obsequii benedictionem daret, alter amore pio propenderet; fraterno quoque iudicio praelatus, cum cibum suum fratri cedendum putasset: delectabatur utique alimento secundum naturam sed secundum pietatem cessit petito. Pastor domino gregis fidus, socero gener sedulus, in labore impiger, in convivio parcus, in satisfactione praevius, in remuneratione largus; denique sic fraternam mitigavit iracundiam ut cuius verebatur inimicitias, adipisceretur gratiam.

112. Quid de Ioseph loquar, qui utique habebat cupiditatem libertatis et suscepit servitii necessitatem? Quam subditus in servitute, quam in virtute constans, quam benignus in carcere, sapiens in interpretatione, in potestate moderatus, in ubertate providus, in fame iustus, ordinem rebus adiungens et opportunitatem temporibus, aequitatem populis officii sui moderatione dispensans!

113. Iob quoque iuxta secundis atque adversis rebus irreprehensibilis, patiens, gratus Deo atque acceptus, vexabatur doloribus sed se consolabatur.

114. David etiam fortis in bello, patiens in adversis, in Hierusalem pacificus, in victoria mansuetus, in peccato dolens, in senectute providus, rerum modos, vices temporum per singularum sonos servavit aetatum, ut mihi videatur non

justice he showed; he fought vigorously in battle; he displayed no greed in victory; he was hospitable at home, and attentive to his wife. **111.** And think of his holy grandson, Jacob. He was quite content to live a quiet life at home, but it was his mother's wish that he should go and live in another country in order to give place to his brother's anger. Her sound counsel overcame his impulse. He was an exile from his home and a fugitive from his parents, yet no matter what his circumstances he maintained an appropriate measure in all his dealings and waited till the time was right. Think how dear he was to his parents at home: his father was so impressed by his promptness in waiting upon him that he granted him his blessing, and his mother was so moved by the love and devotion he displayed that she showed him special favour. He was put first in his brother's estimation as well, for Esau was even ready to give up his own food to him. By nature, of course, Esau loved his food, but he held his brother in such affection that he yielded to his request to give it to him instead. He proved a faithful shepherd of the flock for his master, and a dutiful son-in-law to his father-in-law; he was unstinting in his work, and frugal in his diet. He led the way when it came to making amends, and showed generosity in paying out compensation; in fact, he succeeded in appeasing his brother's anger so much that he actually won his favour—and this after fearing that all he would meet with was his hatred!

112. And what about Joseph? He longed for freedom, of course he did, yet he put up with the harsh bonds of slavery. How submissive he was as a slave, how consistent in the virtue he displayed, how generous in his time in prison—he was wise in the interpretations he gave, moderate in his use of power, far-sighted in times of plenty, and just in times of famine! He brought an order to all his affairs; he timed everything right; and he showed such moderation in discharging his duties that he was able to dispense justice to entire nations at a time.

113. Or look at Job: he remained blameless no matter what his circumstances, in good times and bad; he remained patient through it all, and he was pleasing and acceptable to God. He was plagued with all kinds of troubles, but he found comfort in himself.

114. Take David, too: he was brave in war, patient in all the adversities he suffered, peace-loving in Jerusalem, and mild in the hour of victory; he grieved over his sin; and he proved far-sighted in his old age. He kept due measure in all his affairs and watched his timing carefully so that he always struck the right note for each particular stage of his life. In fact, it seems to me that he poured forth a great immortal melody of his worth just as much in the way he

minus vivendi genere quam canendi suavitate praedulcis immortalem Deo sui fudisse meriti cantilenam.

115. Quod his viris virtutum principalium officium defuit? Quarum primo loco constituerunt prudentiam quae in veri investigatione versatur et scientiae plenioris infundit cupiditatem; secundo iustitiam, quae suum cuique tribuit, alienum non vindicat, utilitatem propriam neglegit ut communem aequitatem custodiat; tertio fortitudinem, quae et in rebus bellicis excelsi animi magnitudine et domi eminet corporisque praestat viribus; quarto temperantiam, quae modum ordinemque servat omnium quae vel agenda vel dicenda arbitramur.

XXV **116.** Haec forsitan aliquis dicat primo loco poni oportuisse, quoniam ab his quattuor virtutibus nascuntur officiorum genera. Sed hoc artis est ut primo officium definiatur, postea certa in genera dividatur. Nos autem artem fugimus, exempla maiorum proponimus quae neque obscuritatem adferunt ad intellegendum neque ad tractandum versutias. Sit igitur nobis vita maiorum disciplinae speculum, non calliditatis commentarium, imitandi reverentia, non disputandi astutia.

117. Fuit igitur in sancto Abraham primo loco prudentia, de quo dicit scriptura: *Credidit Abraham Deo et reputatum est ei ad iustitiam.* Nemo enim prudens qui Dominum nescit. Denique insipiens dixit quia *non est Deus*; nam sapiens non diceret. Quomodo enim sapiens qui non requirit auctorem suum, qui dicit lapidi: *Pater meus es tu*, qui dicit diabolo, ut Manichaeus: 'Auctor meus es tu'? Quomodo sapiens, ut Arianus, qui mavult imperfectum auctorem habere atque degenerem quam verum atque perfectum? Quomodo sapiens, ut Marcion atque Eunomius, qui mavult Dominum malum quam bonum habere? Quomodo sapiens qui Deum suum non timet? *Initium enim sapientiae timor Domini.* Et alibi habes: *Sapientes non declinant de ore Domini sed tractant in confessionibus suis.* Simul quoque dicendo scriptura: *Reputatum est ei ad iustitiam*, alterius virtutis ei gratiam detulit.

118. Primi igitur nostri definierunt prudentiam in veri consistere cognitione. Quis enim illorum ante Abraham, David,

lived as he did in the wonderful sweetness of his singing: it was all one great hymn of praise to God.

115. What duty relating to the chief virtues was missing in these men? The virtue which counted first and foremost for them was prudence, which makes us seek the truth and instils in us a yearning for ever deeper knowledge. The second thing was justice, which allows everyone to have what is rightfully his, and lays no claim to anyone else's property, and disregards what is beneficial for self so as to guarantee fairness for all. The third was courage, which, whether we are dealing with the business of war or the affairs of domestic life, always has the same effect: it manifests itself in loftiness and greatness of spirit, and is evident too in physical strength. And the fourth was temperance, which is all about preserving due measure and proper order in everything we feel we ought to do or say.

116. Perhaps someone will say that these definitions should all have **XXV** been set out at the beginning of our discussion; for whatever category of duty you look at derives from one of these four virtues. It is artificial, though, to start by defining duty and then divide it into fixed categories. We want to shun artificiality: we would rather present the examples of our ancestors, which are neither difficult to understand nor tricky to handle. The life of our ancestors ought to be a mirror of moral instruction for us rather than a record of our own ingenuity, and we should show respect by imitating them instead of looking clever in the way we structure arguments.

117. Prudence certainly came first in the life of holy Abraham. Scripture says this about him: 'Abraham believed God, and it was credited to him as righteousness.' No one can be called prudent who does not know the Lord. It is the fool who has said, 'There is no God', for no wise person could ever say such a thing. How can a person be called wise if he does not seek out his creator, but says to a stone, 'You are my father', or if, as the Manichean does, he says to the devil, 'You are my creator'? How can a person be called wise, if, as the Arian does, he would rather have an imperfect and debased creator than one who is true and perfect? How can a person be called wise, if, as Marcion and Eunomius do, he would rather have a Lord who is evil than one who is good? How can a person be called wise if he does not fear his God? For 'the fear of the Lord is the beginning of wisdom'. And in another place you find it said: 'The wise do not turn away from the word of the Lord, but make mention of him in their confessions.' At the same time, when it says, 'it was credited to him as righteousness', Scripture ascribes to Abraham the grace of the second virtue as well.

118. So then, our people were the first to specify that prudence consists in the knowledge of the truth. Which of the philosophers

Salomonem? Deinde iustitiam spectare ad societatem generis humani. Denique David ait: *Dispersit, dedit pauperibus, iustitia eius manet in aeternum. Iustus miseretur, iustus commodat.* Sapienti et iusto totus mundus divitiarum est. Iustus communia pro suis habet, sua pro communibus. Iustus se ipsum priusquam alios accusat. Ille enim iustus qui nec sibi parcit et occulta sua latere non patitur. Vide quam iustus Abraham: susceperat in senectute filium per repromissionem; reposcenti Domino negandum ad sacrificium, quamvis unicum, non putavit.

119. Adverte hic omnes virtutes quattuor in uno facto. Fuit sapientiae Deo credere nec filii gratiam anteferre auctoris praecepto; fuit iustitiae acceptum reddere; fuit fortitudinis appetitum ratione cohibere. Ducebat hostiam pater, interrogabat filius, temptabatur adfectus patrius sed non vincebatur, repetebat filius appellationem paternam, compungebat paterna viscera sed non minuebat devotionem. Accedit et quarta virtus: temperantia. Tenebat iustus et pietatis modum et exsecutionis ordinem. Denique dum sacrificio necessaria vehit, dum ignem adolet, dum filium ligat, dum gladium educit, hoc immolandi ordine meruit ut filium reservaret.

120. Quid sapientius sancto Iacob qui Deum vidit *facie ad faciem* et benedictionem meruit? Quid iustius, qui ea quae acquisierat oblatis muneribus cum fratre divisit? Quid fortius, qui cum Deo luctatus est? Quid modestius eo qui modestiam ita et locis et temporibus deferebat ut filiae iniuriam mallet praetexere coniugio quam vindicare, eo quod inter alienos positus amori potius consulendum quam odia conligenda censebat?

121. Noe quam sapiens, qui tantam fabricavit arcam! Quam iustus, qui ad semen omnium reservatus solus ex omnibus et

lived before Abraham or David or Solomon? They also insisted that justice has to do with looking after the fellowship of the human race. This is what David tells us when he says: 'He has distributed, he has given to the poor; his righteousness'—or his justice—'endures for ever.' 'A person who is just takes pity on others, a person who is just shows generosity to others.' A person who is wise and just has the entire world for his riches. A person who is just regards common goods as his own property, and his own goods as common. A person who is just accuses himself before he will ever accuse other people, for it is the mark of a just person not to spare himself and not to keep his secrets hidden from view. Look how just Abraham was: in his old age he had received a son according to the promise, yet when the Lord demanded that the boy be given back to him as a sacrifice he did not think to refuse him, even though he was his one and only son.

119. Notice, here, all four virtues in this one deed. There was wisdom in it: he believed God, and he refused to put the attraction of keeping his son before the command of his creator. There was justice in it: what he gave back was what he had received. There was courage in it: he used his reason to restrain his impulses. There he was: a father leading his own son away as a victim; his son was asking him what was happening; his fatherly feelings were being sorely tried but still not overwhelmed; his son kept calling him 'father', piercing his father in the depths of his heart, yet still in no way weakening his pious resolve. And the fourth virtue, temperance, was there too: as a just man, he showed due measure in the affection he felt and kept a proper order in the task he had to perform. In the end, just as he was bringing what was necessary for the sacrifice, just as he was kindling the fire, just as he was binding his son, just as he was drawing his sword, and so performing the sacrifice with proper order, he earned his reward—he was allowed to keep his son.

120. Could any wisdom be greater than the wisdom holy Jacob showed? He saw God 'face to face' and earned a blessing from him. Could any justice be greater than his? By offering gifts, he shared with his brother the things he had acquired. Could any courage be greater that his? He wrestled with God. Could any moderation be greater than his? Look what moderation he showed in his regard for both time and place: he was prepared to draw a veil over the outrage which had been done to his daughter, by offering her hand in marriage, rather than take revenge on her assailants. Surrounded by strangers, he felt it was preferable to have good relations with them rather than let ill-feeling build up between them.

121. How wise Noah was—he built that great ark! How just he was! He was preserved safe and sound, so that the seed of every other

praeteritae generationis superstes est factus et auctor futurae, mundo potius et universis magis quam sibi natus! Quam fortis, ut diluvium vicerit! Quam temperans, ut diluvium toleraverit: quando introiret, qua moderatione degeret, quando corvum, quando columbam dimitteret, quando reciperet revertentes, quando exeundi opportunitatem captaret, agnoverit!

XXVI **122.** Itaque tractant in veri investigatione tenendum illud decorum, ut summo studio requiramus quid verum sit, non falsa pro veris ducere, non obscuris vera involvere, non superfluis vel implexis atque ambiguis occupare animum. Quid tam indecorum quam venerari ligna, quod ipsi faciunt? Quid tam obscurum quam de astronomia et geometria tractare, quod probant, et profundi aeris spatia metiri, caelum quoque et mare numeris includere, relinquere causas salutis, errores quaerere?

123. An non ille eruditus in omni sapientia Aegyptiorum Moyses probavit ista? Sed illam sapientiam detrimentum et stultitiam iudicavit et aversus ab ea intimo Deum quaesivit adfectu ideoque vidit, interrogavit, audivit loquentem. Quis magis sapiens quam ille quem docuit Deus, qui omnem Aegyptiorum sapientiam omnesque artium potentias operis sui virtute vacuavit? Non hic incognita pro cognitis habebat hisque temere adsentiebatur, quae duo in hoc maxime naturali atque honesto loco vitanda dicant qui sibi nec contra naturam esse nec turpe iudicant saxa adorare et a simulacris auxilium petere, quae nihil sentiant.

124. Quanto igitur excelsior virtus est sapientia, tanto magis enitendum arbitror ut adsequi eam possimus. Itaque ne quid contra naturam, ne quid turpe atque indecorum sentiamus, duo haec, id est et tempus et diligentiam, ad considerationem rerum examinandi gratia conferre debemus. Nihil est enim magis quo homo ceteris animantibus praestet quam quod

creature would be saved as well; he was the only person in the entire race to survive from the generation that was past, and he became the progenitor of the one that was to come: he was born far more for the world and for everyone else than he was for himself! What courage he had, to survive the flood! What temperance, to endure the flood! He knew when to go into the ark; he knew the moderation that was necessary to pass the time; he knew when to send out the raven, and when to send out the dove, and when to take them back in again when they returned; and he knew when to watch for and how to recognize the right moment to leave the ark.

122. Now they tell us that when we investigate the truth we must keep **XXVI** a firm hold on what is seemly. This way, they say, we shall pursue the truth with real dedication, and not confuse false ideas with true, or mix up true facts with abstruse speculations, or clutter our minds with things which are pointless or involved or uncertain. They say this— but could anything be more unseemly than to worship pieces of wood, as they do? Could anything be more abstruse than to spend time discussing questions relating to astronomy and geometry, which are the kind of topics they are interested in, or measuring the dimensions of outer space, or reducing the very heavens above us, and the sea as well, to mere figures—and in all of it to leave out the vital issues of salvation, and go off chasing errors?

123. Do you not think that Moses, learned as he was in all the wisdom of the Egyptians, explored all these things? Of course he did; yet he concluded that all such wisdom was loss and folly, and he turned from it and sought God with all his heart—and so it was that he saw him, and asked him questions, and heard him speaking. Who could ever be wiser than he was? He was taught by God, and he confounded all the wisdom of the Egyptians, all their magic arts and powers, by the amazing feats he was able to accomplish. Here was a person who did not treat things which remain unknown as if he knew all about them, or subscribe to such things without thinking. These are the two faults which they tell us we need to avoid when we are trying to discover the truth, this task which is so natural and honourable—and yet they do not consider it at all contrary to nature or shameful to bow down and worship stones themselves, or to seek help from statues which feel nothing whatsoever.

124. The loftier wisdom is as a virtue, then, the more I think we should strive to see if we can attain it. To make sure that we avoid ideas which are contrary to nature, or shameful, or unseemly, there are two essentials which we need to apply in any quest to look into things: one is time, and the other is care. Nowhere is man's superiority to all the other animals more clearly displayed than here: man is the only

rationis est particeps, causas rerum requirit, generis sui auctorem investigandum putat, in cuius potestate vitae necisque nostrae potestas sit, qui mundum hunc suo nutu regat, cui sciamus rationem esse reddendam nostrorum actuum. Nihil est enim quod magis proficiat ad vitam honestam quam ut credamus eum iudicem futurum, quem et occulta non fallant et indecora offendant et honesta delectent.

125. Omnibus igitur hominibus inest secundum naturam humanam verum investigare, quae nos ad studium cognitionis et scientiae trahit et inquirendi infundit cupiditatem. In quo excellere universis pulchrum videtur sed paucorum est adsequi qui volvendo cogitationes, consilia examinando non mediocrem impendunt laborem, ut ad illud beate honesteque vivendum pervenire possint atque operibus appropinquare. *Non enim qui dixerit*, inquit, *mihi: Domine, Domine, intrabit in regnum caelorum, sed qui fecerit ea quae dico.* Nam studia scientiae sine factis haud scio an etiam involvant magis.

XXVII **126.** Primus igitur officii fons prudentia est. Quid enim tam plenum officii quam deferre auctori studium atque reverentiam? Qui tamen fons et in virtutes derivatur ceteras: neque enim potest iustitia sine prudentia esse cum examinare quid iustum, quidve iniustum sit, non mediocris prudentiae sit; summus in utroque error. *Qui enim iustum iudicat iniustum, iniustum autem iustum, exsecrabilis apud Deum. Ut quid abundant iustitiae imprudenti?* Salomon ait. Neque iterum prudentia sine iustitia est: pietas enim in Deum initium intellectus. Quo advertimus illud ab huius saeculi translatum magis quam inventum sapientibus, quia *pietas fundamentum est virtutum omnium*.

127. Iustitiae autem pietas est: prima in Deum, secunda in patriam, tertia in parentes, item in omnes: quae et ipsa secundum naturae est magisterium, siquidem ab ineunte aetate ubi primum sensus infundi coeperit, vitam amamus tamquam Dei munus, patriam parentesque diligimus, deinde aequales quibus sociari cupimus. Hinc caritas nascitur, quae alios sibi praefert, non quaerens quae sua sunt, in quo est principatus iustitiae.

creature to partake of reason, to explore the causes behind things, and to take it as his duty to investigate the creator of his being—the God whose power is so vast that he has the power of life and death over us, the one who rules the world according to his will, the one to whom we know we must give an account of all our actions. Nothing is a greater inducement to live an honourable life than the belief that it is he who will be our judge—he whom no secret can ever escape, he to whom all that is unseemly is an offence, and all that is honourable is a delight.

125. By their very nature as human beings, then, all men have an instinct to investigate the truth, for nature herself impels us to show an enthusiasm for understanding and knowledge and instils in us a yearning for enquiry. To excel in this area is regarded as a great thing by people everywhere; but it is given to only a few to attain it. They are the ones who painstakingly analyse ideas and examine theories and spend no small effort in a quest to reach the life that is happy and honourable and to get close to it by the works they perform. 'For it is not he who says to me, "Lord, Lord," who will enter the kingdom of heaven,' Jesus says, 'but he who does what I say.' In fact, an enthusiasm for knowledge without the actions that should go with it may very well prove more of a hindrance than a help.

126. The first source of duty, therefore, is prudence. What better way **XXVII** of fulfilling our duty could there be than to show devotion and reverence for our creator? But prudence is also the source from which all the other virtues derive. For justice cannot exist without prudence, since it takes no small measure of prudence to determine which is the just course of action and which is the unjust: a mistake on either side is equally serious. 'He who pronounces the just to be unjust, or the unjust to be just, is accursed before God. What use is an abundance of justice to a foolish man?' asks Solomon. But similarly, prudence cannot exist without justice, since piety towards God is the beginning of understanding. We notice here that the wise men of this world simply took over rather than invented the saying: 'Piety is the foundation of all the virtues.'

127. Justice begins with piety: first, towards God, second, towards our country, third, towards our parents, and lastly towards all. Piety is also part of nature's teaching, for from the very earliest age at which sense first begins to be imparted to us, we know what it is to love life as a gift of God, to love our country and our parents, and to love the children of our own age whom we choose as our friends. It is from these beginnings that true love is born, which puts others before itself and does not pursue its own interests; this is where justice has its primary seat.

128. Omnibus quoque animantibus innascitur primo salutem tueri, cavere quae noceant, expetere quae prosint, ut pastum, ut latibula, quibus se a periculo imbribus sole defendant, quod est prudentiae. Succedit quoque ut omnium genera animantium congregabilia natura sint, primo generis sui ac formae consortibus, tum etiam ceteris, ut boves videmus armentis, equos gregibus et maxime pares paribus delectari; cervos quoque cervis et plerumque hominibus adiungi. Iam de procreandi studio et subole vel etiam generantium amore quid loquar, in quo est iustitiae forma praecipua?

129. Liquet igitur et has et reliquas cognatas sibi esse virtutes siquidem et fortitudo, quae vel in bello tuetur a barbaris patriam vel domi defendit infirmos vel a latronibus socios plena iustitiae sit; et scire quo consilio defendat atque adiuvet, captare etiam temporum et locorum opportunitates, prudentiae ac modestiae sit; et temperantia ipsa sine prudentia modum scire non possit; opportunitatem noscere et secundum mensuram reddere, sit iustitiae; et in omnibus istis magnanimitas necessaria sit et quaedam fortitudo mentis plerumque et corporis, ut quis quod velit implere possit.

XXVIII **130.** Iustitia igitur ad societatem generis humani et ad communitatem refertur. Societatis enim ratio dividitur in partes duas: iustitiam et beneficentiam, quam eamdem liberalitatem et benignitatem vocant: iustitia mihi excelsior videtur, liberalitas gratior; illa censuram tenet, ista bonitatem.

131. Sed primum ipsum quod putant philosophi iustitiae munus apud nos excluditur. Dicunt enim illi eam primam esse iustitiae formam ut nemini quis noceat nisi lacessitus iniuria; quod evangelii auctoritate vacuatur: vult enim scriptura ut sit in nobis spiritus filii hominis, qui venit conferre gratiam, non inferre iniuriam.

132. Deinde formam iustitiae putaverunt ut quis communia, id est publica, pro publicis habeat, privata pro suis. Ne hoc quidem secundum naturam: natura enim omnia omnibus in

128. Animals of every kind have an innate instinct to attend to their own safety first of all, to beware of things which might harm them and to go after things which will be advantageous to them, such as food, or places to hide in, where they can take shelter from danger or heavy rains or the sun. This is all evidence of prudence. But then again, we find that animals of every species are also by nature social creatures: they mix first with those which share their own species and type, and then with others as well. So we see that cattle are happy in herds, horses in droves, and so on—like tends to be happy with like. And think of stags: they stick with other stags—not to say with people, too. As for the desire to procreate and the instinct to produce offspring, or the love that parents feel for their young—what is there to say? In all these things the character of justice is there for all to see.

129. It is quite clear, then, that these and all the other virtues are closely related to one another. For courage, the virtue which leads people to protect their country from barbarians in time of war, or which in peacetime makes them defend the weak or protect their friends from robbers, is also full of justice. Then again, in order to know how best to defend people and help them, and to be able to seize the right opportunities of time and place, prudence and moderation are called for. And temperance, for its part, would never know what due measure was were it not for prudence; and it is only thanks to justice that we are able to identify an opportunity, or to repay someone with the appropriate measure. And in every one of these things, greatness of spirit is necessary too, as is a certain mental, not to say physical, courage, to enable a person to carry out his wishes.

130. Justice, therefore, is all about promoting the fellowship of the **XXVIII** human race, and about furthering community. The structure of this fellowship can be divided into two dimensions: first, justice, and second, kindness, which is also called generosity or liberality. Justice seems to me to be the loftier of the two, and generosity the more pleasing; the one maintains a sober judgement about things, the other shows goodness.

131. But the very first role which the philosophers think justice performs is excluded with us. They say the first expression of justice is that a person should do no harm to anyone unless provoked by some injury. This idea is dismissed by the authority of the gospel, for the will of Scripture is that we should have the spirit of the Son of Man in us, and he came to bestow grace, not to inflict injuries.

132. The next expression of justice, they have thought, is that a person who holds common, that is to say public, property should regard it as public, and a person who holds private property should regard it as private. This is not even in line with nature, for nature

commune profudit. Sic enim Deus generari iussit omnia ut pastus omnibus communis esset et terra ergo foret omnium quaedam communis possessio. Natura igitur ius commune generavit, usurpatio ius fecit privatum. Quo in loco aiunt placuisse Stoicis quae in terris gignantur, omnia ad usus hominum creari; homines autem hominum causa esse generatos ut ipsi inter se aliis alii prodesse possint.

133. Unde hoc nisi de scripturis nostris dicendum adsumpserunt? Moyses enim scripsit quia dixit Deus: *Faciamus hominem ad imaginem nostram et secundum similitudinem et habeat potestatem piscium maris et volatilium caeli et pecorum omnium repentium super terram.* Et David ait: *Omnia subiecisti sub pedes eius, oves et boves, universa insuper et pecora campi, volucres caeli et pisces maris.* Ergo omnia subiecta esse homini de nostris didicerunt et ideo censent propter hominem esse generata.

134. Hominem quoque hominis causa generatum esse in libris Moysi repperimus, dicente Deo: *Non est bonum hominem esse solum, faciamus ei adiutorium similem sibi.* Ad adiumentum ergo mulier data est viro quae generaret, ut homo homini adiumento foret. Denique antequam mulier formaretur, dictum est de Adam: *Non est inventus adiutor similis illi*; adiumentum enim homini nisi de homine habere non poterat. Ex omnibus igitur animalibus nullum animal simile et, ut absolute dicamus, nullus adiutor hominis inventus est: muliebris igitur sexus adiutor exspectabatur.

135. Ergo secundum Dei voluntatem vel naturae copulam, invicem nobis esse auxilio debemus, certare officiis, velut in medio omnes utilitates ponere et, ut verbo scripturae utar, adiumentum ferre alter alteri vel studio vel officio vel pecunia vel operibus vel quolibet modo ut inter nos societatis augeatur gratia. Nec quisquam ab officio vel periculi terrore revocetur, sed omnia sua ducat vel adversa vel prospera. Denique sanctus Moyses pro populo patriae bella suscipere gravia non reformidavit nec regis potentissimi trepidavit arma nec

generously supplies everything for everyone in common. God ordained everything to be produced to provide food for everyone in common; his plan was that the earth would be, as it were, the common possession of us all. Nature produced common rights, then; it is greed that has established private rights. In this connection, we are told, the Stoics believed that everything the earth produces is intended for men's benefit, and that men were created for the sake of other men, in order to serve one another.

133. Where do you think they got the idea to say that? From our Scriptures, of course. For Moses wrote that God said: 'Let us make man after our image and according to our likeness, and let him have dominion over the fish of the sea and the birds of the air, over the cattle and all the creatures which creep upon the earth.' And David said: 'You have put everything under his feet: sheep and cattle and all the beasts of the field, the birds of the air and the fish of the sea.' It was from our Scriptures, then, that they learnt that everything has been put under man's authority—that is why they think that everything has been produced for the sake of man.

134. As for the idea that man was created for the sake of his fellow-man—we have found this too in the books of Moses, for God said: 'It is not good for man to be alone: let us make him a helper suitable for him.' So the woman was given to her husband to be a help to him, and to bear children, so that man would be a help to his fellow-man. Indeed, before the woman was formed, it was said of Adam: 'No helper suitable for him could be found,' for there could be no true help for man from any creature other than a fellow-man. Of all the animals, no animal that was suitable for him—or, to quote the exact language, no 'helper' for man—could be found—and so the female sex was awaited as that helper.

135. So, whether we think of it as the will of God or as a bond which nature has established, we have an obligation to be of assistance to one another, to vie with one another in the services we perform, to put all our advantages into a common pile, as it were, and—to employ the scriptural term—to bring 'help' to one another, whether by our devotion or our duty or our money or our good works, or by whatever other means are available to us. This is how our fellowship will be enriched and made more pleasant. No one should be kept back from doing his duty by a fear of danger; each of us must regard every situation as something which concerns him personally, no matter what the circumstances, adverse or favourable. Look at holy Moses: he did not shrink from undertaking the gravest of wars on behalf of his people; he did not tremble at the arms of even the mightiest of kings, or fear the terrible savagery of barbarian peoples: he cast aside

barbaricae immanitatis expavit ferociam, sed abiecit salutem suam ut plebi libertatem redderet.

136. Magnus itaque iustitiae splendor, quae aliis potius nata quam sibi, communitatem et societatem nostram adiuvat; excelsitatem tenet, ut suo iudicio omnia subiecta habeat, opem aliis ferat, pecuniam conferat, officia non abnuat, pericula suscipiat aliena.

137. Quis non cuperet hanc virtutis arcem tenere, nisi prima avaritia infirmaret atque inflecteret tantae virtutis vigorem? Etenim dum augere opes, aggerare pecunias, occupare terras possessionibus cupimus, praestare divitiis, iustitiae formam exuimus, beneficentiam communem amisimus. Quomodo enim potest iustus esse qui studet eripere alteri quod sibi quaerat?

138. Potentiae quoque cupiditas formam iustitiae virilem effeminat. Quomodo enim potest pro aliis intervenire qui alios sibi subicere conatur, et infirmo adversum potentes opem ferre qui ipse gravem libertati adfectat potentiam?

XXIX 139. Quanta autem iustitia sit ex hoc intellegi potest quod nec locis nec personis nec temporibus excipitur, quae etiam hostibus reservatur, ut, si constitutus sit cum hoste aut locus aut dies proelio, adversus iustitiam putetur aut loco praevenire aut tempore. Interest enim utrum aliqui pugna aliqua et conflictu gravi capiatur an superiore gratia vel aliquo eventu: siquidem vehementioribus hostibus et infidis et his qui amplius laeserint vehementior refertur ultio, ut de Madianitis, qui per mulieres suas plerosque peccare fecerant ex plebe Iudaeorum, unde et Dei in populum patrum iracundia effusa est. Et ideo factum est ut nullum Moyses victor superesse pateretur. Gabaonitas autem, qui fraude magis quam bello temptaverant plebem patrum, non expugnaret Iesus, sed conditionis impositae adficeret iniuria. Syros vero Eliseus, quos obsidentes in civitatem induxerat, momentaria caecitate percussos cum quo ingrederentur videre non

all thought of his own safety in order to restore to the people their freedom.

136. What a splendid thing, then, justice is. Born for others rather than itself, it aids the community and fellowship that exist between us. It occupies the moral heights, where it can subject everything to its own judicious scrutiny, bring help to others, give them money, never refuse to fulfil its duties towards them, and assume other people's dangers for them.

137. Who would not want to occupy this citadel of virtue, had not the force of the virtue in all its glory been left weakened and warped by primeval greed? For the fact is, in our desire to extend our own assets, to pile up our own money, to seize people's lands as our own personal possessions, and to outdo others in the wealth that we have, we have removed the character of justice, and we have lost the principle of showing kindness to all in common. How can someone be called if all he longs for is to snatch something from his neighbour because he wants it for himself?

138. The yearning for power is another thing that weakens the manly fibre which is the character of justice. How can someone intervene on behalf of others if he is trying to bring these others under his own control, and how can he bring aid to the weak against the powerful if he is aspiring himself to a power which is injurious to freedom?

139. Here is another measure of the greatness of justice: it is never **XXIX** without relevance, no matter what the place, or the person, or the time. Even warring parties maintain its importance: so, if it has been decided with an enemy that battle will take place at a particular place or on a particular day, it is regarded as a violation of justice to arrive at the place in advance or to bring forward the time. It is one thing for a person to be captured in a battle, after a bitter struggle, and quite another if it happens with the help of a favour from on high or some chance occurrence: for on fiercer enemies, those who prove treacherous and those who are guilty of greater crimes, fiercer vengeance is taken. This was what happened with the Midianites. They had caused most of the Jewish people to sin through the way their women had behaved, and the anger of God was poured out on our fathers' people because of it. The result was that when Moses defeated them, he would not allow a single one of them to be spared. In the case of the Gibeonites, however, who had tried our fathers' people by an act of treachery instead of fighting them in war, Joshua would not crush them: instead, he subjected them to the indignity of being reduced to a vassal status. Or take the case of Elisha. The Syrians were besieging the city, and he had struck them with a temporary blindness and led them in while they could not see anything; but he would not give the

possent, volenti regi Israel percutere non acquiesceret dicens: *Non percuties quos non captivasti in gladio et lancea tua: pone eis panem et aquam, et manducent et bibant et remittantur et eant ad dominum suum,* ut humanitate provocati gratiam repraesentarent. Denique postea in terram Israel venire piratae Syriae destiterunt.

140. Si ergo etiam in bello iustitia valet, quanto magis in pace servanda est! Et hanc gratiam propheta his detulit qui ad eum corripiendum venerant. Sic enim legimus quod in obsidionem eius miserat rex Syriae exercitum suum, cognito quod Eliseus esset qui consiliis et argumentationibus eius obviaret omnibus. Quem videns exercitum Giezi servus prophetae de salutis periculo trepidare coepit. Cui dixit propheta: *Noli timere, quoniam plures nobiscum sunt quam cum illis.* Et rogante propheta ut aperirentur oculi servo suo, aperti sunt. Et vidit itaque Giezi totum montem equis repletum et curribus in circuitu Elisei. Quibus descendentibus ait propheta: *Percutiat Dominus caecitate exercitum Syriae.* Quo impetrato ad Syros dixit: *Venite post me et ducam vos ad hominem quem quaeritis.* Et viderunt Eliseum quem corripere gestiebant, et videntes tenere non poterant. Liquet igitur etiam in bello fidem et iustitiam servari oportere nec illud decorum esse posse si violetur fides.

141. Denique etiam adversarios molli veteres appellatione nominabant ut peregrinos vocarent: hostes enim antiquo ritu peregrini dicebantur. Quod aeque etiam ipsum de nostris adsumptum dicere possumus: adversarios enim suos Hebraei allophylos, hoc est alienigenas, Latino appellabant vocabulo. Denique in libro Regnorum primo sic legimus: *Et factum est in diebus illis, convenerunt alienigenae in pugnam ad Israel.*

142. Fundamentum ergo est iustitiae fides: iustorum enim corda meditantur fidem, et qui se iustus accusat, iustitiam supra fidem conlocat: nam tunc iustitia eius apparet, si vera fateatur. Denique et Dominus per Isaiam: *Ecce,* inquit, *mitto lapidem in fundamentum Sion,* id est Christum in fundamenta ecclesiae. Fides enim omnium Christus; ecclesia autem quaedam forma iustitiae est: commune ius omnium, in commune

king of Israel leave to slay them when he wanted to. 'You must not slay those whom you have not captured with your sword and spear,' he said. 'Set bread and water before them; let them eat and drink, and go back to their master.' His aim was that they would be so inspired by this act of humanity that they would show favour in return. And so it turned out: the Syrian raids on the land of Israel stopped from that time on.

140. If justice is binding like this in war, it is surely all the more necessary to respect it in peacetime. We find that the prophet showed this favour as well, in the way he treated those who had come to seize him. This is what we read. The king of Syria had sent his army to lie in wait for him, for he had discovered that it was Elisha who was thwarting all his schemes and machinations. When Gehazi, the prophet's servant, caught sight of the army, he began to tremble: he was terrified for his life. The prophet said to him: 'Do not be afraid: there are more with us than with them'. Whereupon the prophet prayed that his servant's eyes might be opened, and they were opened. All at once, Gehazi saw the whole mountain filled with horses and chariots, all gathered in a circle around Elisha. As the Syrians came down, the prophet said: 'Lord, strike the Syrian army with blindness.' This prayer was granted, and he then said to the Syrians: 'Come with me, and I will take you to the man you are looking for'. They 'saw' Elisha, the one they so wanted to seize; but even as they saw him, they were quite unable to take hold of him. So, it is quite clear that good faith and justice need to be respected even in war, and there can be nothing seemly about any situation where good faith is violated.

141. People of olden times even used a mild name to describe their foes: they spoke of them as *peregrini*, strangers, for there was an ancient custom of designating *hostes*, enemies, as *peregrini*, strangers. We can say with equal confidence that this, too, was taken from our Scriptures. For the Hebrews used to call their foes *allophyloi*, or, in Latin, *alienigenae*, 'those of another race'. So we read in the first book of the Kings: 'And it came to pass in those days, that *alienigenae*, those of another race, mustered for battle against Israel'.

142. The foundation of justice, then, is faith, for the hearts of the just meditate on faith, and the person who is just, and thus critical of himself, raises the edifice of his justice on the foundation of his faith; indeed, his justice is apparent every time he confesses the truth. This is what the Lord says through Isaiah: 'See, I lay a stone for a foundation in Sion.' That stone is Christ, who is the foundation of the church. For Christ is the faith of us all, and it is the church that reflects the true character of justice. Here, the rights of all are common; the church

orat, in commune operatur, in commune temptatur. Denique qui seipsum sibi abnegat, ipse iustus, ipse dignus est Christo. Ideo et Paulus fundamentum posuit Christum, ut supra eum opera iustitiae locaremus, quia fides fundamentum est: in operibus autem aut malis iniquitas aut bonis iustitia est.

XXX **143.** Sed iam de beneficentia loquamur, quae dividitur etiam ipsa in benevolentiam et liberalitatem. Ex his igitur duobus constat beneficentia ut sit perfecta: non enim satis est bene velle sed etiam bene facere; nec satis est iterum bene facere nisi id ex bono fonte, hoc est bona voluntate, proficiscatur. *Hilarem enim datorem diligit Deus.* Nam si invitus facias, quae tibi merces est? Unde apostolus generaliter: *Si volens hoc ago, mercedem habeo; si invitus, dispensatio, inquit, mihi credita est.* In evangelio quoque multas disciplinas accepimus iustae liberalitatis.

144. Pulchrum est igitur bene velle et eo largiri consilio ut prosis, non ut noceas. Nam si luxurioso ad luxuriae effusionem, adultero ad mercedem adulterii largiendum putes, non est beneficentia ista ubi nulla est benevolentia. Officere enim istud est, non prodesse alteri, si largiaris ei qui conspiret adversus patriam, qui congregare cupiat tuo sumptu perditos qui impugnent ecclesiam. Non est haec probabilis liberalitas si adiuves eum qui adversus viduam et pupillos gravi decernit iurgio aut vi aliqua possessiones eorum eripere conatur.

145. Non probatur largitas si quod alteri largitur alteri quis extorqueat, si iniuste quaerat et iuste dispensandum putet; nisi forte, ut ille Zachaeus, reddas prius ei quadruplum quem fraudaveris et gentilitatis vitia fidei studio et credentis operatione compenses. Fundamentum igitur habeat liberalitas tua.

146. Hoc primum quaeritur ut cum fide conferas, fraudem non facias oblatis, ne dicas te plus conferre et minus conferas. Quid enim opus est dicere? Fraus promissi est: in tua potestate est largiri quod velis. Fraus fundamentum solvit et

prays in common, works in common, and is tempted in common. Wherever you find a person who denies himself, there you have one who is just, and there you have one who is worthy of Christ. This was why Paul also placed Christ at the foundation of everything: it was so that we would build our works of justice upon him, with faith as the foundation. When our works are evil, they reflect injustice; but when they are good, it is justice that is seen.

143. But it is now time for us to say something about kindness. This **XXX** virtue must itself be further divided into goodwill and generosity; kindness has to consist of both of these qualities in order to be perfect. It is not enough to wish well; we must also act well. Nor, again, is it enough to act well unless our action springs from a good source— unless it comes, in other words, from a good will. For 'God loves a cheerful giver'. If you do something unwillingly, what reward do you have for it? So the apostle says, speaking more generally: 'If I do this willingly, I have a reward; if unwillingly, I am simply fulfilling the trust committed to me'. And in the gospel itself we have been given many lessons concerning the kind of generosity that is just.

144. It is a great thing, then, to wish people well, and to give with the intention of doing them good, not harm. If, for instance, you think you should give to an extravagant person in order to fund his extravagance, or to an adulterer to fund his adultery, that is not true kindness, for there is no goodwill in it. Or again, you do more damage than good if you give to a person who is plotting against his country, to someone whose desire is to get together a band of desperate characters at your expense in order to attack the church. Nor is it the kind of generosity of which we can approve if you give assistance to a person who is putting a widow and orphans under severe pressure in a legal dispute, or if you help someone who is trying to seize their goods by some act of violence.

145. We cannot approve of the kind of giving where an individual gives one person money that he has extorted from another, where he acquires funds in an unjust fashion and then imagines that he can distribute them justly—unless, of course, you do what Zacchaeus did, and first pay back fourfold everyone you have defrauded, and make up for the crimes you committed in your pagan days by showing a zeal for the faith and doing the good works of a believer. Your generosity, then, needs to have a foundation.

146. The first requirement is that you give in good faith, and that you do not behave deceitfully when you describe what you are offering: do not say that you are giving more when in fact you are giving less. Is there any need to say anything, in fact? The deceit lies in your promise; it is in your power to give just whatever you wish. The deceit

opus corruit. Numquid Petrus ita indignatione efferbuit ut Ananiam exstingui vellet vel uxorem eius? Sed exemplo eorum noluit perire ceteros.

147. Nec illa perfecta est liberalitas si iactantiae causa magis quam misericordiae largiaris. Adfectus tuus nomen imponit operi tuo: quomodo a te proficiscitur sic aestimatur. Vides quam moralem iudicem habeas: te consulit; quomodo opus suscipiat tuum mentem tuam prius interrogat. *Nesciat*, inquit, *sinistra tua quod facit dextera tua*. Non de corpore loquitur, sed etiam unanimus tuus, frater tuus quod facis nesciat, ne dum hic mercedem quaeris iactantiae, illic remunerationis fructum amittas. Perfecta autem est liberalitas ubi silentio quis tegit opus suum et necessitatibus singulorum occulte subvenit; quem laudat os pauperis et non labia sua.

148. Deinde perfecta liberalitas fide causa loco tempore commendatur ut primum opereris circa domesticos fidei. Grandis culpa si sciente te fidelis egeat, qui praesertim egere erubescat, si scias eum sine sumptu esse, famem tolerare, aerumnam perpeti, si in causam ceciderit aut captivitatis suorum aut calumniae et non adiuves, si sit in carcere et poenis et suppliciis propter debitum aliquod iustus excrucietur (nam etsi omnibus debetur misericordia, tamen iusto amplius), si tempore adflictionis suae nihil a te impetret, si tempore periculi quo rapitur ad mortem, plus apud te pecunia tua valeat quam vita morituri. De quo pulchre Iob dixit: *Benedictio perituri in me veniat*.

149. Personarum quidem Deus acceptor non est, quia novit omnia. Nos autem omnibus quidem debemus misericordiam, sed quia plerique fraude eam quaerunt et adfingunt aerumnam, ideo ubi causa manifestatur, persona cognoscitur,

undermines the foundation and reduces the whole work to ruins. Why was Peter so determined that Ananias and his wife should be destroyed—was it just because he was blazing with anger at them? No, he was making an example of them, because he did not want the others to perish as well.

147. It can hardly be a perfect act of generosity, if when you give you do it with more of an eye to boasting about your good deed than to showing people mercy. The intention of your heart stamps its own mark on your work, and this is how your motive is assessed. Look what a judge of your character you have—he consults you; to see how he should react to your work, he first asks questions of your heart. 'Do not let your left hand know what your right hand is doing,' the gospel says. This verse is not speaking about your body; it is saying that even your closest friend or your own brother should not know what you are about—otherwise, in your quest to get a reward for your boasting in this world, you may well lose the real benefit of recompense in the world to come. An act of generosity is perfect when a person covers his work with silence and when, in trying to meet the needs of this individual or that, he acts secretly. His praise comes from the mouth of the poor, not from his own lips.

148. Then again, a perfect act of generosity commends itself by the faith it shows, by the particular case it helps, and by the time and place at which it does so: first and foremost, you must always act in the interests of those who are of the family of faith. It is a serious fault if one of the faithful is in need—especially if the person is one who finds such need a great embarrassment—and you know about it: say you know, for instance, that someone is without the basic means of life, and is facing starvation and struggling with hardship—or say you fail to give assistance to a person who is the victim of a legal case and faces having his property seized, or being the object of false charges—or say a just man is in prison on account of some debt and is racked with punishments and tortures of every kind (for although everyone deserves mercy, a just man deserves it all the more) and in his time of affliction you do nothing for him; or say that in his time of danger, when he is being dragged away to meet his death, your money matters more to you than the life of someone on the brink of death. Job put it so well when he said: 'May the blessing of the one who is about to perish come upon me.'

149. God is, of course, no respecter of persons, for he knows all things. We ourselves must of course show mercy to everyone; but since there are plenty of people who solicit help by behaving deceitfully and feigning hardship, mercy ought to flow more generously where the legitimacy of the cause is obvious, where the person is recognized, and

tempus urget, largius se debet profundere misericordia. Non enim avarus Dominus est, ut plurimum quaerat: beatus quidem qui dimittit omnia et sequitur eum; sed et ille beatus est qui ⟨secundum⟩ quod habet ex adfectu facit. Denique duo aera viduae illius divitum muneribus praetulit quia totum illa quod habuit, contulit, illi autem ex abundantia partem exiguam contulerunt. Adfectus igitur divitem collationem aut pauperem facit et pretium rebus imponit. Ceterum Dominus non vult simul effundi opes, sed dispensari; nisi forte ut Eliseus boves suos occidit et pavit pauperes ex eo quod habuit, ut nulla cura teneretur domestica sed relictis omnibus in disciplinam se propheticam daret.

150. Est etiam illa probanda liberalitas ut proximos seminis tui non despicias si egere cognoscas. Melius est enim ut ipse subvenias tuis, quibus pudor est ab aliis sumptum deposcere aut alicui postulare subsidium necessitati; non tamen ut illi ditiores eo fieri velint quod tu potes conferre inopibus: causa enim praestat, non gratia. Neque enim propterea te Domino dicasti ut tuos divites facias, sed ut vitam tibi perpetuam fructu boni operis acquiras et pretio miserationis peccata redimas tua. Putant se parum poscere: pretium tuum quaerunt, vitae fructum adimere contendunt! Et accusat quod eum divitem non feceris, cum te ille velit aeternae vitae fraudare mercede!

151. Consilium prompsimus: auctoritatem petamus. Primum neminem debet pudere si ex divite pauper fiat dum largitur pauperi, quia Christus *pauper factus est, cum dives esset*, ut omnes sua inopia ditaret. Dedit regulam quam sequamur, ut bona ratio sit exinaniti patrimonii, si quis pauperum famem repulit, inopiam sublevavit. Unde *et consilium in hoc do*, apostolus dicit: *hoc enim vobis utile est*, ut Christum imitemini. Consilium bonis datur, correptio errantes coercet. Denique quasi bonis dicit quia *non tantum facere sed et velle coepistis ab*

where the time is pressing. The Lord is not so greedy that he wants all that we have. The person who gives up everything and follows him is blessed, of course he is; but the person who gives from the heart in accordance with his means is blessed as well. After all, the Lord rated the two bronze coins of the widow more highly than all the gifts of the rich people, for she gave all that she had, whereas they gave only a tiny amount out of their great wealth. It is the intention of the heart, therefore, that makes a contribution rich or poor, and stamps a value on things. At the same time, the Lord's will is not that we should pour out all our resources at once, but that we should distribute them carefully—at least, this is generally so, though the case of Elisha was different: he slaughtered his oxen and used all that he had to feed the poor. He wanted to make sure that he would not be held back by any domestic concerns, and so he left all these things behind so that he could devote himself to living the life of a prophet.

150. There is another kind of generosity which deserves to be approved as well, and it is this: that you do not look down upon the closest members of your family, if you see them in need. It is better that you should give assistance to your own flesh and blood yourself, for it is a disgrace for them to have to ask others for support or to beg for help when they find themselves in some hour of need. Nevertheless, it should not be done just to satisfy a wish on their part to enrich themselves with money that you could otherwise give to the poor: it is the rightness of a cause, not personal sentiment, that must take priority. Besides, it was not to make your family rich that you dedicated yourself to the Lord: it was to obtain everlasting life for yourself as a reward for your good work, and to atone for your sins by paying the price with your acts of compassion. They think they are only asking for a little—it is the very price of your redemption they are after; they would deprive you of the very reward for your life! Here is a man accusing you of not making him rich, when all he wants is to cheat you out of the recompense of eternal life!

151. We have given advice: let us seek authority for it. To start with, no one should feel ashamed if he once was rich and then ends up poor through giving to the poor. Christ himself, 'though he was rich, yet became poor', that through becoming needy he might enrich us all. He gave us the rule to follow: there needs to be a good reason for someone to use up his entire inheritance—such as the chance of saving the poor from starvation, or alleviating real need. So, 'I give you my advice on this too,' says the apostle: 'This is beneficial for you,' that you should imitate Christ. He is giving advice to those who are good; but there is a note of rebuke there too, to correct those who are going astray. So it is to the good, really, that he goes on to say: 'You began a year ago not

anno praeterito. Perfectorum utrumque est, non pars. Itaque docet et liberalitatem sine benevolentia et benevolentiam sine liberalitate non esse perfectam. Unde ad perfectum hortatur, dicens: *Nunc ergo et facere consummate ut quemadmodum prompta est in vobis voluntas faciendi ita sit et perficiendi ex eo quod habetis. Si enim voluntas proposita est, secundum id quod habet acceptum est, non secundum quod non habet. Non enim ut aliis refectio sit, vobis autem angustia; sed ex aequalitate in hoc tempore vestra abundantia ad illorum inopiam ut et illorum abundantia sit ad vestram inopiam, ut fiat aequalitas sicut scriptum est: Qui multum, non abundavit et qui modicum, non minoravit.*

152. Advertimus quemadmodum et benevolentiam et liberalitatem et modum comprehendit et fructum atque personas. Ideo modum, quia imperfectis dabat consilium: non enim patiuntur angustias nisi imperfecti. Sed et si quis ecclesiam nolens gravare in sacerdotio aliquo constitutus aut ministerio non totum quod habet conferat, sed operetur cum honestate quantum officio sat est, non mihi imperfectus videtur. Et puto quod hic angustiam non animi, sed rei familiaris dixerit.

153. De personis autem puto dictum: *Ut vestra abundantia sit ad illorum inopiam et illorum abundantia ad vestram inopiam*: id est, ut populi abundantia sit bonae operationis ad illorum sublevandam alendi inopiam, et illorum abundantia spiritalis adiuvet in plebe inopiam meriti spiritalis et conferat ei gratiam.

154. Unde exemplum optimum posuit: *Qui multum non abundavit et qui modicum, non minuit.* Bene hortatur ad officium misericordiae omnes homines istud exemplum, quoniam et qui plurimum auri possidet non abundat, quia nihil est quidquid in saeculo est, et qui exiguum habet non minuit, quia nihil est quod amittit. Res sine dispendio est quae tota dispendium est.

only to do this but actually to be willing to do it.' Both elements here are necessary for perfection, not just one of them. So he teaches us that generosity is not perfect without goodwill, and goodwill is not perfect without generosity. Then he exhorts us to go on to perfection, saying: 'Now bring the work to completion as well, then, so that, as your will to do it is keen, you can also find the will to accomplish it, according to your means. For if the will is ready, the gift is accepted in terms of what a person has, not in terms of what he does not have. The aim is not that others will be restored to life at the cost of difficulties for you. There must be equality in this age: your surplus should supply their need and their surplus your need, so that there is equality, just as it is written: "He who gathered much did not have a surplus, and he who gathered little did not lack".'

152. We can see that the apostle includes the importance of goodwill, generosity, and due measure in what he says; he also deals with the question of reward for giving, and the need to consider the persons who are involved. He mentioned the importance of observing due measure simply because his advice was aimed at those who were less than perfect: it is only those who are less than perfect who do experience difficulties. But if a man is appointed to a priesthood or ministry and, unwilling to be a burden to the church, he chooses not to give away all that he has but works away in an honourable fashion, giving whatever is necessary for him to discharge his duty appropriately, it seems to me that he can hardly be described as less than perfect. And I believe that the apostle was not speaking here of difficulties which are spiritual, but of the difficulties a person may experience in retaining enough of his inherited resources.

153. I believe he was also thinking of the need to consider the persons involved in a given situation when he said this: 'So that your surplus will supply their need and their surplus will supply your need.' What he meant was: So that the material surplus which the people have acquired will lead them to do good works to alleviate their brothers' need of food, and so that the spiritual surplus which their brothers have accrued will be of assistance to the people in their lack of spiritual merit, and confer grace upon them.

154. The illustration he gave them, then, was excellent: 'He who gathered much did not have a surplus, and he who gathered little did not lack.' This illustration is a great encouragement to people everywhere to fulfil the duty of mercy. On the one hand, you see, the person who owns plenty of gold has no real surplus, because all that belongs to his world is as nothing; and on the other, the person who possesses very little experiences no real lack, because the thing he misses is nothing in any case. There can be no loss of something if it is all loss anyhow.

155. Est etiam sic intellectus bonus: Qui plurimum habet, etsi non donat, non abundat, quia quantumvis acquirat, eget semper qui plus concupiscit; et qui exiguum habet, non minuit, quia non multum est quod pauperem pascit. Similiter ergo et ille pauper qui confert spiritalia pro pecuniariis, etsi plurimum habeat gratiae, non abundat: non enim onerat gratia sed adlevat mentem.

156. Sed etiam sic potest intellegi: Non abundas, o homo. Quantum est enim quod accepisti, etsi tibi multum est? Iohannes, quo nemo maior est inter natos mulierum, inferior tamen erat eo qui minor est in regno caelorum.

157. Potest et sic: Non abundat Dei gratia corporaliter quia spiritalis est. Quis eius potest aut magnitudinem aut latitudinem comprehendere, quam non videt? Fides si fuerit sicut granum sinapis, montes transferre potest; et non tibi datur ultra granum sinapis. Si abundet in te gratia, non est verendum ne mens tua tanto munere incipiat extolli, quia multi sunt qui ab altitudine cordis sui gravius corruerunt quam si nullam habuissent Domini gratiam? Et qui parum habet non minuit, quia non est corporeum ut dividatur; et quod parum videtur habenti, plurimum est cui nihil deest.

158. Consideranda etiam in largiendo aetas atque debilitas, nonnumquam etiam verecundia quae ingenuos prodit natales, ut senibus plus largiaris, qui sibi labore iam non queunt victum quaerere. Similiter et debilitas corporis et haec iuvanda promptius. Tum si quis ex divitiis cecidit in egestatem, et maxime si non vitio suo sed aut latrociniis aut proscriptione aut calumniis quae habebat amisit.

159. Sed forte dicat aliquis: 'Caecus uno loco sedet et praeteritur . . . et iuvenis validus frequenter accipit'. E verum est, quia obrepit per importunitatem. Non est illu

155. Here is another good way of understanding it. If someone has plenty, even if he gives nothing to anyone, he does not have a surplus, for however much he acquires, he is always in want, for he is forever craving more. At the same time, if someone has very little, he experiences no lack, since it does not take much to feed a poor man. In the same way, the poor person who confers spiritual gifts in exchange for monetary ones, even if he has plenty of grace, does not have a surplus, for grace does not burden the heart—it lightens it.

156. But it can be understood this way, as well. You do not have a surplus, man. What is it all worth, really, all that you have received—however much it may seem to you? No one born of woman is greater than John, yet he was less than the least in the kingdom of heaven.

157. And it can be understood this way: there is no surplus to the grace of God in physical terms, for it is a spiritual thing. Who can fathom its greatness or breadth? These are not properties that can be literally seen. Faith, if it is like a simple grain of mustard-seed, can move mountains—and it is no more than a grain of mustard-seed that is given you. If there were a surplus of grace in you, you would have to spend your time worrying that your mind might become puffed up at the possession of this great gift, would you not? For there are plenty of people who have come to far worse ruin through having a lofty spirit than they would ever have done if they had never possessed an ounce of the grace of the Lord in the first place. But then again, the person who has little does not lack, for grace is not a physical thing that can be divided up; and what seems little to the one who has it is a great deal to one who lacks for nothing.

158. You should take into consideration people's age and weakness when you are contemplating giving to them—and sometimes you need to ask why people show a particular sense of modesty: it can indicate that they come from a good background. You ought to show greater generosity towards the elderly who are no longer in a position to earn their food by their own efforts. The same is true of those who are suffering from weakness of body: they too are cases which deserve particularly prompt assistance. So does anyone who once enjoyed riches but has since fallen on hard times, especially if he has lost what he had through no fault of his own, but by being robbed, or having his goods confiscated, or being the victim of false accusations.

159. But perhaps someone will object at this point. 'Look, here is a blind man, sitting being ignored,' he will say, 'while over there is a young fellow who's hale and hearty, and he's the one getting all the attention.' And it is perfectly true, for the latter presses his claims upon people by being persistent. It is not so much that people judge him to be a more worthy recipient; they are simply wearied by his

iudicii sed taedii. Nam et Dominus ait in evangelio de eo qui iam clauserat ostium suum, si quis ostium eius procacius pulset, quia surgit et dat illi propter importunitatem.

XXXI 160. Pulchrum quoque est propensiorem eius haberi rationem qui tibi aut beneficium aliquod aut munus contulit, si ipse in necessitatem incidit. Quid enim tam contra officium quam non reddere quod acceperis? Nec mensura pari sed uberiore reddendum arbitror, et usum pensare beneficii ut tu subvenias quanto eius aerumnam repellas. Etenim superiorem non esse in referendo quam in conferendo beneficio, hoc est minorem esse, quoniam qui prior contulit, tempore superior est, humanitate prior.

161. Unde imitanda nobis est in hoc quoque natura terrarum, quae susceptum semen multiplicatiore solet numero reddere quam acceperit. Ideo tibi scriptum: *Sicut agricultura est homo insipiens et tamquam vinea homo egens sensu: si reliqueris eum, desolabitur.* Sicut agricultura ergo etiam sapiens, ut tamquam fenerata sibi maiore mensura semina suscepta restituat. Terra ergo aut spontaneos fructus germinat aut creditos uberiore cumulo refundit ac reddit. Utrumque debes quodam hereditario usu parentis ne relinquaris sicut infecundus ager. Esto tamen ut aliquis excusare possit quod non dederit, quomodo excusare potest quod non reddiderit? Non dare cuiquam vix licet, non reddere vero non licet.

162. Ideo pulchre Salomon ait: *Si sederis cenare ad mensam potentis, sapienter intellege ea quae apponuntur tibi et mitte manum tuam sciens quod oportet te talia praeparare. Si autem insatiabilis es, noli concupiscere escas eius: haec enim obtinent vitam falsam.* Quas nos imitari cupientes sententias scripsimus. Conferre gratiam bonum est; at qui referre nescit durissimus. Humanitatis exemplum ipsa terra suggerit: spontaneos fructus ministrat quos non severis, multiplicatum

pestering them. It is just as the Lord himself says in the gospel, when he is describing the man who has already bolted his door when someone comes to call on him: if the person hammers on his door loudly enough, he says, the man will get up and give to him, because of his persistence.

160. It is also good to show a particular indulgence towards someone **XXXI** who has done you a kindness or service at some point, should this person subsequently end up in need himself. What greater contradiction of duty could there be than not to pay back what you have received? I think people should be paid back not with equal but with more generous measure, and you ought to return the benefit of a kindness in such a way that you prove to be of assistance yourself, in so far as you prevent someone from suffering. In reality, if you fail to do more in returning a kindness than was involved in doing it in the first place, you come across as the inferior person, for the one who was the first to give has an advantage over you already in terms of time and has already proved himself to be the first at showing humanity.

161. This is another area where we should imitate the nature of the earth herself: her practice is to give back the seed she has assumed, multiplied far beyond what she first received. It is for your benefit that it is written: 'A foolish man is like a ploughed field, and a man without sense is as a vine: if you leave him, he will become desolate.' Well, a wise man is also like a ploughed field, for he is careful to restore with greater measure—with interest, if you like—the seed he has assumed. So the earth either produces fruits of her own accord, or else she repays and restores with richer abundance what has been entrusted to her. Either way, there is an example for you to follow, if you are going to behave like one who has inherited his mother's ways, and not be abandoned like a field that is barren. Let us suppose someone might just have an excuse for not giving something in the first place—what excuse could there be for not paying back a benefactor for something received? It is scarcely right for a person not to give—it certainly is not right not to pay someone back.

162. This is why the words of Solomon are so apt: 'If you sit down to dine at the table of a ruler, think wisely about what is set before you, and stretch forth your hand, knowing that it is necessary for you to prepare such things. But if you are insatiable, do not desire his delicacies, for these things make for a deceptive life.' Our whole desire in writing is that we should imitate such principles. It is a good thing to do someone a favour, but a person who does not know how to give in return truly has a heart of stone. The earth herself offers you an example of humanity. Entirely of her own accord, she supplies you with fruits you did not sow, and she also returns many times what

quoque reddit quod acceperit. Negare tibi pecuniam numera-
tam non licet: quomodo licet acceptam non referre gratiam?
In Proverbiis quoque habes quod ita plurimum redhibitio ista
gratiae apud Dominum consuevit valere ut etiam in die ruinae
inveniat gratiam quando possunt praeponderare peccata. Et
quid aliis utar exemplis, cum Dominus ipse remunerationem
uberiorem sanctorum meritis in evangelio polliceatur atque
hortetur ut operemur bonum opus, dicens: *Dimittite et
dimittemini; date et dabitur vobis: mensuram bonam, commotam,
superemuentem dabunt in sinum vestrum?*

163. Itaque et illud convivium Salomonis non de cibis sed de
operibus est bonis. Quo enim melius epulantur animi quam
bonis factis? Aut quid aliud tam facile potest iustorum explere
mentes quam boni operis conscientia? Qui autem iucundior
cibus quam facere voluntatem Dei? Quem cibum sibi solum
Dominus abundare memorabat, sicut scriptum est in evangelio: *Meus cibus est ut faciam voluntatem Patris mei qui in
caelo est.*

164. Hoc cibo delectemur, de quo ait propheta: *Delectare in
Domino.* Hoc cibo delectantur qui superiores delectationes
mirabili ingenio comprehenderunt, qui possunt scire qualis
sit munda illa et intelligibilis mentis delectatio. Edamus ergo
panes sapientiae et saturemur in verbo Dei, quia non in solo
pane sed in omni verbo Dei vita est hominis facti ad
imaginem Dei. De poculo vero satis expresse dicit sanctus
Iob: *Sicut terra exspectans pluviam sic et isti sermones meos.*

XXXII **165.** Pulchrum est ergo ut divinarum scripturarum humesca-
mus adloquio et quasi ros sic in nos Dei verba descendant.
Cum igitur sederis ad illam mensam potentis, intellege quis
iste sit potens, et in paradiso delectationis positus atque in
convivio sapientiae locatus considera quae apponuntur tibi.
Scriptura divina convivium sapientiae est; singuli libri singula
sunt fercula. Intellege prius quae habeant ferculorum dapes,
et tunc mitte manum, ut ea quae legis vel quae accipis a
Domino Deo tuo operibus exsequaris et collatam in te
gratiam officiis repraesentes, ut Petrus et Paulus, qui evange-
lizando vicem quamdam largitori muneris reddiderunt, ut
possint singuli dicere: *Gratia autem Dei sum quod sum, et*

she has received. It is not right to deny it if someone has paid you a sum of money; how then can it be right not to return a favour if you have received one? In the Proverbs, you find it put this way. If you repay a favour like this, this is the weight it will carry with the Lord— it will earn his favour even on the day of destruction, when our sins can so easily outweigh everything else. What other examples need I cite? The Lord himself, in the gospel, promises a lavish reward for the merits of the saints, and urges us to perform good works, when he says: 'Forgive, and you will be forgiven; give, and it will be given you: good measure, shaken together and overflowing, they will give into your lap.'

163. So we find that the feast of which Solomon speaks has nothing to do with food, but with good works. What more sumptuous fare could our souls enjoy than the feast of doing things that are good? Is there anything else which can so readily satisfy the minds of the just as the knowledge that they have done a good work? What food is more delicious than to do God's will? This was the only food which the Lord had in plenty, as he told us himself, for it is written in the gospel: 'My food is to do the will of my Father who is in heaven.'

164. Let us delight ourselves with this food, for this is what the prophet is speaking of when he says: 'Delight yourself in the Lord.' The people who delight themselves with this food are those who have been granted a wonderful ability to grasp the higher delights, those who can appreciate what the pure, spiritual delight of the soul is really like. So let us eat the bread of wisdom, and let us be filled with the word of God, for the life of man made in God's image does not consist in bread alone, but in every word of God. As for the cup that is involved, holy Job puts it as clearly as can be when he says: 'As the earth waits for the rain, so they waited for my words.'

165. It is a wonderful thing, then, for us to be refreshed with the **XXXII** language of the divine Scriptures and for the words of God to descend upon us like dew. So when you sit down to dine at that ruler's table, think about who the ruler is; and when you are placed in the paradise of delight and given a seat at the feast of wisdom, consider carefully the things that are set before you. Divine Scripture is this feast of wisdom; individual books are individual courses. Think beforehand about the dishes each course contains, and then stretch forth your hand, so that you put into practice by your good works all that you read or receive from the Lord your God, and by fulfilling your duties offer a return for the favour that has been shown you. This is what Peter and Paul did: by preaching the gospel, they gave something back to the one who had given them the great gift that they had, so they could each say: 'By the grace of

gratia eius egena in me non fuit sed abundantius illis omnibus laboravi.

166. Alius ergo fructum accepti beneficii, ut aurum auro, argentum argento rependit, alius laborem, alius, haud scio an etiam locupletius, solum restituit adfectum. Quid enim si reddendi nulla facultas suppetit? In beneficio referendo plus animus quam census operatur magisque praeponderat benevolentia quam possibilitas referendi muneris. Gratia enim in eo ipso quod habetur refertur. Magna igitur benevolentia quae, etiamsi nihil conferat, plus exhibet et cum in patrimonio nihil habeat, largitur pluribus; idque facit sine ullo sui dispendio, et lucro omnium. Et ideo praestat benevolentia supra ipsam liberalitatem. Ditior haec moribus quam illa muneribus: plures enim sunt qui indigent beneficio quam qui abundant.

167. Est autem benevolentia, et coniuncta liberalitati, a qua ipsa liberalitas proficiscitur, cum largitatis adfectum sequitur largiendi usus, et separata atque discreta. Ubi enim deest liberalitas, benevolentia manet, communis quaedam parens omnium, quae amicitiam connectit et copulat: in consiliis fidelis, in prosperis laeta, in tristibus maesta, ut unusquisque benevolentiae se magis quam sapientis credat consilio, ut David, cum esset prudentior, Ionathae tamen iunioris consiliis acquiescebat. Tolle ex usu hominum benevolentiam: tamquam solem e mundo tuleris ita erit, quia sine ea usus hominum esse non potest ut peregrinanti monstrare viam, revocare errantem, deferre hospitium (non igitur mediocris virtus, de qua sibi plaudebat Iob dicens: *Foris autem non habitabat hospes, ianua mea omni venienti patebat*), aquam de aqua profluenti dare, lumen de lumine accendere. Benevolentia itaque in his est omnibus tamquam fons aquae reficiens

God I am what I am, and his grace towards me was not in vain, but I laboured more abundantly than all of them'.

166. So, one person who benefits from your kindness will repay it in kind, returning gold for gold or silver for silver. Another will repay you with his labour, while yet another will return only a feeling of gratitude; and who knows?—that may well be a more valuable thing. For what if people do not have the means available to pay someone back? When it comes to returning a kindness, the attitude of the heart counts for more than the amount of money a person has, and goodwill matters far more than whether or not someone is able to return a gift. People can return their gratitude in the very act of feeling grateful. Goodwill is a great thing, then: it may have nothing to give, but it has more to offer; it possesses nothing in the way of an inheritance, yet it manages to extend kindness to many—and does so at no loss to itself and to the greater benefit of everyone. And so it is that goodwill is actually more important than generosity itself: it has greater riches in its moral character than generosity has with all its gifts. After all, there are far more people in need of kindness than there are individuals with endless resources to help them.

167. There is such a thing as goodwill, though, and it is closely linked to generosity; generosity itself stems from it, for the actual practice of kindness is secondary to the desire to be kind in the first place. But goodwill is also separate and distinct from generosity. For even where generosity is nowhere to be found, goodwill remains, like the common parent of us all, bringing people together and uniting them in friendship. It is always faithful in giving advice, and it is as ready to share people's joy in times of prosperity as it is to share their sadness in times of grief. There is not a man among us who would not far rather put himself in the hands of someone of goodwill than follow the advice of the wisest of sages. That was how David saw things: he was the one with the greater experience, but he was quite content to trust the advice of Jonathan, his younger friend. Remove goodwill from human behaviour, and it will be as if you have taken the sun from the world. Without it, all kinds of basic elements in human behaviour would simply cease to exist—like showing a stranger the way, or calling somebody back when he is going off course, or offering a visitor hospitality (no small virtue, that—Job could take comfort from the knowledge that he had practised it, and say: 'The guest was not left to stay outside; my door was open to everyone who came'), or giving a passer-by a drink of water from a stream, or kindling a light for your neighbour from your own light. Goodwill is there in all these things: it is like a spring of water that refreshes the thirsty, and like a light that shines for others; and those

sitientem, tamquam lumen quod etiam aliis luceat nec illis desit qui de suo lumine aliis lumen accenderint.

168. Est etiam illa benevolentiae liberalitas, ut, si quod habes debitoris chirographum, scindens restituas, nihil a debitore consecutus debiti. Quod exemplo sui facere nos debere Iob sanctus admonet: nam qui habet, non mutuatur; qui non habet, non liberat syngrapham. Quid igitur, etiam si ipse non exigas, avaris heredibus servas, quam potes cum benevolentiae tuae laude sine damno pecuniae repraesentare?

169. Atque ut plenius discutiamus benevolentiam: a domesticis primum profecta personis, id est a filiis, parentibus, fratribus, per coniunctionum gradus in civitatum pervenit ambitum, et de paradiso egressa mundum replevit. Denique cum in viro et femina benevolentem Deus posuisset adfectum, dixit: *Erunt ambo in una carne*, et in uno spiritu. Unde se Eva serpenti credidit, quoniam quae benevolentiam acceperat esse malevolentiam non opinabatur.

XXXIII **170.** Augetur benevolentia coetu ecclesiae, fidei consortio, initiandi societate, percipiendae gratiae necessitudine, mysteriorum communione. Haec enim etiam appellationes necessitudinum: reverentiam filiorum, auctoritatem et pietatem patrum, germanitatem fratrum sibi vindicant. Multum igitur ad cumulandam spectat benevolentiam necessitudo gratiae.

171. Adiuvant etiam parium studia virtutum, siquidem benevolentia etiam morum facit similitudinem. Denique Ionatha filius regis imitabatur sancti David mansuetudinem, propter quod diligebat eum. Unde et illud: *Cum sancto sanctus eris*, non solum ad conversationem sed etiam ad benevolentiam derivandum videtur. Nam utique et filii Noe simul habitabant et non erat in his morum concordia. Habitabant etiam in domo patria Esau et Iacob sed discrepabant. Non erat enim benevolentia inter eos, quae sibi praeferret alterum, sed magis contentio, quae praeriperet benedictionem. Nam cum alter

who have kindled a light for others from their own find that they have no less light themselves.

168. There is also a particular kind of generosity that derives from goodwill: say, for instance, you have a debtor's bond, and you elect to tear it up and give it back to the debtor, without recovering a penny of the debt from him. This is what holy Job bids us do, by the example he set: he who has does not borrow, he tells us, while he who does not have does not cancel an agreement. Why, then, if you stand in no particular need yourself, do you hold on to a note of agreement, simply to pass it on to your greedy heirs, when you are quite capable of writing it off—especially since, this way, you would win praise for your goodwill, and never miss the money either?

169. If we want to go into the matter more thoroughly, we could say this: goodwill began in the first place with the personal relations which make up the family—in other words, with sons, parents, and brothers—and then, progressing through different levels of relationship, it completed its circuit in the ties which bind us together in our various cities: having set out from paradise, it has filled the whole world. So, when he had placed the spirit of goodwill in the man and the woman, God said: 'The two shall be one in flesh', and one in spirit. This was why Eve believed the serpent: having received the gift of goodwill herself, she simply could not imagine that such a thing as ill-will existed.

170. Goodwill is enhanced by the communal nature of the church, by **XXXIII** our partnership in the faith, by our fellowship as initiates, by our kinship as recipients of grace, and by our communion in the mysteries. These ties can also claim the name of family relationships, for it is the respect of sons, the authority and responsibility of fathers, and the close bonds of brothers that we experience. The relationship which grace brings about does a great deal, then, to build up goodwill between us.

171. It is also helpful when people share a natural inclination towards similar virtues, since goodwill also produces likeness of character. Think of Jonathan, the king's son: he sought to imitate the gentleness shown by holy David, because he loved him. So it would appear that the statement, 'with the holy you will show yourself holy', must be understood to refer not just to manner of life but also to goodwill. Take the case of Noah's sons. They lived side by side, naturally, yet there was no harmony in their characters. Esau and Jacob lived together in their father's house, too, but they were quite different from each other. There was no goodwill between them, to make each put the other before himself; there was only a rivalry as to which of them might manage to snatch the blessing first. The reality was that with one of

praedurus, alter mansuetus esset, inter dispares mores et studia compugnantia, benevolentia esse non poterat. Adde quia sanctus Iacob paternae degenerem domus virtuti praeferre non poterat.

172. Nihil autem tam consociabile quam cum aequitate iustitia, quae velut compar et socia benevolentiae facit, ut eos, quos pares nobis credimus, diligamus. Habet autem in se benevolentia fortitudinem: nam cum amicitia ex benevolentiae fonte procedat, non dubitat pro amico gravia vitae sustinere pericula: *Et si mala*, inquit, *mihi evenerint per illum, sustineo.*

XXXIV **173.** Benevolentia etiam gladium iracundiae extorquere consuevit. Benevolentia facit ut amici vulnera utilia quam voluntaria inimici oscula sint. Benevolentia facit ut unus fiat ex pluribus, quoniam, si plures amici sint, unus fiunt, in quibus spiritus unus et una sententia est. Simul advertimus etiam correptiones in amicitia gratas esse, quae aculeos habent, dolores non habent. Compungimur enim censoriis sermonibus sed benevolentiae delectamur sedulitate.

174. Ad summam, non omnibus eadem semper officia debentur nec personarum semper sed plerumque causarum et temporum praelationes sunt, ut vicinum quis interdum magis quam fratrem adiuverit. Quoniam et Salomon dicit: *Melius est vicinus in proximo quam frater longe habitans.* Et ideo plerumque amici se benevolentiae quisque committit quam fratris necessitudini. Tantum valet benevolentia ut plerumque pignora vincat naturae.

XXXV **175.** Satis copiose iustitiae loco honesti naturam et vim tractavimus. Nunc de fortitudine tractemus, quae velut excelsior ceteris dividitur in res bellicas et domesticas. Sed bellicarum rerum studium a nostro officio iam alienum videtur, quia animi magis quam corporis officio intendimus nec ad arma iam spectat usus noster sed ad pacis negotia. Maiores autem nostri, ut Iesus Nave, Ierobaal, Samson, David, summam rebus quoque bellicis retulere gloriam.

them a hard man and the other gentle by nature, it was impossible that there should be goodwill between such dissimilar characters; their natural inclinations were so different. In addition, it was impossible for holy Jacob to treat someone who was unworthy to be called a son of his father's house as though he mattered more than virtue.

172. But there is nothing quite so social in character as justice combined with fairness. Justice is like a comrade or a companion for goodwill: it makes us love people who are, we believe, like ourselves. Goodwill brings courage with it, too, for since goodwill is the source from which friendship springs, a friend will not hesitate to risk great dangers to life for a friend's sake: 'And if dreadful things befall me on his account,' he will say, 'I bear them.'

173. Goodwill also tends to wrench the sword of anger from our **XXXIV** hands. Goodwill makes wounds inflicted by a friend more beneficial than kisses given freely by an enemy. Goodwill makes those who were many become one, for though friends may be many they do become one, with one spirit and one mind. We see, too, that even rebukes are agreeable when they are delivered in the context of friendship, for while they carry the power to sting, they do not carry real pain. We are stung by the critical words, but we are pleased by the thoughtfulness and goodwill which lie behind them.

174. All in all, we do not always owe the same duties to everyone. It is not always a case of determining priorities according to the persons involved; often we must consider the specific details of cause and time as well. Sometimes a person may find himself giving more help to his neighbour than to his own brother. After all, Solomon also says: 'Better is a neighbour who is near than a brother who lives far away.' That is why it is often the case that someone would far rather put himself in the hands of a friend who shows goodwill than entrust himself to his own brother, for all his natural relationship with him. Such is the power of goodwill: it can often prove stronger than the ties of nature herself.

175. We have now dealt quite fully with the nature and essence of **XXXV** what is honourable from the standpoint of justice. Let us at this point move on to deal with courage. Since it belongs higher up the scale, as it were, than all the other virtues, courage gets divided into two types: one has to do with the business of war, the other with ordinary domestic life. But a taste for the affairs of war appears to be quite alien to the kind of duty which concerns us now, for our interest is in the duty of the soul rather than the body, and our activity has to do not with arms but with the business of peace. All the same, it has to be said that our ancestors, men like Joshua son of Nun, or Jerubbaal, or Samson, or David, won great glory in the affairs of war as well.

176. Est itaque fortitudo velut excelsior ceteris sed numquam incomitata virtus: non enim ipsam committit sibi; alioquin fortitudo sine iustitia iniquitatis materia est. Quo enim validior est, eo promptior ut inferiorem opprimat, cum in ipsis rebus bellicis iusta bella an iniusta sint spectandum putetur.

177. Numquam David nisi lacessitus bellum intulit. Itaque prudentiam fortitudinis comitem habuit in proelio. Nam et adversus Goliam, immanem mole corporis virum, singulari certamine dimicaturus, arma quibus oneraretur, respuit: virtus enim suis lacertis magis quam alienis integumentis nititur. Deinde eminus, quo gravius feriret, ictu lapidis hostem interemit. Postea numquam nisi consulto Domino bellum adorsus. Ideo in omnibus victor proeliis, usque ad summam senectutem manu promptus, bello adversus Titanas suscepto ferocibus bellator miscebatur agminibus, gloriae cupidus, incuriosus salutis.

178. Sed non haec sola praeclara fortitudo est, sed etiam illorum gloriosam fortitudinem accipimus qui per fidem magnitudine animi *obstruxerunt leonum ora, exstinxerunt virtutem ignis, effugerunt aciem gladii, evaluerunt de infirmitate fortes,* qui non comitatu et legionibus succincti communem cum multis victoriam, sed nuda virtute animi singularem de perfidis retulerunt triumphum. Quam insuperabilis Daniel, qui circa latera sua rudentes non expavit leones! Fremebant bestiae, et ille epulabatur.

XXXVI **179.** Non igitur in viribus corporis et lacertis tantummodo fortitudinis gloria est sed magis in virtute animi, neque in inferenda sed depellenda iniuria lex virtutis est. Qui enim non repellit a socio iniuriam, si potest, tam est in vitio quam ille qui facit. Unde sanctus Moyses hinc prius orsus est temptamenta bellicae fortitudinis. Nam cum vidisset Hebraeum ab Aegyptio iniuriam accipientem, defendit ita ut Aegyptium

176. Courage belongs higher up the scale than the other virtues, then; but it is a virtue which never comes unaccompanied, for it does not depend purely on its own resources—at any rate, where courage is without justice, it leads only to wickedness, for the stronger it is, the readier it is to crush an inferior party. Even in the business of war, though, it is considered necessary to assess whether a particular war is just or unjust.

177. David never engaged in war unless he was provoked. This way, he was able to combine courage with prudence when it came to battle. Take the occasion when he was about to go into single-handed combat with Goliath, the man whose physical bulk was so colossal: he spurned the armour offered to him, saying that it would only weigh him down—for bravery depends on its own muscle, rather than on any protection offered by independent resources. Then, remaining at a distance so that he could strike with more deadly force, he felled his foe with the blow of a single stone. From that day forth, he never undertook a war without consulting the Lord first. And so it was that he emerged victorious in every battle he fought, and remained fighting fit and ready to bear arms well into his old age—there he was, engaged in a war against veritable Titans, right in the thick of it, fighting like a true warrior amidst the fierce columns, eager for glory, and quite unconcerned for his own safety.

178. But this is not the only type of courage to be regarded as remarkable. We learn too of the glorious courage of those who, through faith, and with greatness of spirit, 'stopped the mouths of lions, quenched the force of fire, escaped the edge of the sword, and out of weakness grew courageous'. They were not surrounded by comrades-in-arms or by legions, nor were they winning the kind of victory in which a host of others could claim a share; it was by the bare valour of their spirits that they fought and won their triumphs single-handedly over infidels. Look at Daniel, and how invincible he was! He knew no fear even when the lions were roaring right beside him! The beasts were growling furiously, and he remained intent on his food.

179. So the glory of courage does not consist merely in physical **XXXVI** strength or the power of muscle: it is to be found far more in valour of spirit. And the law of valour consists not in doing people an injury but in protecting them from such things. In point of fact, the person who fails to deflect an injury from his neighbour, when he is in a position to do so, is as much at fault as the one who inflicts it. This was where holy Moses took his earliest steps towards proving his courage in war. For when he saw a Hebrew being ill-treated by an Egyptian, he defended him—and did it so successfully that he finished the Egyptian

sterneret atque in arena absconderet. Salomon quoque ait: *Eripe eum qui ducitur ad mortem.*

180. Unde igitur hoc vel Tullius vel etiam Panaetius aut ipse Aristoteles transtulerint, apertum est satis, quamque etiam his duobus antiquior dixerit Iob: *Salvum feci pauperem de manu potentis et pupillum, cui adiutor non erat, adiuvi. Benedictio perituri in me veniat.* Nonne hic fortissimus qui tam fortiter pertulit impetus diaboli et vicit eum virtute mentis suae? Neque vero de eius dubitandum fortitudine, cui dicit Dominus: *Accinge sicut vir lumbos tuos . . . suscipe altitudinem et virtutem . . . omnem autem iniuriosum humiliato.* Apostolus quoque ait: *Habetis fortissimam consolationem.* Est ergo fortis qui se in dolore aliquo consolatur.

181. Et re vera iure ea fortitudo vocatur quando unusquisque se ipsum vincit, iram continet, nullis illecebris emollitur atque inflectitur, non adversis perturbatur, non extollitur secundis et quasi vento quodam variarum rerum circumfertur mutatione. Quid autem excelsius et magnificentius quam exercere mentem, adficere carnem, in servitutem redigere ut oboediat imperio, consiliis obtemperet, ut in adeundis laboribus impigre exsequatur propositum animi ac voluntatem?

182. Haec igitur prima vis fortitudinis, quoniam in duobus generibus fortitudo spectatur animi: primo, ut externa corporis pro minimis habeat et quasi superflua despicienda magis quam expetenda ducat; secundo, ut ea quae summa sunt omnesque res in quibus honestas et illud πρέπον cernitur, praeclara animi intentione usque ad effectum persequatur. Quid enim tam praeclarum quam ut ita animum informes tuum ut neque divitias nec voluptates neque honores in maximis constituas, neque in his studium omne conteras? Quod cum ita adfectus animo fueris, necesse est ut illud honestum ac decorum praeponendum putes illique mentem ita intendas tuam, ut, quidquid acciderit quo frangi animi solent, aut patrimonii amissio aut honoris imminutio aut

off and hid him in the sand. Solomon also says: 'Rescue a man who is being taken to meet his death.'

180. It is quite clear, then, where Cicero—or indeed Panaetius or Aristotle himself—took this idea from. It is equally clear that Job pre-dated even these last two, and he could say: 'I saved the poor from the hand of the powerful, and I gave help to the orphan who had no one to help him. May the blessing of the one who is about to perish come upon me.' Here was a man who epitomized courage, surely—one who showed such courage in enduring all the attacks of the devil, and overcame him by the sheer valour of his heart. In truth, his courage was beyond all doubt, for we read of the Lord saying to him: 'Gird up your loins like a man. . . . Put on true loftiness of spirit, true valour. . . . Let every spirit of injustice be humbled.' And the apostle says: 'You have this consolation, which brings you the greatest of courage.' This, then, is the hallmark of a courageous person: he is one who is able to console himself no matter what grief he is suffering.

181. Real courage, the kind which is truly worthy of the name, is to be seen when an individual masters himself and contains his anger; when he is not weakened or turned aside by any of the alluring things that the world has to offer; when he does not become too dismayed when times are hard or too excited when they are going well, and when he is not carried around, as it were, by every wind of changing circum-stance. To exercise the mind, to control the flesh, to bring it into subjection, so that it obeys the commands of reason and does what wisdom directs, so that in whatever labour it has to undergo it is always ready to carry out the purpose and will of the spirit—what loftier or more magnificent feat could there be than that?

182. Here, therefore, is the first essential character of courage. For courage of spirit needs to be considered in two different dimensions. There is, first, the courage that counts external or physical things for very little and looks upon them as unnecessary, as things to be despised rather than sought after. There is also, in the second place, the courage that applies the best powers of the mind to the pursuit and realization of everything that is truly important, and everything in which what is honourable and what is *prepon*, or seemly, may be clearly discerned. If you train your mind to such a pitch that you attach no great importance to riches or sensual pleasures or honours, and learn not to squander all your enthusiasm on things like these, what could be more glorious than that? When this is your spirit of mind, you need to believe that what is honourable and seemly must come before every-thing else. You need to set your heart upon it so much that if any of the usual things which break people's spirits should happen to you—say you lose an inheritance, or suffer a loss of status, or you are attacked by

obtrectatio infidelium, quasi superior non sentias; deinde ut te salutis ipsius pericula pro iustitia suscepta non moveant.

183. Haec vera fortitudo est quam habet Christi athleta qui *nisi legitime certaverit non coronatur.* An mediocre tibi videtur praeceptum fortitudinis: *Tribulatio patientiam operatur, patientia probationem, probatio autem spem?* Vide quot certamina, et una corona! Quod praeceptum non dat nisi qui est confortatus in Christo Iesu, cuius caro requiem non habebat. Adflictio undique: *foris pugnae, intus timores.* Et quamvis in periculis, in laboribus plurimis, in carceribus, in mortibus positus, animo tamen non frangebatur sed proeliabatur adeo ut potentior suis fieret infirmitatibus.

184. Itaque considera quemadmodum eos qui ad officia ecclesiae accedunt despicientiam rerum humanarum habere debere doceat: *Si ergo mortui estis cum Christo ab elementis huius mundi, quid adhuc velut viventes de hoc mundo decernitis? Ne tetigeritis, ne adtaminaveritis, ne gustaveritis: quae sunt omnia ad corruptelam ipso usu.* Et infra: *Si ergo consurrexistis cum Christo, quae sursum sunt quaerite.* Et iterum: *Mortificate ergo membra vestra quae sunt super terram.* Et haec quidem adhuc omnibus fidelibus; tibi autem, fili, contemptum divitiarum, profanarum quoque et anilium fabularum suadet declinationem, nihil permittens nisi quod te exerceat ad pietatem, quia corporalis exercitatio nulli rei usui est, *pietas autem ad omnia utilis.*

185. Exerceat ergo te pietas ad iustitiam, continentiam, mansuetudinem, ut fugias iuvenilia opera, confirmatus et radicatus in gratia bonum fidei subeas certamen, non te implices negotiis saecularibus, quoniam Deo militas. Etenim si hi qui imperatori militant, susceptionibus litium, actu negotiorum forensium, venditione mercium prohibentur humanis legibus, quanto magis qui fidei exercet militiam, ab omni usu negotiationis abstinere debet, agelluli sui contentus fructibus si habet, si non habet, stipendiorum suorum fructu. Siquidem bonus testis est qui dicat: *Iuvenis fui et senui et non vidi iustum derelictum nec semen eius quaerens panem.* Ea es

unbelievers—you behave as though you are superior to it, and do not feel it. In fact, even dangers to life itself, if endured in the interests of justice, must not disturb you.

183. Here is true courage, the kind possessed by the athlete of Christ, who 'does not receive the crown unless he has competed according to the rules'. Can the law of courage really seem trivial to you? 'Tribulation works patience,' it says, 'patience approval, and approval hope'. Look how many contests there are—but there is only one crown. Who is it that gives us this law? Only the man who knew what it was to be strengthened in Christ Jesus—and his flesh found no rest at all. For him, there was affliction on all sides: 'conflicts without, fears within'. And yet, though constantly in dangers, in countless struggles, in prison cells, and in mortal perils, he remained unbroken in spirit, and kept on in the fight—and so he emerged in the end stronger than his own weaknesses.

184. In the light of this, consider how he teaches those who are entering upon the duties of the church to look with disdain upon the affairs of men: 'If then you have died with Christ from the elements of this world, why do you behave as though you are still alive to them, and judge according to worldly standards? "Do not handle, do not touch, do not taste"—all these things are destined for corruption by their very use.' And later on he says: 'If then you have risen with Christ, seek the things which are above'. And again: 'Put to death, therefore, your members which are on the earth.' These rules are addressed to all the faithful, of course. But to you, my son, the counsel is quite specific. You are to have a contempt for riches, and you are to avoid profane and old wives' tales. You are not allowed anything unless it provides you with the kind of exercise which produces godliness: for bodily exercise is of no real benefit, but 'godliness is beneficial for all things'.

185. So, let godliness provide you with the exercise you need, producing justice, self-control, and gentleness in you, so that you flee the ways of youth and fight the good fight of faith, grounded and rooted in grace, and do not entangle yourself in the affairs of the world, since it is God that you are serving. Look at it this way: if men who serve the emperor are prohibited by human regulations from entering upon lawsuits, engaging in the affairs of the courts, and selling goods for profit, how much more should the man who is committed to the service of the faith keep away from everything to do with business, and be content with the incomes from his own little bit of land, if he has one, or with the income from his stipends, if he does not? Here is a good witness, one who can say: 'I have been young, and now I am old, and I have never seen a just man forsaken, or his offspring begging

enim tranquillitas animi et temperantia, quae neque studio quaerendi adficitur neque egestatis metu angitur.

XXXVII **186.** Ea est etiam quae dicitur vacuitas animi ab angoribus ut neque in doloribus molliores simus neque in prosperis elatiores. Quod si hi qui ad capessendam rem publicam adhortantur aliquos, haec praecepta dant, quanto magis nos qui ad officium ecclesiae vocamur, talia debemus agere quae placeant Deo, ut praetendat in nobis virtus Christi, et ita simus nostro probati imperatori ut membra nostra arma iustitiae sint, arma non carnalia in quibus peccatum regnet, sed arma fortia Deo quibus peccatum destruatur. Moriatur caro nostra ut in ea omnis culpa moriatur et *quasi ex mortuis viventes* novis resurgamus operibus ac moribus.

187. Haec sunt plena honesti et decori officii stipendia fortitudinis. Sed quia in omnibus quae agimus, non solum quid honestum sed etiam quid possibile sit quaerimus, ne forte adgrediamur aliquid quod non possimus exsequi, unde nos tempore persecutionis de civitate in civitatem concedere, immo ut verbo ipso utar, *fugere* vult Dominus, ne temere aliquis, dum martyrii desiderat gloriam, offerat se periculis quae fortasse caro infirmior aut remissior animus ferre ac tolerare non queat.

XXXVIII **188.** Nec rursus propter ignaviam cedere quis ac deserere fidem debet metu periculi. Qua gratia praeparandus est animus, exercenda mens, stabilienda ad constantiam, ut nullis perturbari animus possit terroribus, nullis frangi molestiis, nullis suppliciis cedere. Quae difficile quidem sustinentur, sed quia omnia supplicia graviorum suppliciorum vincuntur formidine, ideo si consilio firmes animum tuum nec a ratione discedendum putes et proponas divini iudicii metum, perpetui supplicii tormenta, potes animi subire tolerantiam.

189. Hoc igitur diligentiae est ut quis ita se comparet; illud ingenii si quis potest vigore mentis praevidere quae futura sunt et tamquam ante oculos locare quid possit accidere et quid agere debeat, si ita acciderit, definire; interdum duo et tria simul voluere animo, quae coniciat aut singula aut

bread.' It is here that we find true tranquillity of spirit, true temperance: the passion for gain does not affect it, nor does the fear of want
cause it anguish.

186. It is here too that we find what is known as the freedom of the **XXXVII**
spirit from anxiety, which ensures that we are neither too feeble in
times of trouble nor too elated when things are going well. If those who
encourage men to take up the reins of state give rules of this sort, how
much more should we who are called to do duty in the church seek to
act in a way that will be pleasing to God? The power of Christ should
be arrayed within us for all to see, and we should be so commendable
to our 'Emperor' that our members function as the weapons of
righteousness—not carnal weapons in which sin reigns, but weapons
that are strong for God, for the destruction of sin. Our flesh must die,
so that in it every fault will die as well, and, like people brought from
death to life, we shall rise again with new works and ways.

187. These are the wages which this duty of courage pays, and they
are full of what is honourable and seemly. But since in everything to
which we put our hand we are interested not simply in what is
honourable but also in what is possible—for we might embark on
some venture and then find ourselves unable to complete it—it is the
Lord's will that in a time of persecution we should pass—or, to use his
precise word, 'flee'—from city to city. For a person might have such a
strong desire for the glory of martyrdom that he exposes himself to
dangers without a thought, only to discover, perhaps, that his flesh is
too weak, or his spirit too slack, and he is unable to cope with them or
endure them.

188. At the same time, it is never right for anyone to give way on **XXXVIII**
account of cowardice, or to desert the faith through fear of danger. To
this end, the spirit needs to be duly prepared and the mind exercised
and trained to stand firm, so that the spirit will not be disturbed by any
kind of fear, or broken by any kind of care, or give way under any kind
of punishment. These are all troubles that are difficult to bear; of
course they are. But since all sufferings can be overcome by a fear of
greater sufferings, if you stiffen your spirit's resolve, if you consider
that it is your duty not to abandon reason, and if you keep before you
the fear of divine judgement and the torments of everlasting punishment, you can find within you an endurance of spirit.

189. All it takes, then, for someone to make himself ready like this is
dedicated preparation. It requires real intelligence, though, for a
person to have the mental power to anticipate the future, to picture
before his eyes, as it were, what might happen, and to determine what
he ought to do if things do turn out like this. Sometimes such an
individual is able to turn over two or three possible scenarios in his

coniuncta accidere posse et aut singulis aut coniunctis disponere actus quos intellegat profuturos.

190. Fortis ergo est viri non dissimulare cum aliquid immi-
neat, sed praetendere et tamquam explorare de specula
quadam mentis et obviare cogitatione provida rebus futuris,
ne forte dicat postea: 'Ideo ista incidi quia non arbitrabar
posse evenire'. Denique nisi explorentur adversa, cito occu-
pant; ut in bello improvisus hostis vix sustinetur, et si
imparatos inveniat, facile opprimit, ita animum mala inex-
plorata plus frangunt.

191. In his igitur duobus illa est animi excellentia, ut primum
animus tuus bonis exercitus cogitationibus mundo corde quod
verum et honestum est videat—*Beati*, enim, *mundo corde quia
ipsi etiam Deum videbunt*—atque id quod honestum est solum
bonum iudicet; deinde nullis perturbetur occupationibus,
nullis cupiditatibus fluctuet.

192. Neque vero id facile quisquam facit. Quid enim tam
difficile quam despicere tamquam ex arce aliqua sapientiae
opes aliaque omnia quae plerisque videntur magna et prae-
celsa? Deinde ut iudicium tuum stabili ratione confirmes et
quae iudicaveris levia tamquam nihil profutura contemnas?
Deinde ut, si quid acciderit adversi idque grave et acerbum
putetur, ita feras ut nihil praeter naturam accidisse putes,
cum legeris: *Nudus sum natus, nudus exibo. Quae Dominus
dedit, Dominus abstulit* (et utique et filios amiserat et facultates), servesque in omnibus personam sapientis et iusti, sicut
ille servavit qui ait: *Sicut Domino placuit, ita factum est: sit
nomen Domini benedictum*; et infra: *Sicut una insipientium
mulierum locuta es: si bona suscepimus de manu Domini, quae
mala sunt non sustinemus?*

XXXIX 193. Non est igitur mediocris nec discreta a ceteris animi

mind simultaneously, surmising that they could come to pass either one at a time or all at once, and he is able to decide which particular course of action he thinks will be most helpful should such eventualities develop, whether one at a time or all at once.

190. So the courageous person sees it as his duty not to look the opposite way when some threat occurs, but knows to focus his attention on it, to explore it carefully from every angle, using his mind almost as though it were a sort of look-out point, and to give careful thought to anticipating all the future contingencies, so that he will not have to say afterwards: 'I fell into these troubles for this reason—I simply did not think they could happen.' The fact is, if we fail to explore adverse possibilities, they can overtake us at a stroke. This is how it is in war: an enemy who has not been spotted in advance is virtually impossible to resist, and if he finds his opposition unprepared, he crushes them without the slightest difficulty. In the same way, evils which have not been explored in advance break the spirit all the more.

191. These, then, are the two features in which excellence of spirit consists. First, your spirit must grow used to the exercise of thinking good thoughts, and must keep a pure heart, to see what is true and honourable—for 'Blessed are the pure in heart, for they shall see God'—and to judge what is honourable to be the sole good. Secondly, it must not be disturbed by any preoccupations or tossed about by any desires.

192. Now there is no doubt about it—this is no easy thing for anyone to achieve. What could be so difficult as to behave as though you are up in a citadel of wisdom, looking down at wealth and all the other things which most people hold to be great and important? Again, what could be so difficult as to stiffen your resolve, to determine that these things are trivial, and to despise them as worthless? Or again, what could be so difficult as to experience a calamity of one kind or another, something which people think is dreadful and cruel, and to bear it, taking the view that what has happened is just part of nature's normal course? For you have read: 'Naked was I born, and naked shall I go from this world. What the Lord gave, the Lord has taken away'—and the man who said this had of course lost his children and all that he had. Or again, what could be so difficult as to maintain the character of a wise and a just person, no matter what your circumstances? This was what that man did, for he said: 'As it has pleased the Lord, so it has come to pass: blessed be the name of the Lord.' And further on he said this: 'You have spoken like one of the foolish women: if we have received good from the hand of the Lord, shall we not also endure evil?'

193. We can see, then, that courage of spirit is no mean quality. Nor **XXXIX**

fortitudo, quae bellum cum virtutibus gerat sed quae sola
defendat ornamenta virtutum omnium et iudicia custodiat, et
quae inexpiabili proelio adversus omnia vitia decernat, invicta
ad labores, fortis ad pericula, rigidior adversus voluptates,
dura adversus illecebras quibus aurem deferre nesciat nec, ut
dicitur, 'Ave' dicat, pecuniam neglegat, avaritiam fugiat
tamquam labem quamdam quae virtutem effeminet. Nihil
enim tam contrarium fortitudini quam lucro vinci. Frequenter pulsis hostibus, inclinata in fugam adversariorum acie,
dum exuviis caesorum capitur proeliator, inter ipsos quos
stravit, miserandus occubuit; et triumphis suis deiectae
legiones, dum spoliis occupantur, hostem in se revocarunt,
qui fugerat.

194. Fortitudo igitur tam immanem pestem repellat et pro-
terat nec temptetur cupiditatibus nec frangatur metu, quia
virtus sibi constat ut fortiter omnia persequatur vitia tamquam virtutis venena; iracundiam velut quibusdam propulset
armis quae tollat consilium, et tamquam aegritudinem vitet;
gloriae quoque caveat appetentiam, quae frequenter nocuit
immoderatius expetita, semper autem usurpata.

195. Quid horum sancto Iob vel in virtute defuit vel in vitio
obrepsit? Quomodo laborem aegritudinis, frigoris, famis pertulit! Quomodo despexit salutis periculum! Numquid rapinis
divitiae coacervatae de quibus tanta inopibus adfluebant?
Numquid avaritiam census aut voluptatis studia cupiditates-
que excitavit? Numquid trium regum iniuriosa contentio vel
servorum contumelia in iram excussit? Numquid gloria sicut
levem extulit, qui imprecabatur gravia sibi si umquam vel
non voluntariam celaverit culpam vel reveritus esset multi-
tudinem plebis quominus adnuntiaret eam in conspectu
omnium? Neque enim consentaneae sunt vitiis virtutes sed
sibi constant. Quis igitur tam fortis quam sanctus Iob? Cui
secundus adiudicari potest, qui parem vix repperit?

XL **196.** Sed fortasse aliquos bellica defixos gloria tenet ut putent

does it exist in isolation from the other virtues: it wages war in company with them, yet in its own strength it defends the honour of all of them and guards their powers of judgement. It fights with implacable hostility against every possible vice; it is indefatigable in hard work of every kind, bold in the face of dangers, resolute and unbending in confronting sensual pleasures, and steadfast and firm when it confronts carnal allurements—it does not know how to lend an ear to them, or even, as it is said, bid them 'Good day'. It has no interest whatsoever in money, and it runs from greed as a deadly disease which weakens the fibre of virtue. For the truth is, there is nothing which runs so contrary to courage as to be overcome by a desire for gain. Many's the time an enemy has been held off and opposition lines have turned and fled—and then some warrior, his attention captivated by the spoils of the slain, has fallen himself, poor fool, in the midst of the very men he has just cut down; and entire legions have been so preoccupied with gathering their booty that they have invited a foe who had fled to come back upon them, and so have been robbed of their triumph.

194. Courage must therefore repel and destroy this plague which is so monstrous, and must not be tempted by desires or broken by fear. For virtue is true to itself, and so it shows courage in going after every vice; to it, every one is like a poison, deadly to virtue. It must as it were take up its arms to drive away anger, for anger supplants sensible thought, and must be avoided as though it were an illness. It must beware of the desire for glory, too, for this is a desire that has often proved harmful when people have wanted it in an excessive measure, and always so when they have found it.

195. Can you identify a single one of these virtues that holy Job lacked, or a single one of these vices that had found its way into him? Look how he endured the struggle of sickness and cold and hunger! Look how he despised the danger to his life! Did he rob people to accumulate his wealth, so much of which poured into the pockets of people who were in need? Did he have a spark of greed in his heart for money, or any tastes or desires for sensual pleasures? Did the arguments of the three leaders, unfair as they were, or the insults of his servants, rouse him to anger? Did glory carry him away like a creature of the wind? He called dread curses to fall on him if he had ever concealed even an involuntary fault, or if he had been too afraid of the ordinary masses to confess it in the sight of all. Virtues have no truck with vices; they are true to themselves. Who, then, could match holy Job for courage? Is there anyone to whom he could be judged second? We can scarcely find his equal.

196. But it may be that glory won in war holds some people so **XL**

solam esse proeliarem fortitudinem et ideo me ad haec
deflexisse quia illa nostris deforet. Quam fortis Iesus Nave,
ut uno proelio quinque reges captos sterneret cum populis
suis! Deinde, cum adversum Gabaonitas surgeret proelium et
vereretur ne nox impediret victoriam, magnitudine mentis et
fidei clamavit: *Stet sol*, et stetit donec victoria consummare-
tur. Gedeon in trecentis viris de ingenti populo et acerbo
hoste revexit triumphum. Ionatha adulescens virtutem fecit in
magno proelio. Quid de Machabaeis loquar?

197. Sed prius de populo dicam patrum qui, cum essent
parati ad repugnandum pro templo Dei et pro legitimis
suis, dolo hostium die lacessiti sabbati, maluerunt vulneribus
offerre nuda corpora quam repugnare, ne violarent sabbatum.
Itaque omnes laeti se morti obtulerunt. Sed Machabaei
considerantes quod hoc exemplo gens omnis posset perire,
sabbato etiam, ipsi cum in bellum provocarentur, ulti sunt
innocentium necem fratrum suorum. Unde postea stimulatus
rex Antiochus, cum bellum accenderet per duces suos
Lysiam, Nicanorem, Gorgiam, ita cum Orientalibus suis et
Assyriis adtritus est copiis ut quadraginta et octo milia in
medio campi a tribus milibus prosternerentur.

198. Virtutem ducis Iudae Machabaei de uno eius milite
considerate. Namque Eleazarus, cum supereminentem ceteris
elephantum, lorica vestitum regia, adverteret, arbitratus quod
in eo rex esset, cursu concitus in medium legionis se proripuit
et abiecto clipeo utraque manu interficiebat bestiam, atque
intravit sub eam et subiecto gladio interemit eam. Itaque
cadens bestia oppressit Eleazarum, atque ita mortuus est.
Quanta igitur virtus animi! Primo, ut mortem non timeret;
deinde, ut circumfusus legionibus inimicorum in confertos
raperetur hostes, medium penetraret agmen et contempta
morte ferocior, abiecto clipeo, utraque manu vulneratae
molem bestiae subiret ac sustineret, post intra ipsam succe-
deret quo pleniore feriret ictu. Cuius ruina inclusus magis
quam oppressus: suo est sepultus triumpho.

enthralled that they imagine courage cannot be found anywhere except in battle; they may feel that I have gone off on this last track simply because that particular quality was missing in our people. Well, look at the courage of Joshua son of Nun. In just a single battle, he captured five kings and laid them low, and their peoples with them. Or again, on the occasion when he was locked in combat with the Gibeonites, he was anxious that night would fall and prevent a decisive victory, so he cried out in faith and with greatness of spirit, 'Let the sun stand still!', and it stood still, until the victory was secured. Gideon, with only 300 men, brought off a triumph over a vast people and a cruel foe. Jonathan, just a young man, proved his bravery in a great battle. As for the Maccabees—where do I begin?

197. But first let me say something about our fathers' people. They were quite ready to stand up for the temple of God and for their laws. But when they were tricked by the enemy and attacked on the Sabbath day, they chose to offer their unprotected bodies to be wounded rather than fight back, so that they would not be guilty of breaking the Sabbath. And so they all gladly offered themselves to death. But the Maccabees decided that if they followed this example the entire nation might perish: so, when they were challenged to join battle, even though it was the Sabbath, they went out and avenged the deaths of their innocent brothers. Then later on, King Antiochus was so enraged at what had been done that he lit the flames of war once more, using his generals, Lysias, Nicanor, and Gorgias: he was completely crushed, and his Eastern and Assyrian forces along with him—48,000 of his men were left lying on the field, cut down by a force of just 3,000.

198. Gauge the bravery of the leader, Judas Maccabaeus, from the bravery of one of his ordinary soldiers. I am thinking of the example of Eleazar. Noticing one particular elephant which towered over the others and was decked out with a cuirass which suggested royal status, he concluded that the king must be riding on it. He ran after it as hard as he could and hurled himself into the midst of the enemy ranks; throwing away his shield, he tried to kill the beast with both hands: he went in beneath it, and finished it off with a blow of his sword from below. Thus, as it fell, the beast crushed Eleazar, and so he died. What bravery of spirit that was! In the first place, he had no fear of death; in the second place, surrounded by legions of hostile forces, he was carried into the thick of the enemy ranks, penetrated their central column, and, all the fiercer in his contempt for death, he threw away his shield, wounded the beast with both hands, and took the full weight of its vast bulk, after he had gone right in beneath it so as to strike it a more deadly blow. He was not so much crushed as trapped by it as it collapsed: he was buried under his own triumph.

199. Nec fefellit opinio virum, quamvis regius fefellerit habitus. Tanto enim virtutis spectaculo defixi hostes inermem, occupatum incursare non ausi, post casum ruentis bestiae sic trepidaverunt ut impares se omnes unius virtuti arbitrarentur. Denique rex Antiochus, Lysiae filius, qui centum viginti hominum milibus armatus venerat et cum triginta duobus elephantis ita ut ab ortu solis per singulas bestias velut montes quidam armorum corusco tamquam lampadibus ardentibus refulgerent, unius territus fortitudine pacem rogaret. Itaque Eleazarus heredem virtutis suae pacem reliquit. Sed haec triumphorum sint.

XLI **200.** Verum quia fortitudo non solum secundis rebus sed etiam adversis probatur, spectemus Iudae Machabaei exitum. Is enim, post victum Nicanorem, regis Demetrii ducem, securior adversus viginti milia exercitus regis, cum nongentis viris bellum adorsus, volentibus his cedere ne multitudine opprimerentur, gloriosam magis mortem quam turpem fugam suasit: *Ne crimen*, inquit, *nostrae relinquamus gloriae*. Itaque commisso proelio, cum a primo ortu diei in vesperam dimicaretur, dextrum cornu, in quo validissimam manum advertit hostium, adgressus facile avertit. Sed dum fugientes sequitur, a tergo vulneri locum praebuit; ita gloriosiorem triumphis locum mortis invenit.

201. Quid Ionatham fratrem eius adtexam? Qui cum parva manu adversus exercitus regios pugnans, desertus a suis et cum duobus tantum relictus reparavit bellum, avertit hostem, fugitantes suos ad societatem revocavit triumphi.

202. Habes fortitudinem bellicam, in qua non mediocris honesti ac decori forma est, quod mortem servituti praeferat ac turpitudini. Quid autem de martyrum dicam passionibus? Et ne longius vagemur, num minorem de superbo rege Antiocho Machabaei pueri revexerunt triumphum quam parentes proprii? Siquidem illi armati, isti sine armis vicerunt.

199. The man was not mistaken in his convictions, either, though he was mistaken in his conclusions about the royal equipment. For the enemy, confronted with such a display of bravery, were rooted to the spot, and could not bring themselves to attack a single, unarmed man, engrossed in his task. When the beast had crashed to the ground dead, they were so overwhelmed at the sight, they decided that, all told, they were no match for this one man in bravery. In fact, the courage of this one man so terrified King Antiochus, the son of Lysias, that he treated for peace, though he had come with an army of 120,000 men and 32 elephants—huge beasts like mountains: when the sun rose upon them as they marched along, one by one, the reflection from their armour was so dazzling, it was like seeing a great line of torches in full blaze. And so it was that Eleazar left peace as the legacy of his bravery. But these are all feats that should count as triumphs.

200. Nevertheless, since courage proves itself not just in times of XLI success but also when circumstances are difficult, let us look at the death of Judas Maccabaeus. After the defeat of Nicanor, king Demetrius' general, Judas behaved fearlessly even though he was facing the king's army of some 20,000 troops, and he entered war with only 900 men. His forces were desperate to retreat, for they were terrified of being crushed by the vast hordes, but he urged them to fight and die with glory rather than flee and bring shame on themselves. 'Let us not leave a stain on our glory,' he said. The battle duly commenced, and the fighting continued from first light until evening. He attacked the right wing of the enemy, where he could see that their strongest force lay, and easily drove it back. But then, while he was going after these troops as they fled, he offered the enemy an opportunity to launch an assault from behind. So he found in death a place of greater glory than his triumphs had afforded.

201. Need I add anything about his brother Jonathan? With just a small force, he fought against the king's armies, and though he was deserted by his soldiers and left with only two men, he went back to war, drove away the enemy, and recalled his men, as they fled, to share in his triumph.

202. Here, then, is courage in war: it offers no small expression of what it means to act in a way that is honourable and seemly, for it prefers death to slavery and disgrace. But what about the martyrs, and the sufferings they endured? To look no further than the family of whom we have just been thinking, let us answer the following question: Did the children of the Maccabees gain any lesser triumph over the proud king Antiochus than their parents had done? Their fathers were armed, after all, but when the children fought their own battle they conquered without arms. There they stood, undefeated, a

Stetit invicta septem puerorum cohors, regiis cincta legionibus: defecerunt supplicia, cesserunt tortores, non defecerunt
martyres. Alius corium capitis exutus speciem mutaverat,
virtutem auxerat; alius linguam iussus amputandam promere
respondit: 'Non solum Dominus audit loquentes qui audiebat
Moysen tacentem. Plus audit tacitas cogitationes suorum
quam voces omnium. Linguae flagellum times, flagellum
sanguinis non times? Habet et sanguis vocem suam qua
clamat ad Deum, sicut clamavit in Abel.'

203. Quid de matre loquar, quae spectabat laeta filiorum quot
funera tot tropaea et morientium vocibus tamquam psallen-
tium cantibus delectabatur, pulcherrimam ventris sui
citharam in filiis cernens et pietatis harmoniam omni lyrae
numero dulciorem?

204. Quid de bimulis loquar, qui ante palmam victoriae
acceperunt quam sensum naturae? Quid de sancta Agne,
quae in duarum maximarum rerum posita periculo, castitatis
et salutis, castitatem protexit, salutem cum immortalitate
commutavit?

205. Non praetereamus etiam sanctum Laurentium qui cum
videret Xistum episcopum suum ad martyrium duci, flere
coepit non passionem illius sed suam remansionem. Itaque his
verbis appellare coepit: 'Quo progrederis sine filio, pater?
Quo, sacerdos sancte, sine diacono properas tuo? Numquam
sacrificium sine ministro offerre consueveras. Quid in me ergo
displicuit, pater? Num degenerem probasti? Experire certe
utrum idoneum ministrum elegeris. Cui commisisti dominici
sanguinis consecrationem, cui consummandorum consortium
sacramentorum, huic sanguinis tui consortium negas? Vide ne
periclitetur iudicium tuum dum fortitudo laudatur. Abiectio
discipuli detrimentum est magisterii. Quid quod illustres,
praestantes viri discipulorum certaminibus quam suis vin-
cunt? Denique Abraham filium obtulit, Petrus Stephanum
praemisit. Et tu, pater, ostende in filio virtutem tuam, offer

little company of seven boys, surrounded by the forces of the king: all the punishments failed, the torturers gave up—but the martyrs never failed. One of them was scalped; he had altered in appearance, but he had grown in boldness. Another was ordered to stick out his tongue so it could be cut off. His reply was: 'It is not only those who speak that the Lord hears: he heard Moses when he was silent. He hears the silent thoughts of his own people more than the voices of all the rest. You are afraid of the scourge of my tongue: are you not afraid of the scourge of blood? Blood, too, has a voice of its own, with which it cries to God, as it cried in the case of Abel.'

203. What about their mother? She could look with joy on the bodies of her sons, seeing them as so many trophies, and take pleasure in the voices of her dying boys: to her ears, they were as charming as airs rendered by the most gifted of singers. There, in her sons, she caught the most marvellous of sounds: it was as if her womb had been a harp, on whose strings was being played a melody of devotion sweeter than any strain of the lyre.

204. And what about those infants who were put to death when they were only two years old? They received the palm of victory before they ever acquired nature's gift of awareness. Or what about holy Agnes? She was faced with a choice between the two things which mattered most to her: her chastity and her life; both were in danger. She chose to preserve her chastity and exchange her life for immortality.

205. And let us not forget holy Lawrence. When he saw his bishop, Sixtus, being led away to be martyred, he began to weep—not for the other man's suffering but because he himself was being left behind. So he began to plead with him, saying: 'Where are you going without your son, father? Where are you hurrying off to, holy priest, without your deacon? Never before has it been your way to offer the sacrifice without your minister present. What is there about me that has displeased you now, father? You did not prove me unworthy, did you? At least see whether you chose a suitable minister. You entrusted me with consecrating the Lord's blood and allowed me to share with you in celebrating the sacraments. Are you now denying me the opportunity to share in *your* blood? Make sure your good judgement isn't cast in question at the very hour when your courage wins you such praise. The rejection of a disciple spells loss for the office of his master. Isn't it true that illustrious men, men of real distinction, win their victories in the contests that their disciples go through, rather than in their own? After all, Abraham offered his son, and Peter sent Stephen on before him. Let it be the same with you, father: demonstrate your bravery in your son: offer the one to whom you have taught so much. This way, you will be confirmed in your

quem erudisti ut securus iudicii tui comitatu nobili pervenias ad coronam.'

206. Tunc Xistus ait: 'Non ego, fili, te relinquo ac desero; sed maiora tibi debentur certamina. Nos quasi senes levioris pugnae cursum recipimus, te quasi iuvenem manet gloriosior de tyranno triumphus. Mox venies, flere desiste: post triduum me sequeris. Sacerdotem et Levitam hic medius numerus decet. Non erat tuum sub magistro vincere, quasi adiutorem quaereres. Quid consortium passionis meae expetis? Totam tibi hereditatem eius dimitto. Quid praesentiam meam requiris? Infirmi discipuli magistrum praecedant, fortes sequantur, ut vincant sine magistro qui iam non indigent magisterio. Sic et Elias Eliseum reliquit. Tibi ergo mando nostrae virtutis successionem.'

207. Talis erat contentio digna sane de qua certarent sacerdos et minister, quis prior pateretur pro Christi nomine. In fabulis ferunt tragicis excitatos theatri magnos esse plausus, cum se Pylades Orestem diceret, Orestes, ut erat, Orestem se esse adseveraret: ille, ut pro Oreste necaretur, Orestes, ne Pyladem pro se pateretur necari. Sed illis non licebat vivere, quod uterque esset parricidii reus: alter qui fecisset, alter qui adiuvisset. Hic Laurentium sanctum adhuc nullus urgebat nisi amor devotionis; tamen et ipse post triduum, cum illuso tyranno impositus super craticulam exureretur: 'Assum est', inquit: 'versa et manduca'. Ita virtute animi vincebat ignis naturam.

XLII 208. Cavendum etiam reor ne, dum aliqui nimia gloriae ducuntur cupiditate, insolentius abutantur potestatibus et plerumque aversos a nobis animos gentilium in studia persecutionis excitent atque inflamment ad iracundiam. Itaque, ut

assessment of me, and you will attain the crown with a proper escort alongside you.'

206. Then Sixtus said: 'I am not leaving or abandoning you, my son, but there are greater contests yet reserved for you. I am an old man, and so I am given an easier fight to finish. But you are young, and for you there is a more glorious triumph over the tyrant awaiting. You will come along soon. Stop your crying! After three days you will be following me: it is only seemly that this interval should come between a priest and his Levite. It wasn't right that you should win the battle under the guidance of your master, as though you needed someone to help you through it. Why are you so keen to share my suffering? I leave its entire inheritance to you. Why do you desire my presence so much? Weak disciples should go before their master, and strong ones should follow, so that they win the battle for themselves, without their master, for they no longer need a master's teaching. That was why Elijah left Elisha behind. It is to you, then, that I am entrusting the legacy of my bravery.'

207. Such was the dispute in which the priest and his minister were engaged, and their rivalry was certainly in a worthy cause, for they were arguing over who should be the first to suffer for the name of Christ. When the tragic plays were being performed, we are told, the audience in the theatre used to burst into great applause at the point where Pylades would say that he was Orestes, and Orestes would insist that this was not so; it was *he* who was Orestes—as of course it was. Pylades' wish was that he should be executed instead of Orestes, while Orestes was determined to prevent Pylades being executed in his place. In their case, though, it genuinely was against all the laws of justice that they should continue to live, for they were both guilty of parricide: one had done the deed; the other had aided and abetted it. In our present example, however, no one pressed holy Lawrence to act in this way—it was down to nothing but his love and devotion. In any event, he too, three days later, was placed on a grid-iron and burnt to death for having made a mockery of the tyrant: 'He's roasted,' he said: 'turn him and eat him.' Such was the bravery of his spirit: he conquered the very nature of fire itself.

208. But caution is necessary as well, I think. For there are some **XLII** people whose desire for glory is too strong, and they become far too arrogant and abusive towards the powers that be. The result is, they arouse in the hearts of the pagans—who are generally hostile towards us anyhow—a determination to persecute us, and they kindle the flames of anger within them. How many persons then end up losing their lives as a result of these people's actions, just so that they

illi perseverare possint et supplicia vincere, quantos perire faciunt?

209. Prospiciendum etiam ne adulantibus aperiamus aurem: emolliri enim adulatione non solum fortitudinis non esse sed etiam ignaviae videtur.

XLIII **210.** Quoniam de tribus virtutibus diximus, restat ut de quarta virtute dicamus, quae temperantia ac modestia vocatur; in qua maxime tranquillitas animi, studium mansuetudinis, moderationis gratia, honesti cura, decoris consideratio spectatur et quaeritur.

211. Ordo igitur quidam vitae nobis tenendus est, ut a verecundia prima quaedam fundamenta ducantur, quae socia ac familiaris est mentis placiditati, proterviae fugitans, ab omni aliena luxu, sobrietatem diligit, honestatem fovet, decorum illud requirit.

212. Sequatur conversationis electio, ut adiungamur probatissimis quibusque senioribus. Namque ut aequalium usus dulcior ita senum tutior est, qui magisterio quodam et ductu vitae colorat mores adulescentium et velut murice probitatis inficit. Namque si hi qui sunt ignari locorum, cum sollertibus viarum iter adoriri gestiunt, quanto magis adulescentes cum senibus debent novum sibi iter vitae adgredi, quominus errare possint et a vero tramite virtutis deflectere? Nihil enim pulchrius quam eosdem et magistros vitae et testes habere.

213. Quaerendum etiam in omni actu quid personis, temporibus conveniat atque aetatibus, quid etiam singulorum ingeniis sit accommodum. Saepe enim quod alterum decet, alterum non decet. Aliud iuveni aptum, aliud seni; aliud in periculis, aliud rebus secundis.

214. Saltavit ante arcam Domini David, non saltavit Samuel; nec ille reprehensus, sed magis iste laudatus. Mutavit vultum contra regem cui nomen Achis; at hoc si remota fecisset

themselves can prove their perseverance and their ability to overcome tortures?

209. We should also beware of offering a ready ear to those who indulge in flattery. If people allow themselves to be won round by flattery, the impression they give is not just that they lack courage, but that they are guilty of cowardice.

210. We have now spoken of three of the virtues, so it remains only for XLIII us to speak of the fourth, which is called temperance or moderation. What we look for or seek here are, above all, a tranquillity of spirit, a desire for gentleness, the grace of moderation, a concern to do what is honourable, and a determination to do what is seemly.

211. We must, then, maintain a certain order in our lives, so that some basic foundations can be established, all of which have modesty as their first premise. Modesty acts like a friend and ally of calmness of mind: it shuns effrontery, it keeps clear of all excess, it loves sobriety, it cherishes what is honourable, and it searches for what is seemly.

212. The next important thing is to choose our company carefully. This means that we need to attach ourselves to older men, to those whose character is thoroughly tried and tested. Think of it this way: it may well be more congenial to associate with those of our own age, but it is by the same token safer to spend time with men who are mature in years. By providing a kind of guidance and direction in life's course, their company lends its own colour to the way in which young men behave; it tinges it, so to speak, with the rich purple of their probity. Or think of it this way: if people who are ignorant of a particular locality make sure to travel in the company of those who have a thorough knowledge of its roads, how much more should young men set out on the road of life, new to them as it is, in the company of mature men, so as to make sure that they do not stray or turn aside from the true path of virtue? There can be no more splendid ideal than to have the same people as both the guides and the witnesses of your life.

213. We also need to consider, in our every action, what is appropriate for particular personalities, circumstances, and stages of life, and what is best suited to the abilities of each of us as an individual. It is often the way that what is seemly for one person is not seemly for another. One thing may be right for a young man, something else for an old man; one thing may be right in time of danger, something else when circumstances are good.

214. David danced before the ark of the Lord; Samuel did not. David was not faulted on that account, but Samuel earned all the more praise. David put on a false appearance in the presence of the king whose name was Achish, but if he had done this in circumstances where he

formidine quominus cognosceretur, nequaquam levitatis reprehensione carere potuisset. Saul quoque vallatus choro prophetarum, etiam ipse prophetavit, et de solo quasi indigno memoratum est: *Et Saul inter prophetas?*

XLIV **215.** Unusquisque igitur suum ingenium noverit et ad id se applicet quod sibi aptum elegerit. Itaque prius quid sequatur, consideret. Noverit bona sua sed etiam vitia cognoscat aequalemque se iudicem sui praebeat ut bonis intendat, vitia declinet.

216. Alius distinguendae lectioni aptior, alius psalmo gratior, alius exorcizandis qui malo laborant spiritu sollicitior, alius sacrario opportunior habetur. Haec omnia spectet sacerdos et quid cuique congruat, id officii deputet. Quod etenim unumquemque suum ducit ingenium aut quod officium decet, id maiore impletur gratia.

217. Sed id, cum in omni vita difficile, tum in nostro actu difficillimum est. Amat enim unusquisque sequi vitam parentum. Denique plerique ad militiam feruntur quorum militaverunt parentes, alii ad actiones diversas.

218. In ecclesiastico vero officio nihil rarius invenias quam eum qui sequatur institutum patris, vel quia gravis deterret actus vel quia in lubrica aetate difficilior abstinentia vel quia alacri adulescentiae videtur vita obscurior; et ideo ad ea convertuntur studia quae plausibiliora arbitrantur. Praesentia quippe plures quam futura praeferunt. Illi autem praesentibus, nos futuris militamus. Unde, quo praestantior causa, eo debet esse cura adtentior.

XLV **219.** Teneamus igitur verecundiam et eam quae totius vitae ornatum adtollit, modestiam. Non enim mediocre est rebus singulis modum servare atque impertire ordinem, in quo vere praelucet illud quod decorum dicitur, quod ita cum honesto iungitur ut separari non queat. Siquidem et quod decet honestum est, et quod honestum est decet, ut magis in

had no fear of being recognized, he would undoubtedly have had to be faulted for carrying on in a frivolous fashion. Or take the case of Saul: he was surrounded by a band of prophets, so he took it upon himself to prophesy as well. Yet it was only of him that people said—implying it was inappropriate for such a person to behave like this—'Is Saul also among the prophets?'

215. Each of us needs to know his own abilities, therefore, and should **XLIV** apply himself to doing whatever he has chosen as right for himself. This means that he must first of all consider what the consequences will be. He should know his good points, but also recognize his faults, and show that he is an honest judge of his own character by concentrating on his good qualities and avoiding his faults.

216. One person may find that he is particularly suited to reading the lessons; another may be better at leading the psalms. One might show especial devotion in conducting exorcisms upon people who are struggling with an evil spirit; another will be more at home doing the work of a sacristan. A bishop should give consideration to all these facts and should appoint each man to the duty to which he is suited. For the truth is, when each person is guided by his own ability, or rather by the kind of duty that is fitting for him, the task is fulfilled with a greater grace.

217. But if this is a difficult principle to observe in any walk of life, then it is extremely difficult in our calling. For each of us is prone to follow the way of life that his parents led. So, most men whose fathers served in the army are drawn towards a military career, and others find the same thing with other occupations.

218. In the office of the church, however, you find nothing more unusual than the case of a man who follows in his father's footsteps. This is either because the severity of the work is off-putting, or because abstinence is more difficult at a treacherous age, or because the way of life appears too obscure to youth with all its energies, and so young men turn to the kind of pursuits which they believe will win them greater applause. Quite simply, the majority of people opt for the realities of this present world in preference to the realities of the world to come. They are engaged in the service of this present world; but we are engaged in the service of the world to come. The more glorious the cause, then, the more care and attention we ought to devote to it.

219. Let us hold fast to modesty, therefore, and to the moderation **XLV** which serves to adorn the whole of life. It is no slight achievement to succeed in maintaining due measure in everything you do and to bestow upon it an order which will truly reflect the splendour of the quality we call seemliness. The standard of seemliness is so closely joined to the standard of what is honourable that it cannot be separated

sermone distinctio sit quam in virtute discretio. Differre enim ea inter se intellegi potest, explicari non potest.

220. Et ut conemur aliquid eruere distinctionis, honestas velut bona valetudo est et quaedam salubritas corporis, decus autem tamquam venustas et pulchritudo. Sicut ergo pulchritudo supra salubritatem ac valetudinem videtur excellere et tamen sine his esse non potest neque ullo separari modo, quoniam nisi bona valetudo sit, pulchritudo esse ac venustas non potest, sic honestas decorum illud in se continet ut ab ea profectum videatur et sine ea esse non possit. Velut salubritas igitur totius operis actusque nostri honestas est et sicut species est decorum, quod cum honestate confusum opinione distinguitur. Nam etsi in aliquo videatur excellere, tamen in radice est honestatis sed flore praecipuo, ut sine ea decidat, in ea floreat. Quid est enim honestas nisi quae turpitudinem quasi mortem fugiat? Quid vero inhonestum nisi quod ariditatem ac mortem adferat? Virente igitur substantia virtutis decorum illud tamquam flos emicat, quia radix salva est; at vero propositi nostri radice vitiosa nihil germinat.

221. Habes hoc in nostris aliquanto expressius. Dicit enim David: *Dominus regnavit, decorem induit.* Et apostolus ait: *Sicut in die honeste ambulate.* Quod Graece dicunt εὐσχήμως, hoc autem proprie significat: bono habitu, bona specie. Deus ergo, primum hominem cum conderet, bona habitudine, bona membrorum compositione formavit et optimam ei speciem dedit. Remissionem non dederat peccatorum; sed posteaquam renovavit eum Spiritu et infudit ei gratiam qui venerat in servi forma et in hominis specie, adsumpsit decorem redemptionis humanae. Et ideo dixit propheta: *Dominus regnavit, decorem induit.* Deinde alibi dicit: *Te decet hymnus, Deus, in Sion*; hoc est dicere: Honestum est ut te timeamus, te diligamus, te precemur, te honorificemus; scriptum est enim: *Omnia vestra honeste fiant.* Sed possumus et hominem

from it, since what is seemly is honourable, and what is honourable is seemly: the distinction between the words is greater than the difference in the virtues they describe. The difference between them can be understood, but it cannot be explained.

220. Still, if we must make an attempt to bring out some kind of distinction, we might say that what is honourable is akin to good health and a basic soundness of body, while what is seemly is like physical grace and beauty. So, just as beauty appears more striking than soundness and health, yet cannot exist without them or be separated from them in any way—for unless there is good health, there can be no such things as beauty and grace—, so doing what is honourable involves doing what is seemly: the one appears to stem from the other, and is unable to exist without it. Honourable behaviour, then, is, if you like, a general soundness in all our work and activity, while conduct that is seemly is, as it were, the external appearance of this reality: it blends in with what is honourable, though notionally it can be distinguished from it. You see, even if in a given case the seemly side appears more striking, it is still dependent on what is honourable. It is like the relationship between a prize flower and its root: without the root, the flower withers; with it, it flourishes. What does it mean to act honourably, other than to flee from everything that is shameful, as though from death itself? And again, what does it mean to act dishonourably, other than to behave in a way that brings barrenness and death? So long as the essence of virtue is green and healthy, then, all that is seemly will burst into bloom like a flower, because its root is sound. But when the root of our life is corrupt, nothing grows from it.

221. You find all this put more clearly in our Scriptures. For David says: 'The Lord has established his kingdom, he has put on a robe of seemly splendour.' And the apostle says: 'Walk honourably, as by day.' In Greek, the word which is used here is *euschemos*, which literally means: 'with a good posture', or: 'with a good appearance'. So, when God created the first man, he gave him a good figure, and good proportion in his limbs, and he granted him a fine appearance. He had not granted him remission of sins, but after he had renewed him by his Spirit and poured grace upon the one who had come in the form of a servant and in the appearance of a man, he assumed the seemly splendour which came with human redemption. This is why the prophet said: 'The Lord has established his kingdom, he has put on a robe of seemly splendour.' Then elsewhere he says this: 'A hymn of praise is seemly for you, O God, in Zion.' What he means, in other words, is: 'It is honourable that we should fear you, and love you, and pray to you, and honour you'; for it is written: 'Everything you do must be done in an honourable manner.' We can fear and love and

timere, diligere, rogare, honorare; hymnus specialiter Deo dicitur. Hoc tamquam excellentius ceteris credere est decorum, quod deferimus Deo. Mulierem quoque *in habitu ornato* orare convenit, sed specialiter eam decet orare velatam et orare promittentem castitatem cum bona conversatione.

XLVI 222. Est igitur decorum quod praeeminet, cuius divisio gemina est. Nam est decorum quasi generale quod per universitatem funditur honestatis et quasi in toto spectatur corpore; est etiam speciale quod in parte aliqua enitet. Illud generale ita est ac si aequabilem formam atque universitatem honestatis in omni actu suo habeat concinentem, cum omnis sibi eius vita consentit nec in ullo aliqua re discrepat; hoc speciale, cum aliquem actum in suis habet virtutibus praeeminentem.

223. Simul illud adverte quod et decorum est secundum naturam vivere, secundum naturam degere, et turpe est quod sit contra naturam. Ait enim apostolus quasi interrogans: *Decet mulierem non velatam orare Deum? Nec ipsa natura docet vos quod vir quidem si comam habeat, ignominia est illi?*, quoniam contra naturam est. Et iterum dicit: *Mulier vero si capillos habeat, gloria est illi.* Est enim secundum naturam, *quoniam quidem capilli pro velamine sunt*: hoc est enim naturale velamen. Personam igitur et speciem nobis natura ipsa dispensat, quam servare debemus: utinamque et innocentiam custodire possemus nec acceptam nostra malitia mutaret!

224. Habes hunc decorem generalem, quia fecit Deus mundi istius pulchritudinem. Habes et per partes, quia cum faceret Deus lucem, et diem noctemque distingueret, cum conderet caelum, cum terras et maria separaret, cum solem et lunam et stellas constitueret lucere super terram, probavit singula. Ergo decorum hoc quod in singulis mundi partibus elucebat, in universitate resplenduit, sicut probat Sapientia dicens: *Ego eram cui applaudebat . . . cum laetaretur orbe perfecto.* Similiter

plead with and honour men as well; but the hymn of praise is addressed to God in particular. It is seemly to believe that what we present to God is, as it were, far superior to everything else. It is also right that a woman should be appropriately dressed when she prays, but in particular it is seemly that she should be veiled when she is at prayer, and that she should pray in a way which assures everyone of her chastity as well as her good conduct.

222. It is conduct which is seemly, then, that makes the greater **XLVI** impression. It too can be divided into two types. There is what we might call seemliness of a general kind: it pervades all that is honourable, and is as it were to be seen in the body as a whole. There is also seemliness of a particular kind: it shines in each individual part of the whole. The general variety is seen when you maintain a consistent character in your every action, or a uniformity which is always in harmony with what is honourable, when your entire life is in accord and there is not a dissonant note anywhere. The particular variety is seen when some particular action stands out in the midst of all the other virtues displayed in such a life.

223. At the same time, take note of this: to behave in a way that is seemly means to live in accordance with nature, and to pass all your days in accordance with nature; to behave in a way that is shameful means to act in any fashion that is contrary to nature. The apostle puts it this way (he is asking a rhetorical question): 'Is it seemly for a woman to pray to God without wearing a veil? Does not nature herself teach you that if a man has long hair, it is a disgrace to him?' Why so? Because it is contrary to nature. And then he adds this: 'But if a woman has flowing hair, it is a glory to her.' Why is that? Because it is in accordance with nature: 'since it is obvious that her flowing hair is given her for a veil'. In other words, the veil is a natural thing. The point is that nature herself endows us with the character and appearance which we ought to maintain. If only we could preserve our innocence as well, and not corrupt, by our wickedness, the gift given to us!

224. You can see the general kind of seemliness all around you, for God made the beauty of this world. You can also see all around you the kind of seemliness that is evident in particular parts of things: for when God made the light, and separated day from night, and when he created the heavens, and divided the earth and the seas, and established the sun, moon, and stars to shine upon the earth, he gave his approval to each of them in turn. So, the seemliness which shone in each of the parts of the world individually was quite dazzling when they were joined together into a complete whole. Wisdom proves this, when she says: 'I was the one he applauded . . . when he rejoiced at the

ergo et in fabrica humani corporis grata est uniuscuiusque membri portio, sed plus in commune compositio membrorum apta delectat, quod ita sibi quadrare et convenire videantur.

XLVII 225. Si quis igitur aequabilitatem universae vitae et singularum actionum modos servet, ordinem quoque et constantiam dictorum atque operum moderationemque custodiat, in eius vita decorum illud excellit et quasi in quodam speculo elucet.

226. Accedat tamen suavis sermo, ut conciliet sibi adfectum audientium gratumque se vel familiaribus vel civibus vel, si fieri potest, omnibus praebeat. Neque adulantem se neque adulandum cuiquam exhibeat: alterum enim calliditatis est, vanitatis alterum.

227. Non despiciat quid de se unusquisque et maxime vir optimus sentiat: hoc enim modo discit bonis deferre reverentiam. Nam neglegere bonorum iudicia vel adrogantiae vel dissolutionis est, quorum alterum superbiae ascribitur, alterum neglegentiae.

228. Caveat etiam motus animi sui: ipse enim sibi et observandus et circumspiciendus est et, ut adversum se cavendus, ita etiam de se tuendus. Sunt enim motus in quibus est appetitus ille qui quasi quodam prorumpit impetu; unde Graece ὁρμή dicitur, quod vi quadam se repente proripiat. Non mediocris in his vis quaedam animi atque naturae est. Quae tamen vis gemina est: una in appetitu, altera in ratione posita, quae appetitum refrenet et sibi oboedientem praestet et ducat quo velit et tamquam sedulo magisterio edoceat quid fieri, quid evitari oporteat, ut bonae domitrici obtemperet.

229. Solliciti enim debemus esse ne quid temere aut incuriose geramus aut quidquam omnino cuius probabilem non possimus rationem reddere. Actus enim nostri causa etsi non omnibus redditur, tamen ab omnibus examinatur. Nec vero habemus in quo possimus nos excusare. Nam etsi vis

completion of the world.' The same thing can be said of the construction of the human body: each member as an individual part is pleasing in itself, but the appropriate way in which all the members are arranged together is more delightful still, for we can then see how well they complement and fit with one another.

225. If a person maintains a consistent character in his life as a whole, **XLVII** and due measure in all his individual actions, with good order besides, and if he preserves a constancy in the words he uses and a moderation in the works he does, then seemliness will be the most striking quality about his life: it will shine like the reflection in a mirror.

226. In addition to that, however, each of us also needs to have a pleasant manner of speaking to people, so that he can win the hearts of his listeners and make himself agreeable to his friends and his fellow-citizens and, if possible, everyone. He must not show himself to be a flatterer, or one who needs to be flattered by anyone—the one is a sign of artfulness, the other of vanity.

227. No one should ever look down on what anyone else thinks of him, especially not on the opinions of a gentleman, for this is how each of us learns to show respect for people who are good. If you pay no attention to the judgements of the good, it suggests either that you are arrogant or that you have adopted a careless attitude: the one is put down to pride, the other to a lack of responsibility.

228. Each of us must also make sure to avoid everything that moves the soul. The inner self must learn to look after itself and take proper care of its instincts: just as it needs to beware of all that is hostile to it, it also needs to keep a close eye on itself. There are a number of ways in which the soul can be moved, and at the heart of all of them lies a deadly impulse which bursts out as though propelled by some strange momentum. This is why the Greek term is *horme*, because the impulse springs out with a particular kind of vigour, and all of a sudden. The kind of force of spirit or nature to be found in these emotions is not to be underestimated. This force, though, is actually twofold in character. One side is to be found in impulse, the other in reason. The job of reason is to restrain impulse, to bring it into subjection, to lead it where it will, and to put it through a process of careful instruction, as it were, to make it understand what it needs to do and what it needs to avoid, so that it becomes submissive to reason, as an animal is submissive to a good trainer.

229. We must be careful to avoid doing anything rashly or carelessly, or anything at all for which we are unable to give a credible reason. We may not be called upon to give an account of our actions to everyone, but our actions are weighed by everyone all the same. And the truth is, we have no possible grounds for excuse. For though there may be a

quaedam naturae in omni appetitu sit, tamen idem appetitus rationi subiectus est lege naturae ipsius et oboedit ei. Unde boni speculatoris est ita praetendere animo ut appetitus neque praecurrat rationem neque deserat, ne praecurrendo perturbet atque excludat, eam deserendo destituat. Perturbatio tollit constantiam, destitutio prodit ignaviam, accusat pigritiam. Perturbata enim mente latius se ac longius fundit appetitus et tamquam efferato impetu frenos rationis non suscipit nec ulla sentit aurigae moderamina quibus possit reflecti. Unde plerumque non solum animus exagitatur, amittitur ratio, sed etiam inflammatur vultus vel iracundia vel libidine: pallescit timore, voluptate se non capit et nimia gestit laetitia.

230. Haec cum fiunt, abicitur illa naturalis quaedam censura gravitasque morum nec teneri potest illa quae in rebus gerendis atque consiliis sola potest auctoritatem suam atque illud quod deceat tenere, constantia.

231. Gravior autem appetitus ex indignatione nimia nascitur, quam acceptae plerumque accendit iniuriae dolor. De quo satis nos psalmi, quem in praefatione posuimus, praecepta instruunt. Pulchre autem et hoc accidit ut, scripturi de officiis, ea praefationis nostrae adsertione uteremur, quae et ipsa ad officii magisterium pertineret.

232. Sed quia supra, ut oportebat, perstrinximus quemadmodum unusquisque cavere possit ne excitetur accepta iniuria, verentes ne praefatio prolixior fieret, nunc de eo uberius disputandum arbitror. Locus enim opportunus est ut in partibus temperantiae dicamus quemadmodum reprimatur iracundia.

XLVIII 233. Tria itaque genera esse hominum iniuriam accipientium in scripturis divinis demonstrare volumus, si possumus. Unum est eorum quibus peccator insultat, conviciatur, inequitat. Iis quia deest iustitia, pudor crescit, augetur dolor. Horum similes plurimi de meo ordine, de meo

certain force of nature in every impulse, that same impulse can still be brought into subjection to reason, just as nature's own law decrees it must, and be obedient to it. A good watchman must stay alert, then, and make sure that impulse neither runs ahead of reason nor leaves it behind: if it runs ahead, it disturbs reason and gets in its way; if it leaves it behind, reason ends up abandoned. When it disturbs reason, constancy of character is undermined; when it abandons it, it proves apathy and points to laziness. Once the mind is disturbed, impulse hurls itself in every direction at once, and in its wild momentum it refuses to submit to the reins of reason or feel any restraint from its driver which might bring it back under control. The result is, very often, that it is not just the soul that is shaken or reason that is lost: the face, too, is affected—it gets inflamed with anger or desire: it grows pale with fear, or it is unable to contain the sense of longing at the sight of sensual pleasure and gets quite carried away with delight.

230. When these things happen, a proper natural judgement and seriousness of character are cast to the winds, and it proves impossible to keep a grip on the only virtue which is able to preserve its own authority and hold on to what is seemly in all our conduct and all our plans—constancy.

231. There is one impulse in particular that is especially virulent: it is the one produced by an excessive sense of indignation, the kind of feeling that is so often kindled by a sense of resentment that one has been the victim of an injustice. On this, the principles given in the Psalm we quoted in the introduction offer us plenty of instruction. In fact, it has turned out to be an excellent thing that we used the clear words of that passage to introduce our theme when we set out to write about duties, for the Psalm is concerned to teach us about duty in its own right as well.

232. But since earlier we merely touched on this question of how each of us can avoid having our feelings aroused when we have been the victim of an injustice—we were obliged to go no further, in case the introduction ended up too lengthy—I think it is now time to discuss the issue more fully. We have come to a suitable stage here, where we are dealing with the kinds of behaviour which temperance requires, to say a little about the ways in which anger can be restrained.

233. We wish to show then, if we can, that there are in the divine **XLVIII** Scriptures three types of person, who all react differently when they are the victims of injustice. One type is to be seen in those who find themselves insulted, abused, and roughly treated by some sinner. With these people, there is very little idea of justice, and so their sense of having been disgraced grows and grows, and their feeling of resentment gets stronger and stronger. A good many from my own

numero. Nam mihi infirmo si quis iniuriam faciat, forsitan,
licet infirmus, ⟨non⟩ donem iniuriam meam. Si crimen obiciat,
non sum tantus ut sim contentus conscientia mea, etiamsi me
eius obiecti alienum noverim; sed cupio abluere ingenui
pudoris notam tamquam infirmus. Ergo *oculum pro oculo et
dentem pro dente* exigo et convicium convicio rependo.

234. Si vero is sum qui proficiam, etsi nondum perfectus,
non retorqueo contumeliam; et si influat ille convicium et
inundet aures meas contumeliis, ego taceo et nihil respondeo.

235. Si vero perfectus sim (verbi gratia loquor, nam veritate
infirmus sum), si ergo perfectus sim, benedico maledicentem,
sicut benedicebat et Paulus qui ait: *Maledicimur et benedici-
mus.* Audierat enim dicentem: *Diligite inimicos vestros, orate
pro calumniantibus et persequentibus vos.* Ideo ergo Paulus
persecutionem patiebatur et sustinebat, quia vincebat et
mitigabat humanum adfectum propositae mercedis gratia, ut
filius Dei fieret si dilexisset inimicum.

236. Tamen et sanctum David in hoc quoque genere virtutis
imparem Paulo non fuisse edocere possumus. Qui primo
quidem, cum malediceret ei filius Semei et crimina obiceret,
tacebat et humiliabatur et silebat a bonis suis, hoc est
bonorum operum conscientia; deinde expetebat maledici
sibi, quia maledicto illo divinam acquirebat misericordiam.

237. Vide autem quomodo et humilitatem et iustitiam et
prudentiam emerendae a Domino gratiae reservaverit. Primo
dixit: *Ideo maledicit mihi quia Dominus dixit illi ut maledicat.*
Habes humilitatem, quia ea quae divinitus imperantur, aequa-
nimiter quasi servulus ferenda arbitrabatur. Iterum dixit: *Ecce
filius meus qui exivit de ventre meo quaerit animam meam.*
Habes iustitiam: si enim a nostris graviora patimur, cur
indigne ferimus quae inferuntur ab alienis? Tertio ait: *Dimitte
illum ut maledicat, quoniam dixit illi Dominus ut videat
humiliationem meam, et retribuet mihi Dominus pro maledicto
hoc.* Nec solum conviciantem pertulit sed etiam lapidantem et

order and from my own rank behave in this way. I am weak, but if someone does me an injustice, the chances are I shall not forgive him for it, even though I am too weak to retaliate effectively. If he starts to make accusations against me, I am not so magnanimous as to be content with the witness of my own conscience, even though I know I am innocent of his charges: weak as I am, I want to expunge this stain upon the honour of a free man. So I exact eye for eye and tooth for tooth, and I repay abuse with abuse.

234. But if I am one who is progressing, even though I am not yet perfect, I refuse to return the insult. Even if the person pours abuse on me and drowns out every other sound in my ears with his insults, I keep silent, and I say nothing in reply.

235. But if I am perfect—I say this only for argument's sake, for the truth is I am weak—if I am perfect, I bless the one who curses me. This was what Paul did, for he says: 'We are cursed, and we bless.' You see, he had heard the One who says: 'Love your enemies; pray for those who slander and persecute you.' That was why Paul endured persecution and put up with it: he was able to conquer and assuage his natural human feelings by concentrating on the reward that was set before him—the promise that he would become a son of God if he had loved his enemy.

236. All the same, we can prove that holy David did not lag behind Paul here: he too displayed this type of virtue. At first, it is true, when the son of Shimei was cursing him and hurling accusations at him, he simply kept quiet, humbled himself, and remained silent about his good deeds, or about the testimony of his conscience as to his good works. But then he went further, and actually expressed a desire to be cursed, for by enduring such curses he was obtaining the mercy of God.

237. Look how he maintained humility, and justice, and prudence, all of which would merit him favour from the Lord. In the first place, he said: 'This is why he is cursing me: the Lord has told him to curse me.' There you have his humility: like the lowliest of servants, he took the view that whatever his divine master commanded, he should bear it with an even temper. And again he said: 'See, it is my son, the one who came from my loins, who is seeking my life.' There you have his justice: if we are prepared to put up with terrible treatment from our own flesh and blood, he reasoned, why should we react with indignation when strangers insult us? And in the third place, he said: 'Leave him to curse, for the Lord has told him to do it; perhaps the Lord will see my humiliation and give me some recompense for this cursing.' Not only did he endure the abuse; he even left the man alone and did him no harm when he came after him and threw stones at him. And

sequentem illaesum reliquit; quin etiam post victoriam petenti veniam libenter ignovit.

238. Quod ideo inserui ut evangelico spiritu sanctum David non solum inoffensum sed etiam gratum fuisse convicianti docerem et delectatum potius quam exasperatum iniuriis, pro quibus mercedem sibi reddendam arbitrabatur. Sed tamen, quamvis perfectus, adhuc perfectiora quaerebat. Incalescebat iniuriae dolore quasi homo, sed vincebat quasi bonus miles; tolerabat quasi athleta fortis. Patientiae autem finis promissorum exspectatio, et ideo dicebat: *Notum mihi fac, Domine, finem meum et numerum dierum meorum qui est ut sciam quid desit mihi.* Finem illum quaerit promissorum caelestium vel illum, quando *unusquisque surgit in suo ordine: primitiae Christus, deinde hi qui sunt Christi, qui in adventum eius crediderunt, deinde finis.* Tradito enim regno Deo et Patri, et evacuatis omnibus potestatibus, ut apostolus dixit, perfectio incipit. Hic ergo impedimentum, hic infirmitas etiam perfectorum, illic plena perfectio. Ideo et dies illos requirit vitae aeternae, qui sunt, non qui praetereunt, ut cognoscat quid sibi desit, quae terra sit repromissionis, perpetuos fructus ferens, quae prima apud patrem mansio, quae secunda et tertia, in quibus pro ratione meritorum unusquisque requiescit.

239. Illa igitur nobis expetenda in quibus perfectio, in quibus veritas est. Hic umbra, hic imago, illic veritas: umbra in lege, imago in evangelio, veritas in caelestibus. Ante agnus offerebatur, offerebatur vitulus; nunc Christus offertur, sed offertur quasi homo, quasi recipiens passionem; et offert se ipse quasi sacerdos ut peccata nostra dimittat, hic in imagine, ibi in veritate, ubi apud Patrem pro nobis quasi advocatus intervenit. Hic ergo in imagine ambulamus, in imagine videmus; illic *facie ad faciem*, ubi plena perfectio, quia perfectio omnis in veritate est.

XLIX 240. Ergo dum hic sumus, servemus imaginem, ut ibi perveniamus ad veritatem. Sit in nobis imago iustitiae, sit imago

that was not all: after his victory, he freely granted him pardon when he asked for it.

238. I have introduced this story to show you that holy David followed the spirit of the gospel: far from displaying resentment, he was actually grateful to the one who hurled abuse at him; and instead of being provoked by the injustices he was suffering he took a pleasure in them, for he believed that he would receive a reward for them. And yet, perfect as he was, he sought still greater perfection. As a man, his sense of resentment at the injustice he was receiving made his blood boil; but as a good soldier he overcame it, and as a courageous athlete he put up with it. Now the final end to which patience looks and for which it faithfully waits is the day when all the promises will be fulfilled, and so he used to say: 'Make me to know, O Lord, my final end, and what the number of my days is, that I may know what I still lack.' The end that he is looking for in these words is the day when all the heavenly promises are fulfilled, or the day 'when each rises in his own order: Christ the first-fruits, then those who are Christ's, who have believed in his coming; and then the end will come'. For 'when the kingdom has been handed over to our God and Father, and all powers have been brought to nothing,' as the apostle has said, perfection begins. So, in this world there are obstacles that remain; in this world there are weaknesses that remain even for those who are perfect—but in the world to come there will be full perfection. That is why he is looking for the days of eternal life, for the days which never pass away but go on and on: he wants to know what he still lacks. What is that promised land, he is asking, which bears the fruits that last for ever? What is the first dwelling-place with the Father, and the second and the third, where each finds rest in accordance with his merits?

239. These, then, are the realities that we should seek, where perfection lies, and where truth lies. Here, what we have is only the shadow, here it is only the image; there, it will be the truth. The shadow is in the law, the image is in the gospel, the truth is in the heavenly realms. In times past, it was a lamb that was offered, or it was a young bull that was offered; now, it is Christ who is offered, but he is offered as a man, as one who submits to suffering; and he offers himself as a priest, to take away our sins, here in the image, but there in the truth, where he intercedes as an advocate with the Father on our behalf. So, here we walk in the image, we see in the image; there, it will be 'face to face', where there is full perfection. For all perfection resides in the truth.

240. While we are here, then, let us make sure that we preserve the image, so that we attain to the truth that awaits us there. Let us have the image of justice in us, and let us have the image of wisdom in us, for **XLIX**

sapientiae, quia venietur ad illum diem et secundum imaginem aestimabimur.

241. Non inveniat in te adversarius imaginem suam, non rabiem, non furorem: in his enim imago nequitiae est. Adversarius enim diabolus sicut leo rugiens quaerit quem occidat, quem devoret. Non inveniat auri cupiditatem, non argenti acervos, non vitiorum simulacra ne auferat tibi vocem libertatis. Vox enim libertatis illa est ut dicas: *Veniet huius mundi princeps et in me inveniet nihil.* Itaque si securus es quod nihil in te inveniat, cum venerit perscrutari, dices illud quod dixit ad Laban Iacob patriarcha: *Cognosce si quid tuorum est apud me.* Merito beatus Iacob, apud quem nihil Laban suum potuit reperire. Absconderat enim Rachel simulacra deorum eius aurea et argentea.

242. Itaque si sapientia, si fides, si contemptus saeculi, si gratia tua abscondat omnem perfidiam, beatus eris, quia non respicis in vanitates et in insanias falsas. An mediocre est tollere vocem adversario, ut arguendi te non possit habere auctoritatem? Itaque qui non respicit in vanitates, non conturbatur; qui enim respicit conturbatur, et vanissime quidem. Quid est enim congregare opes nisi vanum? Quia caduca quaerere vanum est satis. Cum autem congregaveris, qui scias an possidere liceat tibi?

243. Nonne vanum est ut mercator noctibus ac diebus conficiat iter, quo aggerare possit thesauri acervos, merces congreget, conturbetur ad pretium, ne forte minoris vendat quam emerit, aucupetur locorum pretia et subito aut latrones in se invidia famosae negotiationis excitet aut non exspectatis serenioribus flatibus, dum lucrum quaerit, naufragium impatiens morae incidat?

244. An non conturbatur etiam ille vane, qui summo labore coacervat quod nesciat cui heredi relinquat? Saepe quod avarus summa congesserit sollicitudine, praecipiti effusione dilacerat heres luxuriosus et diu quaesita turpis helluo, praesentium caecus, futuri improvidus, quadam absorbet voragine. Saepe etiam speratus successor invidiam partae

that day will come for each one of us, and we shall be assessed according to the measure in which we display that image.

241. Do not allow the enemy to find his image in you, or his rage or his fury, for all that these reflect is the image of wickedness. Your enemy the devil goes about like a roaring lion, looking for someone to destroy, someone to devour. Do not allow him to find in you a desire for gold, or piles of silver, or the idols which are evil vices, or he will deprive you of your claim to be free. You can truly claim to be free when you are able to say: 'The prince of this world will come, and he will find nothing in me.' So, if you are confident that he will find nothing in you when he comes to search you, you will be able to say what the patriarch Jacob said to Laban: 'See if there is anything of yours anywhere in my possession.' No wonder Jacob was called a happy man—Laban could find nothing of his in his possession. For Rachel had hidden the gold and silver idols which were his gods.

242. So, if you have wisdom, if you have faith, if you have a contempt for the world, and if you have your own grace to hide all your faithlessness, you will be happy, for you pay no regard to futile things or to deceitful follies. To deprive the enemy of the opportunity to raise his voice against you; to make sure that he can find no grounds on which to accuse you—that is no small achievement, surely? This is why a person who pays no regard to futile things remains untroubled in his spirit, whereas the person who does pay regard to them knows all about trouble—and all for what? It really *is* all futile! How can it be anything other than futile to pile up riches for yourself? After all, to chase after things that are perishing is futile enough. Even if you succeed in making your pile, how can you be sure you will be allowed to keep it?

243. Is it not futile for a merchant to be always on the go, day and night, amassing piles of treasure, or accumulating great new stocks of merchandise, or worrying himself sick with trouble over the value of it all—what if he has to sell it for less than he paid for it?—or chasing maximum possible prices in this area or that—only to find, all of a sudden, that he incites thieves to rob him because he has made them jealous of his notorious deals, or that, by not waiting for calmer winds, intolerant of the least delay in his relentless quest for profit, he ends up shipwrecked?

244. Do you not think this kind of trouble is futile, too—when a person builds up his wealth through great hard work, and does not know what kind of heir he will be leaving it to? Often, property that a greedy person has taken great pains to amass is squandered with reckless extravagance by an heir who is a spendthrift, and wealth that took a long time to acquire is effectively swallowed up in one gulp

acquirit hereditatis et celeri obitu extraneis aditae successionis transcribit compendia.

245. Quid ergo vane araneam texis quae inanis et sine fructu est, et tamquam casses suspendis inutiles divitiarum copias? Quae, etsi fluant, nihil prosunt; immo exuunt te imaginem Dei et induunt terreni imaginem. Si tyranni aliquis imaginem habeat, nonne obnoxius est damnationi? Tu deponis imaginem aeterni imperatoris et erigis in te imaginem mortis. Eice magis de civitate animae tuae imaginem diaboli et adtolle imaginem Christi. Haec in te fulgeat, in tua civitate, hoc est anima, resplendeat quae oblitterat vitiorum imagines. De quibus ait David: *Domine, in civitate tua ad nihilum deduces imagines eorum.* Cum enim pinxerit Hierusalem Dominus ad imaginem suam, tunc adversariorum omnis imago deletur.

L **246.** Quod si evangelio Domini etiam populus ipse ad despicientiam opum informatus atque institutus est, quanto magis vos Levitas oportet terrenis non teneri cupiditatibus, quorum Deus portio est? Nam cum divideretur a Moyse possessio terrena populo patrum, excepit Levitas Dominus aeternae possessionis consortio, quod ipse illis esset funiculus hereditatis. Unde ait David: *Dominus pars hereditatis meae et calicis mei.* Denique sic appellatur Levita: 'Ipse meus' vel 'Ipse pro me'. Magnum ergo munus eius, ut de eo Dominus dicat: 'Ipse meus', vel quemadmodum Petro dixit de statere in ore piscis reperto: *Dabis his pro me et pro te.* Unde et apostolus, cum episcopum dixisset debere esse sobrium pudicum ornatum hospitalem docibilem, non avarum, non litigiosum, domui suae bene praepositum, addidit: *Diaconos similiter oportet esse graves, non bilingues, non multo vino deditos, non turpe lucrum sectantes, habentes mysterium fidei in conscientia pura. Et hi autem probentur primum et sic ministrent, nullum crimen habentes.*

247. Advertimus quanta in nobis requirantur, ut abstinens sit

by some squandering and shameless fool, blind to the present and heedless of the future. Often, too, a desired inheritor finds himself the victim of envy because of the property he acquires, and dies suddenly under the strain, and the gains of the legacy into which he has just come are signed over to strangers.

245. Why then do you spend your time in these futile ways, weaving this pointless and fruitless web, and suspending all the useless resources of wealth like slender threads in the air? Even if you have plenty of them, they do you no good—in fact, all they do is remove the image of God from you and clothe you with the image of the earthly man. If someone has the image of a tyrant in his possession, he is liable to be condemned under the law, is he not? You are laying aside the image of the eternal Emperor and setting up within yourself the image of death. Instead, cast out the image of the devil from the kingdom of your soul, and raise the image of Christ. This is the image that should shine in you, that should be resplendent in your kingdom, or your soul, the one which effaces all the images of evil vices. This is what David has to say about these things: 'Lord, in your kingdom you shall bring their images to nothing.' When the Lord adorns Jerusalem according to his own image, then every image of his enemies is destroyed.

246. If in the gospel of our Lord even the ordinary people were L trained and taught to despise riches, surely it is all the more encumbent upon you Levites not to allow yourselves to be gripped by earthly desires. For you have God for your portion. When Moses was dividing up the earthly possessions and sharing them out among our fathers' people, the Lord excluded the Levites: they had a share in an eternal possession, for he himself was the lot of their inheritance. This is why David says: 'The Lord is the portion of my inheritance and of my cup.' In fact, this is what the name 'Levite' literally means: 'He himself is mine' (*Ipse meus*), or 'He himself is for me' (*Ipse pro me*). What a great status the Levite has, then, if the Lord says of him: 'He himself is mine', or, as he said to Peter about the silver coin found in the mouth of the fish: 'Give it to them for me and for yourself.' This is also why the apostle, having said that a bishop ought to be sober, chaste, distinguished, hospitable, a good teacher, not greedy, not quarrelsome, and in proper control of his own household, added: 'Deacons, likewise, must be serious, not prone to double talk, not given to much wine, and not devoted to the pursuit of sordid gain, but those who keep the mystery of the faith with a clear conscience. Let them first be proved, and then let them serve, if they are found to be blameless.'

247. We can see how much is required of us. The minister of the Lord

a vino minister Domini, ut testimonio bono fulciatur non solum fidelium sed etiam ab his qui foris sunt. Decet enim actuum operumque nostrorum testem esse publicam existimationem, ne derogetur muneri, ut qui videt ministrum altaris congruis ornatum virtutibus, auctorem praedicet et Dominum veneretur qui tales servulos habeat. Laus enim Domini ubi munda possessio et innocens familiae disciplina.

248. De castimonia autem quid loquar, quando una tantum nec repetita permittitur copula? Et in ipso ergo coniugio lex est non iterare coniugium nec secundae coniugis sortiri coniunctionem. Quod plerisque mirum videtur cur etiam ante baptismum iterati coniugii ad electionem muneris et ordinationis praerogativam impedimenta generentur, cum etiam delicta obesse non soleant si lavacri remissa fuerint sacramento. Sed intellegere debemus quia baptismo culpa dimitti potest, lex aboleri non potest. In coniugio non culpa sed lex est: quod culpae est igitur in baptismate relaxatur, quod legis est in coniugio non solvitur. Quomodo autem potest hortator esse viduitatis qui ipse coniugia frequentaverit?

249. Inoffensum autem exhibendum et immaculatum ministerium nec ullo coniugali coitu violandum cognoscitis, qui integri corpore, incorrupto pudore, alieni etiam ab ipso consortio coniugali, sacri ministerii gratiam recepistis. Quod eo non praeterii, quia in plerisque abditioribus locis cum ministerium ingererent, vel etiam sacerdotium, filios susceperunt, et id tamquam usu veteri defendunt, quando per intervalla dierum sacrificium deferebatur. Et tamen castificabatur etiam populus per biduum aut triduum ut ad sacrificium purus accederet, ut in Veteri Testamento legimus: *et lavat vestimenta sua.* Si in figura tanta observantia, quanta in veritate! Disce, sacerdos atque Levita, quid sit lavare vestimenta tua, ut mundum corpus celebrandis exhibeas sacramentis. Si populus sine ablutione vestimentorum suorum

is to abstain from wine, and he is to be upheld by a good reputation, not just among the faithful but among those who are outside as well. It is seemly that public opinion should bear witness to our actions and our good works: this way, our office will not be disparaged, for the person who sees a minister of the altar adorned with virtues appropriate to his calling will bring praise to the Author of these virtues, and will worship the Lord who has such lowly servants. Praise redounds to the Lord when his possession is pure and the conduct of his household is blameless.

248. As for chastity—what is there to say? All that is permitted is one union and one union only, never to be repeated. So, if we take the actual question of marriage, the law is that you must not remarry or obtain a union with a second wife. A lot of people find this surprising: why should a second marriage, even one contracted before baptism, raise obstacles to a person's election to sacred office and to the privilege of ordination? After all, they reason, even serious crimes are not normally an impediment, once they have been remitted by the sacrament of baptism. But we need to understand this: just because sin can be forgiven through baptism, this does not mean that the law can be abolished. There is no sin in marriage, but there is a law. When we are talking about sin, we are dealing with something that can be relieved in baptism; when we are talking about the law in marriage, we are dealing with something that cannot be annulled. In any case, how can a man encourage other people to remain in a state of widowhood if he has gone through any number of marriages himself?

249. But you are quite aware that you have this obligation to present a ministry that is blameless and beyond reproach, and undefiled by any marital intercourse, for you have received the grace of the sacred ministry with your bodies pure, with your modesty intact, and with no experience at all of marital union. Still, I have had a reason for not passing over this point. In quite a number of out-of-the-way places, men who have been exercising a ministry—even, in some cases, the priesthood itself—have fathered children. They defend this behaviour by claiming that they are following an old custom, one which used to obtain when the sacrifice was offered only at lengthy intervals. Yet the fact is that even the ordinary people used to practise continence for a period of two or three days in order to approach the sacrifice in a state of purity, for we read in the Old Testament: 'And he washes his clothes.' If the standard of observance was this scrupulous in the time of the figure, how much greater it should be now, in the time of the truth! Learn, priest and Levite, what it means to wash your clothes: it means displaying a body that is pure, properly prepared for the celebration of the sacraments. If the ordinary people were forbidden

prohibebatur accedere ad hostiam suam, tu illotus mente pariter et corpore audes pro aliis supplicare, audes aliis ministrare?

250. Non mediocre officium Levitarum, de quibus dicit Dominus: *Ecce eligo Levitas de medio filiorum Israel pro omni primogenito aperiente vulvam filiis Israel: redemptiones eorum erunt isti et erunt mihi Levitae. Mihi enim sanctificavi primogenitum in terra Aegypti.* Cognovimus quia non inter ceteros Levitae computantur sed omnibus praeferuntur, qui eliguntur ex omnibus et sanctificantur ut primogenita fructuum atque primitiae quae Domino deputantur, in quibus est votorum solutio et redemptio peccatorum. *Non accipies*, inquit, *eos inter filios Israel et constitues Levitas super tabernaculum testimonii et super omnia vasa eius adstare et super quaecumque sunt in ipso. Ipsi tollant tabernaculum et omnia vasa eius et ipsi ministrent in eo et in circuitu tabernaculi castra ipsi constituant et promovendo tabernaculum ipsi deponant Levitae et constituendo castra rursum ipsum tabernaculum ipsi statuant. Alienigena quicumque accesserit, morte moriatur.*

251. Tu ergo electus ex omni numero filiorum Israel, inter sacros fructus quasi primogenitus aestimatus, praepositus tabernaculo ut praetendas in castris sanctitatis et fidei, ad quae si alienigena accesserit, morte morietur, positus ut operias arcam testamenti. Non enim omnes vident alta mysteriorum quia operiuntur a Levitis, ne videant qui videre non debent, et sumant qui servare non possunt. Moyses denique circumcisionem vidit spiritalem sed operuit eam, ut in signo circumcisionem praescriberet. Vidit azyma veritatis et sinceritatis, vidit passionem Domini: operuit azymis corporalibus azyma veritatis, operuit passionem Domini agni vel vituli immolatione. Et boni Levitae servaverunt mysterium fidei suae tegmine. Et tu mediocre putas quod commissum est tibi? Primum, ut alta Dei videas, quod est sapientiae; deinde, ut excubias pro populo deferas, quod est iustitiae; castra defendas tabernaculumque tuearis,

to approach their sacrificial victim without washing their clothes, have you the audacity to offer prayers on behalf of others, or have you the audacity to minister to others, with your spirit and body alike unwashed?

250. It is no trivial task, the duty given to the Levites, for the Lord says of them: 'See, I choose the Levites from among the children of Israel, in place of every first-born who opens the womb among the children of Israel: they will serve as a redemption-price for the first-born, and the Levites will be for me. For I consecrated to myself all the first-born in the land of Egypt'. We have seen that the Levites are not counted among all the rest, but are put before all of them, for they are chosen from the whole company and consecrated as the first-born fruits, or the firstlings, destined for the Lord; it is by them that vows are paid and sins are redeemed. 'You shall not include them,' the Lord says, 'among the children of Israel. You shall appoint the Levites to look after the tabernacle of the testimony, and all its vessels, and everything that is in it. Let them be the ones who carry the tabernacle and all its vessels, let them minister in it, and let them pitch camp in the area around the tabernacle. When you move on, let the Levites take down the tabernacle, and when you pitch camp, let them set up the tabernacle again. Any stranger who approaches it must surely be put to death.'

251. It is you, then, who have been chosen out of the entire company of the children of Israel, regarded as the first-born among the sacred fruits, placed in charge of the tabernacle to keep watch over the camp of holiness and faith—and if a stranger approaches this camp, he surely will be put to death—and stationed there in order to keep the ark of the covenant concealed. Not everyone gets to see the depths of the mysteries, for they are concealed by the Levites: this way, those who have no right to see them do not see them, and those who are unable to keep them do not get to handle them. Remember what Moses did: he saw that circumcision was a spiritual thing, but he concealed it, and so prescribed circumcision only as an outward sign. He saw the unleavened bread of truth and sincerity, he saw the passion of our Lord; but he concealed that unleavened bread of truth with literal unleavened bread, and he concealed that passion of our Lord with the sacrifice of a lamb or a young bull. Good Levites have always preserved the mystery behind the shield of their own faith. What about you? Do you think it is a trivial thing, this responsibility with which you have been entrusted? First of all, you get to see the deep things of God: this calls for wisdom. Then, you must keep watch on behalf of the people: this calls for justice. You must defend the camp and look after the

quod est fortitudinis; te ipsum continentem ac sobrium praestes, quod est temperantiae.

252. Haec virtutum genera principalia constituerunt etiam hi qui foris sunt, sed communitatis superiorem ordinem quam sapientiae iudicaverunt, cum sapientia fundamentum sit iustitiae opus sit, quod manere non potest nisi fundamentum habeat. Fundamentum autem Christus est.

253. Prima ergo fides, quae est sapientiae, ut Salomon dicit, secutus patrem: *Initium sapientiae timor Domini.* Et lex dicit: *Diliges Dominum tuum, diliges proximum tuum.* Pulchrum est enim ut gratiam tuam atque officia in societatem humani generis conferas. Sed primum illud decorum, ut quod habes pretiosissimum, hoc est mentem tuam qua nihil habes praestantius, Deo deputes. Cum solveris auctori debitum, licet ut opera tua in beneficentiam et adiumenta hominum conferas, atque opem feras necessitatibus aut pecunia aut officio aut etiam quocumque munere. Quod late patet in vestro ministerio: pecunia, ut subvenias—debito obligatum liberes—officio, ut servanda suscipias quae metuat amittere qui deponenda credidit.

254. Officium est igitur depositum servare ac reddere. Sed interdum commutatio fit aut tempore aut necessitate, ut non sit officium reddere quod acceperis: ut si quis contra patriam opem barbaris ferens, pecuniam apertus hostis reposcat; aut si cui reddas cum adsit qui extorqueat; si furenti restituas, cum servare non queat; si insanienti gladium depositum non neges, quo se ille interimat, nonne solvisse contra officium est? Si furto quaesita sciens suscipias, ut fraudetur qui amiserat, nonne contra officium est?

255. Est etiam contra officium nonnumquam promissum solvere, sacramentum custodire, ut Herodes, qui iuravit quoniam quidquid petitus esset, daret filiae Herodiadis et

tabernacle: this calls for courage. And you must show yourself to be self-controlled and sober: this calls for temperance.

252. Those who are outside have also maintained that these are the principal categories of virtue, but in their judgement community belongs higher up the scale than wisdom. The fact is, however, it is essential that wisdom should be the foundation of justice, since justice cannot remain standing unless it has a foundation. And the foundation is Christ.

253. It is faith, then, that comes first. This is a sign of wisdom, as Solomon says, agreeing with his father: 'The fear of the Lord is the beginning of wisdom.' The Law also says: 'You shall love your Lord, and you shall love your neighbour.' It is a fine thing to contribute your kindness and all your other duties to promote the fellowship of the human race. But here is what is seemly first and foremost: to devote to God the most precious possession you have—your soul. You have nothing more important than this. When you have paid your dues to your Creator, then you can contribute your share of good works to being kind and to helping your fellow-men, and bring your resources to bear on their needs, whether with money, or with your official duty, or with whatever service you are able to render. There is plenty of opportunity for all these things in your ministry. With money, you can offer assistance to people—say by freeing someone who is constrained by a burden of debt. With your official duty, you can, for example, look after valuables which someone is afraid to lose and so has chosen to deposit in your care.

254. It is your duty, therefore, to look after a deposit which has been entrusted to you, and to return it safely. Sometimes, though, a change can occur in people's circumstances or requirements, so that it is no longer your duty to return what you received. Imagine, for example, a situation where a man is giving support to barbarians, to people who are sworn to hostility against his country, and he asks for his money back, having now openly declared himself to be an enemy. Or suppose you return someone's property at a time when a third party is waiting to seize it; or you give something back to a person who is out of his mind and is thus in no position to look after it; or you do not refuse a madman a sword which he has deposited with you, when he is quite likely to kill himself with it—in cases like these, it is surely completely contrary to duty to comply with the person's request. Or say you knowingly accept goods which have been obtained by theft, so that the person who lost them is cheated—surely this too is contrary to duty?

255. It also runs contrary to duty, in certain circumstances, to fulfil a promise or to keep an oath. Take the case of Herod: he swore to give the daughter of Herodias anything she asked for, and ended up being

necem Iohannis praestitit, ne promissum negaret. Nam de
Iephte quid dicam, qui immolavit filiam quae sibi victori
prima occurrerat quo votum impleret quod spoponderat ut
quidquid sibi primum occurrisset, offerret Deo? Melius fuerat
nihil tale promittere quam promissum solvere parricidio.

256. Haec quanti sit consilii prospicere non ignoratis. Et ideo
eligitur Levita qui sacrarium custodiat, ne fallatur consilio, ne
fidem deserat, ne mortem timeat, ne quid intemperantius
gerat, ut specie ipsa gravitatem praeferat; nec solum
animum sed etiam oculos continentes habere quem deceat,
ne vel ipse frontem sobrietatis fortuitus violet occursus,
quoniam: *qui viderit mulierem ad concupiscendum eam, adulter-
avit eam in corde suo.* Ita adulterium non solum facti colluvione sed etiam adspectus intentione committitur.

257. Magna haec videntur ac nimis severa sed in magno
munere non superflua, quando tanta est Levitarum gratia,
ut de his Moyses in benedictionibus diceret: *Date Levi viros
eius, date Levi manifestos eius, date Levi sortem suffragii sui et
veritatem eius viro sancto, quem temptaverunt in temptationibus,
maledixerunt super aquam contradictionis. Qui dicit patri suo et
matri: Non novi te; et fratres suos non cognovit, et filios suos
abdicavit: hic custodit verba tua et testamentum tuum observa-
vit.*

258. Illi ergo viri eius et manifesti eius, qui nihil in corde doli
habeant, nihil fraudis occultent, sed verba eius custodiant et
in corde suo conferant, sicut conferebat et Maria; qui suos
parentes officio suo non noverint praeferendos, qui violatores
oderint castitatis, pudicitiae ulciscantur iniuriam, noverint
officiorum tempora, quod maius sit, quod cui aptum tempori
est, et ut id solum sequantur quod honestum est; sane ubi
duo honesta, id quod honestius est praeponendum putent: hi
iure benedicti.

259. Si quis ergo manifestet iustitias Dei, incensum imponat:
Benedic, Domine, virtutem ipsius, opera manuum eius suscipe, ut
gratiam propheticae benedictionis inveniat.

responsible for the death of John rather than break his promise. And what about Jephthah? He sacrificed his own daughter, who was the first to meet him as he returned home victorious from battle, just to fulfil the vow he had made to offer to God whatever should meet him first. Far better to have made no such promise, than to fulfil the promise with the murder of his own daughter!

256. You are well aware of what good judgement it takes to anticipate possible developments like these. This is why the Levite is chosen to guard the sanctuary: he must not be mistaken in his judgement, he must not desert the faith, he must not fear death, and he must not do anything which suggests a lack of temperance; rather, he must by his very appearance give evidence of a seriousness of character. It is seemly that he should keep a firm control not just of his spirit but of his eyes as well; then not even a casual encounter will bring a blush to his sober cheek, for 'he who looks at a woman lustfully has committed adultery with her in his heart'. As we can see, it is not just in the doing of the foul deed that adultery is committed: it is there even in the intention of a look.

257. These standards may all seem demanding and dreadfully strict, but in those who occupy a role of such responsibility they are not unnecessary. The grace of the Levites is so immense that when Moses blessed the twelve tribes he spoke of them like this: 'Give to Levi his men, give to Levi those who are manifestly his own, give to Levi the lot of his own choice, give his truth to this holy man, the one whom they tested in their temptations and cursed at the waters of rebellion. He it is who says to his father and mother: "I do not know you", who did not recognize his brothers, and disowned his own children: this is the one who guards your words and has kept your covenant.'

258. Here they are, then—his men, those who are manifestly his own, who have no guile in their hearts and harbour no deceit within them, but guard his words and ponder them in their hearts, as Mary did. These are the men who have learned never to put their parents before their duty, the men who detest all who violate chastity, who avenge every outrage to purity, and who have learned to recognize when the time is right for this duty or that, which matters most, and which is right for each specific situation. Their only aim is to do what is honourable; and where there are two possible courses that are both honourable, they hold that whichever is the more honourable should take priority. Rightly are they given a blessing!

259. If, then, a person manifests the works of God's righteousness, he offers him incense: 'Bless, O Lord, his virtue, accept the works of his hands', that he may obtain the grace of the blessing spoken of by the prophet.

LIBER SECUNDUS

I 1. Superiore libro de officiis tractavimus quae convenire honestati arbitraremur, in qua vitam beatam positam esse nulli dubitaverunt quam scriptura appellat vitam aeternam. Tantus enim splendor honestatis est ut vitam beatam efficiant tranquillitas conscientiae et securitas innocentiae. Et ideo, sicut exortus sol lunae globum et cetera stellarum abscondit lumina, ita fulgor honestatis, ubi vero et incorrupto vibrat decore, cetera quae putantur bona secundum voluptatem corporis aut secundum saeculum clara et illustria obumbrat.
2. Beata plane, quae non alienis aestimatur iudiciis sed domesticis percipitur sensibus, tamquam sui iudex. Neque enim populares opiniones pro mercede aliqua requirit neque pro supplicio pavet. Itaque quo minus sequitur gloriam, eo magis super eam eminet. Nam qui gloriam requirunt, his ea merces praesentium umbra futurorum est, quae impediat vitam aeternam, quod in evangelio scriptum est: *Amen dico vobis, perceperunt mercedem suam*; de his scilicet qui velut tuba canenti vulgare liberalitatem suam quam faciunt circa pauperes gestiunt. Similiter et de ieiunio quod ostentationis causa faciunt: *Habent*, inquit, *mercedem suam.*
3. Honestatis igitur est vel misericordiam facere vel ieiunium deferre in abscondito, ut mercedem videaris a solo Deo tuo quaerere, non etiam ab hominibus. Nam qui ab hominibus quaerit, habet mercedem suam; qui autem a Deo, habet vitam aeternam, quam praestare non potest nisi auctor aeternitatis, sicut illud est: *Amen, amen dico tibi, hodie mecum eris in paradiso.* Unde expressius scriptura vitam aeternam appellavit eam quae sit beata, ut non hominum opinionibus aestimanda relinqueretur sed divino iudicio committeretur.
II 4. Itaque philosophi vitam beatam, alii in non dolendo posuerunt, ut Hieronymus, alii in rerum scientia, ut Herillus,

BOOK TWO

1. In the previous book, we discussed the kinds of duty which we thought were appropriate to behaving in a way that is honourable. No one has ever doubted that that is where the happy life, or, as Scripture calls it, 'eternal life', is to be found. Such is the splendour of honourable conduct that peace of conscience and the assurance of innocence make for a happy life. When the sun is high in the sky, it hides the sphere of the moon and all the other lights of the stars—so, in the same way, the brightness of what is honourable, when it shines and glitters with its true, untainted beauty, is so dazzling that it eclipses all the other things which people think are good if they judge by the standards of bodily pleasure, or great and glorious if they go by the standards of the world.

2. A person's life is indeed happy if, instead of being measured by the judgements of other people, he is assessed by his own inner convictions—if he is, as it were, his own judge. Such a life does not court popular opinion as some kind of reward, nor is it afraid of it as a punishment. And so it is that the less it pursues glory, the more it rises above it. In fact, those who go after glory find that the reward it brings in the present is only a shadow of the glory to come, and it is an obstacle to eternal life, as it is written in the gospel: 'Truly I say to you, they have gained their own reward.' The words refer, of course, to people who are so keen to broadcast their generosity towards the poor that they do everything but blow a trumpet to draw attention to it. The same verdict is passed on those who engage in fasting simply for display: they too, the gospel tells us, 'have their own reward'.

3. The honourable course, therefore, is to do your works of mercy and to observe your fasts in secret, so that you may be seen to be seeking a reward only from your God, and not from men as well. For the person who seeks a reward from men has his own reward; the person who seeks it from God has eternal life. This is a gift that only the one who governs eternity can bestow, as he did when he spoke those words: 'Truly, truly I say to you, today you will be with me in paradise'. Scripture has made everything clearer, then, by describing the life that is happy as 'eternal life': this way, the measurement of happiness is not left to the opinions of men, but is entrusted to the judgement of God.

4. The philosophers, of course, have given all manner of answers to the question of what makes for a happy life. Some, like Hieronymus, have said that it is a matter of being free from pain. Others have said it is to be found in the knowledge of things. Herillus, for example, took this position: finding that knowledge was praised to the heights by

qui audiens ab Aristotele et Theophrasto mirabiliter laudatam esse rerum scientiam, solam eam quasi summum bonum posuit, cum illi eam quasi bonum, non quasi solum bonum laudaverint. Alii voluptatem dixerunt, ut Epicurus, alii, ut Callipho et post eum Diodorus, ita interpretati sunt ut alter ad voluptatem, alter ad vacuitatem doloris consortium honestatis adiungerent, quod sine ea non possit esse beata vita. Zenon Stoicus solum et summum bonum quod honestum est; Aristoteles autem vel Theophrastus et ceteri Peripatetici in virtute quidem, hoc est honestate, vitam beatam esse, sed compleri eius beatitudinem etiam corporis atque externis bonis adseruerunt.

5. Scriptura autem divina vitam aeternam in cognitione posuit divinitatis et fructu bonae operationis. Denique utriusque adsertionis evangelicum suppetit testimonium. Nam et de scientia ita dixit Dominus Iesus: *Haec est autem vita aeterna, ut cognoscant te solum verum Deum et quem misisti Iesum Christum.* Et de operibus ita respondit: *Omnis qui reliquerit domum vel fratres aut sorores aut matrem aut filios aut agros propter nomen meum, centuplum accipiet et vitam aeternam possidebit.*

6. Sed ne aestimetur hoc recens esse et prius tractatum philosophis quam in evangelio praedicatum (anteriores enim evangelio philosophi, id est, Aristoteles et Theophrastus vel Zenon atque Hieronymus, sed posteriores prophetis) accipiant quam longe antequam philosophorum nomen audiretur, per os sancti David utrumque aperte videatur expressum. Scriptum est enim: *Beatus quem tu erudieris, Domine, et de lege tua docueris eum.* Habemus et alibi: *Beatus vir qui timet Dominum, in mandatis eius cupiet nimis.* Docuimus de cognitione, cuius praemium aeternitatis fructum esse memoravit propheta, adiciens quia in domo huius timentis Dominum vel eruditi in lege et cupientis in mandatis divinis: *Gloria et divitiae, et iustitia eius manet in saeculum saeculi.* De operibus quoque in eodem psalmo subiunxit vitae aeternae suppetere praemium viro iusto. Denique ait: *Beatus vir qui miseretur et commodat, disponit sermones suos in iudicio: quia in saeculum non*

Aristotle and Theophrastus, he maintained that this, and only this, was the supreme good—despite the fact that those men had esteemed it simply as *a* good, not as *the only* good. Others, such as Epicurus, have said that happiness consists in pleasure; still others, men like Callipho, and Diodorus after him, understood it to involve a combination of honourable conduct and something else as well—one said pleasure; the other, freedom from pain—both of them being convinced that a person's life cannot be happy unless he behaves in an honourable fashion. Zeno the Stoic said that the supreme good, the only good, is to do what is honourable, while Aristotle, Theophrastus, and the other Peripatetics argued that though a happy life undoubtedly consists in virtue, or in behaviour that is honourable, its happiness is nevertheless made complete by the addition of bodily and external advantages.

5. Divine Scripture, however, has specified that eternal life is to be found in the knowledge of the divine, and in the fruit of good works. There is plenty of evidence in the gospel to support both elements of this statement. For example, the Lord Jesus had this to say about knowledge: 'And this is eternal life, that they may know you, the only true God, and Jesus Christ, whom you have sent.' And on the subject of good works, he gave this reply: 'Everyone who has left home, brothers, sisters, mother, children, or lands for my name's sake shall receive a hundredfold, and shall possess eternal life'.

6. But perhaps people will object that this is all recent history and that the subject was discussed by the philosophers long before it was spoken of in the gospel, since the philosophers, men like Aristotle or Theophrastus, or Zeno or Hieronymus, lived far earlier than the gospel, even if they came later than the prophets. Anyone who thinks this way should consider this: long before the name of the philosophers was even heard of, both of these constituents of happiness seem to have been spelt out quite clearly in the words of holy David. For it is written: 'Happy is the man you instruct, O Lord, and teach out of your law.' And in another place we find this: 'Happy is the man who fears the Lord: he will find great joy in his commandments.' We have proved our point, then, about knowledge, and its prize being the reward of an existence that is eternal. This is what the prophet recalled, for he went on to say that this man who fears the Lord, is instructed in his law, and finds great joy in his commandments has 'glory and riches in his house, and his righteousness endures for ever'. And good works are mentioned in the same context, for later on in the same Psalm David added that the prize of eternal life comes to the man who is just. Here are his exact words: 'Happy is the man who shows pity and lends: he orders his words with judgement; nothing shall ever move him. The just shall be in eternal remembrance.' And further on

commovebitur. In memoria aeterna erit iustus. Et infra: *Dispersit, dedit pauperibus: iustitia eius manet in aeternum.*

7. Habet ergo vitam aeternam fides, quia fundamentum est bonum; habent et bona facta, quia vir iustus et dictis et rebus probatur. Nam si exercitatus sit in sermonibus et desidiosus in operibus, prudentiam suam factis repellit; et gravius est scire quid facias nec fecisse quod faciendum cognoveris. Contra quoque strenuum esse in operibus, adfectu infidum, ita est ac si vitioso fundamento pulchra culminum velis elevare fastigia: quo plus struxeris, plus corruit, quia sine munimento fidei opera non possunt manere. Infida statio in portu navem perforat et arenosum solum cito cedit nec potest impositae aedificationis sustinere onera. Ibi ergo plenitudo praemii, ubi virtutum perfectio et quaedam in factis atque dictis aequalitas sobrietatis.

III 8. Et quoniam sola rerum scientia explosa est vel quasi inanis secundum philosophiae disputationes superfluas vel quasi semiperfecta sententia, consideremus quam enodem de eo scriptura divina absolvat sententiam, de quo tam multiplices et implicatas atque confusas videmus quaestiones esse philosophiae. Nihil enim bonum scriptura nisi quod honestum adserit virtutemque in omni rerum statu beatam iudicat, quae neque augeatur bonis corporis vel externis, neque minuatur adversis; nihilque tam beatum nisi quod a peccato alienum sit, plenum innocentiae, repletum gratiae Dei. Scriptum est enim: *Beatus vir qui non abiit in consilio impiorum et in via peccatorum non stetit et in cathedra pestilentiae non sedit, sed in lege Domini fuit voluntas eius.* Et alibi: *Beati immaculati in via qui ambulant in lege Domini.*

9. Innocentia igitur et scientia beatum faciunt. Bonae quoque operationis mercedem esse beatitudinem vitae aeternae superius advertimus. Restat igitur ut spreto patrocinio voluptatis aut doloris metu, quorum alterum quasi infractum et molliculum, alterum quasi eviratum et infirmum despuit, in ipsis doloribus vitam beatam eminere demonstret. Quod facile doceri potest, cum legerimus: *Beati estis cum vobis maledicen*

he says this: 'He has distributed his goods, he has given to the poor: his righteousness'—his justice—'endures for ever.'

7. Eternal life is obtained by faith, then, for faith acts as a good foundation. It is also obtained by good deeds, for a just man earns approval through what he says and does. After all, if a person spends all his time talking but is slow to act, he negates his prudence by his deeds; besides, it is a serious thing if you know what to do and then fail to do what you knew you ought to have done. But then again, if you come across as someone who is always busy doing good works while you have a heart that lacks faith, it is as if you are trying to erect magnificent great domes on top of a building with a faulty foundation: the higher you raise the edifice, the greater its collapse will be, for without the support of faith no works can possibly last. A treacherous berth in a harbour soon holes a ship's hull, and ground that is sandy quickly gives way, unable to sustain the weight of a structure built upon it. Here, then, is where full reward is to be found—where your virtues are seen to be perfect, and where there is as it were a uniform sobriety in what you say and what you do.

8. Since we have totally rejected the argument that everything III depends on knowledge alone—the idea is either hollow, a typical example of the kind of pointless discussions in which philosophy specializes, or it is incomplete as a prescription for happiness—let us consider the simple prescription that divine Scripture offers us on this subject, where, as we see, philosophy has only produced such tortuous, complex, and confused enquiries. Scripture declares that there can be no good whatsoever other than the good of doing what is honourable, and its judgement is that virtuous behaviour makes life happy no matter what its circumstances, for bodily or other external advantages do not make virtue any greater, and outward adversities do not diminish it. Scripture also tells us that there can be no state so happy as the state of being free from sin, full of innocence, and filled with the grace of God. Here is what is written: 'Happy is the man who has not gone in the counsel of the ungodly, or stood in the way of sinners, or sat in the seat of the scornful, but whose desire has been for the law of the Lord.' And in another place we read this: 'Happy are the undefiled in the way, who walk in the law of the Lord.'

9. It is innocence, then, and knowledge that make a person happy. We observed earlier that the happiness of eternal life is also the reward for good works. It remains to prove from Scripture that once we spurn the defence of pleasure or the fear of suffering—and Scripture plainly rejects them both, branding one effete and soft, the other unmanly and feeble—our life can evince happiness even in the midst of sufferings. This can be demonstrated quite easily, for we read: 'Happy are you,

*et persequentur et dicent omne malum adversus vos propter
iustitiam. Gaudete et exsultate quoniam merces vestra copiosa
est in caelo. Sic enim persecuti sunt et prophetas qui erant ante
vos.* Et alibi: *Qui vult venire post me, tollat crucem suam et
sequatur me.*

IV **10.** Est ergo beatitudo et in doloribus, quos plena suavitatis
virtus comprimit et coercet, ipsa sibi domesticis opibus
abundans vel ad conscientiam vel ad gratiam. Neque enim
parum beatus Moyses, cum Aegyptiorum vallatus populis et
mari clausus, per fluctus sibi et populo patrum pedestrem
viam piis meritis invenisset. Quando autem fortior quam
tunc, cum extremis circumventus periculis non desperabat
salutem sed exigebat triumphum?

11. Quid Aaron? Quando beatiorem se credidit quam tunc,
quando medius stetit inter vivos ac mortuos et obiectu sui
statuit mortem, ne ad vivorum transiret agmina a cadaveribus
mortuorum? Quid de puero Daniele loquar, qui tam sapiens
erat ut inter leones fame exasperatos nulla bestialis saevitiae
frangeretur formidine; ita alienus a metu ut posset epulari nec
vereretur ne ad pastum exemplo sui feras provocaret?

12. Est ergo et in dolore virtus, quae sibi bonae suavitatem
exhibeat conscientiae; et ideo indicio est quod non minuat
dolor virtutis voluptatem. Sicut ergo nulla virtuti decessio
beatitudinis per dolorem, ita etiam nulla accessio per voluptatem corporis aut commodorum gratiam. De quibus pulchre
apostolus ait: *Quae mihi lucra fuerunt, haec duxi propter
Christum detrimenta esse.* Et addidit: *Propter quem omnia
damna duxi et aestimo stercora ut Christum lucrifaciam.*

13. Denique Moyses damnum suum credidit thesauros esse
Aegyptiorum et opprobrium dominicae crucis praetulit, nec
tunc dives cum abundaret pecunia nec postea pauper cum
egeret alimento; nisi forte tunc alicui minus beatus videretur
fuisse, cum in deserto cotidiana alimonia sibi et populo suo

when men slander and persecute you, and speak all kinds of evil against you for righteousness's sake. Rejoice and be glad, for great is your reward in heaven. For in the same way they also persecuted the prophets before you.' And in another place we find this: 'Whoever wishes to come after me, let him take up his cross and follow me.'

10. So, happiness can be known even in the midst of sufferings, when IV they are kept under control and held within proper limits by the power of virtue. The attractions of virtue are many, for it has endless riches of its own, whether we think of the value of maintaining a good conscience or the value of obtaining grace. Think of the happiness Moses had—there was nothing meagre about that, was there? There he was, surrounded by the Egyptian hordes, with no way of escape, cut off by the sea—but he earned such favour by the godly spirit he showed that he found a path for himself and our fathers' people to pass through the waves on foot. Did he ever show greater courage than he did at that moment, when he was completely hemmed in, and the dangers could not have been greater? He refused to give up hope of salvation, and in the end he brought off a great triumph.

11. What about Aaron? Did he ever think himself happier than he did at that moment when he stood between the living and the dead, using his own person as a barrier to stop death in its tracks, to prevent it passing from the bodies of the dead to the ranks of the living? Or what about the boy Daniel? Look how wise he was: whichever way he looked, all he could see were lions, starved to the point where they were utterly ravenous, yet he was not in the least overwhelmed with terror at these savage beasts. So undaunted was he that he was even able to eat a meal—with no qualms that in doing so he might give the wild creatures the notion that it was time to start feeding on him!

12. So, virtue exists even in the midst of suffering: by reminding itself of the attractions of maintaining a good conscience, it is able to prove that suffering does not diminish the pleasures of virtue. And just as virtue does not lose in happiness through suffering, neither does it gain in it through bodily pleasure or the enjoyment of other 'advantages'. The apostle puts it all so well when he said: 'The things which were gain to me, those I counted loss for the sake of Christ.' And he added this: 'For his sake I have counted all things as loss, and I regard them as refuse, that I may gain Christ.'

13. Moses, too, considered the treasures of the Egyptians as loss, and preferred to suffer the reproach of the cross of our Lord. He was not rich when he had plenty of money; nor was he poor when, later on, he lacked even basic food. Of course, it appears that he must have been less happy then, when in the desert he and his people were short of the basic supplies which they needed every day; but if we are looking for

deforet. Sed quod summi boni ac beatitudinis nemo negare audeat, manna ei, hoc est *panis angelorum*, ministrabatur e caelo, carnis quoque cotidiana pluvia totius plebis epulis redundabat.

14. Eliae quoque sancto panis ad victum deerat si quaereretur, sed non videbatur deesse quia non quaerebatur. Itaque diurno corvorum obsequio mane panis, caro ad vesperam deferebatur. Numquid ideo minus beatus quia erat pauper sibi? Minime. Immo eo magis beatus quia erat Deo dives. Aliis enim esse quam sibi divitem praestat, ut iste erat, qui tempore famis cibum a vidua petebat, largiturus ut hydria farinae per triennium et sex menses non deficeret, et cotidianos usus olei vas viduae inopi sufficeret ac ministraret. Merito ibi volebat Petrus esse, ubi istos videbat. Merito in monte cum Christo in gloria apparuerunt, quia et ipse pauper factus est cum dives esset.

15. Nullum ergo adminiculum praestant divitiae ad vitam beatam. Quod evidenter Dominus demonstravit in evangelio dicens: *Beati pauperes, quoniam vestrum est regnum Dei. Beati qui nunc esuriunt et sitiunt, quia saturabuntur. Beati qui nunc fletis, quia ridebitis*. Itaque paupertatem famem dolorem, quae putantur mala, non solum impedimento non esse ad vitam beatam sed etiam adiumento evidentissime pronuntiatum est.

v **16.** Sed et illa quae videntur bona, divitias satietatem laetitiam expertem doloris, detrimento esse ad fructum beatitudinis, dominico declaratum iudicio liquet, cum dicitur: *Vae vobis divitibus quia habetis consolationem vestram! Vae vobis qui saturati estis quia esurietis!* Et illis qui rident, quia lugebunt. Sic ergo non solum adminiculo non sunt ad vitam beatam corporis aut externa bona, sed etiam dispendio sunt.

17. Inde enim beatus Nabuthe etiam cum lapidaretur a divite, quia pauper et infirmus adversum opes regias solo erat adfectu et religione dives, ut pecunia regali non commutaret paternae vineae hereditatem; eoque perfectus, quia sanguine proprio defenderet iura maiorum suorum. Inde

evidence of the supreme good, and happiness, here is something no one can deny—manna, the very 'bread of the angels', was supplied from heaven for him, and there were daily showers of meat which provided more than enough to feed the entire company of the people. **14.** And think of holy Elijah. He would have found himself without bread to eat if he had looked for it, but it was precisely because he did not look for it, it seems, that he never went without it. The ravens ministered to him every day; bread was brought to him in the morning, and meat in the evening. Was he any less happy, do you think, because he was poor in and of himself? Far from it. In fact, he was happier than ever, because he was rich towards God. It is better to be rich towards others rather than towards oneself. This was what Elijah was: he could ask a widow for food during a time of famine, only to demonstrate his own generosity by ensuring that her jar of flour never ran out for three years and six months, and seeing to it that the poor widow's jug of oil always had enough to meet her daily needs. No wonder Peter wanted to linger in the place where he could see men like these! No wonder they appeared with Christ himself in glory on the mountain! For he too became poor, though he was rich.

15. Riches provide no assistance, then, in the quest for a happy life. The Lord clearly showed this in the gospel when he said: 'Blessed'—or happy—'are you poor, for yours is the kingdom of God. Blessed are those who hunger and thirst now, for they shall be filled. Blessed are you who weep now, for you shall laugh.' The verdict could not be clearer: poverty, hunger, and suffering, all the things that people imagine are evils, are no obstacle to a happy life—they are in reality an advantage in discovering it.

16. At the same time, things that appear to be good, like riches or abundance or the experience of joy unalloyed by grief, are a disadvantage when it comes to earning the reward of happiness. This is clearly declared to be the Lord's own judgement, for it is said: 'Woe to you who are rich: you have your consolation! Woe to you who are filled: you shall go hungry!' And the same thing is said to those who laugh: they shall mourn. It is clear, then, that bodily or external advantages, far from offering any assistance in the quest for a happy life, actually diminish one's chances of finding it.

17. This was why Naboth was happy even when he was being stoned by a rich man. He was a poor, defenceless individual, confronted with all the resources that the king could muster; his riches lay only in his devotion and in his piety. But he was so rich in these things that he refused to accept the king's money in exchange for the vineyard he had inherited from his fathers. Here was a man who was perfect: he was prepared to defend his ancestral rights even at the cost of his own

quoque miser Achab suo iudicio, quia pauperem necari fecerat ut eius possideret vineam.

18. Certum est solum et summum bonum virtutem esse eamque abundare solam ad vitae fructum beatae, nec externis aut corporis bonis sed virtute sola vitam praestari beatam, per quam vita aeterna acquiritur. Vita enim beata fructus praesentium, vita autem aeterna spes futurorum est.

19. Et sunt tamen qui in hoc corpore tam infirmo, tam fragili, impossibilem vitam beatam putent, in quo necesse est angi dolere deplorare aegrescere; quasi vero ego in corporis exsultatione dicam vitam beatam consistere et non in altitudine sapientiae, suavitate conscientiae, virtutis sublimitate. Non enim in passione esse sed victorem esse passionis beatum est, nec frangi temporalis motu doloris.

20. Pone accidere haec quae gravia ad vim doloris feruntur: caecitatem exsilium famem stuprum filiae, amissionem liberum. Quis neget beatum Isaac, qui non videbat in senectute et beatitudines suis benedictionibus conferebat? An non beatus Iacob, qui profugus patria domo, mercenarius pastor exsilium sustinuit, filiae pudicitiam ingemuit esse temeratam, famem pertulit? Non ergo beati quorum fide Deus accipit testimonium, cum dicitur: *Deus Abraham, Deus Isaac, Deus Iacob*? Misera est servitus, sed non miser Ioseph; immo plane beatus, cum dominae libidines in servitute positus coerceret. Quid de sancto David loquar, qui trium filiorum deploravit obitum et, quod his durius, incestum filiae? Quomodo non beatus, de cuius successione beatitudinis auctor exortus est, qui plurimos fecit beatos: *Beati* enim *qui non viderunt et crediderunt*? Fuerunt et ipsi in sensu infirmitatis, sed evaluerunt de infirmitate fortes. Quid laboriosius autem sancto Iob vel in domus incendio vel filiorum decem interitu momentario, doloribus

blood. And Ahab, for his part, was a miserable wretch, even in his own estimation, for he had caused a poor man to be put to death simply in order to seize possession of his vineyard.

18. It is quite certain that virtue is the only good, the supreme good, and that it and only it enjoys real wealth when it comes to earning the reward of eternal life. It is certain, too, that it is not in the possession of external or bodily advantages that life is rendered happy, but only in the display of virtue, through which eternal life is gained. A happy life is the reward that we have in the present; eternal life is the hope that we have for the future.

19. There are some people, though, who feel it is impossible for life to be happy so long as we remain in this body, so weak and frail, with all its necessary troubles, sufferings, tears, and sicknesses. They seem to imagine me to be saying that a happy life consists in bodily exuberance, rather than in depth of wisdom, peace of conscience, and loftiness of virtue. But it is obvious that happiness is not about finding yourself in a state of suffering: it is about being a victor over that suffering, and not being broken by the emotion of a grief that is only fleeting.

20. Suppose you find yourself confronting the kind of things that are thought to cause people the most terrible grief—the experience of blindness, say, or exile, or famine, or the violation of your daughter, or the loss of your children. Would anyone say that Isaac was not happy? He could not see in his old age, yet he was able to give happiness to others by pronouncing his blessings on them. Or do you think Jacob was not happy? He became a fugitive from his own father's house, and suffered a period of exile working as a hired shepherd; he went through the anguish of discovering that his virgin daughter had been raped; he endured famine. Were they not happy, these men? God himself receives testimony from their faith, for it is said that he is 'the God of Abraham, the God of Isaac, and the God of Jacob'. Slavery is a miserable state to be in; yet Joseph was not miserable. Far from it: he knew what it was to be truly happy, when he found himself reduced to this condition of slavery but able to check the lustful advances of his master's wife. And what about holy David? He experienced the sorrow of the deaths of three of his sons, and, what was even harder to bear, the crime of incest against his daughter. But how could he ever be called unhappy? It was from his lineage that the Author of happiness himself came, the One who has brought happiness to so many. For: 'Happy are those who have not seen, and yet have believed.' These men had an awareness of their weakness, but out of that weakness they grew strong and courageous. What could be more painful than the trials endured by holy Job—the burning of his house, the deaths of his

corporis? Numquid minus beatus quam si illa non pertulisset, in quibus magis probatus est?

21. Esto tamen fuisse in illis aliquid acerbitatis, quem virtus animi non abscondit dolorem. Neque enim profundum mare negaverim quia vadosa litora sunt, neque caelum lucidum quia interdum obtexitur nubibus, neque terram fecundam quia aliquibus locis ieiuna glarea est, aut laetas segetes quia intermixtam solent habere sterilem avenam. Similiter puta beatae messem conscientiae interpellari aliquo acerbo doloris. Nonne totius manipulis vitae beatae, si quid forte adversi accidit atque amaritudinis, tamquam sterilis avena absconditur aut tamquam lolii amaritudo frumenti suavitate obducitur? Sed iam ad proposita pergamus.

VI 22. Superiore libro ita divisionem fecimus ut primo loco esset honestum et decorum, a quo officia ducerentur; secundo loco quid utile. Et quemadmodum in primo diximus quia inter honestum et decorum est quaedam distinctio quae magis intellegi quam explicari possit, sic et cum utile tractamus, considerandum videtur quid utilius.

23. Utilitatem autem non pecuniarii lucri aestimatione subducimus sed acquisitione pietatis, sicut apostolus ait: *Pietas autem ad omnia utilis est, promissionem habens vitae praesentis et futurae.* Itaque in scripturis divinis, si diligenter quaeramus, saepe invenimus quod honestum est utile vocari: *Omnia mihi licent sed non omnia sunt utilia.* Supra de vitiis loquebatur. Hoc ergo dicit: Licet peccare, sed non decet. In potestate sunt peccata sed non sunt honesta. Luxuriari promptum sed non iustum. Non enim Deo esca sed ventri colligitur.

24. Ergo quia quod utile, id etiam iustum: iustum est ut serviamus Christo qui nos redemit; ideo iusti, qui pro eius nomine se morti obtulerunt; iniusti, qui declinaverunt, de

ten children, all at a stroke, and the sufferings that he went through in his body? Was he any less happy, do you think, than he would have been if he had not suffered such troubles? Through all that he endured he was proved all the more.

21. We must grant, certainly, that there was a measure of bitterness in those sufferings, a grief which bravery of spirit cannot conceal. I should not want to deny that the sea is deep because there are such things as shallow reefs, or say that the sky is not bright because it is sometimes interlaced with clouds, or pretend that the earth is not fruitful because in some regions we find only thin gravel, or claim that the corn is not ripe because it often has barren wild oats mixed in with it. In the same way, you may assume that the harvest of a conscience that is happy will have intermingled with it pain or grief of one kind or another. Is it not true, though, that if something hard or bitter does crop up, it is hidden, like those barren wild oats, by all the ripe sheaves which make the overall bundle of life happy, or, like the bitterness of the darnel, is masked by the sweetness of the corn itself? But let us now move on to our actual subject.

22. In the previous book, we divided up our theme like this: in the first **VI** place, we said, there is the principle of doing what is honourable and seemly, which is the source from which all duties are derived; and in the second place there is the principle of doing what is beneficial. In the first of these categories we said that between what is honourable and what is seemly there lies a certain distinction which can be understood better than it can be explained. Well, when we are dealing with what is beneficial, too, it would appear that we need to consider whether one course will be more beneficial than another.

23. Now when we speak of something being 'beneficial', for us this has nothing to do with calculating profit of a monetary kind: it is about attaining godliness. It is as the apostle says: 'Godliness is beneficial for all things, for it holds promise both for the present life and for the life to come.' So, in the divine Scriptures, if we look diligently, we often find that what is honourable is called beneficial: 'All things are permissible for me, but not all things are beneficial.' In the preceding context, the apostle was speaking about various vices. Here, then, is what he means: it is permissible to sin, but it is not seemly. It is within our powers to commit this sin or that, but it is not honourable. It is easy to live a life of extravagance, but it is not just. We do not take food for God: we take it for our stomach's sake.

24. Therefore, because what is beneficial is also just, it is just that we should serve Christ who redeemed us. So, those who have sacrificed themselves to death for his name's sake are just, whereas those who have declined to do so are unjust. Christ is thinking of people like these

quibus dicit: *Quae utilitas in sanguine meo?*, id est: qui iustitiae meae profectus? Unde et illi: *Adligemus iustum quia inutilis est nobis*, id est iniustus, qui nos arguit condemnat corripit. Licet hoc possit etiam ad avaritiam impiorum hominum derivari, quae perfidiae vicina est, sicut in Iuda proditore legimus, qui avaritiae studio et pecuniae cupiditate laqueum proditionis incurrit atque incidit.

25. De hac igitur tractandum est utilitate, quae sit plena honestatis, sicut ipsis verbis definivit apostolus dicens: *Hoc autem ad utilitatem vestram dico, non ut laqueum iniciam vobis, sed ad id quod honestum est.* Liquet igitur quod honestum est utile esse, et quod utile, honestum, et quod utile, iustum, et quod iustum, utile. Neque enim mihi ad mercatores lucri cupidine avaros sed ad filios sermo est, et sermo de officiis quae vobis, quos elegi in ministerium Domini, inculcare gestio atque infundere, ut ea quae mentibus ac moribus vestris usu atque institutione inolita atque impressa sunt, etiam sermone ac disciplina aperiantur.

26. Itaque de utilitate dicturus, utar illo versiculo prophetico: *Declina cor meum in testimonia tua et non in avaritiam*, ne utilitatis sonus excitet pecuniae cupiditatem. Denique aliqui habent: *Declina cor meum in testimonia tua et non ad utilitatem*, hoc est illam quaestuum nundinas aucupantem utilitatem, illam usu hominum ad pecuniae studia inflexam ac derivatam. Vulgo enim hoc solum dicunt utile quod quaestuosum; nos autem de ea tractamus utilitate quae damnis quaeritur, ut Christum lucremur, cuius *quaestus est pietas cum sufficientia.* Magnus profecto quaestus quo pietatem acquirimus, quae apud Deum dives est, non caducis facultatibus sed muneribus aeternis, in quibus non tentatio lubrica sed constans et perpetua sit gratia.

27. Est igitur utilitas alia corporalis, alia pietatis, sicut divisit

when he says: 'What benefit is there in my blood?' What he means, in other words, is: 'What interest has my justice gained?' So they also say: 'Let us bind the just man, for he is of no benefit to us.' Put in different words, what they are saying is this: 'Anyone is unjust, if he dares to criticize us, or condemn us, or rebuke us.' The same point could be applied equally well to the greed that ungodly men display, for greed is a near neighbour to treachery. We can see that when we read the story of the traitor Judas: it is through eager greed and a love of money that he thrusts his neck into the noose of treachery and falls.

25. We need to look at this question of how to behave in a way that is beneficial, then, for such behaviour is full of what is honourable. The apostle has actually defined things in these very terms, for he says this: 'I say this for your benefit, not so as to put a noose around your neck, but to encourage you to do what is honourable.' It is clear, then, that what is honourable is beneficial, and what is beneficial is honourable, and what is beneficial is just, and what is just is beneficial. I say this, because I am not speaking to merchants, to men who are obsessed with greed and whose only desire is for profit; I am speaking to my own sons, and I am speaking to you about the kinds of duties that I long to impress upon you and impart to you, since I have chosen you for the Lord's service. My desire is that the standards which have been implanted and ingrained in your minds and characters by practice and training will be opened up to you by words and instruction as well.

26. Since I am going to speak about what it means to behave in a way that is beneficial, allow me to make use of the little verse the prophet gave us: 'Incline my heart to your testimonies, and not to greed [*avaritia*]'—just in case the sound of the word *utilitas*, 'what is beneficial', should excite a desire for money. There are certain versions, you see, which render it this way: 'Incline my heart to your testimonies and not to what is beneficial [*utilitas*]'. Put differently, this means: 'not to the kind of view of what is beneficial that makes people always on the lookout for lucrative openings in business, not to the kind of perspective that is so distorted and perverted by the ways of men that it has been turned into a longing for money'. In popular parlance, something is called 'beneficial' only if it is lucrative in these financial terms; but we are talking here about the kind of benefit that is sought precisely through the loss of all these things, in order to gain Christ, whose gain is 'godliness with contentment'. And this really is great gain—to attain to godliness. Godliness is rich in the sight of God, not with resources which perish but with privileges which are eternal—and here we have none of the temptations in which we can so easily lose our footing: only a grace that is firm and enduring.

27. So, 'beneficial' means one thing when it is used of bodily things,

apostolus: *Corporalis enim exercitatio ad modicum*, inquit, *utilis est, pietas autem ad omnia est utilis.* Quid autem tam honestum quam integritas? Quid tam decorum quam immaculatum servare corpus et inviolatum atque intaminatum pudorem? Quid etiam tam decorum quam ut vidua uxor defuncto coniugi fidem servet? Quid etiam hoc utilius, quo regnum caeleste acquiritur? *Sunt* enim *qui se castraverunt propter regnum caelorum.*

VII **28.** Est igitur non solum familiare contubernium honestatis et utilitatis, sed eadem quoque utilitas quae honestas. Ideo et ille qui regnum caelorum volebat omnibus aperire non quod sibi utile quaerebat sed quod omnibus. Unde ordo quidam nobis et gradus faciendus est etiam ab his usitatis et communibus ad ea quae sunt praecellentia, ut ex pluribus utilitatis colligamus profectum.

29. Ac primum norimus nihil tam utile quam diligi, nihil tam inutile quam non amari; nam odio haberi exitiale ac nimis capitale arbitror. Itaque id agamus ut omni sedulitate commendemus existimationem opinionemque nostram; ac primum placiditate mentis et animi benignitate influamus in adfectum hominum. Popularis enim et grata est omnibus bonitas nihilque quod tam facile humanis illabatur sensibus. Ea si mansuetudine morum ac facilitate, tum moderatione praecepti et adfabilitate sermonis, verborum honore, patienti quoque sermonum vice modestiaeque adiuvetur gratia, incredibile quantum procedit ad cumulum dilectionis.

30. Legimus enim non solum in privatis sed etiam in ipsis regibus quantum facilitas blandae adfabilitatis profecerit aut superbia verborumque obfuerit tumor, ut regna ipsa labefactaret et potestatem solveret. Iam si quis consilio usu ministerio officiis popularem comprehendat gratiam, aut si quis periculum suum pro universa plebe offerat, non est dubium

and something quite different when it is used of godliness. This distinction was made by the apostle himself: 'For bodily exercise,' he says, 'is of limited benefit, but godliness is beneficial in every way.' What could be more honourable than chastity? What could be more seemly than to keep your body untainted, and to maintain your honour unsullied and undefiled? What could be more seemly than for a widowed woman to keep faith with her dead husband? What could be more beneficial than that by which the kingdom of heaven is obtained? For 'there are some who have made themselves eunuchs for the sake of the kingdom of heaven'.

28. There is not just a close relationship, then, between what is VII honourable and what is beneficial: what is beneficial is in fact the same thing as what is honourable. Thus, even the one whose desire it was to open the kingdom of heaven to all sought to do not what would be of benefit to himself only but what would be of benefit to all. So we need to establish a kind of sequence and gradation covering everything we do, starting with familiar and ordinary actions and going right the way up to those that are truly outstanding. If we do this, we shall reap more and more benefit from more and more opportunities.

29. First and foremost, we need to realize that there is nothing more beneficial than to be loved, and nothing more devoid of benefit than not to be loved—to be hated is, I think, fatal and quite deadly. Let us make sure, therefore, that we take all possible care to commend our good name and reputation; and by showing calmness of mind and liberality of heart first and foremost let us seek to gain a place in people's affections. For benevolence is a popular quality, welcome to all, and there is nothing that more readily strikes a chord in human hearts. If it is promoted by a gentleness and affability of character, and if you show a degree of moderation in telling people what to do and speak to them courteously, using deferential language, and display a patient willingness to engage in conversation with them, and reflect the grace of modesty, it is incredible how much affection can be built up towards you.

30. This is true not just in the lives of private individuals, but also, we read, in the case of kings themselves: an affable and courteous manner has often proved to be of great value there, while, on the other hand, pride and conceited language have frequently done tremendous harm, causing entire kingdoms to fall and bringing regimes to a speedy end. After all, if someone succeeds in capturing popular favour by the advice he gives, by the way he operates, by the services he does for people, and by the duties he undertakes for them, or if someone exposes himself to danger on behalf of the nation as a whole, the outcome can hardly be in doubt: he will be so greatly loved by the

quod tantum caritatis a plebe in eum refundatur ut populus salutem eius et gratiam sibi praeferat.

31. Quantas Moyses a populo inlatas absorbebat contumelias! Et cum Dominus in insolentes vindicare vellet, se tamen pro populo offerebat frequenter ut indignationi divinae plebem subduceret. Quam miti sermone post iniurias appellabat populum, consolabatur in laboribus, deliniebat oraculis, fovebat operibus! Et cum Deo constanter loqueretur, homines tamen humili et grata appellatione adfari solebat. Merito aestimatus est supra homines, ut et vultum eius non possent intendere et sepulturam eius non repertam crederent, quia sic totius plebis mentes devinxerat ut plus eum pro mansuetudine diligerent quam pro factis admirarentur.

32. Quid? Eius imitator sanctus David, electus ex omnibus ad plebem regendam, quam mitis et blandus, humilis spiritu, sedulus corde, facilis adfectu! Ante regnum se pro omnibus offerebat; rex cum omnibus aequabat suam militiam et partiebatur laborem; fortis in proelio, mansuetus in imperio, patiens in convicio, ferre magis promptus quam referre iniurias. Ideo tam carus erat omnibus ut iuvenis ad regnum etiam invitus peteretur, resistens cogeretur, senex ne proelio interesset a suis rogaretur, quod mallent omnes pro ipso periclitari quam illum pro omnibus.

33. Ita sibi gratis officiis plebem obligaverat, primum ut in discordiis populi exsulare in Hebron mallet quam regnare in Hierusalem; deinde ut etiam in hoste positam virtutem diligeret, iustitiam etiam his qui arma contra se tulerant aeque ac suis praestandam putaret. Denique fortissimum adversae partis propugnatorem Abner ducem et inferentem proelia miratus est et orantem pacis gratiam non aspernatus honoravit convivio; interemptum insidiis doluit et flevit,

whole nation that the people will be quite ready to put his safety and happiness before their own.

31. Think of the insults Moses swallowed, all the charges the people hurled at him! Yet despite it all, when the Lord was about to take vengeance on them for their rebellion against him, he repeatedly offered himself on behalf of the people, in order to save the nation as a whole from the divine anger. What gentle words he used when he addressed the people, even in the wake of all the wrongs they had done him, comforting them in their troubles, calming them with his prophetic revelations, and encouraging them with the works that he performed! He was forever speaking with God, yet he could always keep a humble and gracious tone when he spoke to men. No wonder he was thought to belong far above the ranks of ordinary mortals, such that they could not even look on his face, and believed that his tomb was never found. He had won the hearts of the entire nation so successfully that they held him in affection for his gentleness even more than they admired him for his deeds.

32. Then again, look at the case of holy David, who followed in his footsteps. This one man was chosen out of the entire populace to govern the nation: how gentle and amiable he was, how humble in spirit, how diligent in heart, and affable in character! Even before he came to the throne, he offered himself on behalf of them all. As king, he served in the army as much as anyone, and took his share of the labour; he was courageous in battle, mild in authority, patient when abused, always far readier to put up with injustices than to return them. This is how dear he was to them all—as a young man, he was invited to take the throne: he had no intention of it himself and had to be forced into it reluctantly; as an old man, they pleaded with him not to take part in battle, for they were all far happier to put themselves at risk for him than to watch him putting himself at risk for all of them.

33. He had put the nation firmly in his debt by performing duties which won their favour. Think, first, of the time when the people were divided into opposing factions: he was quite prepared to go and live as an exile in Hebron rather than reign in Jerusalem. Or again, think of the value he set on bravery, even in an enemy: he believed that men who had taken up arms against him should be treated with the same justice that he would show to his own forces. Indeed, he held the general Abner in the highest esteem, as the bravest defending champion on the enemy side, even though it was he who was directing the campaign against him; instead of rebuffing him when he sued for peace, he held a banquet in his honour. He mourned and wept when the man was killed as a result of treachery; he walked behind him at his funeral procession and paid him due honour; and in seeking to avenge

prosecutus exsequias honestavit, mortem ultus conscientiae fidem praestitit, quam filio inter hereditaria iura transcripsit, magis sollicitus ne innocentis mortem inultam relinqueret quam quo suam mortem doleret.

34. Non mediocre istud, praesertim in rege, sic obire humilitatis munia ut communem se exhiberet etiam infimis, alieno periculo cibum non quaerere, potum recusare, peccatum fateri seque ipsum pro populo offerre morti ut in se divina indignatio converteretur eum ferienti angelo offerens se diceret: *Ecce sum, ego peccavi et ego pastor malum feci, et iste grex quid fecit? Fiat manus tua in me.*

35. Nam quid alia dicam? Quod dolum meditantibus non aperiebat os suum et tamquam non audiens nullum sermonem referendum putabat; non respondebat conviciis; cum sibi derogaretur, orabat; cum malediceretur, benedicebat. Ambulans in simplicitate, superborum fugitans, sectator immaculatorum, qui cinerem miscebat alimentis suis cum peccata propria deploraret, et potum suum temperabat fletibus. Merito sic expetitus est ab universo populo ut venirent ad eum omnes tribus Israel dicentes: *Ecce nos ossa tua et caro tua sumus: heri et nudius tertius, cum esset Saul et regnaret super nos, tu eras qui producebas et inducebas Israel. Et dixit tibi Dominus: Tu pasces populum meum.* Et quid plura de eo dicam, de quo huiusmodi Dei processit sententia ut de eo diceret: *Inveni David secundum cor meum?* Quis enim in sanctitate cordis et iustitia sicut iste ambulavit ut impleret voluntatem Dei, propter quem et delinquentibus posteris eius venia data et praerogativa est reservata heredibus?

36. Quis igitur non diligeret eum quem videbat ita carum amicis ut, quia ipse sincere amicos diligebat, aeque diligi se a suis amicis arbitraretur? Denique parentes eum filiis suis, filii praeferebant parentibus. Unde graviter indignatus Saul percutere Ionatham filium hasta voluit, quia pluris apud eum valere David amicitiam iudicabat quam vel pietatem vel auctoritatem paternam.

37. Etenim ad incentivum caritatis communis plurimum proficit si quis vicem amantibus reddat nec minus redamare

his death he proved the commitment that he felt in his conscience, and handed on to his son the task of fulfilling it, among all the other legal responsibilities that he left him. He was more concerned that the death of an innocent man should not be left unavenged than that his own death should be duly mourned.

34. It is no small achievement for anyone, especially a king, to behave like this—to discharge his responsibilities with such humility that he renders himself like the lowliest of all; or to take no food when someone else's life is in danger; or to refuse a drink; or to confess his sin; or to offer himself to die for his people, asking that the anger of God against them might be turned upon him, as he did when he offered himself to the destroying angel and said: 'See, I am the one, it is I who have sinned, it is I the shepherd who have done evil—this flock, what has it done? Let your hand fall upon me.'

35. What more is there to say? To those who were plotting guile he would not open his mouth: he acted as if he did not hear them. He felt no need to give any reply, and he did not answer their abuse. When people belittled him, he prayed; when they cursed him, he blessed them. He walked in simplicity of heart; he kept clear of the proud; he maintained company with those who were spotless in their ways; he mixed ashes with his food when he wept over his private sins, and he mingled his drink with tears. No wonder he was so sought after by all the people, so that all the tribes of Israel came to him and said: 'See, we are your bones, your flesh. Yesterday and the day before, when Saul was alive and reigned over us, you were the one who led Israel out and in. And the Lord said to you: "You shall feed my people."' What more shall I say about him? The judgement of God himself went so far as to say of him: 'I have found David a man after my own heart'? Did anyone ever walk in the holiness of heart and justice that he did, so fulfilling the will of God? On his account his successors were granted pardon when they sinned, and his heirs were allowed to keep their rights and privileges.

36. How could anyone not have loved him, seeing how dear he was to his friends? Anyone would have concluded that a man who had such genuine love for his friends himself must be loved with equal measure by his friends. Why, parents put him before their own children, and children before their parents. The result was that Saul became furiously angry, and resolved to kill his son Jonathan with his spear, for he thought that David's friendship meant more to Jonathan than did proper affection or due respect for his own father's authority.

37. As we can see, it is the greatest possible incentive towards being held in popular affection if a person shows love in return to those who love him, and if he demonstrates that he loves no less in return than he

se probet quam ipse amatur idque amicitiae fidelis faciat exemplis. Quid enim tam populare quam gratia? Quid tam insitum naturae quam ut diligentem diligas? Quid tam inolitum atque impressum adfectibus humanis quam ut eum amare inducas in animum, a quo te amari velis? Merito sapiens dicit: *Perde pecuniam propter fratrem et amicum.* Et alibi: *Amicum salutare non erubescam et a facie illius non me abscondam.* Siquidem vitae et immortalitatis medicamentum in amico esse Ecclesiasticus sermo testetur; et summum in caritate praesidium nemo dubitaverit, cum apostolus dicat: *Omnia suffert, omnia credit, omnia sperat, omnia sustinet, caritas numquam cadit.*

38. Ideo David non cecidit quia carus fuit omnibus et diligi a subiectis quam timeri maluit. Timor enim temporalis tutaminis servat excubias, nescit diuturnitatis custodiam. Itaque ubi timor decesserit, audacia obrepit, quoniam fidem non timor cogit sed adfectus exhibet.

39. Prima ergo ad commendationem nostri est caritas. Bonum est ergo testimonium habere de plurimorum dilectione. Hinc nascitur fides, ut committere se tuo adfectui non vereantur etiam alieni, quem pluribus carum adverterint. Similiter etiam per fidem ad caritatem pervenitur, ut qui uni aut duobus praestiterit fidem, tamquam influat in animos universorum et omnium acquirat gratiam.

VIII 40. Duo igitur haec ad commendationem nostri plurimum operantur, caritas et fides, et tertium hoc si habeas quod in te admiratione dignum plerique existiment et iure honorandum putent.

41. Et quia consiliorum usus maxime conciliat homines, ideo prudentia et iustitia in unoquoque desideratur, et ea exspectatur a pluribus ut in quo ea sint, illi deferatur fides quod possit utile consilium ac fidele desideranti dare. Quis enim ei se committat, quem non putet plus sapere quam ipse sapiat qui quaerit consilium? Necesse est igitur ut praestantior sit a quo consilium petitur quam ille est qui petit. Quid enim

is loved himself, and makes it clear by exemplifying faithful friendship. What is more likely to win popular favour than to offer people
gratitude? What instinct is more natural than to show love to someone
who shows love to you? What inclination is more deeply implanted and
ingrained in human hearts than the urge to devote all your energies to
loving a person from whom you want to receive love yourself? No
wonder the wise man says: 'Lose money for a brother and a friend'.
And in another passage: 'I will not blush to greet a friend, and I will
not hide myself from his face', since in a friend there is 'the medicine of
life and of immortality', as the words of Ecclesiasticus testify; and no
one should be in any doubt that it is in love that our strongest defence
lies, for the apostle says: 'It bears all things, believes all things, hopes
all things, endures all things; love never fails.'

38. This was why David did not fall: he was dear to everyone, and he
thought it preferable to be loved rather than feared by his subjects.
Fear can provide the sort of vigilance that offers temporary security,
but it is unable to give the kind of protection that lasts. Once fear has
subsided, boldness soon creeps in; for confidence cannot be compelled
by fear, it can only be guaranteed by affection.

39. The first way to commend ourselves to others, then, is by showing
them love. It is a good thing, then, to have the testimony of being loved
by the majority of people around you. This is how confidence in you is
born: even strangers have no hesitation in entrusting themselves to
your affection, when they see that you are dear to so many. Then, by
the same process, people pass beyond the stage of confidence to the
feeling of love, so that someone who has repaid the confidence of one
or two manages as it were to steal the hearts of all around him, and
wins the favour of everyone.

40. These, then, are the two most effective ways of commending **VIII**
ourselves to others—by showing them love and by earning their
confidence. There is a third way, too, and it is this: it is where you
possess some quality which most people consider worthy of admiration, something which they believe deserves to be respected.

41. Since one particularly good way of winning people over is by
giving them good advice, prudence and justice are desirable in every
situation. Indeed, this is just what most people are looking for: they
want to place their confidence in someone who possesses these virtues,
for they know that he is in a position to give useful and reliable advice
to anyone desiring it. Who is likely to entrust himself to someone
whose wisdom, so far as he can see, is no greater than his own, when he
is the one wanting the advice? It is essential that the person from
whom the advice is being sought is abler than the person who is doing
the seeking! What would be the point in consulting a man if you

consulas hominem quem non arbitreris posse melius aliquid
reperire quam ipse intellegis?

42. Quod si eum inveneris qui vivacitate ingenii, mentis
vigore atque auctoritate praestet et accedat eo ut exemplo et
usu paratior sit, praesentia solvat pericula, prospiciat futura,
denuntiet imminentia, argumentum expediat, remedium ferat
in tempore, paratus sit non solum ad consulendum sed etiam
ad subveniendum, huic ita fides habetur ut dicat qui consilium petit: *Et si mala mihi evenerint per illum, sustineo.*

43. Huiusmodi igitur viro salutem nostram et existimationem
committimus, qui sit, ut supra diximus, iustus et prudens.
Facit enim iustitia ut nullus sit fraudis metus; facit etiam
prudentia ut nulla erroris suspicio sit. Promptius tamen nos
iusto viro quam prudenti committimus, ut secundum usum
vulgi loquar. Denique sapientum definitione, in quo una
virtus est, concurrunt ceterae nec potest sine iustitia esse
prudentia. Quod etiam in nostris invenimus: dicit enim
David: *Iustus miseretur et fenerat.* Quid feneret iustus, alibi
dicit: *Iucundus vir qui miseretur et fenerat, disponit sermones
suos in iudicio.*

44. Ipsum illud nobile Salomonis iudicium nonne sapientiae
plenum ac iustitiae est? Itaque spectemus illud si ita est.
Duae, inquit, mulieres in conspectu regis Salomonis steterunt
et dixit una ad eum: 'Audi me, Domine. Ego et haec mulier in
uno habitantes cubiculo, ante diem tertium partu edito,
singulos filios suscepimus et eramus una, arbiter nullus
domi nec ulla alia nobiscum femina nisi nos solae, et mortuus
est filius eius hac nocte ut obdormivit super eum; et surrexit
media nocte et accepit filium meum de sinu meo et collocavit
eum in gremio suo et filium suum mortuum posuit in sinu
meo. Et surrexi mane ut lactarem parvulum, et inveni
mortuum. Et consideravi illum diluculo et non erat filius
meus.' Et respondit altera: 'Non, sed filius meus est hic qui
vivit; filius autem tuus qui mortuus est.'

45. Et haec erat contentio, cum utraque sibi filium vindicaret
superstitem, defunctum autem suum negaret. Tum rex iussit

thought he was incapable of seeing into something any better than you could understand it yourself?

42. Now if you find a person who shows a lively intellect and a real strength of mind and authority—someone who is, in addition, well-qualified to help you by virtue of his practical experience, capable of delivering you from present dangers, anticipating your future circumstances, warning you of problems which lie on the horizon, explaining the meaning of things, and bringing the kind of relief that is right for the situation in which you find yourself; someone who is qualified not just to offer you advice but to give you real help—this is the type of individual in whom you will feel confidence. Indeed, anyone who seeks advice from such a man might put it like this: 'And if dreadful things befall me on his account, I bear them.'

43. This, then, is the sort of man to whom we are prepared to entrust our life and reputation—the sort who, as we have said, is just and prudent. His justice guarantees that we have no fear of being deceived by him, and his prudence guarantees that we have no suspicion he might be mistaken. All the same, we are far readier to entrust ourselves to someone who is just than to someone who is prudent, to use the common way of putting it. Now if we follow the judgement of the wise, we are told that where we see one virtue, the other virtues are present as well, and so prudence cannot exist without justice. We find the same point made in our Scriptures as well, for David says: 'The just man shows compassion and lends.' What it is that the just man lends, he tells us elsewhere: 'Happy is the man who shows compassion and lends: he measures his words with judgement.'

44. Take the famous judgement of Solomon: here, surely, is a scene full of wisdom and justice. Well, let us look at it, to see if it is so. Two women, Scripture says, came and stood before King Solomon, and one said to him: 'Please hear me, my lord. This woman and I live in the same room, and not three days ago we each had a baby boy. There were just the two of us together at the time—there was no other witness in the house or any other woman present with us; we were on our own. Just last night, her boy died, for she fell asleep on top of him and smothered him. She got up in the middle of the night, and took my boy from my breast and laid him in her bosom, and she put her own dead boy at my breast. I got up in the morning to feed my little one, and I found him lying there, dead! I looked at him carefully in the early morning light, and I could see he was not my boy.' But the other woman said: 'Not at all! This is *my* boy here, alive and well; it is *your* boy that is dead.'

45. This was their dispute—each tried to claim the surviving child as her own, and rejected the one who was dead. The king then gave

adferri machaeram et infantem dividi ac singulas partes dari singulis: dimidiam uni et dimidiam alteri. Exclamat mulier quae vero erat adfectu percita: 'Nequaquam, Domine, infantem dividas: detur potius illi et vivat et non interficias eum'. At illa respondit altera: 'Neque meus neque huius sit infans: dividite eum'. Et statuit rex dari infantem ei mulieri quae dixerat: 'Nolite interficere eum, sed date eum illi mulieri,' quia mota sunt, inquit, viscera eius in filio suo.

46. Itaque non immerito aestimatus est intellectus Dei in eo esse. Quoniam quae occulta sunt Deo? Quid autem occultius internorum viscerum testimonio? In quae sapientis intellectus velut quidam pietatis descendit arbiter et velut quamdam genitalis alvi vocem meruit, qua maternus patuit adfectus qui eligeret filium suum vel apud alienam vivere, quam in conspectu matris necari.

47. Sapientiae igitur fuit latentes distinguere conscientias, ex occultis eruere veritatem et, velut quadam machaera, ita spiritus gladio penetrare non solum uteri sed etiam animae et mentis viscera; iustitiae quoque, ut quae suum necaverat, alienum non tolleret sed vera mater reciperet suum. Denique etiam scriptura hoc pronuntiavit: *Audivit*, inquit, *omnis Israel hoc iudicium quod iudicavit rex, et timuerunt a facie regis, eo quod intellectus Dei in eo esset, ut faceret iustitiam*. Denique et ipse Salomon ita poposcit sapientiam ut daretur sibi cor prudens audire et iudicare cum iustitia.

IX **48.** Liquet igitur etiam secundum scripturam divinam, quae antiquior est, sapientiam sine iustitia esse non posse, quia ubi una earum virtutum, ibi utraque est. Daniel quoque, quam sapienter alta interrogatione fraudulentae accusationis deprehendit mendacium ut calumniatorum sibi responsio non conveniret! Prudentiae igitur fuit vocis suae testimonio reos prodere; iustitiae quoque nocentes supplicio dare, innocentem subducere.

49. Est ergo individuum sapientiae atque iustitiae contubernium, sed vulgi usu dividitur una quaedam forma virtutum,

orders that a sword be brought, and instructed that the baby be cut in two and a piece be given to each of them, half to one and half to the other. One woman, overwhelmed with genuine maternal love, cried out: 'No, my lord! Don't cut the baby in two! Let her have him, so long as he lives! Don't kill him!' But the other replied: 'I don't care if the baby is mine or hers: cut him in two.' So the king ruled that the baby be given to the woman who had said, 'Don't kill him! Let the woman have him!'—because, he said, she could only be moved with such compassion for one who was her own boy.

46. No wonder people concluded that 'the understanding of God was in him'! For what is hidden from God? What is more hidden than the witness that lies deep in the recesses of a person's own heart? It was right down into these depths that this wise man's understanding descended, like a judge of motherly love, where it could detect the sound that came from the life-giving womb itself, giving voice to the real mother's instinct: the real mother would far rather see her boy live and be looked after by someone else than watch him being put to death before her eyes.

47. It took wisdom to discern the secrets of the woman's conscience, to bring out the truth from the hidden depths of her being, and to take the sword of the Spirit as a blade to penetrate not just the innermost yearnings of a mother's womb but the very depths of her heart and soul. And it took justice, too, to make sure that a woman who had been responsible for the death of her own child did not make off with someone else's, and to see that the true mother received her child back. This is what Scripture itself declared on the matter: 'All Israel,' it says, 'heard of this judgement which the king gave, and they feared the face of the king, for the understanding of God was in him to administer justice.' Solomon himself had asked for such wisdom: he had prayed that he would be given a prudent heart so that he would be able to hear and judge with justice.

48. So divine Scripture itself makes it clear—and it is a far older IX witness—that wisdom cannot exist without justice: for where one of these virtues is to be found, there the other is too. If you want another example, take the case of Daniel. Look at the wisdom he showed when he asked those penetrating questions and thus uncovered the lies which lay behind those spurious charges, showing that the answers given by those bringing the false accusations did not square up. It took prudence to expose the culprits by the testimony of their own words; and it took justice, too, to hand over the guilty to be punished and to rescue the one who was innocent.

49. There is therefore an inseparable association between wisdom and justice. All the same, in popular usage each of the virtues is identified

ut temperantia sit in despiciendis voluptatibus, fortitudo spectetur in laboribus et periculis, prudentia in delectu bonorum, sciens commoda et adversa distinguere, iustitia, quae sit bona custos iuris alieni et vindex proprietatis, suum cuique conservans. Sit ergo nobis communis opinionis gratia quadripartita haec facta divisio, ut ab illa subtili disputatione philosophiae sapientiaeque, quae limandae veritatis causa quasi ex adyto quodam eruitur, retrahentes pedem, forensem usum ac popularem sensum sequamur. Hac igitur divisione servata revertamur ad propositum.

X **50.** Prudentissimo cuique causam nostram committimus et ab eo consilium promptius quam a ceteris poscimus. Praestat tamen fidele iusti consilium viri et sapientissimi ingenio frequenter praeponderat. *Utilia* enim *vulnera amici quam aliorum oscula.* Deinde quia iusti iudicium est, sapientis autem argumentum: in illo censura disceptationis, in hoc calliditas inventionis.

51. Quod si utrumque conectas, erit magna consiliorum salubritas quae ab universis spectatur admiratione sapientiae et amore iustitiae, ut omnes quaerant audire sapientiam eius viri in quo utriusque virtutis copula sit, sicut quaerebant omnes reges terrae videre faciem Salomonis et audire sapientiam eius, ita ut Saba regina veniret ad eum et tentaret eum in quaestionibus: *Et venit et omnia locuta est quae habebat in corde suo, et audivit omnem sapientiam Salomonis nec ullum verbum praeterivit eam.*

52. Quae sit ista quam nihil praetereat nec sit aliquid quod ei non adnuntiaverit verus Salomon, cognosce o homo, ex his quae audis loquentem: *Verus est,* inquit, *sermo quem audivi in terra mea de sermonibus tuis et de prudentia tua, et non credidi his qui dicebant mihi, donec veni et viderunt oculi mei; et nunc non est nec dimidia quidem pars secundum ea quae adnuntiabant mihi. Apposuisti bona super omnia quae audivi in terra mea. Beatae mulieres tuae et beati pueri tui qui adsistunt tibi, qui audiunt omnem prudentiam tuam.* Intellege convivium veri Salomonis, et quae apponuntur in eo convivio, intellege sapienter et considera in qua terra congregatio nationum audierit famam sapientiae verae atque iustitiae et quibus

with a particular characteristic: so, temperance is a matter of despising sensual pleasures; courage can be seen when people undergo toils and dangers; prudence consists in the choice of what is good, the knowledge of how to distinguish banes and blessings; and justice is about being a good guardian of another person's rights, a defender of people's property, and the kind of person who preserves for each what is rightfully his own. In deference to popular opinion, let us retain this fourfold division as a working principle. If we thus withdraw from all the pointless discussions of philosophy and of 'wisdom' so-called—brought out from some inner shrine so as to refine truth—we can follow everyday usage and the meaning intended by ordinary people. Maintaining this division, then, let us return to our subject.

50. We entrust our interests to the most prudent person we can find, **X** and we are more prepared to seek advice from such an individual than from anyone else. At the same time, it is particularly important to receive advice that is faithful from a man who is just; this can often be of greater weight than the abilities of the wisest of men, for 'Better are the wounds of a friend than the kisses of others.' And since the person who is just has the ability to come to a right decision while the person who is wise has the power to think through an argument carefully, the one offers the good sense that is necessary to settle disputes and the other the cleverness that is required to come up with ideas.

51. If you put the two sides together, the advice that is given will be sound indeed; people everywhere look on it with admiration for its wisdom and with love for its justice, and everyone will seek to hear the wisdom of a man in whom these two virtues are combined, just as all the kings of the earth sought to see the face of Solomon and hear his wisdom. This was what the queen of Sheba did: she came to him and plied him with all sorts of questions: 'And she came and told him all that was in her heart, and heard all the wisdom of Solomon, and not a word escaped her.'

52. Be clear, man, who this woman is, this one whom nothing escapes, this one to whom the true Solomon declared everything, when you hear what she has to say: 'It was true,' she said, 'the report that I heard in my own land about your words and your prudence, though I did not believe those who told me of it until I came and saw it with my own eyes. As it is, not even the half was declared to me. You have served up good things far beyond what I heard of in my country. Happy are your women, and happy are your servant-boys who wait upon you and hear all your prudence.' Recognize what the feast of the true Solomon is, and what is served up in that feast. Be wise, recognize it, and think about that land where all the nations will hear the fame of his true wisdom and justice, and the eyes with which they will see him, gazing

eum viderit oculis, contemplantibus utique quae non videntur. Quoniam *quae videntur temporalia sunt, quae autem non
videntur aeterna.*

53. Quae sunt beatae mulieres, nisi illae de quibus dicitur
quia multae verbum Dei audiunt et faciunt? Et alibi: *Quicumque enim fecerit verbum Dei, ipse meus et frater et soror et
mater est.* Qui etiam pueri tui beati qui adsistunt, nisi Paulus
qui dicebat: *Usque in hunc diem sto protestans minori ac maiori;*
Simeon qui exspectabat in templo ut videret consolationem
Israel? Quomodo enim dimitti posceret nisi quia adsistens
Domino, discedendi habere facultatem non poterat, nisi
voluntatem Domini adeptus esset? Exempli causa propositus
nobis Salomon est, a quo certatim, ut audiretur eius sapientia,
postulabatur.

54. Ioseph quoque nec in carcere feriatus erat quominus de
rebus incertis consuleretur. Cuius consilium Aegypto universae profuit, ut non sentiret septem annorum sterilitatem
aliosque populos miserae famis levaret ieiunio.

55. Daniel ex captivis regalium consultorum arbiter factus,
consiliis suis emendavit praesentia, adnuntiavit futura. Ex his
enim quae frequenter interpretatus ostenderat vere se esse
adnuntiatum, fides ei in omnibus deferebatur.

XI **56.** Sed etiam tertius locus de his qui admiratione digni
aestimarentur Ioseph et Salomonis et Danielis exemplo
decursus videtur. Nam quid de Moyse loquar, cuius omnis
Israel cotidie consilia praestolabatur? Quorum vita fidem
faciebat prudentiae admirationemque eius augebat. Quis se
non committeret consilio Moysi, cui seniores, si qua supra
suum intellectum et virtutem esse arbitrarentur, diiudicanda
servabant?

57. Quis Danielis consilium refugeret, de quo Deus ipse
dixit: *Quis Daniele sapientior?* Aut quomodo homines de
eorum dubitare mentibus possent, quibus Deus tantam conferebat gratiam? Moysi consilio bella conficiebantur; Moysi
meritis de caelo adfluebat alimonia, potus e petra.

58. Quam purus Danielis animus, ut mulceret barbaros
mores, mitigaret leones! Quae in illo temperantia! Quanta
animi et corporis continentia! Nec immerito mirabilis factus

upon things that are unseen. For 'the things that are seen are temporal, but the things that are unseen are eternal'.

53. Who are the 'happy women'? Are they not those of whom it is said that there are many who hear the word of God and put it into practice? And in another place we read this: 'For whoever puts the word of God into practice is my brother and my sister and my mother.' Who are 'your happy servant-boys who wait upon you'? Are they not men like Paul, who could say, 'To this very day, I stand and testify to great and small alike'; or Simeon, who waited in the temple to see the consolation of Israel? He could never have asked to be dismissed, could he, unless he was a servant of the Lord? For such a person has no right to depart without first obtaining the Lord's permission. Solomon has been presented to us as an example: people vied with each other in demanding to hear his wisdom.

54. And think of Joseph: even when he was in prison, he could get no rest from being consulted about things that were uncertain. His advice proved so valuable to the whole of Egypt that the country did not feel those seven barren years, and was even in a position to alleviate the plight of other peoples who were suffering in the grip of the terrible famine.

55. Or take Daniel: though one of the captives, he was appointed chief of the royal advisers. By giving the advice that he did he improved conditions in the present and declared what would happen in the future. Since he had shown time and again by his ability to interpret things that what he declared came true, people were ready to put their confidence in him in every situation.

56. But the third point, the one about people being considered worthy XI of admiration, also seems to have been raised by these examples of Joseph, Solomon, and Daniel. For what about Moses? All Israel waited for his advice day after day. The character of these men's lives inspired confidence in their prudence, and increased people's admiration for it. Who would not have entrusted himself to Moses' advice? The elders themselves left it to him to decide everything that they considered was beyond their own understanding and ability.

57. Who would have hesitated to take the advice of Daniel? God himself said of him: 'Who is wiser than Daniel?' Or how could men have felt any doubts about the minds of these individuals to whom God granted such grace? Moses' advice brought wars to an end; Moses' merits were such that food rained from the sky and drink flowed out of the rock.

58. What purity of spirit Daniel showed! He could temper the ways of barbarians; he could tame lions! What temperance there was in him! What self-control he had, in body and spirit! No wonder he became

omnibus, quando, quod vehementer admirantur homines, regalibus fultus amicitiis, aurum non quaerebat nec delatum sibi honorem plus faciebat quam fidem. Quin etiam periclitari malebat pro lege Domini quam pro gratia hominis inflecti.

59. Nam de sancti Ioseph, quem paene praeterieram, castimonia et iustitia quid dicam? Quarum altera illecebras heriles respuit, refutavit praemia, altera mortem contempsit, metum reppulit, carcerem praeoptavit. Quis hunc privatae causae ad consulendum idoneum non iudicaret, cuius ferax animus et mens fertilis temporis sterilitatem quodam consiliorum et cordis ubere fecundavit?

XII 60. Advertimus igitur quod in acquirendis consiliis plurimum adiungat vitae probitas, virtutum praerogativa, benevolentiae usus, facilitatis gratia. Quis enim in caeno fontem requirat? Quis e turbida aqua potum petat? Itaque ubi luxuria est, ubi intemperantia, ubi vitiorum confusio, quis inde sibi aliquid hauriendum existimet? Quis non despiciat morum colluvionem? Quis utilem causae alienae iudicet quem videt inutilem suae vitae? Quis iterum improbum malevolum contumeliosum non fugiat et ad nocendum paratum? Quis non eum omni studio declinet?

61. Quis vero, quamvis instructum ad consilii opem, difficili tamen accessu, ambiat, in quo sit illud tamquam si qui aquae fontem praecludat? Quid enim prodest habere sapientiam, si consilium neges? Si consulendi intercludas copiam, clausisti fontem, ut nec aliis influat nec tibi prosit.

62. Pulchre autem et de illo convenit qui habens prudentiam, commaculat eam vitiorum sordibus, eo quod aquae exitum contaminet. Degeneres animos vita arguit. Quomodo enim potes eum iudicare consilio superiorem quem videas inferiorem moribus? Supra me debet esse cui me committere paro.

the object of everyone's admiration, for he showed a spirit that men will always greatly admire—though he had all the support of friendships with royalty, he did not chase after gold, or imagine that the honour he was granted mattered more than his faith. Quite the reverse, in fact: he was prepared to put himself in danger for the law of the Lord rather than be deflected from his devotion simply to obtain the favour of man.

59. And what about holy Joseph, and the chastity and justice he displayed? I had almost passed him by. As for his chastity—he rejected the seductive advances of his master's wife, and turned down all the rewards. As for his justice—he showed a contempt for death, banished his fear, and opted for a life in prison. Who would not have regarded such a man as the right individual to consult on a personal matter? His spirit was fruitful, his mind was fertile—he was able to enrich that barren period by the very profusion of sound counsel in his heart.

60. As we can see, then, when it comes to obtaining good advice, it is **XII** uprightness of life, an obvious preference for all the best virtues, a steady practice of goodwill, and a pleasant and courteous manner that are the qualities which matter most. After all, who would look for a spring in a patch of mud? Who would try to slake his thirst with water that is polluted? If all we find in an individual is decadence, a lack of temperance, and a medley of every imaginable vice, who would suppose there should be a single good draught to be drawn from such a source? Who would not despise that kind of pollution of character? Who would consider a person likely to be of any benefit to the interests of a third party if he sees that the man is incapable of doing anything of benefit to his own life? And again, who would not go out of his way to avoid a dishonest or spiteful or abusive character, with every necessary qualification to do him harm? Who would not make every effort to steer clear of him?

61. But then again, who would ask assistance from an individual if, however well-equipped he might be to give advice, he remained difficult to approach? Someone like that is like a spring of water with its channels all sealed up. What advantage is there in possessing wisdom, if you refuse to give advice? If you shut off every opportunity for anyone to get your advice, you have closed off a spring, so that it neither flows to others nor does you any good yourself.

62. The same could equally well be said of a person who possesses prudence but pollutes it with the filth of various vices, and so contaminates the water at its source. It is people's lives that provide evidence that their hearts are degenerate. How can you consider a man to be better than you when it comes to giving advice if you see that he is worse than you when it comes to morality? If I am going to entrust

An vero eum idoneum putabo qui mihi det consilium quod non det sibi, et mihi eum vacare credam qui sibi non vacet, cuius animum voluptates occupent, libido devincat, avaritia subiuget, cupiditas perturbet, quatiat metus? Quomodo hic consilio locus, ubi nullus quieti?

63. Admirandus mihi et suspiciendus consiliarius quem propitius Dominus patribus dedit, offensus abstulit. Huius imitator debet esse qui potest consilium dare et alienam a vitiis custodire prudentiam, quoniam *nihil inquinatum in illam incurrit.*

XIII 64. Quis igitur tamquam vultu speciem praeferat pulchritudinis et beluinis posterioribus ac ferinis unguibus formae superioris dehonestet gratiam, cum tam admirabilis et praeclara forma virtutum sit et specialiter pulchritudo sapientiae? Sicut series scripturae indicat: *Est enim speciosior sole et super omnem stellarum dispositionem: luci comparata invenitur prior. Lucem etenim hanc suscipit nox, sapientiam autem non vincit malitia.*

65. Diximus de eius pulchritudine et scripturae testimonio comprobavimus. Superest ut doceamus scripturae auctoritate nullum ei contubernium cum vitiis esse sed individuam cum ceteris virtutibus coniunctionem: *Cuius spiritus est disertus, sine inquinamento, certus sanctus amans bonum acutus, qui nihil vetet benefacere benignus stabilis certus securus, omnem habens virtutem, omnia prospiciens.* Et infra: *Sobrietatem docet et iustitiam et virtutem.*

XIV 66. Omnia igitur operatur prudentia, cum omnibus bonis habet consortium. Nam quomodo potest utile consilium dare nisi habeat iustitiam, ut induat constantiam, mortem non reformidet, nullo terrore, nullo revocetur metu, nulla adulatione a vero deflectendum putet, exsilium non refugiat, quae noverit sapienti patriam mundum esse, egestatem non timeat, quae nihil deesse sapienti sciat cui totus mundus divitiarum est? Quid enim praecelsius eo viro qui auro moveri nesciat, contemptum habeat pecuniarum et velut ex

myself to someone, he has to be a better man than I am. Am I really to think that someone is fit to give advice to me when he evidently does not give it to himself, and am I really to believe that he has time for me when he evidently does not have time for himself—when it is quite clear that his mind is taken up with sensual pleasures, or controlled by desire, or a slave to greed, or driven mad with desire, or shaken rigid by fear? How can there be any place for the giving of advice where there is none for calmness of spirit?

63. The kind of adviser who deserves my admiration and respect is the sort of person whom the Lord granted to our fathers when he was favourably inclined towards them and took away when they offended him. This is the example we must each strive to imitate—to be the kind of person who is able to give good advice and keep his prudence free from every evil vice, since 'nothing that is defiled enters into her'.

64. Who would want to present a fine impression of beauty in his face **XIII** while at the same time disfiguring the elegance of his upper body by giving himself the hind quarters of a animal and the hooves of a wild beast? Well, the appearance of the virtues all together as a body is every bit as splendid and magnificent; and the beauty of wisdom is the most special part of all. The whole course of Scripture shows us this. 'She is more dazzling than the sun itself,' we read, 'and brighter than any constellation. Compare her with the light—she is found superior far. For the night carries away their light, but evil does not overcome wisdom.'

65. We have spoken of wisdom's beauty, and confirmed it by citing the testimony of Scripture. What we must now do is show from the authority of Scripture that wisdom has no association with evil vices but is connected inseparably with all the other virtues. 'Her spirit is shrewd, undefiled, sure, holy, and loves all that is good; she is sharp-witted; she forbids no good deed; she is kind, steadfast, sure, and untroubled; she possesses every virtue; she foresees all things.' And further on we read this: 'She teaches sobriety, justice, and virtue.'

66. Prudence is at work in everything, then, for it is closely associated **XIV** with all that is good. For how could prudence give advice that is beneficial without embracing justice as well? It clothes itself in steadfastness of spirit; it holds no fear of death; it is not held back by the slightest terror or the slightest fear; it is convinced that it must never be diverted from the truth by the faintest of flatteries; it does not shrink from the prospect of exile—for it is assured that the whole world is the wise man's country—and it does not fear want, for it knows that the wise man lacks for nothing, since he has the entire world of riches as his own. What sight could be more impressive than that of the individual who finds himself quite unmoved at the prospect

arce quadam despiciat hominum cupiditates? Quod qui
fecerit, hunc homines supra hominem esse arbitrantur: *Quis
est*, inquit, *et laudabimus eum? Fecit enim mirabilia in vita sua.*
Quomodo enim non admirandus qui divitias spernit, quas
plerique saluti propriae praetulerunt?

67. Decet igitur omnes censura frugalitatis, continentiae
auctoritas, et maxime eum qui honore praestet, ne praeeminentem virum thesauri possideant sui et pecuniis serviat qui
praeest liberis. Illud magis decet ut supra thesaurum sit
animo et infra amicum obsequio. Humilitas enim auget
gratiam. Haec plena laudis et digna primario viro: non
communem cum Tyriis negotiatoribus et Galaaditis merca-
toribus habere turpis lucri cupidinem nec omne bonum locare
in pecunia et tamquam mercenario munere cotidianos numer-
are quaestus, calculari compendia.

xv 68. Quod si ab his sobrium animum gerere laudabile est,
quanto illud praestantius, si dilectionem multitudinis liberalitate acquiras neque superflua circa importunos neque
restricta circa indigentes!

69. Plurima autem genera liberalitatis sunt: non solum coti-
diano sumptu egentibus quo vitam sustinere suam possint,
disponere ac dispensare alimoniam, verum etiam his, qui
publice egere verecundantur, consulere ac subvenire, quatenus
communis egenorum alimonia non exhauriatur. De eo enim
loquor qui praeest alicui muneri, ut si officium sacerdotis gerat
aut dispensatoris, ut de his suggerat episcopo nec reprimat si
quem positum in necessitate aliqua cognoverit aut deiectum
opibus ad inopiae necessitatem redactum, maxime si non
effusione adulescentiae sed direptione alicuius et amissione

of gold, who treats money with contempt, and who looks down on all
the desires of men as though he is up in a citadel above them all? Men
regard anyone who behaves this way as more than a man: 'Who is he?'
Scripture asks, 'and we shall praise him. He has done marvellous
things in his time'. How could we fail to admire someone who despises
riches? After all, most people have been prepared to put them before
their own salvation.

67. Well then, the sober judgement that is indicated by a frugal
lifestyle and the proper authority that is evidenced by self-control
are seemly for people everywhere, and especially so for a person who
occupies a position of honour. They prove that the man who is in the
public eye is not held spellbound by his own treasures and that the
man who has charge over free people is no slave to money himself.
Rather, the seemly thing for someone in such a position is to be
superior to treasure in his spirit while in his willingness to serve he is
lower than a friend; for humility increases the esteem in which a
person is held. Here is what is genuinely praiseworthy and appropriate
in a man of the first rank: he must have no desire at all to pursue
dishonourable gain, as do traders from Tyre or merchants from
Gilead; he must not treat money as the source of every possible
good; and he must not behave as though he were merely being paid
to do a job, totting up his gains at the end of every day and calculating
the profits he has made.

68. If it is praiseworthy to show that your spirit is unaffected by such **XV**
desires, it is far more impressive still to win the affection of the masses
by displaying a generosity which is neither prodigal towards those who
are simply persistent in their requests nor miserly towards those who
really are in need.

69. There are many kinds of generosity. It is not simply a matter of
organizing and distributing food to those who lack the basic daily
supplies to stay alive. There is also an obligation to give aid and
assistance to those who are ashamed to show their needs openly—so
long as the resources set aside for the needy as a whole are not
exhausted in the process. I am speaking here of a responsibility
which needs to be shouldered by someone who is in a responsible
position, such as a priest or an almoner. Such a man should inform his
bishop of people who fall into this category, and he should not hold
back if he sees that a person is experiencing some need or other, or has
by a reverse of fortune been reduced from a position of wealth to a state
of hardship and poverty. This is especially important if the person has
landed in this plight not as a result of youthful extravagance but
because someone has stolen from him or because he has lost his

patrimonii in eam reciderit iniuriam, ut sumptum exercere diurnum non queat.

70. Summa etiam liberalitas captos redimere, eripere ex hostium manibus, subtrahere neci homines, et maxime feminas turpitudini, redimere parentibus liberos, parentes liberis, cives patriae restituere. Nota sunt haec nimis Illyrici vastitate et Thraciae. Quanti ubique venales erant toto captivi orbe! Quos si revoces, unius provinciae numerum explere non possint? Fuerunt tamen qui et quos ecclesiae redemerunt, in servitutem revocare vellent, ipsa graviores captivitate qui inviderent alienam misericordiam. Ipsi si in captivitatem venissent, servirent liberi? Si venditi fuissent, servitutis ministerium non recusarent? Et volunt alienam libertatem rescindere, qui suam servitutem non possent rescindere, nisi forte pretium recipere emptori placeret: in quo tamen non rescinditur servitus, sed redimitur.

71. Praecipua est igitur liberalitas redimere captivos, et maxime ab hoste barbaro qui nihil deferat humanitatis ad misericordiam nisi quod avaritia reservaverit ad redemptionem; aes alienum subire si debitor solvendo non sit atque artetur ad solutionem quae sit iure debita et inopia destituta; enutrire parvulos; pupillos tueri.

72. Sunt etiam qui virgines orbatas parentibus tuendae pudicitiae gratia conubio locent, non solum studio sed etiam sumptu adiuvent. Est etiam illud genus liberalitatis, quod apostolus docet ut: *Si quis fidelis habet viduas, subministret illis ut earum alimoniis ecclesia non gravetur, ut his quae vere viduae sunt, sufficiat.*

73. Utilis igitur huiusmodi liberalitas, sed non communis omnibus. Sunt enim plerique etiam viri boni qui tenues sint censu, contenti quidem exiguo ad sui usum sed non idonei ad subsidium levandae paupertatis alienae; tamen suppetit aliud beneficentiae genus quo iuvare possint inferiorem. Est enim duplex liberalitas: una, quae subsidio rei adiuvat, id est usu

inheritance, so that he is no longer in a position to meet his basic daily needs.

70. Another great act of generosity is to ransom prisoners, to snatch people from the hands of the enemy, to deliver men from death and—especially—women from dishonour, to hand children back to their parents and parents back to their children, and to restore citizens to their own country. We saw this all too clearly in the devastation of Illyricum and Thrace. How many prisoners were put up for sale, all over the world—if you could bring them all back, they would match the population of an entire province. And yet there were those who would have taken the very individuals whom the churches ransomed and brought them into slavery again. These people were more severe than the captivity itself: they begrudged mercy to others. If they had ended up in slavery themselves, would they be happy to behave like slaves, free men that they are? If they had been sold, would they not be refusing to serve as slaves? Yet they want to put an end to the freedom of others, when they are quite unable to put an end to their own slavery—unless of course a buyer would like to receive a payment; in which case slavery is not being brought to an end: rather, people are being ransomed from it.

71. It is a special act of generosity to ransom prisoners, then, particularly if they are in the hands of a barbarian enemy, who shows no regard for humanity and no interest in mercy, except in so far as his greed has kept an eye to the profit that might be made from the receipt of ransom-money. It is also a good thing to assume responsibility for a person's debts if he is not in a position to pay them himself, and to supply money which is legally owed but which a person has despaired of ever being able to pay on account of his poverty. It is great, too, to feed little children and to extend protection to orphans.

72. There are also people who endeavour to protect the honour of young women who have lost their parents, by arranging marriages for them, helping them not just with kind feelings but with practical support as well. There is another type of generosity that the apostle teaches, too, and it is this: 'If a believer has widows in his family, he must take care of them himself, so that the church is not burdened by their upkeep, but has enough for those who truly are widows.'

73. Well, generosity of this kind is beneficial, but it is not commonly to be found everywhere you look. For there are lots of people, good people too, who are of only slender means, and while they remain quite content with very little for their own requirements they are in no position to alleviate the poverty of anyone else. However, there is another type of kindness available to them, by which they can help someone worse off than themselves. For there are two kinds of

pecuniae; altera, quae operum collatione impenditur, multo frequenter splendidior multoque clarior.

74. Quanto illustrius Abraham captum armis victricibus recepit nepotem quam si redemisset! Quanto utilius regem Pharaonem sanctus Ioseph consilio providentiae iuvit quam si contulisset pecuniam! Pecunia enim unius civitatis non redemit ubertatem; prospicientia totius Aegypti per quinquennium famem reppulit.

75. Facile autem pecunia consumitur, consilia exhauriri nesciunt. Haec usu augentur; pecunia minuitur et cito deficit atque ipsam destituit benignitatem, ut quo pluribus largiri volueris, eo pauciores adiuves, et saepe tibi desit quod alii conferendum putaveris. Consilii autem operisque collatio, quo in plures diffunditur, eo redundantior manet et in suum fontem recurrit. In se enim refluit ubertas prudentiae et quo pluribus fluxerit, eo exercitius fit omne quod remanet.

XVI **76.** Liquet igitur debere esse liberalitatis modum ne fiat inutilis largitas. Sobrietas tenenda est, maxime a sacerdotibus, ut non pro iactantia sed pro iustitia dispensent. Nusquam enim maior aviditas petitionis. Veniunt validi, veniunt nullam causam nisi vagandi habentes, et volunt subsidia evacuare pauperum, exinanire sumptum; nec exiguo contenti, maiora quaerunt, ambitu vestium captantes petitionis suffragium et natalium simulatione licitantes incrementa quaestuum. His si quis facile fidem deferat, cito exhaurit pauperum alimoniis futura compendia. Modus largiendi adsit ut nec illi inanes recedant neque transcribatur vita pauperum in spolia

generosity: one which offers material help, or the assistance of money, and another which is shown when people contribute their good works. And the latter is often far more splendid and far more noble.

74. Abraham did a far more glorious thing when he recovered his nephew from captivity by armed conquest than he would have done if he had merely ransomed him. Holy Joseph did a far more beneficial thing when he helped Pharaoh the king with his advice and his foresight than he would have done if he had simply given him money. A gift of money would not have restored plenty to a single city, whereas his foresight kept hunger from the whole of Egypt for five years.

75. In any case, money is soon used up, but advice can never be exhausted. It actually grows with use, whereas money is only diminished, and quickly runs out, and has to abandon the whole business of liberality, so that the more people you set out to show kindness to, the fewer you end up helping, and often you find yourself short of funds that you had intended to give to someone else. But when it is advice and good works that you contribute, the more people there are on whom the kindness is poured out, the more abundantly it flows and the more the tide rushes back to its own source. For the rich stream of prudence replenishes itself, and the more people there are to whom it flows, the more effective it renders everything that is left.

76. It is clear, therefore, that we must observe due measure when we **XVI** show generosity, so that we do not bestow the kind of largesse that is of no benefit to anyone. It is essential to maintain moderation, and doubly so for priests: they must distribute alms not for the sake of show but in the interests of justice. Nowhere are greed and begging a more serious problem than they are here. There are people who come along—people who are in perfectly good health—and they come along with no good reason other than the fact that they spend their lives wandering from place to place, and their intention is to use up the supplies intended for the poor, and to reduce to nothing the resources that have been collected for them. Nor are they content with just a little, but they keep on asking for more: they attempt to substantiate their claims by parading around in poor clothes, and they make a bid for greater rewards by pretending that they were born into high social surroundings. If anyone is naive enough to give credence to their claims, before he realizes it he drains the savings which were meant to provide food for the poor. There must be due measure in the generosity we show: that way, people will not go away with their pockets completely empty, but nor will the money collected for the basic subsistence of the poor be handed over to the fraudulent so that they can make off with it like plunder. We need to keep this sense of

fraudulentorum. Ea ergo mensura sit, ut neque humanitas deseratur nec destituatur necessitas.

77. Plerique simulant debita: sit veri examen. Exutos se per latrocinia deplorant: aut iniuria fidem faciat aut cognitio personae, quo propensius iuvetur. Ab ecclesia relegatis sumptus impertiendus si desit eis alendi copia. Itaque qui modum servat, avarus nulli sed largus omnibus est. Non enim solas aures praebere debemus audiendis precantum vocibus sed etiam oculos considerandis necessitatibus. Plus clamat bono operatori debilitas quam vox pauperis. Neque vero fieri potest ut non extorqueat amplius importunitas vociferantum; sed non semper impudentiae locus sit. Videndus est ille qui te non videt; requirendus est ille qui erubescit videri. Ille etiam clausus in carcere occurrat tibi, ille adfectus aegritudine mentem tuam personet qui aures non potest.

78. Quo plus te operari viderit populus, magis diliget. Scio plerosque sacerdotes qui plus contulerunt, plus abundasse, quoniam quicumque bonum operarium videt, ipsi confert quod ille suo officio dispenset, securus quod ad pauperem sua perveniat misericordia: nemo enim vult nisi pauperi proficere suam collationem. Nam si quem aut immoderatum aut nimis tenacem dispensatorem viderit, utrumque displicet, si aut superfluis erogationibus dissipet alieni fructus laboris aut recondat sacculis. Sicut igitur modus liberalitatis tenendus est, ita etiam calcar. Plerumque adhibendus videtur modus ideo ut quod benefacis, id cotidie facere possis, ne subtrahas necessitati quod indulseris effusioni; calcar propterea quia melius operatur pecunia in pauperis cibo quam in divitis

proportion: we must not forget a sense of humanity for people, but genuine hardship must not be left to fend for itself.

77. There are plenty of people who pretend to have debts. We need to look into the truth of their circumstances. They tell us tearfully that they have been stripped of everything by robbers: if their injury is obvious, or if you recognize who they are, this should make you trust them, and they should be given help all the more speedily. Those who have been removed from the church deserve to be given basic supplies, if they do not have the means to feed themselves. The person who maintains this kind of measure in his giving is miserly towards no one but generous towards all. It is not enough for us simply to offer a listening ear, to hear the voices of those who plead with us: we must also use our eyes, to look into their real needs. To the person whose mission it is to do good works, the weakness of a poor man cries out far more powerfully than his voice does. Of course, we cannot always ensure that people who are persistent and vociferous will not extort more, but let us not invariably give way to those who resort to effrontery. It is the person who does not see you that you must see; it is the person who is ashamed to be seen that you must seek out. You must give a thought, too, to the man who is shut up in prison, and the plight of the person who is laid low by illness ought to strike a chord in your heart, even if it cannot strike a chord in your ears.

78. The more the people see you doing good deeds, the more they will love you. I know of many priests who have found that the more they have given, the more plentiful their resources have been. The simple fact is, if anyone sees a man busily engaged in good deeds he is happy to give him something to distribute in his round of duty, for he is confident that his charity will reach the poor—after all, nobody wants his contribution to profit anyone other than the poor. Now if a person sees an almoner behaving in a fashion that is immoderate on the one hand or too sparing on the other, he is displeased either way: in the one case, the fruit of someone else's labour is being thrown away on excessive handouts; in the other, it is being hoarded in people's own pockets. So, just as it is essential when showing generosity to maintain a sense of due measure, it is equally necessary sometimes to be spurred into action. More often than not, it would appear, it is due measure that is called for, to ensure that you are able to perform your acts of kindness day after day and that you do not end up depriving someone in genuine need because you have chosen to indulge somebody else in a way that is extravagant. But there are also times when you need to be spurred into action, for money is put to better use when it feeds the poor than it is when it fills the pockets of the rich. Make sure that you are not drawing the string on the salvation of the needy when you draw

sacculo. Cave ne intra loculos tuos includas salutem inopum et tamquam in tumulis sepelias vitam pauperum.

79. Potuit donare Ioseph totas Aegypti opes et effundere thesauros regios; noluit tamen de alieno effusus videri: maluit frumenta vendere quam donare esurientibus, quia si paucis donasset, plurimis defuisset. Eam liberalitatem probavit quo abundaret omnibus. Patefecit horrea, ut omnes emerent subsidium frumentarium, ne gratis accipiendo cultus terrarum relinquerent, quoniam qui alieno utitur, suum neglegit.

80. Itaque primo omnium coacervavit pecunias, deinde instrumenta cetera, ad postremum iura terrarum regi acquisivit, non ut omnes exueret suo sed fulciret publicum: tributum constitueret quo sua tutius habere possent. Quod ita fuit gratum omnibus quibus terras ademerat, ut non venditionem sui iuris sed redemptionem salutis putarent. Denique dixerunt: *Sanasti nos, invenimus gratiam in conspectu domini nostri*. Nam et de proprietate nihil amiserant qui ius receperant, et de utilitate nihil perdiderant qui acquisierant perpetuitatem.

81. O virum magnum, qui non largitatis superfluae temporalem captavit gloriam sed perpetuam commoditatem constituit providentiae! Fecit enim ut tributis populi se iuvarent suis nec in tempore necessitatis aliena subsidia desiderarent. Melius enim fuit conferre aliquid de fructibus quam totum de iure amittere. Quintam portionem collationis statuit et in providendo perspicacior et in tributo liberalior. Denique numquam postea Aegyptus huiusmodi famem pertulit.

82. Quam praeclare autem collegit futura! Primum, quam argute regalis interpres somnii veritatem expressit! Somnium regis primum hoc fuit. Septem iuvencae ascendebant de flumine, visu decorae, et pingues corpore, et ad oram

the string on your purse, and that you are not burying the poor alive in there just as much as you would if you laid them in a tomb.

79. Joseph could have given away all the wealth of Egypt and squandered the royal treasures; but he did not want to be seen as one who had squandered someone else's property. He preferred to sell the corn rather than give it to the hungry, for if he had given it all to the few there would not have been enough for the many. He adopted this pattern of generosity in order to ensure that there would be plenty for everyone. He opened the grain-stores so that they could all buy their own supply of corn. This was to avoid a situation where, having received it for nothing, they simply gave up cultivating their land; for a person who is able to exploit someone else's assets ceases to bother with his own.

80. First of all, then, he collected up everyone's money, followed by the rest of their goods and livestock, and finally he acquired for the king the rights to their land. His intention was not to deprive all the people of their own property, but to build up the stock of property which lay in the public domain, and to establish a tribute-system which would actually enable them to hold their property with greater security. Those from whom he had taken the land were very pleased with the result: as far as they were concerned, they had not been forced to sell off their rights—they had had their future salvation bought back. This was what they said: 'You have restored us to life; we have found favour in our lord's sight.' They had lost nothing that really belonged to them, for they had received a new right, and they had forfeited nothing that was of benefit to them, for they had gained lasting security.

81. What a great man he was! He did not chase the fleeting glory which can be won by displays of excessive largesse; instead, by exercising foresight, he gave them advantages that would last. By getting the people to pay tribute in this way, he made sure that they helped themselves and in their time of need did not go looking for help from others. It was better for them to give up a portion of their produce than to lose the whole of their rights. He fixed the contribution at a fifth of their total harvest; and so he showed himself to be both clear-sighted in the provision he made for the future and generous in the tribute he imposed. And here was the result: Egypt never suffered such a famine again.

82. Think what remarkable insight it took to anticipate the future as he did! In the first place, think what a clever mind it took to interpret the king's dream and reveal the truth behind it. This was the king's first dream. Seven heifers came up out of the river, fine-looking animals, with well-fed bodies, and began to graze at the river-bank.

pascebantur fluminis. Aliae quoque vitulae visu deformes ac
ieiunae corpore, post illas iuvencas ascendebant de flumine et
iuxta eas in ipso riparum toro pascebantur; et visae sunt eae
vitulae tenues atque exiles devorare illas quae praestabant et
forma et gratia. Et somnium secundum hoc fuit. Septem
spicae pingues, electae et bonae de terra surgebant et post
eas septem spicae exiles et vento corruptae ac madidae se
subicere moliebantur; et visum est quod laetas et uberes
spicas spicae steriles et tenues devoraverunt.

83. Hoc somnium ita aperuit sanctus Ioseph eo quod septem
iuvencae septem anni forent et septem spicae similiter anni
septem forent, ex fetu et fructu interpretatus tempora. Fetus
enim iuvencae annum exprimit et fructus segetis annum
consummat integrum. Quae ideo ascendebant de flumine,
quod dies, anni ac tempora fluminum praetereunt modo et
cursim labuntur. Annos itaque septem priores uberis terrae
fertiles ac fecundos declarat futuros, posteriores autem alios
septem annos steriles atque infecundos quorum sterilitas
adsumptura foret ubertatem superiorum. Qua gratia prospiciendum admonuit ut uberioribus annis congregaretur subsidium frumentarium quod sustentare posset inopiam futurae
infecunditatis.

84. Quid primum mirer? Ingenium quo in ipsum veritatis
descendit cubile, an consilium quo tam gravi atque diuturnae
prospexit necessitati, an vigilantiam atque iustitiam, quarum
altera imposito sibi tanto munere congregavit tam multiplices
commeatus, altera aequalitatem per omnes servavit? Nam de
magnanimitate quid loquar? Quod venditus a fratribus in
servitutem non retulit iniuriam sed famem depulit. Quid de
suavitate? Quod dilecti fratris praesentiam pia fraude quaesivit, quem simulato per elegantiam furto reum statuit rapinae,
ut obsidem teneret gratiae.

85. Unde merito ei a patre dicitur: *Filius ampliatus meus
Ioseph, filius ampliatus meus, zelotes filius meus adulescentior.
. . . Adiuvit te Deus meus et benedixit te benedictione caeli a
summo, benedictione terrae, terrae habentis omnia, propter benedictiones patris tui et matris. Praevaluit super benedictiones*

Then another group of cows, ugly-looking beasts with bodies that were half-starved, came up out of the river after the heifers, and began to graze alongside them on the same stretch of bank. These gaunt and lean cows then appeared to devour the heifers which looked so splendid in their shape and form. And this was the second dream. Seven ears of corn came up from the ground, full and ripe, excellent specimens; then, after them, seven ears that were weak and slender, shrivelled by the wind and sodden wet, sought to take their place. And it seemed that the barren and thin ears devoured the ripe and fruitful ones.

83. Holy Joseph explained this dream as follows. The seven heifers were seven years, and the seven ears likewise were seven years. These periods were worked out according to the time that it takes for gestation, from fertilization to maturity, for the calving of a heifer takes a year, and the ripening of a crop also occupies a full year. The reason why the beasts came up out of the river was that days, years, and seasons pass by like rivers in full flow, and they roll on just as quickly. So the first seven years to come in that fertile land would, he declared, be rich and fruitful, but the following seven years would be barren and unfruitful, and the times would be so hard that all the plentiful produce of the earlier years would be used up. With this in mind, he warned them to see to it that a reserve of corn was amassed during the richer years, which would be sufficient to sustain them through the poverty of the unfruitful period which lay ahead.

84. What should I admire first? The intelligence that enabled him to penetrate right into the innermost depths of the chamber of truth? The vision with which he could foresee that the need would be so severe and prolonged? His watchfulness and justice? It was his watchfulness that made him gather such vast supplies, when the task in all its magnitude was laid upon him, and it was his justice that ensured he treated everyone with the same fairness. And what about his greatness of spirit? He had been sold into slavery by his brothers, yet he took no revenge for the injustice they had done him, but chose to banish their hunger instead. What about his gentleness? To make sure that his much-loved brother stayed with him, he arranged for a piece of trickery to be perpetrated, which showed his devotion: he cleverly staged an act of theft and then accused his brother of it, so that he could keep him as a hostage at his pleasure.

85. Little wonder, then, that his father said to him: 'My son Joseph has become great, my son has become great; a zealous man is my youngest son. . . . My God has helped you and blessed you with the blessing of heaven above, and with the blessing of the earth below, the earth that provides us with all that we enjoy, in accordance with

montium manentium et desideria collium aeternorum. Et in
Deuteronomio: *Qui visus es,* inquit, *in rubo, ut venias super
caput Ioseph et super verticem ipsius. Honorificus inter fratres:
primitivus tauri decus eius, cornua unicornui cornua ipsius: in
ipsis gentes ventilabit simul usque ad extremum terrae. Ipsi decem
milia Ephraim et ipsi milia Manasses.*

XVIII **86.** Talis itaque debet esse qui consilium alteri det, ut se
ipsum formam aliis praebeat ad exemplum bonorum operum,
in doctrina, in integritate, in gravitate, ut sit eius sermo
salubris atque irreprehensibilis, consilium utile, vita honesta,
sententia decora.

87. Talis erat Paulus, qui consilium dabat virginibus, magisterium sacerdotibus, ut primum se ipsum formam nobis
praeberet ad imitandum. Ideo et humiliari sciebat, sicut
scivit et Ioseph, qui summo ortus patriarcharum genere,
non dedignatus degenerem servitutem, exhibebat eam obsequiis, illustrabat virtutibus. Scivit humiliari, qui et vendi-
torem et emptorem passus est et dominum appellabat eum.
Audi humiliantem se: *Si dominus meus propter me nihil scit in
domo sua et omnia quaecumque habet dedit in manus meas neque
subtractum est a me quidquam praeter te, quia uxor illius es,
quomodo faciam verbum malum hoc et peccabo coram Domino?*
Plena vox humilitatis, plena castimoniae: humilitatis, quia
domino deferebat honorificentiam, quia referebat gratiam;
plena quoque castimoniae, quia turpi flagitio contaminari
grave peccatum putabat.

88. Talis igitur debet esse consiliarius, qui nihil nebulosum
habeat, nihil fallax, nihil simulatum, quod vitam eius ac
mores refellat, nihil improbum ac malevolum, quod avertat
consulentes. Alia sunt enim quae fugiuntur, alia quae con-
temnuntur. Fugimus ea quae possunt nocere, quae malitiose
possunt in noxam serpere, ut si is qui consulitur dubia sit fide
et pecuniae avidus, ut possit pretio mutari; si iniuriosus, hic
fugitur ac declinatur. Qui vero voluptarius, intemperans, etsi

the blessings given you by your father and mother. Greater it is than all the blessings of the enduring mountains, than all the desires of the eternal hills.' And in Deuteronomy we read this: 'O You who appeared in the bush, come upon the head of Joseph and upon his crown. Honoured among his brothers, his glory is like the glory of the first-born of the bull, his horns are as the horns of the unicorn: with them he shall scatter the nations, even to the ends of the earth. His are the ten thousands of Ephraim, his the thousands of Manasseh.'

86. This is what a person's character ought to be like, therefore, if he **XVII** is going to give advice to his neighbour: he must present himself as a model to others, as 'an example of good works, in doctrine, in purity, in seriousness of life'; his language must be wholesome and blameless; his advice beneficial, his life honourable, and his opinions seemly.

87. This is what the character of Paul was like—and look at the advice he gave to virgins and the teaching he gave to priests—he presented himself above all as a model for us to imitate. Thus it was that he knew what it was to be humble—as did Joseph, who though he had come from the highest line of the patriarchs, did not think it beneath him to endure the most menial form of slavery, but bore it submissively and adorned it with the virtues he displayed. He knew what it was to be humble: he suffered at the hands of both buyer and seller and called his buyer 'master'. Listen to this for humility: 'If my master relies on me, and gives nothing in his house a thought but has placed in my hands everything he possesses, and if nothing whatsoever has been withheld from me except you, for you are his wife, how can I do this evil deed, and sin in the Lord's sight?' His words are full of humility and full of chastity—of humility, for he showed such deep respect for his master and revealed such gratitude to him; full of chastity, too, for he believed he would be guilty of a terrible sin if he defiled himself by committing such a shameful crime.

88. This then is what the character of one who gives advice ought to be like: there must be nothing shady about him, nothing deceitful, nothing false, such as would give the lie to his whole life and character, and nothing dishonest or malign, such as would put people off if they were looking for advice. For there are some things which people run from, and others which they despise. We run from anything which might do us harm or which might in some subtle way turn out to be harmful. If, for instance, we find that we are seeking advice from someone who turns out to be of doubtful integrity or greedy for money, and thus quite capable of being induced by a bribe to change his mind, or if we find we are dealing with someone who behaves in a way that is harmful to others, we will run from him and keep well away from him. Or again, if a person is interested only in

alienus a fraude, tamen avarus et cupidior lucri turpis, hic contemnitur. Quod enim specimen industriae, quem fructum laboris edere potest, quam recipere animo curam ac sollicitudinem, qui se torpori dederit atque ignaviae?

89. Ideo boni vir consilii dicit: *Ego enim didici in quibus sim sufficiens esse.* Sciebat enim *omnium malorum radicem esse avaritiam*, et ideo suo contentus erat, alienum non requirebat. Satis mihi est, inquit, quod habeo: sive parum sive plurimum habeam, mihi plurimum est. Expressius aliquid dicendum videtur. Signato verbo usus est: Sufficit mihi, inquit, in quo sum, id est, nec deest nec superfluit. Non deest, quia nihil quaero amplius; non superfluit, quia non solum mihi habeo sed pluribus. Hoc de pecunia.

90. Ceterum de omnibus dici potest quia sufficiebant illi praesentia, hoc est non honorem maiorem, non obsequia uberiora desiderabat, non gloriae immodicae cupidus aut gratiam indebite quaerebat, sed debiti finem certaminis, patiens laboris, securus meriti praestolabatur: *Scio*, inquit, *et humiliari.* Non ergo indocta humilitas, sed quae habeat sui modestiam et scientiam, laudi datur. Est enim humilitas formidinis, est imperitiae atque ignorantiae; et ideo scriptura ait: *Et humiles spiritu salvabit.* Praeclare ergo dixit: *Scio et humiliari*: id est, quo in loco, qua moderatione, quo fine, in quo officio, in quo munere. Nescivit Pharisaeus humiliari, ideo deiectus; scivit publicanus, ideo iustificatus est.

91. Sciebat et abundare Paulus, quia animam habebat divitem, etsi thesaurum divitis non habebat. Sciebat abundare, qui non quaerebat datum in pecunia sed requirebat fructum in gratia. Possumus et sic intellegere, quia sciebat abundare

sensual pleasures and lacks restraint, and if, however innocent of actual deception he may be, he is greedy and all too keen on a bit of dishonourable gain, we will despise him. After all, what example of hard work and what evidence of real labour can a person produce, and what serious care and attention can he entertain in his heart, if he has given himself up to a life of inactivity and laziness?

89. This is why the man who gives good advice says: 'I have learnt what it is to know that I have sufficient, whatever my circumstances.' He was well aware, you see, that greed is 'the root of all evils', and so he was content with what he had himself, and did not chase after things that belonged to other people. 'It is enough for me,' he said, 'that I have what I have: whether I have little or plenty, it is plenty to me.' But perhaps we need to make the point clearer still. The precise word that he used is significant: 'There is sufficient for me,' he said, 'whatever my circumstances'. What he meant, in other words, was this: 'I neither find myself in want, nor do I find that I have too much. I am not in want, because I am not looking for anything more; I do not have too much, because what I have is not just for my own good: it is for the good of many.' He was speaking about money.

90. But he could equally well have been speaking about anything in his life, for he always considered that he had sufficient, whatever his lot. So, he had no desire to receive greater honour or to gain more fulsome praise, he had no yearning for infinite glory, and he sought no favour that he did not deserve. No, he endured all his troubles, remained quietly confident about his own merits, and was content to wait for the end of the contest through which he had to pass. 'I know also,' he says, 'what it is to be humble.' The kind of humility that earns praise, then, is not the kind that indicates a basic lack of understanding; it is a humility that reflects due modesty and self-knowledge. For there is a humility which stems from fear, but there is also a humility which derives from inexperience and ignorance, and that is why Scripture says: 'And he will save the humble in spirit.' He put it beautifully, then, when he said: 'I know also what it is to be humble.' In other words, 'I know in what circumstances, with what measure, with what end, in what duty, and in what role to be humble.' The Pharisee did not know what it was to be humble, and so he was rejected; the publican did know, and so he was justified.

91. Paul also knew what it was to have plenty, because he had a soul that was rich, even if he did not possess any of the treasure that a rich person has. He knew what it was to have plenty, for instead of seeking the gift of money he looked rather for the reward of grace. There is another way of understanding his claim that he knew what it was to have plenty, as well, for he could also say this: 'Our mouth

qui poterat dicere: *Os nostrum patet ad vos, o Corinthii, cor nostrum dilatatum est.*

92. In omnibus erat imbutus et saturari et esurire. Beatus qui sciebat saturari in Christo. Non ergo illa corporalis sed spiritalis est satietas quam operatur scientia. Et merito scientiae est opus, quia *non in pane solo vivit homo sed in omni verbo Dei.* Ergo qui sic sciebat saturari et sic esurire, sciebat ut semper nova quaereret, esuriret Deum, sitiret in Dominum. Sciebat esurire qui sciebat quia esurientes manducabunt; sciebat et poterat abundare qui nihil habebat et possidebat omnia.

XVIII 93. Egregie itaque viros alicui praesidentes muneri commendat iustitia et contra iniquitas destituit atque impugnat. Exemplo nobis est scriptura, quae dicit quia cum populus Israel post mortem Salomonis rogasset filium eius Roboam ut relevaret cervices eorum a servitute dura et paterni imperii temperaret austeritatem, illum spreto senili consilio de suggestione adulescentium responsum dedisse huiusmodi, quia et onus adiceret super patrium iugum et leviora gravioribus suppliciis mutaret.

94. Quo responso exasperati responderunt populi: *Non est nobis portio cum David neque hereditas in filiis Iesse. Revertere unusquisque in tabernacula tua, Israel,* quoniam hic homo neque in principem neque in ducem erit nobis. Itaque desertus a populo ac destitutus, vix duarum tribuum propter David meritum habere potuit societatem.

XIX 95. Claret ergo quoniam aequitas imperia confirmet et iniustitia dissolvat. Nam quomodo potest malitia regnum possidere, quae ne unam quidem privatam potest regere familiam? Summa igitur benignitate opus est, ut non solum publica gubernacula sed etiam privata iura tueamur. Plurimum iuvat benevolentia, quae omnes studet beneficiis amplecti, devincere officiis, oppignerare gratia.

96. Adfabilitatem quoque sermonis diximus ad conciliandam

speaks freely to you, people of Corinth, our heart is wide open to you.'

92. In every circumstance of his life, he had learned what it was both to be filled and to be hungry. Here was a man who was truly happy, for he knew what it was to be filled with Christ. The fulness which that knowledge brings is not a physical thing: it is spiritual. It is right to feel the need for such knowledge, for 'man does not live by bread alone, but by every word of God'. Well, this man who knew what it was to be filled this way also knew what it was to experience this kind of hunger, for he was always seeking new things, hungering for God, and thirsting after the Lord. He knew what it was to experience hunger, for he knew that the hungry will eat; and he knew what it was to enjoy plenty, and was able to enjoy it too, for though he had nothing, he possessed all things.

93. Justice, therefore, is a wonderful commendation for men who **XVIII** occupy any kind of responsible position; injustice, on the other hand, induces people to desert them and turn against them. Scripture gives us an example of this. It tells us how, after the death of Solomon, the people of Israel pleaded with his son Rehoboam to release them from their slavery, which was like a burden around their necks, and to moderate the severity of the regime that his father had instituted. But he rejected the advice older people gave him and chose to follow the proposals of young men. He replied that he would do no such thing: rather, he would increase the weight of the yoke his father had imposed, and replace the light afflictions he had given them with ones that were heavier by far.

94. Provoked by this response, the people replied: 'We have no portion with David, no inheritance among the sons of Jesse. To your tents, each of you, O Israel!'—this man will be no ruler or leader for us. So, deserted and forsaken by the people, he only just managed to hold the two tribes together—and even that was achieved only on account of the merits of David.

95. It is clear, then, that fairness imparts strength to any political **XIX** system, and injustice reduces it to ruins. How can corrupt practice possibly hold an entire kingdom together, when it cannot even keep a grip on the private order of a single family? Real kindness is what is called for, so that we can guarantee not just the sound government of public affairs but the rights of private individuals as well. Goodwill is of great assistance here, for it makes us eager to embrace people everywhere with acts of kindness, to capture their hearts by performing services for them, and to win their allegiance by showing them favour.

96. A courteous way of speaking, too, as we have said already, is of

gratiam valere plurimum. Sed hanc volumus esse sinceram ac sobriam, sine ulla adulatione, ne simplicitatem ac puritatem adloquii dedeceat sermonis adulatio. Forma enim esse debemus ceteris non solum in opere sed etiam in sermone, in castitate ac fide. Quales haberi volumus, tales simus, et qualem adfectum habemus, talem aperiamus. Neque dicamus in corde nostro verbum iniquum quod abscondi putemus silentio, quia audit in occulto dicta qui occulta fecit, et cognoscit secreta viscerum qui sensum visceribus infudit. Ergo tamquam sub oculis constituti iudicis, quidquid gerimus in luce positum putemus, ut omnibus manifestetur.

XX 97. Plurimum itaque prodest unicuique bonis iungi. Adulescentibus quoque utile ut claros et sapientes viros sequantur, quoniam qui congreditur sapientibus, sapiens est; qui autem cohaeret imprudentibus, imprudens agnoscitur. Et ad instructionem itaque plurimum proficit et ad probitatis testimonium. Ostendunt enim adulescentes eorum se imitatores esse quibus adhaerent, et ea convalescit opinio quod ab his vivendi acceperint similitudinem cum quibus conversandi hauserint cupiditatem.

98. Inde tantus Iesus Nave quod eum non solum erudivit ad legis scientiam Moysi copula verum etiam sanctificavit ad gratiam. Denique cum in eius tabernaculo divina refulgere praesentia videretur maiestas Domini, solus erat in tabernaculo Iesus Nave. Moyses cum Deo loquebatur, Iesus pariter nube sacra tegebatur. Presbyteri et populus deorsum stabant; Iesus cum Moyse ad accipiendam legem ascendebat. Omnis populus intra castra erat; Iesus extra castra in tabernaculo testimonii. Cum columna nubis descenderet et loqueretur cum Moyse, quasi fidus adstabat minister nec exibat de tabernaculo iuvenis, cum seniores longe positi divina trepidarent miracula.

99. Ubique igitur inter admiranda opera et reverenda secreta sancto Moysi individuus adhaerebat. Unde factum est ut qui fuerat socius conversationis, fieret successor potestatis. Merito vir huiusmodi evasit ut sisteret fluminum cursus, diceret: *Ste*

great importance in winning people's favour. But we want this to be a sincere and sober thing, without the least trace of flattery: the simplicity and purity of our conversation must not be marred by flattery. We are to be a model for everyone around us, not just in our actions but also in our speech, in our chastity, and in our faith. Let us be what we should wish others to think us, and let us show our feelings as they really are. We should never mutter a single word that is unjust, even in our own heart, thinking to ourselves that it is hidden under a veil of silence; for the One who made the secret places hears words that are spoken in secret, and the One who implanted the power of thought in our innermost parts knows the hidden things which those innermost parts contain. So, as people who live under the eyes of their Judge, let us remember that everything we do is exposed to the light, and in this way it will be manifest to all.

97. It is therefore of great advantage to each one of us to associate with people who are good. For younger men in particular, it is beneficial to follow in the steps of gentlemen whose distinction and wisdom are obvious, for 'he who associates with the wise is wise, but he who is ever in the company of fools is seen to be a fool'. There is great value here, not just in terms of the lessons you can learn but also as a witness that your life is upright. Young men show themselves to be the imitators of the people to whom they attach themselves. The evidence in support of this theory is that their lives begin to look just the same as those of the people in whose company they have taken pleasure.   XX

98. This was why Joshua son of Nun went on to be the great man that he was. His bond with Moses not only provided him with instruction in the knowledge of the Law; it also brought him sanctification and growth in grace. So, when the majesty of the Lord appeared, reflecting the glory of the divine presence in his tabernacle, only Joshua son of Nun was there in the tabernacle. When Moses spoke with God, Joshua was covered by the sacred cloud at the same time. The priests and the people stood down below; Joshua went up with Moses to receive the Law. All the people were inside the camp; Joshua was there outside the camp in the tabernacle of the covenant. When the pillar of cloud descended and God spoke with Moses, Joshua stood beside him as his faithful attendant. Though he was only a young man, he would not leave the tabernacle, though even the old men who were stationed at a distance trembled at the wonders God was doing.

99. In every situation, then, throughout all the amazing things that were done and all the awesome secrets that were divulged, he stuck close by holy Moses, his inseparable companion. The consequence was that having been his companion in life, he became his successor in power. No wonder the man turned out as he did—one who could

sol, et staret sol, quasi eius spectator victoriae noctem differ-
ret, diem produceret. Quid? Quod Moysi negatum est, solus
eligeretur ut populum introduceret in terram repromissionis.
Magnus vir fidei miraculis, magnus triumphis. Illius augus-
tiora opera, huius prosperiora. Uterque igitur divina subnixus
gratia ultra humanam processit conditionem: ille mari, hic
caelo imperavit.

100. Pulchra itaque copula seniorum atque adulescentium.
Alii testimonio, alii solatio sunt; alii magisterio, alii delecta-
tioni. Omitto quod Abrahae adhaesit Loth adulescentulus
etiam proficiscenti, ne forte hoc propinquitatis magis fuisse
aestimetur et necessariae potius quam voluntariae adiunctio-
nis. Quid Eliam atque Eliseum loquamur? Licet non expresse
Eliseum iuvenem scriptura significaverit, advertimus tamen et
colligimus iuniorem fuisse. In Actibus Apostolorum Barnabas
Marcum adsumpsit, Paulus Silam, Paulus Timotheum,
Paulus Titum.

101. Sed illis superioribus videmus divisa officia ut seniores
consilio praevalerent, iuniores ministerio. Plerumque etiam
virtutibus pares, dispares aetatibus, sui delectantur copula,
sicut delectabantur Petrus et Iohannes. Nam adulescentem
legimus in evangelio Iohannem et sua voce licet meritis et
sapientia nulli fuerit seniorum secundus: erat enim in eo
senectus venerabilis morum et incana prudentia. Vita enim
immaculata bonae senectutis stipem pendit.

XXI 102. Adiuvat hoc quoque ad profectum bonae existimationis,
si de potentis manibus eripias inopem, de morte damnatum
eruas, quantum sine perturbatione fieri potest, ne videamur
iactantiae magis causa facere quam misericordiae et graviora
inferre vulnera dum levioribus mederi desideramus. Iam si
oppressum opibus potentis et factione magis quam sceleris sui

halt rivers in their course, or say, 'Let the sun stand still', so that it stood still, postponing the night and extending the day as if to witness his final victory for itself. What is more—and this was a favour denied even to Moses himself—it was he and he alone who was chosen to lead the people into the promised land. He was a great man in the miracles that his faith performed, a great man in the triumphs that he won. Moses' achievements may have been more majestic in their character, but Joshua's were more successful in their final outcome. So, with the enabling of God's grace, each of them attained a level of authority far beyond the normal human condition: the one could command the sea, the other the heavens.

100. The bond between old and young is a beautiful thing, then. One party provides testimony of good conduct, the other gives comfort; one offers instruction, the other brings pleasure. I shall say nothing of Lot, who, as a very young man, stuck close by Abraham even when he was setting out on his great journey: it is possible, I suppose, for people to put all this down to kinship and to a relationship that was obligatory rather than voluntary. But what about Elijah and Elisha? Even though Scripture has not explicitly specified that Elisha was a young man, we are clearly right to infer that he was the younger of the two all the same. In the Acts of the Apostles, Barnabas took Mark with him, Paul took Silas, Paul took Timothy, and Paul took Titus.

101. But in all the cases we have mentioned, we notice that there was a division of labour when it came to the respective services which they performed: it was the prerogative of the older men to give advice and of the younger men to serve. We also find very often that people who are as one in the virtues they possess but are quite different in age enjoy a bond together. Peter and John show us this; for we read in the gospel that John was a young man, and he tells us so himself; yet he was second to none of his elders in his merits and in the wisdom he displayed. He possessed the kind of venerable maturity of character which usually comes only with old age, and the kind of prudence which is normally found only in the grey-haired. For a life that is unblemished brings the reward of a good old-age.

102. Here is something else which helps you to gain a good reputation: **XXI** rescuing someone in need from the hands of the powerful, or saving a condemned person from death. The way to go about this, as far as possible, is without making a fuss: we must avoid giving the impression that we are acting with more of an eye to boasting about it than to showing people mercy, for in our very desire to heal light wounds we can end up inflicting ones that are more serious still. If you manage to secure the release of someone who has been crushed by the influence of a powerful foe and is facing ruin not as a consequence of his own

pretio gravatum liberaveris, egregiae convalescit opinionis testimonium.

103. Commendat plerosque etiam hospitalitas. Est enim publica species humanitatis ut peregrinus hospitio non egeat, suscipiatur officiose, pateat advenienti ianua. Valde id decorum totius est orbis existimationi, peregrinos cum honore suscipi, non deesse mensae hospitalis gratia, occurrere officiis liberalitatis, explorari adventus hospitum.

104. Quod Abrahae laudi est datum qui ante ianuam suam speculabatur, ne forte praeteriret peregrinus aliqui, et diligenter praetendebat excubias, ut occurreret, ut praeveniret, ut rogaret ne transiret hospes, dicens: *Domine, si inveni gratiam ante te, ne praeterieris puerum tuum.* Et ideo pro hospitalitatis mercede fructum posteritatis recepit.

105. Loth quoque, nepos eius, non solum genere sed etiam virtute proximus, propter hospitalitatis adfectum Sodomitana a se suisque supplicia detorsit.

106. Decet igitur hospitalem esse, benignum, iustum, non alieni cupidum; immo de suo iure cedentem potius aliqua, si fuerit lacessitus, quam aliena iura pulsantem; fugitantem litium, abhorrentem a iurgiis, redimentem concordiam et tranquillitatis gratiam. Siquidem de suo iure virum bonum aliquid relaxare, non solum liberalitatis sed plerumque etiam commoditatis est. Primum dispendio litis carere non mediocre est lucrum; deinde accedit ad fructum quod augetur amicitia, ex qua oriuntur plurimae commoditates. Quae contemnenti aliqua in tempore, postea fructuosa erunt.

107. In officiis autem hospitalibus omnibus quidem humanitas impertienda est, iustis autem uberior deferenda honorificentia: *Quicumque enim iustum receperit in nomine iusti, mercedem iusti accipiet,* ut Dominus pronuntiavit. Tanta autem est apud Deum hospitalitatis gratia ut ne potus

wrongdoing but on account of the sheer weight of a group's interests, it strengthens people's high opinions of you, and your reputation grows. **103.** Hospitality is another point of commendation, as far as most people are concerned. It is a form of humanity which everyone can see, when the stranger does not go without a place to stay but is received by you as duty decrees, and when your door is open to anyone who knocks. Ask people anywhere in the world, and they will all say the same—it is only seemly that strangers should be received with honour, that they should be deprived of no kindness or hospitality which our table can afford but should meet with all the services which generosity prescribes, and that we should always keep an eye out for people coming to us and be ready to entertain them as guests.

104. This was what Abraham did, and much to his credit it was too. He was always on the lookout outside his door, to make sure that no stranger passed by unnoticed, and he constantly kept watch to see if there was anyone to whom he might offer hospitality, stopping him and asking him to go no further. 'My lord, if I have found favour with you,' he would say, 'please do not pass your servant by.' And this was how he came to be given the line of descendants after him as the return for his hospitality.

105. And look at his nephew, Lot: he was close to him not just as a blood-relation but also in the virtue he displayed. He was so ready to show people hospitality that he saved his guests as well as himself from the punishment visited upon the people of Sodom.

106. It is a seemly thing, then, to be hospitable, kind, and just, and not to crave other people's possessions—or, I should say, to give up some of your own rights if you are provoked, instead of infringing upon the rights of someone else—to avoid lawsuits, to turn away from quarrels, and so to reap the benefits of cordial relations with others and the blessings of a quiet life. For the reality is this: if a gentleman gives up some of his own rights, not only is he displaying generosity; very often he has a lot to gain as well. In the first place, it is no small advantage to be spared the expense of a lawsuit. In the second place, there is the added benefit that friendship grows as a result—and think how many gains derive from that. If a person is prepared to put his own interest on one side just a little for a moment, he will find in due course that they bring him plenty of benefits of their own.

107. When it comes to carrying out the duties of hospitality, we have an obligation to show humanity to everyone without exception; but we should show particular respect to people who are just. For 'whoever receives a just man in the name of a just man shall receive a just man's reward', as the Lord himself has decreed. Here is how much hospitality matters to God: even a gesture as small as giving someone

quidem aquae frigidae a praemiis remunerationis immunis sit. Vides quia Abraham Deum recepit hospitio dum hospites quaerit. Vides quia Loth angelos recepit. Unde scis ne et tu, cum suscipis hominem, suscipias Christum? Licet in hospite sit Christus quia Christus in paupere est, sicut ipse ait: *In carcere eram, et venistis ad me, nudus eram et operuistis me.*

108. Suave est igitur non pecuniae sed gratiae studere. Verum hoc malum iamdudum humanis influxit mentibus, ut pecunia honori sit et animi hominum divitiarum admiratione capiantur. Inde se immersit avaritia velut quaedam bonorum ariditas officiorum, ut homines damnum putent quidquid praeter morem impenditur. Sed etiam in hoc adversus avaritiam, ne quod adferre possit impedimentum, prospexit scriptura venerabilis dicens quia: *Melior est hospitalitas cum oleribus . . . .* Et infra: *Melior est panis in suavitate cum pace.* Non enim prodigos nos docet esse scriptura, sed liberales.

109. Largitatis enim duo sunt genera: unum liberalitatis, alterum prodigae effusionis. Liberale est hospitio recipere, nudum vestire, redimere captivos, non habentes sumptu iuvare; prodigum est sumptuosis effluescere conviviis et vino plurimo: unde legisti: *Prodigum est vinum et contumeliosa ebrietas.* Prodigum est popularis favoris gratia exinanire proprias opes, quod faciunt qui ludis circensibus vel etiam theatralibus et muneribus gladiatoriis vel etiam venationibus patrimonium dilapidant suum, ut vincant superiorum celebritates, cum totum illud sit inane quod agunt, quandoquidem etiam bonorum operum sumptibus immoderatum esse non deceat.

110. Pulchra liberalitas erga ipsos quoque pauperes mensuram tenere ut abundes pluribus, non conciliandi favoris gratia ultra modum fluere. Quidquid ex adfectu puro ac sincero promitur, hoc est decorum: non superfluas aedificationes adgredi nec praetermittere necessarias.

111. Et maxime sacerdoti hoc convenit, ornare Dei templum decore congruo, ut etiam hoc cultu aula Domini resplendeat,

a drink of cold water can earn you favour and reward. You see Abraham looking for guests to entertain, and receiving God himself as his guest. You see Lot receiving angels. So what about you? How can you be sure you are not entertaining Christ when you are entertaining some ordinary man? It is quite possible that Christ might come to us in the form of a guest, for Christ comes to us in the form of a poor person, as he tells us himself: 'I was in prison and you came to me; I was naked and you clothed me.'

108. What a beautiful sight it is, then, to see someone whose heart is set not on making money but on being kind to others. Of course, the evil of chasing wealth first infiltrated the human spirit long ago, so that people think money is something to be valued and the hearts of men are gripped by an admiration for riches. This was how greed found its way into the depths of our being, and under its influence every duty that we associate with being good to others has withered away, so that if people spend anything over and above a token amount they feel they have suffered a loss. But here again holy Scripture has already warned us against greed and sought to check its power to hinder us, for it says: 'Better is hospitality, even when it is only a meal of vegetables . . .'. Or, as we read further on: 'Better is bread taken in pleasantness, with peace.' Scripture teaches us not to be wasteful, but to be generous.

109. There are two forms of giving, you see: one stems from generosity, the other from wasteful extravagance. It is generous to take someone in as your guest, to clothe someone who is naked, to ransom prisoners, and to help people in need by giving them money. It is wasteful to spend exorbitant amounts on sumptuous dinners and endless wine—you have read it yourself: 'Wine is wasteful and drunkenness is abusive.' It is wasteful to exhaust all your personal resources in order to gain popular favour, like men who squander their legacies on circus entertainments, or theatrical performances and gladiatorial shows, or hunting displays, in a bid to outdo the reputations of their predecessors. Their whole effort is utterly pointless, for there can be nothing seemly about any activity which involves a lack of moderation, even if it is expenditure on good works.

110. For generosity to be right, you need to keep a sense of due measure even when you are dealing with the poor, so that you retain adequate resources to help more people besides these; do not squander funds without measure simply to win people's favour. Anything which comes from a pure and sincere motive is seemly; but it is not seemly to get involved in unnecessary building-projects, or to ignore ones that are genuinely necessary.

111. Here is what is appropriate for a priest in particular: to deck out the temple of God with a splendour that is suitable, making the courts

impensas misericordiae convenientes frequentare, quantum oporteat largiri peregrinis non superflua sed competentia, non redundantia sed congrua humanitati, ne sumptu pauperum alienam sibi quaerat gratiam, ne restrictiorem erga clericos aut indulgentiorem se praebeat. Alterum enim inhumanum, alterum prodigum, si aut sumptus desit necessitati ⟨eorum⟩ quos a sordidis negotiationis aucupiis retrahere debeas, aut voluptati superfluat.

XXII **112.** Quin etiam verborum ipsorum et praeceptorum esse mensuram convenit, ne aut nimia remissio videatur aut nimia severitas. Plerique enim remissiores malunt esse ut videantur boni esse, sed nihil simulatum et fictum verae virtutis esse certum est; quin etiam diuturnum esse non solet. In principio vernat, in processu tamquam flosculus dissipatur et solvitur; quod autem verum ac sincerum, alta fundatur radice.

113. Et ut exemplis adsertionis nostrae probemus, quoniam quae simulata sunt diuturna esse non possunt sed tamquam ad tempus virentia cito decidunt, ex ea familia, ex qua nobis plurima ad virtutis profectum exempla arcessivimus, unum simulationis et fraudis proferamus testimonium.

114. Absalon erat David regis filius, decore insignis, egregius forma, praestans iuventa, ita ut vir talis in Israel non reperiretur, a vestigio pedis usque ad verticem immaculatus. Is fecit sibi currus et equos et viros quinquaginta qui procurrerent ante eum. Surgebat diluculo et stabat ante portam in via et si quem advertisset regis iudicia quaerentem, accedebat ad eum dicens: 'Ex qua civitate es tu?' Respondebat: 'Ex tribu una sum de tribubus Israel, servus tuus'. Referebat Absalon: 'Verba tua bona sunt et directa, et qui te audiat non est tibi datus a rege. Quis constituet me iudicem? Et quisquis ad me veniet, cuicumque fuerit iudicium necessarium, iustificabo illum.' Talibus deliniebat singulos sermonibus. Et cum accederent adorare eum, extendens manus suas apprehendebat atque osculabatur eos. Sic convertit in se corda omnium,

of the Lord resplendent by giving them a particular finery; to make sure that money is always being spent in accordance with the obligations that mercy imposes; to give strangers what they genuinely require, not sums that are unnecessary but amounts that are suited to their actual needs, so that things do not go beyond what humanity demands but are in keeping with its constraints. If a priest conducts himself this way, he will not go about seeking other people's favour for himself through his expenditure upon the poor; nor will he come across as either too miserly or too indulgent in his dealings with other clergy. To be too miserly is to lack humanity; to be too indulgent is to be wasteful. One way, you end up with no resources left to meet the needs of people whom you ought to be keeping from the moneylenders and all their sordid schemes; the other, you have so much left over that you can spend it on your own selfish pleasures.

112. What is more, it is right to keep a sense of due measure even in **XXII** the choice of language we use and in the guidelines we prescribe: we need to avoid giving the impression that we are either too relaxed or too severe. Most people prefer to be fairly relaxed in order to look good, but if there is one thing certain it is that falsehood and hypocrisy of every kind have nothing to do with virtue that is true. In fact, more often than not, an image cultivated that way does not even last. It may flourish to start with, but in the course of time it gets dispersed and scattered like blossom. An attitude that is true and sincere, however, is well grounded, and has deep roots.

113. If we must adduce examples to support our claim that gestures that are false can never last but are like flowers which flourish for a time then quickly wither away, let us look at just one instance of falsehood and deceit, and see what it produced. It comes from the same family from which we have already drawn so many examples that encourage us to progress in virtue.

114. Absalom was the son of king David. He was renowned for his good looks; he had an exceptional physique; and he was in the peak of his youth. His like was not to be found anywhere in Israel: there was not a single blemish in him from the sole of his foot to the crown of his head. This man provided himself with chariots and horses, and fifty men to run before him. He would get up at dawn and stand in the road in front of the city gate, and if he saw someone coming to bring a case before the king for judgement he would go up to him and say: 'Which city do you come from?' The person would answer: 'I your servant am from one of the tribes of Israel.' Absalom would reply: 'Your claims are right and fair, but the king has not provided anyone to listen to you. Who would like to make me such a judge? If anyone comes to me, anyone with a case needing to be judged, I will see that he gets justice.'

dum blanditiae huiusmodi intimorum tangunt viscerum sensum.

115. Sed delicati isti et ambitiosi elegerunt honorabilia et grata ad tempus et iucunda. Ubi parva processit dilatio, quam prudens omnium propheta paulisper cedendo interponendam putavit, non potuerunt tolerare ac sustinere. Denique non dubitans de victoria David commendabat filium dimicaturis ut ei parcerent. Ideoque nec proelio interesse maluit, ne vel referre arma, parricidae licet, videretur, sed tamen filio.

116. Liquet igitur ea esse perpetua ac solida quae vera sunt et quae sincere potius quam dolo congregantur; ea vero, quae simulatione atque adsentatione parata sunt, non posse diu perseverare.

XXIII 117. Quis igitur vel illos qui pecunia ad oboedientiam redimuntur, vel eos qui adsentatione invitantur, fidos sibi arbitretur? Nam et illi frequenter se vendere volunt et isti imperia dura ferre non possunt. Levi adsentatiuncula facile capiuntur; si perstrinxeris verbo, immurmurant, deserunt, infesti abeunt, indignantes relinquunt: imperare malunt quam oboedire; quasi obnoxios beneficio, subiectos sibi debere esse existimant, quos praepositos sibi habere debeant.

118. Quis igitur sibi fideles putet quos vel pecunia vel adulatione sibi obligandos crediderit? Nam et ille qui pecuniam acceperit, vilem se et despectum iudicat nisi saepe redimatur. Itaque frequenter exspectat pretium suum; et ille qui obsecratione ambitus videtur, vult semper se rogari.

XXIV 119. Ergo bonis actibus et sincero proposito nitendum ad honorem arbitror, et maxime ecclesiasticum, ut neque resupina adrogantia vel remissa neglegentia sit neque turpis adfectatio et indecora ambitio. Ad omnia abundat animi directa simplicitas satisque se ipsa commendat.

With this sort of talk he charmed them all, one by one. And when they came to pay their respects to him, he would take them in his arms and kiss them. So he soon won the hearts of everyone, for this kind of obsequious behaviour touches people's deepest emotions.

115. But those spoilt and ostentatious people chose things that brought them honour, passing gratification, and pleasure. After a short time had passed (the prophet could foresee everything, and thought it would be best to allow a breathing-space, so he withdrew for a little while), they could not stand or endure the treatment any longer. David was in no doubt that he would win in the end, and he urged his men, as they went into battle, to spare his son. In fact, he chose not to take part in the battle himself for this reason: he did not want people to think he was taking up arms against one who, murderous traitor that he was, was still his own son.

116. It is clear, then, that the relationships which last and are solid are the ones that are true, the ones that are forged with sincerity rather than guile; and it is equally clear that no relationship which is engineered by pretence and flattery can endure for long.

117. What person is going to believe that people are loyal to him if **XXIII** their devotion is being bought with money or induced by flattery? If money is the instrument, people are always ready to sell their favours. If it is flattery that is used, they will never abide any orders which make demands upon them. They are easily won round with a little smooth talk, but if you utter a word of correction to them, they grumble about it, they desert you, they get upset and leave, they take offence and disappear. They are happier to give orders than to obey them, and the people they ought to regard as their leaders should actually, by their way of things, be subject to them instead, for they imagine that they are beholden to them for their kindness.

118. What person is going to imagine that people are faithful to him if he has felt it necessary to capture their loyalty by giving them money or heaping flattery upon them? The man who has received money like this feels that he has been won too cheaply and is being slighted unless he keeps getting bought over again and again, and so he expects his payment frequently; and the man whose support is openly canvassed with cringing appeals wants to be solicited this way all the time.

119. So, in my judgement, the way to strive for preferment is by doing **XXIV** things that are good and doing them with an aim that is sincere; and this is especially true within the church. This way, we avoid arrogant presumption or careless complacency on the one hand, and dishonourable pretension and unseemly ambition on the other. A straight and single-minded attitude is more than adequate at all times, and serves as its own commendation.

120. In ipso vero munere neque severitatem esse duram convenit nec nimiam remissionem, ne aut potestatem exercere aut susceptum officium nequaquam implere videamur.

121. Enitendum quoque ut beneficiis atque officiis obligemus plurimos et collatam reservemus gratiam, ne iure beneficii fiant immemores qui se graviter laesos dolent. Saepe enim usu venit ut quos gratia foveris vel aliquo superiore cumulaveris gradu, avertas si indigne aliquem ei praeponendum iudices. Sed et sacerdotem beneficiis suis vel iudiciis favere convenit, ut aequitatem custodiat, et presbytero vel ministro deferre ut parenti.

122. Neque hos, quia semel probati sunt, adrogantes esse oportet, sed magis tamquam memores gratiae, humilitatem tenere; neque offendi sacerdotem si aut presbyter aut minister aut quisquam de clero, aut misericordia aut ieiunio aut integritate aut doctrina et lectione existimationem accumulet suam. Gratia enim ecclesiae laus doctoris est. Bonum, opus alicuius praedicari; ita tamen si nullo studio fiat iactantiae. Laudent enim unumquemque proximorum labia et non suum os, et commendent opera, non studia sua.

123. Ceterum si quis non oboedit episcopo, ⟨et⟩ extollere atque exaltare sese desiderat, obumbrare merita episcopi simulata adfectatione doctrinae aut humilitatis aut misericordiae, is a vero devius superbit, quoniam veritatis ea est regula ut nihil fuci facias commendandi tui causa quo minor alius fiat, neque, si quid boni habeas, id ad deformationem alterius et vituperationem exerceas.

124. Non defendas improbum et sancta indigno committenda arbitreris neque iterum urgeas et impugnes cuius crimen non deprehenderis. Nam cum in omnibus iniustitia cito offendat,

120. When it comes to the actual exercise of our duties, harshness and severity or an excessively relaxed approach are equally inappropriate. In the one case, it can look as if we are wielding power tyrannically, and in the other as if we have taken on the responsibilities of an official position but are quite inept at discharging them.

121. We must also make every effort to capture the loyalty of as many people as possible with the acts of kindness we do and the duties we carry out, and seek to maintain their favour once we have acquired it. Understandably, people soon forget the kindness you may have done them if they start to feel resentful that you have gone on to hurt them badly. Experience proves that this is often the way: you can so readily alienate the very persons you have supported with your influence or those you have promoted to some higher grade if you then decide, unfairly, to put someone else before them. It is right that a bishop should show people favour, whether through the acts of kindness he performs or the formal decisions he makes, but he needs to maintain fairness at all times, and show the same respect to a priest or a minister as he would to a member of his closest family.

122. Those who have earned approval at some time ought not to behave in an arrogant fashion because of it; on the contrary, they should bear in mind that they have been given a great privilege, and remain humble. A bishop must not take it as a personal offence if a priest or minister or any other cleric increases his reputation by his works of mercy, or his fasting, or his purity, or his teaching and reading. The praise of any teacher brings honour to the church as a whole. It is a good thing if someone's work earns him this kind of acclaim, so long as it is done without any desire on his part to boast about it. For every one of us, our praise should come from our neighbours' lips, not from our own mouth, and our commendation should stem from the works that we do, not the desires that we entertain ourselves.

123. If, however, a man refuses to obey his bishop and is desperate to promote and exalt himself, and to eclipse his bishop's own merits by feigning an ardent devotion to teaching or humility or works of mercy, his pride is taking him far off the path of truth. The rule of truth dictates that you should never behave in a way that is false so as to win commendation at a cost to someone else, and it says that if there is any good in you, you are not to exploit it to denigrate or disparage your neighbour in any way.

124. Do not defend someone who is dishonest, and do not think of entrusting holy things to someone who is unworthy of them. Again, do not harass or set about criticizing a person if you have not clearly established the crime of which you accuse him. If it is true that

tum maxime in ecclesia, ubi aequitatem esse oportet, ubi aequalitatem haberi decet, ut nihil sibi potentior vindicet, nihil plus usurpet ditior (sive enim pauper sive dives, in Christo unum sunt), nihil sanctior plus sibi adroget: ipsum enim par est esse humiliorem.

125. Sed nec personam alterius accipiamus in iudicio: gratia absit, causae merita decernant. Nihil sic opinionem, immo fidem gravat, quam si in iudicando potentiori dones causam inferioris vel pauperem innocentem arguas, divitem excuses reum culpae. Pronum quidem est genus hominum favere honoratioribus, ne laesos sese putent, ne victi doleant. Sed primum, si offensam vereris, non recipias iudicium; si sacerdos es aut si quisquam alius, non lacessas. Licet tibi silere in negotio dumtaxat pecuniario, quamquam sit constantiae adesse aequitati. In causa autem Dei, ubi communionis periculum est, etiam dissimulare peccatum est non leve.

XXV 126. Quid autem tibi prodest favere diviti? An quia citius amantem remuneratur? His enim favemus frequentius a quibus referendae vicem speramus gratiae. Sed eo magis infirmo et inopi nos studere convenit, quia pro eo qui non habet, remunerationem speramus a Domino Iesu, qui sub specie convivii generalem virtutum edidit formam, ut his potius nostra conferamus beneficia qui nobis ea non possint repraesentare, docens ad convivium atque epulas non eos qui divites sunt sed pauperes invitandos. Divites enim rogari videntur ut ipsi quoque nobis reddant convivium; pauperes,

injustice is a sure way to cause offence anywhere, then it is doubly true in the church, where there ought to be fairness, and where it is seemly that the same treatment should apply to all. The man who commands more power than his neighbour should not assert his rights in any way; the man who enjoys more money than his neighbour should not try to get his hands on any more (for whether rich or poor, his neighbour and he are one in Christ); and the man who is holier than his neighbour should not make any great claims for himself—indeed, he ought to be all the more humble.

125. On the contrary, when we are forming a judgement on a particular case, we must not be swayed by the identity of a third party. There must be no trace of partiality in our deliberations; it must be the specific merits of the case that are decisive. There is nothing which so lowers people's estimation of you, or indeed their trust in you, as the situation in which, in giving judgement on a case, you sacrifice the cause of an individual who is weak to the interests of one who is more powerful—say by condemning a poor man who is innocent, or excusing a rich man who is guilty of a crime. Of course, the entire human race has a tendency to show favour to people who are in positions of greater honour, and is keen to ensure that they do not consider themselves wronged and do not feel aggrieved that they have been beaten. If it is causing offence that you are afraid of, though, you should never agree to adjudicate in the first place. If you are a priest— or if you are anyone else either, for that matter—you are not to go about provoking quarrels. It is quite legitimate for you to keep silent where a case turns on nothing more than financial affairs—though in the interests of consistency it is important that you always uphold what is fair. Where the cause of God is concerned, however, and the communion of the church is at stake, even to turn a blind eye is no small sin.

126. In any case, what advantage is there to you in showing favour to a **XXV** rich man? Does it all come down to the fact that you know he will be quicker to repay someone who shows him love? We do more often show favour to people from whom we hope to receive a favour in return. But the right thing to do, actually, is to devote our attentions to the person who is weak and in genuine need: for though such an individual may have no means to repay us himself, we may be confident that the Lord Jesus will reward us on his behalf. Using the illustration of what to do when inviting people to a dinner, he gave us the general principle that we should follow when we are weighing up one virtuous deed against another: it is better that we should bestow our acts of kindness on those who are unable to repay us. We should make sure, he teaches us, that it is not the rich that we invite when we

quia non habent quod restituant, cum acceperint, remunera-
torem nobis faciunt Dominum, qui se pro paupere obligan-
dum obtulit.

127. Ad ipsum quoque saeculi usum collatio beneficii facta in
pauperes magis quam in locupletes plus iuvat, quia dives
dedignatur beneficium et pudet eum debitorem esse gratiae.
Quin etiam id quod collatum est sibi, meritis suis adrogat,
quod velut debitum acceperit vel ideo datum sit eo quod qui
dedit reddendum sibi a divite uberius aestimaverit. Ita in
accipiendo beneficio, eo ipso quod acceperint, divites dedisse
magis quam accepisse existimant; pauper vero, etsi non habet
unde reddat pecuniam, refert gratiam. In quo certum est
quod plus reddat quam acceperit: pecunia enim nummo
solvitur, gratia numquam exinanitur. Reddendo vacuatur
pecunia; gratia autem et habendo solvitur et solvendo retine-
tur. Deinde quod dives refugit, pauper fatetur, quod sit
obligatus debito, sibique subventum, non honori suo delatum
putat: donatos sibi arbitratur filios, vitam redditam, servatam
familiam. Quanto igitur melius apud bonos quam apud
ingratos locare beneficium!

128. Unde Dominus ad discipulos ait: *Nolite possidere aurum
neque argentum neque pecuniam.* Qua velut falce pullulantem in
pectoribus humanis succidit avaritiam. Petrus quoque claudo
qui ex utero matris suae portabatur, ait: *Argentum et aurum
non habeo, sed quod habeo do tibi. In nomine Iesu Christi
Nazarei, surge et ambula.* Itaque pecuniam non dedit, sanita-
tem dedit. Quanto melius est salutem habere sine pecunia
quam pecuniam sine salute! Surrexit claudus, quod non
sperabat; pecuniam non accepit, quam sperabat. Sed haec
vix in sanctis Domini reperiuntur, ut divitiae contemptui sint.

XXVI 129. Ceterum ita incubuerunt mores hominum admirationi
divitiarum ut nemo nisi dives honore dignus putetur. Neque

hold a dinner or a banquet, but the poor. If we ask the rich, it looks as if our aim is to get them to hold a dinner for us in return. If we ask the poor, they may not have the means to return the kindness when they receive it, but they ensure that it is the Lord himself who rewards us—for he offered himself to take the liabilities of the poor.

127. Besides, this is advantageous in worldly terms as well: a kindness done to the poor is more helpful than a kindness done to the rich, for the rich person looks scornfully at kindness and considers it a disgrace to owe anyone a favour. In fact, when anyone does him a kindness, he puts it all down to his own merits: he thinks he has received it because he deserved it, or that it has been given to him simply because the giver imagined he would be repaid more lavishly by someone so rich. So, in the very act of receiving a kindness, the rich believe that the simple fact they have received it proves they have given more than they have received. With the poor man, it is all different—he has no money with which to pay you back, but what he gives you in return is his gratitude. And there is no doubt about it: this way he gives back far more than he received. For where money is concerned, a mere coin settles the score; gratitude, though, is never exhausted. Money is used up when people are repaid; but a debt of gratitude is both paid when it is shown and retained once it is paid. Moreover, a poor man is quite willing to admit that he is obliged and indebted to you—the very thing that is so distasteful to a rich man—and instead of thinking he has been paid an honour because his status warrants it, he feels he has been given help because he needs it. As he sees it, his children have been given back to him, his life has been restored, and his family has been saved. How much better it is, then, to invest your kindness in those who are good than in those who are ungrateful!

128. That is why the Lord said to his disciples: 'Do not possess gold or silver or money'—and in saying it it was as if he took a sickle to the greed that sprouts so profusely in the hearts of men. And remember what Peter said to the lame man, who from his mother's womb had had to be carried everywhere: 'Silver and gold I do not have, but what I do have I give you. In the name of Jesus Christ of Nazareth, get up and walk!' So he did not give him money, but he gave him a sound body. It is a lot better to have health without money than to have money without health! The gift the lame man had not dared to hope for, he was given—he got up. The gift he did hope for—money—he did not receive. But it is rare to find these things among the saints of the Lord, as they hold riches in contempt.

129. Generally speaking, however, human behaviour has devoted **XXVI** itself to the admiration of riches—so much so that people think someone is not worthy of honour unless he is rich. This is not a

hic recens usus, sed iamdudum, quod peius est, inolevit hoc vitium humanis mentibus. Siquidem cum Hiericho magna civitas tubarum sacerdotalium sono corruisset et Iesus Nave potiretur victoria, cognovit infirmatam esse virtutem populi per avaritiam atque auri cupiditatem. Nam cum de spoliis urbis incensae sustulisset Achar vestem auream et ducenta argenti didrachma et linguam auream, oblatus Domino negare non potuit sed prodidit furtum.

130. Vetus igitur et antiqua avaritia est quae cum ipsis divinae legis coepit oraculis, immo propter ipsam reprimendam lex delata est. Propter avaritiam Balac putavit Balaam praemiis posse temptari ut malediceret populum patrum, et vicisset avaritia, nisi Dominus maledicto eum abstinere iussisset. Propter avaritiam praecipitatus Achar, in exitium deduxerat totam plebem parentum. Itaque Iesus Nave, qui potuit solem statuere ne procederet, avaritiam hominum non potuit sistere ne serperet. Ad vocem eius sol stetit, avaritia non stetit. Sole itaque stante confecit Iesus triumphum; avaritia autem procedente paene amisit victoriam.

131. Quid? Fortissimum omnium Samson, nonne Dalilae mulieris avaritia decepit? Itaque ille qui rugientem leonem manibus discerpsit, qui vinctus et alienigenis traditus, sine ullo adiutore solus dissolutis vinculis mille ex his peremit viros, qui funes intextis nervis velut mollia sparti fila dirupit, is super genua mulieris inflexa cervice truncatus, invicti crinis ornatum, praerogativam suae virtutis, amisit. Influxit pecunia in gremium mulieris et a viro discessit gratia.

132. Feralis igitur avaritia, illecebrosa pecunia, quae habentes contaminat, non habentes non iuvat. Esto tamen ut aliquando adiuvet pecunia inferiorem, tamen et ipsum desiderantem. Quid ad eum qui non desiderat, qui non requirit, qui auxilio eius non indiget, studio non flectitur? Quid ad alios, si sit ille

view that has come to the fore only in recent times; far from it: it is an evil tendency that implanted itself in men's hearts long ago—and that makes it worse. So, when the great city of Jericho had fallen, as it did when the priests blew their trumpets, and Joshua son of Nun had secured his victory over the enemy, he discovered that the people's bravery was weakened by greed and by a desire for gold. For while the city was still burning, Achar had helped himself to some of the spoils: a golden robe, 200 shekels of silver, and a wedge of gold. He was brought before the Lord, and he could not deny it, but had to confess his theft.

130. Greed then is an old evil, existing from the most ancient of times. It began right back with the oracles of the divine law—or rather, the law was given in order to bring it under control. It was because of greed that Balak thought Balaam could be induced with the promise of rewards to place a curse on our fathers' people—and greed would have overcome him, if the Lord had not ordered him to abstain from cursing them. It was because of greed that Achar was cast into destruction: he had brought the whole company of our fathers' people to ruin. And so Joshua son of Nun, the man who could halt the sun itself in its course, could not arrest the greed of men from creeping on in its insidious way. At the sound of his voice, the sun stood still, but greed would not stand still. So, when the sun stood still, Joshua brought off his triumph, but when greed kept on going, he very nearly lost the victory.

131. Or what about Samson, the most courageous man of them all? What was it that deceived him? It was the greed of the woman Delilah, was it not? And so, the same man who could tear apart a roaring lion with his bare hands—who, bound hand and foot and delivered into the clutches of foreigners, could, all on his own and with help from no one, break his bonds and destroy 1,000 of their men—who could burst apart ropes woven from the toughest bowstrings as if they were thin strands of thread—this was the man whose head was shorn as he reclined on a woman's knees. He lost the glory of the hair that had made him invincible, and with it the privilege of his great strength. Money flowed into the lap of the woman, and the grace of God departed from the man.

132. Greed is a deadly thing, then, and money is seductive: it defiles those who have it and affords no help to those who do not. Even if we say that money is helpful on some occasions, even then it is only helpful to someone who is in reduced circumstances and really cries out for it. What does it do for a person who does not cry out for it, who does not seek it, who does not require its assistance, and who is not overwhelmed with longing for it? What does it do for other people, if the one who has it is already richer? Is a man's character really more

copiosior qui habet? Numquid idcirco honestior, quia habet
quo honestas plerumque amittitur, quia habet quod custodiat
magis quam quod possideat? Illud enim possidemus quo
utimur; quod autem ultra usum est non utique habet possessionis fructum, sed custodiae periculum.

XXVII 133. Ad summam novimus quod pecuniae contemptus iustitiae forma sit, et ideo avaritiam declinare debemus et omni
studio intendere ne quid faciamus umquam adversus iustitiam
sed in omnibus gestis et operibus custodiamus eam.

134. Si volumus commendare nos Deo, caritatem habeamus,
unanimes simus, humilitatem sequamur, alterutrum existimantes superiorem sibi. Haec est humilitas, si nihil sibi
quis adroget et inferiorem se esse existimet. Episcopus ut
membris suis utatur clericis, et maxime ministris qui sunt
vere filii: quem cuique viderit aptum muneri, ei deputet.

135. Cum dolore amputatur etiam quae putruit pars corporis,
et diu tractatur si potest sanari medicamentis; si non potest,
tunc a medico bono absciditur. Sic episcopi adfectus boni est
ut optet sanare infirmos, serpentia auferre ulcera, adurere
aliqua, non abscidere; postremo, quod sanari non potest,
cum dolore abscidere. Unde pulcherrimum illud praeceptum
magis eminet, ut cogitemus non quae nostra sunt sed quae
aliorum. Hoc enim modo nihil erit quod vel irati nostro
indulgeamus adfectui vel faventes nostrae plus iusto tribua-
mus aliquid voluntati.

XXVIII 136. Hoc maximum incentivum misericordiae, ut compatiamur alienis calamitatibus, necessitates aliorum, quantum
possumus, iuvemus, et plus interdum quam possumus.
Melius est enim pro misericordia causas praestare vel invidiam perpeti quam praetendere inclementiam, ut nos aliquando in invidiam incidimus, quod confregerimus vasa
mystica ut captivos redimeremus, quod Arianis displicere
potuerat; nec tam factum displiceret quam ut esset quod in
nobis reprehenderetur. Quis autem est tam durus immitis
ferreus, cui displiceat quod homo redimitur a morte, femina

honourable if he has something which more often than not prevents him living an honourable life, if he has something that he has to look after rather than something that he can truly possess? After all, we possess something if we use it; but if it is beyond our ability to use a thing, there is clearly nothing to be gained from possessing it: all we have is the risk of looking after it.

133. All in all, we know that contempt for money is an essential **XXVII** expression of justice, and so we ought to avoid greed and make every effort to ensure that we never do anything that is contrary to justice, but seek to preserve it in all our actions and all our works.

134. If we want to commend ourselves to God, let us possess love for one another, let us be of one mind, and let us strive to show humility, each of us regarding his neighbour as better than himself. This is real humility, when a person makes no claims for himself and considers himself to be the one who is inferior. A bishop should treat his clerics as the members of his own body, and especially so where he is dealing with those ministers who truly are his sons; he should allocate each man to the task to which he sees he is suited.

135. It is a distressing thing to have to amputate any part of the body, even if it is gangrenous, and it is normal to treat it for a long time to see if it can be cured with medicines; if it cannot, then a good physician will cut it off. In the same way, it is always the earnest desire of a good bishop to heal members of the church body who are sick, to eliminate ulcers which are spreading, and to cauterize this or that part rather than cut it off—but, as a last resort, if a part cannot be cured, he will cut it off, at great distress to himself. Here we have a shining illustration of the principle that we should each think not of our own interests but of the interests of others. If we follow this principle, we shall never give in to our feelings when we are angry, or concede any more than is just as a favour to our own wishes.

136. The greatest encouragement to show mercy comes from sharing **XXVIII** in others' misfortunes and endeavouring to bring help to our neighbours when they are going through times of need, helping as much as we can, and sometimes more than we can. After all, it is better to give people grounds to criticize you or to suffer their disapproval for seeking to show mercy than to display a lack of compassion. This was what happened to us on one occasion: we incurred disapproval because we had broken up sacred vessels in order to ransom prisoners—the act was enough to annoy the Arians. In actual fact, it was not so much the deed itself that annoyed them; they had simply come upon something for which they could criticize us. But who could be so hard-hearted, so unfeeling, and so insensitive as to be annoyed to see a man being saved from death, or to see a woman being saved from being

ab impuritatibus barbarorum, quae graviores morte sunt, adulescentulae vel pueruli vel infantes ab idolorum contagiis, quibus mortis metu inquinabantur?

137. Quam causam nos etsi non sine ratione aliqua gessimus, tamen ita in populo prosecuti sumus ut confiteremur multoque fuisse commodius adstrueremus, ut animas Domino quam aurum servaremus. Qui enim sine auro misit apostolos, ecclesias sine auro congregavit. Aurum ecclesia habet non ut servet, sed ut eroget, ut subveniat in necessitatibus. Quid opus est custodire quod nihil adiuvat? An ignoramus quantum auri atque argenti de templo Domini Assyrii sustulerint? Nonne melius conflant sacerdotes propter alimoniam pauperum, si alia subsidia desint, quam sacrilegus contaminata asportet hostis? Nonne dicturus est Dominus: 'Cur passus es tot inopes fame emori? Et certe habebas aurum, ministrasses alimoniam. Cur tot captivi deducti in commercio sunt, nec redempti ab hoste occisi sunt? Melius fuerat ut vasa viventium servares quam metallorum.'

138. His non posset responsum referri. Quid enim diceres: 'Timui ne templo Dei ornatus deesset'? Responderet: 'Aurum sacramenta non quaerunt neque auro placent, quae auro non emuntur.' Ornatus sacramentorum redemptio captivorum est. Vere illa sunt vasa pretiosa quae redimunt animas a morte. Ille verus thesaurus est Domini, qui operatur quod sanguis eius operatus est. Tunc vas dominici sanguinis agnoscitur, cum in utroque viderit redemptionem, ut calix ab hoste redimat quos sanguis a peccato redemit. Quam pulchrum ut, cum agmina captivorum ab ecclesia redimuntur, dicatur: 'Hos Christus redemit! Ecce aurum quod probari potest, ecce aurum utile, ecce aurum Christi quod a morte liberat, ecce aurum quo redimitur pudicitia, servatur castitas!'

139. Hos ergo malui vobis liberos tradere quam aurum reservare. Hic numerus captivorum, hic ordo praestantior est quam species poculorum. Huic muneri proficere debuit aurum redemptoris, ut redimeret periclitantes. Agnosco infusum auro sanguinem Christi non solum irrutilasse verum

violated by barbarians—a fate worse than death itself—or to see young people and small boys and infants being saved from the pollution of idols, which was the defilement to which they were being reduced in their fear of death?

137. We had every reason to handle the matter as we did, but we put it to the people this way. We argued with all our powers that it was far more advantageous to preserve souls for the Lord than to preserve gold. For the One who sent the apostles out without gold assembled the churches without gold. The church has gold, not to preserve it for itself but to dispense it, to provide people with assistance in times of need. What is the point of guarding something which brings no help to anyone? Have we forgotten how much gold and silver the Assyrians took from the temple of the Lord? Is it not better for the priests to melt it down to provide food for the poor, if other sources of relief fail, than for a sacrilegious enemy to desecrate it and carry it off? Is not the Lord himself going to say to us: 'Why did you allow so many needy people to die of hunger? You had gold, after all: you should have provided them with food. Why were so many prisoners taken away to be sold, and why were so many not ransomed but left to be killed by the enemy? Far better to have preserved vessels that were living than to have kept ones made of metal.'

138. To such charges there could be no reply. How could you say: 'I was afraid that the temple of God would lack its proper glory'? The response would be this: 'The sacraments have no need of gold; they take no pleasure in gold, for they are not bought with gold. The glory of the sacraments lies in the ransom of prisoners.' Here are vessels that really are precious—the vessels that ransom souls from death. Here is the real treasure of the Lord—the treasure that achieves just what his blood itself achieved. It is then that the vessel of the Lord's blood is recognized, when you see redemption in the vessel as well as in its contents, and the chalice redeems from the enemy those whom his blood has redeemed from sin. What a wonderful sight—to see whole lines of prisoners ransomed by the church, and to hear it said: 'These are the ones Christ redeemed!' Here is gold that we can really approve; here is gold that is truly beneficial; here is the gold of Christ that delivers from death; here is the gold by which virtue is redeemed and chastity is preserved!

139. Well, these were the people I chose to hand over to you as free individuals rather than keep back gold. The glory of this great company of prisoners, of this train, is greater than the beauty of any cups. This was the very function for which the gold of the Redeemer deserved to be of value—ransoming those in danger. I see it now: when poured into the gold, the blood of Christ did more than make it glow

etiam divinae operationis impressisse virtutem redemptionis munere.

140. Tale aurum sanctus martyr Laurentius Domino reservavit: a quo cum quaererentur thesauri ecclesiae, promisit se demonstraturum. Sequenti die pauperes duxit. Interrogatus ubi essent thesauri quos promiserat, ostendit pauperes dicens: 'Hi sunt thesauri ecclesiae.' Et vere thesauri, in quibus Christus est, in quibus fides est. Denique apostolus ait: *Habentes thesaurum in vasis fictilibus.* Quos meliores thesauros habet Christus quam eos in quibus se esse dixit? Sic enim scriptum est: *Esurivi, et dedistis mihi manducare; sitivi, et dedistis mihi bibere; hospes eram, et collegistis me. . . . Quod enim uni horum fecistis, mihi fecistis.* Quos meliores Iesus habet thesauros quam eos in quibus amat videri?

141. Hos thesauros demonstravit Laurentius, et vicit, quod eos nec persecutor potuit auferre. Itaque Ioachim, qui aurum in obsidione servabat nec dispensabat alimoniae comparandae, et aurum vidit eripi et in captivitatem deduci. Laurentius, qui aurum ecclesiae maluit erogare pauperibus quam persecutori reservare, pro singulari suae interpretationis vivacitate sacram martyrii accepit coronam. Numquid dictum est sancto Laurentio: 'Non debuisti erogare thesauros ecclesiae, vasa sacramentorum vendere'?

142. Opus est ut quis fide sincera et perspicaci providentia munus hoc impleat. Sane, si in sua aliquis derivat emolumenta, crimen est; sin vero pauperibus erogat, captivum redimit, misericordia est. Nemo enim potest dicere: 'Cur pauper vivit?' Nemo potest queri quia captivi redempti sunt; nemo potest accusare quia templum Dei est aedificatum; nemo potest indignari quia humandis fidelium reliquiis spatia laxata sunt; nemo potest dolere quia in sepulturis Christianorum requies defunctorum est. In his tribus generibus vasa ecclesiae etiam initiata confringere, conflare, vendere licet.

143. Opus est ut de ecclesia mystici poculi forma non exeat, ne ad usus nefarios sacri calicis ministerium transferatur. Ideo intra ecclesiam primum quaesita sunt vasa quae initiata non essent; deinde comminuta, postremo conflata, per minutias

crimson red; it also stamped upon it the virtue of the divine work itself, and gave it a similar redemptive function.

140. This was the kind of gold that the holy martyr Lawrence kept back for the Lord. He was given an ultimatum to produce the treasures of the church, and he promised that he would present them. On the following day, he led out the poor. Asked where the treasures were that he had promised, he pointed to the poor and said: 'These are the treasures of the church.' And so they are, real treasures, for Christ lives in them, and faith lives in them. It is as the apostle says: 'We have our treasure in earthen vessels.' What better treasures does Christ have than those in whom he has said that he lives himself? For this is what is written: 'I was hungry and you gave me something to eat, I was thirsty and you gave me something to drink, I was a stranger and you took me in. . . . What you did for one of these, you did for me.' What better treasures does Jesus have than those in whom he loves to appear?

141. These were the treasures that Lawrence presented, and the victory was his, for not even the persecutor could take them away. But remember Jehoiachin, too: when his city was being besieged, he held on to his gold and refused to distribute it to buy food, and the result was he saw both the gold snatched away and himself carried off into captivity. Lawrence, who chose to spend the church's gold on the poor rather than keep it back for the persecutor, received the sacred crown of martyrdom as a reward for the unique and brilliant way that he dealt with the situation. Do you really think it was said to holy Lawrence: 'You should not have spent the treasures of the church or sold the sacramental vessels'?

142. It is necessary, to discharge a responsibility like this, that a person should have genuine faith and a clear sense of foresight. Naturally, if someone siphons off profits for his own gain, it is a crime; but if he spends them on the poor and ransoms a prisoner, it is an act of mercy. No one can say: 'Why is this poor man alive?' No one can complain if prisoners have been ransomed; no one can object if the temple of God has been built; no one can be upset if spare ground has been released for the burial of the faithful; no one can be sorry if the dead are being laid to rest in Christian tombs. For these three purposes, it is quite permissible to break up, melt down, or sell the church's vessels even when they have already been consecrated.

143. It is necessary to ensure that the form of the sacramental cup is not lost to the church: we cannot allow the service of the sacred chalice to be turned over to profane uses. So, in the first instance we looked within the church for vessels which had not as yet been consecrated; then we crushed these up; and finally we melted them down, divided the resulting material up into small quantities and distributed it to the

erogationis dispensata egentibus, captivorum quoque pretiis profecerunt. Quod si desunt nova et quae nequaquam initiata videantur, in huiusmodi, quos supra dixi, usus, omnia arbitror pie posse converti.

XXIX **144.** Illud sane diligenter tuendum est ut deposita viduarum intemerata maneant, sine ulla serventur offensione, non solum viduarum sed etiam omnium: fides enim exhibenda est omnibus, sed maior est causa viduarum et pupillorum.

145. Denique hoc solo viduarum nomine, sicut in libris Machabaeorum legimus, commendatum templo omne servatum est. Nam cum indicium factum esset pecuniarum quas in templo Hierosolymis maximas reperiri posse Simon nefarius Antiocho regi prodidit, missus in rem Heliodorus ad templum venit et summo sacerdoti aperuit indicii invidiam et adventus sui causam.

146. Tunc sacerdos deposita esse dixit viduarum victualia et pupillorum. Quae cum Heliodorus ereptum ire vellet et regis vindicare commodis, sacerdotes ante altare iactaverunt se, induti sacerdotales stolas, et Deum vivum qui de depositis legem dederat, flentes invocabant custodem se praeceptorum praestare suorum. Vultus vero et color summi sacerdotis immutatus declarabat dolorem animi et mentis intentae sollicitudinem. Flebant omnes quod in contemptum locus venturus foret si nec in Dei templo tuta fidei servaretur custodia, accinctaeque mulieres pectus et clausae virgines pulsabant ianuam; ad muros alii currebant, per fenestras alii prospectabant, omnes ad caelum tendebant manus orantes ut suis Dominus adesset legibus.

147. Heliodorus autem nec his territus, quod intenderat, urguebat et satellitibus suis aerarium saepserat, cum subito apparuit illi terribilis eques armis praefulgens aureis; equus autem eius erat insigni ornatus opertorio. Alii quoque duo iuvenes apparuerunt in virtute inclita, decore grato, cum splendore gloriae, speciosi amictu, qui circumsteterunt eum et utraque ex parte flagellabant sacrilegum sine ulla

poor. It also provided a contribution towards the sums required for the ransoming of prisoners. But if new vessels or ones which appear never to have been consecrated cannot be found, I think it is quite legitimate to put any vessels to the kinds of uses I have just mentioned, without doing anything irreverent.

144. We must naturally take great care to ensure that property XXIX deposited into our care by widows remains inviolate and is preserved without mishap—indeed, this applies not just to the property of widows, but to the property of anyone. For good faith should be shown to all, though the cause of widows and orphans must take priority.

145. We read in the Books of the Maccabees of how all the property entrusted to the temple was saved because it was registered there only in the interests of widows. When the information got out that there was plenty of money to be found in the temple at Jerusalem (Simon, traitor that he was, had told King Antiochus that there was no end of it, ready for the taking), Heliodorus was sent to look into the matter. He came to the temple, and told the high priest the terrible information he had been given and the reason for his coming.

146. In reply, the priest said that the only items deposited there were stocks of food, to supply the needs of widows and orphans. Heliodorus wanted to go and seize them and requisition them for the king's use. But the priests threw themselves down in front of the altar, with all their priestly finery on, and with tears of anguish began to call upon the living God, who had given the law which told them to look after deposited property, pleading with him to intervene to defend his own precepts. The change in the high priest's countenance and colour showing the distress he felt in his heart, the anxiety and tension that were in his mind. They all wept: 'Surely the place will fall into a state of contempt,' they thought, 'if we can no longer guarantee security and command confidence when we look after property even in the temple of God!' The women put on sackcloth, and the virgins who were normally confined indoors started to beat at the doors. Some ran to the walls, others looked out of the windows; all of them stretched their hands to heaven, crying to the Lord to stand by his own laws.

147. Heliodorus was undeterred by any of it, though, and pressed on with his plans. He had surrounded the treasury with his guards when, all of a sudden, a mighty horseman, terrifying to behold, appeared right in front of him. He was a dazzling sight, clad in armour of gold; even his horse was arrayed in a magnificent caparison. Another two young men appeared with him: they too were wondrously strong and strikingly handsome, glorious in their splendour and brilliant in their apparel. They surrounded him and began to beat him for the sacrilege

intermissione continuato verbere. Quid multa? Circumfusus caligine in terram concidit et evidenti divinae operationis indicio exanimatus iacebat, nec ulla spes in eo residebat salutis. Oborta est laetitia metuentibus, metus superbis, deiectique ex amicis Heliodori quidam rogabant vitam poscentes ei, quoniam supremum gerebat spiritum.

148. Rogante itaque sacerdote summo iidem iuvenes iterum Heliodoro apparuerunt, iisdem amicti vestibus, et dixerunt ad eum: 'Oniae summo sacerdoti gratias age propter quem tibi vita est reddita. Tu autem expertus Dei flagella, vade et nuntia tuis omnibus quantam cognoveris templi religionem et Dei potestatem.' His dictis, non comparuerunt. Heliodorus itaque recepto spiritu hostiam Domino obtulit, Oniae sacerdoti gratias egit et cum exercitu ad regem revertit dicens: 'Si quem habes hostem aut insidiatorem rerum tuarum, illuc illum dirige et flagellatum recipies eum.'

149. Servanda est igitur, filii, depositis fides, adhibenda diligentia. Egregie hinc vestrum enitescit ministerium, si suscepta impressio potentis, quam vel vidua vel orphani tolerare non queant, ecclesiae subsidio cohibeatur, si ostendatis plus apud vos mandatum Domini quam divitis valere gratiam.

150. Meministis ipsi quotiens adversus regales impetus pro viduarum, immo omnium depositis certamen subierimus. Commune hoc vobiscum mihi. Recens exemplum ecclesiae Ticinensis proferam, quae viduae depositum quod susceperat, amittere periclitabatur. Interpellante enim eo qui sibi illud imperiali rescripto vindicare cupiebat, clerici contendebant auctoritatem. Honorati quoque et intercessores dati non posse praeceptis imperatoris obviari ferebant. Legebatur rescripti forma directior, magistri officiorum statuta; agens in rebus imminebat. Quid plura? Traditum erat.

151. Tamen communicato mecum consilio obsedit sanctus

he had committed; they kept at it constantly, one on each side, without letting up for a single moment. So, to cut things short, darkness overwhelmed him, and he fell to the ground and lay there half-dead at this clear manifestation of the work of God, and no hope of salvation was left within him. Joy welled up in the hearts of the people who had been so afraid, terror in the hearts of those who had been so proud. Some of Heliodorus' friends, quite distraught, pleaded with Onias to pray that his life might be spared, for he was almost at his last breath. **148.** Then, while the high priest was pleading for this, the same young men appeared again to Heliodorus, clothed in the same attire, and said to him: 'Give thanks to Onias the high priest: it is because of him that your life has been restored to you. As for you, you have felt the scourge of God: go and tell all your people how great is the sanctity of the temple and the power of God, of which you have learnt.' With these words, they disappeared. So Heliodorus, having had his life restored to him, offered a sacrifice to the Lord, gave thanks to Onias the priest, and went back to the king with his army, saying: 'If you have any enemies, my lord, or anyone plotting against your authority, there is the place to send him: you will receive him back well and truly scourged!'

149. So, my sons, we must keep faith with people when they have deposited property with us, and take proper care of it. Your ministry shines all the brighter if, when someone with power makes an assault on the property of a widow or an orphan, issuing a challenge that is more than the victim can bear, it is resisted with the help of the church, and if you show that the commandment of the Lord means more to you than the favour of the rich.

150. You will recollect yourselves the number of times we have withstood attacks from powers and authorities, and taken up the cudgels to defend property deposited by widows—and not just by widows, indeed, but by all kinds of people. This is something in which you and I have shared. Let me cite the recent example from the church at Pavia. Here was a case where there was a real danger that a deposit received from a widow would be lost. In the face of the demand from the person who was endeavouring to claim it in accordance with an imperial rescript, the clergy fought for the authority of the church. The local notables and appointed executors all maintained that they could not possibly go against the orders of the emperor. The terms of the rescript were read out: they were perfectly clear. The chief magistrate had given orders to execute it; the official charged with carrying out the business was pressing to go ahead. What more could be said? The property was handed over.

151. However, after consulting with me, the holy bishop blocked the

episcopus ea conclavia ad quae translatum illud depositum viduae cognoverat. Quod ubi non potuit auferri, receptum sub chirographo est. Postea iterum flagitabatur ex chirographo: praeceptum imperator iteraverat, ut ipse per semetipsum nos conveniret. Negatum est, et exposita divinae legis auctoritate et serie lectionis et Heliodori periculo, vix tandem rationem imperator accepit. Post etiam temptata fuerat obreptio, sed praevenit sanctus episcopus, ut redderet viduae quod acceperat. Fides interim salva est, impressio non est formidini; quia res, non fides, periclitabatur.

XXX 152. Filii, fugite improbos, cavete invidos. Inter improbum et invidum hoc interest: improbus suo delectatur bono, invidus torquetur alieno: ille diligit mala, hic bona odit, ut prope tolerabilior sit qui sibi vult bene quam qui male omnibus.

153. Filii, ante factum cogitate et cum diutius cogitaveritis, tunc facite quod probatis. Laudabilis mortis cum occasio datur, rapienda est illico: dilata gloria fugit, nec facile comprehenditur.

154. Fidem diligite, quoniam per fidem et devotionem Iosias magnum sibi ab adversariis amorem acquisivit, quoniam celebravit pascha Domini, cum esset annorum decem et octo, quemadmodum nemo ante eum. Zelo itaque ut vicit superiores, ita et vos, filii, zelum Dei sumite. Exquirat vos Dei zelus et devoret, ut unusquisque vestrum dicat: *Exquisivit me zelus domus tuae.* Apostolus Christi zelotes dictus. Quid de apostolo dico? Ipse Dominus ait: *Zelus domus tuae comedit me.* Si ergo Dei zelus, non iste humanus, invidiam generat, sit inter vos pax, quae superat omnem sensum.

155. Amate vos invicem. Nihil caritate dulcius, nihil pace gratius. Et vos ipsi scitis quod prae ceteris vos semper dilexi et diligo: quasi unius patris filii coaluistis in adfectu germanitatis.

156. *Quae bona sunt tenete* et *Deus pacis et dilectionis erit vobiscum* in Domino Iesu, cui est honor gloria magnificentia potestas, cum Spiritu sancto, in saecula saeculorum. Amen.

way to the strongroom to which he knew that the widow's deposit had been taken. Since it was not possible for them to remove it physically, it was recovered in the form of a written bond. Later on, they demanded it once more on proof of the bond. The emperor had reiterated his order, but this time he promised to meet us himself in person. The request was refused. The authority of the divine law was set out, and a list of scriptural passages, including the one which speaks of the plight of Heliodorus, was added: finally, and reluctantly, the emperor listened to reason. Some time later, an attempt was made to seize the property by surprise, but the holy bishop forestalled it by returning to the widow all that she had given into his keeping. Good faith, meantime, was kept, and the assault engendered no serious fear, for it was only the object itself, not good faith, that was in danger.

152. My sons, keep away from people who are dishonest, and beware XXX
of those who are envious. Here is the difference between someone who is dishonest and someone who is envious: a dishonest person is happy so long as he is enjoying good fortune himself, while an envious person is tortured so long as someone else is. The one loves all that is evil, the other hates all that is good, and in the end a person who wishes good only on himself is almost more bearable than a person who wishes evil on everyone.

153. My sons, think before you act, and when you have thought long and hard do what you consider to be right. Should the opportunity arise to die a death that will bring you great praise, seize it there and then: glory which is put off flies away and is not easily captured again.

154. Love faith, for it was through his faith and devotion that Josiah earned great affection from his enemies, for at the age of eighteen he celebrated the Lord's Passover like no one before him. So, just as he surpassed his predecessors in zeal, you too, my sons, show zeal for God. Let zeal for God take you over and devour you, so that each of you can say: 'The zeal of your house has taken me over'. One of Christ's apostles was called 'the zealot'. But why am I talking about an apostle? The Lord himself said: 'The zeal of your house has eaten me up.' If it is zeal for God, then, not ordinary human zeal, that produces the rivalry, there should be peace among you, the peace which passes all understanding.

155. Love one another. Nothing is sweeter than love, nothing is more pleasant than peace. And you know yourselves that I have always loved you and do love you above all others: like the sons of one father, you have grown together in the fondness of brotherhood.

156. 'Hold fast to all that is good', and 'the God of peace and love will be with you' in the Lord Jesus, to whom be honour, glory, majesty, and power, together with the Holy Spirit, for ever and ever. Amen.

LIBER TERTIUS

I 1. David propheta docuit nos tamquam in ampla domo deambulare in corde nostro et conversari cum eo tamquam cum bono contubernali, ut ipse sibi diceret et loqueretur secum, ut est illud: *Dixi, custodiam vias meas.* Salomon quoque filius eius dicit: *Bibe aquam de tuis vasis et de puteorum tuorum fontibus*; hoc est: tuo consilio utere: *Aqua enim alta, consilium in corde viri. Nemo,* inquit, *alienus particeps sit tibi. Fons aquae tuae sit tibi proprius, et iucundare cum uxore quae est tibi a iuventute. Cervus amicitiae et pullus gratiarum confabulentur tecum.*

2. Non ergo primus Scipio scivit solus non esse cum solus esset nec minus otiosus cum otiosus esset: scivit ante ipsum Moyses, qui cum taceret clamabat, cum otiosus staret, proeliabatur; nec solum proeliabatur, sed etiam de hostibus quos non contigerat, triumphabat. Adeo otiosus ut manus eius alii sustinerent, nec minus quam ceteri negotiosus, qui otiosis manibus expugnabat hostem quem non poterant vincere qui dimicabant. Ergo Moyses et in silentio loquebatur et in otio operabatur. Cuius autem maiora negotia quam huius otia, qui quadraginta diebus positus in monte totam legem complexus est? Et in illa solitudine qui cum eo loqueretur, non defuit. Unde et David ait: *Audiam quid loquatur in me Dominus Deus.* Et quanto plus est si cum aliquo Deus loquatur, quam ipse secum?

3. Transibant apostoli et umbra eorum curabat infirmos. Tangebantur vestimenta eorum et sanitas deferebatur.

4. Sermonem locutus est Elias, et pluvia stetit nec cecidit super terram tribus annis et sex mensibus. Iterum locutus est, et hydria farinae non defecit et vas olei toto famis diurnae tempore non est exinanitum.

5. Et quoniam plerosque delectant bellica, quid est praestantius: exercitus magni lacertis an solis meritis confecisse proelium? Sedebat Eliseus in uno loco, et rex Syriae

BOOK THREE

1. The prophet David taught us that we should walk around in our $\quad$ I
heart as though we were in a spacious house, and commune with it as
we would with a good companion. This is what he did himself. He
used to talk to himself and hold conversations with himself, as he tells
us in his own words: 'I have said: I will guard my ways.' His son
Solomon also says: 'Drink water from your own cisterns, and from the
springs of your own wells'. In other words, use your own counsel.
'The counsel that lies in the heart of man is deep water. Let no stranger
share it with you,' he says. 'Let the spring from which your water
comes be all your own, and take delight in the wife who has been yours
from your youth. Like a loving hind and a graceful doe, let her
fellowship be only with you.'

2. Scipio was not the first, then, to know that he was not really alone
when he was alone, and never less at leisure than when he was at
leisure. Moses knew it long before him. When he was silent, he was
crying out, and when he was resting and at leisure, he was fighting
battles—and not just fighting, but triumphing too, conquering foes
without so much as touching them. He was so much at leisure that he
even had other people to support his arms and hold up his hands for
him, yet he was as active as the rest of them, for he was using these
hands which were at leisure to fight against the enemy, when those
who were in the actual battle could not defeat them on their own. Thus
Moses spoke when he was silent and worked when he was at leisure.
Who, even at his most active, ever accomplished greater feats than this
man? And he did it all when he was at leisure! There on the mountain
for forty days, he received the whole of the law. And in that time of
solitude he was hardly without anyone to talk to! This is why David
also says: 'I will hear what God the Lord is saying within me.' It is a far
greater thing, is it not, to think of God talking with someone than to
think of someone talking with himself?

3. When the apostles passed by, their very shadow brought healing to
the sick. People simply touched their clothes, and had their health
restored to them.

4. Elijah simply spoke the word, and the rain stood still: not a drop fell
on the earth for three and a half years. He spoke once more, and the jar
of flour never failed and the jug of oil never ran out for a single day
right through that long famine.

5. Many people find a particular attraction in military glories: well,
which is a more magnificent feat—to win a battle with all the might of a
great army, or to do it solely by virtue of your own merits? Elisha was

magnam belli molem inferebat populo patrum diversisque consiliorum acervabat fraudibus et circumvenire insidiis moliebatur. Sed omnes eius apparatus propheta deprehendebat et vigore mentis per gratiam Dei ubique praesens cogitationes hostium suis adnuntiabat et monebat quibus caverent locis. Quod ubi regi Syriae manifestatum est, misso exercitu clausit prophetam. Oravit Eliseus et omnes eos caecitate percuti fecit et captivos intrare in Samariam, qui venerant obsidere eum.

6. Conferamus hoc otium cum aliorum otio. Alii enim requiescendi causa abducere animum a negotiis solent et a conventu coetuque hominum subtrahere sese et aut ruris petere secretum, captare agrorum solitudines aut intra urbem vacare animo, indulgere quieti et tranquillitati. Eliseus autem in solitudine Iordanem transitu suo dividit ut pars defluat posterior, superior autem in fontem recurrat; aut in Carmelo resoluta difficultate generandi inopina sterilem conceptione fecundat, aut resuscitat mortuos, aut ciborum temperat amaritudines et facit farinae admixtione dulcescere, aut decem panibus distributis reliquias colligit plebe saturata, aut ferrum securis excussum et in fluvii Iordanis mersum profundo, misso in aquas ligno facit supernatare, aut emundatione leprosum, aut siccitatem imbribus aut famem mutat fecunditate.

7. Quando ergo iustus solus est qui cum Deo semper est? Quando solitarius est qui numquam separatur a Christo? *Quis nos separabit,* inquit, *a dilectione Christi? Confido quia neque mors neque vita neque angelus.* Quando autem feriatur a negotio, qui numquam feriatur a merito quo consummatur negotium? Quibus autem locis circumscribitur, cui totus mundus divitiarum possessio est? Qua aestimatione definitur, qui numquam opinione comprehenditur? Etenim quasi ignoratur et cognoscitur, quasi moritur et ecce vivit, quasi tristis et semper laetior, aut egenus et largus, qui nihil habeat

sitting in one place, while the king of Syria was bearing down upon our fathers' people with his vast military machine, making matters worse by resorting to all kinds of treacherous schemes and doing everything in his power to cut them off by laying ambushes for them at every turn. But the prophet found out all the preparations he was making; by the grace of God he was so quick-witted that he managed to be present everywhere at once, and he was able to advise his people of all the enemy's plans and warn them as to where they needed to be on guard. When the king of Syria discovered this, he sent an army and blocked off the prophet's way. Elisha prayed, and caused all of them to be struck with blindness, so that the men who had come to besiege him ended up entering Samaria as prisoners themselves.

6. Let us compare the way in which he spent his leisure-time with the way in which other people spend theirs. Other people tend to seek rest by leaving the cares of everyday activity behind and retiring from the hustle and bustle of human company. They perhaps seek retreat in the country, where they can appreciate the solitude of the open fields; or they may stay in the city but give their minds a little relaxation and enjoy a period of peace and quiet. But look at Elisha: when he has a time of solitude, he divides the Jordan and passes through it on foot, making the lower part continue on its course and the upper part return to its source. Or he is there on Carmel, helping a woman who is unable to bear children, making her barren womb fruitful by predicting that she will yet conceive, even though she has given up hope of it ever happening. He brings the dead to life again. He takes food that tastes bitter and flavours it, making it sweet simply by mixing flour in with it. He distributes just ten loaves, and gathers up fragments left over, with the people all more than satisfied. An iron axe-head falls off and sinks in the depths of the river Jordan: a stick is thrown into the water, and he makes the axe-head float. He turns a leper's life around by cleansing him, turns drought into rain, turns famine into fruitfulness.

7. So, when is the just man ever alone? He is always with God. When is he ever on his own? He is never separated from Christ. 'Who shall separate us,' asks the apostle, 'from the love of Christ? I am confident that neither death nor life nor angel can ever do so.' And when does he take a day off from serious activity? He never takes a day off from showing his true merit, and it is because he has such merit that he can complete so much serious activity. What boundaries can ever hem him in? He has an entire world of riches as his possession. How can he ever be summed up in any definition? There is no judgement that can ever fully comprehend him. He is like someone who is unknown yet recognized, who dies yet still lives on, who experiences sorrow yet is always truly joyful, who knows want yet remains generous—a man

et possideat omnia. Nihil enim spectat vir iustus nisi quod constans et honestum est. Et ideo, etiamsi alii videatur pauper, sibi dives est, qui non eorum quae caduca sed eorum quae aeterna sunt aestimatione censetur.

II **8.** Et quoniam de duobus superioribus locis diximus in quibus honestum illud et utile tractavimus, sequitur utrum honestatem et utilitatem inter se comparare debeamus et quaerere quid sit sequendum. Sicut enim supra tractavimus utrum honestum illud an turpe esset, et secundo loco utrum utile an inutile, similiter hoc loco utrum honestum sit an utile nonnulli requirendum putant.

9. Nos autem movemur ne haec inter se velut compugnantia inducere videamur, quae iam supra unum esse ostendimus, nec honestum esse posse nisi quod utile, nec utile nisi quod honestum: quia non sequimur sapientiam carnis, apud quam utilitas pecuniariae istius commoditatis pluris habetur, sed sapientiam quae ex Deo est, apud quam ea quae in hoc saeculo magna aestimantur, pro detrimento habentur.

10. Hoc est enim κατόρθωμα, quod perfectum et absolutum officium est; a vero virtutis fonte proficiscitur. Cui secundum est commune officium, quod ipso sermone significatur non esse arduae virtutis ac singularis, quod potest plurimis esse commune. Nam pecuniae compendia captare familiare multis, elegantiore convivio et suavioribus delectari epulis usitatum est; ieiunare autem et continentem esse paucorum est, alieni cupidum non esse, rarum; contra autem detrahere velle alteri et non esse contentum suo, nam in hoc cum plerisque consortium est. Alia igitur prima, alia media officia: prima cum paucis, media cum pluribus.

11. Denique in iisdem verbis frequenter discretio est. Aliter enim bonum Deum dicimus, aliter hominem; aliter iustum Deum appellamus, aliter hominem. Similiter et sapientem

who has nothing yet possesses all things. The just man has no interest in anything except what is lasting and honourable. That is why, though he may look poor to anyone else, he is rich in his own eyes, since he calculates his worth not by the measure of the things that are perishing but by the measure of the things that are eternal.

8. Since we have mentioned the two themes that have occupied our II foregoing discussion of what is honourable and what is beneficial, we are now faced with another question: how do we compare conduct that is honourable with conduct that is beneficial, and decide which to aim for? We have already discussed how we are to ascertain whether a course of action is honourable or shameful, and, in the second place, how we are to tell whether something is beneficial or not beneficial. Well, the idea is just the same here: there are those who believe that we need to determine whether a particular way of behaving is honourable on the one hand or beneficial on the other.

9. For our own part, though, we are rather uneasy about this. We do not want it to look as if we are now introducing some kind of conflict between patterns of behaviour that we have already shown to be one and the same. We said that nothing can be honourable unless it is beneficial, and nothing can be beneficial unless it is honourable. For we are not following the wisdom of the flesh, which can think of no higher benefit than financial gain: we are following the wisdom which comes from God, which counts the things that are considered great in this world as loss.

10. What we are speaking of here is *katorthoma*, or the kind of duty which can be described as 'perfect' or 'complete': it proceeds directly from the true source of virtue. After it comes 'common' duty, and it is clear from its very name that it does not require a particularly arduous or exceptional dedication to virtue, for it can be common to a great many people. Think of it this way. It is an everyday habit for plenty of people to try to make money, and it is perfectly normal to take pleasure in a dinner that has been prepared with special care and dishes that are especially succulent. But the practices of fasting and self-control are observed by only a few, and it is a rare thing to find a person who does not entertain desires for other people's property—whereas the kind who would love to grab his neighbour's possessions and who is never content with his own lot finds himself with plenty of company. So, some duties are of the first rank, and others are 'middle', or common. Duties of the first rank are to be found only among the few, whereas 'middle' duties can be identified in the conduct of the many.

11. The point is that the same words are often used with different meanings. For example, it is one thing to say that God is 'good', and another to say that a man is 'good'; it is one thing to call God 'just', and

Deum aliter dicimus, aliter hominem. Quod et in evangelio docemur: *Estote ergo et vos perfecti sicut et Pater vester, qui in caelis est, perfectus est.* Ipsum Paulum lego perfectum et non perfectum. Nam cum dixisset: *Non quod iam acceperim aut iam perfectus sim; sequor autem si comprehendam,* statim subiecit: *Quicumque ergo perfecti sumus.* Duplex enim forma perfectionis: alia medios, alia plenos numeros habens; alia hic, alia ibi; alia secundum hominis possibilitatem, alia secundum perfectionem futuri. Deus autem iustus per omnia, sapiens super omnia, perfectus in omnibus.

12. Inter ipsos quoque homines distantia est. Aliter Daniel sapiens, de quo dictum est: *Quis Daniele sapientior?* Aliter alii sapientes, aliter Salomon, qui repletus est sapientia super omnem sapientiam antiquorum et super omnes sapientes Aegypti. Aliud est enim communiter sapere, aliud sapere perfecte. Qui communiter sapit, pro temporalibus sapit, pro se sapit ut alteri detrahat aliquid, et sibi adiungat. Qui perfecte sapit, nescit sua spectare commoda sed aliud quod aeternum est, quod decorum atque honestum, toto adfectu intendit, quaerens non quod sibi utile est sed quod omnibus.

13. Itaque haec sit formula, ut inter duo illa, honestum atque utile, errare nequeamus: eo quod iustus nihil alteri detrahendum putet nec alterius incommodo suum commodum augere velit. Hanc formam tibi praescribit apostolus dicens: *Omnia licent sed non omnia expediunt, omnia licent sed non omnia aedificant. Nemo quod suum est quaerat sed quod alterius*; hoc est: nemo commodum suum quaerat, sed alterius; nemo honorem suum quaerat, sed alterius. Unde et alibi dicit: *Alter alterum existimantes superiorem sibi, non quae sua sunt singuli cogitantes sed quae aliorum.*

14. Nemo etiam suam gratiam quaerat, nemo suam laudem, sed alterius. Quod evidenter etiam in Proverbiis declaratum

another to call a man 'just'. Similarly, we speak of God as 'wise' in one sense, and of a man as 'wise' in another. This is just what we are taught in the gospel: 'You too, then, be perfect, just as your Father in heaven is perfect.' Paul himself, I read, was perfect and yet not perfect. For when he said, 'Not that I have already attained this or am already perfect, but I press on, in the hope that I shall yet hold of it,' he immediately added: 'For all of us who are perfect . . . '. So the form of perfection is twofold: one satisfies some of the criteria, the other, all of them; one relates to this world, the other to the world beyond; one is measured in terms of the capacity of man, the other in terms of the perfection of the age to come. But God himself is just throughout all things, wise over all things, and perfect in all things.

12. There is also a difference between men themselves. Daniel was wise in one sense; for it was said of him: 'Who is wiser than Daniel?' Others are wise in another sense. Solomon was wise in another sense, for he was filled with wisdom greater than all the wisdom of the ancients and greater than that of all the wise men of Egypt. It is one thing to be wise in the common sense of the word, and another to be perfectly wise. Someone who is wise in the common sense of the word is wise with regard to temporal things; he is wise with regard to his own interests—so he is prepared to take something from his neighbour and add it to his own possessions. Someone who is perfectly wise simply does not know how to look out for his own advantage. He concentrates all his attention on something else entirely—on what is eternal, on what is seemly and honourable—and he is not interested in what will be of benefit to himself but in what will be of benefit to all.

13. Let us then take this principle as our rule of procedure, and there will be no chance of our losing our way between the two ideals of acting in a way that is honourable and acting in a way that is beneficial. For the just man must never think of taking anything away from another person, or desire to boost his own advantage at the cost of disadvantage to his neighbour. This is the principle that the apostle prescribes for you when he says: 'All things are permissible, but not all things are beneficial; all things are permissible, but not all things are edifying. No one should seek his own good, but the good of his neighbour.' What he means, in other words, is: no one should seek his own advantage, but the advantage of his neighbour; no one should seek his own honour, but the honour of his neighbour. So he also says elsewhere: 'Each considering his neighbour better than himself, each looking not to his own interests but to the interests of others'.

14. Similarly, no one should seek to win popularity for himself, no one should seek to win esteem for himself; everyone should aim to increase the popularity and esteem of his neighbour. We find this clearly stated

esse advertimus, dicente sancto per Salomonem Spiritu: *Fili, si sapiens fueris, tibi sapiens eris et proximis; si autem malus evaseris, solus hauries mala.* Sapiens enim aliis consulit, sicut iustus, quando quidem consors sui est utriusque forma virtutis.

III 15. Si quis igitur vult placere omnibus, per omnia quaerat non quod sibi utile sed quod multis, sicut quaerebat et Paulus. Hoc est enim conformari Christo: alienum non quaerere, nihil alteri detrahere ut acquirat sibi. Christus enim Dominus, cum esset in Dei forma, exinanivit se, ut formam susciperet hominis, quam operum suorum locuple-taret virtutibus. Tu ergo spolias quem Christus induit! Tu exuis quem vestivit Christus! Hoc enim agis quando alterius detrimento tua commoda augere expetis.

16. Considera, homo, unde nomen sumpseris: ab humo utique, quae nihil cuiquam eripit sed omnia largitur omnibus, et diversos in usum omnium animantium fructus ministrat. Inde appellata humanitas specialis et domestica virtus homi-nis, quae consortem adiuvet.

17. Ipsa te doceat forma tui corporis membrorumque usus. Numquid membrum tuum alterius membri officia sibi vindi-cat, ut oculus officium oris aut os oculi, ut manus pedum ministerium aut pes manuum? Quin etiam ipsae manus dextera ac sinistra dispertita habent officia pleraque, ut, si usum commutes utriusque, adversum naturam sit, priusque totum hominem exuas quam membrorum tuorum ministeria convertas, si aut de sinistra cibum suggeras aut de dextera fungaris ministerio sinistrae, ut reliquias ciborum abluat, nisi forte poscat necessitas.

18. Finge hanc et da oculo virtutem, ut possit detrahere sensum capiti, auditum auribus, menti cogitationes, odoratum naribus, ori saporem, et sibi conferat: nonne omnem statum dissolvet naturae? Unde pulchre apostolus ait: *Si totum corpus*

in the book of Proverbs, where the Holy Spirit says through Solomon: 'My son, if you are wise, your wisdom will be to your own benefit and to the benefit of your neighbours; but if you turn out evil, you shall reap the evil consequences on your own.' The wise man thinks of the interests of others, and so does the just man, for, like him, the just man displays the form of both virtues at once.

15. If, therefore, a person wishes to please everyone, he should seek in **III** every situation not to take the course that will bring benefit only to himself but the one that will bring benefit to many, as Paul himself did. This is what it means to be conformed to Christ. It means that you do not go after other people's belongings, and do not take your neighbour's property so as to have it for yourself. For Christ the Lord, though he was in the form of God, emptied himself, and took the form of man, so that he could enrich that form through the mighty works he would perform in it. Think of it, then—you are robbing the one whom Christ has put on! You are stripping the one whom Christ has clothed! This is what you are doing when you attempt to boost your own advantages at your neighbour's expense.

16. Think, man, how you acquired your name, *homo*, 'man'. It comes, of course, from *humus*, 'the earth'. Now the earth takes nothing from anyone—far from it: she shows great generosity in giving everything to everyone alike, and she supplies all her different fruits to be enjoyed by all living things. So the quality called *humanitas*, 'humanity', is the virtue that is specific and natural to man, for it is all about man helping those who share the same nature as himself.

17. The very form of your body and the roles which your limbs all perform should teach you this. Can any one of your members claim the functions of any other? Can, say, the eye claim the function of the mouth, or the mouth the function of the eye; or can the hand take over the work of the feet, or the foot the work of the hands? Far from it: even our right and left hands perform many different functions, and if you change the normal role of either one of them, you are going against nature. Indeed, you would need to jettison your entire human structure before you could alter the respective tasks that your members naturally perform—by using your left hand to take food, say, or trying to get your right hand to do something normally done by your left, like wiping traces of food from your lips—unless, of course, necessity demands it.

18. Use your imagination for a moment: let us suppose that you could give the eye the power to take away intelligence from the head, or hearing from the ears, or thinking from the mind, or the sense of smell from the nose, or taste from the mouth, and to assume these capacities itself. This would destroy the whole order of nature, would it not? The

oculus, ubi auditus? Si totum auditus, ubi odoratus? Omnes ergo unum corpus sumus et diversa membra, sed omnia corpori necessaria; non enim potest membrum de membro dicere: 'Non est mihi necessarium.' Quin etiam ipsa quae videntur infirmiora membra esse, multo magis necessaria sunt et maiorem plerumque tuendi se requirunt sollicitudinem. Et si cui dolet membrum unum, compatiuntur ei membra omnia. **19.** Unde quam grave est ut detrahamus aliquid ei cui nos compati oportet, et cui debemus consortium ministerii, ei fraudi et noxae simus! Haec utique lex naturae est, quae nos ad omnem stringit humanitatem, ut alter alteri tamquam unius partes corporis invicem deferamus. Nec detrahendum quidquam putemus, cum contra naturae legem sit non iuvare. Sic enim nascimur ut consentiant membra membris et alterum alteri adhaereat et obsequantur sibi mutuo ministerio. Quod si unum desit officio suo, impediantur cetera. Quod si eruat oculum manus, nonne sibi operis sui usum negabit? Si pedem vulneret, quantorum sibi actuum profectum inviderit? Et quanto gravius est totum hominem quam unum membrum detrahi! Iam si in uno membro totum corpus violatur, utique in uno homine communio totius humanitatis solvitur: violatur natura generis humani et sanctae ecclesiae congregatio, quae in unum conexum corpus atque compactum unitate fidei et caritatis adsurgit. Christus quoque Dominus, qui pro universis mortuus est, mercedem sanguinis sui evacuatam dolebit.

20. Quid? Quod etiam lex Domini hanc formam tenendam edocet, ut nihil alteri detrahas tui commodi servandi gratia, cum dicit: *Non transferas terminos quos statuerunt patres tui,* cum vitulum errantem fratris tui reducendum praecipit, cum furem mori iubet, cum vetat mercenarium debita mercede fraudari, cum pecuniam sine usuris reddendam censuit. Subvenire enim non habenti humanitatis est, duritiae autem plus extorquere quam dederis. Etenim si ideo tuo auxilio erat opus quia non habuit unde de suo redderet, nonne impium est ut sub humanitatis simulatione amplius ab eo poscas, qui non

apostle puts it so well: 'If the whole body were an eye, where would our hearing be? If the whole body had the gift of hearing, where would our sense of smell be?' So we are all one body and different members, but all are necessary to the body, for one member cannot say of another: 'I do not need you.' Far from it: those members which appear to be weaker are in fact much more necessary, and they often require greater care and attention. And if someone suffers pain in one member, all his other members suffer along with it.

19. We can see what a serious thing it is, then, to take anything away from a person when we ought to be sympathizing with him in his suffering, and how serious it is to act deceitfully and harmfully towards a person when we ought to be offering him whatever service we can. This is undoubtedly the law of nature, which binds us to all humanity: we must show respect to one another, since we are all part of one body. And we must never think of taking anything away from our neighbour, for it is an infringement of nature's law if we even fail to give him assistance. We are born in such a way that members fit with other members, and each attaches itself to another, and all serve one another. If one fails in its duty, the rest are impeded. If the hand tears out the eye, all it does, surely, is deny itself the benefit of the function which that instrument performed? If it were to wound the foot, think of all the activities of which it would deny itself the pleasure. Well, it is far worse to take away the entire man than to take away just one of his members! If when one member is treated that way the entire body is violated, then it stands to reason that when one whole man is treated that way it is the community of the whole of humanity that is destroyed. It is the nature of the human race that is violated—and so too is the congregation of the holy church, for it rises into one body, joined and bound together in the unity of faith and love. And Christ the Lord, who died for all, will be grieved, for it will seem that the price of his blood has been paid in vain.

20. Furthermore, the law of the Lord also teaches you to maintain this principle of never taking anything from your neighbour in order to serve your own interests, for it says: 'Do not remove the boundary-stones which your fathers set up.' It stipulates that you should bring back your brother's ox if you find it wandering; it decrees that a thief must be put to death; it forbids the cheating of a hired man out of his due pay; and it has declared that money must be returned without interest. It is an act of humanity to give help to someone who is without means of his own; but it is an act of callousness to extort more in return than you gave in the first place. Look at it this way: if a person has needed your help to begin with because he did not have enough himself to repay a debt, is it not wicked if, under the guise of humanity,

habebat unde minus solveret? Absolvis igitur alteri debitorem ut condemnes tibi: et hanc humanitatem vocas, ubi est iniquitatis auctio?

21. Hoc praestamus ceteris animantibus, quod alia genera animantium conferre aliquid nesciunt: ferae autem eripiunt, homines tribuunt. Unde et psalmista ait: *Iustus miseretur et tribuit.* Sunt tamen quibus et ferae conferant. Siquidem collatione sobolem suam nutriunt et aves cibo suo pullos satiant suos; homini autem soli tributum est ut omnes tamquam suos pascat. Debet istud ipso naturae iure. Quod si non licet non dare, quomodo detrahere licet? Nec ipsae leges nos docent? Ea quae detracta sunt alicui cum iniuria personae aut rei ipsius, cumulo restitui iubent, quo furem a detrahendo aut poena deterreat aut multa revocet.

22. Pone tamen quod aliquis possit aut poenam non timere aut multae illudere: numquid dignum est ut aliqui alteri detrahant? Servile hoc vitium et familiare ultimae conditioni; adeo contra naturam ut inopia magis hoc extorquere videatur quam natura suadere. Servorum tamen occulta furta, divitum rapinae publicae.

23. Quid autem tam contra naturam quam violare alterum tui commodi causa, cum pro omnibus excubandum, subeundas molestias, suscipiendum laborem naturalis adfectus persuadeat et gloriosum unicuique ducatur, si periculis propriis quaerat universorum tranquillitatem, multumque sibi unusquisque arbitretur gratius excidia patriae repulisse quam propria pericula praestantiusque esse existimet quod operam suam patriae impenderit, quam si in otio positus tranquillam vitam voluptatum copiis functus egisset?

IV 24. Hinc ergo colligitur quod homo, qui secundum naturae

you go on to demand a larger sum from him yourself, when he did not have enough to clear off even the smaller amount? You are freeing the debtor from his obligations to someone else only to put him under obligation to you. How can you call that humanity? The injustice of the situation is only increased!

21. It is here that we are superior to all other living things, for other species of living things do not know what it is to give anything at all: wild animals snatch things for themselves, but men share them with others. So we find the psalmist saying: 'The just man shows pity and shares.' There are some, admittedly, to whom the wild animals show some kindness. They make sure to feed their young with whatever they can gather. Birds, too, satisfy their brood with food. But only man has been given the instinct to offer food to all as if they were his own children. This certainly ought to be the way things are, if we follow nature's own law. Well, if it is not right that we should fail to give, how can it be right for us to take? The laws themselves tell us this, do they not? They decree that items which have been taken from someone at the cost of injury to the person or to the property itself must be restored with additional compensation. The intention is to deter the potential thief from taking in the first place by establishing a penalty for doing so, or to dissuade him by levying a fine on such behaviour.

22. Even if we say that a person might be made of such stuff that he feels no fear of any penalty and laughs at every fine—does that make it right for some people to take from others just the same? What we are talking of here is a vice that is found only in the worst of slaves, a habit that is common only among the lowest of the low. In fact, it is so contrary to nature that people have to be driven to it by need, it would appear; they cannot be led this way by nature. Yet the kind of thieving slaves go in for is done in secret, while the pillaging in which the rich engage is open for all to see.

23. What could be so contrary to nature as to do violence to your neighbour for the sake of furthering your own advantage? Our natural instinct, after all, prompts us to be ever-vigilant in the interests of everyone around us, to put up with real troubles for them, and to go to great lengths to serve them. And we all think it a glorious thing if an individual is prepared to face personal dangers in order to guarantee peace for all; if a man feels he has done something far more valuable in saving his country from destruction than he could possibly have done if he had spared himself these dangers; and if he considers it far better that he devoted his energies to the service of his country instead of remaining at leisure, passing a quiet life enjoying whatever pleasures took his fancy.

24. What we conclude from all this is that if man has been designed by IV

formatus est directionem, ut oboediat sibi, nocere non possit alteri; quod, si qui nocet, naturam violet; neque tantum esse commodi quod adipisci sese putet quantum incommodi quod ex eo sibi accidat. Quae enim poena gravior quam interioris vulnus conscientiae? Quod severius iudicium quam domesticum, quo unusquisque sibi est reus seque ipse arguit quod iniuriam fratri indigne fecerit? Quod non mediocriter scriptura commendat dicens: *Ex ore stultorum baculum contumeliae.* Stultitia igitur condemnatur quia contumeliam facit. Nonne hoc magis fugiendum quam mors, quam dispendium, quam inopia, quam exsilium, debilitatis dolor? Quis enim vitium corporis aut patrimonii damnum non levius ducat vitio animi et existimationis dispendio?

25. Liquet igitur id exspectandum et tenendum omnibus, quod eadem singulorum sit utilitas quae sit universorum, nihilque iudicandum utile nisi quod in commune prosit. Quomodo enim potest uni prodesse? Quod inutile sit omnibus, nocet. Mihi certe non videtur qui inutilis est omnibus, sibi utilis esse posse. Etenim si una lex naturae omnibus, una utique utilitas universorum, ad consulendum utique omnibus naturae lege constringimur. Non est ergo eius qui consultum velit alteri secundum naturam, nocere ei adversum legem naturae.

26. Etenim si hi qui stadium currunt, ita feruntur praeceptis informari atque instrui ut unusquisque celeritate non fraude contendat cursuque, quantum potest, ad victoriam properet, supplantare autem alterum aut manu deicere non ausit. Quanto magis in hoc cursu vitae istius sine fraude alterius et circumscriptione gerenda nobis victoria est?

27. Quaerunt aliqui si sapiens in naufragio positus insipienti naufragio tabulam extorquere possit, utrum debeat? Mihi quidem, etsi praestabilius communi videatur usui sapientem

nature's direction to obey the norm within himself, he cannot do harm to his neighbour. Equally, if someone does do harm to his neighbour, he is violating nature, and the advantage he thinks he has gained is not as great as the disadvantage that has in reality befallen him. What punishment could be more serious than the wound of our own conscience within? What judgement could be more severe than the private condemnation of our own heart? By it, each of us stands accused and convicted in his own eyes: we know that we have done wrong in doing an injustice to our brother. Scripture leaves us in no doubt about this, for it says: 'Out of the mouth of fools comes the rod of insult.' Folly is condemned, then, because it leads to insulting behaviour. This is surely something we ought to flee with all our might—more than death or loss or want or exile or pain and sickness. Who would not willingly accept that a blemish in his body or the loss of an inheritance matters far less than a blemish in his soul or the loss of his reputation?

25. It should be obvious, then, that we are speaking of a principle which needs to be observed and maintained by everyone: what is beneficial for the individual is beneficial for all, and nothing can be judged to be beneficial unless it promotes the common good. How can something be beneficial if it only promotes the good of one individual? Anything that is not beneficial to all is harmful. In my judgement, certainly, a person who is not of benefit to all cannot possibly be of benefit to himself. If there really is one law of nature for all, clearly there must be one standard of what is beneficial for all, and clearly we are bound by this law of nature to consider the interests of all. It cannot then be right for a man who wishes to follow nature's norm and consider the interests of his neighbour to transgress the law of nature by doing him harm.

26. Those who run in athletic races, we are told, have it drummed into them from their very earliest training that they must each compete entirely on the basis of speed, and not by any kind of foul play, that they must go for victory simply by covering the distance as quickly as they can, and never think of tripping their neighbour up or pushing him aside with their hand. Well, what about the race we are in in this present life? Surely in this contest it is all the more important that we aim for victory without doing anything treacherous to our neighbour and without cheating him in any way?

27. Some people ask whether it is right for a wise man, if he finds himself involved in a shipwreck, to grab a plank out of the hands of a fellow-victim who is just a fool, if he is in a position to do it. My own view, I have to say, is that although it undoubtedly seems more advantageous to the common good that a wise man should survive a

de naufragio quam insipientem evadere, tamen non videtur quod vir Christianus et iustus et sapiens quaerere sibi vitam aliena morte debeat; utpote qui, etiam si latronem armatum incidat, ferientem referire non possit, ne, dum salutem defendit, pietatem contaminet. De quo in evangelii libris aperta et evidens sententia est: *Reconde gladium tuum: omnis enim qui gladio percusserit, gladio ferietur.* Quis latro detestabilior quam persecutor qui venerat ut Christum occideret? Sed noluit se Christus persecutorum defendi vulnere, qui voluit suo vulnere omnes sanare.

28. Cur enim te potiorem altero iudices, cum viri sit Christiani praeferre sibi alterum, nihil sibi adrogare, nullum sibi honorem adsumere, non vindicare meriti sui pretium? Deinde cur non potius tolerare incommodum quam alienum commodum diripere adsuescas? Quid tam adversus naturam quam non esse contentum eo quod habeas, aliena quaerere, ambire turpiter? Nam si honestas secundum naturam (omnia enim Deus fecit bona valde), turpitudo utique contraria est. Non potest ergo honestati convenire et turpitudini, cum haec inter se discreta naturae lege sint.

V **29.** Sed iam ut etiam in hoc libro ponamus fastigium, in quod velut finem disputationis nostrae dirigamus sententiam: ut nihil expetendum sit nisi quod honestum. Nihil agit sapiens nisi quod cum sinceritate, sine fraude sit, neque quidquam facit in quo se crimine quoquam obliget, etiamsi latere possit. Sibi enim est reus priusquam ceteris, nec tam pudenda apud eum publicatio flagitii quam conscientia est. Quod non fictis fabulis, ut philosophi disputant, sed verissimis iustorum virorum exemplis docere possumus.

30. Non igitur ego simulabo terrae hiatum quae magnis quibusdam dissiluerit soluta imbribus, in quem descendisse

shipwreck rather than a fool, nevertheless, a Christian man, a just and a wise man, ought never to try to save his own life at the cost of death to someone else. Indeed, even if he encounters an armed robber, he is not at liberty to hit back when his assailant hits him, lest in his anxiety to defend his own life he mar the sense of obligation he ought to feel towards the man. The principle given to us about this in the gospel records is crystal clear: 'Put away your sword: for everyone who strikes with the sword shall perish by the sword.' Could any robber ever be more loathsome than the persecutor who had come to slay Christ? Yet Christ would not let anyone defend him by inflicting wounds on those who persecuted him: his desire was to heal all by being wounded himself.

28. After all, what right have you to consider yourself to be a better person than your neighbour? A Christian man has an obligation to put his neighbour before himself, to make no claims for himself, to take no honours to himself, and to expect no immediate reward for whatever merits he has. Besides, why not learn to put up with disadvantage yourself instead of trying to seize an advantage which belongs to someone else? What attitude could be so at odds with nature as not to be content with what you have, and to be always chasing after things that belong to other people, and showing no shame in your desire to solicit them? If conduct that is honourable is conduct that is in accordance with nature—since everything God made was 'very good'—conduct that is shameful is certainly contrary to it. So it is quite impossible for there ever to be any congruence between what is honourable and what is shameful, for the two categories are opposed to each other by nature's own law.

29. But we now need to place a capstone on this book as well, to act as V a final conclusion towards which we can direct the substance of our discussion. Let us say this: there is no ideal ever to be sought other than the ideal of doing what is honourable. A wise man never does anything unless it can be done with real sincerity and without falsehood, and he never undertakes anything that might involve him in any activity that is sinful, even if he could escape detection in the process. For he senses his own guilt long before other people realize that he is guilty, and he is not half so ashamed to discover that his crime has become public knowledge as he is to hear the voice of his own guilty conscience. We can easily demonstrate this, not with the aid of fictitious tales, like the kind the philosophers use when they are developing their arguments, but with the true and factual examples of men who are just.

30. I am not going to draw pretend pictures about a chasm in the earth opening up after a few heavy showers of rain had softened the ground.

Gyges atque ibi fabulosum illum equum aeneum offendisse a
Platone inducitur, qui in lateribus suis fores haberet; quas ubi
aperuit, animadvertit anulum aureum in digito mortui hominis cuius illic exanimum corpus iaceret, aurique avarum
sustulisse anulum. Sed cum se ad pastores recepisset regios,
de quorum ipse numero foret, casu quodam, quod palam eius
anuli ad palmam converterat, ipse omnes videbat atque a
nullo videbatur; deinde, cum in locum suum revocasset
anulum, videbatur ab omnibus. Cuius sollers factus miraculi,
per anuli opportunitatem reginae stupro potitus necem regi
intulit ceterisque interemptis quos necandos putaverat ne sibi
impedimento forent, Lydiae regnum adeptus est.

31. Da, inquit, hunc anulum sapienti ut beneficio eius possit
latere cum deliquerit: non minus fugiet peccatorum contagium quam si non possit latere. Non enim latebra sapienti
spes impunitatis sed innocentia est. Denique *lex non iusto sed
iniusto posita est,* quia iustus legem habet mentis suae et
aequitatis ac iustitiae suae normam, ideoque non terrore
poenae revocatur a culpa sed honestatis regula.

32. Ergo, ut ad propositum redeamus, non fabulosa pro veris
sed vera pro fabulosis exempla proferam. Quid enim mihi
opus est fingere hiatum terrae, equum aeneum anulumque
aureum in digito defuncti repertum, cuius anuli tanta sit vis
ut pro arbitrio suo qui eum sit indutus anulum, appareat cum
velit; cum autem nolit, e conspectu se praesentium subtrahat
ut praesens non possit videri? Nempe eo tendit istud, utrum
sapiens, etiamsi isto utatur anulo quo possit propria flagitia
celare et regnum adsequi, nolitne peccare et gravius ducat
sceleris contagium poenarum doloribus an vero spe impunitatis utatur ad perpetrandum scelus? Quid, inquam, mihi
opus est figmento anuli, cum possim docere ex rebus gestis
quod vir sapiens cum sibi in peccato non solum latendum sed

This is where Plato introduces us to Gyges: he descended into this chasm, he tells us, and there he came upon the fabled bronze horse with doors in its flanks. Opening them up, his eye lit on a gold ring on the finger of a dead man who was lying there, a lifeless corpse. Greedy for the gold, he took the ring. But after he had made his way back to the company of the king's shepherds (he belonged to their number, you understand), by sheer chance he happened to turn the bezel of the ring towards the palm of his hand. Instantly, he could still see all of them, but he had become invisible himself. Then, when he had returned the ring to its normal position, he became visible to them all again. He practised this feat a number of times until he became an expert at it, and then he proceeded to make full use of the advantage which the ring afforded. He seduced the queen and slept with her; he murdered the king; and so, after doing away with all his potential challengers (he thought it best to kill them to stop them getting in his way), he obtained the throne of Lydia.

31. Give this ring to a wise man, Plato says, with all its advantages, so that he could escape detection any time he committed a crime: he would flee the pollution of sin just as much as if he had no such power to escape detection. For the wise man finds his hiding-place not in any hope of impunity, but in the knowledge of his own innocence. In any case, 'the law was given not for the just but for the unjust,' for the just man possesses the law of his own soul and the standard of his own fairness and justice, and so it is not fear of punishment that keeps him from sin; it is the rule of doing what is honourable.

32. So, to return to our theme, I am not going to produce examples from fables in place of illustrations that are true: I can offer you true stories instead of tales from fables. What need have I to invent a chasm in the earth, or a bronze horse, or a gold ring found on the finger of a dead man, or to say that this ring has such power that a man who puts it on can choose to be visible when he wants to be, and when he does not can withdraw from the sight of those around him so that it seems as if he is no longer there? The point of the story, of course, is to settle this question: would a wise man, even if he had the use of such a ring that enabled him to conceal any crimes he might commit and so help himself to the throne of a country, refuse to sin, and would he consider the pollution of the crime itself more severe than the pains which any punishment could inflict? Or would he, on the other hand, exploit the chance of impunity in order to carry out the evil deed? I repeat: what need have I to invent something like that ring, when I can show from actual historical events what would happen? The wise man, even if he saw that he would not only be able to escape detection if he committed the sin but would also be in a position to take over the throne if he

etiam regnandum videret si peccatum admitteret, contra autem periculum salutis cerneret si declinaret flagitium, elegerit tamen magis periculum salutis ut vacaret flagitio, quam flagitium quod sibi regnum pararet?

33. Denique David, cum fugeret a facie regis Saul, quod eum rex cum tribus milibus virorum electorum ad inferendam necem in deserto quaereret, ingressus in castra regis, cum dormientem offendisset, non solum ipse non percussit sed etiam protexit ne ab aliquo qui simul ingressus fuerat, perimeretur. Nam cum diceret ei Abisai: *Conclusit Dominus hodie inimicum tuum in manibus tuis: et nunc occidam eum?* respondit: *Non consumas eum, quoniam quis iniciet manum suam in christum Domini et purus erit?* Et addidit: *Vivit Dominus, quoniam nisi Dominus percusserit illum aut nisi hora illius venerit ut moriatur, aut in pugnam descenderit et apponatur, mihi non sit a Domino inicere manum meam in christum Domini.*

34. Itaque non permisit necari eum sed solam lanceam, quae erat ad caput eius, et lenticulam sustulit. Itaque dormientibus cunctis, egressus de castris transivit in cacumen montis et coarguere coepit stipatores regios et praecipue principem militiae Abner, quod nequaquam fidam adhiberet custodiam regi et domino suo, denique demonstraret ubi esset lancea regis vel lenticula quae erat ad caput eius. Et appellatus a rege lanceam reddidit: *Et Dominus*, inquit, *restituat unicuique iustitias suas et fidem suam, sicut tradidit te Dominus in manus meas et nolui vindicare manu mea in christum Domini.* Et cum haec diceret, timebat tamen insidias eius et fugit, sedem exsilio mutans. Nec tamen salutem praetulit innocentiae, cum iam secundo facultate sibi tributa regis necandi noluisset uti occasionis beneficio, quae et securitatem salutis metuenti et regnum offerebat exsuli.

35. Ubi opus fuit Iohanni Gygeo anulo, qui, si tacuisset, non esset occisus ab Herode? Praestare hoc illi potuit silentium suum ut et videretur et non occideretur; sed quia non solum peccare se propter salutis defensionem passus non est sed ne alienum quidem peccatum ferre ac perpeti potuit, ideo in se causam necis excitavit. Certe hoc negare non possunt potuisse

yielded to the sin; and even if, on the other hand, he could sense that his life would be in danger if he resisted the crime—even then, he would still choose to put his life in danger in order to stay clear of the crime rather than commit the crime in order to secure the throne.

33. Consider the case of David, when he was fleeing from the presence of King Saul. The king, accompanied by 3,000 of his best troops, was pursuing him in the wilderness, with the aim of putting him to death. He entered the king's camp and found him asleep: not only did he refuse to strike him dead himself; he actually protected him from being slain by any of the men who had entered along with him. Abishai said to him: 'This day the Lord has delivered your enemy into your hands. Shall I kill him here and now?' And he replied: 'Do not destroy him, for who shall lay his hand upon the Lord's anointed and remain guiltless?' And he added: 'As the Lord lives, unless the Lord strikes him or unless his hour comes for him to die, or unless he goes down into battle and is delivered into my hands, may the Lord keep me from laying my hand upon the Lord's anointed one.'

34. So he would not allow him to be killed, but removed only his spear, which lay beside his head, and his jug of water. So, while they were all still sleeping, he left the camp, crossed over to the top of the mountain opposite, and began to call out to them, rebuking the royal attendants, especially Abner, the leader of the force, for his utter failure to keep faithful watch over his king and master, and asking him to show him where the king's spear was, or his water-jug, which had lain beside his head. When the king called to him, he returned the spear: 'May the Lord reward each one of us according to his acts of justice and his faithfulness,' he said, 'for the Lord delivered you into my hands and I refused to wreak vengeance with my own hand on the Lord's anointed.' And yet, even as he said it, he was still afraid that he would be ambushed by the king, and he fled, exchanging his rest for exile. And still he would not put the safety of his life before the knowledge of his innocence, for when he was given a second chance to kill the king he again refused to exploit the opportunity, even though it offered him the security of safety instead of fear and the throne instead of exile.

35. When did John ever need Gyges' ring? If he had kept silent, he would not have been put to death by Herod. He could well have remained silent in the king's presence, and been seen and not heard— or seen and not executed. But it was not just that was he unable to sin himself in order to ensure his own safety: he could not abide or tolerate sin in anyone else, either. In this way he acted contrary to his own interests, for he gave his enemies a motive to get rid of him. No one could say that this could not have happened—quite obviously, John

fieri ut taceret, qui de illo Gyge negant potuisse fieri ut anuli beneficio absconderetur.

36. Sed fabula, etsi vim non habet veritatis, hanc tamen rationem habet ut, si possit celare se vir iustus, tamen ita peccatum declinet quasi celare non possit, nec personam suam indutus anulum sed vitam suam Christum indutus abscondat, sicut apostolus ait quia: *Vita nostra abscondita est cum Christo in Deo.* Nemo ergo hic fulgere quaerat, nemo sibi adroget, nemo se iactet. Nolebat se Christus hic cognosci, nolebat praedicari in evangelio nomen suum cum in terris versaretur: venit ut lateret saeculum hoc. Et nos ergo simili modo abscondamus vitam nostram Christi exemplo, fugiamus iactantiam, praedicari non exspectemus. Melius est hic esse in humilitate, ibi in gloria: *Cum Christus*, inquit, *apparuerit, tunc et vos cum illo apparebitis in gloria.*

VI **37.** Non vincat igitur honestatem utilitas, sed honestas utilitatem; hanc dico utilitatem quae aestimatur secundum vulgi opinionem. Mortificetur avaritia, moriatur concupiscentia. Sanctus in negotiationem introisse negat, quia pretiorum captare incrementa non simplicitatis sed versutiae est. Et alius ait: *Captans pretia frumenti maledictus in plebe est.*

38. Definita est sententia, nihil disputationi relinquens quale controversum genus solet dicendi esse, cum alius adlegat agriculturam laudabilem apud omnes haberi, fructus terrae simplices esse, plus qui seminaverit eo probatiorem fore, uberiores reditus industriae non fraudari, neglegentiam magis et incuriam ruris inculti reprehendi solere.

39. 'Aravi,' inquit, 'studiosius, uberius seminavi, diligentius excolui, bonos collegi proventus, sollicitius recondidi, servavi fideliter, provide custodivi. Nunc in tempore famis vendo, subvenio esurientibus, vendo frumentum non alienum sed meum; non pluris quam ceteri, immo etiam minore pretio.

could perfectly well have remained silent. In the case of Gyges, a person might well say that it could not have happened—a man simply could not hide himself merely with the aid of a ring.

36. But even if the fable does not contain the force of truth, it does contain this important principle all the same: if a just man were in a position to conceal himself, he would still avoid sin just as much as if he were not, and instead of hiding his person by putting on a ring, he would hide his life by putting on Christ, as the apostle says: 'Our life is hidden with Christ in God.' So let no one strive to shine in this world, let no one make great claims for himself, and let no one boast about himself. Christ had no wish to be recognized in this world; he had no wish for his name to be proclaimed in the gospel while he lived on earth; he came with a desire to remain unnoticed in this world. Let us then take the same path, and hide our life, following the example of Christ; let us have nothing to do with boasting; and let us not expect to have our virtues broadcast to the world. It is better to live in humility in this world and in glory in the next. 'For when Christ appears,' the apostle says, 'then you too shall appear with him in glory.'

37. What is beneficial, then, must not take priority over what is **VI** honourable, but what is honourable must take priority over what is beneficial. By 'beneficial', I mean here the kind of thing which ordinary people regard as beneficial. Let greed be put to death, and lust die. The saint insists that he has had no involvement in business; for when a man is forever chasing higher and higher prices, it is a sign not of openness and honesty but of cunning. And another witness says this: 'He who pursues high prices for grain is cursed among the people.'

38. The statement is quite precise: it leaves no room at all for the kind of dispute that is standard in the set-piece debates of professional rhetoric. There, one person will argue that people everywhere regard agriculture as a skill that deserves high praise. 'The fruits of the earth are produced naturally,' he will say, 'and the more a person has sown, the more people are bound to admire him. There is nothing dishonest about earning richer returns through extra hard work. Why, most people are all too ready to condemn the neglect and lack of care that are evident when land is left uncultivated.

39. 'I have taken pains over my ploughing,' he will say. 'I have sown my seed liberally. I have tended my land diligently. I have gathered good crops. I have stored them carefully, I have looked after them faithfully, I have kept them with an eye to the future. Now, in a time of famine, I am selling them, and I am bringing relief to the hungry. It is my own grain that I am selling, no one else's, and I am not selling it at a higher price than anyone else is asking—in fact, mine is actually

Quid hic fraudi est, cum multi possent periclitari si non
haberent quod emerent? Num industria in crimen vocatur?
Num diligentia reprehenditur? Num providentia vituperatur?'
Fortasse dicat: 'Et Ioseph frumenta in abundantia collegit, in
caritate vendidit. Num carius aliqui emere compellitur? Num
vis adhibeatur emptori? Omnibus defertur emendi copia, nulli
irrogatur iniuria.'

40. His igitur quantum cuiusque fert ingenium disputatis,
exsurgit alius dicens: 'Bona quidem agricultura quae fructus
ministrat omnibus, quae simplici industria accumulat terrarum fecunditatem, nihil doli, nihil fraudis interserens.
Denique si quid vitii fuerit, plus dispendii est quam si bene
aliquis seminaverit. Melius metet si sincerum tritici granum
severit: puriorem ac sinceram messem colligit. Fecunda terra
multiplicatum reddit quod acceperit; fidelis ager feneratos
solet restituere proventus.'

41. De reditibus igitur uberis glaebae exspectare debes tui
mercedem laboris, de fertilitate pinguis soli iusta sperare
compendia. Cur ad fraudem convertis naturae industriam?
Cur invides usibus hominum publicos partus? Cur populis
minuis abundantiam? Cur adfectas inopiam? Cur optari facis
a pauperibus sterilitatem? Cum enim non sentiunt beneficia
fecunditatis, te auctionante et ⟨propter⟩ pretium condente
frumentum, optant potius nihil nasci quam te de fame publica
negotiari. Ambis frumentorum indigentiam, alimentorum
penuriam, uberis soli partus ingemiscis, fles publicam fertili-
tatem, horrea frugum plena deploras, exploras quando steri-
lior proventus sit, quando exilior partus. Votis tuis gaudes
adrisisse maledictum ut nihil cuiquam nasceretur. Tunc
messem tuam venisse laetaris, tunc tibi de omnium miseria
congeris opes: et hanc tu industriam vocas, hanc diligentiam
nominas, quae calliditatis versutia, quae astutia fraudis est; et

cheaper. What could be dishonest about that, when all these people would be in peril of their lives if there were nothing for them to buy? Is hard work to be made a crime? Is diligence something to be condemned? Is foresight to be attacked?' Or perhaps he will say: 'What about Joseph? He gathered grain in a time of plenty and sold it when it was dear. No one is being forced to buy it at too dear a price, is he? There's no pressure being put on the buyer, is there? Everyone is being given the opportunity to buy; no injustice is being done to anyone.'

40. When this has all been said, and one person has taken the theme as far as his ability will carry him, another man will get up and say: 'Oh yes, agriculture is a good thing all right. It supplies bounty for everyone—with nothing but sheer hard work it is able to enhance the earth's own fertility without introducing a seed of falsehood or a grain of dishonesty. What is more, if anyone engages in any kind of wrongdoing, he suffers greater loss this way than he does if he takes care to sow his crop properly. If somebody sows a grain which is pure wheat, he reaps a better harvest: he gathers a cleaner and purer crop. The fruitful earth gives back many times what she has received; a reliable field will generally yield its produce with interest.'

41. Well now, it is quite right to expect that the returns of a rich soil will provide a reward for your labour, and to look for fair profits from the fruitfulness of fertile ground. But why do you pervert nature's hard work by turning the proceeds into schemes that are dishonest? Why do you begrudge men the use of produce that is intended for public consumption? Why do you reduce the stock that is available to all the people? Why do you pretend that there is a shortage? Why do you make the poor wish that the season had been barren? For when they cannot feel the benefits of the earth's fruitfulness, because you are busy trying to conduct a public auction and hiding the grain you really have so as to boost prices, they would far rather that nothing at all had been produced—better this than seeing you trafficking in people's hunger. You are always desperate to see a scarcity of grain and a shortage of food. You get all upset when the produce of the ground is lavish; you weep and wail when there is plenty for everyone; you are devastated when the granaries are full of corn. You are constantly watching to see if this time the crop is going to be meagre and the produce sparse. You are thrilled when there is a blight: it is an answer to your prayers that there should be no produce at all for anyone. Then you're delighted that your own harvest-time has come; then you're quick to amass riches for yourself on the back of everyone's suffering. And this is what you call 'hard work', this is what you term 'diligence'—it is nothing but low cunning and rank dishonesty! This

hoc tu remedium vocas, quod est commentum nequitiae. Latrocinium hoc an fenus appellem? Captantur tamquam latrocinii tempora, quibus in viscera hominum durus insidiator obrepas. Augetur pretium tamquam sorte cumulatum fenoris quo periculum capitis acervetur. Tibi conditae frugis multiplicatur usura: tu frumentum quasi fenerator occultas, quasi venditor auctionaris. Quid imprecaris male omnibus, quasi maior futura sit fames, quasi nihil frugum supersit, quasi infecundior annus sequatur? Lucrum tuum damnum publicum est.

42. Ioseph sanctus omnibus aperuit horrea, non clausit, nec pretia captavit annonae sed perenne subsidium collocavit; nihil sibi acquisivit sed quemadmodum fames etiam in posterum vinceretur, provida ordinatione disposuit.

43. Legisti quemadmodum hunc frumentarium pretii captatorem exponat in evangelio Dominus Iesus, cuius possessio divites fructus adtulit, et ille quasi egens dicebat: *Quid faciam? Non habeo quo congregem: destruam horrea et maiora faciam*, cum scire non posset utrum sequenti nocte anima sua ab eo reposceretur. Nesciebat quid faceret: quasi ei alimenta deessent, haerebat ambiguo. Non capiebant annonam horrea, et ille se egere credebat.

44. Recte igitur Salomon: *Qui continet*, inquit, *frumentum, relinquet illud nationibus*, non heredibus, quoniam avaritiae emolumentum ad successorum iura non pervenit. Quod non legitime acquiritur, quasi ventis quibusdam, ita extraneis diripientibus dissipatur. Et addidit: *Captans annonam maledictus in plebe est; benedictio autem eius qui participat*. Vides ergo quod largitorem frumenti esse deceat, non pretii captatorem. Non est igitur ista utilitas in qua plus honestati detrahitur quam utilitati adiungitur.

VII 45. Sed et illi qui peregrinos urbe prohibent, nequaquam probandi: expellere eo tempore quo debent iuvare, separare a commerciis communis parentis, fusos omnibus partus

is what you call 'aid'—it is just a situation engineered by sheer wickedness! What should I call it? Usury? Daylight robbery? You seize these opportunities as if they are seasons specially designed for robbery, and you stalk them like a heartless highwayman, waiting to ambush the stomachs of men. You inflate the price, bumping up the interest according to the amount of the capital, as it were, and the risk to life is increased by the same token. You multiply the interest on the corn you have stored; you stash away the grain as though you're a moneylender, and when you sell it you carry on like an auctioneer. Why do you put an evil curse on everyone, making out that the famine will only get worse, that there will be no corn left, and that next year is set to be even worse for crops? Your gain is the public's loss.

42. Holy Joseph opened the granaries to all; he did not shut them up. Instead of chasing the higher prices that could be had from one year's crop, he built up a reserve for the years to come. Rather than getting anything for himself, he had the foresight to make arrangements which enabled the people to deal with the famine that would recur in the years ahead.

43. You have read how the Lord Jesus in the gospel tells of the grain-merchant who was forever chasing profit. The man's property brought him rich pickings; but thinking he still did not have enough, he said to himself: 'What shall I do? I do not have room in which to gather my goods. I shall pull down my barns and build larger ones.' This is what he said—and yet he could not know whether that very night his soul would be required of him. He did not know what to do: somehow he imagined he still did not have enough to live on, and he hesitated, unable to make up his mind. His granaries could not even hold the harvest he took in every year, and he thought he was still in need!

44. How right Solomon was, then, when he said: 'He who hoards grain shall leave it to heathen nations'—he will not leave it to his heirs, for profits made through greed never become the legal inheritance of our successors. Anything that is not rightfully obtained ends up scattered by strangers who plunder it: it might as well be carried away by the four winds. And Solomon added this: 'He who pursues the year's harvest with a grasping spirit is cursed among the people, but blessing belongs to him who shares it.' As you can see, then, the seemly thing is to be the kind of person who distributes grain, not the sort who chases profit. Consequently, there can be nothing truly beneficial about any situation where the loss to what is honourable is greater than the gain to what is beneficial.

45. At the same time, we cannot possibly approve of people trying to VII bar foreigners from the city. They banish them at the very hour when they ought to be helping them; they separate them from the trade of

negare, inita iam consortia vivendi averruncare: cum quibus
fuerint communia iura cum his nolle in tempore necessitatis
subsidia partiri. Ferae non expellunt feras, et homo excludit
hominem! Ferae ac bestiae communem putant omnibus
victum quem terra ministrat; illae etiam conformem generis
sui adiuvant: homo impugnat qui nihil a se alienum debet
credere quidquid humani est!

46. Quanto ille rectius qui, cum iam provecta processisset
aetate et famem toleraret civitas atque, ut in talibus solet,
peterent vulgo ut peregrini urbe prohiberentur, praefecturae
urbanae curam ceteris maiorem sustinens, convocavit honoratos et locupletiores viros, poposcit ut in medium consulerent,
dicens quam immane esse peregrinos eici, quam hominem ab
homine exui qui cibum morienti negaret. 'Canes ante mensam
impastos esse non patimur et homines excludimus.' Quam
inutile quoque tot populos mundo perire quos dira conficiebat
tabes; quantos urbi suae perire qui solerent adiumento esse
vel in conferendis subsidiis vel in celebrandis commerciis;
neminem famem alienam iuvare; protrahere ut plurimum
diem posse, non inopiam repellere; immo tot cultoribus
exstinctis, tot agricolis occidentibus, occasura in perpetuum
subsidia frumentaria. Hos igitur excludimus qui victum nobis
inferre consuerunt; hos nolumus in tempore necessitatis
pascere qui nos omni aetate paverunt. Quanta sunt quae ab
ipsis nobis hoc ipso tempore ministrantur! *Non in solo pane
vivit homo.* Nostra illic familia, plerique etiam nostri parentes
sunt. Reddamus quod accepimus.

47. 'Sed veremur ne cumulemus inopiam. Primum omnium
misericordia numquam destituitur sed adiuvatur. Deinde
subsidia annonae, quae his impertienda sunt, collatione redi-
mamus, reparemus auro. Numquid his deficientibus, non alii

their common parent, deny them a share in the produce provided for all, and avert relationships of life already entered into: they are not prepared in an hour of need to share their resources with those who have enjoyed all the same rights that they have themselves. Even wild beasts do not banish other wild beasts, yet man banishes his fellow-man! Wild beasts and animals regard the food which the earth supplies as something that belongs to everyone without exception; and, what is more, they give assistance to their own kind. Man, who ought to believe that nothing to do with human life is beyond his concern, attacks his own.

46. But let us look at a far better approach—the example set by a man you may remember. He was already well on in years when the city found itself in famine, and, as is so often the way in such situations, there was strong popular clamour for foreigners to be barred from the city. As he held the post of prefect of the city, the highest office of all, he called together the notable people and the men of more substantial means and demanded that they give serious consideration to what would be best for the common welfare. 'This business of throwing out foreigners is monstrous,' he argued. 'It is like stripping a man of all that it means to be a man, to refuse food to the dying! We do not allow dogs to come to our table and go away unfed, yet we are prepared to shut out men. What benefit could there be in allowing all these people to be lost to the world, carried off by some deadly consumption? Look at the vast numbers being lost to their own city! These were people who, as things were, provided all kinds of helpful services for us, contributing their fair share of resources and engaging in their various trades. It is no help to anyone if another person is hungry: you can prolong your day as long as possible but you cannot avert a shortage in the end. The fact is, with so many of those who cultivated the soil already wiped out, and with so many farmers still dying, our supply of grain could well be lost for ever. Think about it: we are shutting out the very people who have up to now been the ones to put the food in *our* mouths! In their hour of need, we are refusing to feed the people who have fed *us* all along. Look at all they are doing for us even as we speak! "Man does not live by bread alone." We are talking here about our own family: many of them are our own parents. We must make some return for all that we have received.

47. 'But we are afraid that this might make the general shortage worse. My answer is this. First, those who show mercy to all are never left in want; they always find that help is provided for them. Secondly, if you ask how we are to find the corn to give them, let us have a public subscription to pay for it and let us use our gold to buy it. If we are deprived of these people, don't you see, we should have to hire other

nobis redimendi cultores videntur? Quanto vilius est pascere quam emere cultorem? Ubi etiam repares, ubi etiam invenias quem reformes? Adde, si invenias, quod ignarum et alieni usus, numero possis substituere, non cultui.'

48. Quid plura? Collato auro coacta frumenta sunt. Ita nec abundantiam urbis minuit et peregrinis alimoniam subministravit. Quantae hoc commendationis apud Deum fuit sanctissimo seni, quantae apud homines gloriae! Hic magnus vere probatus qui vere potuit imperatori dicere, demonstrans provinciae totius populos: 'Hos tibi omnes reservavi, hi vivunt beneficio tui senatus, hos tua curia morti abstulit'.

49. Quanto hoc utilius quam illud quod proxime Romae factum est: eiectos esse urbe amplissima, qui plurimam illic iam aetatem transegerant, flentes cum filiis abiisse, quibus velut civibus amoliendum exsilium deplorarent, interruptas complurium necessitudines, direptas adfinitates! Et certe adriserat anni fecunditas, invecticio urbs sola egebat frumento: potuisset iuvari, peteretur ab Italis frumentum quorum filii expellebantur. Nihil hoc turpius: excludere quasi alienum et exigere quasi suum. Quid illum eicis qui de suo pascitur? Quid illum eicis qui te pascit? Servum retines, trudis parentem! Frumentum suscipis nec adfectum impertis! Victum extorques nec rependis gratiam!

50. Quam deforme hoc, quam inutile! Quomodo enim potest utile esse quod non decet? Quantis corporatorum subsidiis dudum Roma fraudata est! Potuit et illos non amittere et evadere famem, exspectatis ventorum opportunis flatibus et speratarum commeatu navium.

skilled workers to cultivate the land? It is far cheaper to feed one of these workers than to hire one! Where are you going to be able to buy—indeed, where are you even going to be able to find—someone to do a job like this? Suppose you did find somebody—he would be ignorant of all the right techniques and used to different practices, and all you would really be doing would be filling a place in statistical terms, rather than filling it with someone who would actually be able to cultivate the land.'

48. Need I say more? Gold was collected and grain was brought in. So the prefect did not deplete the city's stocks, but he made sure that food was provided for the foreigners. What favour with God it earned this saintly old man to act as he did, and what glory it brought him in the eyes of men! Here was a man who proved himself to be truly great: he could show the emperor the people of an entire province and say of them: 'I have preserved all these for you. These people are alive thanks to the kindness of your senate; these are the ones your council rescued from death.'

49. The outcome in this case was far more beneficial than it was in that recent situation at Rome. People were thrown out from that great city with all its assets—people who had already spent most of their lives there. They went away, weeping pitifully, and their children went with them. They were broken-hearted for them; they ought to have been treated like proper citizens and spared such exile, they said, instead of seeing so many relationships broken off and so many family ties severed. And the truth was, the land had known the blessing of fruitfulness that year: the only place that required any grain to be imported was the city itself. Help was at hand, if they had been prepared to seek grain from the same Italians whose children they were banishing. Nothing could be more shameful than this: to exclude a person as an alien while making demands on him as though he were one of your own. Why throw out someone who provides his own food out of his own resources? Why throw out someone who feeds *you*? You hold on to your slave but send your own parent packing! You take his grain, but show him no affection! You take your food from him by force, yet offer him no gratitude!

50. What a ghastly situation it was! How devoid of what was beneficial! For how can anything that is unseemly ever be beneficial? Just think of all the provisions Rome was deprived of then, provisions which these members of the commercial guilds would have been well able to supply. It was perfectly possible for the city not to lose these people and still escape serious famine; all they had to do was wait until the winds were right, and fresh supplies would arrive, for they were expecting the ships to come in at any time.

51. Quam vero illud superius honestum atque utile! Quid enim tam decorum atque honestum quam collatione locupletum iuvari egentes, ministrare victum esurientibus, nulli cibum defore? Quid tam utile quam cultores agro reservari, non interire plebem rusticanorum?

52. Quod honestum igitur, et utile est; et quod utile, honestum. Et contra, quod inutile, indecorum; quod autem indecorum, id etiam inutile.

VIII 53. Quando maiores nostri servitio exire potuissent, nisi id non solum turpe sed etiam inutile credidissent regi servire Aegyptiorum?

54. Iesus quoque et Caleb, missi ad explorandam terram, uberem quidem terram, sed a ferocissimis inhabitari gentibus nuntiaverunt. Terrore belli populus infractus recusabat terrae eius possessionem. Suadebant missi exploratores Iesus et Caleb terram esse utilem: indecorum putabant cedere nationibus; lapidari potius eligebant, quod minabatur populus, quam decedere de honestate. Dissuadebant alii: plebs reclamabat dicens adversus diras et asperas gentes bellum fore, cadendum sibi in proelio, mulieres suas et pueros direptioni futuros.

55. Exarsit Domini indignatio, ut omnes vellet perdere, sed rogante Moyse temperavit sententiam, ultionem distulit, satis esse perfidis supplicii iudicans: etsi parceret interim nec percuteret incredulos, ad eam tamen terram quam recusaverant, propter incredulitatis suae pretium non pervenirent, sed pueri et mulieres qui non immurmuraverant, vel sexu vel aetate veniabiles, caperent eius terrae promissam hereditatem. Denique quicumque erant a vicesimo anno et supra, in deserto eorum membra ceciderunt; sed aliorum dilata poena est. Qui autem ascenderunt cum Iesu et dissuadendum

51. The first case was so much better as an illustration of behaviour that is both honourable and beneficial. For what could be more seemly or more honourable than this? People who had been in need were helped with the aid of a public subscription, which raised funds from those who were wealthy; people who had been going hungry were provided with sustenance; and there was no lack of food for anyone. And what could be more beneficial? Skilled workers were kept, men who could cultivate the land properly, and the people who had a proper grasp of country ways did not die off.

52. We can see, then, that what is honourable is beneficial, and what is beneficial is honourable. And, conversely, what is not beneficial cannot be seemly either, and what is not seemly cannot be beneficial.

53. When would our ancestors ever have been able to escape from their bondage, if they had not believed that service for the king of Egypt was shameful—and not only shameful, but without benefit as well? **VIII**

54. Joshua, and Caleb along with him, was sent to spy out the land: they reported that it was a rich land, just as they had been told, but inhabited by nations who were fierce savages. The people were so afraid of getting involved in a war that they went to pieces and refused to take possession of the land before them. Joshua and Caleb, who had been sent as spies, tried to persuade them that the land offered all kinds of benefits: to them, it was not seemly to give way at the sight of mere heathen like these. They were prepared to be stoned to death rather than retreat from taking the honourable course—and the people were on the verge of doing it to them, too. The other spies all argued against it, and the people protested against the whole enterprise. They would get entangled in a war against wild and terrible nations, they said; they were bound to be wiped out in battle, and their women and children would be taken as spoils.

55. The Lord blazed with anger, and he was determined to destroy them all. But when Moses interceded with him, he elected to temper his judgement and defer his vengeance. There was already adequate punishment for the faithless, he decided: though he would spare those who had no faith and would not destroy them straight away, he decreed that in return for their unbelief they would never reach this land which they had chosen to reject. Their women and children, however, who had not murmured against the enterprise, excused on the grounds of either their sex or their age, would receive the promised inheritance of the land before them. So, all the men who were twenty years old or more fell in the wilderness, but the punishment of the others was deferred. Those who had gone up with Joshua and had thought fit to dissuade the people died there and then as a result of a

putaverunt, plaga magna statim mortui sunt; Iesus vero et Caleb cum innoxia aetate vel sexu in terram promissionis intrarunt.

56. Pars igitur melior gloriam praetulit saluti, deterior salutem honestati. Divina autem sententia eos probavit qui honesta utilibus praestare arbitrabantur, eos vero condemnavit apud quos ea quae videbantur saluti potius quam honestati accommoda praeponderabant.

IX **57.** Nihil itaque deformius quam nullum habere amorem honestatis et usu quodam degeneris mercaturae, quaestu sollicitari ignobili, avaro aestuare corde, diebus ac noctibus hiare in alieni detrimenta patrimonii, non elevare animum ad honestatis nitorem, non considerare verae laudis pulchritudinem.

58. Hinc nascuntur aucupio quaesitae hereditates, continentiae atque gravitatis simulatione captatae, quod abhorret a proposito Christiani viri: omne enim quod arte elicitum et fraude compositum est caret merito simplicitatis. In ipsis qui nullum ecclesiastici ordinis officium receperint, incongrua iudicatur adfectatae ambitio hereditatis: in supremo fine vitae positos suum habere iudicium, ut libere testentur quod sentiunt qui postea non sunt emendaturi, cum honestum non sit competentia compendia aliis vel debita vel parata avertere, cum vel sacerdotis vel ministri sit prodesse, si fieri potest, omnibus, obesse nemini.

59. Denique, si non potest alteri subveniri nisi alter laedatur, commodius est neutrum iuvari quam gravari alterum. Ideoque in causis pecuniariis intervenire non est sacerdotis, in quibus non potest fieri quin frequenter laedatur alter qui vincitur, quoniam intercessoris beneficio se victum arbitratur. Sacerdotis est igitur nulli nocere, prodesse velle omnibus; posse autem solius est Dei. Nam in causa capitis nocere ei quem iuvare debeas periclitantem, non sine peccato est gravi; in causa autem pecuniae odia quaerere insipientiae est, cum

great plague, while Joshua and Caleb, and all those who were innocent, either because of their age or their sex, went on to enter the promised land.

56. The better element among them, then, were ready to put true glory before their own safety, while the poorer element chose to put their own safety before what was honourable. In the judgement of God, those who believed that the honourable course had to take priority over the course that was 'beneficial' earned approval, but those who adopted a position more likely to guarantee their own safety than it was to guarantee what was honourable incurred condemnation.

57. There is nothing more odious than to have no love for what is IX honourable, to have an enthusiasm for the kind of practices that belong with the lowest of trades and for dishonest gain, to have a heart that burns with greed, to spend day and night in open-mouthed pursuit of the chance to inflict damage on another person's inheritance, and never to lift the spirit to focus on the splendour of what is honourable, and never to contemplate the beauty of true glory.

58. This is how some people succeed in obtaining inheritances: they go after them like hunters pursuing their quarry, and win them by pretending to show how restrained and serious they are. Such behaviour is repugnant to the purpose of a Christian man, for anything that has been elicited by artifice and contrived by deceitful behaviour is bereft of the merit of honesty. Even people who have never assumed any office in a church order believe it inappropriate to solicit an inheritance by putting on an affected manner. Those who are at the end of life ought to be left to come to their own decisions, and given freedom to make their wills as they see fit—they are not going to be able to alter them thereafter. For it is not honourable to divert hard-earned savings which may be due to others or set aside for them. The obligation of the priest or minister is to be helpful to everyone, if possible, and harmful to no one.

59. In the end, if it is not possible to offer assistance to one person without injuring another, it is better to help neither of them than to cause problems for either one. Since this is so, it is not for a priest to get involved in cases which concern financial affairs: in these situations, it is very often impossible to avoid an outcome at which the defeated party takes offence, for he assumes that his defeat has been aided and abetted by the person who has been acting as mediator. So the priest's task is to harm no one, but to be ready to help everyone—though the power to put this into practice belongs to God alone. Think of it this way. In a case of life and death, it is a grave sin if you cause harm to someone who is in danger and whom you ought to help. But in a case concerned with money, it is sheer folly to invite people's hatred

pro salute hominis graves frequenter fiant molestiae, in quo etiam periclitari gloriosum sit. Proposita igitur forma in sacerdotis officio teneatur, ut nulli noceat, ne lacessitus quidem et aliqua iniuria offensus. Bonus enim est vir qui dixit: *Si reddidi retribuentibus mihi mala.* Quae enim est gloria, si eum non laedimus qui nos non laeserit? Sed illa virtus est, si laesus remittas.

60. Quam honestum quod, cum potuisset regio inimico nocere, maluit parcere! Quam etiam utile, quia successori hoc profuit ut discerent omnes fidem regi servare proprio, nec usurpare imperium sed vereri! Itaque et honestas utilitati praelata est et utilitas secuta honestatem est.

61. Parum est quod pepercit; addidit quod etiam in bello doluit occisum et flebiliter deploravit dicens: *Montes qui estis in Gelboe, neque ros neque pluvia cadat super vos. Montes mortis, quoniam ibi sublata est protectio potentium, protectio Saul. Non est unctus in oleo et sanguine vulneratorum et ex adipe belligerantium. Sagitta Ionathae non est reversa retro et gladius Saul non est reversus vacuus. Saul et Ionatha speciosi et carissimi, inseparabiles in vita sua et in morte non sunt separati. Super aquilas leviores, super leones potentiores. Filiae Israel, plorate super Saul, qui vestiebat vos vestimenta coccinea cum ornamento vestro, qui imponebat aurum super vestimenta vestra. Quomodo ceciderunt potentes in media pugna? Ionatha in morte vulneratus est. Doleo in te, frater Ionatha, speciosus mihi valde. Ceciderat amor tuus in me sicut amor mulierum. Quomodo ceciderunt potentes et perierunt arma concupiscenda?*

62. Quae mater sic unicum defleret filium, quemadmodum hic deflevit inimicum? Quis gratiae auctorem tantis prosequeretur laudibus, quantis iste prosecutus est insidiatorem capitis sui? Quam pie doluit, quanto ingemuit adfectu! Aruerunt montes prophetico maledicto et divina vis sententiam

by getting involved—though bitterness and animosity will very often be generated by anyone who tries to defend a man's life, and it is a glorious thing if you are actually prepared to expose yourself to danger in those circumstances. Let us then observe the principle which should govern the duty of a priest: that he should harm no one, not even when provoked or offended by an injustice of any kind. A truly good man says this: 'If I have repaid evil to those who rendered good to me . . . '. After all, what glory is there in merely refraining from injuring somebody who has not injured us? It really is a virtue, though, if, when you *have* been injured by someone, you show him forgiveness.

60. And what an honourable course that good man took: when he was quite capable of doing harm to his enemy the king, he chose to spare him. And look how beneficial it turned out to be, too: it proved advantageous to him when he succeeded to the throne, for all the people learned to show loyalty to their king and realized that power is a thing to be respected, not usurped. So, when the honourable course was put before the 'beneficial' one, a beneficial situation followed upon that honourable course.

61. Perhaps it was just a small thing for him to spare his enemy. But that was not all he did. He mourned for him when he was slain in war, and lamented him with real tears: 'You mountains in Gilboa,' he said, 'may neither dew nor rains ever fall upon you again! You mountains of death—there the shield of the mighty ones was removed, the shield of Saul! No more is it anointed with oil, with the blood of the wounded, with the fat of warriors. The arrow of Jonathan did not turn back, and the sword of Saul did not return empty. Saul and Jonathan were so splendid, so precious: inseparable they were in life, and in death itself they were not separated. Swifter than eagles they were, more powerful than lions. O daughters of Israel, weep over Saul, the one who clothed you in your garments of scarlet and all your rich embroideries, who adorned your costumes with gold. How are the mighty fallen in the midst of the battle? Jonathan was wounded to the point of death. I grieve for you, Jonathan my brother, you who were once so splendid in my eyes! Your love had come upon me like the love of women. How are the mighty fallen, and the weapons so dearly desired now perished?'

62. What mother would ever weep like this for her only son, the way this man wept for his enemy? Who would ever offer a benefactor such lavish praises as this man did to the foe who had lain in wait for his life? Look at the feeling he showed as he poured out his grief, and the love with which he lamented! The mountains dried up in response to his prophetic curse, and the power of God carried out the judgement he

maledicentis implevit. Itaque pro regiae necis spectaculo poenam elementa soluerunt.

63. Quid vero sancto Nabuthe? Quae fuit causa mortis nisi honestatis contemplatio? Nam cum ab eo vineam rex posceret, pecuniam daturum se pollicens, indecorum pretium pro paterna recusavit hereditate maluitque morte declinare huius-modi turpitudinem: *Non mihi*, inquit, *faciat Dominus ut dem tibi hereditatem patrum meorum*; hoc est: Tantum mihi oppro-brium non fiat, non permittat Deus tantum extorqueri flagi-tium. Non utique de vitibus dicit: neque enim de vitibus cura est Deo neque de terreno spatio; sed de iure loquitur patrum. Potuit utique alteram vineam de vineis regis accipere et amicus esse, in quo non mediocris saeculi huius utilitas aestimari solet; sed quod turpe erat, iudicavit non videri utile maluitque periculum cum honestate subire quam utili-tatem cum opprobrio; vulgarem utilitatem loquor, non illam in qua etiam honestatis gratia est.

64. Denique et ipse rex potuit extorquere, sed impudens arbitrabatur, sed occisum doluit. Dominus quoque mulieris immanitatem, quae honestatis immemor turpe antetulit lucrum, congruo supplicio plectendam adnuntiavit.

65. Turpis itaque omnis est fraus. Denique etiam in rebus vilibus exsecrabilis est staterae fallacia et fraudulenta men-sura. Si in foro rerum venalium, in usu commerciorum fraus plectitur, potestne irreprehensibilis videri inter officia virtu-tum? Clamat Salomon: *Pondus magnum et exiguum, et men-surae duplices, immunda sunt coram Domino*. Supra quoque ait: *Statera adultera abominatio est Domino, pondus autem aequum acceptabile est illi.*

x **66.** In omnibus igitur decora est fides, iustitia grata, mensura aequitatis iucunda. Quid autem loquar de contractibus ceteris, ac maxime de coemptione praediorum vel transactionibus atque pactis? Nonne formulae sunt dolum malum abesse

had pronounced upon them. And so it was that the elements themselves paid a price for having witnessed the death of the king.

63. And what about holy Naboth? Why was it that he met his end?
Only because of his determination to do the honourable thing. For
when the king demanded his vineyard from him and promised to give
him money for it, he refused to exchange the inheritance of his fathers
for any such unseemly sum, and he would have nothing to do with
such a shameful scheme, even though this response meant certain
death. 'The Lord forbid,' he said, 'that I should give you the inheritance of my fathers.' Put differently, what he said was this: 'May no
such disgrace ever befall me, may the Lord never allow me to be forced
into such a wicked deal.' Obviously he is speaking here about more
than just vines; God is not interested, of course, in vines or in any
particular areas of land. He is speaking, rather, about the rights of his
fathers. Obviously he could easily have been given another vineyard
from all the vineyards the king had, and been his friend—and most
people would think this the sort of benefit not to be treated lightly in
this world. But because it was shameful, he felt it did not look
beneficial, and he chose to do the honourable thing and face danger
for it rather than behave in a dishonourable fashion and gain something 'beneficial' in the process. I use the word 'beneficial' here in the
popular sense, not in the sense which conveys the distinction that one
has also done something that is honourable.

64. Besides, the king himself could easily have taken the vineyard by
force, but he considered that would be shameless—indeed, he was
upset at Naboth's death. Equally, the Lord declared that the punishment inflicted on the woman had to be of a severity to match her
cruelty; for she had put shameful gain before everything else, heedless
of what was honourable.

65. Deception of any kind is a shameful thing. Even in everyday
business transactions, the use of crooked balances and fraudulent
measures is deplorable. If sharp practice is severely dealt with in the
commercial realm and among those who engage in trade, how can we
claim it is harmless when we find it among those whose duties lie in
fulfilling virtues? Solomon cries: 'The weight that is too great and the
weight that is too small, and double measures—all these are unclean in
the sight of the Lord.' And earlier on he also says: 'A false balance is an
abomination to the Lord, but a just weight is acceptable to him.'

66. In everything, then, good faith is seemly, justice is pleasing, and to X
give fair and just measure is the agreeable course to take. As for all the
other kinds of business contracts, like the terms which cover the sale of
real estate, or deals and agreements of that kind—there is really
nothing to be said, is there? We find, do we not, that there are rules

eumque cuius dolus fuerit deprehensus duplici poenae obnox-
ium fore? Ubique igitur honestatis praeponderat consideratio,
quae dolum excludit, fraudem eicit. Unde recte generalem
David prompsit sententiam dicens: *Nec fecit proximo suo
malum.* Non solum itaque in contractibus, in quibus etiam
vitia eorum quae veneant prodi iubetur, ac nisi intimaverit
venditor, quamvis in ius emptoris transcripserit, doli actione
vacuantur, sed etiam generaliter in omnibus dolus abesse
debet: aperienda simplicitas, intimanda veritas est.

67. Veterem autem istam de dolo, non iurisperitorum formulam sed patriarcharum sententiam scriptura divina evidenter expressit in libro Testamenti Veteris, qui Iesu Nave
scribitur. Nam cum exisset fama per populos siccatum esse
mare in Hebraeorum transitu, fluxisse aquam de petra, de
caelo diurnam ministrari alimoniam tot populi millibus abun-
dantem, corruisse muros Hiericho sacro tubarum sono, ictu et
ululatu plebis arietatos, Geth quoque regem victum et sus-
pensum in ligno usque ad vesperam, Gabaonitae metuentes
validam manum venerunt cum versutia simulantes se de terra
longinqua esse, diu peregrinatos dirupisse calceamenta, detri-
visse amictus vestium quarum veterascentium indicia mon-
strarent: causam autem tanti laboris emerendae pacis et
ineundae cum Hebraeis esse amicitiae cupiditatem, et coeper-
unt a Iesu Nave poscere ut secum firmaret societatem. Et quia
adhuc erat ignarus locorum atque incolarum inscius, non
cognovit fraudes eorum neque Deum interrogavit sed cito
credidit.

68. Adeo sancta erat illis temporibus fides eorum ut fallere
aliquos posse non crederetur. Quis hoc reprehendat in sanctis,
qui ceteros de suo adfectu aestimant? Et quia ipsis amica est
veritas, mentiri neminem putant, fallere quid sit ignorant,
libenter credunt quod ipsi sunt nec possunt suspectum habere

of procedure which banish malicious fraud and state that anyone found guilty of fraud shall be liable to double punishment? Everywhere we look, then, a regard for what is honourable takes priority over everything else: it outlaws fraud and bans deception. David summed up the idea in general so well when he put it this way: 'And he has done no evil to his neighbour.' So it is not just in business contracts that this matters (and in transactions like these you are even obliged to disclose any faults there may be in goods which are for sale; if the seller does not declare them, the deal is nullified by an action for fraud, even if the goods have already been handed over to the purchaser)—but in every area of our behaviour, we must make sure to banish fraud, show honesty, and declare the truth.

67. Since we are speaking of fraud, there is, of course, an ancient principle on the matter, laid down by the patriarchs long ago—I call it a 'principle' rather than a 'rule of procedure', since it is not like a formula devised by legal experts. It is clearly set out for us in divine Scripture, in the Old Testament book ascribed to Joshua son of Nun. The amazing story had spread among the nations—they had heard how the sea had dried up to allow the Hebrews to cross over; how water had flowed out of rock; how, day after day, there was more than enough food supplied from heaven to satisfy all the people in their thousands; how the walls of Jericho had fallen down at a blast from their sacred trumpets and crumbled to dust at the sheer force of the people's war-cry; and how the king of Gath had been defeated, and his body had been hung on a tree until evening. So the Gibeonites, terrified at the thought of this mighty force arriving on them, came with a ruse. They pretended that they belonged to a far-distant land, and said they had been travelling for a very long time, so long that their sandals were torn and their clothes were worn away. And they offered proof that their things really were getting old. They claimed that they had gone through all this effort for one reason, namely the desire they had to obtain peace and to enter into friendly relations with the Hebrews; and they began to appeal to Joshua son of Nun to enter into an alliance with them. And because he was still ignorant of the region and knew nothing of the people who lived there, he did not see through their deceit, but was quite prepared to believe them.

68. Good faith was such a sacred thing to the Hebrews in those days, they could not imagine that anyone would be capable of acting deceitfully. And who would want to fault them for it? People who are holy judge others by their own standards and attitudes. Because the truth is such a dear friend to them, they think that no one is a liar, and they have no idea what it means to deceive. They are quite willing to believe that other people are just like themselves, and they are unable

quod non sunt. Hinc Salomon ait: *Innocens credit omni verbo.*
Non vituperanda facilitas sed laudanda bonitas. Hoc est
innocentem esse, ignorare quod noceat: etsi circumscribitur
ab aliquo, de omnibus tamen bene iudicat qui fidem esse in
omnibus arbitratur.

69. Hac igitur mentis suae devotione inclinatus ut crederet,
testamentum disposuit, pacem dedit, confirmavit societatem.
Sed ubi in terras eorum ventum est, deprehensa fraude, quod,
cum essent finitimi, advenas se esse simulaverunt, circum-
scriptum sese populus patrum indignari coepit. Iesus tamen
pacem quam dederat revocandam non censuit, quia firmata
erat sacramenti religione, ne dum alienam perfidiam arguit,
suam fidem solveret. Multavit eos tamen vilioris obsequio
ministerii. Clementior sententia sed diuturnior: manet enim
officiis poena veteris astutiae, hereditario in hunc diem
ministerio deputata.

XI **70.** Non ego in hereditatibus adeundis digitorum percus-
siones et nudi successoris saltationes notabo (nam haec
etiam vulgo notabilia) non simulatae piscationis compositas
copias ut emptoris illiceretur adfectus. Cur enim tam studio-
sus luxuriae ac deliciarum repertus est ut huiusmodi fraudem
pateretur?

71. Quid mihi tractare de Syracusano illo amoeno secretoque
secessu et de Siculi hominis calliditate, qui, cum peregrinum
aliquem reperisset, cognito quod cupidus esset hortorum
venalium, ad cenam in hortos rogaverit: promisisse invitatum,
postridie venisse, offendisse illic magnam piscatorum multi-
tudinem, exquisitis copiis adornatum convivium, in prospectu
cenantium ante hortulos composito piscatores, ubi numquam
ante iaciebant retia. Unusquisque quod ceperat certatim
offerebat epulantibus: supra mensam pisces ingerebantur,

to entertain the suspicion that it might not be so. That is why Solomon says: 'An innocent man believes every word.' Rather than censuring such a readiness to believe people, we ought to admire the goodness that lies behind it. It is of the essence of innocence to be ignorant of anything which could prove harmful to others: even when an innocent person is taken in by someone, he still holds a good opinion of people in general, for he believes that good faith exists in everyone.

69. So, since Joshua had such a generous nature that he was inclined to trust these people, he made an agreement with them, granted them peace, and established an alliance with them. But when he came into their territories he discovered that they had deceived him: though they had pretended to be strangers to the area, they were in fact near neighbours. Our fathers' people began to get angry that they had been taken in. Joshua, however, was convinced that the peace he had granted must not be revoked—it had been confirmed under the sanction of an oath. To him, revoking it would be tantamount to breaking his own promise of good faith while denouncing other people for their treachery. Nevertheless, he punished them by reducing them to the status of vassals and giving them menial tasks to perform. The sentence was lenient, but its effects were long-lasting: the penalty for having behaved cunningly so long ago still remains as part of their duties; they have to offer this service in every generation, right to this very day.

70. I am not going to refer to some of the things people will do to find **XI** their way into inheritances—such as snapping their fingers or dancing stark naked if it will earn them the right to be an heir. Behaviour like that is notorious even among the common crowd. Nor am I going to talk about somebody fabricating resources and pretending that they come from a nearby fishing-ground so as to sway the emotions of someone interested in buying his property. After all, why did the buyer show himself so set on extravagant pleasures as to fall victim to such deception in the first estate?

71. Why should I narrate the well-known story, about the charming, secluded retreat at Syracuse, and the cunning behaviour of the man from Sicily? Coming upon a stranger one day, and discovering that he was keen to buy an estate, he invited him to dinner at his place. The stranger accepted the invitation, and came the next day. There he found a great crowd of fishermen, and a vast meal lavishly set out with the most exquisite provisions. Within full view of the diners, just opposite the estate, groups of fishermen had been positioned, in a spot where no one had ever previously thought to lay nets. They vied with one another as they offered the diners what they had caught. The fish were placed on the table, and, since they were fresh and still jumping,

oculos recumbentium resilientes verberabant. Mirari hospes tantam copiam piscium tantumque numerum cymbarum. Responsum quaerenti aquationem illic esse, dulcis aquae gratia innumerabiles eo pisces convenire. Quid multa? Pellexit hospitem ut sibi extorqueret hortos: vendere volens cogitur, pretium gravatus suscipit.

72. Sequenti die ad hortos emptor cum amicis venit, navigium nullum invenit. Percontanti num aliqua piscatoribus eo esset die feriarum sollemnitas, respondetur nulla nec umquam illic praeter hesternum diem piscari solitos. Quam hic redarguendi habet auctoritatem doli, qui tam turpe captarit aucupium deliciarum? Qui enim alterum peccati arguit, ipse a peccato debet alienus esse. Non ergo huiusmodi nugas ego in hanc ecclesiasticae censionis auctoritatem vocabo, quae generaliter condemnat omnem lucri turpis appetentiam brevique sermonis compendio excludit levitatem ac versutiam.

73. Nam de illo quid loquar, qui de eo testamento quod ab aliis licet factum falsum tamen cognoverit, hereditatem sibi aut legatum vindicet et lucrum quaerat alieno crimine, cum etiam leges publicae eum qui sciens falso utitur, tamquam reum facinoris adstringant? Regula autem iustitiae manifesta est: quod a vero declinare virum non decet bonum et damno iniusto adficere quemquam, nec doli aliquid adnectere fraudisve componere.

74. Quid evidentius eo quod Ananias? Qui fraudavit de pretio agri sui quem ipse vendiderat, et portionem pretii tamquam summae totius numerum ante pedes posuit apostolorum, sicut reus fraudis interiit. Licuit utique illi nihil offerre et hoc sine fraude fecisset; sed quia fraudem admiscuit, non liberalitatis gratiam reportavit, sed fallaciae poenam exsoluit.

75. Et Dominus in evangelio cum dolo accedentes repudiabat dicens: *Vulpes foveas habent*, quoniam in simplicitate cordis et innocentia nos iubet vivere. David quoque ait: *Sicut novacula acuta fecisti dolum*, nequitiae arguens proditorem, eo quod

they made an impressive sight for the diners as they reclined at their meal. The chief guest was amazed that there was such a vast supply of fish and such a large number of boats. When he asked for an explanation, he was told there was a freshwater stream nearby, and the fish congregated around it in countless numbers because the water was sweet. Well, to cut a long story short, the man so enticed his guest that the latter pressed him to let him have the estate for himself. He willingly allowed himself to be induced to sell it, but he accepted the money with the appearance of a heavy heart.

72. On the following day, the buyer came to the estate with his friends, but he found no boat of any kind there. When he enquired if that day was some kind of holiday strictly observed by fishermen, he was told no, not at all; and indeed, except for the previous day, no one had ever thought of fishing there. What grounds did he have to take action against the fraud, for he had been so shameless himself in his desire to get his hands on a great catch of juicy pleasures? The person who charges his neighbour with sin must be free from sin himself. So I am not going to submit nonsense of this sort to the official censure of the church: it invariably condemns everyone who chases after shameful gain, and, in words that are brief and to the point, it prohibits all trickery and cunning.

73. What about the person who presents a will which he knows has been falsified, even if it has been falsified this way by others, and claims an inheritance or a legacy as his own, seeking to profit through a crime committed by a third party? Even the public laws convict a man who knowingly makes use of a will that is false: according to them, he is guilty of a criminal offence. The rule of justice is clear: for a good man, it is unseemly ever to deviate from the truth in the slightest, or to inflict any unjust loss on anyone, or to be involved in any kind of fraudulent activity, or to engineer any kind of deception.

74. What could be clearer than the case of Ananias? He acted deceptively over the price he had received for a piece of land he had sold: he laid only a part of the price at the apostles' feet, pretending it was the entire sum. So, guilty of deception, he perished. He could just as well have offered them nothing, and done so without being culpable of any deception. But, because there was deception mixed in with what he did, instead of winning favour for his generosity he paid the penalty for his deceit.

75. The Lord himself, in the gospel, rebuked those who came to him with fraudulent intentions in their hearts, saying: 'The foxes have holes.' For his command is that we should live in simplicity of heart and in innocence. And David says this: 'Your fraud is like a sharp razor's slice.' He is accusing the one who betrayed him of showing real

instrumentum huiusmodi ad hominis adhibetur ornatum et plerumque ulcerat. Si quis igitur praetendat gratiam et dolum nectat proditoris exemplo ut eum quem protegere debeat, prodat ad mortem, instrumenti istius comparatione censetur, quod ebriae mentis et titubantis vitio manus vulnerare consuevit. Sicut iste malitiae ebrius vino per funestae proditionis indicium Ahimelech sacerdoti necem detulit, eo quod prophetam hospitio recepisset quem rex invidiae accensus stimulis persequebatur.

XII 76. Purum igitur ac sincerum oportet esse adfectum, ut unusquisque simplicem sermonem proferat, vas suum in sanctitate possideat nec fratrem circumscriptione verborum inducat, nihil promittat inhonestum; ac si promiserit, tolerabilius est promissum non facere quam facere quod turpe sit.

77. Saepe plerique constringunt se ipsi iurisiurandi sacramento et, cum ipsi cognoverint promittendum non fuisse, sacramenti tamen contemplatione faciunt quod spoponderunt, sicut de Herode supra scripsimus, qui saltatrici praemium turpiter promisit, crudeliter solvit: turpe, quod regnum pro saltatione promittitur; crudele, quod mors prophetae pro iurisiurandi religione donatur. Quanto tolerabilius tali fuisset periurium sacramento! Si tamen periurium posset dici, quod ebrius inter vina iuraverat, quod eviratus inter saltantium choros prompserat. Infertur disco prophetae caput et hoc aestimatum est fidei esse, quod amentiae fuit.

78. Neque umquam adducar ut credam non incaute promisisse principem Iephte ut immolaret Domino quidquid sibi revertenti intra limen domus suae occurreret, cum et ipsum voti paenituerit sui postquam filia occurrit sibi. Denique conscidit vestimenta sua et dixit: *Heu me! Filia, impedisti me: in stimulum doloris facta es mihi.* Qui licet pio metu ac

evil, for he compares him to an instrument which is used to improve a man's appearance but which can often cut him badly. If someone puts on an appearance of being favourably disposed to a person while in reality he contrives to behave in a manner that is fraudulent, following the example of this traitor and delivering over to death the very person he ought to protect, this is the judgement passed upon him. This is the instrument to which he is likened—one that inflicts no end of wounds when wielded by a man who is suffering from the vice of a drunken mind and a trembling hand. And here was a man who was indeed drunk with the wine of malice, when he delivered the priest Ahimelech over to death and denounced him in an act of deadly treachery, because he had shown hospitality to the prophet at the time when the king, stung by the pangs of jealousy, was pursuing him.

76. We must therefore keep our hearts pure and sincere: then each of **XII** us will speak with words that are honest and true, will control his body in a way that is holy, will not mislead his brother with words that are false, or promise anything that is dishonourable. If we ever find that we have made such a promise, it is better for us not to keep it if keeping it involves doing what is shameful.

77. Very often people commit themselves to doing something by swearing a solemn oath that they will see it through, and though they realize that they should never have made any such promise, nevertheless, when they think about their oath, they are prepared to carry out what they promised. This is what Herod did, as we mentioned earlier. He made a promise that was quite shameful, undertaking to reward a girl just because her dancing had taken his fancy; and he kept his word, though it meant behaving cruelly. The shameful thing was that he was prepared to give a promise to hand over a whole kingdom in return for a dance; the cruel part was that he was quite willing to sacrifice a prophet's life just to uphold the sanctity of an oath. How much better to have perjured himself instead of honouring his oath! Indeed, perhaps it should not even be called perjury in such a case, for the promise was only an oath sworn by a drunkard in his cups, the word of an effeminate waster given when the dancing was in full swing around him. A prophet's head was brought in on a dish, and this was supposed to be a proof of the man's good faith! All it proved was that he was out of his mind!

78. No one shall ever persuade me that the ruler Jephthah did not speak rashly when he promised to sacrifice to the Lord whatever should meet him at the threshold of his house when he went home—he rued the vow himself, when it was his own daughter who met him. Indeed: he tore his clothes and cried out: 'Ah, my daughter, how you have trapped me! What a thorn of sorrow you have become to me!' In

formidine acerbitatem durae solutionis impleverit, tamen luctum annuum etiam posteris statuit deplorandum ac dereliquit. Dura promissio, acerbior solutio, quam necesse habuit lugere etiam ipse qui fecit! Denique factum est praeceptum et decretum in Israel ex diebus in dies: *Ambulabant*, inquit, *filiae populi Israel, lugentes filiam Iephte Galaaditidis quattuor diebus in anno*. Non possum accusare virum qui necesse habuit implere quod voverat, sed tamen miserabilis necessitas quae solvitur parricidio.

79. Melius est non vovere quam vovere id quod sibi cui promittitur nolit exsolvi. Denique in Isaac habemus exemplum, pro quo arietem Dominus statuit immolari sibi. Non semper igitur promissa solvenda omnia sunt. Denique ipse Dominus frequenter suam mutat sententiam, sicut scriptura indicat. Nam in eo libro qui scribitur Numeri, proposuerat percutere morte et perdere populum; sed postea rogatus a Moyse, reconciliatus est populo suo. Et iterum ad Moysen et Aaron ait: *Dividite vos de medio synagogae eius et consummabo eos simul*. Quibus discedentibus de coetu, Dathan et Abiron subito impios terra praerupto soluta hiatu absorbuit.

80. Praecellentius et antiquius istud exemplum de filia Iephte quam illud quod memorabile habetur apud philosophos de duobus Pythagoreis, quorum alter, cum a tyranno Dionysio capitis damnatus esset, praescripto mortis die poposcit ut domum pergendi ei facultas daretur ut commendaret suos, ac, ne revertendi nutaret fides, vadem mortis obtulit ea conditione ut si ipse deforet ad constitutum diem, vas eius sibi pro eo moriendum agnosceret. Nec qualitatem sponsionis qui offerebatur recusavit constantique animo diem necis praestolabatur. Itaque alter se non subtraxit, alter ad diem

fear and trembling he did his duty, and carried out the bitter task of fulfilling the promise, with its terrible consequences. But he also designated an official period of grief and mourning for his daughter, and gave orders that it was to be observed every year by each succeeding generation. The promise was terrible, but the fulfilling of it was more bitter still. He was the one who had to do it, and even he found it was almost more than he could bear. And it became a rule and a law in Israel ever after to lament the girl for a period of several days on end: 'The daughters of the people of Israel used to walk around,' Scripture tells us, 'mourning the daughter of Jephthah the Gileadite for four days in the year.' I cannot censure a man who felt it necessary to honour the vow he had made, but the necessity was nevertheless a tragic one if it was fulfilled at the price of the slaughter of his own child.

79. It is better not to make a vow at all than to make a vow which the one to whom you are making the promise has no desire should be paid. We have a clear illustration of this in the case of Isaac, for in the end the Lord appointed that a ram was to be sacrificed to him in the young man's place. It is not always right, therefore, to fulfil every promise you make. Even the Lord himself changes his mind about things quite often, as Scripture shows us. In the book of Numbers, for example, he had declared that he was going to strike all the people dead and destroy them completely; but after Moses had prayed, he was reconciled to his people. But then again he said to Moses and Aaron: 'Separate yourselves from the midst of this assembly, and I shall consume them in a moment.' As they left the company, all of a sudden the earth split open and swallowed up Dathan and Abiram into a great chasm for the blasphemy they had committed.

80. The example of Jepthah's daughter is far more remarkable and far more ancient than that story the philosophers think is so memorable, about the two Pythagoreans. There were two men, they tell us: one of them had been condemned to execution by the tyrant Dionysius, and the day of his death had been fixed. He requested permission to go home to make arrangements for the interests of his family after he was gone. As a guarantee that there was no question of his breaking his word that he would return, he offered security for his life: if he failed to turn up himself on the appointed day, he said, the one who stood surety for him would understand that he had to die in his place. The other man, the one being proposed as guarantor, did not challenge these terms, but awaited the day of execution with a calm mind. So the second man did not shirk his obligations, and the first returned on the specified day. What they had done was so astonishing that the tyrant

recepit. Quod eo usque fuit mirabile ut tyrannus eos sibi in amicitiam asciceret, quorum urgebat periculum.

81. Quod ergo in spectatis et eruditis viris plenum miraculi, hoc in virgine multo magnificentius multoque illustrius deprehenditur, quae ingemiscenti patri ait: *Fac mihi ut exivit de ore tuo.* Sed spatium duorum poposcit mensium ut cum aequalibus conventum ageret in montibus, quae virginitatem eius praedestinatam neci pio adfectu prosequerentur. Nec fletus aequalium movit puellam nec dolor flexit nec gemitus retardavit nec dies praeteriit nec fefellit hora. Rediit ad patrem quasi ad votum rediret, et voluntate propria cunctantem impulit fecitque arbitratu spontaneo, ut quod erat fortuitum impietatis fieret pietatis sacrificium.

XIII **82.** Ecce tibi Iudith se offert mirabilis, quae formidatum populis virum Holophernem adit, Assyriorum triumphali saeptum caterva. Quem primo formae gratia et vultus decore perculit, deinde sermonis circumscripsit elegantia. Primus triumphus eius fuit quod integrum pudorem de tabernaculo hostis revexit, secundus quod femina de viro reportavit victoriam, fugavit populos consilio suo.

83. Horruerunt Persae audaciam eius. Utique quod in illis Pythagoreis duobus mirantur, non expavit mortis periculum, sed nec pudoris, quod est gravius bonis feminis; non ictum carnificis sed nec totius exercitus tela trepidavit. Stetit inter cuneos bellatorum femina, inter victricia arma, secura mortis. Quantum ad molem spectat periculi, moritura processit; quantum ad fidem, dimicatura.

84. Honestatem igitur secuta est Iudith et, dum eam sequitur, utilitatem invenit. Honestatis enim fuit prohibere ne populus Dei se profanis dederet, ne ritus patrios et sacramenta proderet, ne sacras virgines, viduas graves, pudicas

adopted them as his friends—having previously placed them in peril of their lives.

81. Well now, let us take this attitude that is regarded as so amazing in the case of these respected and learned men: we can find the very same spirit displayed, and in a far more striking and remarkable way, in the case of a virgin girl. Here is what she said to her father as he grieved: 'Do to me just what your lips decreed.' All she requested was a delay of two months to have a last meeting in the hills with the girls of her own age, so that they could show their devotion by mourning for her virginity, which was now destined to be consecrated in death. All the tears of her companions were not enough to move the girl; no grief that they showed would cause her to bend; and none of their laments could hold her back. She would not let the day go by, or allow the hour to escape her notice. She returned to her father as if she was the one returning to fulfil a vow, and with her own strength of will she urged him on when he hesitated to see the business through. By her own free determination, she ensured that what had begun as an impious accident ended as a pious sacrifice.

82. Think of Judith, and the amazing example she gives you. She went **XIII** to find Holophernes. People everywhere stood in awe of this man; he had all the victorious forces of the Assyrians around him. First she impressed him with the elegance of her figure and the beauty of her face; then she captivated him with the elegant way she spoke. Her first triumph was that she returned from the enemy's tent with her honour intact; her second was that as a woman she carried off a victory over a man, and put nations to flight through the plan she devised.

83. The Persians were terrified at her daring. Obviously she possessed the same quality that people so admire in the case of those two Pythagoreans—like them, she showed not a trace of fear at the danger of death. But with her there was more: she showed no fear at the danger to her honour, and that is a matter of graver concern to women of good character. Like them, she did not quake at the prospect of the executioner's knife. But she went further: she did not quake at the prospect of a whole army and all its weaponry. There she stood, a defenceless woman surrounded by all those ranks of warriors, surrounded by all their conquering arms, not in the least afraid of death. Viewed in terms of the scale of danger she faced, she went out to die; in terms of the faith she had, she went out to fight a battle.

84. Judith's aim, then, was to do the honourable thing, and in aiming for this she discovered at the same time an outcome that was beneficial. She did the honourable thing indeed—she stopped the people of God surrendering to the heathen; stopped them giving up their ancestral rites and mysteries; stopped them handing over their consecrated

matronas barbaricae subiceret impuritati, ne obsidionem deditione solveret; honestatis fuit se malle pro omnibus periclitari ut omnes eximeret a periculo.

85. Quanta honestatis auctoritas ut consilium de summis rebus femina sibi vindicaret nec principibus populi committeret! Quanta honestatis auctoritas ut Deum adiutorem praesumeret! Quanta gratia ut inveniret!

XIV 86. Quid vero Eliseus nisi honestatem secutus est, cum exercitum Syriae, qui ad obsidendum eum venerat, capitivum introduxit in Samariam, cuius oculos caecitate obduxerat, et dixit: *Domine, aperi oculos eorum ut videant*? Itaque cum rex Israel percutere ingressos vellet eamque sibi dari a propheta facultatem posceret, respondit non percutiendos quorum captivitatem non esset manu operatus armisque bellicis, sed magis subsidio alimentorum iuvandos. Denique epularibus refecti copiis numquam postea in terram Israel piratae Syriae revertendum putarunt.

87. Quanto hoc sublimius quam illud Graecorum, quod, cum duo populi adversus se de gloria imperioque decertarent et alter ex his haberet copiam quemadmodum naves alterius populi clanculo exureret, turpe credidit maluitque minus posse honeste quam plus turpiter. Et isti quidem sine flagitio hoc facere nequibant, ut eos qui consummandi belli Persici gratia in societatem convenerant, hac fraude deciperent: quam licet possent negare, non possent tamen non erubescere. Eliseus autem non fraude deceptos licet sed potestate Domini percussos, maluit tamen servare quam perdere, quia decorum foret hosti parcere et adversario donare vitam quam potuisset auferre nisi pepercisset.

88. Liquet igitur id quod decorum est, semper esse utile. Nam et Iudith sancta decoro contemptu propriae salutis solvit obsidionis periculum et publicam honestate propria acquisivit

virgins, venerable widows, and chaste matrons to be defiled by barbarians; and stopped them bringing the siege to an end by simply surrendering to the enemy. She did the honourable thing—she exposed herself to danger for all of them to rescue them all from danger.

85. What an honourable thing it was, that a woman should venture to make decisions on matters of such importance instead of leaving it to the official leaders of the people! What an honourable thing it was, that she should have such confidence that God would be her helper! And what grace there was, that she should find it to be so!

86. And what about Elisha? His aim was just the same, was it not? He **XIV** too pursued the honourable course. Think of the time when he brought a veil of blindness over the eyes of the entire Syrian army and led them into Samaria as prisoners—the very force that had come to cut him off—and then said: 'Lord, open their eyes, and let them see.' And then, when the king of Israel was all set to wipe out these visitors, and asked the prophet for permission to do so, Elijah replied that it was not right to slay men who had not been taken prisoners by force or by the weapons of war; instead, they should help them by giving them a meal. So they provided them with refreshments, a generous dinner with as much as they could eat. And never again did any Syrian raiders think of making an incursion into the land of Israel.

87. This is a far better example than that story of what the Greeks did, when the two peoples were at war, each vying with the other for glory and dominion, and one side discovered an opportunity to set fire to the other's fleet by stealth: they decided that this would be a shameful thing to do, and they preferred to act honourably and have less power than to behave shamefully in order to acquire more. And it would have been shameful, too: they could not have behaved like this without bringing great disgrace on themselves, for they would have been acting in a deceitful and underhand fashion against a people who had been their allies when they were at war with Persia. They could have denied the deception, perhaps, but they could not have failed to blush. In Elisha's case, however, no deception had been involved; the troops had been struck by the power of the Lord. Even so, he preferred to save them rather than see them destroyed, for he felt that it would be seemly to spare an enemy and to grant life to an adversary, when that life might have been taken had he not been so sparing.

88. It is clear, then, that whatever is seemly is always beneficial. Take the case of holy Judith again. By showing such a seemly disregard for her own safety, she brought the siege with all its dangers to an end, and by acting so honourably in a personal capacity she secured an outcome that was beneficial for the people as a whole. In Elisha's case, too, there

utilitatem; et Eliseus gloriosius ignovit quam perculit et utilius servavit hostes quam ceperat.

89. Quid autem aliud Iohannes nisi honestatem consideravit, ut inhonestas nuptias etiam in rege non posset perpeti, dicens: *Non tibi licet illam uxorem habere*? Potuit tacere nisi indecorum sibi iudicasset mortis metu verum non dicere, inclinare regi propheticam auctoritatem, adulatione subtexere: utique moriturum sibi esse quia regi adversabatur; sed honestatem saluti praetulit. Et tamen quid utilius quam quod passionis viro sancto advexit gloriam?

90. Sancta quoque Susanna denuntiato falsi testimonii terrore, cum hinc se videret urgeri periculo, inde opprobrio, maluit honesta morte vitare opprobrium quam studio salutis turpem vitam subire ac sustinere. Itaque, dum honestati intendit, etiam vitam reservavit; quae, si id quod sibi videbatur ad vitam utile praeoptavisset, non tantam reportasset gloriam: immo etiam, id quod non solum inutile sed etiam periculosum foret, poenam criminis forsitan non evasisset. Advertimus igitur quia id quod turpe est, non possit esse utile neque rursus id quod honestum est inutile, quia complex honestatis est semper utilitas et utilitatis honestas.

XV 91. Memorabile ferunt rhetores quod dux Romanorum, cum ad eum adversarii regis medicus venisset pollicens daturum se regi venenum, vinctum eum ad hostem miserit. Et revera praeclarum ut qui virtutis certamen susceperat, nollet fraude vincere. Non enim in victoria honestatem ponebat sed ipsam, nisi honestate quaesitam, victoriam turpem praenuntiabat.

was far greater glory for him in pardoning the enemy than there would have been in destroying them, and far more benefit to be gained from saving the enemy than there would have been from taking them prisoner.

89. Or think of John—he too had no desire but to do the honourable thing, had he? He could not turn a blind eye to a union which was dishonourable, even if it involved a king, but said to him: 'It is not lawful for you to have her as your wife.' He could well have kept silent; but he concluded it would be unseemly to fail to speak the truth simply out of fear for his own life, or to put the authority of a prophet below the authority of a king, or to hide his views under a mask of obsequiousness. He was well aware, of course, that he would die if he opposed the king. But, to him, doing the honourable thing mattered more than looking after his own life. And in any case, what could be more beneficial than the course he took? It brought him, this holy man, the glory of a martyr's suffering.

90. And remember holy Susanna. She was confronted with the terror of false evidence, and could see no escape, for she was faced with danger on the one hand and disgrace on the other. But she was quite ready to die an honourable death to avoid disgrace: better this, she thought, than survive and have to live a life of shame because she had been so anxious to save herself. So she concentrated on doing the honourable thing, and in the process she was able to save her life as well. If she had opted for the course which looked as though it would be beneficial, or more likely to preserve her life, she would never have won the great glory that she did. In fact (and there would have been nothing beneficial about this: indeed, it would have been dangerous), she might well have found no escape from being punished for the crime. We can see, then, that anything that is shameful cannot be beneficial, and, by the same token, anything that is honourable cannot be without benefit, for what is beneficial is always closely tied to what is honourable, and what is honourable to what is beneficial.

91. The orators tell us of a particular incident which they think is **XV** memorable, concerning a Roman general. He was engaged in fighting a king, and the king's physician came to see him and offered to administer poison to his master. Instead of accepting his offer, he had the man put in chains and sent back to his own side. Well, this certainly was a remarkable thing to do: here was a person who had undertaken to defeat his opponent by strength alone, and he was not prepared to gain the upper hand by fraudulent means. For him, it was not honourable to win the victory at any price. He gave clear notice that victory itself was shameful unless it was won by honourable means.

92. Redeamus ad nostrum Moysen atque ad superiora revertamur, ut quanto praestantiora tanto antiquiora promamus. Nolebat Aegypti rex populum dimittere patrum. Dixit Moyses sacerdoti Aaron ut extenderet virgam suam super omnes aquas Aegypti. Extendit Aaron, et conversa est aqnesque Aegyptii siti peribant, sincera autem fluenta patribus abundabant. Iactaverunt favillam in caelum, et facta sunt ulcera et vesicae candentes in hominibus et quadrupedibus. Deduxerunt grandinem in igne flammeo: contrita erant supra terram omnia. Rogavit Moyses, et universa in suam gratiam reverterunt: grando sedata est, sanata ulcera, potus solitos flumina praebuerunt.

93. Iterum caligantibus tenebris operta erat terra per triduum, ex quo Moyses manum levaverat et tenebras infuderat. Moriebatur omne primogenitum Aegypti, cum Hebraeorum omnis esset inoffensa progenies. Rogatus Moyses ut his quoque finem exitiis daret: oravit et impetravit. In illo praedicandum quod a fraudis consortio temperaverit; in hoc mirabile, quoniam divinitus intenta supplicia virtute propria etiam ab hoste detorserit: vere nimium, sicut scriptum est, mansuetus et mitis. Sciebat quod fidem rex non servaret promissi, tamen honestum putabat ut rogatus oraret, laesus benediceret, appetitus remitteret.

94. Proiecit virgam, et serpens factus est, qui devoravit serpentes Aegyptiorum, significans quod Verbum caro fieret, quae serpentis diri venena vacuaret per remissionem et indulgentiam peccatorum. Virga est enim Verbum directum, regale, plenum potestatis: insigne imperii. Virga serpens facta est, quoniam qui erat Filius Dei, ex Deo Patre natus, Filius hominis factus est, natus ex Virgine: qui quasi serpens exaltatus in cruce, medicinam vulneribus infudit humanis. Unde ipse Dominus ait: *Sicut Moyses exaltavit serpentem in deserto, ita exaltari oportet Filium hominis.*

95. Denique et alterum signum ad Dominum Iesum pertinet quod fecit Moyses: *Misit manum suam in sinum, et protulit eam, et facta est manus eius sicut nix. Iterum misit et protulit eam, et erat sicut carnis humanae species*, significans Dominum

92. Let us return to our own Moses, and let us go back to events which took place earlier in history: this way, we can show that the more ancient deeds are also the more outstanding ones. The king of Egypt refused to let our fathers' people go. Moses told Aaron the priest to take his staff and stretch it out over all the waters of Egypt. Aaron did so, and the water of the river was turned into blood. No one could drink the water, and the Egyptians were all dying of thirst; but our fathers still had all the pure running water they could possibly need. They threw hot ashes into the air, and festering sores and terrible burning boils broke out on both men and beasts. They caused hail to fall, and great streaks of lightning, and everything on the ground was utterly destroyed. Moses prayed, and everything was restored to its former order: the hail ceased, the sores were healed, and the rivers provided normal drinking-water once more.

93. Then again, the land was covered with thick darkness for three days, when Moses had raised his hand and spread the darkness. Every first-born creature in the land of Egypt died, yet all the offspring of the Hebrews remained unharmed. They pleaded with Moses to bring these disasters to an end: he prayed, and his request was granted. In the story of the general, the man deserved praise because he would have no part in an act of deception. In Moses's case, the remarkable thing was that he was able by the force of his own virtue to avert judgements which God himself had designed, and to avert them even from his enemy. He was indeed 'gentle and mild', just as it is written. He knew that the king would not keep faith with his promise, yet he thought it an honourable thing to pray for these people when they pleaded with him to do so, to bless them when they did him harm, and to forgive them when they attacked him.

94. He threw down his staff, and it became a serpent, which devoured all the serpents of the Egyptians. This was signifying that the Word would become flesh, and would rid us of the poisons instilled in us by the dread serpent, by granting us the remission and forgiveness of sins. For the staff is the Word—it is straight, kingly, full of power: the emblem of authority. The staff became a serpent, since he who was the Son of God, born of God the Father, became the Son of Man, born of the Virgin, and lifted up on the cross like the serpent, he poured his healing balm into the wounds of mankind. This is why the Lord himself says: 'Just as Moses lifted up the serpent in the wilderness, so must the Son of Man be lifted up.'

95. The other sign which Moses gave refers to the Lord Jesus as well: 'He put his hand into the fold of his cloak, and brought it out again, and his hand had become like snow. He put it in once more, and brought it out, and it had the appearance of human flesh.' This was

Iesum primum fulgorem divinitatis postea susceptionem carnis, in qua fide credere omnes gentes populosque oporteret. Merito manum misit, quia dextera Dei Christus est, in cuius divinitate et incarnatione si quis non crediderit, quasi reprobus flagellatur, sicut iste rex qui, quoniam signis non credidit evidentibus, postea flagellatus orabat ut veniam mereretur. Quantus igitur honestatis adfectus esse debeat, et his probatur et eo maxime quod se obiciebat pro populo dicens ut remitteret populo Deus aut certe de libro viventium se deleret.

XVI **96.** Tobias quoque formam expressit honestatis evidentius, cum relicto convivio mortuos sepeliret et ad cibos pauperis mensae invitaret inopes. Raguel praecipue, qui contemplatione honestatis, cum rogaretur ut filiam suam in coniugium daret, vitia quoque filiae non tacebat, ne circumvenire petitorem videretur tacendo. Itaque cum Tobias filius Tobis posceret ut sibi eam daret puellam, respondit lege quidem ipsi eam deberi tamquam propinquo, sed dedisse se eam iam sex viris et omnes eos esse mortuos. Iustus itaque vir plus alienis timebat et malebat innuptam sibi manere filiam quam propter nuptias eius extraneos periclitari.

97. Quam breviter absolvit omnes quaestiones philosophorum! Illi de vitiis tractant domorum, tegenda an prodenda a venditore videantur; noster nec filiae vitia celanda arbitratus est. Et certe non ipse adfectabat ut eam traderet, sed rogabatur. Quanto utique iste honestior sit illis dubitare non possumus, si conferamus quanto praestantior sit filiae causa quam rei venalis pecunia.

XVII **98.** Consideremus aliud quod in captivitate gestum, summum tenuit honestatis decorem. Nullis enim adversis honestas impeditur: quae in his eminet et magis praecellit quam in

signifying, first, the splendour which characterized the divinity of the Lord Jesus, then, secondly, the fact that he assumed human flesh. This is the faith in which all nations and all peoples must believe. Rightly did Moses put his hand into his cloak, for Christ is the right hand of God. Anyone who will not believe in his divinity and in his incarnation is lost, punished just as that king was. He would not believe in the signs that were so clear right before his eyes, and so he was punished; only then did he pray for pardon. These things show us, then, what devotion we ought to have for the aim of doing the honourable thing— and so too in particular does the occasion when Moses offered to sacrifice himself on behalf of the people, crying to God either to forgive the people or else to blot him out of the book of the living.

96. Tobit also very clearly expressed the form of what is honourable. **XVI** He would interrupt his dinner to go and bury the dead, and invite the needy to share the food of his own table, though he was poor himself. Or think of Raguel in particular. He had such a determination to do the honourable thing that when he was asked for his daughter's hand in marriage, he would not even keep quiet about her faults, in case such silence should be construed as an attempt to mislead the girl's suitor. So, when Tobias the son of Tobit requested if he could have the girl, Raguel replied that as a blood-relative he was certainly entitled to her according to the letter of the law, but he had given her to six husbands already, and every one of them had died. And so this just man feared more for other people than he did for himself. He would rather see his daughter remain unmarried than have other men's lives put in danger by marrying her.

97. What a simple solution he gave to all the questions which preoccupy the philosophers! They argue about things such as defects in houses, and about whether it seems right for a seller to cover them up or disclose them; our man believed it was not right to conceal defects even where it was his own daughter he was dealing with. And what is more, it was not that he was looking to give her away in marriage: he was being asked to do it. We can be in no doubt that he was far more concerned than they about doing the honourable thing: we only need to compare the significance of a daughter's future with the purely monetary value of an item for sale to know which matters more.

98. Let us look at another example, an incident from the time of the **XVII** captivity, which scaled the heights as a case of honourable behaviour. For there is no adversity powerful enough to check honourable behaviour; in fact, it is seen all the more in circumstances like that and is even more prominent then than it is in times of prosperity. So, even when they faced chains on every side; when all they could see

prosperis. Inter vincula itaque, inter arma flammas servitutem, quae liberis omni supplicio gravior est, inter poenas
morientium, excidia patriae, vivorum formidinem, peremp-
torum sanguinem, non excidit tamen cura honestatis maioribus nostris, sed inter eversae patriae cineres et favillas in
adfectibus piis resplenduit et refulsit.

99. Nam cum in Persidem ducerentur patres nostri, qui tunc
Dei omnipotentis cultores erant, acceptum ignem de altari
sacerdotes Domini occulte in valle absconderunt. Erat illic
velut puteus patens, aquae secessu infrequens nec populari
usui patens, ignoto et ab arbitris remoto loco: ibi obsignaver-
unt indicio sacro pariter ac silentio ignem reconditum. Non
illis studio fuit aurum defodere, argentum abscondere, quod
servarent posteris suis; sed inter extrema sua honestatis curam
habentes sacrum ignem servandum putaverunt ne eum vel
impuri contaminarent vel defunctorum sanguis exstingueret
vel deformium ruinarum acervus aboleret.

100. Abierunt itaque in Persidem, sola religione liberi, quoniam sola illis per captivitatem extorqueri nequivit. Post vero
plurimum temporis, quando placuit Deo, dedit hanc mentem
regi Persarum ut restaurari in Iudaea templum et legitimos
reparari Hierosolymis ritus iuberet. Cuius gratia muneris
Nehemiam sacerdotem rex Persarum direxit. At ille secum
deduxit illorum sacerdotum nepotes, qui profecturi de patrio
solo sacrum, ne periret, ignem absconderunt. Venientes
autem, ut patrum sermone est proditum, non invenerunt
ignem, sed aquam. Et cum deesset ignis quo adolerent altaria,
haurire eos aquam Nehemias sacerdos sibique deferre et
aspergere super ligna praecepit. Tunc, visu mirabile, cum
esset caelum intextum nubibus, sol repente illuxit, accensus
est magnus ignis ita ut omnes in tam evidenti Domini gratia
factum stupentes laetitia perfunderentur. Orabat Nehemias,
psallebant sacerdotes hymnum Deo. Utque consumptum est
sacrificium, iussit iterum Nehemias residua aqua maiores
perfundi lapides; quo facto flamma accensa est, lumen
autem refulgens ab altari consummatum illico est.

were arms and flames and slavery (and that, for free people, is worse than any punishment); when they were confronted at every turn with the torments of the dying, the ruins of their country, the terror of the living, and the blood of the slain—even then, our ancestors never lost their concern to do the honourable thing. Even when they were surrounded by the dust and ashes of their shattered country, that concern shone forth, it radiated, in their faithful desires to do what was right.

99. When our fathers were carried away into Persia, those who were at that time the true worshippers of Almighty God, the priests of the Lord took fire from the altar and buried it secretly in a valley. There was a kind of open well in the place, seldom visited because the water had receded and was no longer accessible to most people, for it lay in a remote spot, hidden from the sight of any onlookers. There they hid the fire, and sealed it up with a sacred sign and with strict silence. These men had no desire to bury gold or hoard silver to preserve it for their descendants. No, even in the extreme circumstances in which they found themselves, they maintained their concern to do the honourable thing, and felt that they had an obligation to preserve the sacred fire, to ensure that it was not defiled by people who were unclean, or extinguished by the blood of the dead, or buried beneath a heap of miserable ruins.

100. So they went away into Persia, free only in their religion, for this was the only thing that could not be taken from them in their captivity. But after a very long time, when it pleased God, he put it into the heart of the king of the Persians to order the restoration of the temple in Judaea and the re-establishment of the proper rites prescribed by the Law at Jerusalem. Nehemiah the priest was appointed by the Persian king to carry out this task, but he took with him the grandsons of those priests who had hidden the sacred fire to prevent it from dying out when they left their country. When they arrived at the place, however, we are told in the account of our fathers, it was not fire they found, but water. Well, since there was no fire to burn on the altars, Nehemiah the priest ordered them to draw the water, bring it to him, and sprinkle it upon the wood. Then—an amazing sight!—though the sky was laced with clouds, the sun suddenly broke through and a tremendous fire was ignited. They were all quite awestruck at what had happened: here was a true manifestation of the Lord's favour! They were filled with joy. Nehemiah offered a prayer, and the priests sang a hymn to God. When the sacrifice had been consumed, Nehemiah again ordered them to pour the remainder of the water over the larger stones. When this was done, a flame was ignited, but the light that shone from the altar immediately went out.

101. Hoc patefacto indicio rex Persarum eo loco in quo ignis fuerat absconditus et postea reperta est aqua, templum fieri mandavit cui inferebantur dona plurima. Appellaverunt autem illud qui erant cum sancto Nehemia 'Epathar', quod interpretationem habet purificationis; a plurimis 'Nepthe' vocatur. Invenitur autem in descriptionibus Ieremiae prophetae quod iusserit accipere de igne eos qui postea essent futuri. Hic est ignis qui cecidit super sacrificium Moysi et consumpsit illud, sicut scriptum est quia: *Exivit ignis a Domino et consumpsit universa quae erant super altare holocausta.* Hoc igne oportebat sanctificari sacrificium, ideoque filios Aaron, qui alienum ignem inferre voluerunt, exivit iterum ignis a Domino et consumpsit eos ita ut mortui extra castra proicerentur.

102. Veniens autem Ieremias in locum invenit domum in modum speluncae et tabernaculum et arcam et altare incensi intulit illuc et obstruxit ostium; quod cum hi qui simul venerant curiosius perscrutarentur ut notarent sibi locum, nequaquam comprehendere atque invenire potuerunt. Ut autem cognovit Ieremias quod adfectassent, dixit: *Ignotus erit locus donec congreget Deus congregationem populi et propitius fiat. Tunc Deus ostendet haec et apparebit maiestas Domini.*

XVIII **103.** Congregationem populi tenemus, propitiationem Domini Dei nostri agnoscimus, quam propitiator in sua operatus est passione. Arbitror quod nec ignem istum possimus ignorare, cum legerimus quia baptizat Dominus Iesus in Spiritu sancto et igni, sicut in evangelio dixit Iohannes. Merito consumebatur sacrificium, quoniam pro peccato erat. Ille autem ignis typus Spiritus sancti fuit, qui descensurus erat post Domini ascensionem et remissurus peccata omnium, qui quasi ignis inflammat animum ac mentem fidelem. Unde ait Ieremias accepto Spiritu: *Et factum est in corde meo ut ignis ardens, flammigerans in ossibus meis, et dissolutus sum undique et ferre non possum.* Sed et in Actibus Apostolorum cum decidisset Spiritus super apostolos et plerosque qui exspectabant promissa Domini, tamquam ignem dispersas esse linguas legimus. Denique sic vaporabatur animus singulorum ut musto repleti esse aestimarentur, qui acceperant linguarum diversitatem.

101. When the story of this sign was told to others, the Persian king gave orders that a temple be built on the spot where the fire had been hidden and where the water had subsequently been found, and to this temple people brought vast gifts. Those who were with holy Nehemiah called it 'Epathar', which means 'purification'; most people call it 'Naphtha'. In the records of the prophet Jeremiah, we find that he instructed all those who were to come after him to take some of the fire. This is the same fire which fell on Moses's sacrifice and consumed it, for it is written: 'Fire came out from the Lord and consumed the entire burnt-offerings upon the altar.' It had to be this fire which consecrated the sacrifice, and that is why fire came out from the Lord another time and fell upon the sons of Aaron when they wanted to introduce a different fire, totally consuming them, so that they were thrown outside the camp, dead.

102. Another time, Jeremiah came upon a certain spot and found a chamber-shaped cave, and he brought the tabernacle, the ark, and the altar of incense into it, and blocked up the entrance. Those who had come with him looked closely to see if they could locate the spot for themselves, but they were quite unable to pick it out and could not identify it. And indeed, when Jeremiah heard that they had been trying to find it, this is what he said: 'The place will remain unknown until God shall gather the congregation of his people and show them favour once more. Then God shall reveal these things, and the majesty of the Lord shall appear.'

103. We are the congregation of his people, and we know the favour of XVIII the Lord our God—our Redeemer secured that favour for us through his passion. I think we can hardly be in doubt as to the identity of the fire, for we have read that the Lord Jesus baptizes with the Holy Spirit and with fire, as John tells us in the gospel. How appropriate it was that the sacrifice was consumed, for it was offered for sin. But that fire was a type of the Holy Spirit, who was to descend after the Lord's ascension, and forgive the sins of all: he is like fire, for he sets ablaze the heart and mind of the believer. So, when Jeremiah had received the Spirit, he said: 'And it became in my heart like a burning fire, blazing in my bones. I am utterly ruined! I cannot bear it!' But this is not all. In the Acts of the Apostles we read that when the Spirit fell upon the apostles and upon all the others who were waiting for the Lord's promises to be fulfilled, tongues like flames of fire were scattered among them. Then each of them found his soul warmed within him—people thought they were full of new wine, when what had really happened was that they had received the gift of other tongues.

104. Quid ergo sibi vult esse quod ignis aqua factus est et aqua ignem excitavit nisi quia spiritalis gratia per ignem exurit, per aquam mundat peccata nostra? Eluitur enim peccatum et exuritur. Unde et apostolus ait: *Uniuscuiusque opus quale sit, ignis probabit*; et infra: *Si cuius opus arserit, detrimentum patietur; ipse autem salvus erit, sic tamen quasi per ignem.*

105. Quod ideo posuimus ut probaremus per ignem exuri peccata. Notum est ergo hunc esse vere ignem sacrum qui tunc in typo futurae remissionis peccatorum descendit super sacrificium.

106. Hic igitur ignis absconditur captivitatis tempore, quo culpa regnat; tempore autem libertatis promitur. Et licet in aquae speciem mutatus, tamen servat ignis naturam, ut consumeret sacrificium. Nec mireris, cum legeris quia Pater Deus dixit: *Ego sum ignis consumens*; et alibi: *Me dereliquerunt fontem aquae vivae.* Ipse quoque Dominus Iesus, quasi ignis, inflammat audientium corda, quasi fons refrigerat: nam ipse in evangelio suo dicit quod ideo venerit ut ignem in terras mitteret et potum sitientibus aquae vivae ministraret.

107. Eliae quoque tempore descendit ignis, quando provocavit prophetas gentium ut altare sine igne accenderent. Et cum illi nequissent facere, hostiam suam tertio ipse perfudit aqua et manabat aqua in circuitu altaris et exclamavit et cecidit ignis a Domino de caelis et consumpsit holocaustum.

108. Hostia illa tu es. Considera tacitus singula. In te descendit vapor Spiritus sancti, te videtur exurere cum tua peccata consumit. Denique quod consumptum est sacrificium Moysi tempore, sacrificium pro peccato erat. Unde Moyses ait, sicut in Machabaeorum scriptum est libro, eo quod non sit manducatum quod erat pro peccato, consumptum est. Nonne tibi consumi videtur, quando in baptismatis sacramento interit homo totus exterior? Vetus homo noster confixus est cruci, apostolus clamat. Illic, sicut Patrum exempla te docent, Aegyptius demergitur, Hebraeus resurgit, sancto renovatus Spiritu, qui etiam per mare Rubrum inoffenso transivit vestigio, ubi baptizati sunt patres sub nube et in mari.

104. What could it mean that fire was turned into water and water caused fire to ignite? Surely this: that the grace of the Spirit burns up our sins with fire and cleanses them with water. For sin is washed away and burnt up. That is why the apostle also says: 'The fire shall prove the quality of each person's work.' And further on in the same passage he says this: 'If a person's work burns, he shall suffer loss, but he himself shall be saved, albeit by fire.'

105. We have cited these passages to show that sins are burnt up by fire. They prove that it really was sacred fire which came down upon that sacrifice, and it was a type of the remission of sins that was yet to be given.

106. This fire is hidden in the time of our captivity, then, when sin reigns over us, but it is revealed in the time of our freedom. It may have changed its appearance to that of water, but it preserves the nature of real fire, so that it can consume the sacrifice. You should not be surprised at this, for you have read that God the Father has said: 'I am a consuming fire,' and, in another place, 'They have forsaken me, the fountain of living water.' The Lord Jesus himself is like a fire, too, for he sets ablaze the hearts of those who hear him; and he is like a fountain, for he refreshes them. In fact, he says himself in his gospel that this is why he came—to send fire on the earth and to give living water to the thirsty.

107. The fire came down in Elijah's time as well, when he challenged the heathen prophets to kindle a flame on the altar without fire. And when they were quite unable to do it, he drenched the offering with water three times, making the water run out around the altar on all sides, and cried out, and fire fell from the Lord from heaven and consumed the burnt-offering.

108. You are that offering. Consider each detail silently. It is upon you that the breath of the Holy Spirit descends; it is you who appear to be burnt up when he consumes your sins. For the sacrifice that was consumed in Moses' time was a sacrifice for sin. This was why Moses said these words we find written in the book of Maccabees: 'Because the sacrifice was not to be eaten, but was a sacrifice for sin, it was consumed.' Is it not consumed when our entire outer man perishes in the sacrament of baptism? 'Our old man has been crucified,' cries the apostle. It is there, as the examples of our fathers teach you, that the Egyptian is swallowed up and the Hebrew rises again, renewed by the Holy Spirit, just as he passed through the Red Sea itself on foot without stumbling, where our fathers were baptized under the cloud and in the sea.

109. In diluvio quoque Noe tempore mortua est caro omnis, iustus tamen cum sua progenie servatus est. Annon consumitur homo, cum absolvitur mortale istud a vita? Denique exterior corrumpitur, sed renovatur interior. Nec solum in baptismate sed etiam in paenitentia fit carnis interitus ad profectum spiritus, sicut apostolica docemur auctoritate dicente sancto Paulo: *Iudicavi ut praesens eum qui sic operatus est, tradere huiusmodi Satanae in interitum carnis, ut spiritus salvus sit in die Domini nostri Iesu Christi.*

110. Prolixior excursus admirandi gratia mysterii factus videtur, dum studemus revelatum plenius sacramentum pandere, quod eo usque plenum honestatis est ut sit plenum religionis.

XIX **111.** Quanta autem honestatis cura maioribus fuit, ut unius mulieris iniuriam stupro illatam intemperantium bello persequerentur et victo populo tribus Beniamin obtestarentur in coniugium se eis proprias filias non daturos! Remanserat tribus sine ullo posteritatis subsidio, nisi fraudis necessariae accepisset licentiam. Quae tamen indulgentia congruo intemperantiae supplicio non videtur vacare, quando illis hoc solum permissum est ut rapto inirent coniugia, non connubii sacramento. Et revera dignum fuit ut qui alienum contubernium solverant, ipsi nuptiarum amitterent solemnitatem.

112. Quam plena autem miserationis historia! Vir, inquit, Levita acceperat sibi iugalem (quam a concubitu concubinam appellatam arbitror), quae aliquanto post quibusdam, ut fieri solet, offensa rebus, ad patrem se contulit et fuit illic quattuor mensibus. Exsurrexit vir eius et abiit ad soceri sui domum, ut cum sua iugali repararet gratiam et revocaret eam ac reduceret. Occurrit ei mulier atque in domum patris sui introduxit maritum.

113. Laetatus est adulescentulae pater, venit obviam et sedit cum eo tribus diebus et epulati sunt et quieverunt. Et sequenti die surrexit Levita diluculo et retentus est a socero, ut tam cito non desereret convivii iucunditatem. Et

109. In the flood, too, in Noah's time, all flesh died, yet that just man himself was saved, and his descendants along with him. Man is consumed, is he not, when that which is mortal is removed from his life? For the outer man is destroyed, but the inner man is renewed. And it is not just in baptism that the destruction of the flesh produces gain for the spirit: the same is true of penance as well. We are taught this by apostolic authority, for Saint Paul tells us: 'As though I were actually present with you, I have judged the man who has committed this act: such a person is to be delivered over to Satan for the destruction of the flesh, so that his spirit may be saved on the day of our Lord Jesus Christ.'

110. It looks as if we have now digressed some way from our subject, in marvelling at this great mystery—so keen have we been to expound more and more fully the sacrament that has been revealed to us, which is as full of what is honourable as it is full of religious profundity.

111. But what a concern our ancestors had to do the honourable thing! **XIX** To avenge an outrage perpetrated upon just one woman by a group of depraved men, they were prepared to embark on all-out war. And then, after they had defeated the people of the tribe of Benjamin, they took a solemn oath never again to give their daughters to them in marriage. The tribe would have had no prospect of survival, if they had not allowed them to engage in an essential act of deception. Nevertheless, the fact that they were granted this concession does not appear to do away with the principle that there must be appropriate punishment for such depravity, for the Benjamites were only permitted to form unions by taking girls by force; they were not allowed the sacrament of marriage. And rightly so, for they had destroyed someone else's partnership, so they deserved to forfeit the right to a proper marriage ceremony themselves.

112. But what a tragic story it is all the same. A certain man, Scripture says, a Levite, had taken a wife—strictly speaking, I believe, she was called his concubine, from the word *concubitus*, meaning that she shared his bed. Some time later, she was upset by something or other, as is often the way, and she took herself off to her father, where she stayed for four months. Her husband got up and went to his father-in-law's house, intending to make things up with his wife, ask her to come back to him, and take her home again. The woman came out to meet him, and brought him into her father's house, introducing him as the husband she loved after all.

113. The young woman's father was very pleased, and came to meet him. He stayed with him for three days, and they ate and relaxed together. The following day, the Levite got up at dawn to leave, but he was detained by his father-in-law, who asked him not to go and

alio et tertio die non permisit pater adulescentulae proficisci
generum suum donec laetitia inter eos et gratia omnis con-
summaretur. Sed die septimo, cum iam ad vesperum declinaret dies, post mensas et laeta convivia, cum praetexeret
finitimae noctis viciniam ut apud suos potius quam apud
extraneos requiescendum putaret, nequivit tenere et dimisit
una cum filia sua.

114. Verum ubi facta est aliqua progressio, cum vesper iam
propior urgeret et appropinquatum foret ad urbem Iebu-
saeorum, dicente servulo ut ad eam dominus suus deflecteret,
non acquievit dominus suus, quia non erat ea civitas filiorum
Israel, sed intendit pervenire usque Gabaa, quae habitabatur
a populo tribus Beniamin. Nec erat quisquam qui advenientes
reciperet hospitio, nisi vir peregrinus progressa aetate. Qui,
cum aspexisset eos et interrogasset Levitam: 'Quo vadis vel
unde venis?' quo respondente quod esset viator et montem
repeteret Ephraim et non esset qui colligeret eum, hospitium
ei obtulit et adornavit convivium.

115. At ubi satietas epulandi facta est et mensae remotae,
irruerunt pestilentes viri, circumierunt domum. Tunc senior
filiam suam virginem et coaequalem eius, cum qua cubitare
solita esset, offerebat viris iniquitatis, tantum ne vis irrogar-
etur hospiti. Verum ubi parum ratio processit et vis praevaluit, cessit Levites iugali sua: et cognoverunt eam et tota nocte
illuserunt ei. Qua atrocitate vel dolore victa iniuriae, ante
hospitium hospitis quo vir suus deverterat, proiecit se atque
exhalavit spiritum, supremo licet vitae munere adfectum
bonae coniugis servans, ut exsequias saltem sui funeris
marito reservaret.

116. Quo cognito (ne multis morer) omnis prope populus
Israel in bellum exarsit, dubioque eventu cum anceps maneret
proelium, tertia tamen proeliandi vice, traditus est populus

deprive him of the pleasure of his company so soon. And the next day and the day after that, the young woman's father still would not let his son-in-law set off until they had made the most of each other's company and enjoyed their friendship to the full. On the seventh day, when the evening was already drawing in and they had finished their meal and their good time had come to an end, the host offered the excuse that the night was fast approaching and suggested that the man would be better spending the night with his own family rather than with strangers, but he was unable to detain him any longer, so he let him go, and his daughter with him.

114. After they had gone a short distance, the darkness was almost upon them. By this time they were close to the city of the Jebusites, so the servant suggested his master should turn off into the city. His master, though, would not hear of it, for it was not a city of the children of Israel; he was determined to make it as far as Gibeah, where the people of the tribe of Benjamin lived. On arriving there, however, they could not find anyone who would show them hospitality, except for one rather elderly man who did not belong to those parts himself. As soon as he noticed them, he asked the Levite: 'Where are you going—or should I say, where have you come from?' The Levite replied that he was on a journey and was going back to the hill-country of Ephraim, but could find no one to take him in for the night. Whereupon the old man offered him hospitality and prepared him a meal.

115. But when they had eaten their fill and the tables had been cleared, a number of the very worst characters in the town rushed up and laid siege to the house. At once the old man offered to give these evil men his own daughter, who was still a virgin, and another girl of the same age as well, a friend of hers with whom she often shared her bed, if only they would do no harm to his guest. But attempts to use reason with them got nowhere; brute force was the mood of the moment. The Levite handed over his wife, and they were intimate with her and abused her the whole night long. Completely overcome, whether as a result of the atrocities she had endured or out of sheer horror at the outrage that had been done to her, she threw herself down at the door of the man with whom her husband was lodging, and breathed her last. Even in this, the final task of her life, she still managed to show the devotion that a good wife should, for she at least saved her mortal remains for her husband to bury.

116. When the news spread of what had happened (I must be brief), the people of Israel, virtually to a man, were so incensed that they declared war on the Benjamites. The outcome was uncertain, for the conflict remained evenly matched. However, when they joined in

Beniamin populo Israel et divina iudicatus sententia poenas intemperantiae luit, et condemnatus quoque ne quis ei ex numero pater filiam suam daret in uxorem idque confirmatum iurisiurandi sacramento est. Sed compuncti quod tam acerbam in fratres tulissent sententiam, ita severitatem eius temperaverunt ut orbatas parentibus virgines in coniugium sibi adsciscerent, quarum patres pro delicto perempti forent, vel rapto copulam sociarent, quia pro tam turpis commissi facinore, quia alieni matrimonii ius violaverant, indignos se impetrando exhibuere matrimonio. Sed ne periret una populo tribus, fraudis indulta est coniventia.

117. Quanta igitur honestatis cura maioribus fuerit, hinc proditur ut quadraginta milia virorum stringerent gladium adversus fratres suos de tribu Beniamin dum ulcisci volunt iniuriam pudicitiae, quia temeratores castitatis non sufferebantur. Itaque in eo bello caesa sunt utrimque sexaginta quinque milia bellatorum et exustae urbes. Et cum inferior primo fuisset populus Israel, tamen nec adversi metu belli percitus vindicandae castitatis sequestravit dolorem. Ruebat in proelium vel sanguine suo parans commissi flagitii diluere notam.

XX **118.** Et quid mirum si populo Dei decorum illud atque honestum curae fuit, quando etiam leprosis, sicut in libris Regnorum legimus, honestatis non defuit consideratio?

119. Fames erat magna in Samaria, quia obsederat eam Syrorum exercitus. Rex militares excubias supra murum sollicitus revisebat, interpellavit eum mulier dicens: 'Persuasit mihi haec mulier ut adferrem filium meum et attuli et coximus et comedimus eum et promisit ut et ipsa postea suum filium adferret et carnes illius simul manducaremus; nunc autem filium suum abscondit et non vult eum adferre'. Motus rex quod non solum humanis sed etiam parricidalibus

battle the third time, the people of Benjamin were delivered into the hands of the people of Israel: they were judged by the sentence of God himself, and they paid the price for their depravity. In addition, a decree was passed forbidding any father anywhere among the Israelites to give his daughter to a Benjamite in marriage, and they confirmed this by swearing an official oath. After they had done this, though, they began to feel a measure of regret that they had laid such a harsh sentence upon people who were still, after all, their own brothers, and so they decided to reduce the severity of it. They allowed them to marry virgins who had lost their parents, girls whose fathers had been slain for the sins they had committed; and they let others establish unions by taking girls by force. In committing such a shameful crime—they had violated another person's marriage rights—these men had shown that they had no right to expect proper marriage for themselves. But, to prevent an entire tribe being lost to the nation, the Israelites were prepared to connive at an act of deception.

117. Here, then, is the proof of what a concern our ancestors had to do the honourable thing: 40,000 men were prepared to take up the sword against their brothers from the tribe of Benjamin. That is how determined they were to avenge an outrage to purity; they would not tolerate people violating chastity like this. And what a war it was! sixty-five thousand fighting men were cut down on both sides, and whole cities were burnt. And though initially the people of Israel suffered the worst of it, they remained steadfast and never feared that the war would go against them in the end; they put aside all thoughts of how much it cost them to avenge chastity. They rushed into battle, prepared to shed their own blood if it would wash away the stain of the crime that had been committed.

118. It is no surprise, surely, to find that the people of God had such a **XX** concern to behave in this seemly and honourable fashion? After all, we read in the books of the Kings of how even the lepers were determined to do the honourable thing.

119. There was a great famine in Samaria, for the Syrian army had been laying siege to the city. The king, deeply troubled at the situation, was going round inspecting the military guards posted on the ramparts. He was approached by a woman, who said to him: 'This woman here persuaded me to give up my son, and I did it: we cooked him and ate him. She promised that she would then give up her own son, so the two of us could make a meal out of his flesh as well. But now she has taken her son and hidden him, and she is refusing to give him up.' The king was appalled: not only had the women apparently been living off the flesh of human bodies—they had been eating the bodies

cadaveribus mulieres pastae viderentur, et tam atrocis cala-
mitatis exemplo percitus, Eliseo prophetae denuntiavit necem,
cuius in potestate fore crederet ut obsidionem solveret,
propulsaret famem, vel quia non permiserat regi ut percuteret
Syros quos caecitate perfuderat.

120. Sedebat Eliseus cum senioribus in Bethel et priusquam
introiret ad eum regis nuntius, ait ad seniores viros: *Si vidistis
quoniam filius homicidae illius misit auferre caput meum?* Et
introivit nuntius et mandatum regis pertulit. denuntianti
praesens capitis periculum. Cui respondit propheta: *Hac
hora die crastina mensura similaginis siclo et duae mensurae
hordei sic in porta Samariae.* Et cum missus a rege nuntius
non credidisset dicens: *Si pluerit Dominus de caelo abundantiam frumenti, nec sic quidem id possit effici,* dixit ad eum
Eliseus: *Quia non credidisti, oculis tuis videbis et non mandu-
cabis.*

121. Et factus est subito in castris Syriae velut quadrigarum
sonus et vox multa equitum et vox magna virtutis atque
ingens belli tumultus, et arbitrati sunt Syri quod rex Israel
in societatem advocasset proelii regem Aegypti et regem
Amorrhaeorum, et fugerunt diluculo, relinquentes tabernacula sua, quoniam verebantur ne improviso adventu novorum
opprimerentur hostium et coniunctis regum viribus non
possent resistere. Id incognitum Samariae erat, quoniam
victi metu et fame tabidi nec praetendere audebant.

122. Erant autem leprosi quattuor ad portam civitatis quibus
vita erat supplicium et mori lucrum et dixerunt ad se invicem:
'Ecce nos hic sedemus et morimur. Si ingredimur urbem,
moriemur fame; si manemus hic, nullum subsidium vivendi
suppetit nobis: eamus in castra Syriae, aut compendium
mortis erit aut salutis remedium.' Perrexerunt itaque et
intraverunt in castra: et ecce omnia nuda hostium. Ingressi
tabernacula, primum repertis alimentis fugaverunt famem,
deinde auri et argenti quantum potuerunt, diripuerunt. Et
cum soli praedae incumberent, disposuerunt tamen nuntiare

of their own children! Enraged at this example of the terrible depths to which the people had sunk, he issued a decree that the prophet Elisha must die, for he believed that the prophet had it in his power to bring the siege to an end and stop the famine—though he may have felt as he did because Elisha had not allowed him to destroy the Syrians when he had struck them blind.

120. Elisha was sitting with the elders in Bethel. Before the king's messenger even entered his presence, he said to these venerable elders: 'Have you noticed that that son of a murderer has sent someone to behead me?' Next thing, the messenger entered and relayed the king's orders, which made it clear that his life was indeed in immediate danger. The prophet answered him: 'At this hour tomorrow, a measure of wheat-flour will sell for a shekel and two measures of barley will sell for the same at the gate of Samaria.' The messenger sent by the king did not believe him: 'Even if the Lord should send showers of corn from heaven,' he said, 'this could not happen!' So Elisha said to him: 'Since you have not believed, you will see it with your eyes, but you will not eat of it.'

121. All of a sudden, a sound was heard in the Syrian camp, like the sound of chariots, and the great noise of horsemen, like the vast noise of an armed force, and all the tremendous commotion of warfare at full pitch. The Syrians concluded that the king of Israel had entered into a battle-alliance with the king of Egypt and the king of the Amorites, and they fled at first light, abandoning their tents, terrified that they might be faced with new enemies at any moment and be utterly crushed, unable to withstand the combined might of these other kings. All this was unknown at Samaria, for the people were so overwhelmed with fear and so weak with hunger that they did not venture out at all, and had even given up keeping watch.

122. There were four lepers at the gate of the city. Life for them was nothing but misery, and death itself would have been gain. They said to one another: 'Look, we are dying sitting here. If we go into the city, we shall die of hunger, and if we stay here, there is nothing to keep us alive here either. Let us go to the Syrian camp: at worst it will shorten our wait for death, and at best it could prove to be our salvation.' So they went and entered the camp, and there it was, completely empty, with not a member of the enemy in sight. They went into the tents. The first thing thing they did, on finding food, was to drive away their hunger; then they plundered as much gold and silver as they could carry with them. But though they were the only people to have discovered these spoils, they decided to give the king the news that the Syrians had fled, for they felt that this was the honourable thing to

regi fugisse Syros, quia id honestum arbitrabantur quam represso indicio fovere fraudis rapinam.

123. Quo indicio egressus est populus et diripuit castra Syriae et commeatus hostium abundantiam fecit: annonae vilitatem reddidit, secundum propheticum dictum, ut mensura similaginis siclo et duae mensurae hordei pari pretio constarent. In hac laetitia plebis nuntius ille, in quo requiescebat rex, contritus inter exeuntium festinationem et remeantium exsultationem conculcatus a plebe, mortuus est.

XXI **124.** Quid Esther regina, nonne ut populum suum periculo exueret, quod erat decorum atque honestum, morti se obtulit nec immitis regis trepidavit furorem? Ipse quoque rex Persarum, ferox atque tumido corde, tam decorum iudicavit indici insidiarum quae sibi paratae forent, gratia repraesentare populumque liberum a servitute eripere, eruere neci nec parcere ei qui tam indecora suasisset. Denique quem secundum a se, praecipuum inter omnes amicos haberet, cruci tradidit, quod dehonestatum se eius fraudulentis consiliis animadvertisset.

125. Ea enim amicitia probabilis quae honestatem tuetur, praeferenda sane opibus honoribus potestatibus; honestati vero praeferri non solet, sed honestatem sequi. Qualis fuit Ionathae, qui pro pietate nec offensam patris nec salutis periculum refugiebat. Qualis fuit Ahimelech, qui pro hospitalis gratiae officiis necem potius sui quam proditionem fugientis amici subeundam arbitrabatur.

XXII **126.** Nihil igitur praeferendum honestati; quae tamen ne amicitiae studio praetereatur etiam hoc scriptura admonet. Sunt enim pleraeque philosophorum quaestiones: utrum amici causa quisquam contra patriam sentire necne debeat, ut amico oboediat; utrum oporteat ut fidem deserat, dum indulget atque intendit amici commoditatibus?

do. To withhold the information and keep the plunder for themselves, they thought, would be deceitful.

123. When they got this information, the people went out and plundered the Syrian camp. With these supplies of the enemy, they now had more than enough: the corn became cheap again, just as the prophet had said it would, and a measure of wheat-flour was sold for a shekel, and two measures of barley went for the same price. In the midst of all the public rejoicing, that same messenger, the one on whose arm the king had leant, found himself caught in the stampede as one crowd rushed eagerly to get out and another came back full of the joys of what they had found: he was trampled upon by the throng, and died.

124. What about queen Esther? She exposed herself to death, and XXI never quaked, even at the fury of a savage king. And why? It was in order to do the seemly and honourable thing of rescuing her people from danger, was it not? And that is not all: the Persian king himself, fierce character and proud in heart though he was, still considered that it was seemly to show gratitude to a man who had informed him of a plot which had been laid against him; to rescue a free people from slavery; to snatch them from the jaws of death; and to show no mercy to the one who had urged him to execute such unseemly crimes. So he sent to the gallows the man who had been his second-in-command, the man he had counted chief among all his friends, for he had seen that by giving him such deceitful advice he had treated him in a dishonourable fashion.

125. Friendship is only commendable, you see, when it preserves what is honourable. Friendship must come before wealth, or honour, or power, certainly, but it is not normal that it should come before what is honourable; rather, it should follow it. This was the kind of friendship that Jonathan showed. He had such a sense of loyalty, he did not shrink from incurring his father's displeasure or from endangering his own life for the sake of it. This was the kind of friendship that Ahimelech showed. He had such firm ideas about the importance of showing generous hospitality to his guests, he believed he should undergo death himself rather than betray his friend when he was in flight.

126. Nothing, therefore, must ever be allowed to come before what is XXII honourable. In case we become so enthusiastic about friendship that we forget this, though, Scripture gives us plenty of reminders on this very point. For here again there are endless questions over which the philosophers argue. Is it ever right, they ask, for someone to plot against his country for the sake of a friend, to please him, or is it not? Is it ever right to abandon good faith, when you are doing a favour for a friend and seeking to further his advantage?

127. Et scriptura quidem ait: *Clava et gladius et sagitta ferrata, sic homo est testimonium dans falsum adversus amicum suum.* Sed considera quid adstruat. Non testimonium reprehendit dictum in amicum, sed falsum testimonium. Quid enim si Dei causa, quid si patriae cogatur aliquis dicere testimonium? Numquid praeponderare debet amicitia religioni, praeponderare caritati civium? In his tamen ipsis rebus requirenda est veritas testimonii, ne amicus appetatur amici perfidia cuius fide absolvi debeat. Amicus itaque neque noxio gratificari debet neque innocenti insidiari.

128. Sane si necesse sit dicere testimonium, si quid in amico vitii cognoverit, corripere occulte; si non audierit, corripere palam. Sunt enim bonae correptiones et plerumque meliores quam tacita amicitia. Et si laedi se putet amicus, tu tamen corripe; et si amaritudo correptionis animum eius vulneret, tu tamen corripe; ne verearis. *Tolerabiliora sunt* enim *amici vulnera quam adulantum oscula.* Errantem igitur amicum corripe, innocentem amicum ne deseras. Constans enim debet esse amicitia, perseverare in adfectu: non puerili modo amicos mutare vaga quadam debemus sententia.

129. Aperi pectus tuum amico, ut fidelis sit tibi et capias ex eo vitae tuae iucunditatem: *Fidelis* enim *amicus medicamentum est vitae,* immortalitatis gratia. Defer amico ut aequali nec te pudeat ut praevenias amicum officio: amicitia enim nescit superbiam. Ideo enim sapiens dicit: *Amicum salutare non erubescas.* Nec deseras amicum in necessitate nec derelinquas eum neque destituas, quoniam amicitia vitae adiumentum est. Ideo in ea onera portamus, sicut apostolus docuit: dicit enim his quos eiusdem complexa est caritas. Etenim si amici secundae res amicos adiuvant, cur non et in adversis amici rebus amicorum adiumentum suppetat? Iuvemus consilio, conferamus studia, compatiamur adfectu.

130. Si necesse est, toleremus propter amicum etiam aspera. Plerumque inimicitiae subeundae sunt propter amici innocentiam, saepe obtrectationes, si restiteris vel responderis cum

127. Well, Scripture does say this: 'Like a club, a sword, or an arrow of sharpened iron, so is the man who bears false evidence against his friend.' But notice what Scripture is declaring here. It is not the giving of evidence against a friend as such that is being condemned: it is the giving of *false* evidence. For what if the cause of God or the interests of our country compel a person to give evidence? Should friendship count for more than religion? Should it count for more than love for your fellow-citizens? Even then, however, it is essential to ascertain that the evidence is true: a man should never find himself on the receiving end as a result of a friend's disloyalty; he ought rather to be acquitted by virtue of his friend's faithful support. So a friend should not turn a blind eye if a person is guilty, nor should he set a trap for him if he is innocent.

128. Of course, if it does prove necessary to give evidence against your friend, if you know that there is something wrong in his life, you should rebuke him in secret. If he refuses to listen, you should rebuke him openly. Such friendly rebukes are valuable, and often they are better than the type of friendship that stays silent. Even if your friend feels hurt, rebuke him just the same. Even if your rebuke is bitter and hurts his feelings, rebuke him just the same; do not be afraid. For 'the wounds of a friend are more bearable than the kisses of flatterers.' So, rebuke a friend who is going astray, and do not forsake a friend who is innocent. Friendship ought to be constant, and its feelings ought to last. We must not behave like children, changing our friends just on the basis of a vague whim.

129. Open your heart to your friend, so that he will be faithful to you, and so that you will know joy in your own life from him: For 'a faithful friend is the medicine of life,' the grace of immortality. Show deference to your friend as an equal, and do not be ashamed if you outstrip your friend in the duties you perform, for friendship knows nothing of pride. That is why the wise man says: 'Do not blush to greet a friend.' Do not forsake a friend in need, do not desert him, do not fail him, for friendship is an aid to life. That is how we bear one another's burdens, as the apostle taught us to do—for his words are addressed to those who have been embraced by the same love of friendship. If friends help one another when things are going well, why should not friends also help one another when times are hard? We should support them by offering them our advice; we should devote our best efforts to helping them; and we should sympathize with them with all our heart.

130. If necessary, we should even be prepared to put up with things that are hard for a friend's sake. Quite often, you will have to incur feelings of resentment because your friend is innocent, and frequently you will have to put up with abuse if you object or answer back when

amicus arguitur et accusatur. Nec te paeniteat eiusmodi offensionis; iusti enim vox est: *Et si mala mihi evenerint propter amicum, sustineo.* In adversis enim amicus probatur; nam in prosperis amici omnes videntur. Sed ut in adversis amici patientia et tolerantia necessaria est, sic in prosperis auctoritas congrua est, ut insolentiam extollentis se amici reprimat et redarguat.

131. Quam pulchre in adversis positus Iob dicit: *Miseremini mei, amici, miseremini.* Non quasi abiecta vox ista est, sed quasi censoria. Nam cum iniuste arguitur ab amicis, respondit: *Miseremini mei, amici*; hoc est: Misericordiam debetis facere; opprimitis autem vos et impugnatis hominem cuius aerumnis compati pro amicitia vos oportebat.

132. Servate igitur, filii, initam cum fratribus amicitiam, qua nihil est in rebus humanis pulchrius. Solatium quippe vitae huius est ut habeas cui pectus aperias tuum, cum quo arcana participes, cui committas secretum pectoris tui, ut colloces tibi fidelem virum qui in prosperis gratuletur tibi, in tristibus compatiatur, in persecutionibus adhortetur. Quam boni amici Hebraei pueri, quos a sui amore nec fornacis ardentis flamma divisit! De quo loco supra diximus. Bene ait sanctus David: *Saul et Ionatha, speciosi et carissimi, inseparabiles in vita sua, et in morte non sunt separati.*

133. Hic est amicitiae fructus, non ut fides propter amicitiam destruatur. Non potest enim homini amicus esse, qui Deo fuerit infidus. Pietatis custos amicitia est et aequalitatis magistra, ut superior inferiori se exhibeat aequalem, inferior superiori. Inter dispares enim mores non potest esse amicitia, et ideo convenire sibi utriusque debet gratia: nec auctoritas desit inferiori, si res poposcerit, nec humilitas superiori. Audiat quasi parem, quasi aequalem; et ille quasi

your friend is attacked and accused of things. Feel no regret if you incur this kind of reproach. Remember what the just man says: 'And if dreadful things befall me on a friend's account, I bear them.' It is when times are hard that a friend can be properly proved: when things are going well everyone seems to be your friend. But just as a friend needs patience and endurance to stand by his companion in the hard times, it is equally appropriate for him to sound a note of authority in the days when things are going well. This way he can stop his friend becoming arrogant and developing too high an opinion of himself, and show him that this is wrong.

131. Job makes this point so beautifully, if we think of how he reacted when he was going through hard times: 'Have pity on me, my friends, have pity on me,' he said. This is not the cry of a man who has lost heart: it is a word of censure. He gives this response, you see, when he is being unjustly attacked by his friends: 'Have pity on me, my friends.' What he is saying, in other words, is this: 'When you ought to be showing me compassion, you condemn and attack me. And you are doing this to someone for whom you ought to show sympathy in times of trial: that is what friendship is supposed to be about.'

132. So, my sons, take good care of the friendship you have entered into with your brothers: in the whole range of human life, there is nothing more wonderful than this. It really is a comfort in this life to have someone to whom you can open your heart, someone with whom you can share your innermost feelings, and someone in whom you can confide the secrets of your heart; to have at your side a man who will always be faithful to you, someone who will rejoice with you when things are going well, sympathize with you when circumstances are hard, and encourage you in times of persecution. Think of those Hebrew boys, and what good friends they were! Not even the flames of the fiery furnace could sever them from their love for one another. We have referred to that story already. Well did holy David say: 'Saul and Jonathan were so splendid, so precious: inseparable they were in life, and in death itself they were not separated.'

133. Such is the fruit that friendship produces. It is never right to break faith for the sake of friendship. No one can be a true friend to man if he has been unfaithful to God. Friendship is the guardian of loyalty and the teacher of equality: it makes the superior prove himself equal to the inferior, and the inferior equal to the superior. There cannot be friendship among people who are quite different in character, so there needs to be a similar measure of goodwill on both sides. The inferior must not lack authority if the occasion demands, and the superior for his part must not lack humility. He needs to listen with the attitude that the inferior is just as significant as he is himself, that he is

amicus moneat, obiurget, non iactantiae studio sed adfectu caritatis.

134. Neque monitio aspera sit neque obiurgatio contumeliosa: sicut enim adulationis fugitans amicitia debet esse, ita etiam aliena insolentiae. Qui est enim amicus nisi consors amoris, ad quem animum tuum adiungas atque applices et ita misceas ut unum velis fieri ex duobus, cui te alteri tibi committas, a quo nihil timeas, nihil ipse commodi tui causa inhonestum petas? Non enim vectigalis amicitia est, sed plena decoris, plena gratiae. Virtus est enim amicitia, non quaestus, quia non pecunia paritur, sed gratia, nec licitatione pretiorum sed concertatione benevolentiae.

135. Denique meliores amicitiae sunt inopum plerumque quam divitum, et frequenter divites sine amicis sunt quibus abundant pauperes. Non est enim vera amicitia ubi est fallax adulatio. Divitibus itaque plerique adsentatorie gratificantur: erga pauperem nemo simulator est. Verum est quidquid defertur pauperi; huius amicitia invidia vacat.

136. Quid amicitia pretiosius, quae angelis communis et hominibus est? Unde Dominus Iesus dicit: *Facite vobis amicos de iniquo mammona, qui recipiant vos in aeterna tabernacula sua.* Ipse nos Deus amicos ex servulis facit, sicut ipse ait: *Iam vos amici mei estis, si feceritis quae ego praecipio vobis.* Dedit formam amicitiae quam sequamur, ut faciamus amici voluntatem, ut aperiamus secreta nostra amico quaecumque in pectore habemus, et illius arcana non ignoremus. Ostendamus illi nos pectus nostrum et ille nobis aperiat suum. *Ideo,* inquit, *vos dixi amicos quia omnia quaecumque audivi a Patre meo, nota feci vobis.* Nihil ergo occultat amicus, si verus est: effundit animum suum, sicut effundebat mysteria Patris Dominus Iesus.

137. Ergo qui facit mandata Dei amicus est, et hoc honoratur nomine. Qui est unanimis, ipse amicus est quod unitas animorum in amicis sit, neque quisquam detestabilior quam qui amicitiam laeserit. Unde in proditorem Dominus hoc

an equal, and when the inferior voices words of warning and makes critical observations he needs to do it with the air of a friend, motivated not by a desire to score points, but by genuine concern and real love. **134.** The warnings must never be harsh, and the criticisms never impertinent. If friendship must avoid flattery, it must equally be a stranger to arrogance. What is a friend, in fact, but a partner in love? You unite your innermost being to his, you join your spirit to his, you blend so thoroughly with him that your aim is to be no longer two, but one. You entrust yourself to him as to another self; you fear nothing from him; and you do not ask anything dishonourable of him for your own ends. Friendship is not about taking in sums of money; it is all about pleasing one another, all about treating one another with consideration. Friendship is a virtue, not a means to material gain: it is produced not by offering someone cash but by showing him the consideration he deserves; not by one party offering higher prices than the other but by the one endeavouring to outdo the other in the display of goodwill.

135. In fact, the friendships of people who are needy are very often better than the friendships of the rich, and frequently the rich find themselves without friends while the poor have many. For there can be no true friendship where there is flattery or deceit. There are lots of people ready to fawn upon the rich and do favours for them, but no one makes any pretence with somebody who is poor. Any deference paid to a poor person is genuine; friendship, for him, is free from envy.

136. Is there anything more precious than friendship? It is shared by both men and angels. So the Lord Jesus says: 'Use unjust mammon to make friends for yourselves, so that they will receive you into their eternal tabernacles.' God himself makes us his friends, though we are really the very lowliest of his servants. He says himself: 'Now you are my friends, if you do what I command you.' He has given us the pattern of friendship we should follow: we are to do whatever our friend wishes, open up to our friend every last secret we have in our heart, and not be unaware of his innermost thoughts either. We must show him our heart, and he must open his heart to us. 'I have called you friends,' Jesus says, 'because everything I have heard from my Father I have made known to you.' A friend hides nothing, then, if he is true: he pours out his heart, just as the Lord Jesus poured out the mysteries of the Father.

137. So the person who keeps the commandments of God is his friend, and is honoured with this name. He who is one with him in spirit is also his friend, for there is a unity of spirits among friends, and there is no one more detestable than the individual who damages this friendship. So, when the Lord confronted the one who betrayed him,

gravissimum invenit quod eius condemnaret perfidiam, quod gratiae vicem non repraesentaverit et conviviis amicitiae venenum malitiae miscuerit. Itaque sic ait: *Tu vero, homo unanimis meus et dux meus et notus meus qui semper mecum dulces capiebas cibos.* Hoc est: Non potest sustineri istud quia unanimis appetisti eum qui tibi donaverat gratiam: *Nam si inimicus meus maledixisset mihi, sustinuissem utique et ab eo qui me oderat, absconderem me.* Inimicus vitari potest, amicus non potest, si insidiari velit. Illum cavemus cui non committimus consilia nostra, hunc cavere non possumus cui commisimus. Itaque ad acervandam peccati invidiam non dixit: *Tu vero servus meus, apostolus meus,* sed *unanimis meus*; hoc est: non meus sed etiam tuus proditor es, qui unanimum prodidisti.

138. Dominus ipse, cum a tribus regibus offensus esset qui sancto Iob non detulissent, ignoscere his per amicum maluit, ut amicitiae suffragium remissio fieret peccatorum. Itaque rogavit Iob, et Dominus ignovit. Profuit illis amicitia quibus obfuit insolentia.

139. Haec apud vos deposui, filii, quae custodiatis in animis vestris: quae utrum aliquid profectus habeant, vos probabitis. Interim copiam multam exemplorum adferent; nam prope omnia maiorum exempla, plurima quoque dicta his tribus inclusa libris tenentur, ut, si sermo nihil deferat gratiae, series tamen vetustatis quodam compendio expressa plurimum instructionis conferat.

this was the thing he found worst of all about his treachery, this was the crime he condemned most of all—the man had shown no gratitude at all for all that he had received, but had mixed his evil poisons while sitting at the very table of friendship. This was why the Lord spoke as he did: 'But it was you, a man who was one with me in spirit, my guide and my companion, you who always took sweet food with me.' His point, in other words, was this: 'This is what I find so unbearable: it was *you* who lay in wait for me—*you* who were one with me in spirit! You lay in wait for the one who had shown you such goodwill.' 'For if it had been my enemy who had cursed me, I would have been able to bear it, and I would hide myself from the one who hated me.' An enemy can be avoided; a friend cannot, if he wants to set a snare for you. We are used to being on our guard against the kind of person in whom we would never confide our thoughts; but we cannot be on our guard against a person in whom we have already confided. It was to emphasize how hateful the sin was, then, that the Lord Jesus put it as he did. He did not say: 'But it was you, my servant, my apostle.' He said: 'But it was you, a man who was one with me in spirit.' In other words: 'I am not the one who is betrayed: you have betrayed yourself, for you have betrayed a man who was one with you in spirit.'

138. The Lord himself was angry with the three rulers, for they had failed to show respect for holy Job; but he chose to pardon them when their friend interceded for them, so that friendship's voice might secure the remission of sins. So Job prayed, and the Lord pardoned them. Arrogance did them nothing but harm; friendship brought them nothing but good.

139. And now, my sons, I have left you these thoughts with the desire that you will guard them in your hearts. Whether there is any value in them you will have to prove for yourselves. Whatever the case, they offer you a large stock of examples, for almost all the examples of our ancestors, and a great many of their words too, can be found within these three books. So, while the style may hold no particular charm, the course of ancient history which I have sought to sketch for you here in this abridged form should afford you a good deal of instruction all the same.